Communications in Computer and Information Science 1206

• *Commenced Publication in 2007*
Founding and Former Series Editors:
Phoebe Chen, Alfredo Cuzzocrea, Xiaoyong Du, Orhun Kara, Ting Liu,
Krishna M. Sivalingam, Dominik Ślęzak, Takashi Washio, Xiaokang Yang,
and Junsong Yuan

More information about this series at http://www.springer.com/series/7899

Pradeep Kumar Singh · Sanjay Sood ·
Yugal Kumar · Marcin Paprzycki ·
Anton Pljonkin · Wei-Chiang Hong (Eds.)

Futuristic Trends in Networks and Computing Technologies

Second International Conference, FTNCT 2019
Chandigarh, India, November 22–23, 2019
Revised Selected Papers

 Springer

Editors
Pradeep Kumar Singh ⓘ
Jaypee University of Information
Technology
Waknaghat, Himachal Pradesh, India

Yugal Kumar ⓘ
Jaypee University of Information
Technology
Solan, Himachal Pradesh, India

Anton Pljonkin ⓘ
Southern Federal University
Rostov-on-Don, Russia

Sanjay Sood ⓘ
CDAC
Mohali, India

Marcin Paprzycki ⓘ
Polish Academy of Sciences
Warsaw, Poland

Wei-Chiang Hong ⓘ
Jiangsu Normal University
Xuzhou, China

ISSN 1865-0929   ISSN 1865-0937 (electronic)
Communications in Computer and Information Science
ISBN 978-981-15-4450-7   ISBN 978-981-15-4451-4 (eBook)
https://doi.org/10.1007/978-981-15-4451-4

This Springer imprint is published by the registered company Springer Nature Singapore Pte Ltd.
The registered company address is: 152 Beach Road, #21-01/04 Gateway East, Singapore 189721, Singapore

Preface

The Second International Conference on Futuristic Trends in Networks and Computing Technologies (FTNCT 2019) targeted researchers from different domains of Networks and Computing Technologies to showcase their research ideas at one single venue. The main four technical tracks of conference included: Network and Computing Technologies, Wireless Networks and Internet of Things (IoT), Futuristic Computing Technologies and Communication Technologies, and Security and Privacy. FTNCT was proposed with the intention of becoming an annual ongoing event at which researchers could gather and exchange their latest research results and ideas. The conference will evolve into an intellectual asset in the long term. FTNCT 2019 was jointly hosted by C-DAC Mohali, Jaypee University of Information Technology (JUIT), and HP India during November 22–23, 2019, in Mohali, India, in association with Southern Federal University, Russia; Sciences and Technologies of Image and Telecommunications (SETIT) of Sfax University, Tunisia; and technically supported by the CSI Chandigarh Chapter, India. FTNCT 2019 received funding from three leading government institutions, including AICTE, DRDO, and ISRO (all Government of India).

We are thankful to our valuable authors for their contributions and our Technical Program Committee for their immense support and motivation towards making the second version of FTNCT a grand success. We are also grateful to our keynote speakers: Prof. Arpan Kumar Kar (IIT Delhi, India), Dr. Sanjay Sood (Assoc. Director at C-DAC Mohali, India), Dr. MaheshKumar Kolekar (IIT Patna, India), Dr. Jitender Kumar Chhabra (Professor at NIT Kurukshetra, India), and Mr. Priyank Mistry (Zonal Head – North, M/s PeopleLink) for sharing their technical talks and enlightening the delegates of the conference.

Conference Inaugural was done by Honorable Shri. Balbir Singh Sidhu, Health and Family Welfare Minister, Government of Punjab, India; Dr. P. K. Khosla, Executive Director, C-DAC Mohali, India; Prof. Vinod Kumar, Vice Chancellor, JUIT, India; in presence of other guests and media persons.

We express our sincere gratitude to our publication partner, Springer (CCIS series), for believing in us. We are thankful to Ms. Kamiya Khatter, Associate Editor, Springer, and Sanja Evenson, Editorial Team, CCIS Springer, for extending their help from time to time in the preparation of these proceedings.

November 2019

Pradeep Kumar Singh
Sanjay Sood
Yugal Kumar
Marcin Paprzycki
Anton Pljonkin
Wei-Chiang Hong

Organization

Committee Members

Chief Patrons

Shri Jaiprakash Gaur Ji (Founder Chairman)	Jaypee Group, India
Shri Manoj Gaur Ji (Executive Chairman)	Jaypee Group and Pro-Chancellor JUIT, India

Patrons

Vinod Kumar (Vice Chancellor)	JUIT, India
P. K. Khosla (Executive Director)	C-DAC Mohali, India

Co-patrons

Samir Dev Gupta (Director and Academic Head)	JUIT, India
Veselov Gennady Evgenievich (Director)	Southern Federal University, Russia

Advisory Committee

Abhijit Sen	Kwantlen Polytechnic University, Canada
Ioan-Cosmin Mihai	Alexandru Ioan Cuza Police Academy, Romania
Pelin Angin	Purdue University, USA
Marcin Paprzycki	Systems Research Institute, Polish Academy of Sciences, Poland
Sanjay Sood (Joint Director)	C-DAC Mohali, India
Arti Noor (Joint Director)	C-DAC Noida, India
Bharat Bhargava	Purdue University, USA

Principal General Chairs

Satya Prakash Ghrera	JUIT, India
Sanjay Sood (Joint Director)	C-DAC Mohali, India

Executive General Chairs

Pradeep Kumar Singh   JUIT, India
Pljonkin Anton   Institute of Computer Technologies and Information
                             Security, Southern Federal University, Russia

Honorary Chairs

Maria Ganzha   Warsaw University of Technology, Poland
Pao-Ann Hsiung   National Chung Cheng University, Taiwan
Wei-Chiang Hong   Jiangsu Normal University, China

Program Chairs

Jitender Kumar Chhabra   NIT Kurukshetra, India
Narottam Chand Kaushal   NIT Hamirpur, India
Konstantin Rumyantsev   Southern Federal University, Russia
Samoilov Aleksey   Southern Federal University, Russia
  Nikolaevich

Organizing Secretariats

Yugal Kumar   JUIT, India
Amit Kumar   JUIT, India

Technical Program Committee Coordinator

Vivek Kumar Sehgal   JUIT, India

Conference Web Admin

Rohit   JUIT, India

Funded and Supported By

AICTE, Government of India, India   DRDO, Government of India, India

ISRO, Government of India, India

Academic Collaborators

CSI JUIT Student Chapter, India

ACM JUIT Student Chapter, India

Sothern Federal University, Russia

SETIT, Tunisia

Organized By

C-DAC Mohali, India

JUIT, India

Other Supporters for FTNCT 2019

Conference Alerts as technical promoters, IAC Education, IGI Global as special issues partner, and many more.

Contents

Futuristic Computing Technologies

Communication Technologies, Security and Privacy

Network and Computing Technologies

A Review of LEACH Successors Using Single-Hop and Multi-Hop Communication Model

Avinash Bhagat$^{(\boxtimes)}$ and G. Geetha

Lovely Professional University, Phagwara, India
{avinash.bhagat,geetha.15484}@lpu.co.in

Abstract. LEACH model was proposed 19 years back and research community from the field of WSN has been exploring LEACH variants. To discover unseen areas in the field of WSN it is a great idea to study approved variants of LEACH through the time. Present paper studies the popular and approved versions of LEACH. The study categorizes all the variants in single and multi-hop communication mode, depends upon packets transmitted from the CH and the BS. The paper makes a comparative analysis based on parameters like cluster formation, complexity, energy efficiency, overhead, and scalability. Advantages and disadvantages of all the variants are discussed. Finally, the paper suggests upcoming research in the field of WSN.

Keywords: Cluster · Cluster head · Clustering algorithm · Energy efficiency · LEACH · Routing algorithm · Motes · Wireless sensors

1 Introduction

WSN or wireless sensors network is defined as a group of small sensing nodes also called motes are deployed in an area with one or more leading nodes called base stations. These motes are very small in terms of physical size, sensing, processing, and communication capabilities [1–5]. WSN has widespread application possibilities, such as air pollution monitoring, area monitoring, commercial applications, environmental/ earth sensing, forest fire detection, health care monitoring, home applications industrial monitoring landslide detection military applications and water quality monitoring [2, 5, 6]. Limited power, the low processing power of nodes, low bandwidth, and absence of conventional addressing technique makes designing of routing algorithm challenging task.

Heinzelman et al. [4] in the year 2000 proposed the first-ever hierarchical algorithm named LEACH, "Low energy adaptive clustering hierarchy". Based on LEACH many hierarchical algorithms have been developed, some of them are EECS [5], HEED [6], PEGASIS [7], TEEN [8] and T-LEACH [9].

The objective of LEACH and its variants are to increase the energy efficiency, increase coverage area, scalability, effective data aggregation, minimum delay, provide security to data and robustness. The most common and significant aim of these algorithms is to reduce energy dissipation [10].

© Springer Nature Singapore Pte Ltd. 2020
P. K. Singh et al. (Eds.): FTNCT 2019, CCIS 1206, pp. 3–13, 2020.
https://doi.org/10.1007/978-981-15-4451-4_1

1.1   LEACH "Low Energy Adaptive Clustering Hierarchy" Algorithm

Clustering is the technique of effectively arranging mote and control approach which can be used to improve the network lifetime and scalability of networks. Energy efficiency in LEACH clustering algorithm for WSN is achieved by selecting CH randomly. The operation of LEACH has multiple rounds as in Fig. 1. All the rounds constitute two phases set-up and steady-state phase as shown in Fig. 2 redrawn from [4]. During the setup phase, CHs are elected, motes associate themselves with CH to create a cluster.

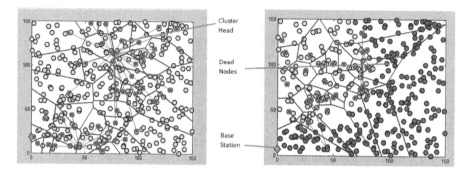

Fig. 1. Leach algorithm, the illustration of two rounds.

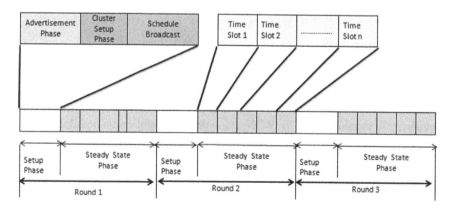

Fig. 2. LEACH operations

In the process of CH election, all the motes produce a random number between 0 and 1, if the random number is less than threshold *Th (rnd)*, the mote becomes CH for the current round; the threshold value is selected using selection Eq. (1) as follows:

$$Th_{(rnd)} = \begin{cases} \frac{p}{1-p*\left(rnd\,mod\frac{1}{p}\right)}, & if \ n \in G \\ 0, & otherwise \end{cases} \qquad (1)$$

Where P indicates the sought after % of motes to be elected as CHs from all the motes, rnd means the present round and G are the numbers of motes which were not part of the process of cluster head election in last $1/P$ rounds. The mote which turns into cluster head in round rnd will not be participant mote for next $1/P$ rounds. Thus, all the mote gets a chance to become the CH, leading to a uniform distribution of energy consumption by motes. When a mote is chosen as CH, it broadcast an ad message to all the motes. Contingent upon the strength of the signal, motes join one of the clusters. New ad message is based on Eq. 1. After forming the cluster, in order to avoid collision CHs plans and follows the TDMA aired to all the motes of the concerned cluster. Motes which are not active go into sleep mode.

Steady-state phase follows the setup phase. During this phase data sensed by motes is transmitted to CH, data gathered by CH is further sent to the base station following the TDMA schedule. While one mote is sending data to CH other motes remains in sleep mode resulting in a reduction in the intracluster collision which enhances the battery life of motes.

As cluster head is chosen randomly, so the same mote may be cluster head again and again. After a few rounds, none of the motes have enough energy to become CH. In LEACH formation of clusters is random. The positioning of the CH is not well defined in LEACH, CHs as CHs may be positioned near the center of the member clusters, while in another scenario the location cluster head may be near the boundaries of the concerned clusters, resulting in higher energy dissipation during intracluster communication. Resulting in degradation in the overall performance of the network. To improve the performance single-hop and multi-hop communication model is used.

2 LEACH Successors Using Single Hop Communication Model

In LEACH, CH receives data from member motes of the concerned cluster, gathered data is then transferred to the BS. Communication process plays an important role in attaining efficiency. If the area of the network is small, single-hop communication is beneficial as overhead, cost and delay are reduced, resulting increased network lifetime. In the variants of LEACH, researchers focused on cluster head selection, creation of clusters and communication within the cluster. This section discusses major LEACH variants which have an improvement over LEACH.

2.1 LEACH-C

Although in the year 2002 Heinzelman et al. [11] proposed LEACH-centralized, an algorithm using central control algorithms in the creation of clusters during the setup and steady-state phase like basic LEACH algorithm. Whereas LEACH-C distributes the cluster head evenly over the entire area of the network thus excellent cluster are formed. Overhead do not increase as the steady-state phase is executed by the base station. The average energy contained by the network E_{avg} is given in Eq. 2.

$$E_{avg} = \frac{\sum_{i=1}^{N} E_i}{n} \tag{2}$$

Where the remaining energy of the ith mote is E_i. And the total motes is denoted by n. If the average distance between elected CH and the BS is d_{tBS}, e_{fs} is transmission fields and e_{mp} receiving fields for both free space and multipath respectively and if there are n motes uniformly deployed in an area then K can be determined using Eq. 3,

$$K = \sqrt{\frac{N}{2\pi} \frac{e_{fs}}{e_{mp}} \frac{M}{d_{tBS}^2}} \tag{3}$$

In LEACH-C, is centralized so it is less scalable, as cluster head selection is done by BS so it is energy efficient than LEACH. In LEACH-C we need to define position so we require GPS to define location and GPS is a costly device.

2.2 DCHS-LEACH

In the year 2002 Handy et al. [12] proposed a modification in LEACH Deterministic Cluster Head Selection LEACH where CH selection is changed to reduce energy dissipation for prolonging the network lifetime, achieved by modifying the threshold T (n) value for electing the cluster head as in Eq. 4 and using a deterministic approach of CH selection resulting low energy consumption.

$$T(n)_{new} = \frac{P}{1 - P\left(r \bmod \frac{1}{P}\right)} \frac{E_{ncurrent}}{E_{nmax}} \tag{4}$$

Where $T(n)_{new}$ is modified threshold value $E_{ncurrent}$ represents the current energy of the node and E_{nmax} is the initial energy of the mote. Initially, this worked out but later on after a few rounds the network stopped. The problem is solved by providing another energy model as in Eq. 5.

$$T(n)_{new} = \frac{P}{1 - P\left(r \bmod \frac{1}{P}\right)} \left[\frac{E_{ncurrent}}{E_{nmax}} + \left(r_s div \frac{1}{P}\right)\left(1 - \frac{E_{ncurrent}}{E_{nmax}}\right)\right] \tag{5}$$

With these modifications, the lifetime of the network is enhanced by 30%. The lifetime of microsensor networks can be obtained but overall performance is degraded due to frequent cluster formation.

2.3 Unequal Clustering LEACH (U-LEACH)

In the single-hop model method, the cluster head sends the aggregated date directly to the base station causing more energy consumption by the distant base station, thus energy consumed is directly proportional to distance. In the year 2010, a clustering algorithm based on unequal LEACH that contains more setup phases was proposed by Ren et al. [13]. The paper proposes a different cluster heads selection phase. Present work suggests two elements of competitive distance and residual energy percentage for any mote to be a part of the cluster head election. Authors have taken the unequal size of circular clusters, cluster nearer to base station are larger than the cluster at a far distance.

Proposed clustering mechanism minimizes the hotspot problem of LEACH Algorithm also balances the energy and enhances the lifetime of the network. The disadvantage of the proposal is intracluster data transmission between clusters nearer to the base station.

2.4 Genetic Algorithm-Based LEACH

In the year 2011 Singh et al. [14] in their survey found Nature-inspired computing (NIC) i.e. Bio-Inspired, Evolutionary Computing, and Swarm Intelligence algorithms can be utilized to tackle complicated problems in modest ways. Liu et al. [15] proposed a genetic algorithm based LEACH (LEACH-GA) which suggested probability-based cluster head selection. In the beginning, all motes are CCH (candidate for cluster head selection process) they generate a random number Rnd which in-turn is compared with threshold value Threshold(s) and if Rnd is less than Threshold(s) and probability value PROBsat is 0.5 the mote becomes cluster head. Rest of the motes send theirs sends its id and location information to the base station. Base station uses a genetic algorithm, evolutionary optimization process, probability transitions, non-deterministic rules, mutation operators and crossover. Probability $PROB_{OPT}$ for n motes and K_{OPT} clusters is defined by relations of Eq. 6

$$PROB_{OPT} = \frac{K_{OPT}}{n} \tag{6}$$

The performance of LEACH-GA is superior to LEACH regarding energy efficiency but overhead cost and scalability is an issue.

2.5 Energy Potential LEACH (EP-LEACH)

In the year 2013 Xiao et al. [16] EP-LEACH used energy harvest technique [17] to improve the lifetime of LEACH motes have rechargeable energy bank which gathers energy from its atmosphere. It is different from LEACH in CH selection phase. The motes with more energy have more probability to become CH and mote can become a CH many times. Accordingly, the threshold equation of LEACH is reformulated in Eq. 7 [16] based on the proposed two modifications.

$$T_k(i) = \frac{F_k(i)}{\sum_{r \in N_k} F_r(i)} X P X |N_k| \tag{7}$$

Where $N_k = \{r|D(r,k) < D_t\}$ D(r, k) is a distance between nodes k and r, D_t is threshold distance between neighboring nodes.

2.6 Improved LEACH (I-LEACH)

In the year 2013 Beiranvand et al. [18] proposed a new idea in the CH section for improvement in LEACH. CH is selected by considering parameters like distance from BS, the number of neighboring motes and their remaining energy. Motes find these parameters from Eqs. 8 and 9 [18]. The number of motes in the neighborhood is defined by its coverage area of radius R_{ch}, which is given by Eq. 8.

$$R_{ch} = \sqrt{\frac{(M * M)}{(\pi * K)}} \tag{8}$$

$$T(n) = \begin{cases} \left(\frac{p}{1-p*\left(rmod\frac{1}{p}\right)} * \frac{E_c}{E_{avg}} * \frac{Nbr_n}{Nbr_{avg}} * \frac{dt_oBS_{avg}}{d_{to}BS_n} \right), & if\ S \in G \\ 0, & otherwise \end{cases} \tag{9}$$

Where K number of clusters are deployed in $M*M$ area. Improved threshold $T(n)$ is shown in Eq. 9. Randomly generated number is compared with $T(n)$, the mote whose randomly generated number is less than the threshold becomes the cluster head for the present round. Arrangement of motes in the given network reduces energy dissipated per mote thus increases network lifetime.

2.7 Vice Cluster LEACH (VC-LEACH)

In the year 2015 Sasikala et al. [19] proposed a concept of vice CH in V-LEACH. Because of poor CH selection in LEACH, some of the CHs die before completing its the current round, vice cluster head will take over the role of cluster head when the original CH dies before the completing its present round. There are three types of motes in VLEACH, CH, member motes of cluster and VCH which works as CH in case CH dies. Thus V-LEACH results more efficient in data delivery and energy efficiency.

3 LEACH Successors Using Multi Hop Communication Model

Data transfer between the BS and CH situated at far distances is done via relay nodes or motes which are now cluster heads. Radio model interprets that energy consumed by motes is proportional to the distance between sender and receiver. Energy consumption is proportional to d^4 if the distance is more than the threshold distance. As the distance between transmitter and receiver is a major factor, researchers aimed their research on cluster formation and size of the cluster. Present section confers about popular multi-hop communication.

3.1   LEACH-B

In the year 2003 Depedri Mahmood *et al.* [20] proposes new strategies for cluster creation and selecting cluster head from motes. The proposed algorithm uses multihop approach, the clusters chosen by the researchers is N_a the motes are N_{TOTAL} distributed uniformly in area of consideration i.e. SXS square meter. Average motes in each cluster are N_{TOT}/N_a non-cluster head motes are $((N_{TOTAL}/N_a) - 1)$ of all the cluster heads is dissipated while transmitting their own packets, retransmitting the packets received from other cluster heads to next cluster head until it reached the base station and energy consumed in advertising. The threshold value is calculated by Eq. 10:

$$T_p(t_i) = \begin{cases} \left(\dfrac{N_a}{N_{TOTAL} - N_a \left(r mod \left[\frac{N_{TOTAL}}{N_a} \right] \right)} \right), & : C_p(t_i) = 1 \\ 0, & : C_p(t_i) = 0 \end{cases} \tag{10}$$

Node p's selection as cluster head depend upon chosen number in between 0 and 1. Node is eligible to become cluster head if it is less than a threshold Tp(ti). Network lifetime in LEACH-B is better than LEACH but it does not perform well in data aggregation task.

3.2   LEACH-ME

In the year 2008 Kumar et al. [21] proposed an extended version of [22], LEACH-ME primary focus of the protocol is on the election of CH. Motes change their clusters and cluster heads as motes are mobile. Relative motions of the nodes among each other, a function defining relativity measure wrt its immediate neighbors are given as in Eq. 12:

$$M_x(t) = \frac{1}{n-1} \sum_{y=0}^{n-1} \left| D'_{xy}(t) \right| \tag{11}$$

Where Dxy is the distance of node x^{th} to all y^{th} neighboring nodes. Motes aggregate data according to TDMA schedule issued by corresponding cluster heads, if presently a node is not sending data to cluster head it goes in sleep mode to save energy.

3.3   C-LEACH

In the year 2010 Asaduzzaman et al. [23] have proposed a cross-layer cooperative diversity protocol for LEACH based WSN. Multiple input multiple output framework based on cooperation is proposed. Multiple CHs are within a single cluster across a layer. After aggregation of data from the motes of the cluster, all the CHs cooperatively send data towards the sink.

3.4   LEACH-Density

In the year 2010 Liu et al. [24] proposed LEACH-D (LEACH based on Density of node distribution) to attain improved network lifetime, the researcher proposed that threshold value as in Eq. 12 is a function of node distribution density to improve connectivity and electing cluster head. Formation of a cluster depends upon the degree of connectivity. Thus, motes join the cluster by looking into the energy attained by cluster head.

$$Th(i) = \frac{p}{1 - p\left(rmod\frac{1}{p}\right)} \cdot \frac{E_{iresidual}}{E_{initial}} \cdot \frac{D_i}{D_{avg}} \tag{12}$$

Where Th(i) is the threshold for i^{th} round $E_{iresidual}$ is present residual energy of mote, $E_{initial}$ is initial energy of the mote, D_i is the degree of connectivity and $D_{average}$ is average connectivity degree of the network.

3.5   SAGA-LEACH

In the year 2012 Zhaou *et al.* [25] proposed the LEACH-SAGA ("Simulated Annealing and Genetic Algorithms"). SAGA LEACH and LEACH are different by the process of CH selection process. The proposed method uses a simulated annealing and genetic algorithm to elect CH while normal LEACH uses random approach. Factors considered are the residual energy of motes, the distance of CH from the cluster center and the average energy of the cluster. The controller algorithm is implemented at the BS. Performance of the proposed protocol is better in terms of network lifetime, CHs are evenly distributed and the energy requirement is less. The proposed protocol can not handle scalability and overhead is high due to complexity.

4   Analysis LEACH Successors

A subjective analysis of LEACH successors is introduced in Table 1 these algorithms are arranged in chronological order. All the mentioned algorithms are compared on various parameters like cluster formation techniques, complexity, delay, energy efficiency, overhead, and scalability. Basic LEACH algorithm has some limits as discussed in Sect. 1. These limitations are addressed in LEACH successors in Sects. 2 and 3. These algorithms show better performance than LEACH in several features like complexity, delay, energy efficiency, overhead, scalability, etc. following conclusion is made from the survey.

(1) Few of the LEACH variants addressed security-related issues but the algorithm proposed increases energy consumption, latest lightweight cryptography techniques can be used to save energy.
(2) Optimization techniques are proposed only on finding the number of cluster and CH selection. Optimization of routing and data aggregation needs to be looked upon.

(3) Renewable energy is a promising research area in WSN. None of the variants utilized renewable energies. Solar power, thermal energy, wind energy, etc. can be used to increase energy efficiency.

(4) Mobility and network coverage is not discussed in any of the LEACH variants.

(5) GPS is the only tool used as location finder in LEACH and its variants. GPS requires a big volume of energy resulting in increased cost.

Table 1. Analysis of LEACH successors.

LEACH successor	Year	Communication model	Cluster formation	Complexity	Delay	Energy efficiency	Overhead	Scalability
LEACH C	2002	Single hop	Centralized	Lo	Lo	Hi	Lo	Lo
LEACH DCHS	2002	Single hop	Distributed	Moderate	Lo	Hi	Hi	Lo
LEACH B	2003	Multi-hop	Distributed	Moderate	Lo	Hi	Hi	Lo
SLEACH	2005	Single hop	Distributed	Complex	Lo	Very Hi	Hi	Moderate
TL-LEACH B	2006	Multi-hop	Distributed	Lo	Lo	Hi	Lo	Lo
LEACH-ME	2008	Multi-hop	Distributed	Complex	Hi	Moderate	Hi	Hi
U LEACH	2010	Single hop	Distributed	Complex	Lo	Hi	Lo	Lo
C LEACH	2010	Multi-hop	Distributed	Complex	Hi	Hi	Hi	Lo
LEACH D	2010	Multi-hop	Distributed	Complex	Lo	Very Hi	Hi	Very Hi
LEACH GA	2011	Single hop	Distributed	Complex	Lo	Hi	Hi	Lo
EP LEACH	2013	Single hop	Distributed	Complex	Lo	Very Hi	Hi	Lo
I LEACH	2013	Single hop	Distributed	Complex	Lo	Hi	Moderate	Lo
SAGA LEACH	2014	Multi-hop	Distributed	Complex	Lo	Hi	Moderate	Hi
V LEACH	2015	Single hop	Distributed	Complex	Lo	Very Hi	Hi	Lo

5 Conclusion

The present paper presents a comprehensive survey of single-hop communication in LEACH and its successors. Cluster formation technique, delay, energy efficiency, overheads cost, scalability, etc. are comparatively analyzed for LEACH and its variants. It is proved by the researchers that LEACH variant algorithms are an improvement over the basic LEACH algorithm. The main achievement of any newly proposed algorithm in WSN is to enhance energy efficiency. According to this survey major of the mentioned algorithms are distributed in nature. While CH selection, energy is a major parameter considered by all the researchers apart from this researcher has looked into other parameters like distance from the BS, the density of motes, location of motes, renewable energy usage, the minimum number of CHs. Many of the researchers have used probabilistic clustering approaches, presently deterministic approaches are also becoming popular, the drawback of deterministic approaches is that they consume more energy and are complex in nature. All variants discussed in the paper claimed to be better than LEACH. Some of the areas of scope are discussed in Sect. 6.

6 Future Scope

LEACH routing algorithm was proposed 19 years back to enhance the lifespan of the wireless sensor networks. It was done by distributing the load equally for data collection from motes, data aggregation from CH to BS. Absence of proper algorithm to process the selection of CH randomly, placing it in the cluster and single-hop communication mode from CH to BS causes hindrance to network lifetime. Further, several alterations are proposed on basic LEACH to overcome these issues. Many variants of LEACH are working on energy efficiency, the need of the day is to do research on security and renewable energy techniques developments for WSN. A new variant of LEACH which uses a hybrid approach, in which cluster head selection is done by Hopfield neural network, data aggregation is done using NSGA and routing is done by swarm intelligence method.

References

1. Arjunan, S., Sujatha, P.: A survey on unequal clustering protocols in wireless sensor networks. J. King Saud Univ. Comput. Inf. Sci. **31**, 304–317 (2019)
2. Arjunan, S., Sujatha, P.: Lifetime maximization of wireless sensor network using fuzzy based unequal clustering and ACO based routing hybrid protocol. Appl. Intell. **48**(8), 2229–2246 (2018)
3. Alkhatib, A.A.A., Baicher, G.S.: Wireless sensor network architecture. In: International Conference on Computer Networks and Communication Systems, CNCS, vol. 35, pp. 11–15 (2012)
4. Li, C., Zhang, H., Hao, B., Li, J.: A survey on routing protocols for large-scale wireless sensor networks. Sensors **11**(4), 3498–3526 (2011)
5. Ilyas, M., Mahgoub, I.: Handbook of Sensor Networks: Compact Wireless and Wired Sensing Systems. CRC Press, Boca Raton (2005)
6. Pino-Povedano, S., Arroyo-Valles, R., Cid-Sueiro, J.: Selective forwarding for energy-efficient target tracking in sensor networks. Sig. Process. **94**(1), 557–569 (2014)
7. Heinzelman, W.R., Chandrakasan, A., Balakrishnan, H.: Energy-efficient communication protocol for wireless microsensor networks. In: Hawaii International Conference on System Sciences (2000)
8. Ye, M., Li, C., Chen, A.G., Wu, J.: EECS: an energy efficient clustering scheme in wireless sensor networks. In: 24th IEEE International Performance, Computing and Communications Conference, IPCCC 2005, pp. 535–540 (2005)
9. Younis, O., Fahmy, S.: HEED: a hybrid, energy-efficient, distributed clustering approach for ad hoc sensor networks. IEEE Trans. Mob. Comput. **3**(4), 366–379 (2004)
10. Lindsey, S., Raghavendra, C.S.: PEGASIS: power-efficient gathering in sensor information systems. In: IEEE Aerospace Conference Proceedings, vol. 3, pp. 1125–1130 (2002)
11. Hong, J., Kook, J., Lee, S., Kwon, D., Yi, S.: TEEN: a routing protocol for enhanced efficiency in wireless sensor networks. Inf. Syst. Front. **11**(5), 513–521 (2009)
12. Hong, J., Kook, J., Lee, S., Kwon, D., Yi, S.: T-LEACH: the method of threshold-based cluster head replacement for wireless sensor networks. Inf. Syst. Front. **11**(5), 513–521 (2009)
13. Singh, S.K., Kumar, P., Singh, J.P.: A survey on successors of LEACH protocol. IEEE Access **5**, 4298–4328 (2017)

14. Heinzelman, W.B., Chandrakasan, A.P., Balakrishnan, H.: An application-specific protocol architecture for wireless microsensor networks, vol. 1, no. 4, pp. 660–670 (2002)
15. Handy, M.J., Haase, M., Timmermann, D.: Low energy adaptive clustering hierarchy with deterministic cluster-head selection. In: 4th International Workshop Mobile Wireless Communication Network, pp. 368–372
16. Ren, P., Qian, J., Li, L., Zhao, Z., Li, X.: Unequal clustering scheme based LEACH for wireless sensor networks. In: Proceedings of the 4th International Conference on Genetic and Evolutionary Computing, ICGEC 2010, pp. 90–93 (2010)
17. Singh, A., Kaur, R., Sharma, B., Acharjee, A.: Literature review of nature inspired computing based search & optimization approaches, vol. 4, pp. 1151–1158 (2018)
18. Liu, J., Ravishankar, C.V.: LEACH-GA: genetic algorithm-based energy-efficient adaptive clustering protocol for wireless sensor networks, vol. 1, no. 1, pp. 79–85 (2011)
19. Xiao, M., Zhang, X., Dong, Y.: An effective routing protocol for energy. In: IEEE Wireless Communications and Networking Conference (WCNC), pp. 2080–2084 (2013)
20. Lattanzi, E., Regini, E., Acquaviva, A., Bogliolo, A.: Energetic sustainability of routing algorithms for energy-harvesting wireless sensor networks. Comput. Commun. 30(14–15), 2976–2986 (2007)
21. Beiranvand, Z., Patooghy, A., Fazeli, M.: I-LEACH: an efficient routing algorithm to improve performance & to reduce energy consumption in wireless sensor networks. In: 2013 5th Conference on Information and Knowledge Technology, IKT 2013, pp. 13–18 (2013)
22. Sasikala, S.D., Sangameswaran, N., Aravindh, P.: Improving the energy efficiency of LEACH protocol using VCH in wireless sensor network. PS - Polit. Sci. Polit. 3(2), 918–924 (2015)
23. Depedri, A., Zanella, A., Verdone, R.: An energy-efficient protocol for wireless sensor networks. In: Autonomous Intelligent Networks and Systems (AINS), Menlo Park, CA, USA (2003)
24. Kumar, G.S., Vinu, P.M., Jacob, K.P.: Mobility metric based LEACH-mobile protocol, pp. 248–253 (2008)
25. He, S., Dai, Y., Zhou, R., Zhao, S.: A clustering routing protocol for energy balance of WSN based on genetic clustering algorithm. IERI Procedia 2(2), 788–793 (2012)

DELBMRFS: Design of Efficient Load Balanced Multicast Routing Protocol for Wireless Mobile Ad-hoc Network Based on Fibonacci Sequence Approach

Ajay Kumar Yadav[1] and Rohit Kumar Yadav[2(✉)]

[1] Department of Computer Science and Engineering, Banasthali Vidyapith,
Jaipur 304022, Rajasthan, India
ajay.iitdhn@gmail.com
[2] Institute of Information Technology Management, D-29, Institutional Area,
Janakpuri 110058, New Delhi, India
rohit.ism.123@gmail.com

Abstract. In a mobile Ad-hoc network, the conservation of resources is a very important issue. So, in order to save the same, information should be send using multicast technique. But, multicasting in mobile Ad-hoc network is a very difficult task due to affecting various factors like dynamic topology nature, large variation of signal strength, lack of battery power, network congestion and so on. In this proposal we have lighted over the network congestion in order to utilize the network resource properly. So, this paper proposes an Efficient Load Balanced Multipath Multicast Routing Protocol using Fibonacci Sequence (ELB-MMRFS) approach to balance the overhead/congestion. In this proposal the source node send the information over different routing paths using the Fibonacci sequence number. Such transmission of the information might be balance the network overhead that leads to better performance. The proposed scheme is be simulated on very popular simulator NS-2 and the results are measured in terms of the PDR and $E2E$, finally the outcomes are compared with some present routing protocol like MAODV and RMAODV.

Keywords: Wireless ad-hoc network · Mobility · Load · Multicast routing · Fibonacci sequence · Multipath

1 Introduction

A mobile ad-hoc network (MANETs) is a wireless network without existing a permanent infrastructure and base station, here the devices can move all over the shop in any direction. The main aim of such network is required to save the data at each devices that are used to propagate the data from source node to target nodes at a time [1–4]. Recently, there are a lots of application of MANET

© Springer Nature Singapore Pte Ltd. 2020
P. K. Singh et al. (Eds.): FTNCT 2019, CCIS 1206, pp. 14–21, 2020.
https://doi.org/10.1007/978-981-15-4451-4_2

[5–9], the suitable applications of the MANETs is used in the areas where quick dilation, dynamic assortment are needed. It have like army battlefields, state of emergency search operation and liberation operation etc. [7,10,11].

During the previous few years, several analysis papers are printed over multicast routing for mobile ad-hoc network and numerous multicast routing protocols are developed [10,12–17] for cluster communication up to currently. The present multicast routing protocols square measure essentially categorized in to several categories like tree, mesh and hybrid based routing protocols that are expostulated later. The entire assortment of the multicast protocols is summarized in a given literature [9].

The main disadvantage of using such multicast routing protocols as discussed above leads to the congestion problem when the wireless network is heavily loaded. It has been discussed already, that the overcrowding is one of the most prominence factor of data packet loss in wireless mobile ad-hoc network. Therefore, multipath based multicast routing protocols provide an excellent solution for such issues [18]. However, an algorithm is used to find the entire all possible multicast routing path to send the data packets optimally over these searched routing paths. After facing all these issues, we have motivated to developed a Load Balanced Multipath Multicast Routing Protocol using Fibonacci sequence approach in order to reduce the network congestion.

The remaining part of the paper is managed as follows. Section 2 describe the contribution of the proposed method. The explanation of proposed protocol "Design of an Efficient Load Balanced Multicast Routing Protocol using Fibonacci Sequence (DELBMRFS)" approach is shown in Sect. 3. The simulation outcomes, performance evaluation and analysis of the proposal is compared with some other e multicast routing protocols such as ($MAODV$) [19] and ($RMAODV$) in Sect. 4 and finally the Sect. 5 describe conclusions. Abbreviation that are considered in proposal is tabulated in Table 1.

Table 1. Symbol table

S	Source
MCD	Multicast destination
U_{id}	Unique id
RPI	Routing path information
ReP	Reverse routing path information
RT	Routing table
RQ	Request packet
RP	Reply packet

2   Contribution

Referring congestion issue in a ad-hoc network, this paper proposes Design of an Efficient Load Balanced Multicast Routing Protocol using Fibonacci Sequence (DELBMMRFS) that decreases the congestion/network overhead with finding the many routing paths and diffuse the transmitted information over these routing paths following the concept of *Fibonaccisequence*. Such dispensation decrease packets loss and renovate the network performance. Due to that fact the proposed protocol suggested the shortest paths more efficiently and get better load balance in a wireless network as described in Sect. 3. Mathematically, Fibonacci sequence is one of the most famous formulas in mathematics that is defined as *"Each number in the sequence is sum of two numbers that precede it"*, as shown by the following equation:

$$F(n) = \begin{cases} 0, & \text{if } n = 0. \\ 1, & \text{if } n = 1. \\ f_{n-2} + f_{n-1} & \text{otherwise if } n > 2 \end{cases} \tag{1}$$

3   Proposed Methodology

3.1   Basic Idea

In this section, we have discussed our proposed methodology "Design of an Efficient Load Balanced Multicast Routing Protocol using Fibonacci Sequence (DELBMRFS) approach" that reduces the network overhead and renovate the network performance. In order to explain the proposed idea, we consider a network as depict in Fig. 1, where S is origin node and M, N are target nodes. Let the node S want to send the information to a group of target nodes say M and N, there is four possible routes are available between them which are $SAEMN, SBFMN, SBGMN$ and $SCDGMN$. In our proposed algorithm it has been assumed that if the network consist of P number of routes then all the paths are arranged in the increasing order according to having the intermediate hops and each routing path are allocated a weight which depends upon number of hopes associated with that particular routes. Therefore the proposed algorithm allocate the different weights for these paths as: Fib$P$, Fib$(P - 1)$, Fib$(P - 2)$...... Fib(2) and Fib(1) respectively according to number of intermediate hop in the routing path.

3.2   Routing Mechanism

Let the origin node want to send the packet, route discovery mechanism is to be executed. Every nodes in the network contains a routing table (RT). This table holds various information about its nearby node such as source address, muticast destination address, next hop address etc.

3.3   Route Discovery Phase

When the origin device wish to send information to a group of target nodes, it will effort to discover an efficient routing paths. To get the same, it will begin the route search process where the (RQ) packets has been broadcasted through out the network. The nodes that are coming under its transmission range will get it. While the (RQ) packets have been transmitted in a wireless mobile network it carried out many information in its header: $\{S,\ MCD,\ U_{id},\ RP\}$, where S refer the origin node, MCD refer destination address, U_{id} refer message unique id that is used to identify the duplicate RQ packets, RP is used to store the entire routing path information while traversing across the network.

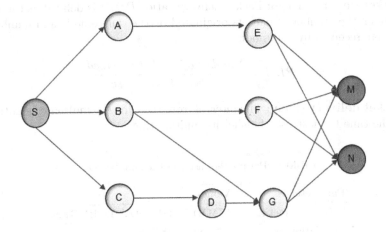

Fig. 1.

In Fig. 1, the source node S wish to transmit the packets so, it broadcast the $RREQ$ packets across the network in order to find the relevant routing path, let the node A, B, and C have received the $RREQ$ packets. After getting this by the node A, B, and C it again through the same packet further across the network to its neighbouring nodes E, F, D and G and receive the $RREQ$ packets, this forwarding operation is carried out until destination nodes (M, N) received the packets. After receiving the $RREQ$ packets the destination node send the reply packet $(RREP)$ to the source node S, after receiving the reply packet by the source node S it decided to transmit the data packets over the relevant multicast routing path that is discovered by using the concept of Fibonacci Sequence approach. Therefore, the proposed protocol reduces the network congestion as well as it also renovate the network performance in term of packet delivery ratio and delay.

4   Performance Evaluation

This part introduces the metrics that are used in our simulation and the outcome of designed protocol is be collated with some extant multi-cast routing methods.

The experiment is run over NS-2 [20] simulator. The size of network area in our experiment is 100 m × 100 m having 40 mobile devices. The speed of each mobile nodes are from 1 to 25 m/s. The forwarding range was 150 m. The size of data packets is 225 bytes. The CBR has been consider as a traffic type in our experiment. The parameters that are considered in our experiment are mentioned in Table 2. The results and execution evaluation of designed protocol is explained with the help of following metrics:

1. **Packet delivery ratio:** Packet delivery ratio (PDR) is defined as the ratio between the number of packets originated by the source node and number of packets received by sink node.

$$PDR = \frac{Number\ of\ packet\ received}{Number\ of\ packet\ sent}$$

2. **Packet delivery delay:** The interval from the time the multicast is initiated to the time the last host finishes its multicasting.

Table 2. Parameters used in the simulations

Parameters	Values
Examined methods	MAODV, RMAODV, DLBMRFS
Simulation area	1000 m × 1000 m
Number of nodes	40
Multicast group size	5–40
Speed of mobility	1–25 m/s
Mobility model	Random waypoint model
Propagation models	Free space propagation model
Transmission ranges	150 m
Packet size	225 bytes

4.1   Simulation Analysis

The simulation depict, the effect of mobility speed over PDR and $E\ 2\ E$ delay of the MAODV, RMAODV, and the proposed technique (DELBMRFS). These protocols have been rum for PDR ratio and $E-2E$ delay against several mobility speed. The simulation depict the performance of the same under multiple mobility speeds.

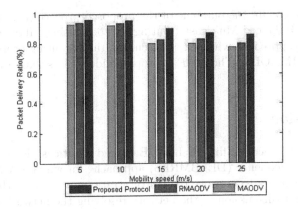

Fig. 2. Packet delivery ratio against mobility speed

The Fig. 2, shows the PDR decreases as speed of the node increases. Because of having high speed of a nodes, leads to communication gap between the mobile devices. The result is loss of information during broadcasting the same. The simulated graph show that the PDR is high when speed of the node is low. The proposed protocol i.e. "Design of an Efficient Load Balanced Multicast Routing Protocol using Fibonacci Sequence (DELBMRFS) approach" gains best PDR in compare to MAODV, RMAODV. Thus, outcome of the proposed mechanism in terms of PDR is better in compare to above protocols as discussed.

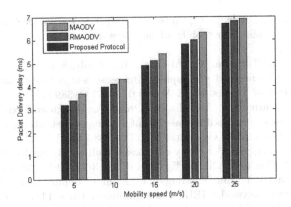

Fig. 3. Packet delivery delay (ms) against mobility speed

Figure 3 depict that the speed of a node increases, the end to end delay also increases due to having high mobility speed. Because, while the information is to be transmitted from origin node to a group of target nodes there is more probability to disjoin the communication Chanel among the mobile devices due to having high speed. We collate the outcome of the proposed protocol i.e. "Design of an Efficient Load Balanced Multicast Routing Protocol using Fibonacci Sequence (DELBMRFS) approach" with some present multicast routing protocols such as MAODV and RMAODV. The PDR of proposed idea is less than other protocols as discussed above.

5   Conclusion

The proposed protocol "Efficient Load Balanced Multicast Routing Protocol using Fibonacci Sequence (DELBMRFS) approach" for wireless MANETs. The proposed protocol try to improve the delivery ratio and decrease the delay during information transmission in the network resolving the network traffic issues using proposed mechanism. Simulation outcome show that the proposed technique is good in compare to MAODV and RMAODV in terms of the PDR and $E2E$ delay. Moreover, the network traffic is to be reduces by distributing the data packet over different discovered routing path as well as it also improve the network lifetime.

References

1. Junhai, L., Liu, X., Danxia, Y.: Research on multicast routing protocols for mobile ad-hoc networks. Comput. Netw. **52**(5), 988–997 (2008)
2. Cheng, H., Cao, J., Fan, X.: Gmzrp: geography-aided multicast zone routing protocol in mobile ad hoc networks. Mobile Networks and Applications **14**(2), 165–177 (2009)
3. Moussaoui, A., Semchedine, F., Boukerram, A.: A link-state QoS routing protocol based on link stability for mobile ad hoc networks. J. Netw. Comput. Appl. **39**, 117–125 (2014)
4. Hasan, M.Z., Al-Turjman, F., Al-Rizzo, H.: Analysis of cross-layer design of Quality-of-Service forward geographic wireless sensor network routing strategies in green Internet of Things. IEEE Access **6**, 20371–20389 (2018)
5. Jagannath, J., Furman, S., Melodia, T., Drozd, A.: Design and experimental evaluation of a cross-layer deadline-based joint routing and spectrum allocation algorithm. IEEE Trans. Mob. Comput. **18**, 1774–1788 (2018)
6. Santhi, G., Nachiappan, A.: Fuzzy-cost based multiconstrained QoS routing with mobility prediction in MANETs. Egypt. Inf. J. **13**(1), 19–25 (2012)
7. Junhai, L., Danxia, Y., Liu, X., Mingyu, F.: A survey of multicast routing protocols for mobile ad-hoc networks. IEEE Commun. Surv. Tutor **11**(1), 78–91 (2009)
8. Yadav, A.K., Das, S.K., Tripathi, S.: EFMMRP: design of efficient fuzzy based multi-constraint multicast routing protocol for wireless ad-hoc network. Comput. Netw. **118**, 15–23 (2017)
9. Torkestani, J.A., Meybodi, M.R.: Mobility-based multicast routing algorithm for wireless mobile ad-hoc networks: a learning automata approach. Comput. Commun. **33**(6), 721–735 (2010)
10. Wang, T., Wen, C.-K., Wang, H., Gao, F., Jiang, T., Jin, S.: Deep learning for wireless physical layer: opportunities and challenges. China Commun. **14**(11), 92–111 (2017)

11. Biradar, R.C., Manvi, S.S.: Review of multicast routing mechanisms in mobile ad hoc networks. J. Netw. Comput. Appl. **35**(1), 221–239 (2012)
12. Thiagarajan, R., Moorthi, M.: Efficient routing protocols for mobile ad hoc network. In: 2017 Third International Conference on Advances in Electrical, Electronics, Information, Communication and Bio-informatics (AEEICB), pp. 427–431. IEEE (2017)
13. Chen, X., Feng, J., Zhou, Z., Jun, W., Perera, C.: Cross-layer optimization for cooperative content distribution in multihop device-to-device networks. IEEE IoT J. **6**(1), 278–287 (2017)
14. Yadav, A.K., Tripathi, S.: QMRPRNS: design of QoS multicast routing protocol using reliable node selection scheme for MANETs. Peer-to-Peer Netw. Appl. **10**(4), 897–909 (2017)
15. Meghanathan, N.: A location prediction based routing protocol and its extensions for multicast and multi-path routing in mobile ad hoc networks. Ad Hoc Netw. **9**(7), 1104–1126 (2011)
16. Chang, C.-Y., Wang, Y.-P., Chao, H.-C.: An efficient mesh-based core multicast routing protocol on MANETs. J. Internet Technol. **8**(2), 229–239 (2007)
17. Singh, J., Singh, A., Shree, R.: An assessment of frequently adopted unsecure patterns in mobile ad hoc network: requirement and security management perspective. Int. J. Comput. Appl. **24**(9), 0975–8887 (2011)
18. Tashtoush, Y., Darwish, O., Hayajneh, M.: Fibonacci sequence based multipath load balancing approach for mobile ad hoc networks. Ad Hoc Netw. **16**, 237–246 (2014)
19. Royer, E.M., Perkins, C.E.: Multicast operation of the ad-hoc on-demand distance vector routing protocol. In: Proceedings of the 5th Annual ACM/IEEE International Conference on Mobile Computing and Networking, pp. 207–218. ACM (1999)
20. The network simulator 2. http://www.isi.edu/nsnam/ns/index.html/

Analytical Study of Wireless Ad-Hoc Networks: Types, Characteristics, Differences, Applications, Protocols

Sadiq Ghalib[1(✉)], Abdulghani Kasem[2], and Aleem Ali[1]

[1] Department of Electronics and Communications Engineering,
Gautam Buddha University, Greater Noida, UP, India
sadiqmohmah@gmail.com, aali3@jmi.ac.in
[2] Department of Electronics and Communications Engineering,
University of Science and Technology, Khartoum, Sudan
Alhaidari72@gmail.com

Abstract. Ad Hoc usually relates to an explanation of planning to address a particular issue or function, which although not generic, but also is inappropriate for the achievement of the other objectives. The ad-hoc networks have been particularly designed for establishing communications in environments where they are extremely complicated or infeasible for creating the specific network infrastructure. Most of these ad hoc networks are spontaneously formed by the consumers. The astounding reality is that the number of devices which are able to maintain wireless communications is increasing on a daily basis. Ad hoc networks are beneficial for implementation in considerable sets of scenarios, for instance, in universities, museums, emergency relief or investigation tasks, where the ability to allocate resources and services is one of the primary attentions. In this paper detailed clarifications of the wireless ad-hoc networks, their historical reviews and application in present scenarios. It clarifies several types of such networks like, mobile ad hoc networks (MANETs), wireless sensor networks (WSNs), wireless mesh networks (WMNs), and vehicular ad hoc networks (VANETs). Then, it also concentrates primarily on the utilization of the MANET, besides achieving the crucial task of classifications, characteristics, challenges, potential fields for the implementation of the ad hoc, differences and the developments of routing protocols.

Keywords: Ad-Hoc · MANET · VANET · WMN · WSN · Protocol

1 Introduction

The initial creation of the ad-hoc network returns to 1972. During this time period, it was named as packet radio network (PRNET). In order to synchronize with areal locations having uncertain conditions, medium access control (MAC) methods such as (ALOHA) [9] and carrier sense medium access (CSMA) [48] and distance vector routing protocols such as PRNETs were utilized on an experimental foundation for providing network capacities to environments where building infrastructure was not possible [10]. The second version of ad hoc networks appeared in 1980s when the

© Springer Nature Singapore Pte Ltd. 2020
P. K. Singh et al. (Eds.): FTNCT 2019, CCIS 1206, pp. 22–40, 2020.
https://doi.org/10.1007/978-981-15-4451-4_3

ad-hoc network system was likely more improved and performed like a section of the existing adaptive radio networks (SURAN) plan. This assisted in the creation of a packet switched network in environments where infrastructures are not available. In 1990s, the notion of trade ad hoc networks emerged with proliferation of laptops and other such communication devices. Simultaneously, the concept of a set of mobile nodes was being suggested at various research conferences. The sub-committee of IEEE 802.11 used an expression "Ad hoc network" and the research society began examining the chance of expanding the ad-hoc network in civil applications. Later in the middle of the 1990s, within the Internet engineering team forces IETF, the mobile ad hoc network working groups were created for standardizing routing path protocols of ad hoc network. The evolution of the routing paths inside the workgroup and the wider society caused creating the protocol of the reactive routing path and the protocol of the proactive routing path. After a brief period, the sub-committee of IEEE 802.11 standardized a protocol regarding medium access which relied on evading the collision and tolerance of hidden stations to build models with mobile ad hoc networks, thereby provisioning its application beyond laptops and PCMCIA compatible 802.11b wireless PC card. Radio local area networks of high-performance (HYPERLAN) and Bluetooth were some of the other ad hoc networks standards which have systematized and advanced ad hoc networks [1]. Potential fields for implementing the ad hoc [8, 12]:-

Disaster Zones: emergency actions and relief procedures in areas where communication infrastructure is not available.

Civilian environment: a multimedia network can be automatically created for circulating data among conference associates, attendances at a conferences or lectures, etc.

Personal district networks: also famous as PAN, they consist of a node that may be a laptop, a mobile phone, personal digital assistant, etc.

Tactical and governmental utilizations: it allows communication between agents, major offices & means of transportation.

Reconnaissance task: for creating a network in regions where infrastructure is not available.

Environment monitoring: to effortlessly deploy in large regions for monitoring natural parameters, for instance, temperature or moisture.

2   Classification of Ad-Hoc Networks

An ad-hoc network is created by means of group of wireless nodes which are able to communicate with one another. They do not have a steady network infrastructure or managerial support. Due to the restricted communication range of the wireless networks, various intermediate nodes most likely need at least one node for transferring information to another node within the network. Every one of the nodes may function like a terminal host or a router for forwarding data to the other mobile terminals. Nodes may either change position arbitrarily or empty their storage cells so as to generate variations in the topology of the network. Eventually, the ad-hoc network should be dynamically adjusted for sustaining the transmissions regardless of these variations.

Simultaneously, due to limited storage cells and restricted coverage region, the energy consumed should be kept minimal, as under certain situations, the storages cells are not replaceable. Based on the dependability of nodes on the coverage region, the ad-hoc networks are categorized the following:

- *Body area networks (BANs):* such as MP3 players, portable phones, and healthcare equipments.
- *Personal area networks (PANs):* it interconnects the BAN network with the environment (printers, at shows or presentations…).
- *Local area networks (LANs):* computer devices, personal digital assistants (PDAs), portable phones.
- *Wide area networks (WANs):* ad hoc networks between buildings which require access to additional networks.

In Fig. 1 a diagrammatic association of one network with another network is shown. Based on their utilizations, these networks are categorized into: Mobile ad-hoc networks (MANET), wireless sensor networks (WSN), wireless mesh networks (WMN) and vehicular ad hoc networks (VANET). The major features and uses of these networks are illustrated for the coming sections. For this work, we have concentrated on MANETs in detail.

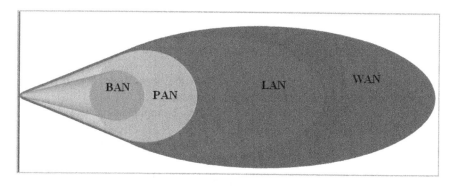

Fig. 1. Ad-hoc network coverage regions

2.1 Wireless Mesh Network

Wireless mesh network (WMNs) [2] is local area network (LANs) which uses one of the two link methods: complete mesh topologies or incomplete mesh topologies. In the complete mesh topology, every one of nodes (workstations or other such devices) is instantaneously linked to every one of others nodes, whereas in incomplete mesh topology, only a number of the nodes are linked to those other nodes that share the most of the information.

A mesh network is trustworthy network and it presents repetitions so that, if a single node is not able to work a long period, all other neighboring nodes are able to connect with one another, either immediately or through one or more of middle nodes. The construction of the mesh network is an initial stage in the direction of presenting a high bandwidth network through a particular transmission region. It is constructed from peer wireless devices which must not be established into a wired gateway as done at conventional wireless LAN entrance locations. Mesh construction provides signal intensity by means of disintegrating long distances into sequences of short hops. Depending on their awareness of the network, middle nodes not only support the signal but also provide routing in a cooperative manner. This architecture when done with precise designing can present high bandwidth, better spectral competence, and efficient economic use through the transmission region. For providing one example, wireless mesh network enables customers to form mesh networks with other wireless mesh networks in addition to wired network entries. A mesh network generally has a comparatively steady topology excluding of cases such as that incidental failure of the nodes or the increase in the number of novel nodes.

The data is apparently assembled at the massive customers' and where the change is irregular. In practice, all the data required in the establishment of mesh networks is either sent to or from the port. However, inside the ad-hoc networks or wireless mesh networks, traffic usually streams between random pairs of customers. These kinds of infrastructures are able to be either decentralized (no main server) or centralized handling system (existing of a main server) since both of them are comparatively lower at cost and flexible since every one of nodes requires just for transmitting as much as the following node is. The nodes operate like routers for transmitting information from close nodes to peers which are very distant for joining in an individual hop and performing a network which is able to cross larger ranges. The properties of the mesh network are trustworthy as every node is linked to various other additional nodes. In case one of the nodes falls outside the network because of the equipment failure or any other cause, its neighbors are able to discover another route through the use of a routing protocol. Mesh network can be incorporated either in stationary or portable devices. Certain distinct solutions to the transmission requirements, for instance in complex environments like emergencies, subways, and petroleum equipment, high-speed uti- lizations of mobile video, on-board general transportation. An important utilization of

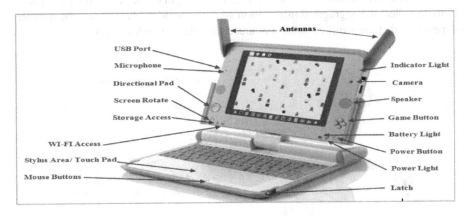

Fig. 2. OLPC laptop with mesh network abilities

the wireless mesh network is Voice over Internet protocol (VoIP) that enhances a quality of service (QoS) of a system.

A wireless mesh can boost regional phone calls when routed through the mesh network. Relation to the manifold uses of the mesh network, the project of One Laptop Per Child (OLPC) as in the Fig. 2 utilizes this technology at the present time. It creates inexpensive laptops that are able to provide routing data demands (for example, internet access) in undeveloped regions where building network infrastructure is not possible/feasible.

2.2 Wireless Sensor Network

A wireless ad-hoc sensor network (WSN) [3] comprises of a number of sensors that are distributed over a geographical region. Every one of the sensors has wireless transmission abilities and a certain level of intelligence to handle the signal and the networking of the information. Generally, a large number of small and weightless wireless nodes are created for observing the environment of a scheme by measuring natural parameters for example temperature, pressure, moisture, motion, …etc. Two methods for classifying wireless ad hoc sensor network are: if the nodes are separately addressable or not, and if information is collected in the network. A single sensor has a restricted sensing area, faster power processing, and energy; whereas, a sensor network is more powerful, dependable and encompasses a larger coverage area. As soon as numerous nodes sense the same proceedings, a wireless sensor network features its error toleration ability. Also when the nodes cooperate with their information; a precise and a longer existing wireless sensor network is established. The major processes involved in the sensor network are that the transmission of the information from the sensors to the sink and the collection of such information before transferring it back to the sink. It is our responsibility to imperatively consider optimum placement and control of sensor node, for example, the network sensor nodes employed inside a closed region such as a car garage must be handled separately so that no hindrance is encountered while defining sensor networks in open areas. If any node requires determining the temperature in the nook of a room, in that case addressability may not be very significant. Every one of nodes in a certain area is able to reply. The strength of the sensor network lies in ability to collect the aggregated information so as to considerably decrease the number of messages that are required to be forwarded over the network (Fig. 3).

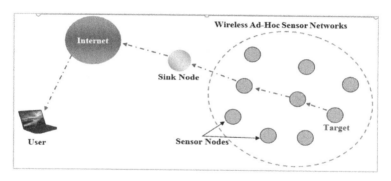

Fig. 3. A wireless sensor network

WSN is Used in the Domains

- *Environment:* detecting woods blaze, flood discovery, ecosystem comprising of chemical, physical, acoustic, image sensors that follow the parameters of universal change, floats for warning swimmers about unsafe bacteria levels, prediction of earthquakes, sensing the natural environment.
- *Home uses:* for domestic purposes such as controlling of ovens and refrigerators remotely, controlling of light and atmospheric conditions, security and monitoring, automatic watering of plants and pet feeding…etc.
- *Uses of weather:* Assessment of rainfall, storms with thunder, and hurricane forecasts.
- *Governmental uses:* monitoring and control of battlefield, and in discovery of chemical or biological weapon.
- *Office uses:* mechanical administration of air flow, a temperature of various portions of the building, deployment of water sprayers that operate after detecting fire.
- *Industrial uses:* inventory monitoring of repositories by placing sensors devices on the products for tracking their motion.
- *Visitor room control and monitoring:* light and climate monitoring, mini-bar administration.
- Seed germination administration: effective cultivation.
- *Monitoring of health care:* diagnosis of patients and surveillance of conditions such as heart rate, blood pressure. WSNs can be utilized for evading the adverse effects of cables around the sick person (notice Fig. 4).

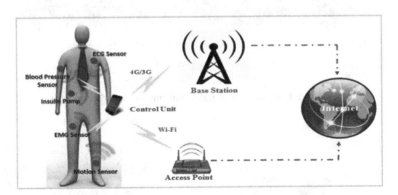

Fig. 4. Sensors network of a sick person (healthcare use)

2.3 Vehicular Ad Hoc Networks

Vehicular ad hoc networks (VANETs) [4] are a modern type from beneficial networks that provide an exchange of traffic data in a cooperative context between vehicles. It is envisioned to be a great revolution in driving, and also presents novel services for instance:-

- *Road integrity:* it also enhances protection in serious or unforeseen driving cases such as fog, accident, and includes effective techniques for preventing the accidents.
- *Traffic administration:* dynamic route planning through cooperative information exchange between vehicles that increases road space and decreases travelling time.
- *Multimedia:* download the content of the multimedia straight from vehicles and also exchange the contents among them.
- *Pollution decrease:* driving improves competence which causes the pollution.
- *Low cost in the vehicle security establishment:* the system process bare minimum maintenance costs and thus collaborates to increase its distribution.
- *Common transport:* improves competence which attracts customers.

Applications founded on VANETs are expanding today. Traffic view is a vehicle that uses a vehicle for actual route designing. Vehicles disseminate beneficial traffic data using short range communications through the use of additional vehicles like routers, as shown in Figs. 5 and 6. This approach, when enforced, can help drivers with

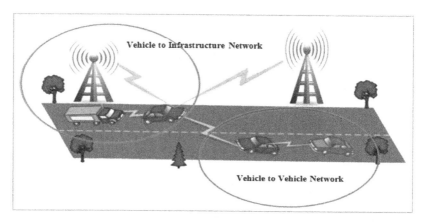

Fig. 5. VANET application of traffic information from a main base

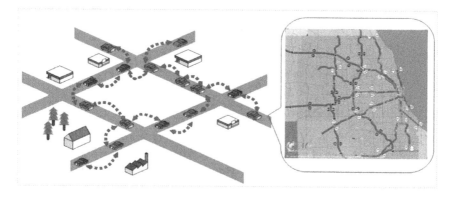

Fig. 6. Disseminating traffic information in VANETs for other users

data regarding accidents and optimum route determination. It can also be used for accessing Taxi from portable devices such as phones, PDAs. Relying on its effective execution, one can also adapt the lights of traffic as per the intensity of the traffic. In addition, the allocation of a particular frequency band is provided to comply with the foundation of worldwide communications standards between cars.

In VANET, the coordinative speed amongst the nodes is much considerable and therefore the link life is much less than for a MANET.

For avoiding the individual results due to minimum life connectivity, the routing protocols must be quick and effective. There is no requirement for a stationary infrastructure as only some ports of Internet are required over the path for accessing the network if and when necessitated. It is a scalable, inexpensive and simple network for implementation by various types of users. Some features of VANETs in comparison with the established infrastructure based and cellular communications are presented in Table 1.

Table 1. VANET vs. the established infrastructure and the cellular communication

	Vehicular communication		
Parameter	Infrastructure based	Cellular systems	VANETs
Delay	Medium	High	Low
Link availability	Low	Low-Medium	Medium-High
Data rate	Medium-High	Low-Medium	High
System availability			
Local	High	High	High
Global	Low	Medium	High
Connection flexibility	Low	Low	High
Costs			
Initial	High	High	Medium-High
Operation	Medium	Medium-High	Null-Low
Service coverage area	Medium	High	Low-Medium
Geographical data?	No	No	Yes
Driving security application support?	Low-Medium	Low	High

VANETs are able to present a wide range of services and hence contribute towards establishing a secure leadership, with minimum cost. The European Commission, a powerful supporter of the technology, is able to stop the accidents through the use of smart car integrity systems, such as, airbag, seatbelt, ABS brake along with VANET that are able to enhance security at a minimal cost. Also, safety awareness attempts at accelerating the market introduction of such type of life-saving technologies (Table 2).

Table 2. The major differences between MANETs and VANETs

MANET	VANET
No infrastructures	Network nodes are vehicle well equipped
Random movements	Nodes follow guidelines (roads, streets)
Restricted battery life	No energy restrictions

2.4   Mobile Ad-Hoc Networks

Mobile ad hoc networks (MANETs) are set of two or more devices or nodes called terminals that are linked through wireless connections and also have ability to configure a network that can connect together in the absence of any central administrative support. In addition to this, the wireless nodes are dynamically able to create a network for exchanging data without utilizing any existing stationary network infrastructure. It also provides an independent system in which movable hosts are linked using wireless connections that are free to be dynamic and sometimes operate like routers simultaneously. Each node within the wireless ad hoc network operates like a router and a host. The topology of network is dynamic since the connection between the nodes may change over time, and as a result, some the nodes deserts and some new nodes connected. These particular characteristics of mobile Ad-hoc networks (MANETs) have

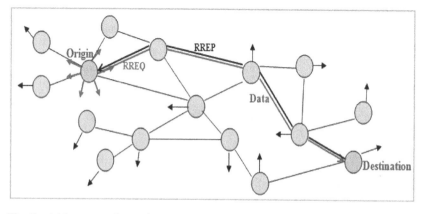

Fig. 7. Ad-hoc networks: nodes move at random in different ways and various speeds

Fig. 8. MANET in a Tokyo crossway

fetched of this technology substantial purposes along with some actual challenges [5, 6]. Each one of the nodes or devices in charge of organizing themselves dynamically, i.e. for establishing connection between each other and for providing the required operating network without any installation of fastened infrastructure or ventral administration. Figure 8 shows random nodes with a dissimilar orientations and velocities [5, 7].

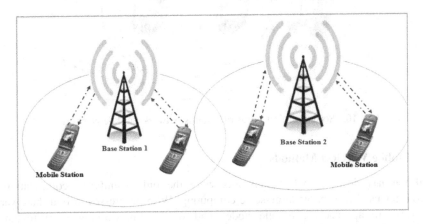

Fig. 9. Scenario of an infrastructure network

MANETs [1, 8] have drawn much consideration from the research societies in the previous years, as a result of which significant technical progress has been achieved. Recently, it is seen that the multi-hop networks have envisioned as significant access to the next-generation network where the request of multimedia services via the end user are in demand. In Fig. 9, an illustration of crossway in a city is visualized in which the users fetch wireless nodes that automatically create a MANET for cooperating distribution of information. The provisions of these multimedia services necessitate guaranteed QoS providing, that is still an open argument in ad-hoc networks.

Salient features of MANETs, like, ability to move, dynamic change of structure of network, limitations of energy, absence of central infrastructure and variable connection capacity, makes the yielding of QoS from this network a challenging task. These queries created due to self-arrangement and system adjustments are matters of key significance in a MANET. As a consequence, instead of assigning alternative stationary network arrangement parameters, the reformed process must be capable of modifying the structure as per on the fly scheme, which is in proportion to the present environmental parameters. The QoS achieved through the use of the network does not rely on outcome from all individual network layers. Nevertheless, concerning organized efforts from every one of layers, it is indeed desirable to improve effective solutions founded on cross layer methods that are also capable of taking into consideration various technical designations of the protocol stack (Fig. 7).

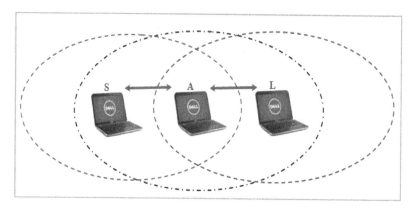

Fig. 10. Scenario of an infrastructureless network (ad-hoc Network)

2.5   Mobile Wireless Methods

Until the last decade, mobile networks were the only significant computational approaches used to support large-scale computing. With progresses in both hardware and software approaches, mobile nodes and wireless networking were together employed for implementing familiar and diverse network environments. At present we consider a very significant method for enabling movable wireless network or IEEE 802.11 that helps a connection amongst many mobile nodes [5, 9, 10]. First the infrastructure of wireless network and then of the ad-hoc network (infrastructureless wireless network) is discussed. We will explain both of the following:

(a) Wireless Networks with Infrastructure

This architecture enables wireless terminals to create a connection with each other. This architecture depends upon the third steady party called the Base Station (BS), as illustrated in Fig. 10. The base station (BS) delivers the presented data from one station to another one, and the same entity is organized for distribution to the other wireless resources. Once the node of the source desires linking to the node of the target, the former informs the base station. At this time, the communicating nodes do not require to have the knowledge of route taken from node to another one. All that matters is that both the origin node and the target nodes fall within the communication area of the base station and then if any node fails to be a part of this situation, the connection will be lost or failed.

(b) Infrastructure-Less Wireless Networks

The mobile wireless networks are popular in MANETs, and, as earlier explained these are a set of two or more devices called as mobile nodes or terminals which are wireless connected and have the ability of structuring a network where they are in contact with each other without the help of any central administrative architecture.

In addition the wireless nodes are able to create a dynamic network for sharing information without utilizing any present stationary network infrastructure, and it's an independent scheme which in the nodes is linked through the use of wireless connections, theses nodes are free to be vital and sometimes operate as routers simultaneously [11, 12]. Infrastructureless architecture apparently requires an imperative implementation in this generation of communication technology since it effortlessly supports extensive computing techniques. Generally, since more of contextual data is required for interchange of information between the mobile units, it is not feasible for a network to depend on the steady network infrastructure. However, at the present time the wireless communication system have made advances quite rapidly. In Fig. 10, we discuss a small example of the ad hoc network for the explanation of such the network. There are three nodes that form the ad-hoc network (S, A, L), the origin node (S) engages the connection with the node of the target (L), both S and L don't occupy the same communication region, and, both utilize node (A) for transmitting/receiving or delivering the packets from the origin to the target, i.e., from one node to another. The node (A) is the node that works as a host and a router simultaneously. In addition, we define of the router as an entity which specifies the route that has to be taken for transmitting the packets to the last target node, and subsequently, the router also selects the next node that will send the packets according to its present knowledge of the network.

The Kinds of the Traffic in the Ad-Hoc Network

The kind of traffic in an ad-hoc network is extremely dissimilar from that present in the wireless networks infrastructure. These are namely: Peer-to-Peer (P2P), remote to remote and dynamic traffic. We will now review each of these traffics [13]:

(a) *Peer-to-Peer:* It appears when transmission between two nodes is in the same region, or when fall occurs within a single hop. The traffic of network is generally constant (bit per second).

(b) *Remote to Remote:* It results when transmission between two nodes require more than one hop. However, a steady routing path is maintained amidst them. This probably either happens due to the presence of a number of nodes that remain in one another's region or perhaps when the nodes proceed in alliance/league. The motion of the traffic is analogous to the normal network traffic.

(c) *Dynamic traffic:* it occurs due to dynamic movement of nodes that also cause reorganization of routers. This leads to a weak connection and as an outcome, the network bursts.

(1) Wireless Local Area Network (LAN) Infrastructures

In this networking as presented in Fig. 11, the framework of any network structure will have an Access Point. The purpose of the Access Point is to connect one or more of the wireless LAN with the present cable network system so that the terminals in the wireless LAN and the remote nodes are able to communicate to each other. It is distinguished by a constant base station which is favourably pre-positioned such as, the topology that provides an effective environment for steady communication. The base station performs robustly/proficiently when it to prepare of comprehensive policies [14, 49].

(2) Ad-Hoc Wireless Local Area Network

It functions in the absence of wireless LAN infrastructure, and aims to merely establish local area network within the construction of every one of devices that can be connected to network despite of the connection with the external world, thus this construction, either one or two customers are able to connect immediately together and this construction is formed as at least of two or additional work stations. It does not require fastened base station, and the network is quite dynamic in nature. It is a fundamental network topology as when subjected to intervention, it automatically forms and adapts to topology changes, even in the absence of infrastructure. Figure 12, further diagrammatically explains an ad-hoc wireless network [49].

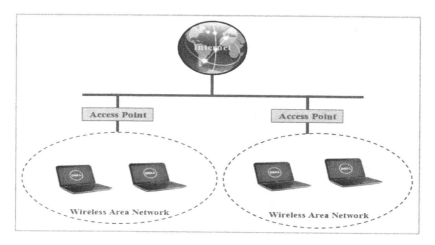

Fig. 11. Wireless LAN infrastructure

The Basic Principles of the Mobile Ad-Hoc Networks

The basic principles of the mobile ad hoc network can be described as follows:

- *Distributed administration:* network monitoring and administration are divided between nodes. No principal entity controls the network procedures.
- *Dynamic topology:* the network topology is able to change rapidly and in an unforeseeable method. The MANET can be adjusted dynamically to the traffic, the motion models and the propagation circumstance.
- *Capability of variable link:* The channel of communication relies on noise level, attenuation factor and interventions. Every one of the links can participate in various sessions. Additionally, accessible routes are able to change continuously.
- *Energy consumption:* nodes are supported by restricted batteries, thus, power consumption is a significant matter in MANET.

There are a number of matters that have been studied extensively in the current years because of its importance to the ultimate conduct as well as its relevance in the performance of MANET. Optimizing these parameters still deal as difficult matters:

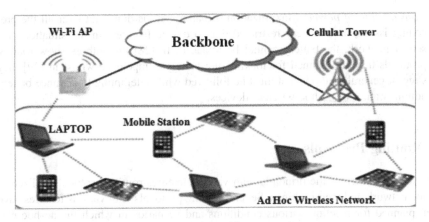

Fig. 12. Wireless ad-hoc networks

- *Routing path:* routing is a critical feature of the network, and there are several associated researches on it, that can be seen in [15–21]. The author in [15] presents a survey of the routing path protocols that also explains their functioning. Whilst, the author in [16, 17] presents a comparison between the protocols. In [18, 19] the author suggests routing protocol of a mobility-aware to enhance the competence in ad hoc networks. In [22], the proposition offered trying to provide routing of a QoS aware to the ad-hoc network.

- *Efficiency:* It is significant for selecting a suitable routing protocol for optimizing the performance of network. It is desirable recognizing and conserving routing paths that have the same velocity as that of the changes in the network that occurs because of intrinsic dynamics. This will help conserve the battery power as well.

- *Quality of Service:* There are numerous suggestions that support the necessity to ensure Quality of Service (QoS). In [23] the authors suggest a structure through IEEE 802.11e that allocates dynamic transmission chance values for the data that relies on the situation of network. In [24] the authors explain the problems of QoS routing paths in MANET. Additionally, the categorization of the QoS routing algorithm is accomplished in accordance with the best effort-related algorithm, the pattern and surroundings they support, and, the layer of the transmission through which it operates.

- *Robustness and security:* It involves techniques, such as, consumer authenticity and principal administration. Several researches associated with confidence and self-interest of have been achieved in the nodes, for instance [25–27]. The authors in [25] show various algorithms and routing protocols that improve reliability and generate a trust aware method for the ad hoc network. [26] and [27] represent reputation techniques that attempt at implementing cooperation between nodes. Every one of nodes specifies a qualification for every other node in the network which grows when cooperation is sensed and reduces otherwise.

- *Consumption of power:* Maximization of battery life is dominant over all the preceding issues, as it is very restricted due to device features. In the situation of a sensor network, the battery cannot be replaced. In [28] the authors show routing protocols that are planned for maximizing battery competence whilst in [29] they suggest general methods that must be followed while attempting to advance battery administration of ad hoc wireless devices.

3   Routing Protocols

This section describes the principle with various features routing protocols utilized in ad hoc network and their rankings. Several routing protocols with various features have been planned for meeting various conditions and scenarios in which the ad-hoc network is capable of working. For achieving specific levels of attributes through this network, quality of service structure has been planned. First, the fundamental function of the routing protocols is discussed in Sect. 3.1 and then the classification is shown in the Sect. 3.2.

3.1   The Functionality of Routing Protocols

Nowadays, several routing protocols have been improved for MANET that concentrates on enhancing the performance parameters of one or more points for the network. The protocols of the routing path for the ad-hoc network are supposed to pursue the following suggestions in its layout:

(a) *Minimum signaling:* The decrease in control information assists in saving the capacity of the battery and thus increases the competence of the transmission.
(b) *Minimal procedure time:* Low power protocols are required that compute less arithmetic time and increase the lifetime of the battery.
(c) *The free of the loop:* Time to live (TTL) is allocated to packets is short for avoiding the packets loops during simulation of the network.
(d) *An inactive process method:* Routing protocols have to be prepared for long passive periods created due to inactive nodes.
(e) *Distributed operation method:* Because of the inherent features in an ad-hoc network, routing protocols utilize various methods for finding a routing path from one node to the other nodes. These methods are defined as source routing path, link state and distance vector.
(f) *Distance vector:* It requires no flooding technique. The routing packets recursively exchange short messages containing data about targets and ranges. The shortest route from where the cost of the connection to the target is less, established. The procedure is easy but not fast, when adjustments in topology are slowly distributed over the nodes. Hence, it is not appropriate for the extensive networks.

(g) *Routing of source:* When a packet is generated by the origin node, its header already contains the entire route information, which consequently elevates the possibility of network overhead in the system. This mechanism generated of loop is not feasible for scenarios that are extensively mobile, since, a crack route may be incurred while the transmission of packets that haven't yet reached target.

(h) *State of link:* considering flood techniques, the path information of every node is provided in the routing path table of each node. The shortest path from where the cost of the link is minimum, utilized for reaching the target. Each node must recognize the entire network topology. The data is collected by distance vector algorithms which makes it appropriate for implementation in large-scale networks.

(i) *Routing path of hop-by-hop:* The packet header doesn't contain the complete path address of the packet but includes address from the target node and the next hop. For this reason, it becomes necessary for every intermediate node to look into its routing table for the next hop of transmitting the packets. One of the significant features of the source routing protocols is that the header size in the packet is small. As a consequence, routes are better able to effectively adapt to the topology of the changing network of these networks. The nodes don't recognize ways to each of the targets. However, they are conscious of the methods of continuous transmissions. As a drawback, every node requires continuous updating of its routing table during the transmission of the routing packets amongst its neighbors.

3.2   Classification of Routing Path Protocols

The routing path protocols with their examples can be classified as:

a. *Proactive Routing Protocols:* These protocols keep updated lists of targets, and their method of functioning is through the periodic distribution of the routing tables through the network. Models of these routing protocols are Destination-Sequenced Distance Vector routing protocol (DSDV) [30] and Optimized Link State Routing Protocol (OLSR) [31].

b. *Reactive Routing Protocols:* No routing path tables are kept. The techniques for discovering the route being only where there is a need for a path to the target. Models are dynamic source routing (DSR) [32] and ad-hoc on-demand distance vector (AODV) [33].

c. *Hybrid Routing Protocols:* These protocols combine the characteristics of proactive routing protocols, and reactive routing protocols. The protocols that recognize the situation, act proactively for short distances and reactively for long distances. The models are temporally-ordered routing algorithm routing protocol (TORA) [34] and zone routing protocol (ZRP) [35].

d. *Hierarchical Routing Protocols:* The selection of the proactive or reactive routing protocols relies on the hierarchical order of the node. The models are core-extraction distributed ad-hoc routing protocol (CEDAR) [36] and hierarchical state routing protocol (HSR) [37].

e. *Geographical Routing Protocols:* These protocols consider the physical distances and the distribution of the nodes for improving the performance of the network. The models are GPS ant-like routing algorithm (GPSAL) [38] and zone-based hierarchical link state routing (ZHLS) [39].

f. *Power Aware Routing Protocols:* These protocols may prefer to select longer routes to avoid excessive energy utilization instead of sending straight to a far node. Examples are: PARO (Power-aware routing optimization protocol) [40] and PAMAS (Power aware multi access protocol with signaling ad-hoc networks) [41].

g. *Multicast Protocols:* The models are adaptive demand-driven multicast routing (ADMR) [42] and ad-hoc QoS Multicast [43] (AQM).

h. *Geographical Multicast Protocols:* These protocols involve geographic data for establishing a multicast routing protocol. The models are location-based multicast (LBM) [44] and mobile Just-in-time multicasting (MOBICAST) [45].

i. *Quality of Service Aware Protocols:* These protocols consider the quality of service (QoS) parameters of the paths for establishing the forwarding route. Examples include in-band signaling support for QoS in mobile ad-hoc networks (INSIGNIA) [46] and flexible QoS model for MANET (FQMM) [24, 47].

4   Conclusion

The ad hoc networks are infrastructure-less networks which send data from source to destination without establishing any connection of wires, which means that the source node and destination is known but the path of the transmission is not specified, each time different routing path is selected. The devices can be operating independently or otherwise connected to the internet.

This paper clarified analytical study of wireless ad hoc networks in the detail. It discussed their histories and the uses in the present scenarios. It also explained the several other types of these networks, for instance, mobile ad-hoc Networks, wireless sensor networks, wireless mesh networks and vehicular ad hoc networks. In addition to, the paper clarified and concentrated on the most important characteristics, challenges and differences of ad hoc networks, routing protocols, different applications.

References

1. Aguilar, M.: Contribution to provide QoS over Mobile Ad Hoc Networks for Video-Streaming Services based on Adaptive Cross-Layer Architecture. Diss (2009)
2. Akyildiz, I.F., Wang, X.: A survey on wireless mesh networks. IEEE Communications Magazine 43(9), S23–S30 (2005). http://www.ece.gatech.edu/~wxudong/Xudong_Wang_commesh.pdf
3. Zhao, F., Guibas, L.: Wireless Sensor Networks: An Information Processing Approach. Morgan Kaufmann, Burlington (2004). http://research.microsoft.com/%7Ezhao/wsnbook.html. ISBN:1-55860-914-8
4. Kosch, T., Adler, Ch., Eichler, S., Schroth, Ch., Strassberger, M.: The scalability problem of vehicular Ad Hoc networks and how to solve it. IEEE Wireless Commun. Magazine 13(5), 22–28 (2006)

5. Al-Omari, S.A.K., Sumari, P.: An overview of mobile Ad Hoc networks for the existing protocols and applications (2010). arXiv preprint arXiv:1003.3565
6. In conclusion, health, free wireless network multi-path redundant mechanisms, June 2008
7. Perkins, C.E.: Ad Hoc Networking. Addison-Wesley, Boston (2001)
8. IEEE Computer Society LAN MAN Standards Committee, Wireless LAN medium access control (MAC) and physical layer (PHY) specifications, IEEE standard 802.11, 1997. The Institute of Electrical and Electronics Engineers, New York (1997)
9. IEEE Computer Society. IEEE standard for information technology telecommunications and information exchange between systems – local and metropolitan networks – specific requirements – part. 11: Wireless LAN medium access control (MAC) and physical layer (PHY) specifications: Higher speed physical layer (PHY) extension in the 2.4 GHz band (1999)
10. Frodigh, M., Johansson, P., Larsson, P.: Wireless Ad Hoc networking: the art of networking without a network. Ericsson Rev. **4**, 248–263 (2000)
11. IETF Working Group: Mobile Adhoc Networks (manet). http://www.ietf.org/html.charters/manetcharter.html
12. Ad Hoc Networking Extended Research Project. http://triton.cc.gatech.edu/ubicomp/505
13. Li, X.: Multipath routing and QoS provisioning in mobile Ad hoc Networks. Department of Electronic Engineering, Queen Mary, University of London, April 2006
14. Abolhasan, M., Wysocki, T., Dutkiewicz, E.: A review of routing protocols for mobile Ad Hoc networks. Ad Hoc Netw. **2**, 1–22 (2004)
15. Clausen, H.T., Jacquet, P., Viennot, L.: Comparative study of routing protocols for mobile Ad Hoc networks. INRIA, Project Hipercom, France (2001)
16. Xu, Yuwei: Optimising Video Streaming Over Multi-hop Wireless Networks: A Queueing Model Analytical Approach. University of Otago, Diss (2013)
17. Tung, T., Jia, Z., Walrand, J.: A Practical Approach to Qos Routing for Wireless Networks. University of California, Berkeley (2004)
18. Chakrabarti, S., Mishra, A.: Quality of service for wireless mobile Ad Hoc networks. Wireless Commun. Mob. Comput. **4**, 129–153 (2004)
19. Michiardi, P., Molva, R.: CORE: a collaborative reputation mechanism to enforce node cooperation in mobile Ad Hoc networks. In: 6th IFIP Communications and Multimedia Security Conference, pp. 107–121 (2002)
20. Bansal, S., Baker, M.: Observation-based Cooperation Enforcement in Ad Hoc Networks (OCEAN). arXiv:cs.ni/0307012v2. Technical report, Stanford University (2003)
21. Chiasserini, C.F., Rao, R.R.: Routing Protocols to Maximize Battery Efficiency. IEEE MILCOM 2000, October 2000
22. Chiasserini, C.F., Rao, R.R.: Energy efficient battery management. IEEE JSAC **19**(7), 1235–1245 (2001)
23. Perkins, C.E., Bhagwat, P.: Highly Dynamic Destination-Sequenced Distance-Vector Routing (DSDV) for Mobile Computers (1994)
24. Optimized Link State Routing (OLSR), RFC 3626 (2003). http://www.faqs.org/rfcs/rfc3626.html
25. Dynamic Source Routing Protocol (DSR) for Mobile Ad Hoc Networks, RFC 4728, February 2007. ftp://www.ftp.rfc-editor.org/in-notes/rfc4728.txt
26. Park, V., Corson, S.: TORA (Temporally-Ordered Routing Algorithm). IETF MANET Working Group, June 2001. Functional Specification, Internet Draft
27. ZRP. Zone Routing Protocol, July 2002. Draft work in progress http://tools.ietf.org/id/draft-ietf-manetzone-zrp-04.txt
28. Sivakumar, R., Sinha, P., Bharghavan, V.: Core Extraction Distributed Ad Hoc Routing (CEDAR), Internet Draft (2000). http://draft-ietf-manet-cedar-spec-00.txt

29. HSR (Hierarchical State Routing protocol), . Allan o'NeillHongyi Li, Internet Draft (2000). http://alternic.net/drafts/drafts-o-p/draft-oneill-li-hsr-00.txt

30. Camara, D., Alfredo, A., Loureiro, F.: A novel routing algorithm for Ad Hoc networks. Baltzer J. Telecommun. Syst. **18**(1–3), 85–100 (2001)

31. Ng, J., Tai, I.: Zone-based hierarchical link state routing. IEEE J. Select. Areas Commun. **17** (8), 1415–1425 (1999)

32. Gomez, J., Campbell, A.T., Naghshineh, M., Bisdikian, C., Watson, T.J.: Power-Aware Routing Optimization protocol (PARO). Internet Draft, draft-gomez-paro-manet-00.txt, work in progress, June 2001

33. Singh, S., Raghavendra, C.S.: Power aware multi access protocol with signaling Ad Hoc networks (PAMAS). PAMAS & PAMAS-Power Aware Multi Access Protocol with Signaling Ad Hoc Networks

34. Jetcheva, J.G., Johnson, D.B.: Adaptive demand-driven multicast routing in multi-hop wireless Ad Hoc networks (ADMR). In: 2nd ACM International Symposium on Mobile and Ad-Hoc Networking & Computing (MobiHOC), pp. 33–44, October 2001

35. Bur, K., Ersoy, C.: Ad Hoc quality of service multicast routing (AQM). Elsevier Sci. Comput. Commun. **29**(1), 136–148 (2005)

36. Huang, Q., Lu, C., Roman, G.-C.: Mobicast: Just-in-time multicast for sensor networks under spatiotemporal constraints (MOBICAST). Lect. Notes Comput. Sci. **2634**, 442–457 (2000)

37. Lee, S.B., Ahn, G.S., Zhang, X., Campbell, A.T.: INSIGNIA: an IPbased quality of service framework for mobile Ad Hoc networks. J. Parallel Distrib. Comput. **60**(4), 374–406 (2000)

38. Xiao, H., Winston, K.G., Lo, S.A., Chua, K.C.: A flexible quality of service model for mobile Ad Hoc networks. In: VTC2000 IEEE Vehicular Technology Conference, pp. 445–449, May 2000

39. http://www1.i2r.a-star.edu.sg/~winston/papers/VTC2000Spring-FQMM.pdf. Tokyo, Japan

40. Igartua, M.A., Frias, V.C.: Self-configured multipath routing using path lifetime for video-streaming services over Ad Hoc networks. Elsevier Comput. Commun. **33**(145), 1879–1891 (2010)

41. Ancillotti, E., Bruno, R., Conti, M., Pinizzotto, A.: Load-aware routing in mesh networks: models algorithms and experimentation. Comput. Commun. **34**, 948–961 (2011). 14, 64, 81 Ad Hoc Wireless Distribution Service - Layer 2 wireless mesh routing protocol, 2007

42. HSR (Hierarchical State Routing protocol), Allan o'Neill, Hongyi Li, Internet Draft (2000). http://alternic.net/drafts/drafts-o-p/draft-oneill-li-hsr-00.txt

43. Bellur, B., Ogier, R.G., Templin, F.L.: (TBRPF) Topology Dissemination based on Reverse-Path Forwarding routing protocol, February 2004

44. RFC 3684 http://tools.ietf.org/html/rfc3684.html

45. Boppana, R.V., Konduru, S.P.: An adaptive distance vector routing algorithm for mobile Ad Hoc networks (ADV) (Adaptive Distance Vector routing), April 2001

46. Perkins, C.E., Bhagwat, P.: Highly Dynamic Destination-Sequenced Distance-Vector Routing (DSDV) for Mobile Computers (1994). http://www.cs.virginia.edu/~cl7v/cs851-papers/dsdv-sigcomm94.pdf

47. Bergano, M.: MMWN (Mobile Multimedia Wireless Network). Technical report, DARPA project DAAB07-95-C-D156, October 1996

48. Chettibi, S., Chikhi, S.: Dynamic fuzzy logic and reinforcement learning for adaptive energy efficient routing in mobile Ad-Hoc networks. Appl. Softw. Comput. **38**, 321–328 (2016)

49. Srinivasan, A., Teitelbaumy, J., Liangz, H., Wuyand, J., Cardei, M.: Algorithms and Protocols for Wireless Ad Hoc and Sensor Networks. Wiley, Hoboken (2007)

Experimental Study of the Millimeter Wave Range Receiver

Anatoliy Zikiy[✉], Pavel Zlaman[✉], and Konstantin Rumyantsev[✉]

Southern Federal University, Taganrog, Rostov Region, Russian Federation
zikiy50@mail.ru, fmymail@mail.ru, rke2004@mail.ru

Abstract. A study of the millimeter wavelength range receiver are presented. A description of the circuit features and results of field tests of a radio signal mixer and a logarithmic detector is given. The conversion characteristic and frequency response of the sensitivity of the logarithmic detector are given, as well as the dependence of the mixer conversion loss on the signal frequency.

Keywords: Radio receiver · Millimeter wave band · Mixer · Logarithmic detector

1 Introduction

The improvement of radio receivers of the millimeter wave range, the creation of new generations of radio receivers are the important tasks of modern radio engineering. A significant number of monographs and articles [1–10] is devoted to the problems of receiving radio signals in the millimeter wave range. Interest in the receivers of this class confirms the patent search.

However, much less attention is paid to the design of small-sized radio receivers for communication systems between mobile objects, which would meet the following requirements:

- wavelength range - about 8 mm;
- sensitivity 10^{-8} ... 10^{-9} W;
- dynamic range of signals 50 dB;
- selectivity on the adjacent channel 50 dB;
- selectivity on the image channel 30 dB;
- selectivity on the channel of direct leakage 50 dB;
- dimensions and weight are minimal;
- power supply - 24 V.

P. K. Singh et al. (Eds.): FTNCT 2019, CCIS 1206, pp. 41–51, 2020.
https://doi.org/10.1007/978-981-15-4451-4_4

2 The Structure of the Superheterodyne Millimeter Wave Range Receiver

Traditionally, this problem is solved using a superheterodyne receiver. Due to the low specified sensitivity, you can do without a low-noise amplifier. Due to the small frequency tuning range, a non-tunable wideband preselector can be used. In this case, the entire receiver tuning is carried out by changing the frequency of the local oscillator - frequency synthesizer. Its functional diagram is shown in Fig. 1.

The radio receiver consists of a protective device 1, a path filter 2, a controlled attenuator 3, gates 4 and 14, a mixer 5, an intermediate frequency filter 6, a logarithmic detector 7, Schmitt trigger 8, frequency synthesizer 9, frequency multipliers by two 10 and 11, frequency multipliers by four 13, peak detector 15 and voltage regulator 16. Units 1–5 and 13, 14 are waveguides. Below is a description of the circuit features and results of field tests only radio signal mixer and a logarithmic detector. A detailed description of the remaining functional units of the radio receiver and the results of their experimental tests can be found in [11, 12, 14–19]. Brief specifications are shown in Table 1.

Table 1. Units parameters.

Наименование параметра, размерность	Значение параметра
Attenuator	
Frequency range, GHz	26...37,5
Attenuation range, dB	1...36
Control current, mA	0...28
Design - waveguide	
Filter EHF	
Lower cutoff frequency of bandwidth, GHz	32,7
Upper cutoff frequency of bandwidth, GHz	34,3
Bandwidth loss, dB (including losses in two cables and two transitions)	6,5
Stopband loss, dB	34
Design – waveguide with two longitudinal diaphragms in the E - plane	
Frequency synthesizer	
Frequency range, GHz	1,85...2,15
Frequency grid step, kHz	100
Relative frequency instability	10^{-6}
Output power, dBm	0
Frequency multiplier	
Frequency multiplicity factor	4
Input frequency range, GHz	~ 8
Output frequency range, GHz	~ 32
Input power, dBm	10
Output power, dBm	$-1...6$
Input – coaxial, SRG50-751FV	
Output – waveguide, Section 7,2 × 3,4 mm	

(continued)

Table 1. (*continued*)

Наименование параметра, размерность	Значение параметра
Centimeter range oscillator	
Output frequency range, GHz	~8
Frequency grid step, kHz	400
Output power, dBm	6...12
Level of non-harmonic spectral components, no more than, dB, with respect to the useful signal	minus 45
Power amplifier centimeter range for the heterodyne path	
Frequency range, GHz	8...10
Output power, mW	10...15
Gain, dB	10...14
Input and output impedance, Ohm	50
SAW intermediate frequency filter	
Bandwidth center frequency, MHz	1575
Bandwidth loss, dB	8
Bandwidth, MHz	20
Input and output wave impedance, Ohm	50
Attenuation on $2f_0$, dB	21
Attenuation at offset ±100 MHz, dB	30
Protective device	
Frequency range, GHz	26...40
Loss at low power level, dB	3
Output restriction level, dBm	9...13
Design – waveguide-slot (finline)	
Gate	
Frequency range, GHz	32...35
Direct loss, dB	0,3
Reverse loss, dB	20
Design – waveguide with flanges 7,2 × 3,4 mm	

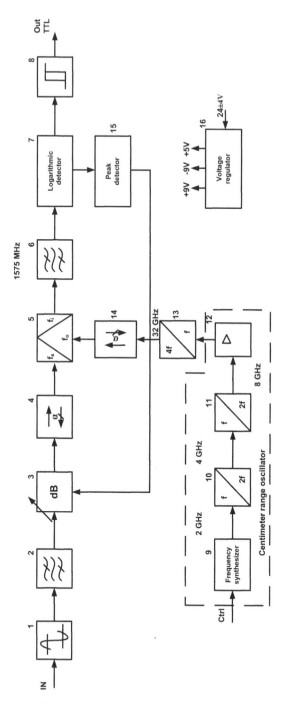

Fig. 1. Functional diagram of the receiver.

3   Protective Device Tests

The object of study in this section is the serial device M54403, manufactured by the enterprise "Svetlana". Figure 2 shows the schematic diagram of the protective device (PD). The PD contains 6 diodes, of which 4 diodes perform limiting functions, and 2 diodes serve as detectors to energize the limit diodes. In this way, it is possible to lower the level of limitation.

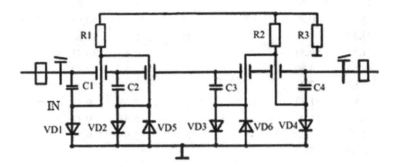

Fig. 2. Schematic diagram of the protective device

The M54403 module has overall dimensions of $43 \times 25 \times 41$ mm. Flanges 7.2×3.4 mm. In the plane E of the rectangular waveguide there is a dielectric insert on which 6 diodes and three resistors are installed. At the input and output of the PD there is a adapter from a standard to a narrowed section. To protect against moisture, both flanges are covered with sealed transparent windows. The module is conveniently mounted in the receiver with four pins. The taken measures allow the PD to operate in harsh climatic conditions.

The purpose of this section is to measure the amplitude characteristics of the protective device. Often such a task is impossible due to the lack of sufficiently powerful sources of microwave signals. In this case, a microwave signal generator with a guaranteed output power of 20 dBm (100 mW) type E8267D from Agilent Technologies is used. Agilent Technologies spectrum analyzer type 8564EC is used as an output power meter. The block diagram of the measuring installation is shown in Fig. 3.

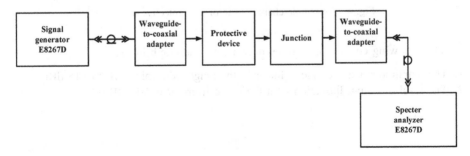

Fig. 3. Blok diagram of the measuring installation

The results of measurements of the amplitude characteristics are shown in Table 2 and in Fig. 4.

Table 2. The amplitude characteristic of the protective device

P_{in}, dBm	P_{out}, dBm	P_{out}, dBm after deducting cable losses	P_{in}, dBm	P_{out}, dBm	P_{out}, dBm after deducting cable losses
−10	−29,50	−14,50	12	−8,00	7,00
−8	−27,50	−12,50	14	−6,00	9,00
−6	−25,50	−10,50	16	−4,17	10,83
−4	−23,33	−8,33	18	−2,50	12,50
−2	−21,33	−6,33	20	−4,47	10,53
0	−19,50	−4,50	21	−5,63	9,37
2	−17,83	−2,83	22	−5,63	9,37
4	−16,83	−1,83	23	−5,63	9,37
6	−14,00	1,00	24	−5,63	9,37
8	−12,00	3,00	25	−5,63	9,37
10	−10,00	5,00			

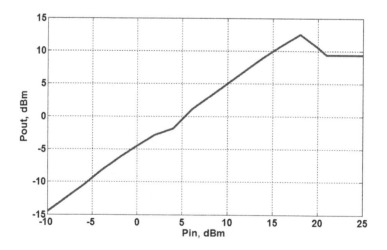

Fig. 4. Amplitude characteristic of the protective device

The following conclusions can be drawn from the graph in Fig. 4:

1. The amplitude characteristic is linear in the range from minus 10 to +18 dBm.
2. The level of output limitation is in the range from +9 to +13 dBm.

4 Mixer Tests

A block diagram of an installation for testing a radio signal mixer is shown in Fig. 5.

The mixer is built according to a balanced scheme on a waveguide-slot line on diodes with a Schottky barrier. The signal and heterodyne inputs are waveguide with a cross section of 7.2 × 3.4 mm flanges. The output of the intermediate frequency signal is through the coaxial connector SRG50-751FV.

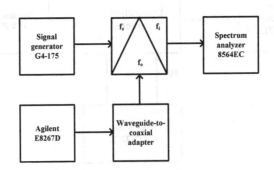

Fig. 5. Block diagram of the measurement installation.

As a signal source, a generator of standard signals of the type G4-175 was used. As a source of heterodyne power applied signal generator type E8267D company Agilent Technologies. As an indicator of output power and frequency applied a spectrum analyzer of the type 8564 EC of the same company serves. The measurements were carried out in the frequency range of signals 32 … 37 GHz and intermediate frequency 2 GHz. The measurement results of the conversion loss are shown in Fig. 6. It can be seen that the conversion loss does not exceed 10 dB, and the loss unevenness was 4 dB.

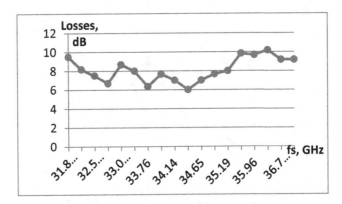

Fig. 6. Dependence of conversion loss on the signal frequency.

5   Experimental Study of a Logarithmic Detector

The investigated logarithmic detector is implemented on the chip AD8313. A block diagram of an installation for experimental testing of a logarithmic detector is shown in Fig. 7.

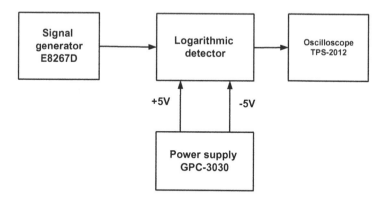

Fig. 7. Block diagram of the measurement installation.

As the source of the signal was used generator E8267D. A digital oscilloscope such as TPS-2012 from Tektronix was used as an indicator of the output signal. The power source is the GPC-3030 unit. The conversion characteristic of the logarithmic detector at a frequency of 1500 MHz is shown in Fig. 8. The average steepness of the characteristic is 54 mV/dB. This characteristic is close to the logarithmic curve.

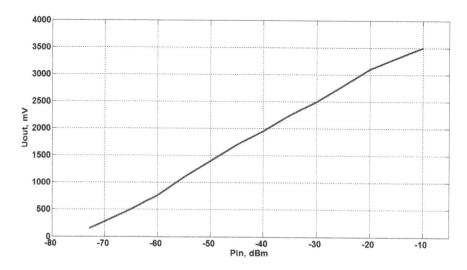

Fig. 8. Conversion characteristic of the logarithmic detector.

The frequency response of the sensitivity is shown in Fig. 9. It can be seen that the sensitivity of the logarithmic detector in the frequency range of 1575 ± 20 MHz exceeds minus 75 dBm, and the dynamic range is at least 60 dB. The measured parameters of the logarithmic detector allow you to turn off the automatic gain control (AGC) of the radio receiver, while ensuring the specified dynamic range.

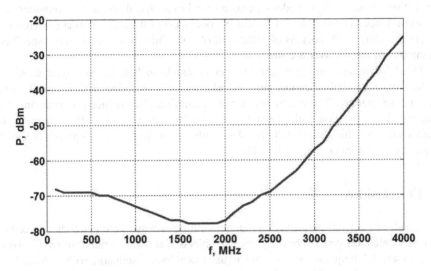

Fig. 9. Frequency response of the sensitivity of a logarithmic detector.

6 The Millimeter Waves Receiver Tests

The tests of the receiver were carried out at the installation, the block diagram of which is shown in Fig. 10.

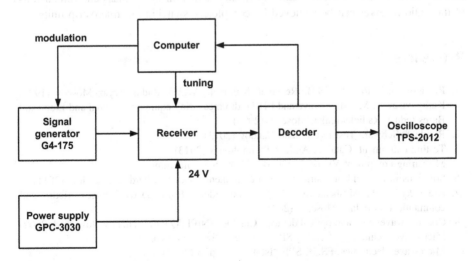

Fig. 10. Block diagram of the measurement installation.

As a source of modulated signals, a generator of standard signals G4-175 was used. The oscilloscope TPS-2012 is used as an indicator of the output signal. The power source is the GPC-3030 unit. The computer generates a coded modulating pulse sequence for applying to the G4-175 modulation input, as well as tuning codes for the frequency of the frequency synthesizer in the receiver.

The decoder provides a comparison of the received sequence of pulses with a given one. If they coincide, the decoder outputs a signal of a logical unit to the computer and the oscilloscope. The criterion of the correct operation of the receiver is considered the correct decoding of 99 packets of pulses out of 100. This ensures that all the specified parameters of the receiver are met.

The disadvantages of the described receiver should include the low dynamic range of the frequency multiplication path. In addition, the receiving path is sensitive to temperature changes. These drawbacks can be eliminated or reduced by reducing the frequency multiplication multiplicity factor from 16 to 2 or 3. Currently its achievable when using the chip ADF41020 for the synthesis of frequencies. The upper cutoff frequency of this microchip is 10 GHz.

7 Conclusions

As a result of the work performed, a tunable millimeter-wave superheterodyne receiver for communication systems between mobile objects was manufactured. In the receiver, the ADF4360-2 frequency synthesizer is used as a local oscillator, with followed by frequency multiplication by 16. The high dynamic range is provided by use an AD8313 logarithmic detector in the intermediate frequency path.

The high selectivity in the adjacent channel is due to the use of a filter on surface acoustic waves in the intermediate frequency path. The required selectivity in the image channel is achieved by selecting a high intermediate frequency of 1575 MHz.

Small dimensions and mass are obtained due to the complete absence of waveguide sections between the functional units. A further reduction in the mass and dimensions of the radio receiver can be achieved by completely switching to microstrip units.

References

1. Rozanov, B.A., Rozanov, S.B.: Receivers Millimeter Waves. Radio i svyaz, Moscow (1989)
2. Kudryavtsev, A.M.: Microwave and EHF radio measuring equipment. Nodal and Elemental Bases (edn.). Radiotekhnika, Moscow (2006)
3. Rohde & Schwarz Test Equipment. Catalog (2013)
4. Testing equipment. Catalog. Agilent Technologies (2013)
5. Measuring equipment VILKOM (2010–2011). www.vilcorn.ni
6. Solutions in the field of instrumentation equipment. Tektronix hardware catalog. (2011)
7. Krenitsky, A.P., Meshchanova, V.P.: Ultra-wideband microwave devices. Radio and communication (edn.), Moscow (2001)
8. Coaxial, waveguide and optical devices. Catalog NNIPI "Quartz", Nizhny Novgorod (2002)
9. Microwave technology. Catalog SPE "Salute", Nizhny Novgorod (1997)
10. Microwave electronics. FSUE SPE "Istok", Fryazino (2003)

11. Zikiy, A.N., Vlasenko, D.V.: Attenuator millimeter range. In: Proceedings of the 4th International Scientific Conference "Modern Problems of Radio Electronics", pp. 315–318 (2012)

12. Zikiy, A.N., Vlasenko, D.V.: Experimental study of EHF filters. Questions Spec. Radio Electron. Ser. Gen. Questions Radio Electron. **2**(12), 116–118 (2012)

13. Zikiy, A.N., Zlaman, P.N., Vlasenko, D.V.: Five octave frequency synthesizer. Electric. Data Process. Facilitiess Syst. **9**, **4**(4), 31–36 (2013)

14. Zikiy, A.N., Zlaman, P.N., Monastyrny, A.S., Shipulin, M.V.: The synthesizer frequency decimeter range. Inf. Countering Threats Terrorism **17**(24), 126–130 (2011)

15. Zikiy, A.N., Zlaman, P.N., Vlasenko, D.V., Shipulin, M.V.: Millimeter frequency multiplier. Inf. Countering Threats Terrorism **17**(24), 140–144 (2011)

16. Zikiy, A.N., Zlaman, P.N., Vlasenko, D.V., Shipulin, M.V.: The local oscillator of the centimeter range. In: Proceedings of the international scientific-practical conference "Fundamental and applied science today", pp. 193–196. Moscow (2013)

17. Zikiy, A.N., Zlaman, P.N., Vlasenko, D.V.: Experimental study of the power amplifier centimeter range. Questions Spec. Radio Electron. Ser. Gen. Questions Radio Electron. **1**(12), 136–139 (2013)

18. Zikiy, A.N., Zlaman, P.N., Vlasenko D.V.: Filter on surface acoustic waves. Electric. Data Process. Facilitiess Syst. **9**, **3**(4), 5–7 (2013)

19. Belyaev, D.V., Zikiy, A.N., Burlachenko, A.A., Rumyantsev, K.E.: Logarithmic detectors. Inf. Countering Threats Terrorism **12**(24), 241–249 (2008)

20. Zikiy, A.N., Bondarenko, L.V., Vlasenko, D.V., Monastyrny, A.S.: Millimeter range safety device. Questions Spec. Radio Electron. Ser. Gen. Questions Radio Electron. **2**(12), 106–109 (2011)

Smart Platforms of Air Quality Monitoring: A Logical Literature Exploration

Pankaj Rahi[1]([⊠]) [iD], Sanjay P. Sood[2], and Rohit Bajaj[3]

[1] University Institute of Computing, Chandigarh University, Mohali, India
pankajrahi@rediffmail.com
[2] Health Informatics, CDAC-Mohali, Mohali, India
spsood@gmail.com
[3] Department of Computer Science and Engineering, Chandigarh University, Mohali, Punjab, India
rohit.rick@gmail.com

Abstract. The emerging platform of smart computing are playing a vital role in revolutionizing the data era via offering massive data collection, information exchange and variable data analytics. Air is the vital nutrients necessarily acquired by all the living beings on the earth. The air quality monitoring is important area largely associated with living beings that are under the espousers of it for longer or short duration of time. The air quality monitoring system support the activities of the measurement of the concentration of hazardous gases and pollutants causing harm to the environment or the living beings directly or indirectly. In this review paper critical view of the smart solution designed, developed for the monitoring of ambient air (outdoor) and indoor air quality are represented.

Keywords: Smart system · Air quality monitoring · Air Quality Index · Cloud computing

1 Introduction

Air is the vital component constituting the atmosphere. The World Health Organization has also defined various standards which are accepted globally for monitoring ambient the air quality. Air quality monitoring is the important area largely associated with complex integration and processes of environmental information processing. There are multiple systems in place for monitoring the air quality which are either introduced by the governmental agencies or by the private organizations for keeping the track of air quality on different geographical areas. But there are many areas still remain untouched and out of reach from such initiatives. The deployment of smart systems for monitoring the environments phenomena have initiated the transformation and derived the multiple matrices of information gathering, for real-time analytics for healthy leaving style.

In current scenario the Internet and Communication Technology (ICT) in integration with physical processes of real-world which are further playing vital role in improving technology assisted living for improving the quality of life in India. Despite of several recent developments, evaluation of real-time air quality analytics and

© Springer Nature Singapore Pte Ltd. 2020
P. K. Singh et al. (Eds.): FTNCT 2019, CCIS 1206, pp. 52–63, 2020.
https://doi.org/10.1007/978-981-15-4451-4_5

pollutants availability in air requires more efforts for policy decisions and computing integrations. Big data described the era of largest growing technology which are offi-cering variable services at high velocity of data capturing methods like environment related systems, storage, discovery and analysis for large scale databases. Deriving the new-analytics by linking the climate changes, weather factors, ambient air quality (indoor and outdoor both) and health aspects, the cloud computing provides new perceptions for improving the human health and wellbeing. It is also underpin the expansions of decision making methods and alert devices which promote the resilience to healthy living environment for all living beings.

The aim of this paper is to study the practices deployed for monitoring the air quality in context to methodology and technology integration and also critically review the indices of system beneficial for measuring the real-time air quality.

2 Background

2.1 Air

Air belongs to the one of four classical elements known as air, water, earth, and fire. It is a clean, colorless and order less gas essentially required by living things to live and breathe [1]. Air has the composition of gases like nitrogen (NO_2) (78%), Oxygen (O_2) (21%), other tiny amount of gases (1%) as carbon dioxide, helium methane, argon etc. and very thin particles of dust, microbes and pollen etc.

2.2 Air Pollutants

The air pollutants have been defined and used as indicators of air quality. The main common pollutants are carbon monoxide, nitrogen dioxide, ozone, particles and sulfur dioxide.

- Carbon Compounds: Oxides of carbon (Carbon dioxide (CO_2) generated form decomposition or burning of fossil fuels, exhale process of human beings etc.
- Carbon monoxide (CO) commonly released from vehicles and burning of fossil fuels.
- Sulphur Compounds: SO_2, NO_2, HNO_3 released from power plants and industrial units.
- Ozone: (O_3) Ozone, a secondary pollutant formed in the atmosphere, has serious health impacts. Ozone is a strong oxidant, and it can react with a wide range of cellular components and biological materials. Ozone can aggravate bronchitis, heart disease, emphysema, asthma and reduce lung capacity. Irritation can occur in res-piratory system, causing coughing, and uncomfortable.

2.3 Air Quality Monitoring Index

The Air Quality Index defines the color coding or numeric value scheme of repre-senting the level of pollutants availability in the ambient air which causes harm to the human plants and other living beings. It is also represented differently by different countries by defining the variable methodology of calculations for measuring the quality of air, defining the availability of harmful gasses. Initially it is also known as Pollution Standard Index (PSI) [1]. There are many countries developed and deployed modeling of Air Quality Index for notifying the pollutants availably in the air for the interest of citizens. Many scientific models have been studies for deriving the comparison in terms of defining the initial and end points of AQI, which has been represented as numeric value but multiple ranges, has been defined for representing the various AQI having the different name in different countries. The most common evaluated Volatile Organic Compounds in air are Ozone (O_3), Particulate Matters (PM_{10} and $PM_{2.5}$), carbon monoxide (CO), Sulphur dioxide (SO_2), Nitrogen dioxide (NO_2), COH, Total Suspended Particulate (TSP), Photochemical Oxidants, Suspended Particulate Matter (SPM) and Carbon dioxide (CO_2). There are many categories of AQI like (Good, Satisfactory, Moderately polluted, Poor, Very Poor, and Severe) defined for easy understanding and representations of air quality [12]. Each of these categories are decided based on ambient concentration values of air pollutants and their linked health impacts (health breakpoints). AQ sub-index and health breakpoints are evolved for eight pollutants (PM_{10}, $PM_{2.5}$, NO_2, SO_2, CO, O_3, NH_3, and Pb) for which short-term (upto 24-h).

Taxonomies Analogy of Air Quality Monitoring Index

Table 1 described the available Air Quality Indexes in use internationally.

Table 1. Comparison of Air Quality Indexes

Author & Year	Index	Measurement scale of index	Measurement units of pollutants	VOC evaluated
Taylor and Green [1, 2]	Green Index (GI)	0–100	ppm	SO_2, COH
Fenstock [3]	Fenstock Air Quality Index		ppm	CO, TSP, SO_2
Inhaber [1]	Canadian Environmental Quality Index	0–0.99	Not defined	Air Quality Index, Water Quality Index, Land Quality Index, Misc Aspects of Environment Quality Index
EPA [6, 7]	Environmental Protection Agency-Pollution Standard Index (PSI)	0–500	ppm, ppb, $\mu g/m^3$	O_3, PM, CO, SO_2, NO_2
EPA [6, 7]	National Ambient Air Quality Standards (NAAQS)	0–500	ppm, ppb, $\mu g/m^3$	O_3, PM, CO, SO_2, NO_2

(continued)

Table 1. (*continued*)

Author & Year	Index	Measurement scale of index	Measurement units of pollutants	VOC evaluated
EPA [6, 7] [6] Bruno and Cocchi [2, 3] Saisana (2005)	National Ambient Air Quality Standards (NAAQS) And Significant Harm Level (SHL)	0–500	ppm, ppb, $\mu g/m^3$	O_3, PM, CO, SO_2, NO_2
Shenfeld (1970)	Air Pollution Index	0–100	ppm	SO2, COH
Babcock and Nagda (1972)	Oak Ridge Air Quality Index (ORAQI)	0.03–7.0 in ppm, 150 in $\mu g/m3$	ppm, $\mu g/m^3$	SO_2, NO_2, PM, CO, Photochemical Oxidants
GVAQI [5]	Greater Vancouver Air Quality Index (GVAQI)	25–50–100	ppm, $\mu g/m^3$	SO_2, NO_2, O_3, TSP, COH, PM_{10}
Ott (1978)	Most Undesirable Respirable Contaminants Index (MURC)	0.3–2.15 (COH) 0–121 (MURC)		COH
CPCB, Ministry of Environment and Forests [12]	National Air Quality Index, Indian-National Air Quality Index (IND-NAQI)	0–500	ppm, ppb, $\mu g/m^3$	CO, NO_2, SO_2, PM of less than 2.5 microns size ($PM_{2.5}$), PM of less than 10 microns size (PM_{10}), O_3, Pb, NH_3, Benzo(a) Pyrene (BaP), Benzene (C6H6), Arsenic (As), and Nickel (Ni)
Singh [9]	Air Quality Depreciation Index	0–10	ppm, $\mu g/m^3$	Suspended Particulate Matter (SPM), SO_2, NOx and (TSP × SO2)
Abbaspour [19]	Air Quality Risk Index (AQRI)	1 - greater than10 (R_H) $0 \geq 10.00$ (R_S) 0–00 (AQI)	ppm, $\mu g/m^3$, R_H, R_S, R_E	NOx, SOx, CO, $PM_{2.5}$ and PM_{10} for Significant damages, R_S, AQHI for health-related risk, R_H, indices define and measure AQRI

Comparison Amongst Air Quality Indexes and Model of Classifications

Table 2. Comparison of Air Quality Indexes

Index	Target Air Pollutants										
	O_3	PM_{10}	$PM_{2.5}$	CO	SO_2	NO_2	COH	TSP	Photo-chemical Oxidants	SPM	Other defines Indices
Green Index(GI) [1]					◯		◯				
Fenstock Air Quality Index[14]				◯	◯			◯			
Canadian Environmental Quality Index[2]											◯
Environmental Protection Agency- Pollution Standard Index(PSI)[6]											◯
National Ambient Air Quality Standards (NAAQS) [6]	◯		◯	◯	◯	◯					
National Ambient Air Quality Standards (NAAQS) And Significant Harm Level (SHL)[6]											
Air Pollution Index[13]	◯	◯	◯	◯	◯	◯					
Oak Ridge Air Quality Index (ORAQI)[12]			◯	◯	◯				◯		
Greater Vancouver Air Quality Index (GVAQI)[5]	◯	◯	◯	◯	◯	◯					
Most Undesirable Respirable Contaminants Index (MURC)[3]							◯				
National Air Quality Index, Indian-National Air Quality Index(IND-NAQI [12]	◯	◯	◯	◯	◯	◯					◯
Air Quality Depreciation Index[9]					◯	◯		◯		◯	◯
Air Quality Risk Index (AQRI)[20]		◯	◯	◯	◯	◯					◯
Total Evaluated (13)	**4**	**4**	**7**	**7**	**9**	**6**	**2**	**2**	**1**	**1**	**5**

The Table 2 describes the commonly known pollutants which are more active in contamination of the air, which are targeted for being observed for keeping the track of daily air quality.

Color Coding Scheme of Indian-National Air Quality Index (IND-NAQI)
To status of the air quality and its effects on living beings in context to the India the IND-AQI [12] is represented in the form of color pattern as:

Good	Satisfactory	Moderately polluted	Poor	Very poor	Severe
(0-50)	(51-100)	(101-200)	(201-300)	(301-400)	(> 401)

3   Cloud Computing and Environmental Benefits

Cloud Computing platform provides manifold benefits in the world of IT like reducing costs, elimination of risk of failure, improving efficiency and support agility and help in saving the natural environmental also [37]. Despite of technological and financial benefits of cloud computing it offers manifold environmental benefits like it reduces energy consumption, harmful carbon emissions and help to reduce the greenhouse gases effect. As per the study conducted by Microsoft cloud computing offers the 93% more energy efficient benefit and 98% more carbon efficiency [44]. The Microsoft study further projected that data centre energy consumption would drop by 31% between 2010 and 2020 as large numbers of organizations are joining the cloud computing platform. The key benefits offered by Cloud Computing in reference to the environmental safety are:

- Reduces energy use
- Decrease Green House Gases (GHG) emissions
- Dematerialization
- Data centre efficiency

The main factors reduce the CO_2 emissions in context to the deployment of the Cloud computing [11] are as follows (Fig. 1):

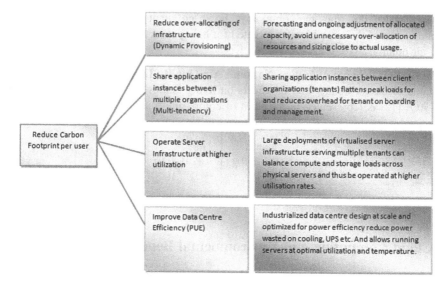

Fig. 1. Key features of Cloud Computing helpful for reducing the Carbon emission [11]

4 Cloud Computing Based Modeling for AQI

Cloud computing plays significant role in ubiquitous living methodology which are globally accepted by the users though multiple cloud computing platforms-social medical platforms like Facebook, Twitter, Weibo etc. The Cloud computing has become as a services to these Online Social Media (OSN) Platform which is extensively utilized may mass numbers of Vusers (Verified Users) on Social Media platform. Cloud computing offers the companies and organizations for reducing the cost in handling pollution.

The comparative of Cloud Computing based platform for Environmental or Air Quality has been analyzed and discussed by various researchers as:

Table 3. Comparison of Air Quality Indexes

Author & Year	Cloud platform	Target parameter	Frequency of measurement	Method/Algorithm
Di Lonardo et al. [17]	Cloud-PaaSwith IoT	$PM_{2.5}$, PM_{10}	Daily	Classification, Crowd-Sourcing Methods
Wang et al. [39]	Yes	$PM_{2.5}$	Daily	Regression Modeling with filtered post frequency
Mei et al. [42]	Yes	AQI	Daily	Regression Modeling with text features

(continued)

Table 3. (*continued*)

Author & Year	Cloud platform	Target parameter	Frequency of measurement	Method/Algorithm
Jiang and Alves et al. [43]	Yes, OSNs	AQI	Daily	Regression Modeling and Parameter Estimation
Chen et al. [44]	Yes	AQI	Not defined	Sentiment analysis, Principal Component Analysis
Tse et al. [40]	Yes, OSNs	$PM_{2.5}$	Two hours	Regression Modeling, Textual data mining
Sammarco, Tse, Pau, Marfia [41]	Yes	$PM_{2.5}$, PM_{10}	Two hours	Regression Modeling
Harkat and Mansouri [47]	Yes	AQI	Daily	Principal Component Analysis, Regression Model, fault detection method

Table 3 represents the cloud computing based models deployed for calculating the air quality. The usage of cloud computing for evaluating the air pollutants is a cost effective method as it offers the services as a clouds' in-build feature. The other scientific systems derived for monitoring the ambient air quality are:

Di Lonardo et al. derived the new method of air monitoring the air using the Sensor Web-Bike (SWB) as a low cost information service designed to support the participative sensing and accuracy for monitoring the air quality [17].

Hochadel explains the global regression models derived for estimating the exposure of traffic generated air pollutants at individual level. This study defines the complete cohort, representing the impact of traffic generated air pollution on respiratory health [22].

Jiang and Jia describes the solution of portable personal air quality monitor PAM which provides real-time air quality monitoring in the local environments. This unit is constructed with two sub units known as cloud-side PAM service and the service side PAM services. Using this an air quality monitoring the has been measured for PM 2.5 to AQI [23].

Liu and Hsu (1998) proposed the technique whereby classification and association rule mining are integrated by focusing on mining special subset of association rules, called class association rules (CARs). This also describe that the classifier built this way is more accurate than that produced by the C4.5 technique [27].

Ciolli and Cemin explains the sensor enabled indoor air quality sensing and automation (IASA) system which is used to monitor the presence of air pollutants percentages continuously in homes, offices. The sensor enabled devices will measure the air quality and espousers' to particulate matter [8].

Yu and James descried the Bus Sensors development network problem and Chemical Reaction Optimization technique is used to detect the pollution level in a grid of geographic area for one hour of the time interval. This technique defines the efficient usage of deployment of sensors to have wise coverage in the area [37].

Yi and Zhang describes the two new approaches utilized for predicting the air quality monitoring upto next 48 h. The new deep neutral network (DNN) approach and deep distributed fusion network (DDFN) and provides the air quality prediction for next 48 h duration [34].

Although large numbers of organisations have derived the Air Quality Index for timely notification of the quality of air in their surroundings. However the large amount of word is required for declaring the Indoor air for precautionary measure etc. It is not even possible to have any assessment of indoor air quality and assessment of pollutants available in the indoor proximity of workplaces or houses on daily.

There is need of having low end, cost effective air quality monitors which will provide the real-time assessments of air quality in both the cases (indoor, outdoor). The variable methods of mobile air pollution monitoring have been elaborated with the architectures of air pollution monitoring systems using the Mobile Devices and Crowd-sourcing method [27]. EMMA (Environmental Monitoring in Metropolitan Air-Enterprises) demonstrates the technique of vehicles fitted sensors (Car2X method of communication is used) for retrieving the data of the geographical area covered by the roaming vehicles. This technique requires less efforts and investments.

Monitoring the real-time pollutants level in the ambient air will improve the quality of life and officers several benefits including the decrease in the occurrences of health hazards. The large scale system of monitoring the data set of air quality systems requires standardization. This will help in generating the real-time air quality index, which will be beneficial for timely interventions for controlling of diseases. The interventions also provide multiple ways for data collections, analytics based on the big data platform of cloud computing.

5 Summary

It is observed from the methodologies adopted for the calculations of AQI (air pollution index), the estimation of critical parameters that the estimates for various months and the different results were observed ranging from good to sever levels for the same set of data. This variations were arises from the eclipsing effect of data values used in the formulas described by many researchers of various countries. The statistical theory used for calculation of AQI itself leading to the variations, as the use of means from simple arithmetic to logarithmic and weighted averages to use of breakpoint concentration as basis of estimation.

Hence the monitoring of air quality and deriving the AQI, the cloud based secured platform will be highly beneficial and cost effective. Technology driven smart system of air quality monitoring leverage numbers of benefits in terms of timely initiation of preventive actions for control of hazard which further improves quality of life, reduce efforts and cost and also improve effectiveness of the system.

The limitation of real-time air quality monitoring (AQM) is as it confined to the area, hence it may require more numbers of data acquisition nodes to be put in place for covering the large geographical areas, which may increase the cost, complexity-in analytics and also increase the response time of the system. This paper also provides insight to the AQI generation which will be cost effective if made operational with integration of Cloud computing.

6 Future Work

The effectiveness of technology driven air quality monitoring systems will only be realized if the standardization of Internet of Things IoT) and Internet of Everything modeling devices be enforced along with the standardization of algorithms for Smart Environmental and eHealth System. Standardization and modeling of data catalogs with semantic indexes for uniform and interoperable data exchange is also necessary. The privacy in friendliness of smart systems needs more refined modeling for information exchange amongst the multiple cohesive phenomena's of systems.

References

1. Inhaber, H.: Environmental quality: outline for a national index for Canada. Science **186**, 798–805 (1974)
2. Inhaber, H.: A set of suggested air quality indices for Canada. Atmos. Environ. **9**, 353–364 (1975)
3. Thom, G.C., Ott, W.: Air Pollution Indices: A Compendium and Assessment of Indices Used in the United States and Canada (1975)
4. Juda-Rezler, K.: Classification and characteristics of air pollution models. In: Pawlowski, L., Lacy, W.J., Dlugosz, J.J. (eds.) Chemistry for the Protection of the Environment. ESRH, vol. 42, pp. 51–72. Springer, Boston (1991). https://doi.org/10.1007/978-1-4615-3282-8_5
5. GVAQI: Greater Vancouver Regional District Air Quality and Source Control Department, Burnaby, BC, Canada (1997)
6. EPA: Guideline for reporting of daily air quality – air quality index (AQI), Environmental Protection Agency, EPA-454/R-99-010, Office of Air Quality Planning and Standards, Research Triangle Park, NC (1999)
7. Schell, E.B., Ackermann, I.J., Hass, H., Binkowski, F.S.: Modeling the formation of secondary organic aerosol within a comprehensive air quality model system. J. Geophys. Res.: Atmos. **106**, 275–293 (2001)
8. Ciolli, M., Cemin, A., Nave, D.: Modeling emission and dispersion of road traffic pollutant for the town of Trento. In: Proceedings of Open Source Free Software GIS - GRASS users Conference, University of Trento, Italy (2002)
9. Singh, G.: An index to measure depreciation in air quality in some coal mining areas of Korba Industrial Belt of Chhattisgarh, India. Environ. Monit. Assess. **122**, 309–317 (2006). https://doi.org/10.1007/s10661-005-9182-5
10. Kampa, M., Castanas, E.: Human health effects of air pollution. Environ. Pollut. **151**(2), 362–367 (2008)
11. Accenture & WPS: Cloud Computing and Sustainability: The Environmental Benefits of Moving to the Cloud (2010)
12. CPCB and Ministry of Environment and Forests: National Ambient Air Quality Status & Trends in India-2010. Central Pollution Control Board, GoI, January 2012
13. Doering, M.: High-resolution large-scale air pollution monitoring: approaches and challenges. In: ACM HotPlanet, pp. 5–9 (2011)
14. Taylor, P., Shenfeld, L.: Ontario's air pollution index and alert system. J. Air Pollut. Control Assoc. **20**, 612 (2012)
15. Taylor, P., Green, M.H.: An air pollution index based on sulfur dioxide and smoke shade. J. Air Pollut. Control Assoc. 37–41 (2012)

16. Ott, W.R., Thorn, G.C.: Air pollution index systems in the United States and Canada. J. Air Pollut. Control Assoc. 460–470 (2012)
17. Di Lonardo, S., et al.: The SensorWebBike for air quality monitoring in a smart city. In: IET Conference on Future Intelligent Cities, pp. 1–4 (2014)
18. Doering, M.: High-resolution large-scale air pollution monitoring: approaches and challenges, . In: HotPlanet 2011, pp. 5–9 (2011)
19. Ahmadi, A., Abbaspour, M., Arjmandi, R., Abedi, Z.: Air Quality Risk Index (AQRI) and its application for a megacity. Int. J. Environ. Sci. Technol. **12**, 3773–3780 (2015). https://doi.org/10.1007/s13762-015-0837-7
20. Corno, F., Montanaro, T., Migliore, C., Castrogiovanni, P.: SmartBike: an IoT crowd sensing platform for monitoring city air pollution. Int. J. Electr. Comput. Eng. **7**(6), 3602–3612 (2017)
21. Bergold, S., Steinmayr, R.: Personality and intelligence interact in the prediction of academic achievement. J. Intell. **6**, 27 (2018)
22. Hochadel, M., et al.: Predicting long-term average concentrations of traffic-related air pollutants using GIS-based information. Atmos. Environ. **40**(3), 542–553 (2006)
23. Jiang, X., Jia, J., Wu, G., Fang, J.: Demo: low-cost personal air-quality monitor, pp. 100–110 (2013)
24. Jiang, Y., et al.: MAQS. In: Proceedings of the 13th International Conference on Ubiquitous Computing - UbiComp 2011, p. 271 (2011)
25. Kaur, P.D.: Optimization of cloud resources for air pollution monitoring devices. In: 16th Proceedings of International Conference on Advances in Information Communication Technology & Computing, vol. 28, pp. 2–7 (2016)
26. Kim, S., Paulos, E., Mankoff, J.: inAir. In: Proceedings of the SIGCHI Conference on Human Factors in Computing Systems - CHI 2013, p. 2745 (2013)
27. Zheng, Y., Liu, F., Hsieh, H.: U-air: when urban air quality inference meets big data. In: KDD, pp. 1436–1444 (2013)
28. Cheng, Y., et al.: AirCloud. In: Proceedings of the 12th ACM Conference on Embedded Networked Sensor Systems - SenSys 2014, pp. 251–265 (2014)
29. Zhuang, Y., Lin, F., Yoo, E., Xu, W.: AirSense: a portable context-sensing device for personal air quality monitoring, pp. 17–22 (2015)
30. Adeleke, J.A., Moodley, D.: An ontology for proactive indoor environmental quality monitoring and control. In: Proceedings of the 2015 Annual Research Conference on South African Institute of Computer Scientists and Information Technologists - SAICSIT 2015, pp. 1–10 (2015)
31. Zhang, C., Yan, J., Li, C., Rui, X., Liu, L., Bie, R.: On estimating air pollution from photos using convolutional neural network. In: Proceedings of the 2016 ACM Multimedia Conference, MM 2016, pp. 297–301 (2016)
32. Asgari, M., Farnaghi, M., Ghaemi, Z.: Predictive mapping of urban air pollution using Apache Spark on a Hadoop cluster (2017)
33. Min, K.T., Lundrigan, P., Patwari, N.: Demo abstract: IASA - indoor air quality sensing and automation, pp. 277–278 (2017)
34. Yi, X., Zhang, J., Wang, Z., Li, T., Zheng, Y.: Deep distributed fusion network for air quality prediction. In: Proceedings of the 24th ACM SIGKDD International Conference on Knowledge Discovery & Data Mining - KDD 2018, pp. 965–973 (2018)
35. Singla, S.: Air quality friendly route recommendation system. In: Proceedings of the 2018 Workshop on MobiSys 2018 Ph.D. Forum - MobiSys PhD Forum 2018, pp. 9–10 (2018)
36. Lin, Y., et al.: Exploiting spatiotemporal patterns for accurate air quality forecasting using deep learning. In: Proceedings of the 26th ACM SIGSPATIAL International Conference on Advances in Geographic Information Systems - SIGSPATIAL 2018, pp. 359–368 (2018)

37. James, J.Q., Yu, S., Lam, A.Y.S.: Sensor deployment for air pollution monitoring using public transportation system, no. 2, pp. 10–15 (2012)
38. Kotsev, A., Schade, S., Craglia, M., Gerboles, M., Spinelle, L., Signorini, M.: Next generation air quality platform: openness and interoperability for the internet of things. Sensors (Switzerland) 16(3), 1–16 (2016)
39. Wang, S., Paul, M.J., Dredze, M.: Social media as a sensor of air quality and public response in china, J. Med. Internet Res. 17(3), e22 (2015)
40. Tse, R., Xiao, Y., Pau, G., Fdida, S., Roccetti, M., Marfia, G.: Sensing pollution on online social networks: a transportation perspective. Mob. Netw. Appl. 21(4), 688–707 (2016). https://doi.org/10.1007/s11036-016-0725-5
41. Sammarco, M., Tse, R., Pau, G., Marfia, G.: Using geosocial search for urban air pollution monitoring. Pervasive Mob. Comput. 35, 15–31 (2017)
42. Mei, S., Li, H., Fan, J., Zhu, X., Dyer, C.R.: Inferring air pollution by sniffing social media. In: Proceedings of IEEE/ACM International Conference on Advances in Social Networks Analysis and Mining, ASONAM 2014, pp. 534–539 (2014)
43. Jiang, S., Alves, A., Rodrigues, F., Ferreira Jr, J., Pereira, F.C.: Mining point-of-interest data from social networks for urban land use classification and disaggregation. Comput. Environ. Urban Syst. 53, 36–46 (2015)
44. Chen, J., Chen, H., Hu, D., Pan, J.Z., Zhou, Y.: Smog disaster forecasting using social web data and physical sensor data. In: Proceedings of IEEE International Conference on Big Data (Big Data), pp. 991–998 (2015)
45. Microsoft: The Carbon Benefits of Cloud Computing (2019)
46. Singh, P., Paprzycki, M., Bhargava, B., Chhabra, J., Kaushal, N., Kumar, Y. (eds.): Futuristic Trends in Network and Communication Technologies, FTNCT 2018. CCIS, vol. 958. Springer, Singapore (2018). https://doi.org/10.1007/978-981-13-3804-5
47. Harkat, M., Mansouri, M.: Enhanced data validation strategy of air quality monitoring network. Environ. Res. 160, 183–194 (2018)
48. Briggs, D.: Environmental pollution and the global burden of disease, no. January, pp. 1–24 (2018)
49. Aujla, G.S., Chaudhary, R., Kumar, N., Das, A.K., Rodrigues, J.J.P.C.: SecSVA: secure storage, verification, and auditing of big data in the cloud environment. IEEE Commun. Mag. 56(1), 78–85 (2018)

An Efficient SIP Authentication Scheme for Multiserver Infrastructure

Brij B. Gupta and Varun Prajapati[(⊠)]

Department of Computer Engineering, NIT Kurukshetra,
Kurukshetra, Haryana, India
Gupta.brij@gmail.com, prajapativarun570@gmail.com

Abstract. Session Initiation Protocol (SIP) is used between user and server to generate and agree upon a new session key through authentication mechanism. Many single server SIP authentication schemes have been proposed, but we need multiserver scheme to make it more realistic and feasible for implementation. It was found that some schemes work only for single server model and are not possible to scale up for multiserver environment. While some models support multiserver architecture but are vulnerable to known attacks. In this paper, we propose a new authentication scheme for SIP which can support multiserver environment. Security evaluation was done against various known attacks to check strength of the proposed scheme. Various functionalities like mutual authentication and user anonymity is also supported by the newly proposed scheme. Further our model is relatively more efficient as we establish connection only by using hash functions which are lightweight operations.

Keywords: SIP · Security · Multiserver scheme · Mutual authentication · AVISPA · User anonymity

1 Introduction

The Internet Engineering Task Force (IETF) designed SIP in 1996. SIP 1.0 was standardized as RFC 2543 in 1999 and accepted as 3GPP communication protocol in 2000. SIP 2.0 was released in 2014 as RFC 3261 [1]. SIP is a client server protocol, so session initiator acts as client and the receiver acts as server. Receiver verifies identity of client before sending reply to received request, and sender verifies identity of server before establishing a secure connection. Thus mutual authentication becomes a key property of SIP. SIP was found vulnerable due to its open-text nature [2].

Many different authentication schemes have been proposed by researchers using different protocols like extensible authentication protocol (EAP) [3], password authentication protocol (PAP) [4], challenge handshake authentication protocol (CHAP) [5] and microsoft challenge handshake authentication protocol (MS-CHAP) [6]. Further different authentication methods can be implemented in EAP framework like EAP-TLS (Transport Level Security), EAP-TTLS (Tunneled Transport Layer Security), EAP-MD5 (Message Digest 5), EAP-PEAP (Private Key Infrastructure EAP), EAP-LEAP (Lightweight EAP), EAP-POTP (Protected One Time Password) and EAP-PSK (Pre-Shared Key) [7].

© Springer Nature Singapore Pte Ltd. 2020
P. K. Singh et al. (Eds.): FTNCT 2019, CCIS 1206, pp. 64–74, 2020.
https://doi.org/10.1007/978-981-15-4451-4_6

A general working mechanism of password is shown in Fig. 1. Initially user sends a login message to the server via an open insecure channel. This message comprises of a challenge which is sent to server. If server can successfully solve the challenge, then the details of user are revealed to server. Server then sends an appropriate response message to user along with a challenge from server. User first verifies authenticity of server based on the received message and after successful identity verification solves the received challenge from server. An appropriate response mechanism is sent to server by user which is used to verify user identity at server. After successful authentication of user and server, a session key is created between server and user which ensures secure exchange of messages on insecure channel.

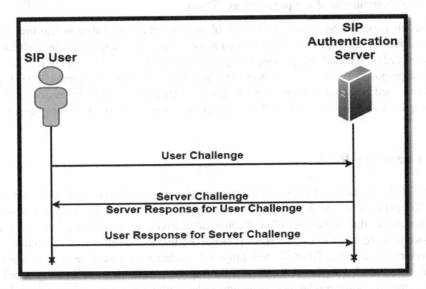

Fig. 1. Working of basic password authentication protocol.

Offline user identity verification is another key property used to identify wrong credentials at an early stage [2]. This enabled server to address only legitimate login attempts as scenarios with wrong credentials were no longer addressed by server. This provided resistance to stolen verifier attack and provided enhanced scalability and increased efficiency by eliminating the need of a verification table.

Rest of this paper is divided as follows: Sect. 2 provides overview of different SIP authentication schemes along with their disadvantages. In Sect. 3, the proposed model is divided into 5 phases and their steps are explained in detail. Section 4 provides formal, informal and comparative security analysis of the proposed model. We conclude our paper in Sect. 5 and provide scope for future work.

2 Motivation and Contribution

Security is backbone of any infrastructure which operates on a large scale. Success or failure of some operations lie in privacy of the tasks carried out to reach the goal. In order to establish a proper security protocols, it is essential to have strong authentication mechanism. Primary goal of authentication mechanism is to ensure that only legitimate parties can access the information stored on the system. Secondary goal of authentication mechanism can be distribution of secure session keys for further communication which is crucial factor for providing security in distributed wired and wireless networks.

Key contributions of the paper are as follows:

1. In this paper we addressed the key problem of synchronizing data in real time on multiserver environments. We proposed a new security mechanism in which all data is stored on the card and provided a dynamic verifier to verify the data in real time.
2. We proposed a system which is extremely efficient in terms of authentication. We have used only lightweight hash functions which leads to efficient processor utilization and provides output with less computations without compromising security.

3 Literature Review

Yoon et al. [8] claimed to develop a scheme which provided perfect forward secrecy but Xie [9] proved that the scheme was vulnerable to password guessing and stolen verifier attacks due to presence of verification table. Zhang et al. [10] proposed a secure password based scheme but Tu et al. [11] proved that the scheme was vulnerable to impersonation attacks, Tu et al. then proposed a scheme to overcome impersonation attack but Farash [12] proved this scheme was vulnerable to masquerading attack. Farash then proposed a scheme to overcome vulnerability but Lu et al. [13] proved this scheme vulnerable to server masquerading attack, password guessing attack and could not provide early detection of wrong passwords.

Chaudhry et al. [14] demonstrated Zhang et al. and Farash's schemes were vulnerable to replay and denial of service attacks. Chaudhry et al.'s scheme was proved to have inefficient login and authentication phase and provided no user anonymity by Maitra et al. [1]. Maitra et al. then proposed a scheme to overcome said vulnerabilities but it consists global clock in login phase which suffers through clock synchronization problem, and contained cipher operations which made system less efficient.

Major identified issues in literature review includes presence of elements which made scheme vulnerable like global clock and verification table. Absence of desired functionalities like early wrong password detection, was also noted. It was observed that using only cryptographic hash functions increased efficiency of the system when compared with cipher operations.

4 Proposed Model

Proposed Scheme consists of 5 different phases. First phase is server initialization phase where we initialize our master server which is responsible for registration of new users and servers. Second phase is server registration phase which is used to register new remote servers by master server. Third phase is used to register new users done by

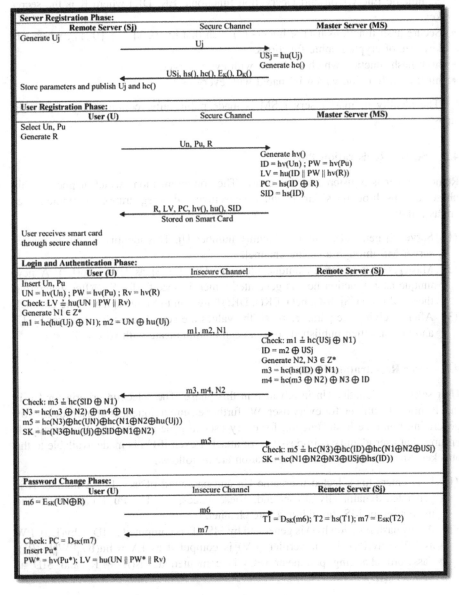

Fig. 2. Different phases of proposed model.

master server. Fourth phase is used for user login and mutual authentication between server and user. Fifth phase is used by user to change their passwords. These phases are explained in detail in Fig. 2.

4.1   A Initiation Phase

Master server SM generates system parameters which are as follows:

- Symmetric Encryption and Decryption functions (EK, DK) where K is the secret key.
- Secure hash functions hs() & hu() $\in$ h() such that h: $\{0, 1\}^* \rightarrow \{0, 1\}^t$, where t is key size of cryptographic functions.
- hs(): hash function which is shared with every server.
- hu(): hash function which is shared with every user.

The identity of master server SM is made public after completion of following steps.

4.2   Server Registration Phase

Remote server is registered in this phase. The communications which happen in this phase happens through a secure channel. Steps involved in registration of remote server are as follows:

(1) Server Sj generates a unique identity number Uj. This identity is sent to master server MS through a secure channel.
(2) Master server generates unique identifier USj for Sj as USj = hu(Uj). A new unique hash function hc() is generated which is specific for Sj. After generating these values, {USj, hs(), hc(), EK(), DK()} are sent to Sj through a secure channel.
(3) After receiving the parameters, all the values are stored securely on server Sj. Uj and hc() are then published so users can communicate with server Sj.

4.3   User Registration Phase

User selects his identity Un in advance in this phase. The selection criteria for Un is that it should be unique for every user. We further ensure uniqueness of user identity by generating a unique hash function for every user to generate identity dynamically. It ensures that user identity is impossible for attacker even if Un is made available to the attacker. Steps involved in user registration are as follows:

(1) User enters his selected username Un and password of user Pu. A number R is generated dynamically at user end. These values, i.e. (Un, Pu, R) are sent to the master server MS through a secure channel.
(2) A new hash function hv() is generated by MS. ID is computed as ID = hv(Un), PW as PW = hv(Pu). Local verifier (LV) is computed as LV = hu(ID||PW||hv(R)). Password changing parameter (PC) is computed as hs(ID $\oplus$ R) and SID as SID = hs(ID).

(3) Values {R, LV, PC, hv(), hu(), SID, EK(), DK()} are stored on smart card and sent securely to user.

4.4 Login and Authentication Phase

We check identity of user locally and then perform mutual authentication in this phase. All the messages are transferred through insecure channel in this phase. A login message is generated by user U and sent to server Sj. Sj provides verification for his identity and sends a challenge message to U. U first verifies identity of Sj and then provides the response to the received challenge to Sj. After successful verification of identities, session key SK is generated on both ends which is then used to communicate securely. SK is generated from the parameters generated dynamically at U and Sj respectively. Steps involved in this phase are as follows:

(1) User U enters Un and Pu in the system after entering smart card in the smart card reader. UN, PW and Rv are generated as $UN = hv(Un)$, $PW = hv(Pu)$ and $Rv = hv(R)$. User credentials are then verified locally and user is authenticated if $LV = hu(UN\|PW\|Rv)$.
(2) After successful user authentication, N1 is generated dynamically as $N1 \in Z^*$. Message m1 is generated as $m1 = hc(hu(Uj) \oplus N1)$. Message m2 is generated as $m2 = UN \oplus hu(Uj)$. Login message is sent to Sj as {m1, m2, N1}.
(3) Primary verification of user identity is done if $m1 = hc(USj \oplus N1)$. If primary verification is successful then user identity ID is generated as $ID = m2 \oplus USj$. N2 and N3 are generated dynamically as $N2, N3 \in Z^*$. Message m3 is generated as $m3 = hc(hs(ID) \oplus N1)$ and m4 as $m4 = hc(m3 \oplus N2) \oplus N3 \oplus ID$. Challenge message is sent from Sj to U as {m3, m4, N2}.
(4) U authenticates Sj if $m3 = hc(SID \oplus N1)$. After successful authentication, N3 is computed by U as $N3 = hc(m3 \oplus N2) \oplus m4 \oplus UN$. Message m5 is generated as $m5 = hc(N3) \oplus hc(UN) \oplus hc(N1 \oplus N2 \oplus hu(Uj))$. Session key SK is computed as $SK = hc(N3 \oplus hu(Uj) \oplus SID \oplus N1 \oplus N2)$. Message m5 is sent as the response message to Sj.
(5) Remote server Sj authenticates user U if $m5 = hc(N3) \oplus hc(ID) \oplus hc(N1 \oplus N2 \oplus USj)$. Session key SK is generated by Sj as $SK = hc(N1 \oplus N2 \oplus N3 \oplus USj \oplus hs(ID))$.

4.5 Password Change Phase

This phase is performed by user when user wants to change his password. Login and authentication phase must be executed by user first to ensure only legitimate user is accessing the card. Steps involved in this phase after execution of login and authentication phase are as follows:

(1) U generates m6 as $m6 = ESK (UNR)$. Message m6 is then sent to the Sj.
(2) Sj computes T1 as $T1 = DSK (m6)$. T2 is then computed as $T2 = hs(T1)$. Message m7 is computed as $m7 = ESK (T2)$.
(3) System prompts U to enter new password Pu* if $PC = DSK (m7)$. PW* is computed as $PW* = hv(Pu*)$. LV is updated as $LV = hu(UN\|PW*\|Rv)$.

5   Security Analysis

In this section, first formal security evaluation is done using AVISPA tool, then proposed scheme is informally evaluated against various known attacks followed by relative analysis against some similar schemes.

5.1   Formal Security Analysis

Automated Validation of Internet Security Protocols and Applications (AVISPA) tool is used for formal security evaluation of scheme. This tool supports High Level Protocol Specification Language (HLPSL) to input the proposed model. After evaluation, results are given as either SAFE or UNSAFE. There are 4 different back-ends which are supported by AVISPA through which we can evaluate our protocol. We will be using OMFC (On-the-fly Model Checker) back-end and ATSE (Constraint-logic-based Attack Searcher) back-end to evaluate our protocol. Figure 3 shows result of protocol evaluation as SAFE with ATSE back-end. Figure 4 shows result of protocol evaluation as SAFE with OFMC back-end.

We evaluate only the login and authentication phase as only this phase is carried out over an insecure channel. Some assumptions are made about entities of system, and they are as follows:

1. All the elements stored in smart card are secure and not accessible to adversary.
2. Adversary can access smart card and modify the outgoing and incoming messages.
3. Adversary cannot verify identity without response from remote server.
4. Adversary cannot alter the internal processing of data within smart card.

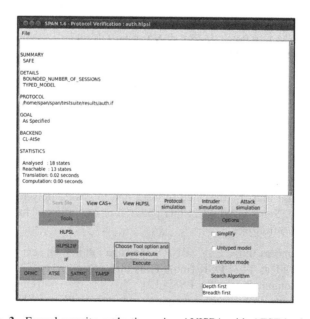

Fig. 3. Formal security evaluation using AVISPA with ATSE backend

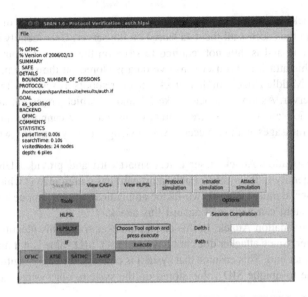

Fig. 4. Formal security evaluation using AVISPA with OFMC backend

5.2 Informal Security Analysis

We informally evaluate security of proposed model against different attacks and functionalities. Attacks like brute force attack, replay attack, stolen smart card attack, insider attack, man-in-the-middle attack and impersonation attack are used for evaluation. Functionalities like mutual authentication, user anonymity, secure session key generation, global clock synchronization and online password changing mechanism are used for evaluation. The informal evaluation of proposed model is as follows:

- Brute Force Attack: In our proposed model, we accept Un and Pu from the user. These parameters are used to generate local verifier token LV which is used to verify user identity. As it is hard to forge two parameters in polynomial time, our system can withstand against this attack.
- Replay Attack: In our proposed model, N1 is dynamically generated at user end and N2 and N3 at server end. These parameters are used for session key generation, and they ensure freshness property of message. By generating dynamic nonce at user and server end, our system can withstand against this attack.
- Stolen Smartcard Attack: User must enter Un and Pu to verify his identity locally. After verification of user identity, UN is generated which is used for generation of session key. As it is impossible to connect with server and verify identity without necessary parameters, our system can withstand this attack.
- Stolen Verifier Attack: In this attack, the details about user identity and password stored on server for verifying user identity is compromised and accessed by the attacker. This provides user with necessary knowledge to pose as a legitimate user and access the system. As we do not store any user specific data on the server which provides direct mapping to user credentials, our system can withstand this attack.

- Insider Attack: In this attack, the malicious attacker is already part of the system. Attacker can thus access all the data stored on the server. User identity is generated at the user end and is thus not required to store on the server. So our system can withstand this attack as no user sensitive data is stored on the system.
- Man-in-the-Middle Attack: In this attack, attacker spoofs as server with user and as user with server. As key parameters like N3 and ID which are essential for session key generation are not transferred directly and attacker cannot extract from the transferred messages without necessary knowledge, our system can withstand this attack.
- User Impersonation Attack: User enters smart card and provides Un and Pu to verify his identity in the system. Each smart card has a unique hv() which is used to generate user identity. Due to two-factor authentication and unique hv() for each user, our system can withstand against this attack.
- Server Impersonation Attack: In this attack, attacker spoofs his identity as genuine remote server. Since attacker does not have real hs(), SID value is not matched from attacker at user end. This ensures that system is connected to only legitimate remote servers. Due to unique SID value stored on the system, our system can withstand this attack.
- Mutual Authentication: In this functionality, both user and server initially verifies their identities before establishing secure connection with each other. User identity is verified from message m5 and server identity is verified through parameter SID. Thus, we provide mutual authentication in our system.
- User Anonymity: In our system, user identity is verified locally by smart card. A unique hv() stored on smart card is used to generate user identity UN. UN is then used by the system to generate session key. Our system provides user anonymity as there is no practical way to map Un to UN for every instance.
- Secure Session Key Generation: In our system, we use dynamically generated parameters i.e. N1, N2, N3 to generate SK thus ensuring that generated SK is also dynamic. SK is generated through ID and N3 which are never transferred in plain text format through insecure channels. This ensures that the generated SK is always random and secure. Thus, our system provides secure session key generation.
- Early detection of wrong passwords: In our system, user identity is verified locally at smart card through LV parameter. If the entered password is incorrect, then user authentication fails and server is not disturbed. Thus, our system provides early detection of wrong parameters using local verifier.
- Online Password Changing Mechanism: Password changing mechanism must first ensure that user identity is properly verified. In order to ensure successful user verification, we perform password change phase after login and authentication phase. We include server in this phase (making the mechanism online) to ensure that user identity is thoroughly verified. PC can be matched only after successful user authentication and establishing a secure channel with remote server. Thus, our system provides online password changing mechanism.

5.3 Comparative Security Analysis

In this section, the proposed scheme is compared with some schemes described in Sect. 2. This comparative analysis is done in Table 1. We observe that the proposed scheme is secure against all attacks. Other desired properties of proposed scheme include Efficient login and password change phase, presence of user anonymity and absence of verification table and global clocks which are not present in every other schemes.

Table 1. Comparative security analysis.

Attack types	Zhang et al.	Tu et al.	Farash et al.	Chaudhry et al.	Maitra et al.	Our model
Insider attack	N	N	N	N	N	N
Replay attack	Y	Y	Y	N	N	N
Impersonation attack	Y	N	N	N	N	N
Efficient login phase	A	A	A	A	P	P
Efficient password change phase	A	A	A	A	P	P
User anonymity	A	A	A	A	P	P
Global clock	A	A	A	A	P	A
Verification table	A	A	A	A	A	A

Y: Vulnerable against attack
N: Secure against attack
P: Functionality present
A: Functionality absent

6 Conclusion and Future Scope

SIP is key component for VoIP communications but was found vulnerable due to its open text nature. Various schemes were proposed for single server environment but it is infeasible to implement system in single server in real world. Major disadvantage of some multiserver environments was storage of data on server and synchronizing them in real time.

So in this paper, we proposed a multiserver SIP authentication scheme. Major advantage of proposed model is that the storage of data is done on cards instead of server. This solves the problem of synchronizing data in real time. Formal evaluation of scheme was done with AVISPA tool and informal evaluation was done for various known attacks. Proposed scheme is highly efficient as only hash operations are performed over cryptographic cipher operations. Further improvement can be done in the scheme so that remote server can verify identity of the user without the presence of shared parameter.

Acknowledgements. This publication is an outcome of the R&D works undertaken under the YFRF project under Visvesvaraya Ph.D. Scheme of Ministry of Electronics & Information Technology, Government of India and being implemented by Digital India Corporation.

References

1. Maitra, T., Giri, D., Mohapatra, R.N.: SAS-SIP: a secure authentication scheme based on ECC and a fuzzy extractor for session initiation protocol. Cryptologia **43**(3), 212–232 (2019). https://doi.org/10.1080/01611194.2018.1548391
2. Dhillon, P.K., Kalra, S.: Secure and efficient ECC based SIP authentication scheme for VoIP communications in internet of things. Multimed. Appl. **78**, 22199–22222 (2019). https://doi.org/10.1007/s11042-019-7466-y
3. Leibovitz, A.M., et al.: Extensible access control architecture (2015)
4. Song, R.: Advanced smart card based password authentication protocol. Comput. Stand. Inter. **32**(5–6), 321–325 (2010)
5. Hussein, K.Q., Ibrahim, A.S.: Client authentication by selected secure password-based on image using challenge handshake authentication protocol. Iraqi J. Inf. Technol. **9**(3), 39–49 (2019)
6. Schneier, B., Wagner, D., et al.: Cryptanalysis of microsoft's PPTP authentication extensions (MS-CHAPv2). In: Baumgart, R. (ed.) Secure Networking—CQRE [Secure] ' 99. CQRE 1999. LNCS, vol. 1740, pp. 192–203. Springer, Heidelberg (1999). https://doi.org/10.1007/3-540-46701-7_17
7. Prakash, A., Kumar, U.: Authentication protocols and techniques: a survey. Int. J. Comput. Sci. Eng. **6**, 1014–1020 (2018)
8. Yoon, E.-J., Shin, Y.-N., Jeon, I.-S., Yoo, K.-Y.: Robust mutual authentication with a key agreement scheme for the session initiation protocol. IETE Tech. Rev. **27**(3), 203–213 (2010)
9. Xie, Q.: A new authenticated key agreement for session initiation protocol. Int. J. Commun. Syst. **25**(1), 47–54 (2012)
10. Zhang, L., Tang, S., Cai, Z.: Efficient and flexible password authenticated key agreement for voice over internet protocol session initiation protocol using smart card. Int. J. Commun. Syst. **27**(11), 2691–2702 (2014)
11. Tu, H., Kumar, N., Chilamkurti, N., Rho, S.: An improved authentication protocol for session initiation protocol using smart card. Peer Peer Netw. Appl. **8**(5), 903–910 (2015)
12. Farash, M.S.: Security analysis and enhancements of an improved authentication for session initiation protocol with provable security. Peer Peer Netw. Appl. **9**(1), 82–91 (2016)
13. Lu, Y., Li, L., Peng, H., Yang, Y.: An anonymous two-factor authenticated key agreement scheme for session initiation protocol using elliptic curve cryptography. Multimed. Tools Appl. **76**(2), 1801–1815 (2017)
14. Chaudhry, S.A., Naqvi, H., Sher, M., Farash, M.S., Hassan, M.U.: An improved and provably secure privacy preserving authentication protocol for SIP. Peer Peer Netw. Appl. **10**(1), 1–15 (2017)

Synchronization of the Quantum Key Distribution System with Priori Information About the Fiber-Optic Line Length

Konstantin Rumyantsev[1](✉) [iD] and H. H.-Sh. Shakir[2]

[1] Southern Federal University, Taganrog,
Rostov Region, Russian Federation
rke2004@mail.ru
[2] Ministry of Education, Baghdad, Iraq
hyder.almansoor@yahoo.com

Abstract. The synchronization is explored for the quantum key distribution (QKD), where photon pulses are utilized as synchronized signals. The analyzed two-stage synchronization algorithm is based on the truth that legitimate users of the QKD system have a priori information with respect to the length of the fiber-optic line. Explanatory expressions are gotten that build up the functional relationship of the energy, probability and time parameters of the single-photon synchronization subsystem with the parameters of the optical fiber, fiber optical transmitter, single-photon avalanche photodiode (SPAD). The necessities for the selection of the least number of frames at the search stage and the allowable number of tests at the testing stage are formulated.

Keywords: Quantum key distribution · Auto-compensation system · Synchronization · Two-stage single-photon algorithm · Fiber-optic line length

1 Introduction

The utilize of quantum key distribution protocols for messages enciphering meets the requirements of absolute secrecy [1–3]. However, in the synchronization process, control of signals transmitted between stations is not provided. However, in the process of joining the QKD system into synchronism, control of signals transmitted between stations is not provided. Hence the removal of energy part at the quantum channel does not influence the operation of the QKD system. Presence of the intruder will not be detected.

To increase security from unauthorized access, the principle of synchronization of receiving-transmitting and coding stations with the help of photon sync signals [4, 5] can be used. Here the photon sync signal represents the optical pulse of the transmitter, attenuated to the level of registration in it on average less than one photon. Notice, that the attenuation of the optical pulse to the photon level is carried out at propagation of the synchronization signal via fiber-optic line from the coding station to the receiving-transmitting station.

© Springer Nature Singapore Pte Ltd. 2020
P. K. Singh et al. (Eds.): FTNCT 2019, CCIS 1206, pp. 75–86, 2020.
https://doi.org/10.1007/978-981-15-4451-4_7

In [6–9], a two-stage synchronization algorithm for receiving-transmitting and coding stations of the QKD system was proposed and investigated. The algorithm is based on the fact that at the receiving end of the search complex, the repetition period T_s and the duration τ_s of the optical sync signals are known. At the 1st synchronization stage (search stage), the equipment registers a photon in the first frame $[0, T_s]$. If there is no photon registration in the 1st frame, the search continues in subsequent frames $[(j - 1)T_s, jT_s], j \geq 2$.

If a photon is registered in the N_T frame, at the time t_{ph}, then the equipment transfers to the 2nd stage (testing stage), at which the photodetector registers photons only in intervals

$$[(k - 1) \cdot T_s + t_{strob1}, (k - 1) \cdot T_s + t_{strob2}], k = \overline{1, N_{T.max}}.$$

The value t_{strob1} corresponds to the beginning moment, and t_{strob2} - to the moment of the end of the gating pulse with a duration τ_{strob} during the testing. The value τ_d represents the time delay between the moments of registration and reception of a photon.

The synchronization algorithm assumes that if a photon is repeatedly registered during the N_{test}-th test, at that point a choice is made about reception a photon pulse within the analyzed frame. If for a permissible number of tests $N_{test.max}$ there is no photon registration, then the equipment returns to the search stage again.

The two-stage synchronization algorithm provides a significant gain in time of synchronization with the use of real SPAD in comparison with the algorithm, which divides the frame into time windows [10]. The algorithm provides the low probability of synchronization error.

In any case, the two-stage algorithm can be effectively applied only to short communication lines (tens of kilometers), while to sufficiently long fiber optic links (around 100 km), its use gets to be impossible due to the probability of synchronization error. Actually, the limitation on the length of the fiber-optic line due to the synchronization subsystem also limit the range of the quantum key distribution.

At the same time, it should be noted that the earlier analysis of the two-stage algorithm is focused on complete a priori uncertainty regarding the fiber-optic line length. From a practical point of view, the users of the QKD system always have a priori information about the length of the fiber optic line. First, the geographical location of users determines the low boundary of the analyzed length of the fiber optic line $L_{TF.min}$. Secondly, there is information about the used optical fiber, which gives information about the upper boundary of the fiber optic line $L_{TF.max}$.

It defines the relevance of the research of a two-stage algorithm of single-photon synchronization of stations in the autocompensation QKD system with a priori information about the length of the fiber-optic line.

2 Algorithm of Two-Stage Single-Photon Synchronization with a Priori Information in Relation to the Length of the Fiber-Optic Line

Let at the moment t = 0 the receiving-transmitting station generates an optical pulse. In case the length of the fiber optic line is $L_{TF.min}$, then the optical pulse reaches the coding station at time t_{1min} (Fig. 1). After phase encoding, the photon (attenuated) pulse is directed toward the receiving-transmitting station. The photon is received by station during the moment t_{2min}. In this case, the photon travels a distance greater than at 2 times of the length of the fiber-optic line.

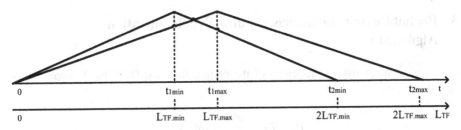

Fig. 1. Illustration of a two-stage time synchronization algorithm

Similarly, if the fiber-optic line length is $L_{TF.max}$ then the optical pulse reaches the coding station at time t_{1max}, and the photon pulse is received by the receiving and transmitting station at time t_{2max}.

The photon propagation velocity in the optical fiber v_{OF} is depended on the refractive index of optical radiation in its core n_{OF} at a wavelength λ_s:

$$v_{OF} = c_{opt}/n_{OF} \tag{1}$$

where c_{opt} = 300 000 km/s is the velocity of radiation propagation in vacuum.

Therefore, from a practical point of view, it is of interest to detect a photon only in the time interval $[t_{2min}, t_{2max}]$.

When oriented to the upper boundary of the fiber-optic line $L_{TF.max}$, the repetition period of the optical sync pulses should satisfy the condition

$$T_s \geq T_{s.min} = \frac{2 \cdot L_{TF.max}}{v_{OF}} \tag{2}$$

The multiplier 2 within the equation takes into account that within the auto-compensation QKD system a photon passes twice a fiber optic line: a receiving and transmitting station → fiber-optic line → an encoding station → a fiber-optic line a receiving and transmitting station (see Fig. 1).

The equipment of two-stage single-photon synchronization with a priori information regarding the fiber-optic line length successively in each frame $[(j-1) \cdot T_s, j \cdot T_s], j \geq 1$ at the search stage registers the reception of a photon or DCP in interval $[(j-1) \cdot T_s + t_{2min}, (j-1) \cdot T_s + t_{2max}], j \geq 1$.

When registering a photon, the equipment transfers to testing, in which a single-photon photodetector is sensitive to receiving a photon only during gating pulse with a duration

$$\tau_{strob} = 2 \cdot \tau_s + 2 \cdot \Delta T_s \tag{3}$$

where ΔT_s is the instability of the sync pulse period.

3 Probabilistic Characteristics of a Synchronization Algorithm

To describe the statistical properties of the photon flux and DCP, the Poisson distribution can be used

$$Pr\{n|\bar{n}\} = \frac{\bar{n}^n}{n!} \cdot \exp(-\bar{n}).$$

Here, the probability of generation of n events decided by the average number of photons and/or DCP during the observation time (duration of a frame, photon pulse or gating pulse) $\bar{n}$.

Let ξ_{DCR} be the frequency of registered DCP. At that point the average number of noise pulses is

$$\overline{n_{DCR.\tau}} = \xi_{DCR} \cdot \tau_{an} \tag{4}$$

during the analysis

$$\tau_{an} = t_{2max} - t_{2min} = 2\frac{L_{TF.max} - L_{TF.min}}{v_{OF}} = 2\frac{\Delta L_{TF}}{v_{OF}}. \tag{5}$$

For the duration of the optical pulse τ_s the average number of DCP will be

$$\overline{n_{DCR.s}} = \xi_{DCR} \cdot \tau_s. \tag{6}$$

The average number of registered photons $\bar{n}_s$ for the photon pulse duration with the real fiber-optic line length L_{TF} is decided by the equation

$$\overline{n_s} = \overline{n_{s0}} \cdot 10^{-\frac{\alpha_{OF}[\text{дБ/км}] \cdot L_{TF}[\text{км}]}{10}}, \tag{7}$$

where $\overline{n_{s0}}$ is the average number of photons within the pulse at the exit of the coding station; α_{OF} is the attenuation loss of the optical fiber.

The moment $t_1 \in [t_{2min}, t_{2max}]$ corresponds to the moment of reception of the photon pulse in the 1st frame $[0, T_s]$. Then the conditional detection probability of photon pulse at the search stage during the analysis of the first frame is equal to

$$P_1\{t_1\} = exp(-\xi_{DCR} \cdot t_1) \cdot P_{Ds}.$$

Here, the value $exp(-\xi_{DCR} \cdot t_1)$ determines the absence probability of DCP in the interval $[0, t_1]$ preceding the reception moment of the photon pulse. The second value P_{Ds} determines the probability of registration of at least one photon or DCP in the interval $[t_1, t_1 + \tau_s]$:

$$P_{\tau s} = 1 - exp(-\overline{n_{DCR.s}} - \overline{n_s}). \tag{8}$$

In case the signal is not detected within the 1st frame, at that point it is possible within the second frame in the interval $[t_1 + T_s, t_1 + T_S + \tau_s]$ with conditional detection probability

$$P_2\{t_1\} = exp(-\xi_{DCR} \cdot t_1) \cdot P_{T0} \cdot P_{\tau s}.$$

The nonattendance probability of photons and DCP P_{T0} is decided by the average numbers of photons during the duration of the photon pulse $\overline{n_s}$ and DCP during the analysis $\overline{n_{DCR.\tau}}$:

$$P_{T0} = exp(-\overline{n_s} - \overline{n_{DCR.\tau}}). \tag{9}$$

Using the method of mathematical induction, we find the conditional detection probability of photon pulse at the search stage in the j-th frame

$$P_j\{t_1\} = exp(-\xi_{DCR} \cdot t_1) \cdot P_{T0}^{j-1} K \cdot P_{\tau s}.$$

The conditional detection probability of photon pulse at the search stage during N_T frames will be

$$P_D\{t_1, N_T\} = \sum_{j=1}^{N_T} P_j\{t_1\} = exp(-\xi_{DCR} \cdot t_1) \cdot P_{\tau s} \cdot \sum_{j=1}^{N_T} P_{T0}^{j-1}.$$

The series $P_1\{t_1\}, P_2\{t_1\}, \ldots, P_{N_T}\{t_1\}$ represents the geometric progression with the denominator of the progression P_{T0}. Utilizing the expression to calculate the sum of the first N_T members of a geometric progression, we discover

$$P_D\{t_1, N_T\} = exp(-\xi_{DCR} \cdot t_1) \cdot \frac{1 - P_{T0}^{N_T}}{1 - P_{T0}} \cdot P_{\tau s}.$$

The unconditional detection probability (hereinafter the probability) of photon pulse at the search stage for N_T frames is found by averaging the probability $P_D\{t_1, N_T\}$ over the probability density of distribution $\omega(t_1)$ of the appearance moment of the photon pulse $t_1 \in [t_{2min}, t_{2max}]$

$$P_D\{N_T\} = \int_{t_{2min}}^{t_{2max}} \omega(t_1) \cdot P_D\{t_1, N_T\} \cdot dt_1.$$

Considering the distribution of the appearance moment of an optical pulse in the interval $t_1 \in [t_{2min}, t_{2max}]$

$$\omega(t_1) = \frac{1}{t_{2max} - t_{2min}} = \frac{1}{\tau_{an}},$$

we find

$$P_D\{N_T\} = \frac{1}{\tau_{an}} \cdot \frac{1 - P_{T0}^{N_T}}{1 - P_{T0}} \cdot P_{\tau s} \cdot \int_{t_{2min}}^{t_{2max}} \exp(-\xi_{DCR} \cdot t_1) \cdot dt_1.$$

After integration we have

$$P_D\{N_T\} = P_{D1} \cdot \frac{1 - P_{T0}^{N_T}}{1 - P_{T0}} \cdot P_{\tau s}, \tag{10}$$

where

$$P_{D1} = \frac{\exp(-\xi_{DCR} \cdot t_{2min}) - \exp(-\xi_{DCR} \cdot t_{2max})}{\xi_{DCR} \cdot \tau_{an}} \tag{11}$$

is the average probability of the absence of DCP in the interval preceding the moment of reception of the photon pulse.

For an infinite number of frames $(N_T \rightarrow \infty)$, taking into account the strict inequality $P_{T0} < 1$, we find the maximum (limiting) detection probability of photon pulses in the search stage

$$P_{D.max} = P_{D1} \cdot \frac{P_{\tau s}}{1 - P_{T0}}. \tag{12}$$

Comparison of Eqs. (10) and (12) shows that the value $1 - P_{T0}^{N_T}$ in (10) determines the allowable fallout of detection probability of photon pulse at the search stage when the number of frames is limited to N_T. The probability deterioration can be given by the coefficient

$$K_D = \frac{P_D\{N_T \rightarrow \infty\}}{P_D\{N_T\}} = \frac{1}{1 - P_{T0}^{N_T}} > 1.$$

This permits us to formulate requirements for the choice of the least allowable number of frames at the search stage:

$$N_T \geq \frac{1}{ln(P_{T0})} \cdot ln\left(\frac{K_D - 1}{K_D}\right). \tag{13}$$

The average number of registered photons and DCP during the pulse duration τ_{strob} is equal to

$$\overline{n_{stob}} = \overline{n_s} + \xi_{DCR} \cdot \tau_{strob}. \tag{14}$$

Then the error probability in making a choice about detecting an optical sync signal at the testing stage can be calculated by the equation

$$P_{err.test} = exp(-N_{test} \cdot \overline{n_{stob}}). \tag{15}$$

The expression permits us to formulate the requirements for the determination of an acceptable number of N_{test} tests to guaranteed error probability $P_{err.test0}$ in making a decision about the detection of a clock signal at the testing stage:

$$N_{test} \geq N_{test.min} = \frac{1}{\overline{n_{stob.min}}} \cdot ln\left(\frac{1}{P_{err.test}}\right). \tag{16}$$

For the described algorithm, the error probability following two stages of synchronization is

$$P_{err.sync} = 1 - P_D\{N_T\} \cdot (1 - P_{err.test}). \tag{17}$$

4 The Change in the Probability of Synchronization Errors Along the Link Length

We study the behavior of probabilistic characteristics within the analyzed fiber-optic line of 20...30 km for the synchronization subsystem.

The results of the probability calculation of a synchronization error are presented in Fig. 2 by a solid line, of the nondetection probability $(1 - P_D\{N_T\})$ at the search stage - by the dashed line, of the probability of testing error $P_{err.test}$ - by the dash-dotted line. Here, the dotted line represents the receiving probability a photon and DCP during the analysis of the fiber-optic line section $1 - P_{T0}$.

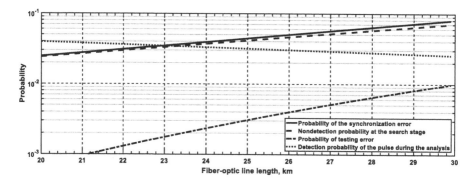

Fig. 2. Changes in probabilistic characteristics within the fiber-optic line section

The dependency analysis in Fig. 2 reveals a important features.

1. By expanding the number of tests, it is possible to provide an arbitrarily low probability of a testing error. This streamlines the expression (17)

$$P_{\text{err.sync}} \cong 1 - P_D\{N_T\}. \tag{18}$$

2. In QKD systems, the condition $\overline{n_{DCR.s}} \ll \overline{n_s} < 0,1$ is always satisfied. Then, to calculate the reception probability of at least one photon or DCP in the interval $[t_1, t_1 + \tau_s]$, we can use the approximate equation

$$P_{\tau s} \cong 1 - \exp(-\overline{n_s}) \cong \overline{n_s} - \overline{n_s}^2/2. \tag{19}$$

3. In the example, the average number of DCP, even during the duration of the frame determined by the line length of 30 km, is $0.002 \ll 1$. This is 3.4 times less than the average number of DCP during the analysis of the fiber optic Section (0.00059). At the same time, even at the end of the fiber-optic line with a length of 100 km, the average number of photons in a photon pulse is 0.001. Then

$$P_{D1} \cong 1 - \xi_{\text{DCR}} \cdot t_{2\min} - 0,5 \cdot \xi_{\text{DCR}} \cdot \tau_{\text{an}}. \tag{20}$$

4. The average number of registered photons and DCP during gating pulse τ_{strob} is determined only by the average number of photons in the photon pulse

$$\overline{n_{\text{stob}}} = \overline{n_s} + \xi_{\text{DCR}} \cdot \tau_{\text{strob}} \cong \overline{n_s}. \tag{21}$$

Then the error probability at the testing stage can be calculated by the equation

$$P_{\text{err.test}} = \exp(-N_{\text{test}} \cdot \overline{n_{\text{stob}}}) \cong \exp(-N_{\text{test}} \cdot \overline{n_s}).$$

Eqs. (18)–(22) can significantly simplify the calculation of synchronization parameters.

In confirmation of established features, on Fig. 3 are presented the results of calculations at 9 values of the minimum fiber-optic line length $L_{TF.min}$. It is assumed that the initial uncertainty in the line length is 10%. For each section, the numbers of frames and tests are calculated using Eqs. (13) and (16).

In Fig. 3, the results of probability calculations of the synchronization error are represented by solid lines, of the nondetection probability at the search stage $(1 - P_D\{N_T\})$ - by dashed lines, and of the probability of testing error $P_{err.test}$ - by dash-dotted lines.

Due to the increase in the length of fiber-optic line sections from 1 to 9 km with an increase in their minimum length $L_{TF.min}$ from 10 to 90 km, the analysis time increases almost at 10 times. At the same time, the average number of DCP during analysis varies at 9 times. But the minimum average number of photons during the analysis drops at 17 times from 0.060 to 0.001. As a result, the ratio of the average number of photons and DCP during the analysis falls more than at 500 times. Naturally, this determines the increase in the probability of synchronization error with an increase in the minimum length of the section.

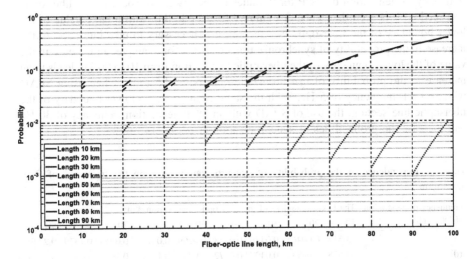

Fig. 3. Changes in the probability characteristics within the sections of fiber-optic line

Dependencies in Fig. 3 confirm the ability to maintain the probability of a testing error of no higher than a given level (in the example, 0.01). Although this requires an increase in the number of tests (Fig. 4). In the example, this will require increasing the number of tests at 58 times from 76 to 4397.

The results of calculations show that the number of frames at the search stage increases almost at 40 times from 50 to 1932. However, even this does not guarantee that the probability of a synchronization error is not above a certain level.

A comparative analysis of the probabilities in Fig. 3 confirms the possibility of using the approximate Eq. (18) to calculate the probability of a synchronization error.

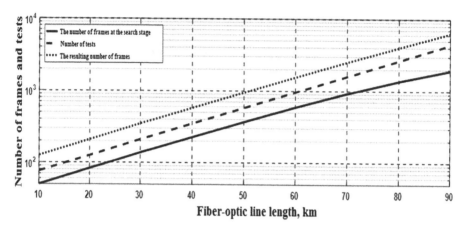

Fig. 4. Dependencies of the number of frames and tests from the section length of the QKD line

Table 1 shows the dependences of the probability of synchronization errors on the frequency of generation of DCP for 9 values of the lower boundary of the fiber-optic line section. It is seen that when designing a fiber-optic line with a large value of the lower boundary of the fiber-optic line section, it is necessary to take into account the increase in the probability of synchronization error. So, for example, an increase in the value of the lower boundary of the fiber-optic line section from 10 to 90 km leads to an increase in the probability of synchronization errors by 4.5 times when using SPAD with an DCP frequency of 5 Hz. With the same changes in the lower boundary of the fiber-optic line section, the use of SPAD with an DCP generation frequency of 30 Hz will increase the probabilities of synchronization errors by 14 times.

Table 1. Dependence of the probability of synchronization error on the frequency of DCP generation

Frequency of generation of DCP, Hz	The lower boundary of the fiber optic line section, km								
	10	20	30	40	50	60	70	80	90
5	0.0517	0.00461	0.0426	0.0438	0.0509	0.0677	0.0995	0.1529	0.2340
10	0.0528	0.0491	0.0497	0.0572	0.0757	0.1109	0.1699	0.2587	0.3765
15	0.0538	0.0520	0.0567	0.0704	0.0996	0.01505	0.2306	0.3417	0.4752
20	0.0549	0.0564	0.0636	0.0833	0.1221	0.1870	0.2834	0.4085	0.5475
25	0.0560	0.0593	0.0705	0.0964	0.1437	0.2206	0.3297	0.4635	0.6028
30	0.0571	0.0622	0.0773	0.1083	0.1645	0.2518	0.3707	0.5095	0.6464

Changing the frequency of generation of DCP practically does not affect the required number of tests to maintain a given probability of testing error. But the required number of frames very much depends on the frequency of DCP generation (Table 2). So, for example, at the lower boundary of the fiber optic line section $L_{TF.min}$ = 90 km, the number of required frames decreases from 2016 at ξ_{DSR} = 5 Hz to 825 at ξ_{DSR} = 30 Hz, i.e. 2.48 times.

Table 2. Dependence of the required number of frames on the frequency of generation of DCP

Number of frames	The lower boundary of the fiber optic line section, km								
	10	20	30	40	50	60	70	80	90
5	50	83	138	277	371	599	943	1429	2046
10	50	83	137	224	361	566	853	1207	1579
15	50	83	136	221	350	537	778	1045	1285
20	50	82	135	218	341	510	715	921	1083
25	50	82	134	214	332	486	662	823	936
30	50	82	133	212	323	464	616	744	825

5 Conclusion

Explanatory expressions for QKD system with initial information about the length of the fiber-optic line are gotten that built up the functional relationship between the characteristics of the single-photon synchronization subsystem and the parameters of the optical fiber, optical transmitter, single-photon avalanche photodiode. The requirements for the determination of the least number of frames at the search stage and the allowable number of tests are formulated.

Acknowledgment. The work was prepared with the support of the Russian Foundation for Basic Research, projects number 16-08-00752.

References

1. Bennett, C., Brassard, G.: Quantum cryptography: public key distribution and coin tossing. In: Proceedings of IEEE International Conference on Computers, Systems and Signal Processing, Bangalore, India, pp. 175–179. IEEE, New York (1984)
2. Gisin, N., Ribordy, G., Tittel, W., Zbinden, H.: Quantum cryptography. Rev. Mod. Phys. **74** (1), 145–195 (2002)
3. Shor, P.W., Preskill, J.: Simple proof of security of the BB84 quantum key distribution protocol. Phys. Rev. Lett. **85**, 441–444 (2000). Quant-ph/0003004
4. Rumyantsev, K.E., Plyonkin, A.P.: Synchronization of the quantum key distribution system when using photon pulses to increase security. Izvestiya SFedU. Eng. Sci. (8), 81–96 (2014)
5. Rumyantsev, K.E., Plyonkin, A.P.: Synchronization of the quantum key distribution system in the single-photon registration mode of pulses to increase security. Radio Commun. Technol. (2), 125–134 (2015)
6. Rumiantsev, K., Rudinsky, E.: Parameters of the two-stage synchronization algorithm for the quantum key distribution system. In: Proceedings of the 10th International Conference on Security of Information and Networks, SIN-2017, Rajasthan, India, 13–15 October 2017, pp. 140–150 (2017)
7. Rumyantsev, K., Rudinsky, E.: Time synchronization method in quantum key distribution system with automatic compensation of polarization distortions. In: Proceedings of the 2nd International Conference on Multimedia and Image Processing, ICMIP 2017. Wuhan, China, 17–19 March 2017, pp. 346–349. https://doi.org/10.1109/icmip.2017.68. 132083

8. Plenkin, A., Rumyantsev, K., Rudinsky, E.: Comparative analysis of single-photon synchronization algorithms in the quantum key distribution system. In: Proceedings of 2017 IEEE East-West Design & Test Symposium, EWDTS-2017, Serbia, Novi Sad, 29 September–2 October 2017 (2017). https://doi.org/10.1109/ewdts.2017. 8110047
9. Rudinsky, E.A., Rumyantsev, K.E.: Graph-analytical method for estimating single-photon synchronization parameters of an auto-compensation quantum key distribution system. In: Proceedings of the Futuristic Trends in Network and Communication Technologies, FTNCT-2018, Waknaghat, India, 9–10 February 2018 (2018). Submission ID 166
10. Rumyantsev, K.E., Rudinsky, E.A.: Two-stage time synchronization algorithm in the system of quantum key distribution with automatic polarization distortion compensation. Izvestiya SFU. Tech. Sci. (5), 75–89 (2017)

Single-Photon Algorithm for Synchronizing the System of Quantum Key Distribution with Polling Sections of a Fiber-Optic Line

Y. K. Mironov[1](✉) and K. E. Rumyantsev[2](✉)

[1] Scientific Design Bureau of Digital Signal Processing,
Southern Federal University, Taganrog, Russia
tmiyapll7@gmail.com
[2] The Department of Information Security of Telecommunication Systems,
Southern Federal University, Taganrog, Russia
rke2004@mail.ru

Abstract. The main idea of the proposed single-photon synchronization algorithm is to split the time frame into intervals. The algorithm involves sequential polling of fiber optic sections with decreasing length. The requirements for the choice of the number of time frames and tests for each fiber optic link are formulated. Relations have been obtained for calculating the energy, probabilistic, and timing parameters of synchronization with sequential polling of a fiber-optic line (FOL).

Keywords: Quantum key distribution · Single-photon synchronization · AutoCompensation · Fiber optic line

1 Introduction

The use of quantum cryptography protocols ensures absolute secrecy when encrypting messages and distributing the secret key among legitimate users [1–3]. However, the technical imperfection of the optoelectronic components of the synchronization system of the quantum key distribution (QKD) simplifies the intruder's organization of unauthorized access to information or introducing interference during the operation of the system [4–7]. To do this, the attacker must have information about the time of strobe photodetectors [8, 9].

In order to increase security against unauthorized access, photon pulses can be used as clock signals [10, 11]. A photon pulse represents a weakened transmitter pulse before registering on average less than one photon.

In [12, 13], the analysis of the one-photon synchronization algorithm of the QKD system stations with the division of a time frame equal to the repetition period of optical pulses into time windows was carried out. The high efficiency of the algorithm is proved when using an ideal single-photon instrument capable of registering all incoming photons. In addition, it is assumed that the photodetector does not need time to recover from the registration of a photon or a dark current pulse (DCP). However, single photon avalanche photodiodes (SAPD) used in QKD systems register only one (first) photon in the photon counting mode. In addition, in the case of a photon

© Springer Nature Singapore Pte Ltd. 2020
P. K. Singh et al. (Eds.): FTNCT 2019, CCIS 1206, pp. 87–97, 2020.
https://doi.org/10.1007/978-981-15-4451-4_8

registration, time is required to restore the working state of the SAPD [14–16]. As a result, the described algorithm takes considerable time to synchronize the stations.

In [17, 18], a two-stage station synchronization algorithm was proposed and investigated without splitting time frames into time windows. The algorithm is based on the fact that at the receiving end the following period is known T_s and the duration τ_s of optical sync signals. The equipment at the search stage (1st stage) registers the reception of a photon or DCP in the first time frame $[0, T_s]$. If a photon is not registered in the frame, the search continues in subsequent intervals. If a photon is accepted when analyzing a time frame, the equipment proceeds to testing (2nd stage), where the second survey is performed only during the gating of the photodetector. Note that at other times, the photo-receiving channel does not respond to the reception of photons and DCP. Since the duration of the time frame is many times longer than the time to restore SAPD operability, the two-stage algorithm provides a significant gain in synchronization time as compared to the algorithm where the time frame is divided into time windows [19].

However, the two-stage synchronization algorithm can only be successfully applied to short links. It is shown that for used SAPD because of DCP, the length of the FOL is limited to 70 km with a synchronization error probability of 0.05.

The latter determines the relevance of the search for new algorithms in order to increase the length of fiber optic links, where a high probability of synchronization of stations is guaranteed.

Article purpose is a proof of advantages of offered single-photon synchronization algorithm with sequential polling of FOL sections with decreasing length.

2 Justification of the Method of One-Photon Synchronization of Autocompensation System of Quantum Key Distribution

Analysis of the two-stage synchronization algorithm [19] shows that, by increasing the number of N_{test} tests, an arbitrarily small probability of testing error $P_{err.test}\{N_{test}\}$ can be made. However, to achieve an arbitrarily close to 1 probability of detecting a photon pulse at the $P_D\{N_T\}$ search stage, increasing the number of N_T frames (analysis time) is impossible.

Consequently, it is impossible for a considerable length of the fiber optic link to get an arbitrarily small probability of an alarm

$$P_{err.sync} = 1 - P_D\{N_{Ts}\} \cdot (1 - P_{err.test}\{N_{test}\})$$

The limitation of the length of the FOL is due to two reasons.

Reason 1: when implementing FOL on a single-mode optical fiber and focusing on the maximum possible $L_{TF.max}$ spacing of the receiving and transmitting and coding stations of the QKD autocompensation system, the repetition period of the optical sync pulses should satisfy the condition

$$T_s \geq T_{s,min} = (2 \cdot L_{TF.max})/v_{OF}$$

The multiplier 2 in the formula takes into account that in the autocompensation system of the QKD a photon passes twice a fiber optic line: a receiving and transmitting station $\rightarrow$ FOL $\rightarrow$ an encoding station $\rightarrow$ a fiber optic link $\rightarrow$ receiving and transmitting station.

The photon propagation velocity in the optical fiber v_{OF} is determined by the core refractive index n_{OF} at the wavelength λ_s : $v_{OF} = c_{opt}/n_{OF}$, where $c_{opt} = 300\ 000$ km/s is the speed of radiation propagation in vacuum.

As a result, the average number of DCP increases over the duration of the time frame T_s (the period of repetition of optical pulses)

$$n_{DCR.T.mid} = \xi_{DCR} \cdot T_s$$

Note that the statistical properties of the photon flux and DCP are described by the Poisson law $P_r\{n|n_{.mid}\}$, where the probability of generating n events is determined by the average number of photons and/or DCP n_{mid} during the observation time (duration of the time frame, optical pulse or gating pulse).

Reason 2: the average number of registered photons $n_{s.mid}$ for the photon pulse duration decreases with increasing length FOL L_{TF}

$$n_{s.mid} = n_{s0.mid} \cdot 10^{-(\alpha_{OF}[dB/km] \cdot L_{TF}[km])/10}$$

where $n_{s0.mid}$ is the average number of photons in the pulse at the output of the coding station; α_{OF} is the specific attenuation of the applied optical fiber.

The probability of detecting the sync pulse $P_D\{N_T\}$ at the search stage during the analysis of the first N_T frames decreases with increasing FOL length:

$$P_D\{N_T\} = [(1 - exp(-n_{DCR.T.mid}))/(n_{DCR.T.mid}) \cdot (1 - P_{DCR}\wedge(N_T))/(1 - P_{DCR})] \cdot P_{Ds}$$

Indeed, with the increase in the length of the FOL, there is a decrease in the probability of the absence of reception of photons and the generation of DCP over a time frame

$$P_{DCR} = exp(-n_{s.mid} - n_{DCR.T.mid})$$

and the probability of registering at least one event during the reception of the photon pulse

$$P_{Ds} = 1 - exp(-n_{DCR.s.mid} - n_{s.mid})$$

Note that in the QKD systems for the average number of DCP for the duration τ_s of the optical pulse

$$n_{DCR.s.mid} = \xi_{DCR} \cdot \tau_s$$

the condition is always satisfied

$$n_{DCR.s.mid} < < n_{s.mid}$$

In order that the synchronization error probability does not exceed the permissible value $P_{err.sync.lim}$, condition must be met

$$n_{s.mid} \geq n_{s.min.mid} = n_{DCR.T.mid} \cdot \left(1 - P_{err.sync.lim}\right)/P_{err.sync.lim} \qquad (1)$$

The condition when $L_{TF} = L_{TF.max}$ determines the maximum length of the FOL $L_{TF.max}$, which is found by solving a transcendental equation

$$L_{TF.max}[km] = L_{TF.lim}[km] \cdot 10^{-(\alpha_{OF}[dB/km] \cdot L_{TF.max}[km])/10}$$

where

$$L_{TF.lim}[km] = [(n_{s0.mid} \cdot v_{OF}[km/s])/(2 \cdot \xi_{DCR})] \cdot \left[P_{err.sync.lim}/\left(1 - P_{err.sync.lim}\right)\right]$$

– FOL maximum length when using optical fiber without loss ($\alpha_{OF} = 0$ dB/km).

The basis of the new synchronization algorithm is the division of fiber-optic lines into N_L sections with decreasing length. Moreover, at the upper boundary of each section, condition (1) must always be met, in which the probability of a synchronization error does not exceed the permissible value $P_{err.sync.lim}$.

3 Synchronization Algorithm with a Sequential Plot FOL with a Losing Length

Let the average number of photons necessary for ensuring safety for the duration of an optical pulse at the output from the Alice coding station, corresponding to the lower boundary of the first plot FOL, is $n_{s0.mid}$. Then the upper boundary of the 1st part of the fiber optic link L_{TF1} is found by solving the transcendental equation

$$L_{TF1}[km] = L_{TF.lim}[km] \cdot 10^{-(\alpha_{OF}[dB/km] \cdot L_{TF1}[km])/10}$$

The equipment at the search stage registers a photon or DCP in the time interval $[0, \tau_{L1}]$ in the first frame $[0, T_s]$. Here $\tau_{L1} = (2 \cdot L_{TF1})/v_{OF}$.

If the photon is not registered in the interval $[0, \tau_{L1}]$ of the first frame, the search continues in the intervals $[(j - 1) \cdot T_s, (j - 1) \cdot T_s + \tau_{L1}]$ of subsequent time frames $[(j - 1) \cdot T_s, j \cdot T_s]$.

Suppose that at time $t_{AD} \in [(N_T - 1) \cdot T_s, (N_T - 1) \cdot T_s + \tau_{L1}]$ a photon was registered by the photoreceiver in the N_T frame. The equipment proceeds to testing. Here the photo detector is re-polled only at intervals

$$[(k - 1)T_s + t_{strob1}, (k - 1)T_s + t_{strob2}], k = (1, N_{test.max})_{mid}$$

Note that, for the rest of the time, the single-photon registration channel does not respond to the reception of photons and the generation of DCP in a photodetector.

The value $t_{strob1} = t_D - \tau_{delay} + T_S - 0.5 \cdot \tau_{strob}$ corresponds to the beginning moment, and $t_{strob2} = t_D - \tau_{delay} + T_S + 0.5 \cdot \tau_{strob}$ - at the end of gating. The value τ_{delay} represents the time delay between the moment of registration t_D and the moment of reception of the photon t_{ph}.

It was established that due to a priori uncertainty regarding the moment of reception of a photon, the duration of the gating pulse τ_{strob} should exceed the duration of the sync pulse τ_s by more than 2 times (the work does not take into account the dispersion properties of optical fiber):

$$\tau_{strob} = 2 \cdot \tau_s + 2 \cdot \Delta T_s$$

where ΔT_s – instability of the period of following sync pulses.

The synchronization algorithm assumes that if a photon is repeatedly registered during the N_{test} test, then the decision is made to receive a photon pulse in the analyzed time frame

$$[(N_{test} - 1) \cdot T_s + t_{strob1}, (N_{test} - 1) \cdot T_s + t_{strob2}]$$

If, for the admissible number of tests $N_{test.max}$, the photon reception is not fixed, then the equipment returns to the search mode again. And now the second plot FOL link with a length of L_{TF2} is being checked by monitoring time intervals

$$[(N_{test} + j) \cdot T_s + \tau_{L1}, (N_{test} + j) \cdot T_s + \tau_{L1} + \tau_{L2}], j \geq 1$$

Using the method of mathematical induction, we find formulas for calculating the synchronization parameters for $j \geq 1$. For example, the length of the j-th FOL section ($j \geq 2$) is found by solving the equation

$$L_{TF.j} = L_{TF.(j-1)} + L_{TF.lim}[km] \cdot 10^{-(\alpha_{OF}[dB/km] \cdot L_{TF.j}[km])/10} \tag{2}$$

To calculate the analysis time of the j-th part of the FOL, the formula is valid

$$\tau_{L.j} = 2 \cdot \left[(L_{TF.j} - L_{TF.(j-1)})/v_{OF} \right]$$

Note that the length of the j-th area is equal to N_L

$$\Delta L_{TF.j} = L_{TF.j} - L_{TF.(j-1)}$$

The total length of FOL of N_L plots is

$$L_{TF} = L_{TF}.N_L$$

4 Probability of Synchronization Error

When calculating the probability of synchronization error with sequential polling of sections with decreasing length, it is necessary to take into account the dependence of energy and time parameters on the number of the section.

Indeed, the calculation of the average number of DCP should be carried out during the analysis of the specific j-th part of the fiber optic link

$$n_{DCR.j.mid} = \xi_{DCR} \cdot \tau_{L.j}$$

The minimum average number of photons per optical pulse duration at the upper edge of the j-th segment is equal to

$$n_{s.j.mid} = n_{s0.mid} \cdot 10^{-(\alpha_{OF}[dB/km] \cdot L_{TF.j}[km])/10} \tag{3}$$

Taking into account (3), the formula for calculating the probability of lack of reception of photons and DCP generation during the analysis of the plot changes $\tau_{L.j}$

$$P_{DCR.j} = exp\left(-n_{s.j.mid} - n_{DCR.j.mid}\right) \tag{4}$$

The calculation of the probability of registration of at least one photon or DCP during the reception of a photon pulse in the analysis of the j-th segment should be carried out according to the formula

$$P_{Ds.j} = 1 - exp\left(-n_{s.j.mid} - n_{DCR.s.mid}\right) \tag{5}$$

As a consequence, the formula is converted to calculate the probability of detection at the search stage during the analysis of N_{Tj} frames of the j-th segment

$$P_D\{N_{Tj}\} = \{[(1 - exp(-n_{DCR.j.mid}))/n_{DCR.j.mid}] \cdot [(1 - P_{DCR.j}\wedge(N_{Tj}))/(1 - P_{DCR.j})]\} \cdot P_{Ds.j} \tag{6}$$

Let during the gating time the smallest average number of registered photons and DCP at the upper boundary of the j-th segment (lower boundary of the (j + 1)-th segment) is

$$n_{strob.j.mid} = n_{sj.mid} + \xi_{DCR} \cdot \tau_{strob} \tag{7}$$

then the highest probability of a testing error (the absence of photon and DCP registration during testing) when analyzing the j-th region can be calculated by the formula

$$P_{err.test.j} = exp\left(-N_{test.max.j} \cdot n_{strob.j.mid}\right) \tag{8}$$

In accordance with (6) and (8), the formula is changed to calculate the probability of an alarm error

$$P_{err.sync.j} = 1 - P_D\{N_{Tj}\} \cdot \left(1 - P_{err.test.j}\{N_{test.j}\}\right) \tag{9}$$

5 Formulation of Requirements for the Selection of the Number of Time Personnel and Tests

From expression (9) it follows that to minimize the probability of a synchronization error, it is necessary to maximize the detection probability at the search stage $P_D\{N_{Tj}\}$, defined by formula (6), and minimize the probability of testing error $P_{err.test.j}\{N_{test.j}\}$ defined by the formula (8).

Assuming the possibility of an infinite number of time frames ($N_{Tj} \to \infty$) in view of the strict inequality $P_{DCR.j} < 1$, the maximum probability of photon pulse detection at the search stage is found

$$P_D\{N_{Tj} \to \infty\} = \left[(1 - exp(-n_{DCR.j}))/n_{DCR.j.mid}\right] \cdot \left[1/(1 - P_{DCR.j})\right] \cdot P_{Ds.j}$$

A comparison of c (8) shows that the deterioration in the probability of detection of a photon pulse at the search stage when the number of frames is limited is determined by the coefficient

$$K_{D.j} = P_D\{N_{Tj} \to \infty\}/P_D\{N_{Tj}\} = 1/(1 - P_{DCR.j} \wedge N_{Tj}) > 1$$

This allows us to formulate the requirements for the choice of the minimum number of frames at the search stage, assuming that

$$K_{D.j} = K_{D.j} = 1, N_{L.mid}$$
$$N_{Tj} \geq ln((K_D-1)/K_D)/ln(P_{DCR.j}) \tag{10}$$

For example, if we accept the permissible degradation of the detection probability by 10% ($K_{D.j} = 1{,}1$) with $P_{DCRj} = 0{,}98$, then the number of N_{Tj} frames at the search stage should be at least 119.

Let during the gating time the smallest average number of registered photons and DCP on the upper border of the j-th segment is (7).

Expressions (7) and (8) allow us to formulate requirements for the selection of an admissible number of tests $N_{test.max.j}$ to ensure a given probability of testing error $P_{err.test.lim}$ during the analysis of the j-th segment:

$$N_{test.max.j} \geq \left(1/n_{strob.j.mid}\right) \cdot ln\left(1/P_{err.test.lim}\right) \qquad (11)$$

From expressions (10) and (11) it can be seen that as the number of a section increases, the required number of time frames and tests increases.

6 Change of Probability of Synchronization Error Length FOL

The results of calculations by formulas (1)–(11) are presented in Fig. 1 by solid lines. The stepwise changes in the function correspond to the transitions to the analysis of the next fiber-optic segment. It also presents a dashed line depending on the length of the FOL skip probability at the search stage $(1 - P_D\{N_{Tj}\})$ and the dotted line indicates the probability of testing error $P_{err.test.j}$.

Note that with increasing fiber optic length within one section, the probability of synchronization error increases, reaching a maximum value at the ends of plots FOL.

It should be remembered that the choice of the borders of the fiber optic sections is focused on ensuring the probability of a synchronization error not higher than 0.05. The realized maximum probability of a synchronization error is 2 times greater. The latter is explained by the introduction of restrictions on the maximum number of frames and tests.

It is important that the difference between the probabilities of synchronization errors at the boundaries of the sites with increasing numbers decreases. So, for example, during the transition from the 1st section to the 2nd, the probability of a synchronization error falls from 0.104 to 0.03, i.e., 3.4 times. But when moving from the 9th section to the 10th, the probability of a synchronization error changes by 26%. Consequently, with increasing fiber optic length, the efficiency of the proposed algorithm decreases. Such a functional dependence is explained by the monotonously falling graph of the function in Fig. 1 (dash-dotted line), corresponding to the probability of the absence of registration of photons and DCP during the analysis of the FOL. Note that the function $1 - P_{DCR.j}$ is determined by the average number of photons per pulse $n_{sj.mid}$ and DCP $n_{DCR.j.mid}$ during the analysis of the segment.

More clearly the features of the proposed single-photon algorithm for synchronizing stations with sequential polling of fiber optic sections with decreasing length can be explained by the graphs in Fig. 2. Here the solid line shows changes in the average number of received pulses (photons and DCP), and the dotted line shows the average number of DCP pulses over time gating.

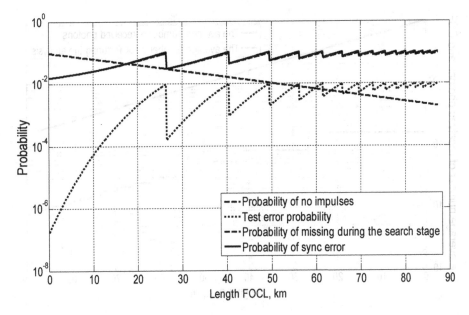

Fig. 1. Synchronization error probability.

Due to the reduction in the time of analysis of each subsequent part of the FOL, there is an abrupt change in the average number of DCP pulses during gating. However, within the site it is permanent. But the average number of received pulses falls monotonously within the FOL. The ratio of the average number of received photons and DCP at the end of all sections is ~ 19. Due to this, the probability of error in making a decision about the detection of an optical clock signal following the results of two stages of synchronization at the end of all sections is the same.

In the transition to the analysis of the neighboring FOL section with a constant average number of received photons, there is a decrease in the average number of pulses of the DCP analysis of the area. Indeed, during the transition from the 1st section to the 2nd, the average number of DCP impulses during the analysis falls from $1{,}6 \cdot 10^{-3}$ to $8{,}2 \cdot 10^{-4}$ (1.9 times), and during the transition from 2-th plot to the 3rd from $8{,}2 \cdot 10^{-4}$ to $5{,}4 \cdot 10^{-4}$ (1.5 times).

Finally, at the end of the FOL, there is practically no change in the average number of DCP pulses during the transition to the neighboring site. Since the average number of photons during the analysis is constant at the boundaries of the plots, the differences between the probabilities of synchronization errors should disappear. This reflects the graph in full line in Fig. 1.

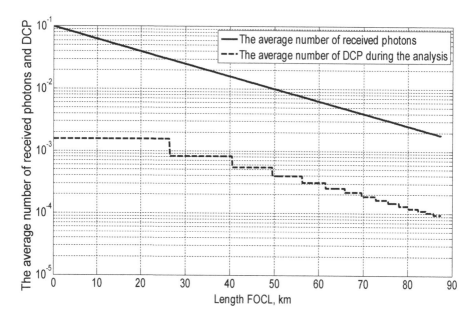

Fig. 2. The average number of received photons and DCP during the analysis.

7   Findings

The main idea of the proposed single-photon synchronization algorithm is to split the time frame into intervals. Each interval corresponds to a particular part of the FOL. The algorithm involves sequential polling of FOL sections with decreasing length. The latter allows to significantly reduce the average number of dark current pulses during the analysis of sections. This significantly increases the signal-to-noise ratio, which implies an increase in the distance at which signal detection becomes possible.

The requirements for the choice of the number of time frames and tests for each FOL are formulated. Relations have been obtained for calculating the energy, probabilistic, and timing parameters of synchronization with sequential polling of FOL. An abrupt change in the probability of a synchronization error along the length of the FOL is explained.

Acknowledgment. The work was prepared with the support of the Russian Foundation for Basic Research, projects number 16-08-00752.

References

1. Bennett, C., Brassard, G.: Quantum cryptography: public key distribution and coin tossing. In: Proceedings of IEEE International Conference on Computers, Systems and Signal Processing, Bangalore, India, pp. 175–179. Institute of Electrical and Electronics Engineers, New York (1984)

2. Gisin, N., Ribordy, G., Tittel, W., Zbinden, H.: Quantum cryptography. Rev. Mod. Phys. **74**(1), 145–195 (2002)
3. Shor, P.W., Preskill, J.: Simple proof of security of the BB84 quantum key distribution protocole. Phys. Rev. Lett. **85**, 441–444 (2000)
4. Gerhardt, I., Liu, Q., Lamas-Linares, A., Skaar, J., Kurtsiefer, C., Makarov, V.: Full-field implementation of a perfect eavesdropper on a quantum cryptography system. Nat. Commun. **2**, 1–6 (2011)
5. Lydersen, L., Wiechers, C., Wittmann, C., Elser, D., Skaar, J., Makarov, V.: Hacking commercial quantum cryptography systems by tailored bright illumination. Nat. Photonics **4**, 686–689 (2010)
6. Makarov, V.: Controlling passively quenched single photon detectors by bright light. New J. Phys. **11** (2009)
7. Gisin, N., Fasel, S., Kraus, B., Zbinden, H., Ribordy, G.: Trojan-horse attacks on quantum-key-distribution systems. Phys. Rev. A **73** (2006)
8. Rumyantsev, K.E.: Synchronization in the system of quantum key distribution with automatic compensation of polarization distortions. Telecommunications **2**, 32–40 (2017)
9. Rumyantsev, K.E.: Protection of the synchronization process in the system of quantum key distribution with automatic compensation of polarization distortion. Telecommunications **3**, 36–44 (2017)
10. Rumyantsev, K.E., Plyonkin, A.P.: Synchronization of the quantum key distribution system when using photon pulses to increase security. Izvestiya SFedU. Eng. Sci. **8**, 81–96 (2014)
11. Rumyantsev, K.E., Plyonkin, A.P.: Synchronization of the quantum key distribution system in the single-photon registration mode of pulses to increase security. Radio Commun. Technol. **2**, 125–134 (2015)
12. Plyonkin, A.P., Rumyantsev, K.E.: Dependence of the probability of photon pulse detection in the synchronization mode of the quantum key distribution system on the duration of the time window. In: Collection of Materials of the International Scientific e-Symposium. Technical and Natural Sciences: Theory and Practice, pp. 59–72 (2015)
13. Pljonkin, A., Rumjantsev, K.: Single-photon synchronization mode of quantum key distribution system. In: Proceeding of the International Conference on Computational Techniques in Information and Communication Technology, pp. 531–534 (2016)
14. ID100 Specifications. www.idquantique.com. Accessed 19 Mar 2019
15. ID230 v2015 04 29. Specifications as of May 2015. www.idquantique.com. Accessed 19 Mar 2019
16. ID280. http://www.idquantique.com/photon-counting/photon-counting-modules/id280/. Accessed 19 Mar 2019
17. Rumiantsev, K., Rudinsky, E.: Parameters of the two-stage synchronization algorithm for the quantum key distribution system. In: Proceedings of the 10th International Conference on Security of Information and Networks (SIN-2017), pp. 140–150 (2017)
18. Plenkin, A., Rumyantsev, K., Rudinsky, E.: Comparative analysis of single-photon synchronization algorithms in the quantum key distribution system. In: Proceedings of 2017 IEEE East-West Design & Test Symposium, EWDTS 2017 (2017)
19. Rumyantsev, K.E., Rudinsky, E.A.: Two-stage time synchronization algorithm in the system of quantum key distribution with automatic polarization distortion compensation. Izvestiya SFedU. Eng. Sci. **5**, 75–89 (2017)

Adaptive Noise Generator for Masking Side Electromagnetic Radiation and Interference

Petr Zemlyanuchin[✉] and Alekcandr Suhoveev

Southern Federal University, Taganrog, Rostov Region, Russian Federation
pazemlyanuchin@sfedu.ru,
Aleksandr.sukhoveev@ictis.sfedu.ru

Abstract. The article analyzes the possibility of constructing a noise signal source of adaptive multichannel noise generators to provide active protection of informative components of side electromagnetic radiation and interference (SERaI). Had reviewed technical solutions of the noise generators to mask SERaI. Domestic and foreign literature, patent documentation confirming the relevance of the creation of adaptive noise generators for masking SERaI were analyzed. It was identified that in current noise generators designed to mask SERaI, there are shortcomings. It is shown that the improvement of the characteristics and expansion of the fields of application of such devices is possible due to the creation of multichannel adaptive noise generators. In such noise generators in each noise masking channel it is proposed to provide both the power adjustment of the emitted signal and frequency band modification. In order to achieve this objective, quasi-harmonic noise signals are used as a carrier and control oscillations for the purpose of forming the initial noise signal in each noise channel by modulation methods.

Keywords: Noise generator · Noise signal · SERaI · Electronic countermeasures · Quasi-harmonic noise signal

1 Introduction

During operation, electronic devices such as monitors, printers, fax machines, etc., emit side electromagnetic radiation and crosstalk (SERaI), carrying information that is processed by electronic devices. These radiations are formed due to the physical processes occurring in these devices at all kinds of switching (changing signal levels). SERaI can spread in the open space, or be aimed at various metal constructions and go beyond the protection zone. With appropriate receiving equipment, an attacker can intercept these emissions from a remote location and then reproduce the intercepted information.

With the advancement of the tools for data processing, storage and transmission of information that has the status of state or commercial secret, the creation of high-efficiency noise signal generators **is relevant** through communication channels. On the one hand, the generators are able to ensure the safety of information emitted through the SERaI channels [1], on the other hand, they can provide electromagnetic

© Springer Nature Singapore Pte Ltd. 2020
P. K. Singh et al. (Eds.): FTNCT 2019, CCIS 1206, pp. 98–103, 2020.
https://doi.org/10.1007/978-981-15-4451-4_9

compatibility of technical measures for active information security with other wireless devices and telecommunication systems.

The relevance of actions taken against side electromagnetic radiation and interference can be traced in [2]. It is shown that on an insulated computer that used the Diffie-Hellman key exchange algorithm on elliptic curves [3], a group of researchers managed to extract the decipher key. It took a few seconds by analyzing the electromagnetic signal that the computer emits. It took 66 iterations to read and analyze SERaI and 3.3 s to extract the key.

There are technical devices that, when connected to a computer, allow to re-transmit electromagnetic radiation, previously amplifying SERaI [4, 5].

The masking interference generators are widely used to protect the technical means of processing, storage and transmission of information from the theft of information by intruders through the channels of SERaI. These generators, as a means of active protection, are a cheaper alternative to shielding objects and the use of shielded equipment (passive protection).

Analysis of scientific and technical literature reveals that the main part of the noise generators available on the market, allow to form a noise signal in the frequency range from several tens of kHz to 1–2.5 GHz [6–8]. That is not enough, since the clock frequencies of the same computers are constantly increasing and the frequency range of SERaI radiation is also expanding.

There are patents that offer ways to implement noise generators with improved characteristics [9]. The patents [10, 11] stipulate the improvement of noise characteristics of noise generators and the reduction of the influence on the electromagnetic environment in the area of the noise generator location. The work of such generators is based on the use of a noise generator and a signal with a clock frequency of the information processing device. These signals are transmitted to a frequency converter [10] or to a non-linear amplifier [11]. However, the patent descriptions do not specify the energy uniformity of the noise signal spectrum in the stipulated frequency range up to 10 GHz.

With regard to the noise generators of the GS series, it is noted [12] that they provide either smooth or discrete control of the output signal level. For example, the noise signal generator GS-1000U has five independent noise generators. The output of one channel is directly connected to the antenna. Additional external devices can be connected to the outputs of 4 other channels: additional antennas, directional couplers to supply a noise signal to the power grid, grounding, etc. Similar functions can be found in a number of other noise generators. At the same time, such noise generators do not provide effective electromagnetic compatibility with other electronic devices.

Sequences of pseudorandom signals can be used to generate a noise signal [13]. However, such sequences are described by deterministic systems of equations, which limits the random nature of the occurrence of such sequences in comparison, for example, with "white noise", which is an equable stochastic process in a wide frequency range.

Analyzing the noise generators, it can be concluded that the frequency range of the presented devices may not cover the entire scope of informative side electromagnetic radiation and interference of modern computer facilities [9]. Accordingly, one can be concluded that there is a necessity to develop a noise generator with a maximum noise frequency up to 5–10 GHz and an output power sufficient to mask SERaI. Since, if the SERaI is located in the frequency span, the length of 10 MHz, the integral power of the known noise generators may not be enough to mask the SERaI [4].

Many challenges inherent in noise generators (electromagnetic compatibility and high power output; extended operating frequency range, up to 10 GHz) can be solved by constructing noise signal generators on the principle of multichannel systems. Such systems would allow:

– to avoid overlapping bands in which there is the operation of technical means of information processing is not observed;
– to provide adjustment of the output power of the noise signal in the required noise channel;
– to provide adjustment of the width of the noise signal spectrum in the required noise channel.

The analysis shows that the development of a multichannel noise generator with a maximum frequency of up to 5–10 GHz is relevant.

The aim is to construct multichannel adaptive noise signal generators with an extended range of operating frequencies and providing electromagnetic compatibility with other electronic devices and telecommunication systems.

2   The Proposals for the Construction of Adaptive Noise Generators

Construction of adaptive noise generators is applicable due to band segmentation [14]. Within the sub-band, the output noise signal is formed and its parameters are controlled: the range of noise frequencies; the integral output power; the linearity of the spectral density of the noise signal; the switching on and off of the noise signal in a particular sub-band.

To ensure the control of noise signal parameters in a given sub-band, it is possible to use a noise signal generator with specified and controlled parameters. Figure 1 shows the block diagram of the initial noise signal generator.

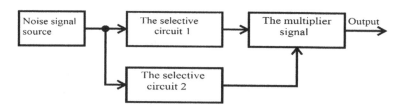

Fig. 1. Block diagram of the initial noise signal generator

The generator has a low-power source of noise signal (generates a noise signal close to the "white noise"). From the source output, the noise signal is received at the inputs of two selective circuits. Two parallel oscillatory circuits are used as an example.

One of them is customized to the central frequency $f_{01} = \frac{\omega_{01}}{2\pi} = 2,45 \cdot 10^5 \, \text{Hz}$ $(\omega_{01} = 1,54 \cdot 10^6 \, \text{rad/s})$, and the other $- f_{02} = \frac{\omega_{02}}{2\pi} = 0,5 \cdot 10^5 \, \text{Hz}$ $(\omega_{02} = 0,315 \cdot 10^6 \, \text{rad/s})$ (see Fig. 2). The first oscillatory circuit, highlighting the spectral components of the noise signal, forms a quasi-harmonic signal $\xi_1(t)$, the spectral density

$$S_1(j\omega) = \int\limits_{-\infty}^{\infty} \xi_1(t) \cdot e^{-j\omega t} dt$$

of which is concentrated at the level of 0.707 in the frequency range $\Delta f_1 = \frac{\Delta\omega_1}{2\pi} = 1 \cdot 10^4 \, \text{Hz}$ $(\Delta\omega_1 = 6,3 \cdot 10^4 \, \text{rad/s})$ relative to the central frequency f_{01}.

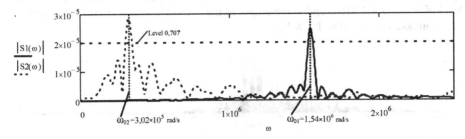

Fig. 2. Spectral densities of noise signal amplitudes at the outputs of the first and second oscillatory circuits

The second oscillatory circuit forms a quasi-harmonic signal $\xi_2(t)$, the spectral density

$$S_2(j\omega) = \int\limits_{-\infty}^{\infty} \xi_2(t) \cdot e^{-j\omega t} dt$$

at the level of 0.707 is concentrated in the frequency range $\Delta f_2 = \frac{\Delta\omega_2}{2\pi} = 0,33 \cdot 10^4 \, \text{Hz}$ $\Delta\omega_2 = 2,1 \cdot 10^4 \, \text{rad/s}$ relative to the central frequency f_{02}.

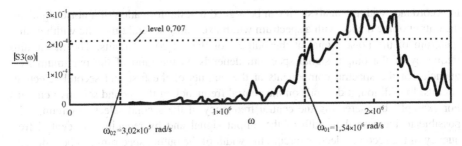

Fig. 3. Spectral density of noise signal amplitudes at signal multiplier output

Then the signals from the first and second selective circuits are come to the signal multiplier. The spectral density of the noise signal at the output of the signal multiplier can be calculated using the convolution integral (Fig. 3)

$$S_3(j\omega) = \int\limits_{-\infty}^{\infty} \xi_1(t) \cdot \xi_2(t) e^{-j\omega t} dt = \frac{1}{2\pi} \int\limits_{-\infty}^{\infty} S_1(jz) \cdot S_2[j(\omega - z)] dz.$$

Figure 4 shows the results of modeling the spectral density of the noise signal. The simulation is carried out in the environment of circuit modeling Micro-Cap 9. In this case, at the output of the signal multiplier, the width of the noise signal spectrum at the level of 0.707 is 15 MHz (the lower diagram in Fig. 4). In doing so, the width of the spectrum at the output of the first selective circuit (the upper diagram in Fig. 4) at the level of 0.707 is 4.4 MHz, and at the output of the second selective circuit (the diagram in the middle in Fig. 4) is 1.2 MHz.

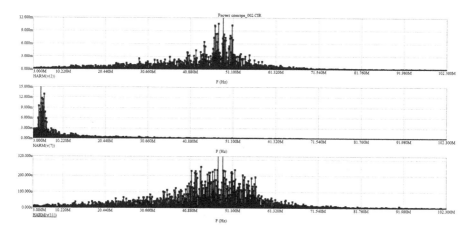

Fig. 4. Results of modeling the spectral density of the noise signal

3 Conclusion

In accordance with the analysis, it can be argued that the formation of a noise signal at the output of the device with a spectrum width exceeding several times the width of the spectrum of the noise signal at the outputs of the selective circuits. The maximum frequency of the output signal spectrum depends on the ratio of the maximum frequencies of the spectral components at the outputs of the first and second selective circuits. In addition, it depends on the central frequency of the second selective circuit. For example, by increasing the central frequency of the second selective circuit, it is possible to increase the width of the output signal and by reducing the central frequency of the second selective circuit, the width of the output spectrum can be reduced. It allows controlling the width of the output signal spectrum in the noise signal generator, which can have a profitable effect on the electromagnetic compatibility of the multichannel adaptive noise generator.

References

1. Barsukov, V.S.: Security: technologies, tools and services. KUDITS, 496 p. (2001)
2. Genkin, D., Pachmanov, L., Pipman, I.: Stealing Keys from PCs using a Radio: Cheap Electromagnetic Attacks on Windowed Exponentiation, 27 February 2015. www.cs.tau.ac.il/~tromer/papers/radioexp.pdf
3. The NSA compromised the Diffie-Hellman Protocol? https://habr.com/ru/post/356870/. Accessed 11 June 2019
4. Williams, E.: TEMPEST: A tin foil hat for your electronics and their secrets, 19 October 2015. http://www.hackaday.com/2015/10/19/tempest-a-tin-foil-hat-for-your-electronics-and-their-secrets. Accessed 12 June 2019
5. Demyanenko, A.V., Ilyin, I.V., Topalov, F.S.: USB modem. Eng. J. of Don 1 (2015). http://www.ivdon.ru/uploads/article/pdf/IVD_62_Demyanenko.pdf_58e80ef25e.pdf. Accessed 12 June 2019
6. Bezrukov, V.A., Ivanov, V.P., Kalashnikov, V.C., Lebedev, M.N.: Device of radio deception. Patent RU № 2170493 Russian Federation, IPC H04K 3/00, declared 15 May 2000, publ. 10 July 2001, BI No. 19
7. System for protection against leak of information on SERaI channels "Grom-ZI-4B". https://pro-spec.ru/catalog/generatory-shuma/sistema-dlya-zashchity-ot-utechki-informatsii-po-kanalam-pemin-grom-zi-4b. Accessed 18 June 2019
8. SEL SP-21 "Barricade" spatial noise generator. http://www.profinfo.ru/catalog/r89/398.html. Accessed 18 June 2019
9. Pavlov, Yu.S.: Method of protection of information exchange in the local radio system. Patent RU № 2114513 Russian Federation, IPC H04K 3/00, declared 25 July 1995; publ. 27 June 1998, BI No. 18
10. Demin, V.M., Lepekha, P., Poyarkov, L.A.: The protection method of an information processing system from side electromagnetic radiation, the device for implementing the method and the generator of the noise signal for the implementation of devices. Patent RU № 2421917 Russian Federation, IPC H04K1/04, H03B29/00, declared 15 April 2010, publ. 20 June 2011, BI No. 17
11. Shcherbakov, V.A., Horev, A.A.: Device for protection of automated systems from information leakage through channels of side electromagnetic radiation. Patent RU № 2669065 Russian Federation, IPC 29/00 H03B, declared 13 December 2017, publ. 08 October 2018, BI No. 28
12. Ivanov, V.P.: Information security, problems of SERaI, radio noise generators. Information counteraction to threats of terrorism. Sci. Pract. J. 13, 125–134 (2009)
13. Loginov, S.S., Zuev, M.Yu.: Statistical characteristics of pseudorandom signals on the basis of the Lorenz system, Chua and Dmitriev-Kislov, implemented over a Galois field. Eng. J. Don 4 (2018). http://www.ivdon.ru/uploads/article/pdf/IVD_182_Loginov_Zuev.pdf_6b531fd17d.pdf. Accessed 18 June 2019
14. Zemlyanuchin, P.A.: Multichannel noise generator to mask SERaI. Izvestiya SFU. Eng. Sci. 9(182) (2016). http://old.izv-tn.tti.sfedu.ru/?cat=486&lang=ru Accessed 20 June 2019

Wireless Networks and Internet of Things (IoT)

A Comparative Analysis of Application of Proposed and the Existing Methodologies on a Mobile Phone Survey

Rajni Bhalla[✉] and Amandeep

Lovely Professional University, Jalandhar, Punjab, India
rajni.b27@gmail.com

Abstract. With the development of the Web, the social media has emerged as the most useful platform where people can share, upload, disseminate their feelings about goods or services, governmental issues, economic movements, recent developments, and a plethora of such social interactions. The problem with the huge numbers of reviews is that we need to sift and retrieve the relevant information. In spite of the fact that there are quantities of arrangements accessible for data extraction, however the precision of their mining procedure is a long way from exact. For accomplishing the most elevated exactness, the problem of zero likelihood, looked by Naive Bayes investigation, should be tended to reasonably. The proposed system means to separate the necessary data with high exactness that could endure the issue of zero likelihood. In this study, RB-Bayes method will be used and implemented on mobile phone survey and compare accuracy with naive Bayes. The result has shown that RB-Bayes procedure yields a more precise result than those of the prevailing algorithms. RB-Bayes accuracy is 90%. For the implementation of the proposal, Python has been used. This technique is sure to supersede Naive Bayes because of the ability to overcome the problem of zero frequency.

Keywords: Mobile phone · Naïve Bayes · RB-Bayes

1 Introduction

In this investigation, capacity of a mobile feature to forecast the importance of the mobile model is predictively identified. A feature of the phone means characteristics of the mobile phone. There can be a number of characteristics of mobile phone like technical features, a brand of mobile, the price of the phone, manufacturer trademark and sales period. As an example, before purchasing a mobile phone end user thinks about a popular feature like an operating system. Operating system plays important role in the popularity of phone. There are a number of operating systems available like android, IOS, Microsoft, RIM, BADA, Symbian and others. The measurement demonstrates the worldwide major part of the overall industry is held by the main cell phone operating system, as far as deals to end clients, from 2009 to 2018. In the second quarter of 2018, 88% of all phones sold to end clients were mobile phones with the Android operating system [1]. But the importance of features depends upon the client to client. Every client having their own priority of features before purchasing a mobile

© Springer Nature Singapore Pte Ltd. 2020
P. K. Singh et al. (Eds.): FTNCT 2019, CCIS 1206, pp. 107–115, 2020.
https://doi.org/10.1007/978-981-15-4451-4_10

phone. It can depend on gender, age, occupation, monthly income, and education level, for instance. Customer goal is to choose mobile phone which satisfies number of constraints and fulfill all conditions. For example, customer satisfy if they get number of features in less price and phone comes in their salary budget. Sometimes specific features of phone become popular because a number of end users have similar preferences and conditions.

The distinction of the telephones can be analyzed with buyer utility development approach, by using surveys or by applying predictive modeling methods. Customer purchases a product to fulfill his/her own requirement. To know that requirement consolidate diffusion impacts and decision impacts in an integrated model could be used. With respect to utility boost strategy for cell phone markets, discrete choice models could be used to get the decision maker over multi-generational item attributes [2]. In any case, as far as anyone is concerned, the discrete decision model has not been utilized for cell phones popularity investigation. Studies can be utilized to catch shoppers' decision criteria. An essential methodology is to lead an investigation where customers are asked for to rank predefined choice criteria into different criticalness levels and subsequently the results can be engineered in perspective of the demand of significance or popularity. Research papers with respect to cell phone decision criteria dependent on surveys started to show up in the mid-2000s. They learn about the decision criteria in nations, for example, Finland, India, Malaysia, Netherlands, South-Korea and the U.S. The assessment of the PDA ubiquity with prescient model systems deduces that information from telephone models with various component packs is amassed, by then respects are mentioned into various prominence break, lastly the fame interims between times are foreseen with assistance of telephone highlights. The outcome based on the analytical demonstrating investigation isn't a rundown of decision criteria, regardless of whether a significant number of the found features (to foresee fame) may have been straightforwardly or in a roundabout way buyer affect decision criteria, be that as it may, yet overview of telephone properties, which are markers for the ubiquity of a particular telephone model.

None of the expected documents separates the dynamic changes in the optimal standards or on the other hand in the consistency of feature popularity. Such a longitudinal examination can perceive new models, examples and essential disruptions that are commonly unnoticeable. This new learning can be used in mobile incorporate positioning and endorsing, or in clearing up variations in the PDA showcase. In this exceptional situation, an example suggests a steady extending or decreasing change however an essential break alludes an amazing contrast in something like one component attributes in predicting product prominence in the midst of a particular time span [3].

Finland is a fascinating concentration for a longitudinal report, since it has been a fundamental market in mobile phone passage and use. In 2001, more than 200 texts for each capita were passed on, in 2006 the PDA entrance in Finland outperformed the masses and in 2012 compact broadband invasion was the most vital in Europe [4].

With respect to the examples and helper breaks, a fascinating period is the ten-year time span starting from the mid-2000s when a strong headway in all parts of phones occurred, cell phones ended up being astoundingly outstanding, and the activity of producers, for instance, Nokia, changed definitely. There are number of strategies utilized by number of creators to foresee the purposes behind fame of mobile phone model.

The examination requests of this item can be characterized as pursues. What is an appropriate prescient model to examine telephone notoriety as a part of its highlights and time? What will be best model for extraction of features that make phone model popular? To know most desirable feature that influences the choice of client is identified.

The rest of this article is organized as follows. Based on literature segment 2 investigate the earlier investigations of cell phone decision criteria.

2   Related Work

In their work, author have introduced the recent work reported on teaching learning based optimization algorithm and also propose a new chaotic version of TLBO algorithm to solve major problem of optimization [5]. Though, numbers of techniques have been developed to solve optimization problem. A vibrating particle system (VPS) is developed and evaluated that provide optimal solutions for constrained optimization problem. Currently, people are very much concern about their health and diseases. They need a system for prior precaution. So, in their work, author introduced a personal health record based decision support model for monitoring diabetes using mobile environment [6]. Number of techniques have been used to find most important features in smart phone discussed in Table 1.

Table 1. Related work

Reference	Data collection method	Year	Data count	Method	Important features
[3]	Interview and questionnaire	2002	66	Factor	Brand, interface and price
[4]	Survey	2002	800	Regression analysis	Brand and price
[7]	Questionnaire	2006	2571	Correlation analysis, multiple regression analysis ANOVA	Color screen, voice activated dialing and wireless connectivity
[8]	Interviews and questionnaire	2004	?	Analytic hierarchy process and TOPSIS method	Battery life, brand name and usability
[9]	Questionnaire + Experiment	2006	99 + 59	Multiple linear regression	Camera, weight, size, slim
[10]	Questionnaire	2012	1928	Non-linear principal component analysis	Operating system, battery life, size, camera
[11]	Questionnaire	2018	515	Descriptive statistics and factor analysis	Physical attributes, apps and sound
[12]	Provided by market research company	2016	570 approx.	Linear test, chow test, tree augmented naïve bayes	Operating system

3 Research Data and Research Methodology

3.1 Dataset

Our Dataset consists of 6 columns of gender, age, occupation, monthly income, education level, and battery backup as shown in the table. One of column battery backup type as a label. Dataset does not contain any missing values.

The exploration information comprise of sexual orientation, age, occupation, month to month pay, instruction level and 32 unique highlights of cell phone like camera, video, Bluetooth, multi-media alternative, shading show, alluring shading, model, brand value, product price, special offers, reliability family opinion, domestic product, Dual Sim option, charging hour…etc. We will predict whether battery backup is important for particular tuple or not. Questionnaire has been created on five point scale.

Naive Bayes

Naïve Bayes basically a probabilistic machine learning model used for classification tasks. Naive Bayes' most importantly used for classification based on Bayes theorem. Using naive Bayes we can find probability of one feature occurring, given that other has already occurred. If one of feature is present, it does not affect the other. It means features are independent. This is reason it is called naïve.

Now let us extend this to our classic mobile phone. The objective here is to estimate the likelihood of popularity of feature of mobile phone. There are 515 records and measured on five point likert scale like not all important, not very important, neutral, somewhat important and very important. Without knowing any of the other data, the naive estimate whether battery backup is not at all important, not very important, neutral, somewhat important or very important. Additionally, we will check accuracy of naïve.

Now we had information regarding battery backup feature as shown in Table 2:

Table 2. Battery backup

Gender	Age	Occupation	Monthly income	Education	Batter backup
Female	Below 18	Student	Below 5000	Undergraduate	Very important
Male	19–25	Student	Below 5000	Undergraduate	Very important
Male	19–25	Student	Below 5000	Postgraduate	Very important
Male	Below 18	Student	5000–20000	Undergraduate	Very important
Male	19–25	Student	Below 5000	Undergraduate	Very important
Male	19–25	Student	Below 5000	Undergraduate	Neutral
Male	19–25	Student	Below 5000	Undergraduate	Very important
Female	19–25	Student	Below 5000	Undergraduate	Neutral

Now the question "Whether battery backup is an important feature or not" for a particular type of tuple. What is the likelihood of feature of battery backup? What is accuracy if we calculate prediction using naive Bayes?

- **RB-Bayes Algorithm**

As it is characterize in our past research RB-Bayes is one of most effortless managed method [13]. It is a gathering structure considering Bayes theory. It is generally used in content order. Naive Bayes is furthermore established on Bayes theory. Regardless, unfit to manage issue of likelihood of zero credibility. RB-Bayes is proposed to comprehend this issue. RB-Bayes estimation gives a technique for finding out desire.

RB-Bayes algorithm steps

1. Each tuple that we wish to classify is represented by $X = (x_1, x_2.........a_n)$.
2. There are n numbers of labels. Given a tuple, X, the classifier will anticipate that X has a place with the label having the highest value from all labels.
3. Checking highest value for labels

$$(P_y F > P_n F) \quad \text{Where } y \neq n$$

Value of y and n are different labels. Maximum value from all labels will do prediction.
4. Maximize

$$\text{Mean} = \frac{T_y}{Total_{Sampleset}}$$

$$P_y F = \text{Mean} * \left(\frac{T_y a + T_y b + T_y c + T_y d..........T_y n}{T_F * T_y} \right)$$

5. T (Y_i), for I = 1, 2, 3....n, is a prior probability value depends on labels. The prior probability of each class can be computed based on training tuples. We calculate $T_y a, T_y b, T_y c,$ and $T_y d.........T_y n$, And this needs to be maximized.
   $T_y a$ is calculated by comparing value with P(y). Count will store in $T_y a + T_y b + T_y c + T_y d...........T_y n$, wherever both values are active. Similarly for $T_y b, T_y c,$ and $T_y d$

$$T_y a = \prod_{k=1}^{n} p(x_k | Y_i)$$
$$= P(x1|Y_i) * P(x_2|Y_i) * ....P(x_n|Y_i)$$

6. Predicting class label depending upon highest value after comparing the value of $P_y F, P_n F$
7. Factors affecting y and n can be n number of factors i.e.

$$T_y a, T_y b, T_y c \text{ and } T_y d.........T_y n$$

8. The classifier predicts that the class label of tuple X is the class $P_y F$ or $P_n F$
   If and only if

$$\frac{T_y}{Total_{SS}} * \left(\frac{T_ya + T_yb + T_yc + T_yd\ldots\ldots\ldots T_yn}{T_F * T_y}\right) > \text{Or} < \frac{T_n}{Total_{SS}}$$
$$* \left(\frac{T_na + T_nb + T_nc + \cdots\ldots\ldots\ldots + T_nn}{T_F * T_n}\right)$$

Proposed classifier has a minimum error rate when contrasted with other algorithms. All factors are thought about.

Time Complexity

The time complexity of an algorithm means the amount of time taken by an algorithm to accomplish a function on the input data. This is also an important factor which can be used to compare the accuracy of algorithms. Here time complexity of both RB-Bayes and Naïve Bayes algorithms are compared for understanding the efficiency of each algorithm in terms of time taken by both of them as shown in Table 3.

Naïve Bayes would output 0.009000629425 s on my computer and RB-Bayes would output 0.00699996948242. Time Complexity/Order of Growth characterizes the measure of time taken by any program regarding the size of the info. Time unpredictability of RB-Bayes calculation is given beneath.

O (N^2) Time Complexity

Table 3. Time complexity

Time complexity of algorithms	
Naïve Bayes algorithm	0.0090000629425
RB-Bayes algorithm	0.00699996948242

4 Results and Comparison

```
In [6]: import numpy as np
   ...: import matplotlib.pyplot as plt
   ...: import pandas as pd
   ...: train = pd.read_csv('ActualNB.csv')
   ...: pred= pd.read_csv('PredictedNB.csv')
   ...: from sklearn.metrics import
confusion_matrix
   ...: confusion_matrix(train,pred)
   ...: from sklearn.metrics import accuracy_score
   ...: accuracy_score(train,pred)
Out[6]: 0.87
```

Fig. 1. Accuracy with Naive Bayes

As shown in Fig. 1 accuracy with naive Bayes comes 87%. In previous research [11] it is shown that battery backup and operating system is one of important feature in mobile phone. It gives great impact on phone popularity. One of the hindrances with Naive-Bayes is that in the event that you have no events of a class label and specific property estimation together then the frequency based likelihood estimate will be zero. RB-Bayes algorithm proposed to overcome problem of Naïve Bayes. RB-Bayes algorithm and Naive Baye's algorithm to identify popular feature and comparing accuracy.

Applying RB-Bayes algorithm to check the importance of battery backup for a particular tuple. At the end we are going to compare value for Pyf and Pnf. Highest values predict the probability. With mobile dataset, we will compare probability value for not at all important, not very important, neutral, somewhat important and very important.

```
In [11]: import numpy as np
    ...: import matplotlib.pyplot as plt
    ...: import pandas as pd
    ...: train = pd.read_csv('Actual.csv')
    ...: pred= pd.read_csv('Predicted.csv')
    ...: from sklearn.metrics import
confusion_matrix
    ...: confusion_matrix(train,pred)
    ...: from sklearn.metrics import
accuracy_score
    ...: accuracy_score(train,pred)
Out[11]: 0.90000000000000002
```

Fig. 2. Accuracy with RB-Bayes algorithm

Accuracy with RB-Bayes is 90% as shown in Fig. 2. When we have datasets where zero values also occur then RB-Bayes perform better.

Table 4 represents the comparative analysis of proposed techniques with naive Bayes. The outcomes indicated that proposed system expels the issue of zero recurrence in credulous Bayes. In RB-Bayes, we split the dataset into preparing and testing at that point applied RB-Bayes on dataset.

Table 4. Comparative analysis of performances

Performance on 515 instances on mobile phone survey	
Classifier	Accuracy
Naive Bayes	87%
RB-Bayes	90%

5 Conclusion

This study provides greater benefit for manufacturer, marketer, consumer and seller to known number of methods to find popularity of feature. All methods are effective to find new patterns from existing data. Manufacturer as well as consumers can take benefits from these data. Manufacturer can find the reason about the popularity of particular brand and work on those features to add on their own production. The main aim of study to present a comparative study of the supervised techniques which permit doing a forecast based on training data. Stress that the proposed calculation considers all variables regardless of whether the likelihood of probability is zero, and yields a surprising precision level. Both the techniques were applied on a dataset of mobile phone survey and a comparative study, of the accuracy of results obtained from both techniques, was done. The comparative study of accuracy shows that RB-Bayes is not only more accurate in comparison to Naive Bayes but has the ability to overcome the drawback of zero probability of Naive Bayes also. Accuracy with RB-Bayes is coming 90% as compared to Naïve Bayes. In future, we will test it on large datasets and will compare with other classification algorithms.

References

1. Mobile OS. Mobile OS market share 2018 | Statista (2018). https://www.statista.com/statistics/266136/global-market-share-held-by-smartphone-operating-systems/. Accessed 1 Jan 2019
2. Bin, J.D., Park, Y.S.: A choice-based diffusion model for multiple generations of products. Technol. Forecast Soc. Change **61**, 45–58 (1999). https://doi.org/10.1016/S0040-1625(98)00049-3
3. Karjaluoto, H., Karvonen, J., Kesti, M., et al.: Factors affecting consumer choice of mobile phones: two studies from Finland. J Euromarketing **14**, 59–82 (2005). https://doi.org/10.1300/J037v14n03_04
4. Liu, C.: The effects of promotional activities on brand decision in the cellular telephone industry. J. Prod. Brand Manag. **11**, 42–51 (2002). https://doi.org/10.1108/10610420210419540
5. Kumar, Y., Singh, P.K.: A chaotic teaching learning based optimization algorithm for clustering problems. Appl. Intell. **49**, 1036–1062 (2019). https://doi.org/10.1007/s10489-018-1301-4
6. Kumar, Y., Yadav, G., Singh, P.K., Arora, P.: A PHR-based system for monitoring diabetes in mobile environment. In: Paiva, S. (ed.) Mobile Solutions and Their Usefulness in Everyday Life. EICC, pp. 129–144. Springer, Cham (2019). https://doi.org/10.1007/978-3-319-93491-4_7
7. Ling, C., Hwang, W., Salvendy, G.: Diversified users' satisfaction with advanced mobile phone features, 239–249 (2009). https://doi.org/10.1007/s10209-006-0028-x
8. Işıklar, G., Büyüközkan, G.: Using a multi-criteria decision making approach to evaluate mobile phone alternatives. Comput. Stand. Inter. **29**, 265–274 (2007). https://doi.org/10.1016/j.csi.2006.05.002
9. Han, S.H., Kim, K.J., Yun, M.H., et al.: Identifying mobile phone design features critical to user satisfaction. Hum. Factors Ergon. Manuf. **14**, 15–29 (2004). https://doi.org/10.1002/hfm.10051

10. Suominen, A., Hyrynsalmi, S., Knuutila, T.: Young mobile users: Radical and individual - not. Telemat Inform. **31**, 266–281 (2014). https://doi.org/10.1016/j.tele.2013.08.003
11. Bhalla, R., Amandeep, A.: A comparative analysis of factor effecting the buying judgement of smart phone. Int. J. Electr. Comput. Eng. **8**, 3057–3069 (2018). https://doi.org/10.11591/IJECE.V8I5.PP3057-3069
12. Kekolahti, P., Kilkki, K., Hämmäinen, H., Riikonen, A.: Features as predictors of phone popularity: an analysis of trends and structural breaks. Telemat. Inform. **33**, 973–989 (2016). https://doi.org/10.1016/j.tele.2016.03.001
13. Bhalla, R.: Opinion mining framework using proposed RB-Bayes. Int. J. Electr. Comput. Eng. **9**(1), 1–12 (2018). https://doi.org/10.11591/ijece.v9i1.pp%25p

A Review on Interoperability and Integration in Smart Homes

Renu Sharma$^{(\boxtimes)}$ and Anil Sharma

Lovely Professional University, Kapurthala (Jalandhar), Phagwara, Punjab, India
renusharma1978@yahoo.com, anil.19656@lpu.co.in

Abstract. Smart Home is a result of the surge of human mind to increase the convenience in living. It is a dwelling having appliances, lighting and other devices that can be handled remotely. Theoretically Smart devices can communicate with each other leading to high-tech functionalities. But if practical applicability is checked, many bottlenecks are there: constrained resources (memory, computational power and power backup), heterogeneity in terms of hardware as well as in terms of software (operating system, communication protocols etc.). Handling these diverse issues creates major issue of interoperability and integration. Interoperability could only be possible, if devices can communicate with each other regardless of their environment and operational detail. Interoperability could be manifested in terms of ease of data exchange among the smart devices or in terms of adding a new device. In this paper various solutions of interoperability and integration have been reviewed and are classified in various categories: network layer based, based on middleware, by gateways, by adapters, based upon framework etc. Paper aims to help researchers to find new directions in integration and interoperability through the classification provided.

Keywords: IoT · Smart Home · Zigbee · Z-wave · SOAP · OSGi

1 Introduction

Smart Home is a dwelling having network of many appliances that can communicate with each other or with outer world through internet. This communication enable a person to manage a home remotely. Internet of things (IoT) refers to a system in which sensors collect data from a network, and then share that data over the Internet, where it can be utilized for various applications [1]. IoT means having devices linked through internet to exchange their information and to create results helpful for mankind. Next era of computing will not be based on desktops but will be of IoT devices [2]. It is the most significant electronic revolution after internet [3]. During the couple of years of progression in remote sensing, "Machine–to–Machine" communication is the answer to most of the automation (M2M undertaking and assembling answers for hardware observing and operation to turn into wide-ranging appreciation). Most of these early M2M suggestions were depended on close function built framework and exclusive on manufacturing–particular principles instead of Internet Protocol (IP) based framework and Internet principles [4]. To associate objects through IP to the web is not a first

© Springer Nature Singapore Pte Ltd. 2020
P. K. Singh et al. (Eds.): FTNCT 2019, CCIS 1206, pp. 116–128, 2020.
https://doi.org/10.1007/978-981-15-4451-4_11

thought. The main Internet gadget is an IP–linked toaster with internet connectivity was used and highlighted in 1990 at an Internet consultation [5], early internet assisted devices like a coke apparatus at the Carnegie Mellon University in the US [6] was developed. With this early development, a strong area of ingenious work has turned into brilliant entity networking helped to make the establishment for now's Internet of Things [7].

According to Gartner, number of smart devices will be 26 billion by 2020. If anyone list, areas of application of IoT, list is keep on expanding to various diverse fields. Some areas of application are: Smart Homes, Remote Health care monitoring, Smart cities, Education, Smart Transport, Smart Agriculture, Business, Energy, Disaster detection etc.

The smart home is a leading application of IoT. From the Amazon Echo to the Nest Thermostat, there are copious devices accessible that customers can be in command of their voices to create their lives more associated than in previous times. The home machines can be partitioned into two classes: (1) Non-schedulable machines for example: lights, PCs and TVs which depends on manual control to work and are required just when the clients are in home [8]. (2) Schedulable home machines, which can be planned for suitable operation or operation according to convenience for example: washing machine, dishwasher, air conditioners, water heaters, heaters etc. The machines which can finish an undertaking with no manual control, for example, ventilation and cooling system and water warmer are schedulable [9]. All these IoT based devices requires following components to operate: Sensors, Middleware, Cloud computing, Internet [10]. (a) Sensors: They are used to detect and react to certain type of input. The base of IoT is various types of sensors. Constraints of sensors are: low energy, constrained computation and small memory. Because of these constraints a system involving sensors are difficult to design. (b) Middleware: In the applications based upon IoT, sensors do have different architectures and working based upon different protocols. So to make communication achievable, we require tools and they are called middlewares. They are used to integrate various devices. (c) Cloud computing: To have an IoT based application we need a cloud. Due to constrained resources of sensors, all the computation required cannot be done in the theses devices, so cloud is required in many applications. (d) Internet: To join different sensors and cloud, Internet is required. In any IoT based application, sensors have very less amount of power, so they cannot afford to be on network all the time. Generally PANs are used and connectivity to internet is provided when required. Next is the architecture used for such a system, for developing network of smart home systems a layered architecture was being discussed by King Bing et al. in [11] as shown in Fig. 1.

This architecture has three layers: sensors layer, network layer and application layer [11]. By using technology, smart home gives a new level of control to the home owners. Smart home concept is mainly to raise level of luxury. But it has given many added advantages, other than luxury. Some of the benefits of Smart Homes are: Remote monitoring, Assisted living for elderly [12], Energy efficiency [13], Comfort etc. Although smart home market is quite positive, in terms of user as well as from market perspective, but many technical as well as social hazards are there in the implementation of the same [8, 14]. In development of smart home applications, many challenges

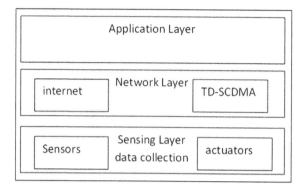

Fig. 1. Smart Home layered architecture [11]

are there. Some of them are: Interoperability and integration [15, 16], Security [16], Privacy [17], Data storage, Constrained resources, Data Analysis.

1.1 Interoperability and Integration

Smart home idea is mostly based upon sensors. Sensors do have varied architectures and their integration is a major challenge. Smart home industry lacks in standardization or in other words so many standards are there. Every company has adopted different standards. While integrating these devices many technological issues got arise. Integration of a new device is having issues at two levels: hardware and software level. To have a new device, its hardware details has to be compatible with the existing devices and its software specification should match with the existing solution. If some compatibility issues are there then many solutions suggested in the literature. This paper is focused on these solutions and in research gaps in the proposed solutions.

1.2 Security

Security is the major challenge for IoT devices. In IoT enabled cars, major possibility of intrusion is there by using server of the company. IoT is based upon network and network is vulnerable to threats. As in home automation system main identity of user is RFID card. Copy of that card is possible. If a person is using GPRS all its travelling pattern can be monitored and that can create major security issues. If we study health monitoring, intruder can create major blunders. Jacobsson et al. [18] have discussed various risks involved in smart home applications. Total 32 risks have been examined. So in all sensitive areas, IoT is quite helpful but its implementation needs security attention to the deeper insights.

1.3 Privacy

Privacy is also major concern. Somebody can study all patterns of someone just by analyzing data of sensors. And that information can be used for criminal activities. GPRS, wearable devices [19] and other sensors used for home can easily tell about daily routine of somebody. Apthorpe et al. [20] have demonstrated by taking some devices of smart home (Amazon Echo, camera, switch and a sleep monitor), how privacy is at threat even if the data is encrypted. Passive fragment of a network like internet service providers can easily analyze the data of the sensors and can tell pattern of the activities of home dwellers. So privacy is a major issue in the implementation of smart home.

1.4 Data Storage

In any smart environment huge data is produced. To process that huge data, traditional data processing techniques cannot be used or in other words they are not capable enough to process that huge data. To overcome this challenge there is a need of need data processing techniques capable to work on high volume and high velocity data. Data mining tools are to be updated.

1.5 Constrained Resources

In IoT devices main components are sensors. These sensors are really constrained as far as processing power, battery life and memory is concerned. Many wireless protocols are available (IEEE 802.11, 802.15, Zigbee, Zwave etc.), but on constraines resources it is not feasible to apply any protocol. In the literature new protocols have been proposed, capable to work on less resources like Constrained Application Protocol (CoAP). Every sensor is different as far as its computational capability is concerned, so to have same solution is not possible. To overcome these constraints are also a big challenge.

1.6 Data Analysis

Using sensors, gigantic data is generated. It is a challenge to handle such a large data. Existing data processing techniques can not be used on this chunk of data. So research is required to have new algorithms which could be based on machine learning, artificial intelligence or some other techniques. For analysis of data produced by IoT sensors, Mohammadi et al. [21] have used deep learning technique of machine learning. Data produced is categorized in two categories: fast data and big data. Need for analysis is different for two. First category needs speedy analysis and second category needs ways to deal huge amount of data.

2 Interoperability and Integration (Literature Review)

The main cost involved in developing smart home is to integrate various IoT devices [22]. IoT devices are based upon various protocols like: Zigbee, Z-Wave, X10, Insteon. All these protocols are having different architectures, they all are not interoperable their interoperability can be summarized as: (a) Zigbee is not interoperable with other protocols [23], (b) Z-wave is interoperable only with Z-wave based Devices [24], (c) X10 is interoperable with insteon and X10, (d) Insteon based devices are interoperable with insteon based devices.

Different approaches can be classified as suggested in literature to handle interoperability in IoT devices. Some of them are: Network layer based D2D communication [24]. Application based interoperability model [25]. By using IoT Middleware [3, 26]. Approach based upon proxy framework [27]. Given solutions for integration and interoperability for smart home are:

Asano et al. have used a framework that act as a proxy which will accept API requests in standard format [27]. And the proposed framework will convert request into device specific request. So an application programmer is not to bother for specific APIs, they have to work on standard APIs. This frame work is comprising of: (a) Device Manager (which will interact with application of devices as well as with devices. It will take service of device profile repository to convert standard format request to device format request. If that device is not in the repository it can further take service of cloud that is vendor specific.) (b) Device Profile Repository (c) Authorization Manager (d) Access Control Manager (to control access) (e) Cloud service hosted by specific vendor.

Perumal et al. have suggested a framework which is based upon SOAP using cloud services for smart home [28]. The proposed framework has following components: (a) Application Interface (this is the main component of this framework. This interface will give service which will locate suitable data ports of the individual device and help that device to integrate into smart home environment. This is also responsible for communication between devices and home automation software. (b) Service Stub (this component will handle requirements of integration of a new device in the system. It contains built in SQL commands that corresponds to the framework organization.) (c) Database Module.

Wu et al. have suggested to have a solution based upon common standards like OSGi (Open service gateway initiative) [29]. It is a service oriented model based on mobile agent technology. In this solution every device has its own OSGi platform. Various components of the proposed model are: Interface Agent, Device Agent, Service Agent, Agent Directory, MAG, Context Agent, Database Agent, Agent Coordinator. (a) Interface Agent: its main function is interaction of the user and components. (b) Device Agent: this is a device dependent component. Main function of this agent is to control, monitor the device as well as to cooperate. (c) Service Agent: It is to control many device agents. This component provides control at higher hierarchical level. (d) Agent Directory: this is repository of registry of various services. (e) Mobile Agent Generator: its main task is to create mobile agents and mobile agent is responsible to perform and schedule the desired task. (f) Context Agent: this component transforms raw data into contextual data based upon specific query. (g) Database Agent: its function is to manage all the data of the system. (h) Preference Agent: it is store preferences of individual users. (i) Agent Coordinator: its function is to coordinate any conflicts among mobile agents.

To provide integration and interoperability Valtchev et al. [30] have suggested an OSGi based platform for smart home. They have chosen OSGi due to its flexibility and extensibility. Their solution can integrate many smart home standards and protocols. In this paper [31], authors have classified interoperability at three levels and levels are: (a) Basic Connectivity Interoperability, (b) Network Interoperability, (c) Syntactic Interoperability. They have suggested some middleware technologies like CORBA,

.NET framework, XML based, J2EE and SOAP. Proposed system is using SOAP to provide scalability and interoperation. In this paper [32], Al Mehairi et al. has proposed a prototype system which is capable to integrate different technologies for smart home. Various components of the purposed system are: network (internal as well as external), appliances, gateway and services. [33] authors in this paper has discussed interoperability on different platforms. Special focus is given on AAL (active and assisted living). In this paper interoperability has been discussed at different levels (device to device, network to network, middleware to middleware, application service to application service and Data and Semantics to Data and Semantics). Two platforms for healthcare has been discussed BodyCloud and universalAAL.

[34] in this paper stress is given on lack of standardization is the main cause in the problem of interoperability. In this paper semantic interoperability has been discussed. A model based translation layer has been introduced for interoperability among various devices in the purposed solution. [35] in this paper key areas of IoT: Health, logistics and transportation have discussed. Various ontologies has been discussed and authors have tried to reach semantic interoperability. Many ontologies are there dealing with various sensors. Mainly W3C SSN ontology is being used. OpenIoT project is based on this ontology. Many other ontologies have been discussed. Authors have suggested to achieve interoperability with middlewares, semantics and agents.

[36] authors has based their research on DHC (Digital Home Compliant) protocol. As lack of standardization is the major cause of interoperability issues in smart home context, DHC communication protocol is one possible solution to standardization. In this paper need of adapters has been discussed for integration and it has been pointed out that maximum code of adapters are common. So by using this property adapters can be generated automatically based upon model driven architecture. This Model Driven Architecture is widely used by OMG group for heterogeneous softwares. Various standard protocols has been discussed for integration of new appliances like UPnP (universal plug and play), Echonet, Jini, OSGi etc. Various tools has been discussed for automatic code generation (Acceleo, Actifsource, Code-g, Jinja, ZumCoder) and their relevance in smart home. To generate automatic adapter following stages has been suggested as depicted in Fig. 2 [36].

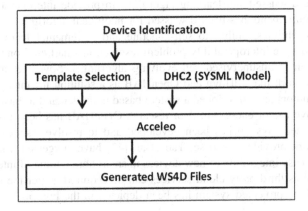

Fig. 2. [36] automatic adapter generation process

[37] in this paper an intelligent gateway is proposed to provide a platform to deal with the heterogeneity of the smart devices. Authors have described a gateway which can detect a new device itself and get that registered and if user discards an old device, gateway automatically deletes its registry. In such an environment it is very convenient to integrate new devices. In this solution a gateway by IoTivity framework has been used which is based on client/server model. It uses CoAP protocol for communication between device to device. It uses following operations for communication: (a) GET, (b) PUT (c) POST (d) DELETE (e) OBSERVE (in this solution observe is modified and a new operation has been created named INIT.) [38] a mobile gateway based upon smart phones have been proposed in this paper as a solution for interoperability in IoT devices. In the heterogeneous field of IoT, lack of standardization is a major fsproblem. And gateways to bridge this heterogeneity can really help. As individual sensors have constrained resources, an efficient gateway can really help to solve problem of interoperability. Purposed application has following modules: (a) Manager (this module act as coordinator of the Entire architecture.) (b) Communication Service Engine (five different services are given by this engine including 3G/LTE, Wi-Fi, Zigbee, Bluetooth and SPINE) (c) IoT Device Management (main functions of this module are data analysis exchange, execution of control commands and to load adapters dynamically of devices) (d) GW database(to store local database on the smart phone based on the library of SQLite. (e) GUI (this interface is used for the interaction with user and to access settings of all the modules.) (f) Application Services (to start various services and to supervise them) [1]. To provide interoperability in IoT devices Kaur et al. [1] has suggested an approach based on MDA model. This model has been introduced in 2001 by OMG group. And it has huge success stories in varies applications. The same approach is suggested for IoT. This model helps to create a system which is capable of interoperability and easy integration. It is based upon stages first computation independent model (CIM) is developed and from that a platform independent model (PIM) is being created. From PIM, a platform specific model can be created. From platform specific model, code can be generated. Di Martino et al. [39] has studied various reference models suggested by Microsoft, Intel, SAP, WS2o in the perspective of security and interoperability in IoT devices. A comparative analysis has been given of proposed frameworks (Standard, commercial and academic proposals). Nawaratne et al. [40] have discussed self-learning algorithms to provide interoperability at data level. Three requirements has been discussed for intelligent algorithms: unsupervised self-learning capabilities, ability to self-generate and incremental learning. Authors stressed upon to have interoperability problem resolved in smart environment the best type of approach is unsupervised self-evolving algorithms. Sowah et al. [41] have suggested framework like AllJoyn and OpenHAB as a solution for interoperability in smart home. Authors have developed a system based upon demand to have an efficient and cost effective use of energy. In their research OpenHAB has been used. A Smart Power Management System has been developed and to resolve issues of interoperability framework provides the base. Tao et al. [42] have suggested a hybrid cloud architecture for easy integration of new devices in smart home. Issue of interoperability can be resolved as third party cloud services can be acquired as per the requirement. Architecture of the projected system has been depicted in the Fig. 3.

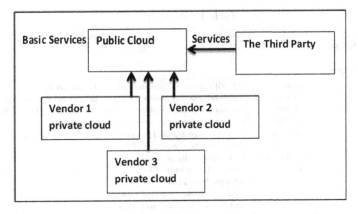

Fig. 3. [42] hybrid cloud architecture

Many solutions have been purposed in the literature. Marica Amadeo et al. have used fog computing for smart home [43]. Jahoon Koo et al. about interoperability in diverse platforms [44]. We have tried to classify these solutions based upon various categories. The classification is given in Table 1. And different solutions are combined.

3 Findings and Research Gaps in the Purposed Solutions for Interoperability and Integration

Table 1. Findings and research gaps

Interoperability & integration solutions purposed in literature based upon	Authors	Findings	Research gaps
Network layer based	Perumal et al. [31] Pace et al. [33]	[31, 33] if we want to achieve interoperability than adaptability in network layer could be the answer. Network layer is mainly responsible for effective communication in a network. And if changes are done at that layer, problem of integration and interoperability can be resolved	In this area only introductory work has been done. There is a scope to have a network model such that it can support integration on these constrained devices
Based upon common standards	Wu et al. [29] Strassner et al. [34]	[29, 34] main issue of interoperability is lack of standardization, if we have common standard, problem can be solved	There should be some central authority to standardize models
Based upon middleware	Pace et al. [33] Ganzha et al. [35]	[33, 35] to provide interoperability an effective middleware can play a significant role. Main focus is on semantic interoperability and AAL (assisted active living)	If middleware can be designed such that it can use artificial intelligence concepts and machine learning than self adaptable middlewares can be created

(*continued*)

Table 1. (*continued*)

Interoperability & integration solutions purposed in literature based upon	Authors	Findings	Research gaps
Based upon framework	Perumal et al. [28] Valtchev et al. [30] Kang et al. [37] Sowah et al. [41]	[28, 30] a common developmental framework can also provide a solution to the interoperability [37] a proxy framework can also be used to convert Standard request to device Specific request [41] commercially available frameworks can be used for interoperability like OpenHAB as used by R. A. Sowah et al. For using such frameworks their capabilities has to be studied well and whether it can be used in our desired environment	Framework is limited to some devices and some protocols. A solution should be such to cover larger horizons
A smart phone based mobile gateways	Aloi et al. [38]	[38] smart phone based gateway can really be great help to provide interoperability	How to create gateways which can work on constrained resources like smart phones to include more devices
Based on model driven architecture automatic generation of adapters	Fernandez et al. [36]	[36] in this automatic adapter generation has been discussed using SysMl model. While adding a new device if adapters could be generated automatically than problem of integration can be resolved. But practically	Limited devices have been covered. Effort can be put forward to add more devices
Mapping from one reference model to another	Di Martino [39]	[39] there must be a possibility of mapping of one model to another model. If practical solution is available for mapping than two diverse devices can be integrated easily. So one solution for integration and interoperability could be effective mapping from one model to another	This is a theoretical concept, for future its practical viability can be checked for various models
Automatic configurable IoT gateway	Kang et al. [37]	[37] an automatic configurable IoT gateway can really help in integrating new devices. If gateway can configure itself according to new needs than when a new device is to be attached, it can prepare itself for change. In such a scenario integration could be easy	It is for some limited devices, further work can be extended to add more
Self-learning intelligent algorithm based approach	Nawaratne et al. [40]	[40] in this artificial intelligence has been used and among the three approaches, authors have proved with their research that unsupervised self-learning algorithm approach is suitable for interoperability in context of data in smart environment. So artificial Intelligence could be the solution for integration and interoperability in smart home	For interoperability using artifical intelligence work has been done on unsupervised self-learning approach, it can be extended to others too

(*continued*)

Table 1. (*continued*)

Interoperability & integration solutions purposed in literature based upon	Authors	Findings	Research gaps
Hybrid cloud architecture	Tao et al. [42]	[42] To provide easy integration of a new device hybrid cloud architecture could be a solution. For a new device, services of the third party can be taken as it is not possible to put all type of services in your system. Third party help can be a quite effective solution	Efficient applications are needed on the cloud to cater all type of needs
Using model driven architecture	Kaur et al. [1]	[1] MDA model has been used in many areas and its success ratio is huge, so we can apply this model in IoT based devices. This model has been used in many areas, due to its layered approach and some layers are generalized for any environment this could be a solution for easy integration of new devices	Till now only concepts have been purposed, this idea can be developed practically

3.1 Conclusion and Future Work

Authors have apprised the interoperability issues in home automation. Literature survey of this paper, highlights the various works done to provide easy integration and interoperability. Findings can be used as a ready reckoner to pick a direction for solution in interoperability and integration. Research gaps can really help researchers to find future directions. Smart home is facing challenges in terms of security [45], privacy [46, 47], energy efficiency and interoperability [48, 49]. Introduction to all these challenges have been covered to whet the appetite of the researchers and comprehensive information is given about interoperability and integration [50], to get an insight. It will further help researchers to decide future course to find the solution of the above challenges. Categorization has been done of solutions provided for interoperability and integration. Various categories are: network layer based [28, 30], based upon common standards [26, 31], middleware based [30, 32], framework based [25, 27, 34, 38], based upon MDA [1, 33], by using artificial intelligence [38], by using hybrid cloud architecture [39] etc. Integration of new device will become an easy task if hardware and software specifications are standardized. If easy integration is possible, smart home will become a huge commercial success and open up future avenues. If plug and play option could be given, integration of new devices will be very easy [35]. A plug and play solution is given for smart cities (P. Misra et al., 2015). On the same pattern if plug and play option is given in smart home, integration issue can be resolved to a large extent. Future scope for this challenge is to have a solution which can result in plug and play.

References

1. Kaur, K., Sharma, A.: Interoperability among Internet of Things (IoT) components using model-driven architecture approach. In: Fong, S., Akashe, S., Mahalle, Parikshit N. (eds.) Information and Communication Technology for Competitive Strategies. LNNS, vol. 40, pp. 519–534. Springer, Singapore (2019). https://doi.org/10.1007/978-981-13-0586-3_52
2. Jayavardhana, G., Buyya, R., Marusic, S., Palaniswami, M.: Internet of Things (IoT): a vision, architectural elements and future directions. J. Future Gener. Comput. Syst. **29**(2), 1645–1660 (2013)
3. Ngu, A.H., Gutierrez, M., Metsis, V., Nepal, S., Sheng, Q.Z.: IoT middleware: a survey on issues and enabling technologies. IEEE Internet Things J. **4**(1), 1–20 (2017)
4. Webpage of automation world. https://www.automationworld.com/cloud-computing/know-difference-between-iot-and-m2m. Accessed 20 Dec 2018
5. Webpage of living internet. http://www.livinginternet.com/i/ia_myths_toast.html. Accessed 18 Dec 2016
6. Webpage of cs. https://www.cs.cmu.edu/~coke/history_long.txt. Accessed 18 Sept 2016
7. Webpage of tools IETF. https://tools.ietf.org/html/rfc7452. Accessed 18 Sept 2016
8. Wilson, C., Hargreaves, T., Hauxwell-Baldwin, R.: Benefits and risks of smart home technologies. Energy Policy **103**, 72–83 (2017)
9. Mitchell, S., Villa, N., Stewart-Weeks, M., Lange, A.: The Internet of everything for cities. Connecting People, Process, Data, and Things to Improve the 'Livability' of Cities and Communities. https://www.cisco.com/c/dam/en_us/about/ac79/docs/ps/motm/IoE-Smart-City_PoV.pdf. Cisco (2013)
10. Lee, I., Lee, K.: The Internet of Things (IoT): applications, investments, and challenges for enterprises. Bus. Horiz. **58**(4), 431–440 (2015)
11. Bing, K., Fu, L., Zhuo, Y., Yanlei, L.: Design of an Internet of things-based smart home system. In: The 2nd International Conference on Intelligent Control and Information Processing, pp. 921–924, July 2011
12. Daraby, S.J.: Smart technology in the home: time for more clarity. Build. Res. Inf. **46**(1), 140–147 (2017)
13. Herrero, S.T., Nicholls, L., Strengers, Y.: Smart home technologies in everyday life: do they address key energy challenges in households. Curr. Opin. Environ. Sustain. **31**, 65–70 (2018)
14. Webpage. https://www.trendmicro.com/vinfo/au/security/news/internet-of-things/threats-and-risks-to-complex-iot-environments. Accessed 05 Apr 2019
15. Raggett, D.: The web of things: challenges and opportunities. IEEE Comput. **48**(5), 26–32 (2015)
16. Elkhodr, M., Shahrestani, S., Cheung, H.: The internet of things: new interoperability, management and security challenges. Int. J. Netw. Secur. Appl. **8**, 85–102 (2016). arXiv:1604.04824v1
17. Notra, S., Siddiqi, M., Gharakheili, H. H., Sivaraman, V., Boreli, R.: An experimental study of security and privacy risks with emerging house-hold appliances. In: Proceedings IEEE Conference on Communications and Network Security, pp. 79–84 (2014)
18. Jacobsson, A., Boldt, M., Carlsson, B.: A risk analysis of smart home automation system. Future Gener. Comput. Syst. **56**, 719–733 (2016)
19. Martin, J.A.: 10 things you need to know about the security risks of wearables. Para 4, 24 March 2017. https://www.cio.com/article/3185946/wearable-technology/10-things-you-need-to-know-about-the-security-risks-of-wearables.html. Accessed 12 Feb 2018

20. Apthorpe, N., Resiman, D., Feamster, N.: A smart home is no castle: privacy vulnerabilities of encrypted IoT traffic. arXiv:1705.06805 (2017)

21. Mohammadi, M., Sorour, S.: Deep learning for IoT big data and streaming analytics: a survey. IEEE Commun. Surv. Tutor. **20**(4), 2923–2960 (2018)

22. Stojkoska, B.L.R., Trivodaliev, K.V.: A review of internet of things for smart home: challenges and solutions. J. Clean. Prod. **140**(3), 1454–1464 (2017)

23. Ray, B.: Z-wave Vs. Zigbee. Para 3,4. 21 November 2017. https://www.link-labs.com/blog/z-wave-vs-zigbee. Accessed 13 Feb 2018

24. Bello, O., Zeadlly, S., Badra, M.: Network layer inter-operation of device-to-device communication technologies in Internet of Things (IoT). Ad Hoc Netw. **57**, 52–62 (2017)

25. Chander, R.V., Mukherjee, S., Elias, S.: An applications interoperability model for heterogeneous internet of things environments. Comput. Electr. Eng. **64**, 163–172 (2017)

26. Bandyopadya, S., Sengupta, M., Maiti, S., Dutta, S.: Role of middleware for internet of things: a study. Int. J. Comput. Sci. Eng. Surv. **2**(3), 94–105 (2011)

27. Asano, S., Yashiro, T., Sakamura, K.: A proxy framework for API interoperability in the internet of things. In: Proceedings of the IEEE 5th Global Conference on Consumer Electronics, October 2016

28. Perumal, T., Ramliand, A.R., Leong, C.Y.: Interoperability framework for smart home systems. IEEE Trans. Consum. Electron. **57**(4), 1607–1611 (2011)

29. Wu, C.L., Liao, C.F., Fu, L.C.: Service-oriented smart-home architecture based on OSGi and mobile agent technology. IEEE Trans. Syst. Man Cybern. **37**(2), 193–205 (2007)

30. Valtchev, D., Frankov, I.: Service gateway architecture for a smart home. IEEE Commun. Mag. **40**(2), 126–132 (2002)

31. Perumal, T., Ramli, A.R., Leong, C.Y., Manso, S., Samsudin, K.: Interoperability for smart home environment using web services. Int. J. Smart Home **2**(4), 1–16 (2008)

32. Al Mehairi, S.O., Barada, H., Al Qutayri, M.: Integration of technologies for smart home applications. In: Proceedings of the IEEE/ACS International Conference on Computer Systems and Applications, pp. 241–246 (2007)

33. Pace, P., et al.: IoT platforms interoperability for active and assisted living healthcare service support. In: Proceedings of the 2017 Global Internet Of Things Summit (GIoTS), pp. 1–6, 2017

34. Strassner, J., Diabl, W.W.: A Semantic Interoperability Architecture for Internet of things Data Sharing and Computing. In Proc. IEEE 3rd World Forum on Internet of Things (WF-IoT), pp. 609–614, Dec. 2016

35. Ganzha, M., Paprzycki, M., Pawlowski, W., Szmeja, P., Wasielewska, K.: Semantic interoperability in the internet of things; an overview from IINTER-IoT perspective. J. Netw. Comput. Appl. **81**, 111–124 (2017)

36. Fernandez, M.R., Alonso, G., Casanova, E.Z.: Improving the interoperability in the digital home through the automatic generation of software adapters from a SysML model. J. Intell. Rob. Syst. **86**(3–4), 511–521 (2017)

37. Kang, B., Choo, H.: An experimental study of a reliable IoT gateway. ICT Express **4**(3), 130–133 (2018)

38. Aloi, G., et al.: Enabling IoT interoperability through opportunistic smartphone-based mobile gateways. J. Netw. Comput. Appl. **81**, 74–84 (2017)

39. Di Martino, B., Rak, M., Ficco, M., Esposito, A., Maisto, S.A., Nacchia, S.: Internet of things reference architectures, security and interoperability: a survey. Internet Things **1**, 99–112 (2018)

40. Nawaratne, R., et al.: Self-evolving intelligent algorithms for facilitating data interoperability in IoT environments. Future Gener. Comput. Syst. **86**, 421–432 (2018)

41. Sowah, R.A., et al.: Demand side management of smart homes using open HAB framework on interoperability of devices. In: Proceedings of IEEE 7th International Conference on Adaptive Science & Technology (ICAST) 2018
42. Tao, M., Qu, C., Wei, W., Zhou, B., Huang, S.: Hybrid cloud architecture for cross-platform interoperability in smart homes. In: Vaidya, J., Li, J. (eds.) ICA3PP 2018. LNCS, vol. 11336, pp. 608–617. Springer, Cham (2018). https://doi.org/10.1007/978-3-030-05057-3_45
43. Amadeo, M., Giordano, A., Mastroianni, C., Molinaro, A.: On the integration of information centric networking and fog computing for smart home services. In: Cicirelli, F., Guerrieri, A., Mastroianni, C., Spezzano, G., Vinci, A. (eds.) The Internet of Things for Smart Urban Ecosystems. IT, pp. 75–93. Springer, Cham (2019). https://doi.org/10.1007/978-3-319-96550-5_4
44. Koo, J., et al.: Device identification interoperability in heterogeneous IoT platforms. Sensors **19**(6), 616–625 (2019)
45. Webpage. https://dzone.com/articles/iot-smart-home-automation-and-its-future-predictio. Accessed 18 May 2019
46. Webpage. https://www.iotforall.com/smart-home-interoperability-fragmented-landscape/. Accessed 21 Apr 2019
47. Zheng, S., Apthorpe, N., Chetty, M., Feamster, N.: User perceptions of Smart Home IoT privacy. https://arxiv.org/1802.08182v2 (2018)
48. Webpage. https://www.safewise.com/home-security-faq/home-automation-features/. Accessed 11 Mar 2019
49. Webpage. http://smarthomegallery.com/insights/integrating-smart-home-devices/. Accessed 12 Jan 2019
50. Pan, L., Lu, C.: Challenges in integrating IoT in smart home. Report Number: (2019). All Computer Science and Engineering Research (2019)

Testbed on MANET (ToM): Private Testbed Facility for MANET Experiment

Farkhana Muchtar[1]([✉]), Mosleh Al-Adhaileh[2],
Ili Najaa Aimi Mohd Nordin[3], Asyikin Sasha Mohd Hanif[4],
Pradeep Kumar Singh[5], Ajoze Abdulraheem Zubair[1],
and Ajibade Lukuman Saheed[1]

[1] School of Computing, Faculty Engineering, Universiti Teknologi Malaysia,
81310 Skudai, Johor, Malaysia
farkhana@gmail.com, ajozeoziadal968@gmail.com,
ajibade.sa@gmail.com
[2] Deanship of E-Learning and Distance Education, King Faisal University,
Al-Ahsa, Kingdom of Saudi Arabia
madaileh@kfu.edu.sa
[3] Faculty of Engineering Technology, Universiti Tun Hussein Onn Malaysia,
84600 Pagoh, Malaysia
ilinajaa@uthm.edu.my
[4] Centre for Artificial Intelligence and Robotics (CAIRO),
Malaysia-Japan International Institute of Technology,
Universiti Teknologi Malaysia, 5400 Kuala Lumpur, Malaysia
asyikinsasha@gmail.com
[5] Department of CSE&IT, Jaypee University of IT, Waknaghat, Solan 17334,
Himachal Pradesh, India
pradeep_84cs@yahoo.com

Abstract. This article aims to share how to create a minimum MANET testbed facility as a requirement for evaluation of MANET research. Testbed facility that we have developed is called as Testbed on MANET or abbreviation ToM. We chose to use single board computer (SBC) to represent mobile devices in MANET. ToM facility and can be used either in a static mesh network or in a dynamic network topology, where each node in the testbed can move according to the needs of the researcher. To realize a real world node mobility in ToM, we use mobile robot technology and mobile robot that we have develop, where we named it as ToMRobot. Our experience in developing a ToM facility proves that with today's technological developments, the private MANET testbed facility can be developed more easily at low cost.

Keywords: MANET · Mobile ad hoc network · Testbed · Mobile robot

1 Introduction

In this literature, we will discuss how we design and implement a private MANET testbed facility that we call Testbed on MANET or a summary of ToM as meeting the requirements of some of our MANET research. Most of the research in the field of

© Springer Nature Singapore Pte Ltd. 2020
P. K. Singh et al. (Eds.): FTNCT 2019, CCIS 1206, pp. 129–145, 2020.
https://doi.org/10.1007/978-981-15-4451-4_12

MANET uses network simulation and network emulation methods rather than real world testbed method for evaluation purposes on conducted research [1–5]. However, not all research can be answered via network simulation or network emulation. At the same time not all the scenarios studied can be translated into network simulation and network emulation.

From there, we observe that there is a need to use a real world testbed method for evaluation purposes in MANET research. In addition, real world testbed is also needed to validate network simulation and network emulation used is accurate in representing the actual situation and scenario. Therefore, there is a need to use the real world testbed method in MANET research and this literature is one of the efforts to share how to create a minimum testbed facility for MANET research needs.

2 Related Work

Based on our research on the development of some of the previous MANET testbed facilities, we can categorize this type based on three testbed facility methods, private based MANET testbed facility, community based MANET testbed facility and public based MANET testbed facility. Private based MANET testbed facility refers to the MANET testbed facility developed specifically for one or more research used by the same individual or research group. The testbed design is only focused on their research needs. An example MANET testbed facility that can only be used privately by the researcher or research group itself are CONE project [6, 7] and Roomba MADNET [8, 9].

Community based MANET testbed facility refers to a testbed facility developed in collaboration with several different research groups for their respective research needs. It is usually a collaboration to combine resources available to each research group such as funds, researchers, skills, technology and existing facilities. Among community based MANET testbed facilities are like MiNT-m [10–12], Mint-2, Proteus, ARUM and Sensei-UU.

Public-based MANET testbed facility refers to MANET testbed facility that is publicly opened for use by any interested researcher or require a testbed facility for their research needs. MANET testbed facility opened publicly are Mobile Emulab [13, 14], ORBIT [15, 16], w-ilab.t [17–20], IoT-Lab [20–22] and NITOS [20, 23–27].

Besides, MANET testbed facility can also be divided based on the implementation method of node mobility which is either by emulation or by real node mobility method. There are several ways to implement virtual or emulated mobility in MANET testbed such as instance migration [15], on/off connection [28], RF matrix switch [29–33] and through virtual machine and network [34]. While real world mobility is implemented in various ways such as cars [35–40], taxis [41], trains [42–48], bicycles [24, 49], humans [2, 36, 50–58] (See Fig. 1), control cars [59] and multiple mobile robots like Mobile Emulab Testbed (also known as TrueMobile) [13], MiNT (miniaturized mobile multi-hop wireless network testbed) [10–12] and PHAROS Testbed [60, 61].

Fig. 1. Real mobility in MANET testbed using human [57]

3 Testbed Management System

Before we touch on the technical topics on other additional components, we first provide focus on the main component of our MANET testbed facilities which is the testbed management system that we called as Testbed on MANET or ToM. ToM is developed to be at its bare rudiment possible created specifically to fulfill the purpose of our research. Therefore, the interface and the usage of ToM is not produced to be generic in nature but rather, it is specific to the experiments carried out in this research (Fig. 2).

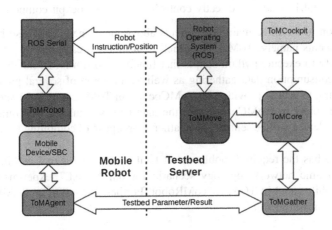

Fig. 2. Testbed on MANET (ToM) system

ToM is a web based testbed management system developed using Flask web framework[1] which is a Python based microframework for web based application. We used Python based web framework to facilitate the integration of mobile robot control

---

[1] http://flask.pocoo.org.

system that uses Robot Operating System (ROS) with the mobile devices used in our testbed facility namely, Banana Pro and Banana Pi M1+ through the use of remote agent which is also developed using Python. ToM consists of three main components designed to fulfill three main requirements of our testbed facility:

i. **ToMCockpit = Testbed Scenario Management.** This is the general setup for the testbed scenario that also includes the parameters on each of the scenarios such as the setting on the number of testbed repetition, the determination of nodes to act as consumer node or producer node, the file to be selected as targeted content during the experiment as well as deciding which congestion control solution that is going to be used.

ii. **ToMGather = Testbed Result Management.** ToMGather functions as testbed result management by remotely collecting all the testbed results from each mobile device in the testbed facility and creates it as spreadsheet format. CSV spreadsheet format is used because this format can be interpreted by most statistical analysis software such as R programming language, Julia Lang and SPSS. ToMGather also performs data checks in the testbed result to ensure that the testbed results obtained is valid and can be used for statistical analysis purposes.

iii. **ToMMove = Mobile Robot/Mobility Control System.** ToMMove is a ToM component developed using Robot Operating System (ROS) framework to control and operate mobile robots in our MANET testbed facility based on the setup made in ToMCockpit. ToMMove is only used in dynamic network topology scenarios that requires mobile robot to provide real mobility mechanisms when experiments are being performed. Whereas for static network topology scenarios, ToMMove is not used but instead it is directly controlled by ToMCockpit components.

In addition to the three main components above mentioned, ToM also has several other components namely, ToMAgent which is installed at each mobile device in the testbed facility to execute python scripts that functions to run NFD, ndndump, power and energy consumption data gathering as well as the setup of several parameters on NFD according to setting provided by ToMCockpit in ToM server. ToMAgent is fully controlled remotely by ToMCockpit and the data that is regulated by TomAgent's at every mobile device will be sent to ToMGather for purpose of compiling testbed results as a whole.

ToM also has the required mobile robot facility needed for real mobility mechanisms in dynamic network topology scenario for our MANET experiment and we called the mobile robot in TOM as ToMRobot. Further discussion on ToMRobot can be referred to in Subsect. 4.3.

4 Hardware Setup for Testbed Facility

Discussions about hardware setup for ToM facilities range from selection of mobile devices to be used in testbed, hardware or tools used for different testbed scenarios as well as some other issues related to hardware setup for ToM facility. The testbed facility we developed supports experiments conducted in static network topology and dynamic network topology. Both scenarios have different setup and requirements and will be discussed in depth in this section. At the same time, we also discussed a few testbed miniaturization approaches that are also important in the testbed facility we develop as a testbed miniaturization allowing our testbed facility to be created internally because it does not require extensive area as practiced by some MANET testbed facility ever developed.

4.1   Single Board Computer (SBC) as Mobile Device in Testbed

Single board computer or SBC, is a type of computer where all of its main components are placed on the same board and it require no additional components to perform basic functions of computer. SBC is commonly used in electronics for product development, prototyping, demonstration, education, hobby projects and in some cases are used in production as embedded computer controller.

SBC became popular among hobbyists and "maker"[2] with the introduction of Raspberry Pi Model A (see Fig. 3) which commemorate to be the first open hardware SBC and the main reason why it became so popular was due to its small, credit card-sized, ease of use and affordable price.

Fig. 3. Raspberry Pi model A

The use of SBC to represent mobile devices in wireless ad-hoc network testbed is not a relatively new practice as it has been applied in Decristofaro et al. [62], Paramanathan et al. [63], Nikhade [64], Oda et al. [65, 66], Oda and Barolli [67] and Barolli et al. [68, 69].

In our opinion, SBC has many other advantages to be used as mobile device for MANET testbed facility compared to any other options such as laptop, smartphone, PDAs (obsolete technology) and mobile tablet. SBC is cheaper, smaller, modular and developer friendly. At the same time SBC also maintain the same advantages with smartphone as mobile device in MANET testbed facility as mentioned by Abdallah et al. [70].

We chose Banana Pro (see Fig. 4) and Banana Pi M1+ (see Fig. 5) to represent the mobile devices in our testbed facility for two main reasons.

The first reason we chose Banana Pro SBC is because of AXP209 PMU IC (see Fig. 12) in Banana Pro and Banana Pi M1+ allows us to get the power consumption

---

[2] https://en.wikipedia.org/wiki/Maker_culture.

readings on the board if battery terminal is used as the source of power source instead of micro USB terminal. AXP209 allows us to perform power and energy consumption data gathering without the need for other external devices especially on experiments that involves with node mobility scenarios. Further discussion on the use of AXP209 chips for power and energy consumption data gathering can be seen in Subsect. 5.1.

The second reason is both SBC is supporting external Wi-Fi antenna setup is one of the critical required feature that needs to exist in the SBC of our choice because it allows us to perform Wi-Fi signal miniaturization with the addition of fixed attenuator (see Fig. 11) on Wi-Fi antenna. Unlike Raspberry Pi 2 and 3 that is produced and comes equipped with included on-board or embedded Wi-Fi antenna, it is virtually almost impossible to perform Wi-Fi signal miniaturization without the necessary use of some dirty hack to replace on-board Wi-Fi antenna with external Wi-Fi antenna. More elaborate details and discussions pertaining to testbed miniaturization can be found in Subsect. 4.4.

Based on the requirements mentioned above, we decided to use of Banana Pro even though it is comparably more expensive than Raspberry PI 2.

Fig. 4. Banana Pro single board computer

Fig. 5. Banana Pi M1+

In the early stages of development, we choose Banana Pro because Banana Pi M1+ is not yet available in the market. We then added the number of mobile nodes in our testbed facility using Banana Pi M1+ since the specifications and the components used are identical to Banana Pro but available at much cheaper price (USD 30) which is less than half the price of Banana Pro (USD 70).

4.2   Hardware Setup for Static Network Topology

In static network topology scenario testbed setup, we are utilizing ESP8266 to serve as mobile robot controller for dynamic topology scenario experiment as the serial transparent bridge over Wi-Fi between Banana Pro/Banana Pi M1+ and ToM server (see Fig. 6). This method combines simplicity of setup and operation of approach number one and low energy consumption communication of approach number two. We can use existing serial transparent bridge for ESP8266 such as esp_link[3] and ESP8266_transparent_ bridge[4]. We can access remote console We can remotely access the console of each Banana Pro/Banana Pi M1+ via web console or through telnet and at the same time trigger testbed scripts in each Banana Pro/Banana Pi M1+ through REST or JSON based web service wirelessly.

Fig. 6. ESP8266 as transparent bridge for wireless serial communication

We choose this method to control each unit of Banana Pro/Banana Pi M1+ when experiments is being conducted in static network topology setup scenario in our MANET testbed facility. As for dynamic topology scenario, we use a slightly different approach although it still uses ESP8266 as the intermediate between Banana Pro/Banana Pi M1+ because it involves real mobility mechanism using mobile robot technology and this will be discussed further in Subsect. 4.3.

4.3   Hardware Setup for Dynamic Network Topology Scenario

We developed an in-house multiple mobile robot that we call as ToMRobot to provide real mobility mechanism in the testbed facility that we are using for our research experiment. We chose to use mobile robot technology since it provides better control and consistency compared to other methods when implementing node mobility in the MANET testbed. At the same time, robotic technology is getting more affordable in line with the current "Maker Culture" that promotes DIY culture among hobbyists and amateurs to create their own robots.

4.3.1   ToMRobot Hardware Architecture

For robot chassis, we used a combination of Tamiya Track and Wheel with Tamiya Twin Motor (see Fig. 7) as the main body chassis for ToMRobot 2.0. Both components are easy to find, reasonably priced, reliable, ideal for both indoor as well as outdoor environment and also because it is one of the most popular options among hobbyist as mobile robot's main body chassis.

---

[3] https://github.com/jeelabs/esp-link.

[4] https://github.com/beckdac/ESP8266-transparent-bridge.

Fig. 7. Tamiya track and wheel and tamiya twin motor

In ToMRobot 2.0, we did not use Tamiya universal plate set but instead we have produced our own robot chassis plate by using 3D printers that allows us to design ToMRobot according to our requirements such as the placement of the batteries, robot controller, mobile nodes, sensors and several other components.

For ToMRobot controller, we chose to utilize ESP8266 NodeMCU microcontroller that we combined with motor shield as the robot controllers for ToMRobot 2.0 shown in Fig. 8.

Fig. 8. ESP8266 NodeMCU with motor shield board

The main reason as to why we choose ESP8266 NodeMCU as the mobile robot controller is due cheaper price and much better capabilities such as higher processing power, larger flash memory size, more IO pin compared to Arduino Uno. More interesting, ESP8266 has a built-in Wi-Fi chip.

Furthermore, the ESP8266 board is much smaller than Arduino Uno board despite having better capabilities. This factor provides us with more room to add other components in the mobile robot chassis such as sensors and batteries.

4.3.2 Indoor Localization and Path Planning for ToMRobot

Based on our research, the combination of 9 DOF IMU GY-85 (see Fig. 9) and ultrasonic based Indoor localization solution from Marvelmind Robotics (see Fig. 10) or also known as Marvelmind 'indoor GPS' is the best indoor localization solution for ToMRobot 2.0.

Marvelmind 'indoor GPS' uses ultrasonic trilateration method to perform indoor localization compared to most existing indoor localization that uses Radio Frequency (RF) based trilateration approach.

Fig. 9. IMU GY-85 sensor

Fig. 10. Marvelmind robotics localization beacons and modem (Hardware Version 4.5)

The advantages of ultrasonic based trilateration compared to RF based trilateration is the nonexistence of wireless signal noise and interference which is an important factor in our choice of indoor localization solution. The main drawback of ultrasonic trilateration solution is the fact that it cannot be used in a room or noisy environment however such issues does not exist in our MANET testbed facility.

4.4 Testbed Miniaturization

Miniaturized testbed in this testbed facility is referring to the miniaturization of wireless signal (radio signal) effective range from its original radio signal range size to the much smaller radio signal range to allow wireless multi-hop ad-hoc network environment even if it is performed in small indoor testbed arena. Testbed miniaturization goal is to enable real MANET testbed to be conducted in the small indoor area since executing MANET testbed using actual area size is very expensive. Additionally, most wireless testbed facilities are outdoor testbed facilities where the experiment to be conducted are affected by weather condition [71]. Among MANET testbed facilities that uses wireless testbed miniaturization method are MiNT [10–12], Kansei [72], Kansei Genie [73, 74], ivynet [71, 75] and Orbit [15].

Wireless signal range miniaturization can be performed through the combination of two methods. The first method is, by reducing to the lowest possible wireless signal transmission power on Wi-Fi transmitter inside the Wi-Fi Chip. However wireless signal range is still big to enable MANET testbed to be performed indoor. Hence, we need the addition of a second method which is achievable by installing fixed radio signal attenuator on the Wi-Fi external antenna as shown in Fig. 11 [10, 12]. The reduction of the radio signal effective range does not affect the nature of the wireless communication of the mobile devices [71].

Fig. 11. Fixed radio signal attenuator

5 Experiment Data Gathering

There are two main categories of experiment data that we want to obtain during the experiment, namely energy consumption data and network traffic statistic data. Each category of these experiment data represents different stochastic factor and it is measured with various different tools and approaches.

5.1 Energy Consumption

AXP209 Power Management Unit Integrated Circuit (PMU IC) as shown in Fig. 12, is a power management chip that is used in most AllWinner ARM chip based mobile devices including Banana Pro and Banana Pi M1+. AXP209 is designed as a highly integrated PMU IC optimized for mobile devices that require single cell lithium ion battery power supply such as smartphone and tablet and it allows intake from multiple power source from DC to DC converter such as 5 V power supply from micro USB port.

Fig. 12. AXP209 integrated circuit

Similar to other PMU ICs for mobile devices, AXP209 also has the ability to monitor voltage, current and power consumption that serves as the indicator on the use of electric energy of mobile devices allowing estimations on the amount of electric power stored in the battery.

We are not using the default AXP209 Linux kernel driver since the default kernel driver only allows data gathering update rate for every two seconds, which is equal to 500 mHz. Therefore, we used a customized AXP209 kernel driver that allows us to modify the data gathering update rate up to every 1/2 of a second, which is equivalent to 2000 mHz. The customized AXP209 kernel driver is obtainable by default when using ARMbian Linux distribution, embedded Linux that is developed specific for ARM based SBC especially SBC that uses AllWinner ARM based SoC such as A20 that is used in Banana Pro and Banana Pi M1+.

5.2 Network Traffic Statistic

In order to obtain MANET traffic statistics, two approaches can be used. The first approach is through network packet analysis using Tcpdump or Wireshark application, and the second through network traffic generator such as Iperf and DIT-G. Both methods have their own purpose and requirement.

In the ToM facility, network traffic analysis is controlled through the ToMGather module that controls the ToMAgent remote running within the SBC. ToMAgent will run either network packet analysis or network traffic generator according to the selected testbed scenario in ToMGather. Once the experiment is completed, network traffic statistic generated by the network traffic generator or by network packet analysis will be collected by ToMAgent on every SBC and then sent to ToMGather for the purpose of data consolidation for all mobile devices in the Fifetestbed. Pre-processing data will be done first by ToMGather and will then be processed into spreadsheet format before the analysis process is done manually.

6 Conclusion

The MANET testbed facility that we develop for our research needs have achieves our set target, i.e. complete testbed facilities and low cost. We have discussed how we designed the testbed facility from the testbed management system, the testbed hardware setup until the testbed result was taken when the experiment was conducted inside the testbed facility. The testbed facility also has a real world mobility mechanism that uses mobile robot technology to ensure that the real world mobility mechanism can be properly controlled to ensure that the experiments are repeatable and reproducible. We also discussed how testbed miniaturization methods are implemented in our testbed facility to allow for smaller spaces and at the same time can be created indoor. From an experimental data gathering point, we have also discussed how the testbed results are taken either in the form of network traffic statistic or energy consumption of each mobile device in testbed.

From our success in establishing this testbed facility, it can be concluded that today's technology development allows MANET testbed facilities to be developed more easily and inexpensively. It is hope that this positive development allows more MANET researchers to choose the real world testbed method as an evaluation tool for their research for the benefit of MANET's development as a practical communication solution in the world.

References

1. Benmoshe, B., Berliner, E., Dvir, A.: Performance monitoring framework for Wi-Fi MANET. In: 2013 IEEE Wireless Communications and Networking Conference (WCNC), pp. 4463–4468 (2013). https://doi.org/10.1109/wcnc.2013.6555297
2. Kulla, E., Sakamoto, S., Ikeda, M., Barolli, L., Xhafa, F., Kamo, B.: Evaluation of a MANET testbed for central bridge and V-shape bridge scenarios using BATMAN routing protocol. In: 2013 Eighth International Conference on Broadband and Wireless Computing, Communication and Applications
3. Do, V.T.M., Landmark, L., Kure, O.: Testbed-based performance evaluation of a connectionless multicast protocol for MANETs. In: 11th International Symposium on Wireless Communications Systems (ISWCS), pp. 276–281 (2014). https://doi.org/10.1109/iswcs.2014.6933361
4. Friginal López, J., Andrés Martínez, D.D., Ruiz García, J.C., Martínez Raga, M.: A survey of evaluation platforms for ad hoc routing protocols: a resilience perspective. Comput. Netw. **75**(Part A), 395–413 (2014). https://doi.org/10.1016/j.comnet.2014.09.010
5. Vessaz, F., Garbinato, B., Moro, A., Holzer, A.: Developing, deploying and evaluating protocols with ManetLab. In: Gramoli, V., Guerraoui, R. (eds.) NETYS 2013. LNCS, vol. 7853, pp. 89–104. Springer, Heidelberg (2013). https://doi.org/10.1007/978-3-642-40148-0_7
6. Vingelmann, P., Pedersen, M., Heide, J., Zhang, Q., Fitzek, F.: Data dissemination in the wild: a testbed for high-mobility MANETs. In: IEEE International Conference on Communications (ICC), pp. 291–296 (2012). https://doi.org/10.1109/icc.2012.6364123
7. Vingelmann, P., Heide, J., Pedersen, M.V., Zhang, Q., Fitzek, F.H.P.: All-to-all data dissemination with network coding in dynamic MANETs. Comput. Netw. **74**(Part B), 34–47 (2014). https://doi.org/10.1016/j.comnet.2014.06.018. http://www.sciencedirect.com/science/article/pii/S1389128614003144
8. Reich, J., Misra, V., Rubenstein, D.: Roomba MADNeT: a mobile ad-hoc delay tolerant network testbed. ACM SIGMOBILE Mob. Comput. Commun. Rev. **12**(1), 68–70 (2008). https://doi.org/10.1145/1374512.1374536. http://doi.acm.org/10.1145/1374512.1374536
9. Reich, J., Misra, V., Rubenstein, D., Zussman, G.: Connectivity maintenance in mobile wireless networks via constrained mobility. IEEE J. Sel. Areas Commun. **30**(5), 935–950 (2012). https://doi.org/10.1109/JSAC.2012.120609
10. De, P., Raniwala, A., Sharma, S., Chiueh, T.C.: MiNT: a miniaturized network testbed for mobile wireless research. In: Proceedings of the 24th Annual Joint Conference of the IEEE Computer and Communications Societies, INFOCOM 2005, vol. 4, pp. 2731–2742. IEEE (2005). https://doi.org/10.1109/infcom.2005.1498556
11. De, P., et al.: MiNT-m: an autonomous mobile wireless experimentation platform. In: Proceedings of the 4th International Conference on Mobile Systems, Applications and Services, MobiSys 2006, pp. 124–137. ACM, New York (2006). https://doi.org/10.1145/1134680.1134694. http://doi.acm.org/10.1145/1134680.1134694
12. De, P.: Mint: a reconfigurable mobile multi-hop wireless network testbed. Ph.D. thesis, State University of New York at Stony Brook, Stony Brook, NY, USA (2007)
13. Johnson, D., Stack, T., Fish, R., Flickinger, D., Ricci, R., Lepreau, J.: TrueMobile: a mobile robotic wireless and sensor network testbed. In: The 25th Annual Joint Conference of the IEEE Computer and Communications Societies. IEEE Computer Society (2006)
14. Johnson, D., et al.: Mobile Emulab: a robotic wireless and sensor network testbed. In: Proceedings of the 25th IEEE International Conference on Computer Communications, INFOCOM 2006, pp. 1–12 (2006). https://doi.org/10.1109/infocom.2006.18

15. Raychaudhuri, D., et al.: Overview of the ORBIT radio grid testbed for evaluation of next-generation wireless network protocols. In: Wireless Communications and Networking Conference, vol. 3, pp. 1664–1669. IEEE (2005)

16. Zhang, F., Reznik, A., Liu, H., Xu, C., Zhang, Y., Seskar, I.: Using ORBIT for evaluating wireless content-centric network transport. In: Proceedings of the 8th ACM International Workshop on Wireless Network Testbeds, Experimental Evaluation & Characterization, WiNTECH 2013, pp. 103–104. ACM, New York (2013). https://doi.org/10.1145/2505469.2508457. http://doi.acm.org/10.1145/2505469.2508457

17. Bouckaert, S., Vandenberghe, W., Jooris, B., Moerman, I., Demeester, P.: The w-iLab.t testbed. In: Magedanz, T., Gavras, A., Thanh, N.H., Chase, J.S. (eds.) TridentCom 2010. LNICST, vol. 46, pp. 145–154. Springer, Heidelberg (2011). https://doi.org/10.1007/978-3-642-17851-1_11

18. Bouckaert, S., Jooris, B., Becue, P., Moerman, I., Demeester, P.: The IBBT w-iLab.t: a large-scale generic experimentation facility for heterogeneous wireless networks. In: Korakis, T., Zink, M., Ott, M. (eds.) TridentCom 2012. LNICST, vol. 44, pp. 7–8. Springer, Heidelberg (2012). https://doi.org/10.1007/978-3-642-35576-9_4

19. Vandenberghe, W., Moerman, I., Demeester, P., Cappelle, H.: Suitability of the wireless testbed w-iLab.t for VANET research. In: 18th IEEE Symposium on Communications and Vehicular Technology in the Benelux (SCVT), pp. 1–6 (2011). https://doi.org/10.1109/scvt.2011.6101301

20. Muchtar, F., Abdullah, A.H., Lati, M.S.A., Hassan, S., Wahab, M.H.A., Abdul-Salaam, G.: A technical review of MANET testbed using mobile robot technology. J. Phys. Conf. Ser. **1049**(1), 012001 (2018). https://doi.org/10.1088/1742-6596/1049/1/012001. http://stacks.iop.org/1742-6596/1049/i=1/a=012001

21. Fleury, E., Mitton, N., Noel, T., Adjih, C.: FIT IoT-LAB: the largest IoT open experimental testbed. ERCIM News (101), 14 (2015). https://hal.inria.fr/hal-01138038

22. Harter, G., Pissard-Gibollet, R., Saint-Marcel, F., Schreiner, G., Vandaele, J.: Demo: FIT IoT-LAB A: large scale open experimental IoT testbed. In: Proceedings of the 21st Annual International Conference on Mobile Computing and Networking, MobiCom 2015, pp. 176–178. ACM, New York (2015). https://doi.org/10.1145/2789168.2789172. http://doi.acm.org/10.1145/2789168.2789172

23. Giatsios, D., Apostolaras, A., Korakis, T., Tassiulas, L.: Methodology and tools for measurements on wireless testbeds: the NITOS approach. In: Fàbrega, L., Vilà, P., Careglio, D., Papadimitriou, D. (eds.) Measurement Methodology and Tools. LNCS, vol. 7586, pp. 61–80. Springer, Heidelberg (2013). https://doi.org/10.1007/978-3-642-41296-7_5

24. Kazdaridis, G., Stavropoulos, D., Maglogiannis, V., Korakis, T., Lalis, S., Tassiulas, L.: NITOS BikesNet: enabling mobile sensing experiments through the OMF framework in a city-wide environment. In: IEEE 15th International Conference on Mobile Data Management (MDM), vol. 1, pp. 89–98 (2014). https://doi.org/10.1109/mdm.2014.17

25. Keranidis, S., et al.: Experimentation on end to-end performance aware algorithms in the federated environment of the heterogeneous PlanetLab and NITOS testbeds. Comput. Netw. **63**, 48–67 (2014). https://doi.org/10.1016/j.bjp.2013.12.026. http://www.sciencedirect.com/science/article/pii/S1389128613004398

26. Keranidis, S., Kazdaridis, G., Passas, V., Korakis, T., Koutsopoulos, I., Tassiulas, L.: NITOS energy monitoring framework: real time power monitoring in experimental wireless network deployments. SIGMOBILE Mob. Comput. Commun. Rev. **18**(1), 64–74 (2014). https://doi.org/10.1145/2581555.2581566. http://doi.acm.org/10.1145/2581555.2581566

27. Pechlivanidou, K., Katsalis, K., Igoumenos, I., Katsaros, D., Korakis, T., Tassiulas, L.: NITOS testbed: a cloud based wireless experimentation facility. In: 26th International Teletraffic Congress (ITC), pp. 1–6 (2014). https://doi.org/10.1109/itc.2014.6932976

28. Yoon, H., Kim, J., Ott, M., Rakotoarivelo, T.: Mobility emulator for DTN and MANET applications. In: Proceedings of the 4th ACM International Workshop on Experimental Evaluation and Characterization, WINTECH 2009, pp. 51–58. ACM (2009). https://doi.org/10.1145/1614293.1614303. http://doi.acm.org/10.1145/1614293.1614303

29. Clancy, T., Walker, B.: MeshTest: laboratory-based wireless testbed for large topologies. In: 3rd International Conference on Testbeds and Research Infrastructure for the Development of Networks and Communities, TridentCom 2007, pp. 1–6 (2007). https://doi.org/10.1109/tridentcom.2007.4444659

30. Seligman, M., Walker, B.D., Clancy, T.C.: Delay-tolerant network experiments on the MeshTest wireless testbed. In: Proceedings of the Third ACM Workshop on Challenged Networks, CHANTS 2008, pp. 49–56. ACM, New York (2008). https://doi.org/10.1145/1409985.1409996. http://doi.acm.org/10.1145/1409985.1409996

31. Walker, B., Clancy, C.: A quantitative evaluation of the MeshTest wireless testbed. In: Proceedings of the 4th International Conference on Testbeds and Research Infrastructures for the Development of Networks & Communities, TridentCom 2008, pp. 29:1–29:6. ICST (Institute for Computer Sciences, Social-Informatics and Telecommunications Engineering), Brussels (2008). http://dl.acm.org/citation.cfm?id=1390576.1390612

32. Walker, B., Vo, I., Beecher, M., Clancy, C.: A demonstration of the meshtest wireless testbed. In: 5th International Conference on Testbeds and Research Infrastructures for the Development of Networks Communities and Workshops, TridentCom 2009, p. 1 (2009). https://doi.org/10.1109/tridentcom.2009.4976234

33. Hahn, D., Lee, G., Kim, Y., Walker, B., Beecher, M., Mundur, P.: DTN experiments on the virtual meshtest testbed. In: Proceedings of the 5th ACM Workshop on Challenged Networks, CHANTS 2010, pp. 79–82. ACM, New York (2010). https://doi.org/10.1145/1859934.1859952. http://doi.acm.org/10.1145/1859934.1859952

34. Kim, Y., Taylor, K., Dunbar, C., Walker, B., Mundur, P.: Reality vs emulation: running real mobility traces on a mobile wireless testbed. In: Proceedings of the 3rd ACM International Workshop on MobiArch, HotPlanet 2011, pp. 23–28. ACM, New York (2011). https://doi.org/10.1145/2000172.2000180. http://doi.acm.org/10.1145/2000172.2000180

35. Maltz, D.A., Broch, J., Johnson, D.B.: Experiences designing and building a multi-hop wireless ad hoc network testbed. Special Purpose Grant in Science and Engineering F19628-96-C-0061, Carnegie Mellon University, USA (1999)

36. Maltz, D., Broch, J., Johnson, D.: Lessons from a full-scale multihop wireless ad hoc network testbed. IEEE Pers. Commun 8(1), 8–15 (2001). https://doi.org/10.1109/98.904894

37. Ramanathan, R., Redi, J., Santivanez, C., Wiggins, D., Polit, S.: Ad hoc networking with directional antennas: a complete system solution. IEEE J. Sel. Areas Commun. 23(3), 496–506 (2005). https://doi.org/10.1109/JSAC.2004.842556

38. Veeravuttiphol, P., Komolkiti, P., Aswakul, C.: MANET testbeds for evaluation of real-time controls in multimedia transmissions. In: 3rd International Conference on Testbeds and Research Infrastructure for the Development of Networks and Communities, TridentCom 2007, pp. 1–6 (2007). https://doi.org/10.1109/tridentcom.2007.4444705

39. Tsukada, M., Ernst, T.: Vehicle communication experiment environment with MANET and NEMO. In: International Symposium on Applications and the Internet Workshops, SAINT Workshops 2007, p. 45 (2007). https://doi.org/10.1109/saint-w.2007.104

40. Yazir, Y., Jahanbakhsh, K., Ganti, S., Shoja, G., Coady, Y.: A low-cost realistic testbed for mobile ad hoc networks. In: IEEE Pacific Rim Conference on Communications, Computers and Signal Processing, PacRim 2009, pp. 671–676 (2009). https://doi.org/10.1109/pacrim.2009.5291291

41. Galati, A., Bourchas, T., Siby, S., Frey, S., Olivares, M., Mangold, S.: Mobile-enabled delay tolerant networking in rural developing regions. In: IEEE Global Humanitarian Technology Conference (GHTC), pp. 699–705 (2014). https://doi.org/10.1109/ghtc.2014.6970359

42. Jetcheva, J., Hu, Y.C., PalChaudhuri, S., Saha, A., Johnson, D.: Design and evaluation of a metropolitan area multitier wireless ad hoc network architecture. In: Proceedings of Fifth IEEE Workshop on Mobile Computing Systems and Applications, pp. 32–43 (2003). https://doi.org/10.1109/mcsa.2003.1240765

43. Pentland, A., Fletcher, R., Hasson, A.: DakNet: rethinking connectivity in developing nations. Computer **37**(1), 78–83 (2004). https://doi.org/10.1109/MC.2004.1260729

44. Kutscher, D., Greifenberg, J., Loos, K.: Scalable DTN distribution over uni-directional links. In: Proceedings of the 2007 Workshop on Networked Systems for Developing Regions, NSDR 2007, pp. 6:1–6:6. ACM, New York (2007). https://doi.org/10.1145/1326571. 1326580. http://doi.acm.org/10.1145/1326571.1326580

45. Coulson, G., et al.: Flexible experimentation in wireless sensor networks. Commun. ACM **55**(1), 82–90 (2012). https://doi.org/10.1145/2063176.2063198. http://doi.acm.org/10.1145/2063176.2063198

46. Zarafshan-Araki, M., Chin, K.W.: TrainNet: a transport system for delivering non real-time data. Comput. Commun. **33**(15), 1850–1863 (2010). https://doi.org/10.1016/j.comcom. 2010.06.008. http://www.sciencedirect.com/science/article/pii/S0140366410002690

47. Nati, M., Gluhak, A., Abangar, H., Headley, W.: SmartCampus: a usercentric testbed for internet of things experimentation. In: 16th International Symposium on Wireless Personal Multimedia Communications (WPMC), pp. 1–6 (2013)

48. Nati, M., Gluhak, A., Domaszewicz, J., Lalis, S., Moessner, K.: Lessons from smartcampus: external experimenting with user-centric Internet-of-Things testbed. Wireless Pers. Commun. **93**(3), 709–723 (2014). https://doi.org/10.1007/s11277-014-2223-z

49. Bromage, S., et al.: SCORPION: a heterogeneous wireless networking testbed. ACM SIGMOBILE Mob. Comput. Commun. Rev. **13**(1), 65–68 (2009). https://doi.org/10.1145/1558590.1558604. http://doi.acm.org.ezproxy.psz.utm.my/10.1145/1558590.1558604

50. Ramanathan, R., Hain, R.: An ad hoc wireless testbed for scalable, adaptive QoS support. In: IEEE Wireless Communications and Networking Conference, WCNC 2000, vol. 3, pp. 998–1002 (2000). https://doi.org/10.1109/wcnc.2000.904763

51. Ritter, H., Tian, M., Voigt, T., Schiller, J.: A highly flexible testbed for studies of ad-hoc network behaviour. In: Proceedings of 28th Annual IEEE International Conference on Local Computer Networks, LCN 2003, pp. 746–752 (2003). https://doi.org/10.1109/lcn.2003. 1243208

52. Lenders, V., Wagner, J., May, M.: Analyzing the impact of mobility in ad hoc networks. In: Proceedings of the 2nd International Workshop on Multi-hop Ad Hoc Networks: From Theory to Reality, REALMAN 2006, pp. 39–46. ACM, New York (2006). https://doi.org/10.1145/1132983.1132991. http://doi.acm.org/10.1145/1132983.1132991

53. Ikeda, M., Kulla, E., Hiyama, M., Barolli, L., Takizawa, M., Miho, R.: A comparison study between simulation and experimental results for MANETs. In: 13th International Conference on Network-Based Information Systems (NBiS), pp. 371–378 (2010). https://doi.org/10. 1109/nbis.2010.75

54. Kulla, E., Hiyama, M., Ikeda, M., Barolli, L.: Comparison of experimental results of a MANET testbed in different environments considering batman protocol. In: Third International Conference on Intelligent Networking and Collaborative Systems (INCoS), pp. 1–7 (2011). https://doi.org/10.1109/incos.2011.69

55. Ikeda, M., Barolli, L., Hiyama, M., Kulla, E., Takizawa, M.: Performance evaluation of MANET routing protocols: simulations and experiments. Comput. Inf. **30**(6), 1147–1165 (2011)
56. Hiyama, M., Kulla, E., Oda, T., Ikeda, M., Barolli, L.: Experimental results of a MANET testbed in a mixed environment considering horizontal and vertical topologies. In: IEEE 26th International Conference on Advanced Information Networking and Applications (AINA), pp. 884–889 (2012). https://doi.org/10.1109/aina.2012.68
57. Hiyama, M., Kulla, E., Ikeda, M., Barolli, L.: Evaluation of MANET protocols for different indoor environments: results from a real MANET testbed. Int. J. Space-Based Situated Comput. **2**(2), 71–82 (2012)
58. Kulla, E., Ikeda, M., Oda, T., Barolli, L., Xhafa, F., Takizawa, M.: Multimedia transmissions over a MANET testbed: problems and issues. In: Sixth International Conference on Complex, Intelligent and Software Intensive Systems (CISIS), pp. 141–147 (2012). https://doi.org/10.1109/cisis.2012.82
59. Alenazi, M.J.F., Cetinkaya, E.K., Rohrer, J.P.: Implementation of the AeroRP and AeroNP protocols in Python. In: Proceedings of the International Telemetering Conference (2012). http://arizona.openrepository.com/arizona/handle/10150/581658
60. Stovall, D., Paine, N., Petz, A., Enderle, J., Julien, C., Vishwanath, S.: Pharos: an application-oriented testbed for heterogeneous wireless networking environments. Technical report TR-UTEDGE-2009-006, The University of Texas at Austin (2009)
61. Fok, C., Petz, A., Stovall, D., Paine, N., Julien, C., Vishwanath, S.: Pharos: a testbed for mobile cyber-physical systems. Technical report TR-ARiSE2011-001, University of Texas at Austin (2011)
62. Decristofaro, M.A., Lansdowne, C.A., Schlesinger, A.M.: Heterogeneous wireless mesh network technology evaluation for space proximity and surface applications. In: SpaceOps Conference. American Institute of Aeronautics and Astronautics (2014). https://doi.org/10.2514/6.2014-1600. https://arc.aiaa.org/doi/10.2514/6.2014-1600
63. Paramanathan, A., Pahlevani, P., Thorsteinsson, S., Hundeboll, M., Lucani, D., Fitzek, F.: Sharing the Pi: testbed description and performance evaluation of network coding on the Raspberry Pi. In: 79th Vehicular Technology Conference (VTC Spring), pp. 1–5. IEEE (2014). https://doi.org/10.1109/vtcspring.2014.7023090
64. Nikhade, S.G.: Wireless sensor network system using Raspberry Pi and Zigbee for environmental monitoring applications. In: International Conference on Smart Technologies and Management for Computing, Communication, Controls, Energy and Materials (ICSTM), pp. 376–381 (2015). https://doi.org/10.1109/icstm.2015.7225445
65. Oda, H., Kulla, E., Ozaki, R., Nishihara, N.: Design of an adhoc testbed for IoT and WSAN applications using Raspberry Pi. BWCCA 2016. LNDECT, vol. 2, pp. 535–546. Springer, Cham (2017). https://doi.org/10.1007/978-3-319-49106-6_53
66. Oda, T., Yamada, M., Obukata, R., Barolli, L., Woungang, I., Takizawa, M.: Experimental results of a Raspberry Pi based wireless mesh network testbed considering TCP and LoS scenario. In: 10th International Conference on Complex, Intelligent, and Software Intensive Systems (CISIS), pp. 175–179 (2016). https://doi.org/10.1109/cisis.2016.86
67. Oda, T., Barolli, L.: Experimental results of a Raspberry Pi based WMN testbed considering CPU frequency. In: IEEE 30th International Conference on Advanced Information Networking and Applications (AINA), pp. 981–986 (2016). https://doi.org/10.1109/aina.2016.146
68. Barolli, A., Oda, T., Barolli, L., Takizawa, M.: Experimental results of a Raspberry Pi and OLSR based wireless content centric network testbed considering OpenWRT OS. In: IEEE 30th International Conference on Advanced Information Networking and Applications (AINA), pp. 95–100 (2016). https://doi.org/10.1109/aina.2016.153

69. Barolli, A., Elmazi, D., Obukata, R., Oda, T., Ikeda, M., Barolli, L.: Experimental results of a Raspberry Pi and OLSR based wireless content centric network testbed: comparison of different platforms. Int. J. Web Grid Serv. **13**(1), 131–141 (2017). https://doi.org/10.1504/IJWGS.2017.082064.   https://www.inderscienceonline.com/doi/abs/10.1504/IJWGS.2017.082064

70. Abdallah, A., MacKenzie, A., DaSilva, L., Thompson, M.: On software tools and stack architectures for wireless network experiments. In: IEEE Wireless Communications and Networking Conference (WCNC), pp. 2131–2136 (2011). https://doi.org/10.1109/wcnc.2011.5779462

71. Su, Y., Gross, T.: Validation of a miniaturized wireless network testbed. In: Proceedings of the Third ACM International Workshop on Wireless Network Testbeds, Experimental Evaluation and Characterization, WiNTECH 2008, pp. 25–32. ACM, New York (2008). https://doi.org/10.1145/1410077.1410084. http://doi.acm.org/10.1145/1410077.1410084

72. Arora, A., Ertin, E., Ramnath, R., Nesterenko, M., Leal, W.: Kansei: a high-fidelity sensing testbed. IEEE Internet Comput. **10**(2), 35–47 (2006). https://doi.org/10.1109/MIC.2006.37

73. Sridharan, M., et al.: From Kansei to KanseiGenie: architecture of federated, programmable wireless sensor fabrics. In: Magedanz, T., Gavras, A., Thanh, N.H., Chase, J.S. (eds.) TridentCom 2010. LNICST, vol. 46, pp. 155–165. Springer, Heidelberg (2011). https://doi.org/10.1007/978-3-642-17851-1_12

74. Sridharan, M., et al.: KanseiGenie: software infrastructure for resource management and programmability of wireless sensor network fabrics. In: Next-Generation Internet Architectures and Protocols. Cambridge University Press (2011). http://dx.doi.org/10.1017/CBO9780511920950.015

75. Su, Y., Heule, M., Gross, T.: Ivynet: a testbed for multihop wireless network research. Technical report. Citeseer (2006). Citation Key: su2006ivynet

ToMRobot 2.0: Real Mobility Mechanism in MANET Testbed Using Mobile Robot

Farkhana Muchtar[1(✉)], Mosleh Al-Adhaileh[2],
Ili Najaa Aimi Mohd Nordin[3], Ajoze Abdulraheem Zubair[1],
Pradeep Kumar Singh[4], Radzi Ambar[5],
and Ajibade Lukuman Saheed[1]

[1] School of Computing, Faculty Engineering, Universiti Teknologi Malaysia,
81310 Skudai, Johor, Malaysia
farkhana@gmail.com, ajozeoziadal968@gmail.com,
ajibade.sa@gmail.com
[2] Deanship of E-learning and Distance Education, King Faisal University,
Al-Ahsa, Kingdom of Saudi Arabia
madaileh@kfu.edu.sa
[3] Faculty of Engineering Technology, Universiti Tun Hussein Onn Malaysia,
84600 Pagoh, Malaysia
ilinajaa@uthm.edu.my
[4] Department of CSE and IT, Jaypee University of IT, Waknaghat, Solan 17334,
Himachal Pradesh, India
pradeep_84cs@yahoo.com
[5] Faculty of Electrical and Electronic Engineering,
Universiti Tun Hussein Onn Malaysia, 86400 Batu Pahat, Malaysia
aradzi@uthm.my

Abstract. This paper is a continuation of our previous paper under the same topic, ToMRobot 1.0. Our main goal of developing ToMRobot 2.0 is to improve the ToMRobot 1.0 that we developed earlier. ToMRobot was developed because we think mobile robot technology is more practical than other approaches as a real world mobility mechanism in MANET testbed. But to develop our own mobile robot at low cost and at the same time not complex is very challenging. The challenge is overcome through the use of easy-to-use components, self-built components using 3D printers and the use of mobile robot designs that have proven to be easily developed, cheap and effective. The use of the Robot Operating System (ROS) as the main robot software framework greatly helps to reduce the complexity of developing control system for mobile robot.

Keywords: MANET · MANET testbed · Mobile robot

1 Introduction

The objective that we have set for ToMRobot 2.0 is to create a real mobility mechanism in MANET testbed facility that can be fully controlled accurately and accurately to clear the mobility pattern used during the experiment to be repeated multiple times and can be reproduced in another testbed facility. Based on this criterion, we think it can

© Springer Nature Singapore Pte Ltd. 2020
P. K. Singh et al. (Eds.): FTNCT 2019, CCIS 1206, pp. 146–163, 2020.
https://doi.org/10.1007/978-981-15-4451-4_13

only be achieved by using mobile robot technology. At the same time we need to ensure the cost of mobile robot components development in our testbed facility is low and also reduce the complexity of the mobile robot development without compromising the quality we need for the mobile robot to be used in the MANET testbed we develop.

We developed an in-house multiple mobile robot that we call as ToMRobot to provide real mobility mechanism in the testbed facility that we are using for our research experiment. We chose to use mobile robot technology since it provides better control and consistency compared to other methods when implementing node mobility in the MANET testbed. At the same time, robotic technology is getting more affordable in line with the current "Maker Culture" boom that promotes DIY culture among hobbyists and amateurs to produce their own robots.

Before we elaborate further on ToMRobot, we first provide a synopsis as to how real mobility is performed in previous MANET testbed and how previous researches have applied mobile robot technology in MANET testbeds that they used for their research.

2 Real Mobility Mechanism in MANET Testbed

Real mobility mechanism in MANET testbed facility is very important in order to obtain results that are accurate and realistic. However, real mobility implementation in MANET testbed can be very challenging. Nonetheless when done correctly, real mobility mechanisms provides accurate result for experiments conducted in MANET testbed [1–3]. Node mobility in network simulator is represented by mobility model that determines the location, velocity and acceleration of the mobile node in MANET [4]. However in real testbed experiment, there are various ways that have previously been used by researchers to create mobility mechanisms in MANET testbed facilities either using virtual mobility or real mobility [5].

Fig. 1. Real mobility in MANET testbed using human [35]

The most obvious difference between virtual mobility and real mobility methods is that, virtual mobility does not involve any physical mobility but rather, those mobility mechanisms are manipulated in several ways such as instance migration [6], on/off connection [7], RF matrix switch [8–12] and the use of virtual machine technology and virtual network [13]. Meanwhile, real mobility method for MANET testbed practiced in previous research can be found in cars [14–19], taxis [20], trains [21–27], bicycles [28, 29], humans [1, 2, 15, 30–37] (see Fig. 1), remote control cars [38] and multiple mobile robots such as Mobile Emulab Testbed (also known as TrueMobile) [39], MiNT (miniaturized mobile multi-hop wireless network testbed) [40–42] and PHAROS Testbed [43, 44].

The main reason we choose mobile robot to be the real mobility mechanism in our testbed is because mobile robot technology provides the highest controllability and accessibility of real mobility mechanism compared to other real mobility mechanisms. Controllability and accessibility of the real mobility mechanism is very important since both of these features produce elements of repeatability and reproducibility of real mobility patterns in our testbed facility so that the experiments conducted qualifies to be credible in scientific research.

We have published several articles namely, Farkhana and Abdul Hanan [5], Muchtar et al. [45–47] which is our study on the use of mobile robot technology as a real mobility mechanism in previous and existing MANET testbed facility. The knowledge that we obtained from the study allows us to expand and develop we utilized it further to develop on our own real mobility mechanism in our MANET testbed facility and this will be described further in the next subsection.

Following we will be discussing in elaborate detail regarding ToMRobot architecture, the technology used behind ToMRobot and how ToMRobot is used to provide real mobility in our MANET testbed facility.

3   ToMRobot Hardware Architecture

We will briefly discuss what are the main hardware components that we have chosen We will now brie y discuss on the main hardware components that we have chosen to develop ToMRobot 2.0 as improvements to our previous ToMRobot 1.0 (see Fig. 3) namely the main body chassis, motor and robot controller. Aspects pertaining to hardware for indoor localization solution will be discussed in Subsect. 5.1.

3.1   Robot Chassis

We used a combination of Tamiya Track and Wheel with Tamiya Twin Motor (see Fig. 2) as the main body chassis for ToMRobot 2.0 since it is easy to and, reasonably priced, stable, ideal for both indoor as well as outdoor environment and also because it is one of the most popular options among hobbyist as mobile robot's main body chassis.

Fig. 2. Tamiya Track and Wheel and Tamiya Twin Motor

When compared, ToMRobot 1.0 make use of RC big wheel car and it has very limited space to include other mobile robot components such as mobile robot controller (ToMDuino), sensors and mobile devices (Banana Pro). At the same time the RC car we previously used has uneven top surface and this makes it very difficult for us to add these additional components while ensuring its stability when the mobile robot moves. Hence, we are forced with the option to create additional platform on the RC car to place those key components on the mobile robot as shown in Fig. 3.

Fig. 3. ToMRobot using RC big wheel car

As for the robot chassis plate for ToMRobot 2.0, we did not use Tamiya universal plate set but instead we have produced our own robot chassis plate by using 3D printers that allows us to design ToMRobot according to the needs that we require such as the placement of the batteries, robot controller, mobile nodes, sensors and several other components.

Tamiya Rail and Wheel based new chassis makes ToMRobot 2.0 movements more maneuverable with much precision compared to ToMRobot 1.0. At the same time the new mobile robot chassis is more development friendly for any additional development and eases the process of modifying the component's layout when ToMRobot 2.0 is developed. ToMRobot 2.0 movement is also much more stable and predictable thus reduces the need to perform position correction when it is operating. Compared to

ToMRobot 1.0 anatomy that incorporates servo at the front tires for left or right motion and single motor at the rear wheels for front or back movements, ToMRobot 2.0 uses twin motor approach to obtain similar movement results with better simplicity and accuracy.

3.2   ToMRobot Controller

We use TomDuino which is an in-house customized version of Arduino board as the robot controller for ToMRobot version 1 by combining Arduino Uno with Motor Controller chip and uses ZigBee XBee Pro Series 1 for wireless communication purposes between robot controller and Mobility Control System server. As the time that we developed ToMRobot version 2.0, we have more and better hardware components options and chose to utilize ESP8266 NodeMCU microcontroller that we combined with motor shield as the robot controllers for ToMRobot 2.0 shown in Fig. 4.

Fig. 4. ESP8266 NodeMCU with motor shield board

The main reason as to why we choose ESP8266 NodeMCU as the mobile robot controller is due to the combination cost which is much cheaper compared to Arduino Uno while at the same time provides us with much better capabilities than Arduino Uno such as higher processing power, larger flash memory size, bigger amount of IO numbers and most importantly is the availability of a built-in Wi-Fi chip. Furthermore, the ESP8266 board is much smaller than Arduino Uno board despite having better capabilities and this factor provide us with more room to add other components in the mobile robot chassis such as sensors and batteries. ESP8266 comes in many variants and we choose ESP8266 NodeMCU variant since it is easier and versatile enough to be used for development purposes aside from the fact that most ESP8266 shield board that are available in the market is ESP8266 NodeMCU variant.

The motor shield board that we use along with ESP8266 NodeMCU comes equipped with L293D dual H-bridge motor driver and provides several number of GPIO pin extensions and some serial communication pins as well as two dedicated terminals for two DC motors (see Fig. 4). This feature facilitates us further to utilize ESP8266 as the mobile robot controller of choice for ToMRobot 2.0. Additionally, the motor shield board also allows same power source to be used between ESP8266 and DC motor whilst at the same time disparate to each other thus prevents interference from occurring. This design allows us to use only one battery pack as the source of electricity and it is shared by both ESP8266 and Tamiya twin motor in ToMRobot 2.0.

4   Testbed Miniaturization

Most wireless testbed facilities are using outdoor testbed facilities where the experiment to be conducted are those that can be affected by weather condition [48]. Some of the previous research are using testbed miniaturization approach in their testbed facilities such as MiNT [40–42], Kansei [49], Kansei Genie [50, 51], ivynet [48, 52] and Orbit [6] to overcome this problem.

MANET testbed miniaturization is referring to the miniaturization of wireless signal (radio signal) effective range from its original radio signal range size to the much smaller radio signal range to allow wireless multihop ad-hoc network environment even if it is performed in small indoor testbed arena. Testbed miniaturization goal is to enable real MANET testbed to be conducted in the small indoor area since executing MANET testbed using actual area size is very expensive.

Fig. 5. Fixed radio signal attenuator

Wireless signal range miniaturization can be performed through the combination of two methods with the first method is, by reducing to the lowest possible wireless signal transmission power on Wi-Fi transmitter inside the Wi-Fi Chip. However wireless signal range is still big to enable MANET testbed to be performed indoor. Hence, we need the addition of a second method which is achievable by installing fixed radio signal attenuator on the Wi-Fi external antenna as shown in Fig. 5 [40–42]. The reduction of the radio signal effective range does not affect the nature of the wireless communication of the mobile devices [48].

5   Indoor Localization and Path Planning for ToMRobot

Indoor localization and mobile robot path planning are important elements in ToMRobot to control the mobility of ToMRobot in order to create real node mobility that can be implemented repeatedly with the same mobility pattern.

5.1   Hardware Components for Indoor Localization

The selection for indoor localization approaches and the technology for ToMRobot 2.0 is very challenging since we want for solutions that is cost effective priced yet at the same time provides high accuracy.

Indoor localization solution used in ToMRobot 1.0 is solely depended on the combination of dead reckoning and odometry methods for indoor localization. This is achieved by incorporating Inertial Measurement Unit (IMU) sensors and wheel encoder sensors.

Based on our experience, the use of dead reckoning and odometry method as a combination was found to be less than accurate as an indoor localization in MANET testbed. There were several occasions where we need to repeat the same experiment because the movement of mobile robot are often overleap from its original path due to wheel slippage and other factors.

Therefore, we decided that indoor localization for ToMRobot 2.0 needs use methods that is much better in terms of accuracy and reliability but yet still maintains the simplicity of design and implementation of ToMRobot 1.0. Based on what we have learned from ToMRobot 1.0 pertaining to indoor localization solution for mobile robot, we set five key indoor localization solutions criteria that needs to be met in ToMRobot 2.0

  i. **Reliable and Accurate.** Indoor localization solution that is going to be used needs to be accurate and reliable for frequent use in MANET testbed.
 ii. **Affordable.** The overall cost of the indoor localization used needs to be reasonable and does not result the cost per unit of the mobile robot to be expensive.
iii. **Available.** The chosen indoor localization solution needs to be either available solution that can be purchased or available solution that can be developed independently.
 iv. **Simple to setup and operate.** The hardware and software for the selected indoor localization solution needs to be easy for use either throughout the calibration process or during experiments that also includes times when it is integrating with other systems.
  v. **Non RF Signal based Wireless Communication.** The indoor localization solution used must not use Radio Frequency (RF) based technology because it will produce RF signal noise and interference to the RF based wireless communication such as Wi-Fi in MANET testbed.

Based on our research, the combination of IMU and ultrasonic based trilateration is the best indoor localization solution for ToMRobot 2.0. For IMU sensors, we used 9 DOF IMU GY-85 (see Fig. 6) that combines three sensors into one single board namely accelerator sensor ADXL345, gyroscope sensor ITG3200 and magnetometer sensor HMC5883. IMU GY-85 is selected because of its low cost, can easily be obtained and accurate enough to be used as part of the indoor localization solution for ToMRobot 2.0.

Fig. 6. DOF IMU GY-85 sensor

Indoor localization solution from Marvelmind Robotics[1] (see Fig. 7) or also known as Marvelmind 'indoor GPS', is the selection of choice for ultrasonic based trilateration as part of indoor localization for ToMRobot 2.0. The advantages of ultrasonic based trilateration is the nonexistence of wireless signal noise and interference which is an important factor in our MANET testbed facility [53] There are several indoor localization solutions that are almost identical to Marvelmind that exist in the market and research worlds such as Pozyx[2], MIT Cricket[3], FIND[4], Indoors[5], OnYourMap[6] and Locatify[7]. Compared to other indoor localization, Marvelmind indoor localization solution provides several advantages in terms of price, accuracy, ultrasonic based localization solution, simplicity and can be easily integrated with other hardware. Marvelmind Robotics indoor localization solution also provides development libraries to facilitate integration with other systems such as Arduino development environment and ROS.

Fig. 7. Marvelmind robotics localization beacons and modem (hardware version 4.5)

5.2   Software Components for Indoor Localization

We chose to utilize ROS Robot Localization node which is a general purpose state estimation solution in ROS to manage mobile robot localization when the experiments is being carried out. By simply using the inputs received from 9 DOF IMU GF-85

---

[1] https://marvelmind.com

[2] https://www.pozyx.io

[3] http://cricket.csail.mit.edu

[4] https://www.internalpositioning.com

[5] https://indoo.rs

[6] http://www.oym.co

[7] https://locatify.com

sensors, and Marvelmind ultrasonic trilateration solution and processed using Extended Kalman Filter algorithm is already sufficient enough for it to be used in ToMRobot 2.0 as shown in the Fig. 8.

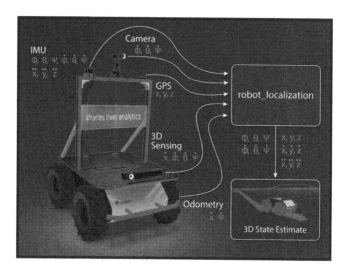

Fig. 8. ROS robot localization approach

ROS Robot Localization node offers a simple yet accurate and reliable localization solution for mobile robot. ROS Robot Localization node does not limit the amount of inputs received from various sensors that is used to generate 15 dimension state space vectors (X, Y, Z, *roll*, *pitch*, *yaw*, X', Y', Z', *roll'*, *pitch'*, *yaw'*, X'', Y'', Z'') to represent pose, linear velocity and linear acceleration of mobile robot (see Fig. 8). 9 DOF IMU sensors providing data for locally accurate state estimation needs and Marvelmind indoor localization solution provides data for global state estimation requirements.

5.3   Path Planning, Trajectory Correction and Collision Avoidance

Path planning for each unit of ToMRobot in our MANET testbed facility is purposely to provide real mobility control mechanism for the experiments conducted in our research. Regardless whether it is done in controlled mobility scenario or random mobility scenario, the path planning approach that is used should be concise and requires no complex workflow. This is because, the main goal of path planning for ToMRobot 2.0 is to create real mobility that can be repeatedly performed in experiments and can also be replicated in other MANET testbed facilities.

To facilitate the implementation of path planning and motion control in ToMMove, we utilized ROS Move Base node as the main component in ToMMove and ROS Global Planner node[8] as path planning engine that provides several path planning algorithms such as A*, Dijkstra and Navfn Behavior to be used in ToMRobot's Mobility Control System. The mobility pattern used in controlled mobility scenarios is performed at specific mobile robot and only for simple forward and backward movements. Mobility pattern for random mobility scenario is first generated at random based on fixed map of the testbed arena for the purpose of path planning in the experiments that is going to be conducted.

Collision avoidance mechanism used in our testbed is more inclined towards ensuring as to how each mobile robot in the testbed does not to collide with each other during the experiments. ROS Multi-Robot Collision Avoidance node[9] or also known as colloid node is used as collision avoidance solution for ToMRobot 2.0. Colloid node uses Collision Avoidance under Bounded Localization Uncertainty (CALU) algorithm [54–56] to ensure that multiple mobile robots do not collide with each other when it is moving in the testbed arena. CALU uses indoor localization information from robot localization component and path planning from the Global Planner component in ROS to perform dynamic collision avoidance between each mobile robot when the experiment is being performed. As a backup, infra-red sensors are placed in front of each mobile robot unit used as early detection for collision avoidance in case CALU is not able to detect possible collision.

6 Mobility Control System (ToMMove) and Robot Operating System (ROS)

One of the reasons why mobile robot technology is less opted as the choice to create real mobility mechanism in MANET testbed is due to the fact that it is quite complex to implement and requires expertise in robotic skills before it can be developed [5]. However, such difficulties can be overcome with the existence of Robot Operating System or in abbreviation ROS[10] which is an open source meta-operating system for robots. ROS contains robots system development framework, libraries and necessary tools that can be used on a wide range of robot platform as well as hardware and this allows researchers and developers to simply focus on the development of robot solutions that are related to what they are conducting in their research as well as the development process that they are pursuing and make use of what is already provided in ROS for the rest of the whole robot system [57].

ROS facilitates us to develop ToMRobot control system since all the requirements that enables ToMRobot to fully function in our MANET testbed facility are already available in the ROS. Our interest is simply to exploit existing and available mobile robot solutions to provide real mobility mechanism in our MANET testbed facility.

---

[8] http://wiki.ros.org/global_planner.

[9] http://wiki.ros.org/multi_robot_collision_avoidance.

[10] https://www.ros.org.

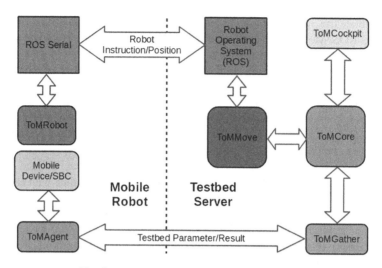

Fig. 9. ToMMove and ROS in testbed system

Therefore, all of the technical requirements for the mobile robot such as localization algorithm, obstacle avoidance algorithm, mobile robot decision making and autonomous navigation, mobile robot communication, sensor data processing, mobile robot positioning correction and so on already exist in ROS and we only need to have general understandings of how each component is used.

Furthermore, we use a centralized mobility control system that we called ToM-Move. Almost all of the processes in ROS are conducted in ToMMove server. The robot controller (ESP8266) at every mobile robot only need to perform movements towards the mobile robot based on decisions provided by ToMMove system and provides feedback in the form of current location of where the mobile robot is situated. We use costumed ROS serial over Wi-Fi for ESP8266[11] for the purpose of communication between ESP8266 as robot controller in each ToMRobot unit and ToMMove server. Testbed results on the other hand is stored in the microSD card that are available at each Banana Pro/Banana Pi M1+ and does not need to be sent to the server during the experiment. Instead, the testbed result is only sent to ToM server via ToMMove system once the experiment is completed. Figure 9 shows how ToMMove and ROS operate inside the testbed system.

If ToMMove architecture is performed as distributed where each path planning and movement decision is conducted individually by each mobile robot on its own, this will increase the cost per unit for each mobile robot since additional computer in the form of SBC is required to run ROS in order to implement the mobility control system at every mobile robot. Concurrently, the integration between ToM and ToMMove can be conducted easier when done centrally. Hence, it is more practical if mobility control logic and decision making are done centralized at ToMMove rather performing it individually at each of the mobile robot itself.

---

[11] https://github.com/agnunez/espros.

Every ROS component used for mobile robot needs to meet our mobile robot requirements in our testbed facility is called as ROS node. In order to facilitate discussion, all of the components to be described in the next subsection will now be called as node instead of components to avoid potential confusion when discussing the next sections.

7 Conclusion

The selection for indoor localization approaches and the technology for ToMRobot 2.0 is very challenging since we want for solutions that is cost effective priced yet at the same time provides high accuracy. Two available options are available to use which is, whether to develop our own local indoor localization for ToMRobot 2.0 from scratch or to use existing solutions that are already available in the market. Although in-house indoor localization solution allows us to lower the cost per unit of each mobile robot but due to certain limitations of our knowledge and expertise in this specific area as well as the time constraint we are faced with to develop our own indoor localization, we therefore decided that it is more practical to use solutions that are already available in the market.

The development of ToMRobot 2.0 facility achieves the objectives we have set to create a real mobility mechanism in the MANET testbed facility using mobile robot technology. At the same time, we need to ensure the cost of mobile robot components development in our testbed facility is low and also reduce the complexity of mobile robot development without sacrificing the quality we need for the mobile robot to be used in the MANET testbed we develop.

To ensure the cost of mobile robot components in the testbed facility remains low, we use three strategies: (1) Using components that are readily available and commonly used by hobbyists in the field of robotic (2) Build own components such as robot chassis (3) Using open hardware component such as microcontroller as the price offered is reasonable.

At the same time, to reduce the complexity of developing a mobile robot component in the testbed facility, we are reusing the existing mobile robotic design which is simple but efficient enough for our real mobility mechanism for MANET testbed facility. We also use existing software tools and libraries that can help us develop mobile robot control systems more easily without the need for deep robot knowledge. Therefore, we chose to use the Robotic Operating System (ROS) which is a set of open source software libraries and tools that help to develop robotic applications.

There are some weaknesses that exist in ToMRobot 2.0 such as

i. **Dependency on niche solution for main indoor localization solution.**
   We chose Marvelmind Robotics indoor localization solution for ToMRobot 2.0 because this solution is the only available indoor localization solution that does not use radio signal based trilateration indoor localization, instead of using ultrasound for that purpose. Marvelmind Robotics indoor localization solution is also chosen because the solution is simple, reliable, accurate and affordable. Even

though there are other indoor localization solutions, they are not all the combinations we have mentioned.

The dependence on only solvable solvents on a single vendor is less practical for the long term. We also think that simple but quality indoor localization can be self-evolved as much as many mobile robot projects have done. But when ToMRobot 2.0 was developed, our knowledge and experience in the field of mobile robot's localization and positioning is still not enough to develop its own indoor localization solution.

ii. **Battery charging for each mobile robot is still done manually.**

After a multiple-run experiment, every mobile robot needs to manually charge before the next experiment can be executed. This method is quite complicated because every mobile robot needs to be installed charging the cable manually and delay the execution of the experiment.

iii. **All the logic process for mobile robot is run in testbed server, not by the mobile robot itself.**

To reduce per unit costs for each mobile robot we do not place the computer as robot processing unit on any mobile robot but the logic process is done on the testbed server. Mobile robot only performs movement and testbed on mobile device according to what has been processed in testbed server. The disadvantage of this method is the delay in logic processed by the actions performed by the mobile robot. The delay will affect the accuracy of mobility for each mobile robot.

For the future, to overcome the weaknesses above we suggest the methods below

i. **Implementing Bluetooth based indoor localization using ESP32 microcontroller.**

When we started developing ToMRobot 2.0, ESP32 was still not in the market. Among the advantages of ESP32 versus ESP8266 we use in ToMRobot 2.0 is it has a Bluetooth function other than Wi-Fi and ESP32 has a dual core processor compared to a single core in ESP8266. This advantage allows us to develop our own Bluetooth based indoor localization using ESP32 and at the same time using ESP32 as the main controller for mobile robot.

ii. **Wireless charging using Qi wireless charging system.**

Qi wireless charging system is widely used for smartphones including iPhone and Android based smartphones. It is easily available and can be found at a cheap price. Therefore, we think Qi wireless charging system is suitable for the next version of ToMRobot to eliminate the manual charging approach we are using now.

iii. **Using cheap single board computer (SBC) to run logic process on each mobile robot individually.**

When ToMRobot 2.0 was developed, we did not have much choice over the single board computer (SBC) that was suitable for the cheap robot controller for our mobile robot. However, at present there are many SBC options that are suitable at low prices (less than USD 20, some even less than USD 10) such as Orange Pi Zero, Raspberry Pi Zero, NanoPi M1 and Pine A64 +. The combination of cheap SBC with ESP32 microcontroller to be used as mobile robot controller is more practical in improving the accuracy of mobility and positioning for each mobile robot.

The rapid development of current including robotic provides new opportunities for the use of mobile robots for various applications including for the needs of MANET testbed with drastic reduction of cost, greater choice of solutions and easier to use by ordinary people. Therefore, we believe the use of mobile robot technology to provide a real mobility mechanism in the MANET testbed and other wireless testbed will be re-established. This allows the real world approach to testbed getting a place other than the network simulator in the field of MANET research.

References

1. Lenders, V., Wagner, J., May, M.: Analyzing the impact of mobility in ad hoc networks. In: Proceedings of the 2nd International Workshop on Multi-hop Ad Hoc Networks: From Theory to Reality, REALMAN 2006, pp. 39–46. ACM, New York (2006). https://doi.org/10.1145/1132983.1132991. http://doi.acm.org/10.1145/1132983.1132991

2. Kulla, E., Hiyama, M., Ikeda, M., Barolli, L.: Comparison of experimental results of a MANET testbed in different environments considering BATMAN protocol. In: 2011 Third International Conference on Intelligent Networking and Collaborative Systems (INCoS), pp. 1–7 (2011). https://doi.org/10.1109/incos.2011.69

3. Kulla, E., Ikeda, M., Barolli, L., Xhafa, F., Iwashige, J.: A survey on MANET testbeds and mobility models. In: Park, J.J.H., Chao, H.-C., S. Obaidat, M., Kim, J. (eds.) Computer Science and Convergence. LNEE, vol. 114, pp. 651–657. Springer, Dordrecht (2012). https://doi.org/10.1007/978-94-007-2792-2_63. http://link.springer.com.ezproxy.psz.utm.my/chapter/10.1007/978-94-007-2792-2_63

4. Vijayavani, G.R., Prema, G.: Performance comparison of MANET routing protocols with mobility model derived based on realistic mobility pattern of mobile nodes. In: 2012 IEEE International Conference on Advanced Communication Control and Computing Technologies (ICACCCT), pp. 32–36 (2012). https://doi.org/10.1109/icaccct.2012.6320729

5. Farkhana, M., Abdul Hanan, A.: Mobility in mobile ad-hoc network testbed using robot: technical and critical review. Robot. Auton. Syst. **108**, 153–178 (2018). https://doi.org/10.1016/j.robot.2018.07.007. http://www.sciencedirect.com/science/article/pii/S09218890183-02458

6. Raychaudhuri, D., et al.: Overview of the ORBIT radio grid testbed for evaluation of next-generation wireless network protocols. In: Wireless Communications and Networking Conference 2005, vol. 3, pp. 1664–1669. IEEE (2005)

7. Yoon, H., Kim, J., Ott, M., Rakotoarivelo, T.: Mobility emulator for DTN and MANET applications. In: Proceedings of the 4th ACM International Workshop on Experimental Evaluation and Characterization, WINTECH 2009, pp. 51–58. ACM, New York (2009). https://doi.org/10.1145/1614293.1614303. http://doi.acm.org/10.1145/1614293.1614303

8. Clancy, T., Walker, B.: MeshTest: laboratory-based wireless testbed for large topologies. In: 3rd International Conference on Testbeds and Research Infrastructure for the Development of Networks and Communities 2007, TridentCom 2007, pp. 1–6 (2007). https://doi.org/10.1109/tridentcom.2007.4444659

9. Seligman, M., Walker, B.D., Clancy, T.C.: Delay-tolerant network experiments on the meshtest wireless testbed. In: Proceedings of the Third ACM Workshop on Challenged Networks, CHANTS 2008, pp. 49–56. ACM, New York (2008). https://doi.org/10.1145/1409985.1409996. http://doi.acm.org/10.1145/1409985.1409996

10. Walker, B., Clancy, C.: A quantitative evaluation of the meshtest wireless testbed. In: Proceedings of the 4th International Conference on Testbeds and Research Infrastructures for the Development of Networks & Communities, TridentCom 2008, pp. 29:1–29:6. ICST (Institute for Computer Sciences, Social-Informatics and Telecommunications Engineering), Brussels (2008). http://dl.acm.org/citation.cfm?id=1390576.1390612

11. Walker, B., Vo, I., Beecher, M., Clancy, C.: A demonstration of the meshtest wireless testbed. In: 5th International Conference on Testbeds and Research Infrastructures for the Development of Networks Communities and Workshops 2009, TridentCom 2009, p. 1 (2009). https://doi.org/10.1109/tridentcom.2009.4976234

12. Hahn, D., Lee, G., Kim, Y., Walker, B., Beecher, M., Mundur, P.: DTN experiments on the virtual meshtest testbed. In: Proceedings of the 5th ACM Workshop on Challenged Networks, CHANTS 2010, pp. 79–82. ACM, New York (2010). https://doi.org/10.1145/1859934.1859952. http://doi.acm.org/10.1145/1859934.1859952

13. Kim, Y., Taylor, K., Dunbar, C., Walker, B., Mundur, P.: Reality vs emulation: running real mobility traces on a mobile wireless testbed. In: Proceedings of the 3rd ACM International Workshop on MobiArch, HotPlanet 2011, pp. 23–28. ACM, New York (2011). https://doi.org/10.1145/2000172.2000180. http://doi.acm.org/10.1145/2000172.2000180

14. Maltz, D.A., Broch, J., Johnson, D.B.: Experiences designing and building a multi-hop wireless ad hoc network testbed. Special Purpose Grant in Science and Engineering F19628-96-C-0061, Carnegie Mellon University, USA (1999)

15. Maltz, D., Broch, J., Johnson, D.: Lessons from a full-scale multihop wireless ad hoc network testbed. IEEE Pers. Commun. 8(1), 8–15 (2001). https://doi.org/10.1109/98.904894

16. Ramanathan, R., Redi, J., Santivanez, C., Wiggins, D., Polit, S.: Ad hoc networking with directional antennas: a complete system solution. IEEE J. Sel. Areas Commun. 23(3), 496–506 (2005). https://doi.org/10.1109/jsac.2004.842556

17. Veeravuttiphol, P., Komolkiti, P., Aswakul, C.: MANET testbeds for evaluation of real-time controls in multimedia transmissions. In: 3rd International Conference on Testbeds and Research Infrastructure for the Development of Networks and Communities 2007, TridentCom 2007, pp. 1–6 (2007). https://doi.org/10.1109/tridentcom.2007.4444705

18. Tsukada, M., Ernst, T.: Vehicle communication experiment environment with MANET and NEMO. In: International Symposium on Applications and the Internet Workshops 2007, SAINT Workshops 2007, p. 45 (2007). https://doi.org/10.1109/saint-w.2007.104

19. Yazir, Y., Jahanbakhsh, K., Ganti, S., Shoja, G., Coady, Y.: A low-cost realistic testbed for mobile ad hoc networks. In: IEEE Pacific Rim Conference on Communications, Computers and Signal Processing 2009, PacRim 2009, pp. 671–676 (2009). https://doi.org/10.1109/pacrim.2009.5291291

20. Galati, A., Bourchas, T., Siby, S., Frey, S., Olivares, M., Mangold, S.: Mobile-enabled delay tolerant networking in rural developing regions. In: 2014 IEEE Global Humanitarian Technology Conference (GHTC), pp. 699–705 (2014). https://doi.org/10.1109/ghtc.2014.6970359

21. Jetcheva, J., Hu, Y.C., PalChaudhuri, S., Saha, A., Johnson, D.: Design and evaluation of a metropolitan area multitier wireless ad hoc network architecture. In: Fifth IEEE Workshop on Mobile Computing Systems and Applications 2003, Proceedings, pp. 32–43 (2003). https://doi.org/10.1109/mcsa.2003.1240765

22. Pentland, A., Fletcher, R., Hasson, A.: DakNet: rethinking connectivity in developing nations. Computer 37(1), 78–83 (2004). https://doi.org/10.1109/mc.2004.1260729

23. Kutscher, D., Greifenberg, J., Loos, K.: Scalable DTN distribution over uni-directional links. In: Proceedings of the 2007 Workshop on Networked Systems for Developing Regions, NSDR 2007, pp. 6:1–6:6. ACM, New York (2007). https://doi.org/10.1145/1326571. 1326580. http://doi.acm.org/10.1145/1326571.1326580

24. Coulson, G., et al.: Flexible experimentation in wireless sensor networks. Commun. ACM 55(1), 82–90 (2012). https://doi.org/10.1145/2063176.2063198. http://doi.acm.org/10.1145/ 2063176.2063198

25. Zarafshan-Araki, M., Chin, K.W.: TrainNet: a transport system for delivering non real-time data. Comput. Commun. 33(15), 1850–1863 (2010). https://doi.org/10.1016/j.comcom. 2010.06.008. http://www.sciencedirect.com/science/article/pii/S0140366410002690

26. Nati, M., Gluhak, A., Abangar, H., Headley, W.: SmartCampus: a usercentric testbed for Internet of Things experimentation. In: 2013 16th International Symposium on Wireless Personal Multimedia Communications (WPMC), pp. 1–6 (2013)

27. Nati, M., Gluhak, A., Domaszewicz, J., Lalis, S., Moessner, K.: Lessons from SmartCampus: external experimenting with user-centric Internet-of-Things testbed. Wireless Pers. Commun. 93(3), 709–723 (2014). https://doi.org/10.1007/s11277-014-2223-z. http://link. springer.com/article/10.1007/s11277-014-2223-z

28. Bromage, S., et al.: SCORPION: a heterogeneous wireless networking testbed. ACM SIGMOBILE Mob. Comput. Commun. Rev. 13(1), 65–68 (2009). https://doi.org/10. 1145/1558590.1558604. http://doi.acm.org.ezproxy.psz.utm.my/10.1145/1558590.1558604

29. Kazdaridis, G., Stavropoulos, D., Maglogiannis, V., Korakis, T., Lalis, S., Tassiulas, L.: NITOS BikesNet: enabling mobile sensing experiments through the OMF framework in a city-wide environment. In: 2014 IEEE 15th International Conference on Mobile Data Management (MDM), vol. 1, pp. 89–98 (2014). https://doi.org/10.1109/mdm.2014.17

30. Ramanathan, R., Hain, R.: An ad hoc wireless testbed for scalable, adaptive QoS support. In: 2000 IEEE Wireless Communications and Networking Conference 2000, WCNC, vol. 3, pp. 998–1002 (2000). https://doi.org/10.1109/wcnc.2000.904763

31. Ritter, H., Tian, M., Voigt, T., Schiller, J.: A highly flexible testbed for studies of ad-hoc network behaviour. In: 28th Annual IEEE International Conference on Local Computer Networks 2003, LCN 2003, Proceedings, pp. 746–752 (2003). https://doi.org/10.1109/lcn. 2003.1243208

32. Ikeda, M., Kulla, E., Hiyama, M., Barolli, L., Takizawa, M., Miho, R.: A comparison study between simulation and experimental results for MANETs. In: 2010 13th International Conference on Network-Based Information Systems (NBiS), pp. 371–378 (2010). https:// doi.org/10.1109/nbis.2010.75

33. Ikeda, M., Barolli, L., Hiyama, M., Kulla, E., Takizawa, M.: Performance evaluation of MANET routing protocols: simulations and experiments. Comput. Inform. 30(6), 1147– 1165 (2011)

34. Hiyama, M., Kulla, E., Oda, T., Ikeda, M., Barolli, L.: Experimental results of a MANET testbed in a mixed environment considering horizontal and vertical topologies. In: 2012 IEEE 26th International Conference on Advanced Information Networking and Applications (AINA), pp. 884–889 (2012). https://doi.org/10.1109/aina.2012.68

35. Hiyama, M., Kulla, E., Ikeda, M., Barolli, L.: Evaluation of MANET protocols for different indoor environments: results from a real MANET testbed. Int. J. Space-Based Situated Comput. 2(2), 71–82 (2012). https://doi.org/10.1504/ijssc.2012.047465. http://www. inderscienceonline.com/doi/abs/10.1504/IJSSC.2012.047465

36. Kulla, E., Ikeda, M., Oda, T., Barolli, L., Xhafa, F., Takizawa, M.: Multimedia transmissions over a MANET testbed: problems and issues. In: 2012 Sixth International Conference on Complex, Intelligent and Software Intensive Systems (CISIS), pp. 141–147 (2012). https://doi.org/10.1109/cisis.2012.82

37. Kulla, E., Sakamoto, S., Ikeda, M., Barolli, L., Xhafa, F., Kamo, B.: Evaluation of a MANET testbed for central bridge and V-shape bridge scenarios using BATMAN routing protocol. In: 2013 Eighth International Conference on Broadband and Wireless Computing, Communication and Applications (BWCCA), pp. 199–205 (2013). https://doi.org/10.1109/bwcca.2013.21

38. Alenazi, M.J.F., Çetinkaya, E.K., Rohrer, J.P.: Implementation of the AeroRP and AeroNP protocols in Python. In: International Telemetering Conference Proceedings (2012). http://arizona.openrepository.com/arizona/handle/10150/581658

39. Johnson, D., Stack, T., Fish, R., Flickinger, D., Ricci, R., Lepreau, J.: TrueMobile: a mobile robotic wireless and sensor network testbed. In: The 25th Annual Joint Conference of the IEEE Computer and Communications Societies. IEEE Computer Society (2006)

40. De, P., Raniwala, A., Sharma, S., Chiueh, T.: MiNT: a miniaturized network testbed for mobile wireless research. In: Proceedings IEEE INFOCOM 2005, 24th Annual Joint Conference of the IEEE Computer and Communications Societies, vol. 4, pp. 2731–2742 (2005). https://doi.org/10.1109/infcom.2005.1498556

41. De, P., et al.: MiNT-m: an autonomous mobile wireless experimentation platform. In: Proceedings of the 4th International Conference on Mobile Systems, Applications and Services, MobiSys 2006, pp. 124–137. ACM, New York (2006). https://doi.org/10.1145/1134680.1134694. http://doi.acm.org/10.1145/1134680.1134694

42. De, P.: MiNT: a reconfigurable mobile multi-hop wireless network testbed. Ph.D. thesis, State University of New York at Stony Brook, Stony Brook, NY, USA (2007)

43. Stovall, D., Paine, N., Petz, A., Enderle, J., Julien, C., Vishwanath, S.: Pharos: an application-oriented testbed for heterogeneous wireless networking environments. Technical report TR-UTEDGE-2009-006, The University of Texas at Austin (2009)

44. Fok, C., Petz, A., Stovall, D., Paine, N., Julien, C., Vishwanath, S.: Pharos: a testbed for mobile cyber-physical systems. Technical report TR-ARiSE2011-001, University of Texas at Austin (2011)

45. Muchtar, F., Abdullah, A.H., Arshad, M.M., Wahab, M.H.A., Ahmmad, S.N.Z., Abdul-Salaam, G.: A critical review of MANET testbed using mobile robot technology. J. Phys. Conf. Ser. 1019(1), 012046 (2018). https://doi.org/10.1088/1742-6596/1019/1/012046. http://stacks.iop.org/1742-6596/1019/i=1/a=012046

46. Muchtar, F., Abdullah, A.H., Lati, M.S.A., Hassan, S., Wahab, M.H.A., Abdul-Salaam, G.: A technical review of MANET testbed using mobile robot technology. J. Phys. Conf. Ser. 1049(1), 012001 (2018). https://doi.org/10.1088/1742-6596/1049/1/012001. http://stacks.iop.org/1742-6596/1049/i=1/a=012001

47. Muchtar, F., Abdullah, A.H., Wahab, M.H.A., Ambar, R., Hana, H.F., Ahmmad, S.N.Z.: Mobile ad hoc network testbed using mobile robot technology. J. Phys. Conf. Ser. 1019(1), 012047 (2018). https://doi.org/10.1088/1742-6596/1019/1/012047. http://stacks.iop.org/1742-6596/1019/i=1/a=012047

48. Su, Y., Gross, T.: Validation of a miniaturized wireless network testbed. In: Proceedings of the Third ACM International Workshop on Wireless Network Testbeds, Experimental Evaluation and Characterization, WiNTECH 2008, pp. 25–32. ACM, New York (2008). https://doi.org/10.1145/1410077.1410084. http://doi.acm.org/10.1145/1410077.1410084

49. Arora, A., Ertin, E., Ramnath, R., Nesterenko, M., Leal, W.: Kansei: a high-fidelity sensing testbed. IEEE Internet Comput. 10(2), 35–47 (2006). https://doi.org/10.1109/mic.2006.37

50. Sridharan, M., et al.: From Kansei to KanseiGenie: architecture of federated, programmable wireless sensor fabrics. In: Magedanz, T., Gavras, A., Thanh, N.H., Chase, J.S. (eds.) TridentCom 2010. LNICST, vol. 46, pp. 155–165. Springer, Heidelberg (2011). https://doi.org/10.1007/978-3-642-17851-1_12.   http://link.springer.com/chapter/10.1007/978-3-642-17851-1_12

51. Sridharan, M., et al.: KanseiGenie: software infrastructure for resource management and programmability of wireless sensor network fabrics. In: Next-Generation Internet Architectures and Protocols. Cambridge University Press (2011). http://dx.doi.org/10.1017/CBO9780511920950.015

52. Su, Y., Heule, M., Gross, T.: IvyNet: a testbed for multi-hop wireless network research. Technical report, Citeseer (2006). Citation Key: su2006ivynet

53. Sanchez, A., Elvira, S., de Castro, A., Glez-de Rivera, G., Ribalda, R., Garrido, J.: Low cost indoor ultrasonic positioning implemented in FPGA. In: 2009 35th Annual Conference of IEEE Industrial Electronics, pp. 2709–2714 (2009). https://doi.org/10.1109/iecon.2009.5415427

54. Hennes, D., Claes, D., Meeussen, W., Tuyls, K.: Multi-robot collision avoidance with localization uncertainty. In: Proceedings of the 11th International Conference on Autonomous Agents and Multiagent Systems - Volume 1, AAMAS 2012, pp. 147–154. International Foundation for Autonomous Agents and Multiagent Systems, Richland (2012). http://dl.acm.org/citation.cfm?id=2343576.2343597

55. Claes, D., Hennes, D., Tuyls, K., Meeussen, W.: Collision avoidance under bounded localization uncertainty. In: 2012 IEEE/RSJ International Conference on Intelligent Robots and Systems, pp. 1192–1198 (2012). https://doi.org/10.1109/iros.2012.6386125

56. van den Berg, J., Guy, S.J., Lin, M., Manocha, D.: Reciprocal n-body collision avoidance. In: Pradalier, C., Siegwart, R., Hirzinger, G. (eds.) Robotics Research. Springer Tracts in Advanced Robotics, vol. 70. Springer, Heidelberg (2011). https://doi.org/10.1007/978-3-642-19457-3_1

57. Boren, J., Cousins, S.: Exponential growth of ROS [ROS topics]. IEEE Robot. Autom. Mag. 18(1), 19–20 (2011). https://doi.org/10.1109/mra.2010.940147

Modified Genetic Algorithm for Resource Selection on Internet of Things

Monika Bharti$^{(\boxtimes)}$ and Himanshu Jindal

Department of Computer Science Engineering/Information Technology,
Jaypee University of Information Technology,
Waknaghat Solan 173234, Himachal Pradesh, India
{monika.bharti,himanshu.jindal}@juit.ac.in

Abstract. With the epidemic progression in resources on *IoT*, discovery emerges as an eminent challenge due to requirement of their self-automation. The traditional resource discovery approaches do not provide efficient methodologies due to continuously changing *IoT* search metrics such as syntax, access, architecture, etc. To address the gap, the paper proposes an optimized technique, *namely*, Modified Genetic Algorithm for Resource Selection (*MGA-RS*) that intends to discover optimum data (resources) is short period of time by considering the bit strings of chromosomes. It is evaluated on datasets of Ionosphere from machine learning repository of university college, London. The best and mean fitness are selected in a way that they should be close to each other at the time when *MGA-RS* reaches termination condition and to minimize classification error from kNN. It is found that *MGA-RS* outperforms well with *kNN* based fitness function and is approximately 14% and 15% better than simple and rastrigin fitnesses, respectively, for selecting the optimal resources in *IoT*.

Keywords: Internet-of-Things · Genetic · Discovery · Resource · Feature

1 Introduction

The Internet of Things (*IoT*) paradigm due to disseminated organization, disseminated intelligibility and conveyance properties on platform poses various challenges to resources with respect to their identification, communication and computation. The resources are expected to grow up to *50 to 100* billion resources by *2020* [16,24] and would produce heterogeneous data which is estimated to grow up to *40* zeta bytes [19]. Such huge amount of heterogeneous data would affect their discovery with respect to search metrics on *IoT* such as data format, access type, type of search, implementation, etc. [4,5,26].

Several models were suggested for real-time discovery [7,23], but they have their limitations due to centralized systems and fail to provide search solution against queries. For example, a centralized system is postulated that stores the

© Springer Nature Singapore Pte Ltd. 2020
P. K. Singh et al. (Eds.): FTNCT 2019, CCIS 1206, pp. 164–176, 2020.
https://doi.org/10.1007/978-981-15-4451-4_14

contact to resources based on prediction model [13,27]. It further calculates the probability of matching query and provides scalability with increase in number of resources. The system has its limitations that it does not store whole information of resources by virtue of which few requests do not get completed and this result into increased traffic on network.

To overcome the shortcoming, new method, *namely*, Social Internet of Things (*SIoT*) has been postulated, which is an integration of *IoT* and social networks [12,37,38]. In this method, each object searches for desired service via friendship connections by virtue of which new resource can dynamically be added to *SIoT* resulting into less consumption of time for search. It is advisable to limit number of resources as social friendship among resources may effect search efficiency and hence, affect negatively the searching time. Few authors have formulated a hierarchical methods to deal with large set of resources [21,28,29]. However, these methods perform well for pseudo-static meta-data but they are not scalable at the time of change of network and frequent data. To select the rightful resource having the maximum similarity match, swarm intelligence is adopted as it provides a new approach to problem solving using an example of social behavior of insects. It helps in resource selection for similarity indexes, hence, reducing the dimensions of clustered resources. An isolated signalized junction is considered for traffic control in Intelligent Transportation System (*ITS*) [22]. Later, it is optimized using historical flow data [14,30]. The optimizer uses Hill-Climbing for selecting best resource [20]. These algorithms have their limitations due to time consumption.

Some of the researchers have presented a method to provide resource selection using Genetic Algorithm (*GA*) [11,31]. The system forms links in network and thus, results in relevant higher quality resource list that can be used for further future links (resource to resource). It is discussed by few authors that high dimensional resource list (having feature set based on its attributes like type, service, location, *etc.*) affects the performance of system due to redundant data [3,36]. In order to overcome this shortcoming, different combinatorial set of resources are suggested to keep best combination to achieve optimal accuracy. Resource selection in machine learning is also called as variable, attribute and subset selection. Existing techniques *namely*, Principle Component Analysis (*PCA*) [6], Particle Swarm Optimization (*PSO*) [17], Genetic Algorithm (*GA*) [25,32] help to obtain such optimal resources. Few researchers have used Waikato Environment for Knowledge Analysis (*WEKA*) software to reduce dimensions. This software has static approach for resource selection methodology and face limitation that the users cannot change the properties or attributes of concerned selected resources [8,35]. It is suggested that *GA* being adaptive and efficient is suited best for optimal resource selection. The Ant Colony Optimization (*ACO*) is proposed for finding optimal signal parameters in coordinated fixed set of link flow [2,33,34]. This algorithm reaches to global optimum solution fairly quickly.

The organization of paper is as follows. Sections 2 and 3 discuss the motivation, contribution and the existing Genetic Algorithm, respectively. The data set considered for proposed approach is described in Sect. 4. Problem statement for minimization is formulated in Sect. 5. Section 6 discusses the proposed *MGA-FS* for *SIoT*. The experimental results and comparison are postulated in Sects. 7 and 8, respectively. Finally, Sect. 9 concludes the paper's outcome.

2 Motivation and Contribution

• With the extensive survey it is found that for resource selection, *GA* is adopted due to its dynamicity properties and easy configuration. However, it faces few limitations for selecting lists of resources with increasing number of resources and results into increased traffic congestion on network due to redundant information. In order to eliminate these gaps, the paper intends to propose an approach *namely*, Modified Genetic Algorithm for Resource Selection (*MGA-RS*) on *IoT*. The approach succinctly selects the optimal resources in less time by considering the bit strings of chromosomes. For testing purpose, the approach has considered Ionosphere dataset from machine learning repository of university college, London. • The proposed technique, *i.e.*, MGA-RS is an optimal method of resource selection. It uses *kNN* based fitness function for describing datasets of genetics of human (population). It further selects the distinguished (optimal) resources from generated population's matrix. *MGA-RS* provides desirable and efficient search with the selection of supreme resources.

3 Preliminaries: Genetic Algorithm

GA is a population search heuristic based optimization technique that imitates the evolution process of human being [1,9,10,15,18]. It manipulates population of resources iteratively to generate new population through functions like crossover and mutation (genetic functions). The terminology between human genetic and *GA* is summarized in Table 1.

Table 1. Terminology among human genetic and *GA*

S. No.	Human genetic	GA
1	Chromosomes	Bit strings
2	Genes	Features
3	Allele	Feature value
4	Locus	Bit position
5	Genotype	Encoded string
6	Phenotype	Decoded genotype

The finesses of chromosomes (solution candidates) are evaluated using objective or fitness function. The fitness function provides numerical values that are used for ranking the given chromosomes in population. The formulation of fitness function depends on problem being solved.

4   Data Set

The dataset used in this paper is of Ionosphere (*see* Table 2). Where, $i = 1$ to 34 features. It is collected from machine learning repository of University College of London, available at https://archive.ics.uci.edu/ml/datasets/ionosphere. The dataset is comprised of *351* observations and *34* attributes having binary class information. The *34* continuous features in this data set are derived from the signals read by a phased array of *16* high frequency antennas in Goose Bay, Labrador [39]. These radar signals are designed to recognize structure in the ionosphere. Received signals were processed using an autocorrelation function whose arguments are the time of a pulse and the pulse number. There were 17 pulse numbers for the Goose Bay system. Instances in this database are described by 2 attributes per pulse number, corresponding to the complex values returned by the function resulting from the complex electromagnetic signal.

Table 2. Features in resources dataset

S. No.	Descriptor	Features	Number
1	ZM	$Fr_{1,i}, Fr_{2,i}, ...Fr_{20,i}$	20
2	LM	$Fr_{21,i}, Fr_{22,i}, ...Fr_{40,i}$	20
3	Hu7M	$Fr_{41,i}, Fr_{42,i}, ...Fr_{47,i}$	7
4	TP	$Fr_{48,i}, Fr_{49,i}, ...Fr_{69,i}$	22
5	GP	$Fr_{70,i}, Fr_{71,i}, ...Fr_{79,i}$	10
6	FDs	$Fr_{80,i}, Fr_{81,i}, ...Fr_{100,i}$	21

5   Problem Formulation

Consider the following optimization problem:

$$Given: n \in z^+, 1 \leq n \leq 100, \ and \ \beta \in R^+ \ni 0 \leq \beta \leq 100, \tag{1}$$

where, n is number of resources in reduced resource's set, β is classification error, R^+ is the reduced resources set and Z^+ tells relation among two sets. It is solved based on dataset described in Table 2 where a subset of features, F_{r_i}, is searched in a way that objective β and n are minimized.

6   Proposed Modified Genetic Algorithm for Resource Selection in Internet-of-Things

MGA-RS uses binary search space of chromosomes, *i.e.*, bit strings to manipulate finite binary resources. At an instance, random population of resources is created and is evaluated using fitness function. In this process, for employed binary chromosome, gene value as '*1*' depicts that particular resource, indexed by position of '*1*' is picked else is not selected for evaluation (gene value as '*0*'). The chromosomes are ranked using positional indexes of resources and the top '*n*' fittest genes are selected for next generation (called as Elite genes). After the elite genes are automatically pushed for next generation, remaining genes are passed genetically to functional crossover and mutation to generate crossover and mutation genes (resources), respectively. These three genes, *i.e.*, elite, crossover and mutation then generate new population of resources. Crossover (genetic function) is combination of two chromosomes to generate crossover genes. Mutation is used for genetic perturbation of genes *via* flipping bits based on mutation probability. The steps for *MGA-RS* are shown in Fig. 1.

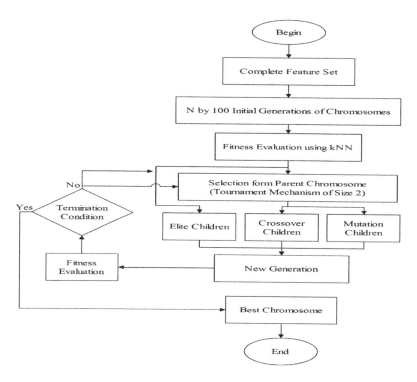

Fig. 1. Steps for modified GA based resource selection

6.1   Generation of Resources as Population

The population is generated as a matrix (*PopulationSize* × *ChromosomeLength*) having random bits. The population size is total chromosomes while chromosome length is total bits in each chromosome. The generation of population is summarized in Algorithm 1.

Algorithm 1. *Population Generation*

1: **begin**
2: *popfunc()*
3: $p_1 \leftarrow binarymatrix$ // $(PopulationSize \times ChromosomeLength)$
4: return p_1 // Population
5: **end**

6.2 Generating Children of New Population

After evaluating fitness, new population of resources is generated using elitism, crossover and mutation. Table 3 shows the configuration of *MGA-RS*.

Table 3. Parameters for *MGA-FS*

S. No.	Descriptor
Size of population	100
Chromosome length	1000
Type of population	Bit strings
Fitness function	kNN based classification error
Crossover	Arithmetic
Crossover probability	0.8
Mutation	Uniform
Mutation probability	0.1
Selection method	Tournament of size 2
Elite count	2

The maximum generation is set at *300* to avoid trapping of *MGA-RS* in local optimal. *MGA-RS* generates new population in sequential order.

(i) *Elite:* In Table 3, the value of elite is *2, i.e.,* top two children with lowest fitness values are pushed for next generation $(E1 = 2)$. Thus, *98 (100 − E1)* are remained for crossover and mutation processes.

(ii) *Crossover:* The function of next generation from remaining children are generated by crossover. Here, the function value used is *0.8*. If the value is set at *1* then there is no crossover child in *MGA-RS*. Therefore, number of children in mutation are, $C1 = round(98 * 0.8) = 78$.

(iii) *Mutation:* The number of mutation children that are selected is, $M1 = 100 − E1 − C1 = 20$.

6.3 Tournament Based Selection Mechanism

The tournament selection mechanism aims to improve new generation population over all fitness values in order to discard bad designs and selecting best individuals, Tournament based selection mechanism enforces higher selection pressures resulting into higher probability of convergence and discarding worst individuals. Value for selection is taken as '*2*' due to its speed and efficiency. Tournament selection uses two functions. First function generates parents needed for tournament function and second function outcomes with winner of tournament. The finesses of selected chromosomes are ranked and best chromosome is selected as winner. The selection is performed iteratively until new population is filled.

6.4   Crossover Function

It genetically combines two parent's chromosomes (taken from tournament selection), to generate children for next generation. *MGA-RS* uses crossover function, *i.e.*, *Cfrac*, to specify children generated by crossover function after removing elite children. Cfrac is bounded by inequality, $0 \leq Cfrac \leq 1$. It performs XOR operation on two parent chromosomes and its value is selected as *0.8*.

6.5   Mutation Function

It ensures genetic diversity and searching broader solution space. It generates chromosome length set of random numbers. Each random numbers' value is linked with position of each gene (bit) of chromosome. The value of random number is compared using mutation probability by scanning each chromosome from left to right and relatable genes are flipped with chromosome else left unflipped. The process is applied to mutation children only.

6.6   New Population

The *MGA-RS* works iteratively till new population is filled. The new population is filled by summing up all individuals from elite, crossover and mutation. The newly generated population is evaluated again and selection reproduction steps are repeated until stopping condition is reached.

6.7   Termination

Once, *MGA-RS* select optimum resources as solution, it stops. The stop function is applicable to two conditions, *i.e.*,

(i) Total maximum generations, *i.e.*, (Generation $\ni Z^+$).
(ii) Generation limit, *i.e.*, ($GenLimit \ni Z^+$).

MGA-RS terminates prematurely if 'Generations' are not set properly. The proposed method uses '*300*' value for maximum generation and '*100*' is used for generation limit. The fitness for *MGA-RS* helps to select best chromosome and consequently converges to provide optimum solution.

7   Experimental Results

For the given dataset and *MGA-RS* configuration (described in Table 3, the fitness function is chosen carefully to minimize classification error from *kNN*. The best and mean fitness are selected in a way that they should be close to each other at the time when *MGA-RS* reaches termination condition. For testing the process, the random generation of *20, 40, 50, 75, 100, and 118* are selected and its simulation graphs are shown in Fig. 2.

Figure 2 shows the iterations for generation of random population. It describes the mean and best fitness value for selected resources by each iteration. The generated values for fitness are shown in Table 4.

Table 4. *kNN* fitness function based *MGA-RS* results

Generation	Best fitness	Mean fitness	Stall generation limit
5	0.001644	0.002997	0
7	0.001266	0.002682	0
10	0.001161	0.002324	0
11	0.001096	0.002268	0
14	0.001055	0.002097	0
18	0.0008766	0.001688	0
20	0.0008766	0.001586	2
40	0.0008766	0.001132	22
50	0.0008766	0.001182	32
75	0.0008766	0.001187	57
100	0.0008766	0.001254	82
118	0.0008766	0.001177	100

Table 4 consists of generation, best fitness, mean fitness and generation's stall limit. It is observed that best fitness varies at generation *5, 7, 10, 11, 14, 18, 20,* respectively and mean fitness is continuously decreasing by each iteration. The best fitness describes the lowest fitness function (optimal) among all members of resources' list. Mean fitness tells the average over all members in current resource list. Therefore, *kNN* based best resources are found at *5, 7, 10, 11, 14, 18 and 20*.

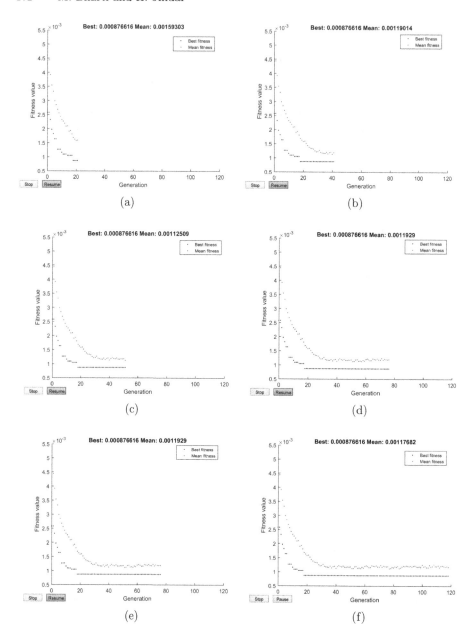

Fig. 2. *MGA-RS* simulations for generations (a) 20 (b) 40 (c) 50 (d) 75 (e) 100 (f) 118

8 Comparison with Existing Data Sets

For validating *MGA-RS*, the results are compared with existing fitness function such as Simple having quadratic equation as:

$$min(f_x) = 100 \times (x_1^2 - x_2)^2 + (1 - x_1)^2 \tag{2}$$

and Rastrigin given as:

$$Ras(x) = 20 + x_1^2 + x_2^2 - 100(cos(2\pi x_1)) + cos(2\pi x_2) \tag{3}$$

The simulation graph for Simple and Rastrigin function is shown in Fig. 3.

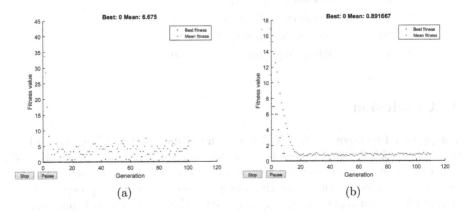

Fig. 3. Simulation graphs for (a) Simple (b) Rastrigin

It is observed that based on chosen fitness function, *MGA-RS* shows convergence but no best feature is selected. The generated values for best fitness and means for both functions are shown in Table 5. It is depicted from Table 5 that the existing feature selection methods do not efficiently optimize the solution as compared with *kNN*. The best and mean fitness values for simple and rastrigin functions are *0, 0.8333 and 0, 0.7667*, respectively. In comparison, *kNN* has best and mean fitness values as *0.0008766 and 0.001177*, respectively. Thus it is concluded that MGA-RS outperforms well with kNN based fitness function and is approximately 14% and 15% better than simple and rastrigin finesses, respectively, for selecting the optimal resources in *IoT*.

Table 5. *kNN* fitness function based *MGA-RS* results

Generation	Best fitness	Mean fitness	Stall generation limit
5	0.001644	0.002997	0
7	0.001266	0.002682	0
10	0.001161	0.002324	0
11	0.001096	0.002268	0
14	0.001055	0.002097	0
18	0.0008766	0.001688	0
20	0.0008766	0.001586	2
40	0.0008766	0.001132	22
50	0.0008766	0.001182	32
75	0.0008766	0.001187	57
100	0.0008766	0.001254	82
118	0.0008766	0.001177	100

9   Conclusion

The proposed technique, *i.e.*, *MGA-RS* is an optimal method of resource selection. It uses *kNN* based fitness function for describing datasets of genetics of human (population). It further selects the distinguished (optimal) resources from generated population's matrix. The proposed technique is processed iteratively for generating contemporary population through the use of functions of elitism, crossover and mutation. Elitism provides discovered resources having lower value of fitness, considered as best resources. Crossover performs XOR operation to genetically combine two parent's chromosomes (population) and mutation ensures ancestral (genetic) diversification and finding expansive result-set (solution) by effectively addition of new resources to outputted population. The *MGA-RS* uses tournament based selection methodology for discarding disquantified resources. It is processed iteratively for finding optimal resultant set. It is found from the evaluation that *MGA-RS* provides desirable and efficient search with the selection of supreme resources.

For the future work, *MGA-RS* will be extended for data synchronization among applications like home automation and intelligent transportation/toll plaza systems.

References

1. Akbari, R., Ziarati, K.: A multilevel evolutionary algorithm for optimizing numerical functions. Int. J. Ind. Eng. Comput. **2**(2), 419–430 (2011)
2. Baskan, O., Haldenbilen, S., Ceylan, H., Ceylan, H.: A new solution algorithm for improving performance of ant colony optimization. Appl. Math. Comput. **211**(1), 75–84 (2009)

3. Bruzzone, L., Persello, C.: A novel approach to the selection of robust and invariant features for classification of hyperspectral images. In: 2008 IEEE International Geoscience and Remote Sensing Symposium, IGARSS 2008, vol. 1, pp. 1–66. IEEE (2008)

4. Datta, S.K., Bonnet, C.: Search engine based resource discovery framework for internet of things. In: 2015 IEEE 4th Global Conference on Consumer Electronics (GCCE), pp. 83–85. IEEE (2015)

5. Datta, S.K., Bonnet, C.: Describing things in the internet of things: from core link format to semantic based descriptions. In: 2016 IEEE International Conference on Consumer Electronics-Taiwan (ICCE-TW), pp. 1–2. IEEE (2016)

6. Fogel, D.B.: Evolutionary Computation: The Fossil Record. Wiley-IEEE Press, New York (1998)

7. Geetha, S.: Social internet of things. World Sci. News **41**, 76 (2016)

8. Hall, M., Frank, E., Holmes, G., Pfahringer, B., Reutemann, P., Witten, I.H.: The weka data mining software: an update. ACM SIGKDD Explor. Newslett. **11**(1), 10–18 (2009)

9. Holland, J.H.: Adaptation in Natural and Artificial Systems: An Introductory Analysis with Applications to Biology, Control, and Artificial Intelligence. MIT Press, Cambridge (1992)

10. Mitchell, M.: An Introduction to Genetic Algorithms. MIT Press, Cambridge (1998)

11. Naruchitparames, J., Güneş, M.H., Louis, S.J.: Friend recommendations in social networks using genetic algorithms and network topology. In: 2011 IEEE Congress on Evolutionary Computation (CEC), pp. 2207–2214. IEEE (2011)

12. Nitti, M., Atzori, L., Cvijikj, I.P.: Network navigability in the social internet of things. In: 2014 IEEE World Forum on Internet of Things (WF-IoT), pp. 405–410. IEEE (2014)

13. Ostermaier, B., Römer, K., Mattern, F., Fahrmair, M., Kellerer, W.: A real-time search engine for the web of things. In: 2010 Internet of Things (IOT), pp. 1–8. IEEE (2010)

14. Robertson, D.I.: 'Tansyt' method for area traffic control. Traffic Eng. Control **8**(8) (1969)

15. Srinivas, M., Patnaik, L.M.: Adaptive probabilities of crossover and mutation in genetic algorithms. IEEE Trans. Syst. Man Cybern. Cybern. **24**(4), 656–667 (1994)

16. Sundmaeker, H., Guillemin, P., Friess, P., Woelfflé, S.: Vision and challenges for realising the internet of things. Clust. Eur. Res. Proj. Internet Things Eur. Comm. **3**(3), 34–36 (2010)

17. Taherdangkoo, M., Paziresh, M., Yazdi, M., Bagheri, M.: An efficient algorithm for function optimization: modified stem cells algorithm. Open Eng. **3**(1), 36–50 (2013)

18. Tian, J., Hu, Q., Ma, X., Han, M.: An improved KPCA/GA-SVM classification model for plant leaf disease recognition. J. Comput. Inf. Syst. **8**(18), 7737–7745 (2012)

19. Vandana, C., Chikkamannur, A.A.: Study of resource discovery trends in Internet of Things (IoT). Int. J. Adv. Network. Appl. **8**(3), 3084 (2016)

20. Wallace, C.E., Courage, K., Reaves, D., Schoene, G., Euler, G.: Transyt-7f user's manual. Technical report (1984)

21. Wang, H., Tan, C.C., Li, Q.: Snoogle: a search engine for pervasive environments. IEEE Trans. Parallel Distrib. Syst. **21**(8), 1188–1202 (2010)

22. Webster, F.: Traffic signal settings, road research technical paper no. 39. Road Research Laboratory (1958)

23. Yap, K.K., Srinivasan, V., Motani, M..: Max: human-centric search of the physical world. In: Proceedings of the 3rd International Conference on Embedded Networked Sensor Systems, pp. 166–179. ACM (2005)

24. Zaslavsky, A., Jayaraman, P.P.: Discovery in the internet of things: the internet of things (ubiquity symposium). Ubiquity **2015**, 1–10 (2015). 2

25. Zhang, J., Chung, H.S.H., Lo, W.L.: Clustering-based adaptive crossover and mutation probabilities for genetic algorithms. IEEE Trans. Evol. Comput. **11**(3), 326–335 (2007)

26. Roopa, M.S., Pattar, S., Buyya, R., Venugopal, K.R., Iyengar, S.S., Patnaik, L.M.: Social Internet of Things (SIoT): foundations, thrust areas, systematic review and future directions. Comput. Commun. (2019)

27. Song, Z., Sun, Y., Wan, J., Huang, L., Xu, Y., Hsu, C.H.: Exploring robustness management of social internet of things for customization manufacturing. Future Gener. Comput. Syst. **92**, 846–856 (2019)

28. Rho, S., Chen, Y.: Social Internet of Things: applications, architectures and protocols (2019)

29. Han, G., Zhou, L., Wang, H., Zhang, W., Chan, S.: A source location protection protocol based on dynamic routing in WSNs for the Social Internet of Things. Future Gener. Comput. Syst. **82**, 689–697 (2018)

30. Meena Kowshalya, A., Valarmathi, M.L.: Dynamic trust management for secure communications in Social Internet of Things (SIoT). Sadhana **43**(9), 1–8 (2018). https://doi.org/10.1007/s12046-018-0885-z

31. Lin, K., Li, C., Fortino, G., Rodrigues, J.J.: Vehicle route selection based on game evolution in social internet of vehicles. IEEE Internet Things J. **5**(4), 2423–2430 (2018)

32. Ning, Z., Wang, X., Kong, X., Hou, W.: A social-aware group formation framework for information diffusion in narrowband Internet of Things. IEEE Internet Things J. **5**(3), 1527–1538 (2017)

33. Chen, Z., Ling, R., Huang, C.M., Zhu, X.: A scheme of access service recommendation for the Social Internet of Things. Int. J. Commun. Syst. **29**(4), 694–706 (2016)

34. Nitti, M., Murroni, M., Fadda, M., Atzori, L.: Exploiting social internet of things features in cognitive radio. IEEE Access **4**, 9204–9212 (2016)

35. Chen, G., Huang, J., Cheng, B., Chen, J.: A social network based approach for IoT device management and service composition. In: IEEE World Congress on Services, pp. 1–8 (2015)

36. Li, Z., Chen, R., Liu, L., Min, G.: Dynamic resource discovery based on preference and movement pattern similarity for large-scale social Internet of Things. IEEE Internet Things J. **3**(4), 581–589 (2015)

37. Atzori, L., Iera, A., Morabito, G., Nitti, M.: The Social Internet of Things (SIoT)-when social networks meet the Internet of Things: concept, architecture and network characterization. Comput. Network. **56**(16), 3594–3608 (2012)

38. Chen, R., Bao, F., Guo, J.: Trust-based service management for social internet of things systems. IEEE Trans. Dependable Secure Comput. **13**(6), 684–696 (2015)

39. Sigillito, V.G., Wing, S.P., Hutton, L.V., Baker, K.B.: Classification of radar returns from the ionosphere using neural networks. Johns Hopkins APL Tech. Digest **10**(3), 262–266 (1989)

A Clustering Based Optimized PEGASIS in Wireless Sensor Networks

Samayveer Singh[1]([⊠]) and Pradeep Kumar Singh[2]([⊠])

[1] Department of Computer Science and Engineering, Dr B R Ambedkar National Institute of Technology, Jalandhar, Punjab, India
samayveersingh@gmail.com
[2] Jaypee University of Information Technology, Waknaghat, HP, India
pradeep_84cs@yahoo.com

Abstract. The wireless sensor network (WSN) is an evolving technology where clustering performs an imperative part in effective utilization of energy dissipation of its batteries for monitoring the physical world. The batteries indicate the effectiveness of the deployed networks in terms of their lifespan. Generally, most of energy of sensors is consumed in the communication process between the sensor nodes and sink. Thus, a effective mechanism is required for balancing the communication load among the sensor. In this work, we propose an optimize PEGASIS protocol for enhancing the lifespan of homogeneous and heterogeneous networks. In the optimization of PEGASIS protocol, a fuzzy system is considered for selecting the cluster head (CH) along with data aggregation and data collection using chain-based process. It considers three parameters for effective clustering namely sensor node residual energy, cluster density, and, sensor and base station distance. The proposed method deliberates a chain based process for efficient data communication within the cluster and outside the cluster. It also introduces a data gathering process which remove the redundancy of the data. The removal of redundancy of the data helps in saving the energy and also decrease the network overheads. The performance of the proposed optimized PEGASIS protocol investigated by using MATLAB and deliberate the simulation matric parameters namely: alive and dead nodes, throughput, and energy consumption. The simulation outcomes of the proposed optimized PEGASIS protocol outperforms than the other existing protocol.

Keywords: Lifetime · Clustering · Wireless sensor networks · Energy efficiency · Fuzzy logic system

1 Introduction

Nowadays, there is a significant development in wireless sensor networks (WSNs) in industry and academia specially in the arena of communication, sensing, and computation. The WSNs retain dissimilar characteristics like the capability to survive unforgiving ecological circumstances, the ease of practice, nodes energy depletion limitations, node failures survivability, scalability in a different category of deployment, cross-layer design, and homogeneity & heterogeneity of nodes [1]. The WSNs consist of different abilities link automatic sensing, computing, and communication and

© Springer Nature Singapore Pte Ltd. 2020
P. K. Singh et al. (Eds.): FTNCT 2019, CCIS 1206, pp. 177–195, 2020.
https://doi.org/10.1007/978-981-15-4451-4_15

these nodes are easy adding into the existing networks because of its self-organizing nature [1]. The WSNs having various characteristics which are as self-organizing capability from various failures, constraints of nodes energies, easy to use, usage of homogeneity and heterogeneity nodes in a defined network, and absorb various harsh environmental conditions. The sensors are positioned in the observing field for gathering the information. These sensors collect information from the deployed filed and forward that gathered information to other sensor node and then next node forward that information to the another nearer node. Then, at last collected information to be communicated to the base-station (BS). BS is unswervingly or indirectly associated to the server with the help of internet [2].

Currently, WSNs are being deployed in numerous solicitation applications for example various fields in health care, water quality monitoring, landslide recognition, industrial and consumer applications, armed reconnaissance, natural disaster deterrence, building/bridge structural health, various type of data centre, forestry fire detection, data classification, and so on. Generally, there are two possible methods to organize/deploy sensors in the monitoring fields namely deterministic and non-deterministic. The sensors are deployed manually in case of deterministic deployment where as in non-deterministic deployment sensors are thrown using aircraft [2].

The sensor systems can be characterized into two comprehensive categories namely homogeneous and heterogeneous depending upon the nodes energy levels and nodes capabilities. The homogeneous networks consist of similar type of nodes means same amount of preliminary vitality, whereas energy is not same of heterogeneous networks. The heterogeneous nodes are positioned in all the possible groups in the observing area. Naming of these groups are called levels or tires. The above discussion is founded on the vitality of the sensors; thus it is called the energy heterogeneity. The energy heterogeneity of only possible in the heterogeneous nodes defined in the networks. There are two more type of heterogeneity in WSNs i.e., link, and computational heterogeneity [2]. In link heterogeneity, sensors have different transmission bandwidth, whereas sensors have different computational resources such as microprocessor in computational heterogeneity as associate to the normal nodes.

The nodes have nearly restrictions due to the limited dimension, vitality, storing and cost of the sensor devices. Therefore, there is dare need to design an energy efficient network to overcome the limitations of the sensor networks up to some extent. The clustering shows a vital role for efficient utilizing of the limited size, power, storage and cost of the sensor devices. It also helps in efficient gathering data from the monitoring filed using size of the cluster, election of CHs, intra and inter cluster announcement, and data aggregation. Thus, this work is attempt to determination the problems and provides the solution of energy efficiency by proposing a threshold based optimize energy efficient routing technique in heterogeneous WSNs.

In this work, we propose an optimize PEGASIS protocol for enhancing the lifespan of homogeneous and heterogeneous networks. In the optimization of PEGASIS protocol, a fuzzy system is considered for selecting the CH along with data aggregation and data collection using chain-based process. It considers three parameters for effective clustering namely sensor node residual energy, cluster density, and, sensor and base station distance. The proposed method deliberates a chain based process for efficient data communication within the cluster and outside the cluster. It also introduces a data gathering process which remove the redundancy of data. The removal of redundancy of data helps in saving the energy and also decrease the network overheads. The various performance matrices centered on the nonfiction evaluation for evaluating the performance are considered which are given as network lifetime and in relationships of steadiness epoch (first node dead), throughput, number of CHs, total energy consumption etc.

The roadmap of the manuscript is given as follows. Section 2 discusses the literature review. In Sect. 3 the energy and radio models are discussed. In Sects. 4 and 5 the proposed models are discussed. Section 6 discusses the simulation result and their deliberations. Finally, Sect. 7 accomplishes the paper.

2 Literature Review

Nowadays, limited power supply, the limited size of sensor nodes, no rechargeable etc. are the major issues in WSN because of these nodes operated by the battery power. Thus, we need to propose some techniques which will be energy efficient for solving such type of problems. In the past few decades there is a lot number of clustering approaches for balancing the load of the sensor networks are discussed. This load balancing strategy provides the solution of instant energy consumption which also helps in extending the lifetime of the networks. A very first protocol is Low energy adaptive clustering hierarchy (LEACH) [3] which is implemented for balancing the load among the sensor nodes. The implementation of LEACH consists of two-phase which are as follows setup phase and steady-state phase. Nodes are divided in regions and corresponding cluster heads are selected in the setup phase. The selection of cluster heads depends on the probability function. Data transmission is performed in the steady-state phase of the LEACH protocol. The LEACH again modified as power-efficient gathering in sensor information systems (PEGASIS) by considering chains for collecting the data [4]. The construction of chains, start from the farthest node and then select the nearby nodes for constructing the chain. After completing the chaining process data collection process starts from the farthest node to nearer node to the BS. This protocol did not work well for the large networks but it works well for the small networks.

To increase the longevity of wireless sensor networks, "heterogeneous stable election protocol (hetSEP)" was introduced for 2-level heterogeneity and 3-level heterogeneity [5]. The hetSEP uses functions namely: weighted election probability and threshold for CH election and cluster members selection. However, hetSEP may increase overhead in case of long-distance transmission. For two-level and multilevel energy heterogeneities, the distributed energy-efficient clustering (DEEC) protocol was proposed [6]. The cluster heads are elected using ratio residual energy of each node and average energy of the network. Nevertheless, additional vitality of superior sensor nodes is not professionally consumed as the vitality is randomly allocated which leads to infeasibility issues. In [7], the CHs are assigned based the remaining essentialness of sensors to heightening life span of the WSN if there should be an occurrence of three-level heterogeneity. However, this system requires extra essentialness to remake the groups in each cycle. The convention may endure information misfortune issues in the event of correspondence issues of group heads with one another. To diminish the entomb bunch vitality, Maheswari et al. presented vitality productive two-level grouping convention dependent on node's degree [8]. The convention utilizes multi-bounce correspondence which thusly experiences surprising burden at the sink.

The papers [9–11] discuss cluster techniques for heterogeneous wireless sensor networks. They have considered the various level of heterogeneity in WSNs. These papers don't consider the chaining approach for data collection and don't consider the data aggregation process among nodes and the CHs. Singh et al. discuss a protocol HEED-FL protocol which considers the basic approach of the HEED [12]. In this the election of CHs based on the different parameters like residual energy, distance, using the fuzzy system. This paper suffers from the load balancing in the CH selection process and data aggregation process at the time of data collection.

Faisal et al. deliberate a zonal-stable election protocol for hybrid routing called Z-SEP for WSNs [13] and Z-SEP uses the same cluster formation as discussed in LEACH [3]. It does not consider normal nodes in the clustering process. The Z-SEP [13] is extended by Khan et al. as AZ-SEP [14] in which Khan et al. discuss a hybrid and multi-hop advanced Z-SEP for WSN that communication of sensors with the BS is hybrid [14]. In this method, certain sensor nodes connect straight while others use clustering mechanism to transfer their information. The complete monitoring field is separated into three dissimilar zones founded on their nodes' energy and introduced a new mechanism of CH selection based on residual energy and distance from the BS. This method suffers the load balancing problem within the cluster sets. Smaragdakis et al. discuss a heterogeneous protocol to increase lifespan before death of the first node called SEP [15]. It also increases the stability period of the networks. In SEP, the election of CHs is based on weighted election probabilities of each node and considers the residual energy of the individual nodes. SEP considers two types of nodes to define the heterogeneity in networks. Tang et al. discuss a routing algorithm based on chain-cluster which divides the network into different chains and divided into two phases [16]. In the first phase, sensor nodes send their data/information to the head node of the respective chain with the help of routing protocol and in the second one, head nodes of the all the chain create a cluster node that performs data aggregation. Some of the work also discussed in [17]. In the following segment, we deliberate the fuzzy logic system which will help in efficient clustering.

3 Network, Energy, and Radio Dissipation Model

In this segment, the first talk about the presumptions finished for the proposed system and afterward examine the system models. The fundamental suspicions are given as pursues:

- All the sensors have an interesting ID and conveyed arbitrarily in the observing zone and they are stationary in nature.
- Nodes can be homogeneous or heterogeneous and their initial energies rely upon the level of heterogeneity.

- Sensors have symmetric connections, comparative capacities, and constrained computational supremacy, memory, and vitality.
- BS is situated in the checking territory and separation among nodes and BS can be determined to utilize got signal quality.
- Nodes make them sort out capacities.

Here, we deliberate a two-tier heterogeneity model which consists of N total number of sensor nodes. The energies of level-1 and level-2 nodes are denoted as E_1 and E_2, respectively, by considering the condition $E_1 < E_2$ and their numbers are denoted as N_1, N_2 respectively, by considering the condition $N_1 > N_2$. The total system energy is determined as follows:

$$E_T = \theta * N * E_1 + (1 - \theta) * N * E_2 \tag{1}$$

where θ is a model parameter.

Level-1 Heterogeneity: For $\theta = 1$, distinct the network has solitary level-1 nodes, i.e. each node has identical energy. Thus, the total system energy is assumed by

$$E_{level-1} = N * E_1 \tag{2}$$

where E_1 is the initial energy of the networks.

Level-2 Heterogeneity: The level-2 comprises 2-type of sensors namely level-1 and level-2 nodes and whole network energy defines in Eq. (1) given by

$$E_{level-2} = \theta * N * E_1 + (1 - \theta) * N * E_2 \tag{3}$$

The number of level-1 and level-2 nodes are given as and indicated by N_1 and N_2, respectively.

$$\left.\begin{array}{l} N_1 = N * \theta \\ N_2 = N * (1 - \theta) \end{array}\right\} \tag{4}$$

The energy of the level-1 and level-2 sensor nodes are given as E_1 and $E_2 = E_1 * (1 + \omega)$, respectively. Let consider the value of constants θ and ω are 0.4 and 0.25, respectively.

Here, we also discuss a radio dissipation energy model to calculate the transmitting and receiving the energy by the sensors during transmission, sensing, and computational process. The transmitting the L-bit message over the distance d the energy exhaustion is specified as follows [3]:

$$E_{TXS} = L * \epsilon_{elec} + L * \epsilon_{fs} * d^2 \qquad \text{if } d \leq d_0 \tag{5}$$

$$E_{TXL} = L * \epsilon_{elec} + L * \epsilon_{mp} * d^4 \qquad \text{if } d > d_0 \tag{6}$$

where $\in_{elec}$, $\in_{fs}$ and $\in_{mp}$ are the energy degenerate and d_0 is threshold distance between a sensor and the BS as particular below:

$$d_0 = \sqrt{\frac{\in_{fs}}{\in_{mp}}} \tag{7}$$

The energies consumed in sensing (E_{Sx}) and in receiving (E_{Rx}) are specified in (8) and (9) as follows:

$$E_{Rx} = L * \in_{elec} \tag{8}$$

$$E_{Sx} = L * \in_{elec} \tag{9}$$

In the next section, we discuss the fuzzy logic system which helps in electing the CHs for load balancing.

4 Fuzzy Logic System for the Proposed Protocol

The fuzzy logic system (FIS) is considered for electing the CHs and their cluster formation process. This section discusses the fuzzy rule set for election of cluster heads depend on different parameters namely node residual energy, cluster node density, and node and BS distance. The FIS comprises of four key steps viz. fuzzifier, rule base, fuzzy interface engine, and defuzzifier [11]. The fuzzifier accepts crisp input as a crisp number i.e., node residual energy, cluster node density, and distance between a node and BS and transforms these values into the fuzzy set by applying functions like trapezoidal, Gaussian and triangular shaped. The fuzzy rule base contains various IF-THEN procedures to choose the fuzzy system outcome by considering different fuzzy operator like AND/OR. The fuzzy interface engine or aggregation is the collective output of all rules i.e. the maximum values to produce the aggregate fuzzy set value. Defuzzification receives inputs from the fuzzy interface and converts them into crisp values as an output value. Defuzzifier procedures used the centroid method for attainment the crisp value also known as the final output probability. In this work, we used the Mamdani model for obtaining the output probability in terms of crisp value. The Mamdani model is the simple, easy, and most widely used model in different applications [11]. The centroid defuzzifier function is computed as follows:

$$\text{Centroid function} = \frac{\int \Psi_\eta(x) * xdx}{\int \Psi_\eta(x)dx} \tag{10}$$

where, $\Psi_\eta(x)$ denotes the membership function of set η for value x.

Here, WSNs deliver three input parameters to the FIS namely sensor residual energy, cluster node density, and distance, and each input parameters contain three membership functions as indicated in Table 1. The output consists of seven membership functions in terms of probability generated by FIS as shown in Table 2. The input variable membership functions consist of one Gaussian and two half trapezoidal shapes and output membership functions consist of five Gaussian and two half trape-zoidal shapes as shown in Figs. 1(a)–(d), respectively. Table 3 indicates the fuzzifi-cation relationship between different input and output variable. We have calculated the outcome probability value for determining the CH based on the three input parameters for a particular round. The maximum probability value helps in finalize the CH out of deployed sensors in the targeting area for the current round. The following formula is given for calculating the outcome probability:

$$\text{Probability} = \frac{w_1 * L_{re} + w_2 * L_{nd} + w_3 * (M_d - L_d)}{w_1 * M_{re} + w_2 * M_{nd} + w_3 * M_d} \tag{11}$$

w_1, w_2, and w_3 are the weights for the fuzzy input variables, initially, all are considered 1. L_{re}, L_{nd}, and L_d indicate the current level values of the residual energy, node density, and distance, respectively. M_{re}, M_{nd}, and M_d represent the maximum level value of the sensor residual energy, cluster node density, and distance among cluster and BS, respectively.

In the next section, we will discuss the data aggregation process of the data which is collected by the respective CH and intermediate CHs which are used to advancing the information to the BS.

Table 1. Illustrations the output in terms of probability generated by FIS

Output value	Membership functions		
Residual energy	Low (0)	Medium (1)	High (2)
Node density	Sparsely (0)	Medium (1)	Densely (2)
Distance	Near (0)	Medium (1)	Far (2)

Table 2. Illustrations the output in terms of probability generated by FIS

Output value	Membership functions
Probability	Very weak (0), weak (1), lower medium (2), medium (3), higher medium (4), strong (5), very strong (6)

Table 3. Illustrations the fuzzy rule base

Residual energy	Node density	Distance	Probability
Low (0)	Sparsely (0)	Near (0)	Lower medium (2)
Low (0)	Sparsely (0)	Medium (1)	Weak (1)
Low (0)	Sparsely (0)	Far (2)	Very weak (0)
Low (0)	Medium (1)	Near(0)	Medium (3)
Low (0)	Medium (1)	Medium (1)	Lower medium (2)
Low (0)	Medium (1)	Far (2)	Weak (1)
Low (0)	Densely (2)	Near (0)	Higher medium (4)
Low (0)	Densely (2)	Medium (1)	Medium (3)
Low (0)	Densely (2)	Far (2)	Lower medium (2)

(continued)

Table 3. (*continued*)

Residual energy	Node density	Distance	Probability
Medium (1)	Sparsely (0)	Near (0)	Medium (3)
Medium (1)	Sparsely (0)	Medium (1)	Lower medium (2)
Medium (1)	Sparsely (0)	Far (2)	Weak (1)
Medium (1)	Medium (1)	Near (0)	Higher medium (4)
Medium (1)	Medium (1)	Medium (1)	Medium (3)
Medium (1)	Medium (1)	Far (2)	Lower medium (2)
Medium (1)	Densely (2)	Near (0)	Strong (5)
Medium (1)	Densely (2)	Medium (1)	Higher medium (4)
Medium (1)	Densely (2)	Far (2)	Medium (3)
High (2)	Sparsely (0)	Near (0)	Higher medium (4)
High (2)	Sparsely (0)	Medium (1)	Medium (3)
High (2)	Sparsely (0)	Far (2)	Lower medium (2)
High (2)	Medium (1)	Near (0)	Strong (5)
High (2)	Medium (1)	Medium (1)	Higher medium (4)
High (2)	Medium (1)	Far (2)	Medium (3)
High (2)	Densely (2)	Near (0)	Very strong (6)
High (2)	Densely (2)	Medium (1)	Strong (5)
High (2)	Densely (2)	Far (2)	Higher medium (4)

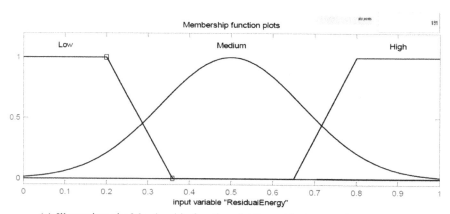

(a) Illustrations the Membership function plot for residual energy input parameter

Fig. 1. (a–d): Illustrations the membership functions plot corresponding to different inputs and output variables

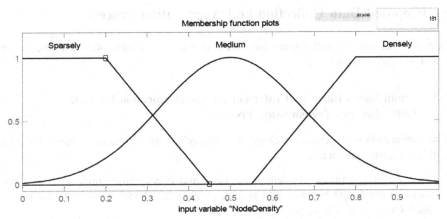

(b) Illustrations the Membership function plot for node density input parameter

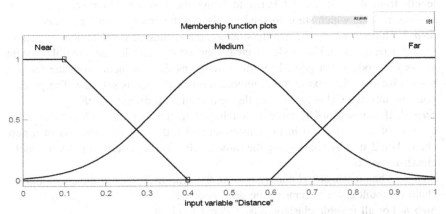

(c) Illustrations the Membership function plot for distance input parameter

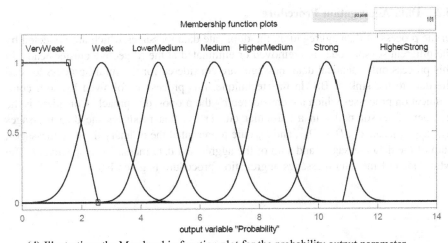

(d) Illustrations the Membership function plot for the probability output parameter

Fig. 1. (*continued*)

5 Proposed Data Collection and Aggregation Process

In this subsection, we will discuss the data aggregation and data collection process for the stable election protocol.

5.1 Chain Based Intra- and Inter-cluster Communication for Data Gathering and Transmission Process

The explanation of the chain development strategy's working process is given for intra and inter-cluster interaction.

Step 1. First, estimate the length for each and every sensor node and CH, and estimate the length between all the nodes within the cluster or estimate the length each CH and the BS in the system across.

Step 2. The Selection of the first sensor node/cluster head depends on the furthest length from the respective CH/BS to being the first intra/inter communication sensor/CH node which starts to send the data to the other sensor/CH node.

Step 3. Through taking the greedy strategy, the farthest sensor/CH node begins to pick the next sensor/CH node to create the string. The lowest possible distant sensor/CH node is considered by this strategy as the next node from the farthest node. Likewise, the next minimal remote sensor/CH node is selected. The process goes on until the CH/networks are the next minimum distant node/CH.

Step 4. If any sensor/CH node is not linked to the respective CH/BS after the creation of the first chain in the cluster/networks, then the construction of a new chain should start by considering the same mechanism as described in Step 3 in the cluster/networks.

Step 5. When a sensor/CH energy is zero, the sensor/CH dies in the chain and the chain is rebuilt again to remove the dead node/CH.

Step 6. For all feasible clusters, repeat step 1 to phase 5.

5.2 Data Aggregation Procedure

In the process of data aggregation, the duplicate data messages which are collected by the different sensor nodes are removed or eliminated at the respective cluster heads. In this process only identical data messages are considered for the future process to send the data to the sink or BS. In this technique, this process is followed by both communication processes which are considered by the proposed approach. Consider δ is the number of sensor nodes in a particular cluster (α) that produces the data messages $\alpha_{p1}, \alpha_{p2}, \alpha_{p3}, \ldots, \alpha_{p\delta}$. D_{A1}, D_{A2}, and D_{A3} are represented the ordinary the data messages, sum of the data messages, and sum of the aggregated data messages, respectively. The whole idea of the data messages aggregation procedure is given below:

Input: Set of Clusters $C = \{\alpha, \beta, \gamma ....\}$ *and BS*
Output: Aggregate data packets at CH or BS

Begin
  for every cluster $C = \{\alpha, \beta, \gamma ....\}$
    $if(\alpha_{p1} = \alpha_{p2} = \alpha_{p3} = \cdots = \alpha_{p\delta})$
      // *all the sensors generated the exact same data packets*
      $$D_{A1} = \left\{ \left(\frac{\alpha_{p1}}{2^{q-1}}\right) + \left(\frac{\alpha_{p2}}{2^{q-1}}\right) + \left(\frac{\alpha_{p3}}{2^{q-2}}\right) + \left(\frac{\alpha_{p4}}{2^{q-3}}\right) + \cdots + \left(\frac{\alpha_{p\delta}}{2}\right) \right\}$$
      // *q is number of nodes generated same data packets*

    else if $(\beta_{p1} \neq \beta_{p2} \neq \beta_{p3} \neq \cdots \neq \beta_{p\delta})$
      // *all the sensors generated the different data packets*
      $$D_{A2} = \beta_{p1} + \beta_{p2} + \beta_{p3} + \cdots + \beta_{p\delta}$$
      // *sum of the data packets*
    else if $(\gamma_{p1} = \gamma_{p4} = \cdots = \gamma_{p\delta-1}) \neq \gamma_{p2} \neq \gamma_{p3} \neq \gamma_{p\delta}$
      // *some sensors generated the exact same data packets and*
      some sensor generated the different data packets
      $$D_{A3} = D_{A1} + D_{A2}$$
      $$D_{A3} = \left\{ \left(\frac{\gamma_{p1}}{2^{q-1}}\right) + \left(\frac{\gamma_{p4}}{2^{q-1}}\right) + \left(\frac{\gamma_{p5}}{2^{q-2}}\right) + \left(\frac{\gamma_{p6}}{2^{q-3}}\right) + \cdots + \left(\frac{\gamma_{p\delta-1}}{2}\right) \right\}$$
      $$+ \left\{ (\gamma_{p2} + \gamma_{p3} + \gamma_{p\delta}) \right\}$$

    end if
  end for
End

6 Simulation Results and Discussions

In this section, the proposed schemes imitation results are compared with the existing Tang et al. [16] and PEGASIS [4] methods by considering alive and dead nodes/round, stability period, energy consumption, throughput and normalized average energy consumption/round. PEGASIS is an optimal chaining approach that minimizes power consumption [4]. The proposed method has also implemented a process for removing redundant data also called data aggregation, a transmission and data gathering process using chaining system for intra-and inter-cluster communication. All the suggested implementations are applied to both protocols networks to estimate performance. The suggested networks are implemented in MATLAB 2014a environment using 100 number of sensor nodes. Initially, entire nodes of the homogeneous networks are deployed with 0.5 J initial energy and BS is positioned at the middle of the targeted region. In two-level of heterogeneity, we considered 70 nodes as the normal and 30 nodes as the advanced nodes with their initial energies 0.414 J and 0.7 J, respectively. The power consumption to run the circuit ($\in_{elec}$), to transmit signal over shorter distance ($\in_{fs}$), and to transmit over longer distance ($\in_{mp}$) is 50 nJ/bit, 10 pJ/bit/m², and 0.0013 pJ/bit/m⁴, respectively. The message size (L), cluster radius (R), and threshold distance (d_0) are 4000 bits, 25 m, and 75 m, respectively. For each experiment, we have taken 25 simulations using randomly sensor deployment and finally, the average of that 25 simulations is considered as the outcome of the results. Two categories are considered for evaluation of the proposed and existing methods namely, performance evaluation for homogeneous and heterogeneous networks. In the next subsection, the simulation results and their analysis for homogeneous networks are deliberated in detail.

6.1 Performance Evaluation for Homogeneous Networks

In this subsection, a comparative result analysis of the PEGASIS [4], Tang. et al. [16] and the proposed method are discussed for a homogeneous network where all the nodes have identical energy by considering alive and dead nodes/round, stability period, energy consumption/round, throughput and normalized average energy consumption/round.

Figure 2 illustrations the alive nodes with reference to the rounds for PEGASIS [4], Tang. et al. [16] and the proposed technique. It is observed that the proposed technique covers 3719 rounds previously exhausts its whole energy whereas Tang et al. [16] and PEGASIS [4] covers 2626 and 2303 rounds, respectively. Thus, Tang et al. [16] and the proposed method increase 14.03%, and 61.49% in the lifespan network in respect of PEGASIS [4], respectively. The proposed method helps in increment in the network lifetime because node density and other parameters reduce the message cost among the BS and sensors. Furthermore, the sensors in the Tang et al. [16] and proposed method die leisurely than the PEGASIS [4] because this method selects the cluster head nodes competently, thus network lifetime prolongs significantly. The Fig. 2 shows the sustainable period of the Tang et al. [16], and proposed method for first node dead outstrips by 26.92%, and 76.92%, as a comparison with the PEGASIS [4] significantly, respectively. Figure 3 illustrations the number of dead nodes per rounds for PEGASIS [4], Tang et al. [16], and the proposed method.

The average energy dissipation of the PEGASIS [4], Tang et al. [16], and proposed method with respect to the number of rounds for homogeneous networks is displayed the Fig. 4. The preliminary network energy is deliberated as 50 J.

The proposed method outperforms as compare to the PEGASIS [4] and Tang et al. [16] because of it concealments a superior number of rounds. The results show the higher energy consumption in PEGASIS [4] because PEGASIS [4] did not consider data aggregation with chaining approach for data transmission among the BS and nodes. Moreover, the proposed method preserves the energy of the sensor in an effective manner. Thus, it diminishes the energy cost of the cluster head nodes for both the proposed networks. The number of information messages received by the BS in respect of the number of rounds till the networks alive using PEGASIS [4], Tang et al. [16], and proposed method for the homogeneous networks are shown the Fig. 5. The number of information packets sent by the proposed method, Tang et al., and PEGASIS are 2.28×10^{-4}, 1.61×10^{-4}, and 1.32×10^{-4}, respectively. It is observed that the proposed method sent a message at an advanced frequency to the BS as related to PEGASIS [4] and Tang et al. [16]. However, the proposed method produces more messages because the sensors in the proposed method persist alive more.

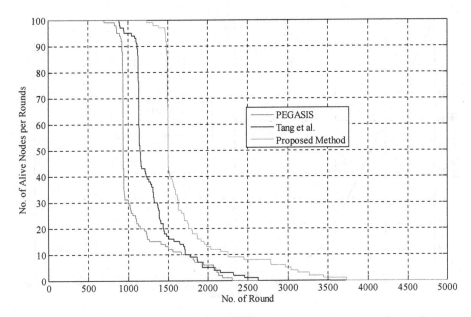

Fig. 2. Shows the comparative analysis of PEGASIS, Tang et al., and proposed a model by considering the number of alive nodes with respect to the number of rounds.

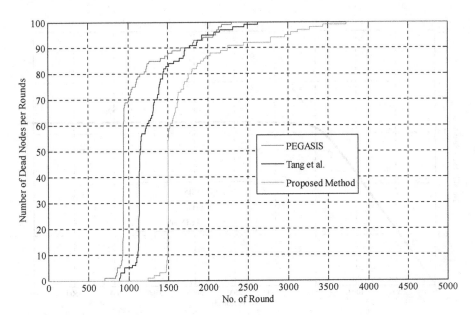

Fig. 3. Shows the comparative analysis of PEGASIS, Tang et al., and proposed a model by considering number of dead sensor nodes with respect to a number of rounds.

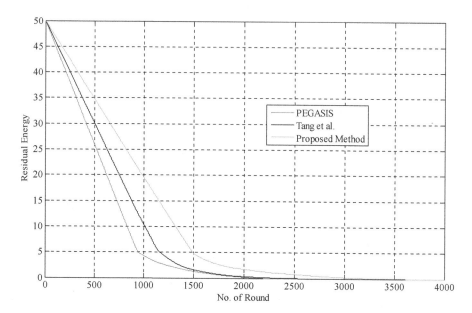

Fig. 4. Shows the comparative analysis of PEGASIS, Tang et al., and proposed model by considering total energy consumption with respect to the number of rounds.

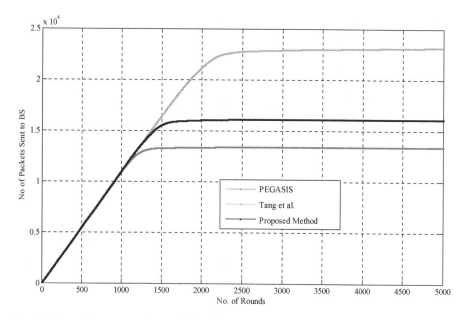

Fig. 5. Shows the comparative analysis of PEGASIS, Tang et al., and proposed a model by considering number of packets sent to BS with respect to the number of rounds.

6.2   Performance Estimation for Heterogeneous Networks

In this sub section, a comparative result analysis of the PEGASIS [4], Tang et al. [16], and the proposed method are discussed for a heterogeneous network where nodes have dissimilar amount of network energy by considering alive and dead nodes per round, stability period, energy consumption per round, throughput.

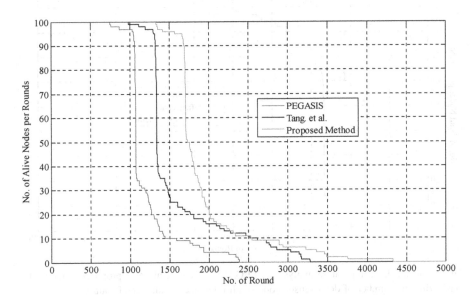

Fig. 6. Shows the comparative analysis of PEGASIS, Tang et al., and proposed model by considering a number of alive sensor nodes with reference to the number of rounds.

Figure 6 illustrations the number of alive nodes with reference to a number of rounds for PEGASIS [4], Tang et al. [16], and the proposed technique. It is observed that the proposed technique covers 4322 rounds before dissipating its energy to zero whereas Tang et al. [16] and PEGASIS [4] covers 3277 and 2381 rounds, respectively. Thus, Tang et al. [16] and the proposed method increase 37.63%, and 81.52% in the network lifespan with respect to PEGASIS [4], respectively. The proposed method helps in increment in the network lifetime because node density and other parameters reduce the message cost among the BS and nodes.

Furthermore, the sensors in the Tang et al. [16] and proposed method die leisurely than the PEGASIS [4] because the selection of the cluster heads is very effective due to the fuzzification. This fuzzification extends the lifespan of the networks. The Fig. 6 also shows the sustainable period of the Tang et al. [16], and proposed method for first node dead outstrips by 29.97%, and 77.19%, as a comparison with PEGASIS [4] significantly, respectively. Figure 7 illustrations number of dead nodes per rounds for PEGASIS [4], Tang et al. [16] and proposed method.

The average energy dissipation of the PEGASIS [4], Tang et al. [16], and proposed method with reference to the number of rounds for heterogeneous networks is shown the Fig. 8. The preliminary network energy is deliberated as 50 J. The proposed method outperforms as compare to the PEGASIS [4] and Tang et al. [16] since it

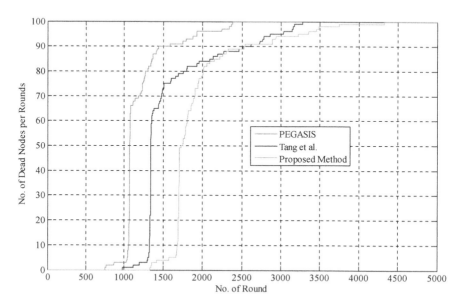

Fig. 7. Shows the comparative analysis of PEGASIS, Tang et al., and proposed a model by considering the number of dead sensor nodes with reference to number of rounds.

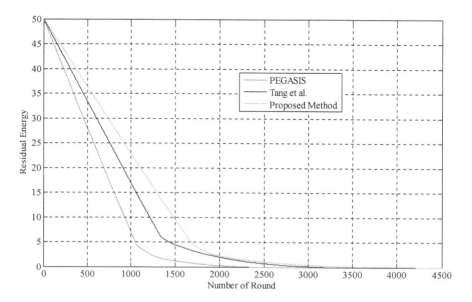

Fig. 8. Shows the comparative analysis of PEGASIS, Tang et al., and proposed a model by considering total energy consumption with reference to the number of rounds.

concealments a greater number of rounds. The outcomes display the sophisticated energy consumption in PEGASIS [4] because this method did not deliberate data aggregation with a chaining approach for transmission of information/data among the BS and sensors. Moreover, the proposed method deliberates both intra- and inter-cluster communication through data aggregation and chain process. It conserves the energy of the sensor nodes in data communication and aggregation using an effective way. Thus, this process moderates the CHs computational energy cost of the networks. Figure 9 shows the number of information packets acknowledged by the BS with reference to the number of rounds till the networks alive using PEGASIS [4], Tang et al. [16], and proposed method for the heterogeneous networks.

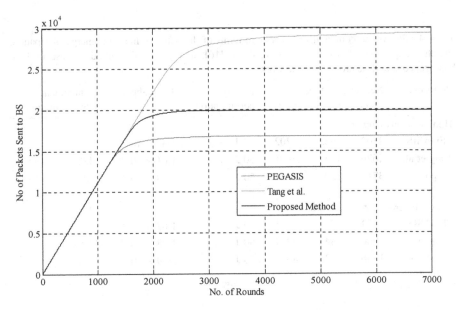

Fig. 9. Shows the comparative analysis of PEGASIS, Tang et al., and proposed model by considering number of packets sent to BS with reference to number of rounds.

The number of packets sent by the proposed method, Tang et al., and PEGASIS are 2.89×10^{-4}, 1.98×10^{-4}, 1.67×10^{-4}, respectively. It is observed that the proposed method sent packets of the data at an advanced frequency to the BS as concomitant with PEGASIS [4] and Tang et al. [16]. However, the proposed method produces the highest number of packets because the nodes in the proposed method persist alive more in terms of the extent of rounds.

Table 4 demonstrations the comparative analysis of network lifespan, energy dissipation, throughput to define the sustainability of the networks, and percentage increment in network lifetime for PEGASIS [4], Tang et al. [16], and proposed a method in case of both homogeneous and heterogeneous networks. In the case of homogeneous networks, throughput is 2.28×10^{-4}, 1.61×10^{-4}, and 1.32×10^{-4}

for the proposed method, Tang et al. [16] and PEGASIS [4], respectively but for heterogeneous networks throughput is 2.89×10^{-4}, 1.98×10^{-4}, 1.67×10^{-4} for the proposed method, Tang et al. [16] and PEGASIS [4], respectively. The proposed methods transmitted a greater number of information packets since the network's lifetime of the proposed is better than the existing ones. The increment in the network lifespan of the Tang et al. [16] and proposed method is 69.21% and 19.88% as compared with the PEGASIS [4] without any increment in the network lifespan, respectively for homogeneous networks, similarly increment in the network lifespan of the Tang et al. [16] and proposed method is 73.43% and 20.31% as compared with the PEGASIS [4] without any increment in the network lifespan, respectively for heterogeneous networks.

Table 4. Shows the comparative analysis in terms of the network lifespan, energy dissipation, and throughput for PEGASIS [4], Tang et al. [16], and proposed method in case of both homogeneous and heterogeneous networks

Protocols	Network lifetime			Energy consumption	Throughput	% increment in network lifetime
	FND	HND	LND			
Homogeneous networks						
PEGASIS	2303	933	702	50 J	1.32×10^{-4}	–
Tang et al.	2626	1147	891	50 J	1.61×10^{-4}	14.03
Proposed method	3719	1501	1242	50 J	2.28×10^{-4}	61.49
2-level heterogeneous networks						
PEGASIS	754	1074	2381	50 J	1.67×10^{-4}	–
Tang et al.	980	1343	3277	50 J	1.98×10^{-4}	37.63
Proposed method	1336	1726	4322	50 J	2.89×10^{-4}	81.52

7 Conclusion

In this paper, a clustering centered optimized PEGASIS protocol for prolonging the network lifespan of the WSNs is proposed. The proposed method deliberated both for identical and different node energies networks for PEGASIS [4], Tang et al. [16], and the proposed technique. The proposed technique used a fuzzy centered clustering technique for the CH determination process and chain-based system for efficient data collection including data aggregation. The proposed method delivers a large sustainable district in the system accomplishment for both type of networks because the selection of nodes for CH selection is efficient which have higher residual energy. The simulation results demonstration lifetime for homogeneous and heterogeneous networks is increased by 14.03%, 61.49% and 37.63%, 81.52% for 50 J network energy in case of Tang et al. and proposed a method with respect of the PEGASIS [4], respectively. The proposed method performs best among the PEGASIS [4] and Tang et al. [16].

References

1. Singh, S., Chand, S., Kumar, B.: Performance investigation of heterogeneous algorithms in WSNs. In: 3rd IEEE International Advance Computing Conference (IACC), pp. 1051–1054 (2013)
2. Singh, Y., Singh, S., Kumar, R.: A distributed energy-efficient target tracking protocol for three level heterogeneous sensor networks. Int. J. Comput. Appl. **51**, 31–36 (2012)
3. Heinzelman, W.R., Chandrakasan, A.P., Balakrishnan, H.: An application-specific protocol architecture for wireless microsensor networks. IEEE Trans. Wireless Commun. **1**, 660–670 (2002)
4. Lindsey, S., Raghavendra, C.S., Sivalingam, K.M.: Data gathering algorithms in sensor networks using energy metrics. IEEE Trans. Parallel Distrib. Syst. **13**, 924–935 (2002)
5. Singh, S., Malik, A.: hetSEP: heterogeneous SEP protocol for increasing lifetime in WSNs. J. Inf. Optim. Sci. **38**, 721–743 (2017)
6. Qing, L., Zhu, Q., Wang, M.: Design of a distributed energy-efficient clustering algorithm for heterogeneous wireless sensor networks. Comput. Commun. **29**, 2230–2237 (2016)
7. Singh, S., Malik, A., Kumar, R.: Energy efficient heterogeneous DEEC protocol for enhancing lifetime in WSNs. Eng. Sci. Technol. Int. J. **20**, 345–353 (2017)
8. Maheswari, D.U., Sudha, S.: Node degree based energy efficient two-level clustering for wireless sensor networks. Wirel. Pers. Commun. **104**, 1209–1225 (2018)
9. Chand, S., Singh, S., Kumar, B.: Heterogeneous HEED protocol for wireless sensor networks. Wirel. Pers. Commun. **77**, 2117–2139 (2014)
10. Singh, S., Chand, S., Kumar, B.: Energy efficient clustering protocol using fuzzy logic for heterogeneous WSNs. Wirel. Pers. Commun. **86**, 451–475 (2016)
11. Singh, S., Chand, S., Kumar, B.: Multilevel heterogeneous network model for wireless sensor networks. Telecommun. Syst. **64**, 259–277 (2017)
12. Singh, S., Chand, S., Kumar, B.: An energy efficient clustering protocol with fuzzy logic for WSNs. In: 5th International Conference-Confluence the Next Generation Information Technology Summit, pp. 427–431 (2014)
13. Faisal, S., Javaid, N., Javaid, A., Khan, M.A., Bouk, S.H., Khan, Z.A.: Z-SEP: zonal-stable election protocol for wireless sensor networks. J. Basic Appl. Sci. Res. 3(5), 132–139 (2013)
14. Khan, F.A., Khan, M., Asif, M., Khalid, A., Haq, I.U.: Hybrid and multi-hop advanced zonal-stable election protocol for wireless sensor networks. IEEE Access **7**, 25334–25346 (2019)
15. Smaragdakis, G., Matta, I., Bestavros, A., SEP: a Stable Election Protocol for clustered heterogeneous wireless sensor networks. Technical report BUCS-TR-2004-022, Boston University Computer Science Department, pp. 1–11 (2004)
16. Tang, F., You, I., Guo, S., Guo, M., Ma, Y.: A chain-cluster based routing algorithm for wireless sensor networks. J. Intell. Manuf. **23**, 1305 (2012)
17. Singh, P.K., Paprzycki, M., Bhargava, B., Chhabra, J.K., Kaushal, N.C., Kumar, Y. (eds.): FTNCT 2018. CCIS, vol. 958. Springer, Singapore (2019). https://doi.org/10.1007/978-981-13-3804-5

M-N Hashing: Search Time Optimization with Collision Resolution Using Balanced Tree

Arushi Agarwal, Sashakt Pathak$^{(\boxtimes)}$, and Sakshi Agarwal

Jaypee Institute of Information Technology, Noida, India
aaruagarwal15@gmail.com, psashakt@gmail.com,
sakshi.agarwal@jiit.ac.in

Abstract. In the field of networking, storing and fast lookup from the large amount of data are two important measures. Hashing is one of the well-known techniques for indexing and retrieving data from the database efficiently. It is mostly used for fast lookups in the fields which require quick results from the database. As the size of the database increases, the number of collisions in the hash table also increases which handled through collision resolution techniques. Traditional algorithms like Separate Chaining, Linear Probing, and Quadratic probing takes linear search time. The tremendous increase of data in recent years requires more profound hash table implementation. In this paper, we have proposed a new and innovative way of implementing hash table to handle collisions more efficiently in logarithmic time i.e. M-N Hashing. To handle the collisions with a scalable sized hash table, the proposed algorithm used the concept of the AVL tree. The performance of the proposed algorithm is analyzed using continuous integer dataset that varies from 0 to 100000. Through experiments, it is depicted that M-N hashing improved the search time up to 99.97% with respect to contemporary algorithms i.e. Separate Chaining, Linear Probing, and Quadratic probing.

Keywords: Hashing · Separate Chaining · Linear Probing · Quadratic Probing · Search time complexity

1 Introduction

In today's world, data is increasing exponentially with respect to time. In the era of digitization, regular up gradation of data and storing the huge amount of data in an organized manner is one of the major requirements for various applications such as banking sector, social networks, newsfeed applications, e-commerce, etc. Therefore, data storage with optimal space requirement and searching an element within optimal time is a challenge for all those applications who deal with a large amount of data very frequently. At present, most of the applications are handling this problem with the help of data structures like arrays, linked lists, hash tables, etc. It has been observed from the literature that Hash table is the most widely used form of storing and searching for data like in the field of password verification [1], storage optimizations [2], IP address lookups [3], networking [11] and more such fields which requires fast searching of data in the large database. In computer networks, the data is stored on more than one node in

© Springer Nature Singapore Pte Ltd. 2020
P. K. Singh et al. (Eds.): FTNCT 2019, CCIS 1206, pp. 196–209, 2020.
https://doi.org/10.1007/978-981-15-4451-4_16

a replicated fashion. One of the measurable technique to maintain the synchronization of such data is hashing and the most commonly used data structure used is Distributed Hash Table.

The aim of hashing is to map every key to a distinct index using an appropriate hash function so that the primitive operations like query, insert and delete take the constant time of $O(1)$. Since the size of data is increasing tremendously, hash collision [4, 5] comes into picture which means more than one key results in the same mapping index from the hash function and hence degrades the performance of the primitive operations. Thus, the optimal hash functions are needed to be designed with a suitable resolution strategy. There are two evaluative parameters that have been used so far to estimate the goodness of any hash function. The first parameter is, it should distribute data uniformly and avoid clustering and the second parameter is, it should be easy to quantify as well as minimize the number of collisions.

In literature, various methods and algorithms have been proposed with respect to the implementation of the hashing technique. These hashing algorithms have been classified into two categories [6] i.e. open addressing and closed addressing. The first category is Open Addressing, in which data is stored inside the hash table and the second one is Closed Addressing in which additional data structure is used to store the data. The examples of open addressing are Linear probing [7], Quadratic probing [7], and Matrix Hashing [8]. Linear probing, in which the next free slot is searched linearly during the collision and Quadratic probing [7] in which the next free slot is searched by adding consecutive values of the quadratic polynomial when a collision occurs. In matrix hashing [8], the two-dimensional hash table is used as a substitute for a one-dimensional array. In the 2D hash table, there are eight choices to put the key in adjacent blocks. If all the eight neighbors are unavailable, then the key is inserted in a separate row known as collision removal block. In open addressing, the size of the hash table is fixed due to which only a limited amount of data can be stored. The example of Closed Addressing is Separate Chaining [4] that uses linked lists to store data at the time of hash collisions. Overall, in closed addressing, extra space is required to handle collision using data structures such as linked lists which requires additional space in the memory.

These classical algorithms are not preferred much in practical applications. The reasons behind it are more space requirements and search time, less efficiency and a large number of collisions because there may exist unused indexes which result in wastage of space and look up time increases when the chain becomes very long. To handle these problems, we proposed an algorithm named M-N hashing. In M-N hashing, two distinct indexes are calculated using two different hash functions which are used in such a way with the tree data structure that it not only decreases the search time of the data but also reduce the number of collisions.

2   Background

2.1   Separate Chaining

In separate chaining [4], the keys are stored both inside and outside the hash table. Initially, keys are stored in the hash table corresponding to their hash function values. When the collision occurs, the linked list is created and the key is added in this list, where the address of the head pointer of the linked list is stored in the hash table corresponding to their hash function value. There is no need to predefine the number of elements to be inserted as the space required is not fixed initially. Space is created at the time of insertion of the element. If there is a long chain of keys at any slot, then the worst case search time complexity is O(L) because it has to traverse the entire linked list. Here, L is the size of the dataset. The cache performance of this algorithm is not satisfactory as the elements are kept in the form of linked lists and the extra space is used for links.

2.2   Linear Probing

In linear probing [7], the keys are stored only inside the hash table. So, the hash table size should be initially fixed and always greater than the number of keys inserted. Each slot stores only one key so when the collision takes place, the algorithm finds the next closest free slot to insert the key. By storing keys at immediate next available slot, clustering of the keys occur, which acts as a barrier to find the required key easily.

2.3   Quadratic Probing

In quadratic probing also [7], the keys are stored only inside the hash table and the hash table size is always greater than the number of keys inserted. When the hash collision happens, the index resulted by the initial hash function is added to a quadratic polynomial to find an empty slot. This may also lead to clustering of the keys and may cause the same issues as in Linear Probing.

Agrawal et al. [8] proposed a new technique for collision resolution based on two-dimensional array. The 2-D array is used to increase the space to store any key in the hash table. If the index generated by the hash function is already occupied, then all the eight neighbors of that index are explored. If none of the neighbors is empty, the second level of collision is activated in which key is placed in collision removal block array and it is sorted every time when the key is inserted because while searching, matrix hashing use binary search algorithm. Sorting the array every time will increase the time complexity of the algorithm.

Pietrzyk et al. [12] presented a new application of linear probing in the field of vectorization. Author has stated that with growing capacities of the memory, data processing become viable. To improve the processing performance of CPU, vectorization is a common approach. They have used linear probing to improve vectorization. Tian et al. [13] proposed a Dynamic Hash Table (DHT) implementation to develop efficient auditing techniques to gain trust and confidence of data owners for cloud services. Tumblin et al. [14] developed a hashing method which is suitable for the parallel computation using quadratic probing as a collision resolution strategy. Zhou et al. [15] improved the existing double hashing technique for multi-pattern matching. The number of comparisons are reduced by storing patterns in a two dimensional array of pointers. The classical algorithms like Linear Probing, Quadratic Probing and Separate Chaining are still being used by many researchers for their recent works [12, 14, 16, 17].

3 Methodology

In the current state of hashing, there is a limitation with respect to time complexity i.e. lookup time required to search a key is high due to large size databases. Therefore, to tackle this issue, in this paper we proposed a distinctive way of implementing the hash tables in a more efficient manner i.e. M-N Hashing. Our proposed algorithm, M-N Hashing is a Closed Addressing approach. Table 1 describes the terminology used in our proposed algorithm. For example, we have X elements in our database. To store these elements in the hash table, we used two bucket layout i.e. primary bucket and secondary bucket. Each block of primary bucket named segments_array is further connected to a secondary bucket named segment_value as shown in Fig. 1. The use of the secondary bucket is able to resolve collision directly without using extra space for the small-sized dataset.

Table 1. Notation table

Variables	Description
X	Number of elements in the dataset
segments_array	Primary bucket
segment_value	Secondary bucket
N	Size of segments_array bucket
M	Size of segment_value bucket
K	Key to be inserted
H1()	Hash function for segments_array
H2()	Hash function for segment_value bucket
index	Block of segments_array
index2	Block of segment_value
K_t	Key to be searched (target key)
$index_t$	Block of segments_array for target key
$index_t2$	Block of segment_value for target key
H	Height of the tree
ptr	Temporary pointer to locate a node in the tree
E	Number of elements inserted in the tree
B	Balance factor of a node in the tree
I	No of testing iteration i.e. 2 Million
T_A	Time in milliseconds required to search a key K_t in the hash table by technique A

Let segments_array is of constant size N and segment_value is of constant size M. Therefore, the initial space required for our algorithm is O(MN) as illustrated in Fig. 1. Further, the size of our hash table is variable and may increase depending on the collision in the hash table, unlike open addressing in which a fixed size hash table is defined to accumulate all elements. Therefore, in open addressing total count of elements should be known in the beginning.

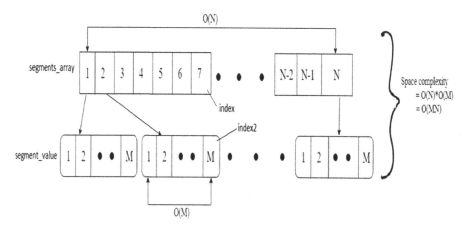

Fig. 1. Initial space complexity

Whereas, the proposed algorithm does not need to know the total number of elements to be inserted. Our proposed methodology is divided into two major components:

- Scalable hash table Generation
- Lookup an element

The detailed description of the proposed algorithm as follows:

3.1   Scalable Hash Table Generation

Open addressing hash techniques require the size of the hash table to be fixed according to input size in beginning. Therefore, if the input size increases, open addressing fails. To handle this limitation, the proposed algorithm extends the size of the hash table depending upon the increase in the input size. This generation process is divided into two modules i.e. the first module is block assignment and the second module is tree generation.

Block assignment is the initial part of the Dynamic hash table Generation, where we assign a block to the input element. The process of block assignment is described in Table 2. Let the size of segments_array be N, the size of each segment_value be M and inserted element is K i.e. key. The proposed algorithm will compute two hash values i.e. index and index2 of the key using two different hash functions H1(K) and H2(K) for segments_array and segment_value respectively. These two hash functions H1 and H2 are calculated using Eqs. (1) and (2) respectively.

$$H1(K) = K\%N \tag{1}$$

$$H2(K) = K\%M \tag{2}$$

Therefore, hash function H1(K) identify the position of key K in segments_array by calculating the hash value i.e. indexing of the key K in segments_array. Similarly, hash function H2(K) discovers the block of key K in segment_value by calculating the hash value i.e. indexing of the key K in the segment_value, where the segment_value bucket is connected to each block of segments_array as shown in Fig. 1.

Table 2. Block assignment

INSERT ELEMENT FUNCTION

```
Start
index <- H1(K)
index2 <- H2(K)
   if isEmpty (segments_array[index] ->
              segment_value[index2]):
       segments_array[index]->
              segment_value[index2] = K

else:
       insert_Node(segments_array[index] ->
segment_value[index2]->next_node, K) Stop
```

Selected block of segment_value will be the position where the key K will be stored. With a large number of insertions, the chance of collision also increases i.e. the probability of our selected block being already occupied increases. When a collision occurs at index2, the proposed algorithm creates a self-balancing tree connected to index2 i.e. AVL Tree data structure to handle collision. Therefore, each index of segment_value bucket points to their self-balancing tree separately. Initially, all AVL tree corresponding to each segment_value bucket is empty. Whenever the collision occurs at the index2 block, a new node is created and inserted in the tree connected to corresponding segment_value block index2.

In this paper, we handled the collision problem in logarithmic time using nonlinear data structure i.e. Tree as shown in Fig. 4. Tree stores the information in a hierarchal manner so that insertion, deletion, and searching occur in moderate time. In this paper, we used the AVL tree which is an extension of BST. In AVL tree, the cost of lookup, insert and delete operations is always in logarithmic time. It also keeps the tree balanced, unlike BST. Therefore, we applied the AVL tree to handle the collision [10].

Whenever a collision occurs for key K, the key is inserted as a new element in the AVL tree connected to the key's corresponding segment_value. The process of insertion in the tree is described in Table 3.

Initially, the root node of the balanced tree is NULL, and it expands as new elements are inserted. Each key is compared to current node key value and thus decides whether to place the key in the left subtree or in the right subtree, and this process is repeated recursively until our key is placed. The process of left rotation and right rotation is described in Table 4.

Table 3. Insertion in balanced tree

insert_node(node, K)

```
Start
if node is NULL:
        node <- newNode(K)
        return node
if K < node->K:
        insert_Node(node->left, K)
else if K > node->K:
        insert_Node(node->right, K)
else:
        return node
if (β > 1) && (K < node->left->K):
        return rightRotate(node)
if (β < -1) && (K > node->right->K):
        return leftRotate(node)
if (β > 1) && (K > node->left->K):
        (node -> left) <- leftRotate(node->left)
        return rightRotate(node)

if (β < -1) && (K < node->right->K):
        (node -> right ) <- rightRotate(node->right)
        return leftRotate(node)
return node
Stop
```

Insertion of K in AVL tree data structure takes $O(H)$ time since it has to keep the tree balanced and thus reducing the Look up time to $O(H)$. Balancing the AVL tree includes two operations i.e. rotation and height up gradation using balance factor β (-1, 0, 1). The balance factor β ensures the height difference of ± 1 or 0 between left and right sub trees to maintain the balanced tree. If not, rotation of the tree is performed to convert it from unbalanced to a balanced tree. Two types of rotations are performed to successfully balance the tree – Left Rotation as shown in Fig. 2 or Right Rotation as shown in Fig. 3 or their combination i.e. Left-Left, Left- Right, Right-Left, Right-Right. If the height of the left subtree is greater, then the right rotation operation is applied and similarly, left rotation operation is applied when the height of the right subtree is greater than the left subtree. Overall, balancing of the AVL tree takes constant time i.e. O(H) where H is the height of the tree with value LogE, where E is the number of elements inserted in the tree. Hence, the insertion in the AVL tree takes O(LogE) time [10].

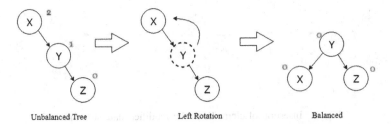

Unbalanced Tree   Left Rotation   Balanced

Fig. 2. Left rotation

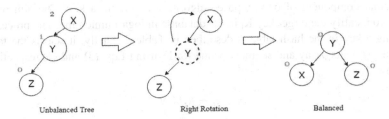

Unbalanced Tree   Right Rotation   Balanced

Fig. 3. Right rotation

Table 4. Rotation in balanced tree

leftRotate(node)	rightRotate (node)
| ```
x <- node
y <-(x -> right)
z <-(y -> left)
(y -> left) <- x
(x -> right)<- z
return y
``` | ```
x <- node
y <- (x -> left)
z <- (y -> right)
(y -> right) <- x
(x -> left) <- z
return y
``` |

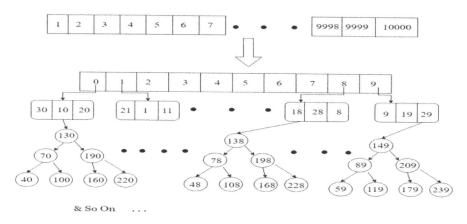

Fig. 4. Insertion of elements in the modified data structure

3.2   Search (Look up) Process

The second component of our proposed algorithm is lookup a key. The aim of the module to identify the target key K_t in the database in logarithmic time. The process of searching a key in the hash table is described in Table 5. Firstly, it selects the target index in segments_array and segment_value for K_t using Eqs. (3) and (4) respectively as follow:

$$index_t = K_t \% N \tag{3}$$

$$index_t = K_t \% M \tag{4}$$

Therefore, $index_t2$ is the target indexing where key K_t is present at the segment_value [$index_t2$] or in its connected AVL tree. If K_t is present at segment_value[$index_t2$], our algorithm will search it in O(1) time. As the size of databases is very large, there is a very low probability of successful search attempts in O(1) time due to the collision. After mismatch of K_t at segment_value[$index_t2$], K_t will be searched in corresponding AVL tree.

The process of searching K_t in the AVL tree is recursive. It starts with the root node of the AVL tree as ptr node and compares K_t with ptr node's value, where ptr is a temporary pointer that is used to point a particular node in a tree. There are two possible outcomes of this comparison either true or false. If the outcome is true, the position of K_t is found otherwise the process will continue recursively. In the recursive process, the search will move towards left subtree or right subtree depending on the value of K_t. If K_t is larger than the ptr node value then the search will be moved to the right subtree otherwise to the left subtree. Our algorithm is also able to handle the unavailability of the K_t in database i.e. it is possible that key K_t is not placed in the hash table. In this case, the proposed approach will return False indicating that the K_t is not present in the hash table in O(H) time.

Overall, the best case complexity of the proposed algorithm is O(1). In the worst case, it takes O(H) lookup time where H is the height of the tree. The height of the AVL Tree is LogE, where E is the number of elements inserted in the tree, this gives the lookup time complexity of O(log E) [10].

Table 5. Locating a key in Hash Table

search_key(K$_t$)

```
Start
indext2 <- H1(Kt)
indext2 <- H2(Kt)
if isEmpty(segments_array[indext]->
                        segment_value[indext2]):
            return False
if segments_array[indext]->segment_value[indext2]-
                            > value== Kt:
            return True
else:
            ptr=segments_array[indext]->
                        segment_value[indext2]->next_node
            if ptr->value == Kt:
                    return True
            while ptr != NULL and ptr->value != Kt:
                    if ptr->value > Kt:
                            ptr = ptr->left
                    else:
                            ptr = ptr->right
                    if ptr->value == Kt

                    return True
 return False
 Stop
```

4   Analysis of Results

In this paper, we proposed a distinctive way of implementing the hash table i.e. M-N Hashing and analyze its performance with respect to traditional hashing techniques i.e. Linear Probing, Quadratic Probing, and Separate Chaining.

4.1   System and Data Description

The system specification used for the experiments is as follow: 4 cores Intel core i7-4720HQ CPU based on Haswell architecture clocked at 2.60 GHz with 8 GB of DDR3 type memory. This CPU has L3 cache of size 6 Mbytes with 64 byte line size. The data set used for the experiment is integer type and ranged between [0 − 100000] i.e. size of the dataset D. As discussed in the previous section, segments_array and segment_value are two key components of M-N Hashing, where N and M are the size of segments_array and segment_value respectively. The value of N and M can vary according to the size of the dataset. To identify the optimal values of N & M we applied parametric tuning and based on experimental results, we used the optimal values of N and M i.e. 10 and 3 respectively in this paper.

4.2   Evaluation Parameters

To analyze the performance of algorithms, we perform I number of search iterations in our testing phase. In each iteration, selection of target key K_t is completely random. Therefore, key selection in the nth iteration is independent of the selection of the target key in other iterations. The evaluation parameter used in this paper is search time and improvement:

$$\textbf{\textit{Search Time }} T_A\left(\textbf{\textit{K}}_t\right) = \textit{Time in milliseconds required to search a}$$
$$\textit{key } K_t \textit{ in the hash table by technique A.} \tag{5}$$

In this work, we represented the total search time i.e. $\sum T_A(K_t)$ for I random keys.

$$\textbf{\textit{Improvement }} (\textbf{\textit{in }}\%) = \left(\left(T_c - T_p\right) * 100.0\right)/T_c \tag{6}$$

Where T_P is the total time taken by the proposed algorithm and T_C is the total time taken by algorithm C. Here, C is the algorithm used for the performance comparison i.e. Separate Chaining, Linear Probing or Quadratic Probing.

4.3   Time Complexity Analysis

Hashing is one of the most practically used techniques to store and retrieve data efficiently. In this technique, a hash function is designed to locate data to an index in the appropriate data structure. The basic operations of the hashing technique are creation, searching, and deletion of the key. Creation of a hash table is a one-time operation and deletion an element from the hash table is also not so frequent as compared to the search operation. Therefore, we compared search time complexity of the proposed algorithm with traditional hashing techniques such as Linear Probing, Quadratic Probing and Separate Chaining for two case scenarios i.e. best case scenario and worst case scenario. The best scenario when there is no collision. Worst case scenario when a collision occurs at every index of hash table i.e. due to the large data set. Traditional hashing techniques take O(1) constant time in the best case scenario and O(L) in the worst case scenario to perform basic operations of hashing techniques. Here, L is the size of the hash table. Whereas, the proposed algorithm takes O(1) constant time in the best case scenario and O(LogL) in the worst case scenario. In the proposed model, the number of collisions is reduced using the segment_value connected to each index of segments_array and the time complexity in searching and insertion of data is reduced to O(LogL) using the self-balancing AVL tree.

Overall, the proposed algorithm performed better than all traditional hashing techniques in worst case scenario when the size of the dataset is very large and the probability of collision is very high.

We also compared the performance of the proposed algorithm with classical algorithms in terms of search time $T_A(K_t)$ as shown in Fig. 5 using Eq. (5). Figure 5 illustrate the tradeoff between search time with respect to the size of data. Where search time is in milliseconds and the size of the dataset D varies from 0 to 100000.

It can also be depicted from Fig. 5 that as the size of the dataset increases, the time T_A required to locate target key K_t in the hash table is also increased for all three algorithms i.e. Separate Chaining, Linear Probing, and Quadratic Probing. Whereas, increment in T_A with respect to the proposed algorithm is better than all other algorithms. This improvement in search time is calculated with respect to 2 million search iterations. Table 6 describes the percentage improvement in search time i.e. calculated using Eq. (6). The proposed algorithm is able to achieve up to 99.97% improvement in search time with respect to compared algorithms.

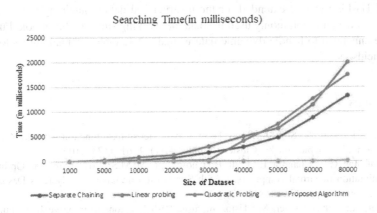

Fig. 5. Search time (in milliseconds)

Table 6. Improvement (in %) of the proposed algorithm in total search time

Size of the dataset (D)	Separate Chaining	Linear Probing	Quadratic Probing
100	65.5	87.13	31.59
1000	87.33	96.86	89.52
5000	95.86	98.93	89.53
10000	97.59	99.07	95.61
20000	98.55	99.34	96.25
40000	99.05	99.53	98.09
80000	99.42	97.97	99.54
100000	99.59	97.93	99.58

5 Conclusion

The exponential increase of data in recent years like in the field of networking, requires more profound hash table implementation. Existing hashing provides an efficient way of implementing search, insert and deletion operation in constant time for small sized datasets. However at large sized dataset the frequency of collisions increases resulting in the rise of time complexity. Therefore, in this paper, we proposed an algorithm to overcome the shortcomings of existing classical hashing techniques i.e. the collision resolution strategy, fixed hash table size, and high time complexity. M-N Hashing provides a scalable solution for collision resolution with respect to different sized datasets. The hash table will increase its size according to the number of keys inserted so, there is no restriction on the size of the dataset. We analyzed the performance of the proposed algorithm through an evaluative parameter i.e. search time complexity. Results demonstrated the considerable progress in the performance of the proposed algorithm up to 99.97% with respect to existing hashing techniques i.e. Separate Chaining, Linear Probing, and Quadratic Probing.

M-N Hashing can be extended for the unstructured data (containing images, text, videos, etc.) which is commonly used in social networking sites like Facebook. Further, it can be enhanced to handle dynamic data to make it suitable for banking sector and similar fields.

References

1. Mun, H.-J., Hong, S., Shin, J.: A novel secure and efficient hash function with extra padding against rainbow table attacks. Cluster Comput. **21**(1), 1161–1173 (2018)
2. Sapuntzakis, C.P., Chandra, R., Pfaff, B., Chow, J., Lam, M.S., Rosenblum, M.: Optimizing the migration of virtual computers. In: 5th Symposium on Operating Systems Design and Implementation, pp. 377–390 (2002)
3. Broder, A., Mitzenmacher, M.: Using multiple hash functions to improve IP lookups. In: IEEE, INFOCOM (2001), pp. 1454–1463
4. Nimbe, P., Frimpong, S.O., Opoku, M.: An efficient strategy for collision resolution in hash tables. Int. J. Comput. Appl. **99**(10), 35–41 (2014)
5. Askitis, N., Zobel, J.: Cache-conscious collision resolution in string hash tables. In: Consens, M., Navarro, G. (eds.) SPIRE 2005. LNCS, vol. 3772, pp. 91–102. Springer, Heidelberg (2005). https://doi.org/10.1007/11575832_11
6. Liu, D., Xu, S.: Comparison of hash table performance with open addressing and closed addressing: an empirical study. Int. J. Network. Distrib. Comput. **3**, 60–68 (2015)
7. Bello, S.A., Liman, A.M., Gezawa, A.S., Garba, A., Ado, A.: Comparative Analysis of Linear Probing, Quadratic Probing and Double Hashing techniques for resolving collision in a Hash table. Int. J. Sci. Eng. Res. 685–687 (2014)
8. Agarwal, A., Bhyravarapu, S., Krishna Chaitanya, N.V.: Matrix Hashing with two level of collision resolution. In: IEEE, pp. 526–532 (2018)
9. Dhar, S., Pandey, K., Premalatha, M., Suganya, G.: A tree based approach to improve traditional collision avoidance mechanisms of hashing. In: International Conference on Inventive Computing and Informatics (2017)

10. Fredman, M.L., Saks, M.E.: The cell probe complexity of dynamic data structures. In: STOC 1989 Proceedings of the Twenty-First Annual ACM Symposium on Theory of Computing, pp. 345–354 (1989)

11. Miller, J.L.: Routing cache for distributed hash tables. U.S. Patent No. 7,808,971. 5 October 2010

12. Pietrzyk, J., Ungethüm, A., Habich, D., Lehner, W.: Fighting the duplicates in hashing: conflict detection-aware vectorization of linear probing. In: Grust, T., et al. (eds.), BTW 2019. Gesellschaft für Informatik, Bonn (2019)

13. Tian, H., et al.: Dynamic- hash-table based public auditing for secure cloud storage. IEEE Trans. Serv. Comput. 10(5), 701–714 (2017)

14. Tumblin, R., Ahrens, P., Hartse, S., Robey, R.W.: Parallel compact hash algorithms for computational meshes. SIAM J. Sci. Comput. 37(1), C31–C53 (2015)

15. Zhou, Y., Gao, C.: Research and improvement of a multi-pattern matching algorithm based on double hash. In: IEEE (2017)

16. Köppl, D.: Separate chaining meets compact hashing. arXiv preprint arXiv:1905.00163 (2019)

17. Maier, T., Sanders, P., Dementiev, R.: Concurrent hash tables: fast and general (?)! ACM Trans. Parallel Comput. (TOPC) 5(4), 16 (2019)

Analysis and Identification of Relevant Variables for Precision Farming Using Harmonic Systems

Daniela López De Luise[1(✉)], Ernesto Ledesma[2], Walter Bel[2],
Eduardo Velazquez[2], and Javier Pirchi[3]

[1] CI2S Labs, Buenos Aires, Argentina
mdldl@ci2s.com.ar
[2] IDTI Lab, FCyT UADER, Oro Verde, Argentina
erneledesma@gmail.com, belwalterv@gmail.com,
eduardoantoniovelazquez@gmail.com
[3] INTA, Oro Verde, Entre Ríos, Argentina
pirchi.hector@inta.gob.ar

Abstract. This paper introduces a proposal for modeling the behavior of rice precision farming. The motivation of this researching is the requirement of an optimum balance between humidity and weather of this type of crops. The model determines patterns representing key conditions for handling specific conditions that must be critical to avoid hydric stress. The focus is on avoiding excess or scarcity of water in the plant. Besides, it is useful for determining the sampling rate. The main contribution, among other findings, is the surprisingly short timing detected (15 min). Other findings include the lack of influence of the air temperature and land temperature to wet conditions. As a consequence, there is no need to measure them. Furthermore, critical relationships were discovered and some others can be discarded due to their lack of influence in the hydric balance between the environment and the water level on land. All these can be used to define main patterns in Harmonics Systems models for making an early prediction of how is the best watering approach in rice crops. As the main contribution, besides the mentioned patterns, there is a reliable determination of sampling cycles and the reduction of relevant variables, taking certain classical measures out of consideration. Consequently, costs can be reduced and weather stations can be simpler and cheaper. At the same time, the lightweight model allows performing quicker decisions and actions on hydric levels, providing better yields and increasing production capacity. The scope of this paper includes the variable selection from the first sampling with a special weather station, variables selection, and patterns derivations but not the statistical testing of such patterns.

Keywords: Data mining · Harmonic systems · Time mining · Precision farming · Hydric balance · Rice crops

© Springer Nature Singapore Pte Ltd. 2020
P. K. Singh et al. (Eds.): FTNCT 2019, CCIS 1206, pp. 210–232, 2020.
https://doi.org/10.1007/978-981-15-4451-4_17

1 Introduction

Precision crops are increasingly being used. The agricultural industry trends to optimize productivity. There are many approaches in the field, some of them include computational intelligence techniques. For instance in Bangladesh [1] a Neuro-Fuzzy system merges Fuzzy Logic (FL) and Neural Networks (NN). It can calculate the crop yield for a given type of vegetable using sampling measures of humidity, temperature, and precipitation. The data-set used to train the system was collected through the official web site of the Bangladesh Statistical bureau.

FL was also used to model the farmer expertise on classification of the goodness of lands. To do that, a Geographical Information System was used (GIS). Classes were defined as Fuzzy Sets (FS) with membership functions for soil texture, soil depth, ground slope and to relate farmer concepts to scientific feature classifications. The defined rules are used to make inferences by combining fuzzy maps with fuzzy operators and creating land capability maps [2]. This model has been applied to asses the capability of the land for poplar hybrids in Canada, to determine the possibility of large-scale afforestation.

In [3] spatial models based on Boolean logic is used along with statistical models from a geographical information system. There is also an integrated model to predict European land usage, called ImpelERO©. It is a hybrid model using NN for decision making. The main approach of ImpelERO© consists in quantifying the land-erosion features, covering the vulnerability of the land, rate of soil loss, type of erosion risk and reduction of soil depth by using sugar beet plants [4].

But the look for watering optimization in rice crops is crucial to obtain the best yield [5–7]. Many technologies and approaches may serve to optimize hydric resources, focusing on it to obtain highest yields and at the same time-saving water [8–13].

This work introduces an approach based on a model that collects signals using a prototype with a low-cost electronic system for sampling and to keep track of different critical factors related to hydric handling in rice crops. This intends to contribute to the analysis and decision making in the risk prediction and watering procedures. The system implemented is a contribution to the local precision farming market, based on Expectation-Maximization and induction Tree J48 to drift-off the induction rules of the model.

The scope of this paper includes information collection by INTA (State Institute for agro-industrial), the problem context, the relevance of real-time control of hydric levels during rice cropping, and the need for proper decision making in order to reduce hydric stress and costs in the cultivation process. The following sections are a description of the prototype (Sect. 2), design, implementation and tests (Sect. 3), statistics and analysis (Sects. 4 and 5), and finally conclusions and future work (Sect. 6).

2 Prototype KRONOS - AGRO

This proposal introduces a prototype under development based on Arduino (c) technology and a tuned weather station to collect data on rice crops. This information is processed at the end of the harvest.

The device also has several sensors for humidity, hydric level, ground temperature, pluviometer, anemometer, ambient air temperature and ultraviolet radiation.

The input hardware is powered by a battery and a solar panel. A local memory records a data log from the activity and status. The architecture is in Fig. 1.

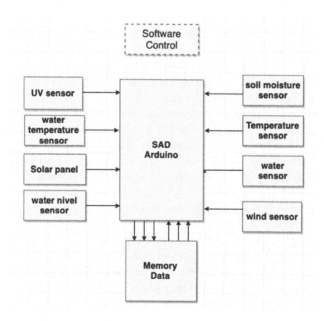

Fig. 1. Circuit architecture

2.1 Hardware and Components

The components used for the data-acquisition system are:

1. Indoor Arduino Ground-humidity sensor Ptec. Supply voltage of 5.5 V 35 mA, producing an analog output voltage that increases with the ground conductivity.
2. Ultra-violet Radiation Adafruit sensor - model ML8511. Light detection range of 280 nm to 390 nm. Provides analogue tension linearly with the UV intensity measured (mW/cm^2).
3. Temperature sensor Dallas Semiconductor DS18B20 waterproofed. Working up to 125 °C, its wire has a PVC wrapping. For that reason, it must be used under 100 °C. As it is digital, it has not any signal degradation at large distances. It can be used with a range of 3.0–5.5 V.
4. Station pluviometer Argent Data System, model WH/WS1081. The pluviometer is a type of automatic oscillating-bucket. Every 0.011″ (0.2794 mm) of rainfall, a transient contact interruption is produced. It can be recorded with a digital counter or by an input interruption in a micro-controller. The switch in the meter is connected to a couple of conducting central cables ended with an RJ11.

5. Station-anemometer Argent Data System, model PN80422. It can measure the wind speed by closing a contact any time a magnet traverses a switch. A wind-velocity of 1.492 MPH (2.4 km/h) makes the switch to close once a second. The switch of the anemometer is connected to a couple of internal connectors of an RJ11 shared with the anemometer and a weather vane (pins 2 and 3).
6. Hydric level sensor KUS, with a 240 Ω resistance floating on top, and 30 Ω on the lower part. Its power supply is 5 V.
7. Micro-controller ATmega328P Arduino© Uno. Working power of 5 V.

2.2 Localization of the Crops Tested

The tests in the field were performed in the rural area of Ubajay city (Entre Ríos province, Argentina). This region is framed in the polygon with latitude 31° 43' 58.4" S, longitude 58° 23' 55.9" W, lot of 16 ha assigned by INTA (Instituto Nacional Tecnológico Agropecuario), Concepción del Uruguay branch. It can be observed in Fig. 2. The irrigation system for the rice crops is named irrigation sleeves system [5]. The samples were collected from December 26th, 2018 until February 14th, 2019. The total number of cases is 2742.

Fig. 2. Geo-localization of the prototype. The Geo-localization is taken from agromonitoring. com.

3 Data Acquisition System

The prototype (Fig. 3) has a white rigid cabinet of size 25 cm × 25 cm made with PVC. It can resist extreme weather conditions, making it able for outdoor tests. Before the outdoor tests, several laboratory tests were performed during a week as can be seen in Fig. 3. Those tests were focused on sensors calibration, and samplings rate determination (the estimated laboratory test rate is 10 min). Data are stored in a micro SD memory, for local data persistence (a requirement for the first stage of the prototype).

3.1   Sensors Calibration

The steps performed for calibration are:

1. The hydric level: calibrated with a multi-tester under resistive modality. Then parameters with a linear transformation from 0 cm to 8 cm length were passed.
2. The anemometer is fed with linear pulses with a digital converter that registers 2 pulses every a complete round of the vane. According to Fabric specifications with a wind speed of 2,5 km/h there is 1 pulse per second.
3. The humidity sensor was calibrated with several samplings of conductivity in humid areas, with a range between 0 mv to 985 mv.
4. The pluviometer is an oscillating-bucket. It registers a pulse every complete cycle. It was calibrated with a test tube of 250 ml. There is a pulse every 0.30 mm of water.

Fig. 3. In-door tests of the acquisition data system (IDTILAB FCyT)

The Fig. 4 is a detail of the circuit implemented int the data acquisition system, designed using the editor NCR Impress©.

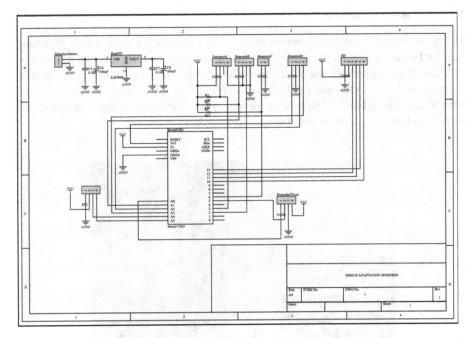

Fig. 4. Design of the printed circuit of the acquisition system

3.2 Electronics

The components were mounted on the pertinax board welded trough hole. The list is in Table 1.

Table 1. Electronic components used in the acquisition unit.

Comment	Description	Designation	Footprint	LibRef	Quantity
0.1 uF	Capacitor	C5, C7	CAP200	CAP	2
100 uF	Polarized capacitor	C6, C8	CAPPOL200	CAPPOL	2
CON2	Connector 2	Arduino input	Bornera2-T	CON2	1
CON4	Connector 4	HumiditySoil	CON4	CON4	1
10 K	Resistance	R1	RES300	RES	1
220 K	Resistance	R2	RES300	RES	1
4K7	Resistance	R3	RES300	RES	1
LM7809	Voltage regulator - positive voltage	Reg09V	TO220P	LM78XX	1
RTC	Connector 4	RTC	CON4	CON4	1
CON6	Connector 6	SD	CON6	CON6	1
CON4	Connector 4	SensorsA, sensorsB, sensorsD	BORNERA4	CON4	3
CON2	Connector 2	SensorsC	BORNERA2	CON2	1
SHIELD UNO		SHIELD UNO	SHIELD UNOS	SHIELD UNO	1

3.3   Assembly Structure

The Assembly for the data acquisition system is in Fig. 5. It has an iron base with four feet, for better stability on the floor. There is also an upper base for the data acquisition data unit. Base support has the solar panel with a telescope that can displace the unit to different angles for better solar radiation absorption. The lower base has tips of 15 cm large to provide stability when it is on the soil, where there can be irregularities of the surface and extreme weather conditions.

Fig. 5. Supporting structure for the data acquisition unit

3.4   Fit Tests

Sensors calibration occurred during the first five days of field tests. The hydric level of the sensor was adjusted by sight (see Figs. 6, 7 and 8). The sensor is on a mobile base that can be vertically displaced over a shaft. It allows several heights above the ground. During tests, a battery failure from 23:00 until 6:00 AM, and therefore there were no recordings in that period.

Fig. 6. Calibration of the sensor of hydric level

Fig. 7. SAD during the test

Fig. 8. Acquisition unit in the rice crop

4 Statistical Analysis

From data obtained in the first field test, a database was obtained. The statistics are performed with software Weka© [14].

The Expectation-Maximization analysis is the clustering technique performed with all the variables and the parameters: maximum number of iterations = 100, maximum number of clusters = −1 (that is, no limit), number of folds for cross validation = 10, ll-cv = 1.0E−6 (threshold the variation of log-likelihood to consider adding a cluster), ll-iter = 1.0E−6 (threshold in variation of log likelihood to consider switching from E and M steps), M 1.0E−6 (minimum standard deviation), number of slots 1, Seed = 100. Results are described in the following subsections.

4.1 Variable

All the variables were considered. They are a total of 12 variables: Mes (month), Día (day), Hora (Time), Minuto (minute), Humedad Ambiente (humidity), Temperatura Ambiente (temperature), Humedad Suelo (soil humidity), Temperatura de suelo (soil temperature), Radiación UV (UV radiation), Sensor nivel hídrico (hydric level), Anemómetro (anemometer), Pluviómetro (pluviometer). All the instances of the recordset were processed.

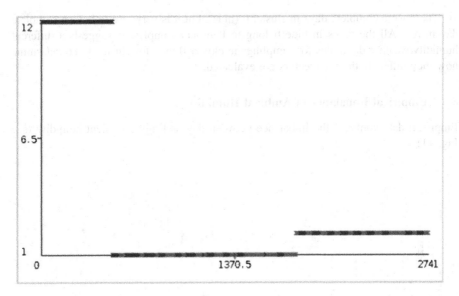

Fig. 9. Clusters obtained with EM (Color figure online)

4.2   Clusters

Two clusters arise from the EM analysis with all the variables (see Fig. 9).

The figure shows with blue cluster 0 and red for cluster 1. All the instances from December are in cluster 0. Months January and February (1 and 2) are alternates of both clusters. This indicates that December had differentiated behavior.

When studying the behavior hour by hour during a month, there is also a typical distribution (see Fig. 10).

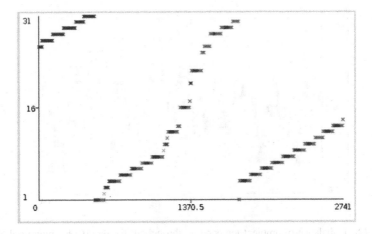

Fig. 10. Hour distribution according to the day in the month (Color figure online)

There were complete days in cluster 0 (blue), but it is very rare to have a complete day in red. All the cases in blue belong to February samples. It suggests a different humidity/weather dynamics for samplings in cluster 0 than for cluster 1. To determine how they differ, both eigenvectors are evaluated.

4.3   Empirical Imbalance of Ambient Humidity

Empirical data confirms the imbalance between day and night ambient humidity (see Fig. 11).

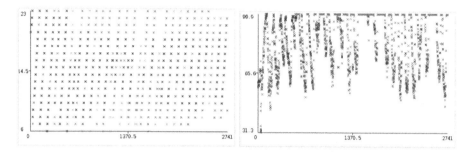

Fig. 11. Unbalance of ambient humidity (Color figure online)

It can be observed that only after December there are red dots (excess water). Humidity indicators fall to lowest levels typical in blue points (hydric stress).

Red points (cluster 1) indicate humidity near 100% (that means high probability of rain).

Figure 12 shows the distribution of ambient temperature along the day.

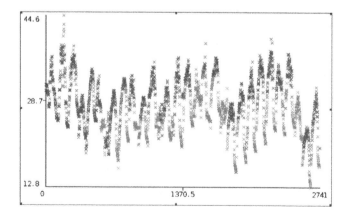

Fig. 12. Unbalance of ambient temperature throughout the day (Color figure online)

Red dots do not correspond to higher temperatures but to days after high temperatures combined with high humidity. Further analysis show there is a correlation between soil temperature and ambient temperature (see Fig. 13).

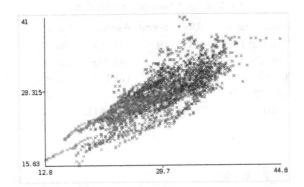

Fig. 13. Correlation between soil temperature and ambient temperature (Color figure online)

4.4   Discussion of Results

From Figs. 9, 10, 11 and 12 it can be said that:

- Cluster distribution indicates independence between ambient and soil temperature
- There is a typical humidity distribution on the day after high temperature and humidity
- There is no dependency between ambient and soil humidity
- There is no direct relationship between temperature and humidity
- Cluster distribution shows a relationship between water excess and a combination of time, radiation and ambient humidity.

Respecting average and standard deviation of variables of both clusters:

- The pluviometer level is quite different
- The anemometer level is different
- Ambient temperature is different
- Hydric level matches
- Radiation level matches
- Soil temperature matches
- Ambient humidity is different
- Times are different: cluster 1 (red dots in figures) represent later hours than in cluster 0 (blue dots)

For both clusters humidity distribution have similar higher scores (above 525 mv, millivolts), but cluster 1 has fewer records with scarce humidity in the ground.

From the listed items, it can be said that EM has determined a model that differentiates the hydric level according to the water level, and found two main behaviors: cluster 1, representing humidity stress in the environment but not in the soil; and cluster

0 with no stress. It appears also that hydric level must be complemented to properly predict changes in the humidity.

Also, soil humidity has an interesting distribution depicted in Table 2 and Fig. 14.

Table 2. Soil humidity distribution.

Lower-bound	Upper-bound	Average	Label
'(−inf–291.75]'	685.5019	391.4981	Blue
'(291.75–535.5]'	816.0633	483.9367	Red
'(535.5–779.25]'	147.8226	161.1774	Turquoise
'(779.25–inf)'	54	10	Green
[total]	1703.3877	1046.6123	

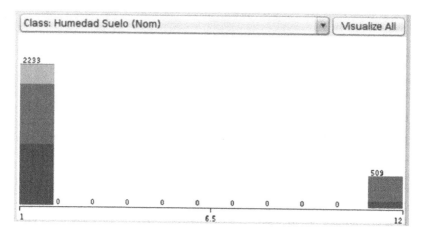

Fig. 14. Soil humidity distribution. (Color figure online)

In the Figure, x-ax represents the soil humidity and the different colors the accumulated hydric level. It shows that hydric level sensor can't discriminate in time when the humidity level is low. Note that there are days with only blue dots and others with red dots (when there is hydric stress).

This can be due to a slow reaction to the different climate factors and its effects in the soil and crop.

Figure 15 shows the minute-by-minute humidity variation, corroborating that the reaction timing is affecting the dryness. In the figure Y-ax represent the hour of the day, and X-ax the humidity variation.

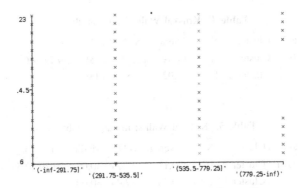

Fig. 15. Variation of the humidity minute-by-minute.

It is important to note that sampling must be reduced from the current dairy or per-hour rate to 15 min. Table 3 shows the Hour and Minute average and Standard Deviations.

Table 3. Distribution of soil humidity.

	Cluster 0	Cluster 1
Hour		
Mean	14.54	16.13
Std. Dev.	3.73	5.56
Minute		
Mean	30.16	30.47
Std. Dev.	17.23	17.40

The difference between clusters is not relevant, then the averaged time in both clusters is the same (15 h 34 min), the time of higher humidity stress. The averaged Minutes is also statistically the same, about 30.31 min, with a Standard deviation of 17.3 min each one.

From the previous statistics it can be said that sampling rate must be about 13 min 1 sec to be able to adjust effectors to rapid changes. During the test certain changes where collected every 10 min along with a total of 1539 h. Due to the battery failure, the sensing stopped from 23 h to 6 h approximately, producing delayed reactions, and temporary humidity stress reflected in the red dots (cluster 1 of the Figs. 9, 10, 11, 12 and 13).

4.5 Validation of the Results - Krustall Wallis on the Original Dataset

The original data distribution was analyzed with Krustall Walls (nonparametric variance on two samples), considering dependent variables the humidity level of the soil. The result is that soil humidity, hydric level, and pluviometer have significant variations (see p-value of every case in Tables 4, 5, 6, 7, 8, 9, 10, 11, 12 and 13).

Table 4. Kruskal Walis: hour variable.

Variable	Cluster	N	Average	S.D.	Median	H	p
TIME	Cluster 0	1675	14,59	3,74	15,00	59,77	<0,0001
	Cluster 1	1067	16,02	5,54	17,00		

Table 5. Kruskal Wallis: minute variable.

Variable	Cluster	N	Average	S.D.	Median	H	p
MINUTE	Cluster 0	1675	30,18	17,21	30,00	0,29	0,5951
	Cluster 1	1067	30,43	17,44	30,00		

Table 6. Krustall Wallis: environment humidity variable.

Variable	Cluster	N	Average	S.D.	Median	H	p
Ambient humidity	Cluster 0	1675	77,11	13,83	76,60	1915,20	<0,0001
	Cluster 1	1067	99,90	1,6E−12	99,90		

Table 7. Kruskal Wallis: room temperature.

Variable	Cluster	N	Average	S.D.	Median	H	p
Ambient temperature	Cluster 0	1675	29,88	4,35	30,00	778,40	<0,0001
	Cluster 1	1067	24,52	4,01	24,40		

Table 8. Kruskal Wallis: soil humidity variable.

Variable	Cluster	N	Average	S.D.	Median	H	p
Soil humidity	Cluster 0	1675	0,74	0,74	1,00	6,23	0,2657
	Cluster 1	1067	0,80	0,72	1,00		

Table 9. Kruskal Wallis: soil temperature variable.

Variable	Cluster	N	Average	S.D.	Median	H	p
Soil temperature	Cluster 0	1675	28,99	3,63	29,00	770,18	<0,0001
	Cluster 1	1067	24,92	2,97	25,38		

Table 10. Kruskal Wallis: radiation ultra violet variable.

Variable	Cluster	N	Average	S.D.	Median	H	p
UV radiation	Cluster 0	1675	2,12	1,55	1,87	336,64	<0,0001
	Cluster 1	1067	1,11	1,22	0,42		

Table 11. Kruskal Wallis: water level variable.

Variable	Cluster	N	Average	S.D.	Median	H	p
Hydric level	Cluster 0	1675	21,83	16,21	21,60	46,11	<0,0001
	Cluster 1	1067	16,24	16,80	9,41		

Table 12. Kruskal Wallis: anemometer variable.

Variable	Cluster	N	Average	S.D.	Median	H	p
Anemometer	Cluster 0	1675	8,53	7,34	7,00	179,08	<0,0001
	Cluster 1	1067	5,57	7,52	2,00		

Table 13. Kruskal Wallis: pluviometer variable

Variable	Cluster	N	Average	S.D.	Median	H	p
Pluviometer	Cluster 0	1675	0,22	0,94	0,00	5,95	0,5799
	Cluster 1	1067	1,46	4,81	0,00		

To perform this analysis Day and Month were not considered.

4.6 Krustall Wallis of Each Cluster

The same analysis was repeated for each cluster. The result is similar in both cases. Despite the Time, Humidity of Soil and Pluviometer have different statistical description, the regression model does not detect those difference as significant for detection the Hydric Level, but they are significant to determine the Hour.

4.7 Conclusions of the Analysis

It was shown that both clusters represent different behavior of humidity and water in soil and raining intensity. Cluster 0 has typically lower levels of pluviometer and soil humidity.

Statistics can't determine the relationships between the rest of the variables in the EM model, because they have a higher bias. A priori it can be said the behaviors in both clusters are different but it remains to verify if the rest of the features are also significant as the preliminary ones.

5 Model for Predicting Water Stress

According to the previous statistics an induction Tree was feed with the relevant variables of the test. The attributes considered were 11, 2742 instances collected during the test.

The data-set was used entirely to build the model of a J48 pruned tree.

Variables considered are: Month (Mes), Day (Días), Hour (Hora), Minute (Minuto), Ambient Humidity (Humedad Ambiente), Ambient Temperature (Temperatura Ambiente), Soil Humidity (Humedad Suelo), Soil Temperature (Temperatura Suelo), Ultra Violet Radiation (Radiación UV), Anemometer (Anemometro) and Pluviometer (Pluviómetro).

The resulting tree is in Figs. 16, 17, 18 and 19 with a number of 57 Leaves and a total size of the tree of 113.

The summary of the model is:

Correctly Classified Instances: 2693 (98.213%)
Incorrectly Classified Instances: 49 (1.787%)
Kappa statistic: 0.9706
Mean absolute error: 0.0165
Root mean squared error: 0.09
Relative absolute error: 5.4258%
Root relative squared error: 23.3%
Total Number of Instances: 2742

The detailed Accuracy By Class is in Table 14, and the confusion matrix in Table 15.

Table 14. Rates of precision and recall for the J48 model

TP rate	FP rate	Precision	Recall	F-measure	MCC	ROC area	PRC area	Class
0.987	0.005	0.992	0.987	0.989	0.982	0.999	0.998	'(−inf–291.75]'
0.988	0.021	0.977	0.988	0.982	0.966	0.994	0.991	'(291.75–535.5]'
0.945	0.004	0.967	0.945	0.956	0.950	0.993	0.961	'(535.5–779.25]'
0.968	0.000	1.000	0.968	0.984	0.983	1.000	0.996	'(779.25–inf)'
Weighted avg.	0.982	0.012	0.982	0.982	0.982	0.971	0.996	0.990

Table 15. Confusion matrix of J48

a	b	c	d	Classified as
1061	14	0	0	a = '(−inf–291.75]'
7	1282	9	0	b = '(291.75–535.5]'
1	16	290	0	c = '(535.5–779.25]'
1	0	1	60	d = '(779.25–inf)'

5.1   Rules Based on Hour and Minute

Due to the lack of historical information about weather conditions in the region, it was not possible to validate the information with external references. Therefore, the model is taken as an a-priory information. It mainly affects the processing of ultraviolet radiation and its effects on the conditions, thus relaying the model on the most biased variables Hour and Minute.

The Table 16 shows the original variable ranges and relationships where each entry represent a branch in the J48 Tree, and therefore a rule and a potential pattern for the predictive Harmonic System (HS) **KRONOS**.

Table 17 has highlighted the most trivial entries that were collapsed to the closest entry conditions in other branches.

Table 18 has the final relationships among variables of the model, there every entry is a pattern in the HS.

Figures 16, 17, 18 and 19 show the tree graph of the J48 model.

Table 16. Original variable distribution and relationships.

TIME	MINUTE	Amb. Humidity	Amb. Temperature	Hydric Level	Soil Temperature	UV Radiation	Anemomet.	Pluviometer	W	Err	Low	Med.	High
>6					<=26.31	<=8			20.0	3.0	SI		
<=7				<=9.2	<=30.63	<=0.61		<=0	13.0		SI		
>7						<=0.61			3.0				
<=8			>25.9		<=18.06	>0.11			52.0			SI	
<=8			>25.9	>9.63	>18.06	<=0.11	<=13		62.0		SI		
<=8			>25.9	<=9.63		<=0.11	>13		911.0	2.0	SI		
<=8	<=18	>90.9		<=21.82					8.0	1.0	SI		
<=8	>18			<=21.82					6.0		SI		
<=8				>21.82					7.0	1.0	SI		
>8			<=25.9						10.0		SI		
>8			>28.8	>21.82		<=4.16			65.0	1.0		SI	
>8			>23.5	<=21.82					7.0			SI	
>8				>21.82					21.0	1.0	SI	SI	
>8			<=16.8		<=19.88		<=1		5.0	1.0		SI	
>8			>16.8				>1		12.0				SI
>8	>48			>36.58	<=20.75				31.0	1.0	SI		
<=9							>19		3.0		SI	SI	
<=9	>48	<=23.5		<=21.6	>21.19				5.0		SI		
<=9	>2		<=26.1				>3		6.0		SI		
<=9				>21.6					3.0		SI		
>9	<=23			<=21.82					8.0		SI		
>9	>2		<=26.1						14.0	3.0		SI	
<=10						<=1.64	>3		2.0		SI		
<=10						>1.64	<=19		22.0		SI		
<=10		<=90.9		>0.23	<=26.25				7.0		SI		

Table 17. Collapsed variable relationships

TIME	MINUTE	Amb. Humidity	Amb. Temperature	Hydric Level	Soil Temperature	UV Radiation	Anemomet.	Pluviometer	W	Err	Low	Med.	High
<=10		<=99.2			<=23.75		>3		2.0			SI	
<=10			>22.7						3.0		SI		
<=10					>23.75				7.0		SI		
<=10									3.0		SI		
>10	<=48			<=36.58	>19.69				103.0			SI	
>10		>99.2				>4.96			16.0		SI		
<=11					>26.31		>8		53.0	1.0	SI		
>11					<=25.5				6.0		SI		
>11		<=98.6	<=28	<=21.82	> 25.5		<=8		2.0	1.0	SI		
>11		>98.6	>28				>8		34.0		SI		
<=12								> 3.35	10.0	2.0	SI		
<=13	>1	> 63.1	>28.5						19.0		SI		
>12								> 3.35	10.0		SI		
<=13			>35.3						8.0			SI	
>13									15.0			SI	
>13	>1				<= 27.5				3.0		SI		
>13				>0.23					11.0		SI		
>13		<=69					>3.36		5.0		SI		
>13		>69							3.0		SI		
<=14				>21.82					2.0			SI	
<=14			>29.2						6.0		SI		
>14				>21.82					11.0		SI		
<=16				>21.82	> 27.56	<= 0.42			5.0		SI		
<=16				>21.82	> 0.42		<=2		4.0	2.0	SI		
<=16				>21.82	<= 27.56				6.0		SI		

Table 18. Aggregation for patterns in the HS

TIME	MINUTE	Amb. Humidity	Amb. Temperature	Hydric Level	Soil Temperature	UV Radiation	Anemomet.	Pluviometer	W	Err	Low	Med.	High
<=16	0	<=85.7	<=29.1	<=0.23		>1.49	>0		64.0	6.0	SI		
<=16	0	>81.2	<=22.5						12.0		SI		
<=16	0			<=21.82					2.0			SI	
<=16	>2	>81.2	>27.3	<=0.0	>25.25	>1.66	>0		248.0	11.0	SI		
>16		>78.1	>32.9		>28.94		>20		48.0		SI		
>16	<2	>80.8	<=22.3	>0.2	<=28.94		<=20		652.0	1.0	SI		
>16	<=37	<=85.4	<=22.7	>21.82	<=24.44				141.0	1.0	SI		
>16		>85.4		>21.82					17.0		SI		
>16			<=29.2		>23.25	<=0.57	>12		21.0	1.0		SI	
>16		<=66.1						> 0.28	29.0	1.0			SI
>16		>66.1		<=21.39				>3.91	99.0		SI		
>16			<=34	<=21.39		<=2.1	<=3	<= 0.56	5.0		SI		
>16			>34	>21.39				<= 3.91	580.0	4.0	SI		
>16			>29.2	<=0.23	>30.63				22.0		SI		
>18	<=1		<= 32.6	>9.83				<= 0.28	20.0		SI		
>18	>1		>26.9	<=21.82	<=29.31	<=0.84			23.0		SI		
>16	>1	<=79.2	<=28.5	<=21.82		>0.84			26.0	1.0		SI	
<=16			>32.7	>0.03	>28.56				215.0	1.0	SI		
<=18			>26.6	<=0.23	<=28.56				31.0	3.0	SI		
>18			<=23.6	<=21.82	<=23.75	<=0.27			54.0	3.0	SI		
>18			>23.6	<=21.82		<=0.27			46.0	3.0	SI		
>18				<=21.82		>0.27			4.0		SI		
<=18		>0.75	<= 32.9	>21.82	>26.19				280.0	3.0	SI		
<=21					>19.88				11.0	1.0		SI	
> 21				<=21.82					15.0			SI	

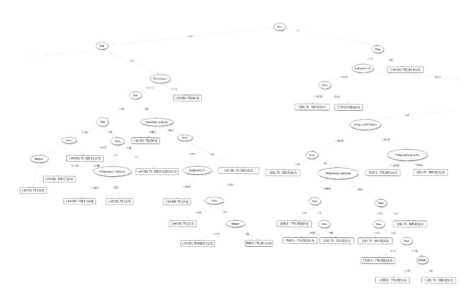

Fig. 16. Root and main nodes of J48 model

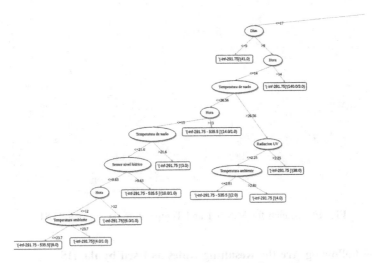

Fig. 17. Branch for Mes <= 1 and Día <= 17

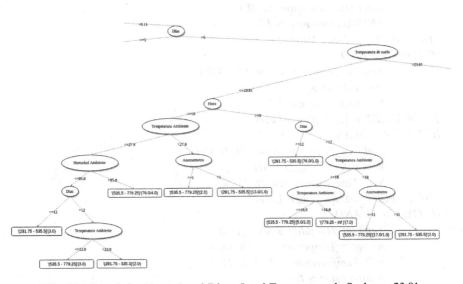

Fig. 18. Branch for Mes > 1 and Día > 5 and Temperatura de Suelo <= 23.81

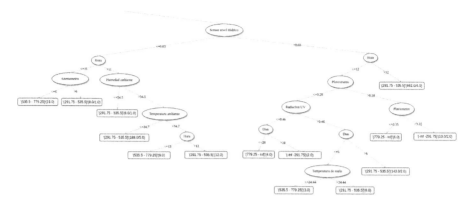

Fig. 19. Branch for Mes > 1 and Temperatura de Suelo > 23.81

5.2 The Following Are the Resulting Rules as Used by the HS

IF TIME <= 8 AND Ambient_Temperature > 25.9 AND
        Water_level <= 9.63
        AND UV_Radiation <= 0.11
        AND Anemometer > 13
THEN ALERT = Low_Water_Level
IF TIME > 8 AND
        Ambient_Temperature > 28.8 AND
        Water_level > 21.82 AND
        UV_Radiation <= 4.16
THEN ALERT = Low_Water_Level
IF TIME <= 10 AND
        Ambient_Temperature <= 90.9 AND
        Water_level > 0.23 AND
        Soil_Temperature <= 28.25
THEN ALERT = Low_Water_Level
IF TIME > 11 AND
        Ambient_Humidity > 98.6 AND
        Ambient_Temperature > 28 AND
        Soil_Temperature > 25.5 AND
        Anemometer > 8
THEN ALERT = Low_Water_Level

IF TIME >= 16 AND
        Ambient_Humidity > 81.2 AND
        Ambient_Temperature > 27.2 AND
        Water_level <= 0.0 AND
        Soil_Temperature > 26.25 AND
        UV_Radiation > 4.66 AND
        Anemometer > 9
THEN ALERT = Low_Water_Level
IF TIME > 16 AND
        Ambient_Humidity > 60.8 AND
        Ambient_Temperature <= 22.3 AND
        Water_level > 9.2 AND
        Soil_Temperature <= 28.94 AND
        Anemometer <= 20 THEN
ALERT = Low_Water_Level
IF TIME > 16 AND
        Ambient_Temperature > 34 AND
        Water_level > 21.39
THEN ALERT = Medium_Water_Level
IF TIME > 18 AND
        Low_Water_Level > 97.6 AND
        Ambient_Temperature <= 32.9 AND
        Water_level > 21.82 AND
        Soil_Temperature > 26.19
THEN ALERT = Low_Water_Level
IF TIME >= 21 AND
        Soil_Temperature > 19.88
THEN ALERT = Medium_Water_Level

6 Conclusions and Future Work

This paper introduces a preliminary field test with the first weather station as a **KRONOS** acquisition module for rice crops. An initial data set was obtained and statistically analyzed. The first rules for HS were derived after the determination of the relevant variables from the test. These variables were processed with a J48 induction tree in order to predict hydric stress based on a reduced and simplified set of variables. The first findings indicate that:

- sampling rate must be dramatically reduced from a daily basis to 15 min
- that radiation can be taken with UV giving results similar to that in the classical papers of the field where global radiation is considered
- that there is a simple combination of soil/ambient temperature that can be used to predict hydric stress (detailed rules of prediction are in Table 18).

There are certain electronic improvements pending like the battery, to get a complete data compilation along all day. The UV sensor must be compared in performance for the model against other radiation sensors, a shield of communication GPRS/3G to send data in a real-time fashion and a PH sensor to complete the parameters. From the first rule set the patterns obtained must be tested and afterward tested against the same data-sets. Also, the variables will be fuzzified to include them in the fuzzy patterns and be able to process also with Fuzzy Harmonic Systems (FHS) and compare scoring against FH and other models.

References

1. Fahim J., et al.: Analysis of optimum crop cultivation using fuzzy system. In: 2016 IEEE ICIS 2016. Okayama, Japan. Department of Electrical and Computer Engineering North South University, Dhaka (2016)
2. Sicat, S., Carranza, M., Nidumolu, U.: Fuzzy modeling of farmers' knowledge for land suitability classification. National Economic and Development Authority (NEDA), Zamboanga City, Philippines (2004)
3. Joss, B., Hall, R., Sidders, D., Keddy, J.: Fuzzy-logic modeling of land suitability for hybrid poplar across the Prairie Provinces of Canada (2017)
4. Afshar, E., Mehrdad, Y., Bagherzadeh, Reza S., Bahram, M.: The effects of cropping systems on soil erosion risks and crop productivity using ImpelERO model and GIS in northeast of Iran. Model. Earth Syst. Environ. 2, 164 (2016). https://doi.org/10.1007/s40808-016-0142-6
5. Bouman, B., Tuong, T.: Field water management to save water and increase its productivity in irrigated lowland rice. Soil and Water Sciences Division, International Rice Research Institute, Makati Central Post Off.Philippines (2000)
6. Domingos, G., Cerri, P., Magalhaes, G.: La Aplicación de la Agricultura de Precisión en Cultivos de Caña de Azúcar en BrasilFacultad de Ingeniería Agrícola – Unicamp – Campinas – SP – Brasil (2001
7. Liu, M., Dannenmann, M., Lin, S., Saiz, G.: Ground cover rice production systems increase soil carbon and nitrogen stocks at regional. College of Resource and Environmental Science, China Agricultural University, Beijing, China (2015)
8. Mauricio González, B., Ana Milena, A.: Tecnologías para ahorrar agua en el cultivo de arroz. Fondo Francisco José de Caldas, Colciencias-SENA, SENAGROTIC, Centro Agropecuario "La Granja", SENA (2016)
9. Yao, Z., et al.: Water-saving ground cover rice production system reduces net greenhouse gas fluxes in an annual rice-based cropping system. State Key Laboratory of Atmospheric Boundary Layer Physics and Atmospheric Chemistry (2013)
10. Yousef, E., Hamouda, M.: Smart Irrigation Decision Support based on Fuzzy Logic using Wireless Sensor Network. Computer Department Al-Aqsa University Gaza, Palestine (2017)
11. Tarange, P.H., Mevekari, R.G., Shinde, P.A.: Web based automatic irrigation system using wireless sensor network and embedded Linux board. In: IEEE International Conference on Circuit, Power and Computing Technologies (ICCPCT) (2015)
12. Ali, M.H.: Practices of Irrigation & On-farm Water Management, vol. 2. Springer, New York (2011). https://doi.org/10.1007/978-1-4419-7637-6
13. Bandeira, S., Böcking, B.: Riego de arroz por mangas Donistar S. en C, Salto-R.O.U. (2014)
14. Witten, I., Frank, E., Hall, M.: Data Mining: Practical Machine Learning Tools and Techniques, vol. 3. Elsevier, Amsterdam (2011)

A Smart Industrial Pollution Detection and Monitoring Using Internet of Things (IoT)

E. Udayakumar[1]([⊠]), S. Tamilselvan[1], K. Srihari[2],
G. Venkata Koti Reddy[2], and S. Chandragandhi[3]

[1] KIT-Kalaignarkarunanidhi Institute of Technology,
Coimbatore, Tamilnadu, India
udayakumar.sujith@gmail.com,
tamilselvanece87@gmail.com
[2] SNS College of Engineering, Coimbatore, Tamilnadu, India
harionto@gmail.com, gvkotireddy@gmail.com
[3] JCT College of Engineering and Technology, Coimbatore, Tamilnadu, India
chandragandhi09@gmail.com

Abstract. In this paper an information securing framework which will gauge certain parameters in every condition is proposed for ventures. WSN has been utilized to gather a physical wonder in shifts application, for example, living space observing. By utilizing Time Division Multiple Access (TDMA) GSM framework was created as advanced framework which is utilized. The IoT empowers physical gadgets, vehicles, home apparatuses, different things Embedded with electronic programming, sensor actuators to interface trade information. The ongoing information from nature is gathered by PIC and sensors. By zigbee show arduino works goes about as a base station which accumulates number of passed on sensor a considerable number reports verifying.

Keywords: WSN · Data acquisition · Zigbee · Time Division Multiple Access · IoT

1 Introduction

Fast assessment of remote sensor system and information obtaining framework, the new circuits permitting increasingly computational power, higher transmission separations and exactness estimations with lower control utilizations. All these raising the need of remote access quickened the reconciliation of remote systems and remote hubs in the developing universe of Internet of Things (IOT). IOT organizations that offer fast return and empower producers to acknowledge computerized change from a few points of view, for example, effectiveness, computerization, client centricity, aggressive advantages [1]. Air pollution is the most concerning issue of every nation, paying little heed to cause medical issues in various industrial areas. The pollution from vehicles and various other sound and noise pollution will lead to the death of humans. So we have to be more cautious and aware to stop these extreme disasters. The rule goal of IOT Air and Sound Monitoring System is that the Air and sound tainting is a creating

© Springer Nature Singapore Pte Ltd. 2020
P. K. Singh et al. (Eds.): FTNCT 2019, CCIS 1206, pp. 233–242, 2020.
https://doi.org/10.1007/978-981-15-4451-4_18

issue these days. It is central to screen air quality and screen it for an unrivaled future and strong living for all. As a result of flexibility and minimal effort Internet of things (IoT) is getting celebrated well ordered. With the urbanization and with the development in the vehicles on road the climatic conditions have stunningly impacted.

Examination of checking information enables us to survey how terrible air contamination and sound contamination is from everyday. The field of ecological parameters checking is of high intrigue these days. Research exercises produce new advancements, arrangements and techniques to expand dependability, straightforwardness and vitality proficiency. The sensor organizes equipment stages are essentially low-control installed frameworks with some various sensors, for instance, on board sensors and straightforward I/O ports to relate sensors. Like gear, programming should in like manner be made, including OS, sensor/hardware drivers, sorting out shows and application-express distinguishing and getting ready figurings. The Zigbee is an anomalous state correspondence shows used to make remote systems. Transmission divisions to 10–100 meters relying on power yield and normal properties, zigBee gadgets can transmit information over long separations by going information through a work sort out topology.

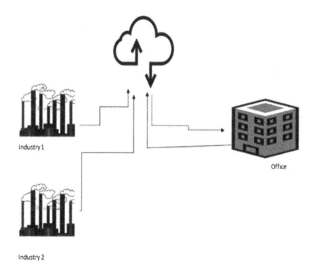

Fig. 1. Schematic diagram

The zigbee transmission information rate is 250 Kbit/s. For transmit and get the information of sensor respects zigbee is utilized [5]. The genuine schematic outline is appeared in the Fig. 1.

The business meters available in the market are Fluke CO-220 carbon monoxide meter for CO, Amprobe CO2 m for CO2, LPG gas spillage sensor alert for LPG spillage distinguishing proof. The investigators in this field have proposed diverse air quality checking structures subject to WSN, GSM Presently every innovation has restricted uses as per the proposed capacity, as Zigbee is intended for clients with Zigbee trans-recipient, Bluetooth. GIS based framework is de-marked, actualized and tried to screen the pinpoints of air contamination of any region. It comprises of a microcontroller, gas sensors, portable unit, a brief memory cushion and a web server with web network which gathers information from various areas alongside facilitate's data at certain time of multi day.

The global position system helps us to avoid various disturbances and pollution issues in the city. The public should be aware of the consequences and impact of the pollution and various hazardous issues. GPRS also helps us to prevent the pollution (Noise and Air). Technologies are applied to prevent the harmful effects in the society. The contamination level of carbon di-oxide, LPG can be prevented.

2 Related Work

In [12] the originator explains that in remote sensor arrange structure, the sensor center sense the data from the sensor and that data assembles the end marks, end names send its data to the switch and change to facilitator and supply multi-clients affiliations including data appear, the whole data will be confirmed in base station and the set away data will send to the cloud (Ethernet) and the client can visit the base station remotely through (site) Ethernet. Such a sensor is temperature, vibration, weight, doused quality, light, and sullying. In [3] the producer screens essentially water parameter. The teaching stage gives fusing frameworks a systems for revealing watched or perceived water sullying occasions by strategies for SMS observes. In [14] the producers present a WSN based water condition checking structure submitted for water quality estimation.

The structure implements WSN sensors, concentrates on base station, far station checking, SMS alerts. The design explains the estimation of transducers, a MSP430 controller is a module and a CC2530 is a remote processor. The alignment explains the detail about CC2530 controllers for third generation technologies along with ARM32 micro controller. In [15] a neat WSN framework is explained and it also explains about raspberry pi which is used for the implementation of various advanced level technology and security. The real time system for various applications of Raspberry is used to implement in the work for the authorization of the work. The IoT implemented system along with controller will provide effective and efficient methods for implementation. So as a result we will get an optimum solution. The IoT system is generally used for many medical and real time applications. The system is also provides many solution in aerospace engineering. Many researchers have concluded that for implementing IoT along with block chain technologies. The security part is handled by block chain. Equilibrium is the software used to implement block chain [12].

As the enthusiasm of limitless wellspring of essentialness has snatched the eye of different industry players and government bodies far and wide, the effort in decreasing sullying and utilization in increasing end-customer sand close-by masses with clean feasible power source have transformed into a benchmark in setting up another time of sensible society that is normally insightful. A bounteous of research has been begun with a moving disposition in examining elective ways to deal with abuse the previously mentioned wellspring of imperativeness. The advantages of centrality get-together have been ordinarily fathomed on an inexorably obvious scale the degree that the bringing down of ozone depleting substance floods, vitality security and the flood impacts, yet the effect of such essentialness structure for a littler scale application, for example. A critical rate ways of thinking will be talked about and looked in the subsequent [14].

This paper incorporates an idea of implanting a controller at the transmitter side. Actually when the defilement level evaluated by the sensor crosses the most extreme zigbee transmit the data to the beneficiary [7]. At the recipient side arduiouno sends data to IOT where the data is taken care of in the cloud similarly as SMS is send to the stress master. Right when this happens for different occasions arduino sends a sign to the transmitter where the PIC sends a control sign to close the power supply of the business similarly as the water supply is in like manner halted [3].

3 System Designs

Remote sensor center points can be part into two fragments as differently featured working area. A center that have static data plan, a fixed model rate and not able to decipher data or execute critical predictions. The programmable sensor hub is taken into consideration. These hubs that have an adaptable information design, an adaptable example rate and can run calculations and fundamental arithmetic capacities. Other than the contributions, in the correspondence between with different hubs or doors the hub edge arrangement and substance can be exclusively characterized. In the transmitter part gas, temperature, sound and pH sensor is utilized. All these sensor re remote sensor in which gas sensor is non-programmable sensor and remaining sensor are programmable sensor. Non-programmable sensor can screen various types of lethal gases, for example, sulfide, alkali gas, benzene arrangement steam and CO_2. The identification range is 10–10,000 ppm with the voltage pace of about 5.0 V $\pm$ 0.1 V AC or DC. The temperature sensor which is a programmable sensor is precision fused circuit temperature devices produces a voltage which can be considered [8].

The low-yield impedance, straight yield and precise trademark modification of the LM35 contraption makes interfacing to readout or control equipment are especially basic. Sound sensor can be utilized for sonic light, with photosensitive sensors go about as sound and light alert, additionally can be utilized in the event of voice control and sound location. The mechanical pH terminal is made of touchy glass film with low impedance. It tends to be utilized in an assortment of PH estimations with quick reaction and fantastic warm soundness. It has great reproducibility, is hard to hydrolysis, and can kill fundamental soluble base mistake. PIC16f877a finds its applications in a huge number of devices. It is used in remote sensors, security and prosperity devices, home automation and in various current instruments [9]. Forget and transmit data zigbee is used as remote correspondence. ZigBee show layers rely upon OSI model.

At the beneficiary side zigbee gets the information and it sends to arduinouno where it contains at mega 328 microcontroller. Arduniouno sends the information to the IOT module where the information is put away consequently in the cloud. At whatever point the information is required it very well may be recovered from the cloud [10]. At the

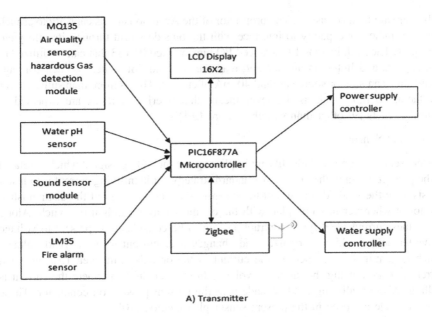

A) Transmitter

Fig. 2. Proposed block diagram of the transmitter

point when the sensor worth crosses the utmost through GSM messages will be send to the worry specialist. At the point when this occurs for multiple times the work that will be done in the business is naturally halted by sending message through zigbee to the transmitter where the water supply is ceased and power is closed down which is constrained by the PIC. The block diagram of transmitter is shown in Figs. 2 and 3.

To accomplish our proposed framework need to utilize Arduino microcontroller 328, current sensor, sunlight based, battery, LCD. Typically burden takes power supply from matrix. DC battery utilized for capacity reason. The square graph of vitality gathering utilizing IoT is appeared in Fig. 1. DC to AC converter is utilized to change over sustainable power source to air conditioning vitality. IOT is utilized to send the determined measure of sustainable power source use. Voltage sensor is utilized to quantify the line voltage. Here current sensor is utilized for shield the gadgets from deficiencies like 1. over voltages 2. under voltage. On the off chance that any of the above issue happens the gadget is consequently offer or turn off the gadget. Controller status and everything is shown in LCD. The entire procedure is constrained by microcontroller. The information sent to the cloud for consistently we can get to the site at anyplace [8].

A. Arduino Microcontroller

The Arduino microcontroller is a simple to utilize yet amazing single board PC that has increased significant footing in the side interest and expert market. The Arduino is open source, which means equipment is sensibly valued and improvement programming is free. This guide is for understudies in ME 2011, or understudies anyplace who are standing up to the Arduino just because [7]. For cutting edge Arduino clients, lurk the web; there are loads of assets. The proprietor of the Arduino isn't its capacity to crunch code, yet rather its capacity to interface with the outside world through its info yield (I/O) pins. The Arduino has 14 advanced I/O pins marked 0 to 13 that can be utilized to turn engines and lights on and off and read the condition of switches. Each computerized stick can sink or source around 40 mA of current. This is more than sufficient for interfacing to most gadgets, however means that interface circuits are expected to control gadgets [9] other than straightforward LED's.

B. Current Sensor

Current sensor is a present identifying implies age of the voltage signal which is related to the present going in the circuit. A standard strategy for identifying current is to insert a resistor in the method for current to be sense. By then we can put the distinguished resistor at wherever in game plan with the circuit it may be weight or switch. Along these lines current identifying contraptions are to be considered as present to voltage converter device which recognizes and changes over current to get a yield voltage, which is genuinely in respect to the current in the organized manner. Exactly when current is experiencing the circuit, a voltage drops over the way where the current is spilling. Also an alluring field is made near the present passing on conductor. These above miracle are used in the present sensor plan method [10].

C. Current Transformer (CT)

Current Transformer (CT) is a transformer is to quantify electric flows and the present high current strong state vitality meters. It can make the grade regarding very high present and devours little power. It is additionally extremely valuable in estimating or checking high current, high voltage and high power circuits. These are utilized in power arrangement of different types, for example, control supplies, engine controls, lighting controls.

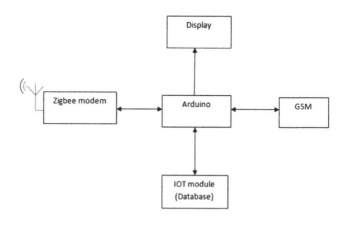

B) Receiver

Fig. 3. Proposed block diagram of the receiver

Arduino is a electronic device uses both hardware and software. It uses more sensors and it is simple and low cost. The web based developing network backing Arduino comprises of software engineers like us that offer their models for others to make it an increasingly dependable stage. It is mostly utilized in RF and IR circuits. These decoders are mostly utilized for remote control applications like criminal alert, vehicle entryway caution, security framework and so forth. The picked pair of encoder and decoder for correspondence ought to have same number of location and information bits.

4 Results and Discussion

In remote sensor mastermind, there are three sorts of contraptions: facilitator, switch and end marks. Open source information arrange for the Internet of Things offers access to a wide degree of inserted contraptions and web associations. As such, here one zigBee is organized as a facilitator, which is connected with the arduino. Here sensor focus point is sorted out as switch and end tag (E52); it will send its constant information to the closest switch [11]. There is just a single facilitator in the structure, which converses with the base station. The yield screen capture is appeared in Figs. 4 and 5.

Fig. 4. Transmitter

Step 1: In WSN structure the sensor focus point sense the information from the sensor. Sense information gets the end stamps and end name search the closest switch. On the off chance that switch it in range than end tag sends the information to the switch.

Fig. 5. Receiver

Step 2: Router to facilitator and organizer direct chat with base station. In base station set away the all information, the customer can visit direct to the base station.
Step 3: Base station sends all information to the cloud or Ethernet. Customers or clients can connect with the web application inside the area.
Step 4: If the cutoff range crosses for multiple occasions, the base station will imply the GSM to send SMS to concern experts.
Step 5: The base station will speak with facilitator that is at the transmitter side the water supply to the business will naturally halted just as the power is closed somewhere around controlling utilizing pic.
Step 6: In remote sensor arrange, there are three sorts of gadgets, every gadget sending and accepting information show on the screen.

5   Conclusion

The present model shows current pollution watching and controlling system using IOT. A plan which is low power and versatile is made for water, air and environmental parameters watching. A remote sensor sort out structure using adurinouno as a base station, zigbee as a frameworks organization show sensor as a blend of sensor center points has used. Unmistakable straightforward data WSN is convert into automated a motivating force by data verifying, the propelled worth is held from the cloud by using IOT. The model in like manner gives a SMS entrance organizations. One essential favored position of the structure lies in the compromise of the entrance center point of remote sensor mastermind, database server and web server into one fundamental traditionalist and low power. It is useful in various present day natural checking and data gathering. More sensors can be connected later on.

6 Future Research Directions

In future the IoT based 5 G will be implemented for monitoring and controlling the pollution. An innovative system which uses advanced sensors and 5 G technologies will be implemented to solve the issue of pollution and other social related issues. The technology can be applied in weather forecasting, flood prediction and to avoid natural calamities to a certain extend. The future of IoT purely depends on the system and technologies revolving over it.

CMX 500 is the new fifth generation technology in the market that provides a dynamic and sustainable environment for implementing IoT. Hence many researches is concentrating in that.

The future research should not harm any human being and also should be useful to the human society. The current 5 G has many faults over the radiation issues that has to be solved and it should be combined with IoT for the benefit of mankind and other living objects in earth. Finally technologies like IoT and 5 G should be used for the benefit of people and it should not harm them.

We have decided to develop an IoT system with 5 G technology that gives an optimal solution for finding terrorist activities, crop prediction in the soil, human trafficking.

References

1. Yang, J., et al.: Integration of WSN in environmental monitoring based on cyber structure. Wirel. Net. **16**, 1091–1108 (2010). https://doi.org/10.1007/s11276-009-0190-1
2. Derbew, Y., Libsie, M.: A WSN framework for large industrial poll monitor. J. Comput. Sci. Tech. **2**, 95–101 (2014)
3. Zakaria, Y., Michael, K.: An integrated cloud on WSN for monitor waste water into water sources. Wirel. Sen. Netw. **9**, 290–301 (2017)
4. Vetrivelan, P., et al.: A NN based automatic crop monitoring based robot for agri. In: The IoT and the Next Revolutions Automating the World, pp. 203–212. IGI Global (2019)
5. Lieping, Z., et al.: Design of water environment monitoring system based on WSN. In: International Conference on Measuring Technical & Mechatronics Automation, pp. 210–213 (2016)
6. Lukas, W., et al.: On the application of IoT: monitor of water level using WSN. IEEE Conference on Wireless Sensors, Melaka, pp. 58–62 (2015)
7. Wang, C., et al.: A self air quality monitor system using WSN. In: International Conference on Computing & Application, Taipei, pp. 1–6 (2012)
8. Vetrivelan, P., et al.: Design of surveillance security system based on sensor network. Int. J. Res. Stud. Sci. Eng. Tech. **4**, 23–26 (2017)
9. Nikhade, S.G.: WSN Communication on Embedded Linux Cirtt, Power & Computing Technology, pp. 1468–1473 (2014)
10. Sheikh Ferdoush: WSN Sys Pi & Arduino of Environmental Monitoring Application Conference on Future Networks and Communications (2014)
11. Santhi, S., et al.: SoS emergency on ad-hoc wireless net. In: Computational Intelligence & Sustainable Systems (CISS), EAI/Springer Innovations in Communication & Computing, pp. 227–234 (2019)

12. Rakhonde, M.A., Khoje, S.A., Komati, R.D.: Vehicle collision detection and avoidance with pollution monitoring system using IoT. In: Global Conf on Wireless Computing and Networking (GCWCN), Lonavala, India, 2018, pp. 75–79 (2018)
13. Muthukumar, S., et al.: IoT based air pollution monitoring and control system. In: 2018 International Conference on Inventive Research in Computing Applications (ICIRCA), Coimbatore, pp. 1286–1288 (2018)
14. Kavitha, B.C., Vallikannu, R.: IoT based intelligent industry monitoring system. In: 2019 6th International Conference on Signal Processing and Integrated Networks (SPIN), Noida, India, pp. 63–65 (2019)
15. Munsadwala, Y., et al.: Identification and visualization of hazardous gases using IoT. In: International Conference on IoT: Smart Innovation and Usages (IoT-SIU), Ghaziabad, India, pp. 1–6 (2019)

Futuristic Computing Technologies

Comparative Analysis of Different Machine Learning Techniques

Nidhi Srivastava[1]([⊠]), Tripti Lamba[2]([⊠]), and Manisha Agarwal[1]([⊠])

[1] Banasthali Vidyapith, Vanasthali, India
nidhi.sv@gmail.com, manishaagarwal18@yahoo.co.in
[2] IITM GGSIPU, New Delhi, India
triptigautam@yahoo.co.in

Abstract. Artificial learning (AI) is one of the areas of computer science which develops the system in a way that our system starts learning and gives the reaction as a human brain does. This paper discussed one of the branches of AI i.e. Machine learning as the name suggests it focuses on the development of the computers especially their programs that access the data that can be used for self-development. The main objective of the paper is to compare the best machine learning model by using the performance parameter R squared and Mean square Error (MSE). The data set was taken from the promise repository for the analysis. Feature selection technique Boruta was applied to find the important/confirmed variables from the dataset which are having information regarding the JAVA projects. This paper finds out that among different algorithms which one outperforms when the comparative analysis was done to find the best model.

Keywords: Machine learning model · Random forest · Software bug detection · Feature selection

1 Introduction

In computer science data mining is the process by which one can easily form relationships and patterns among the various data and collect information which helps in decision making, it further helps in the area of software development [12]. Deep learning is one of the dimensions of machine learning connects to the area of artificial intelligence [13] through machine learning one can easily extract information from problem reports and decide by analyzing through the extracted information. The detection of software bugs and improve software quality can be done by using different machine learning techniques. Machine learning is one of the branches of AI which is used for the correct prediction of outcomes without any explicit programming. Machine Learning also helps in creating a predictive model that is further divided into defective & non-defective Modules [14]. Different machine learning models like linear regression, random forest, decision tree, Support vector machine, decision stump, etc. can be used to predict the software defect. To find out the bugs in software by applying various ML Techniques which can are implemented with different comparative performance analysis like R Squared, Mean square error, Accuracy, adjusted R^2 etc. [13].

© Springer Nature Singapore Pte Ltd. 2020
P. K. Singh et al. (Eds.): FTNCT 2019, CCIS 1206, pp. 245–255, 2020.
https://doi.org/10.1007/978-981-15-4451-4_19

Comparison is done among different Machine Learning models to find out results easily. In this paper comparative analysis is done between the models of Machine Learning i.e. linear Regression, Random Forest by implementing different techniques to get the best model from out of it. The dataset is taken from the well-known repository Github. Feature selection technique Boruta is applied on oryx, titan, mcMMO, neo4j, netty dataset which are the java Projects. The objective of the paper can be achieved by comparing both the models by implementing R square and Mean Square Error on the model and verified by the results. Sections in the paper are as follows: Sect. 2 consists of Literature Review. Section 3 discussed different machine learning models and there are different techniques that can be used to predict software bugs. Section 4 discussed the feature selection technique Boruta which is one of the best techniques as it uses the wrapper method. Mathematical Model MSE and R^2 were discussed in Sect. 5. Experiment and Result is discussed in Sect. 3. Section 6 gives the conclusion of the research [15].

2   Literature Review

Machine Learning technique is useful to detect or predict the bugs in software. Machine learning results in the increase of efficiency of a software, there are different Machine Learning models [1] being discussed in the paper and tried on different datasets to find out the accuracy, F-measure and Mean Absolute Error which helps in find out the best performance of algorithms. It concluded that Support Vector Machine, Multilayer Perception and bagging techniques give good results on bug detection. In the Classification technique there are two major challenges i.e. firstly software data repository must be converted into architecture and secondly, there should not be anyone detector model for the prediction of accuracy [2]. Classification algorithms implement on different types of data sets like share market data, data of patients, financial dataset [3]. Hence these classification techniques show how data can be determined and grouped when a new set of data is available. Each technique has got its features and limitations as given in the paper. Based on the Conditions, corresponding performance and feature each one as needed and selected. In the survey paper different ML Techniques are technique is taken and then compared and find out the False Positive rate, Accuracy F-measure, Precision and recall and tried to find out the best algorithm to be used [4]. They talked about machine learning and finally tried to find out the strength and impact of association with a different explanatory variable to find the performance after the mitigation of the interference introduced by strongly associated observations [5]. Different machine learning techniques are taken and a comparison is done among them by considering the different factors [6]. The discussion is about the software defect using Support vector machine in paper different classifier are taken and made a comparison based on accuracy, recall, and precision [7]. A discussion on two real-time case studies i.e. of Volvo and Ericsson is taken and tried to implement the Machine learning and discussed how to work efficiency will increase if Machine Learning is implemented [8]. This paper discusses that from the meta-analysis it is extremely difficult to predict the software defect through experiment [9]. The factors influence the predictive performance of software defect classifiers by the correlation coefficient and tried to find out the exact position of the bug. In this paper, the author has used different feature selection technique on different dataset and then they have found out the best Machine learning model by the implementation of different performance parameters like accuracy, mean square error, R Square and correlation and concluded that support vector machine was the best model [10].

3 Data Mining Techniques

The data mining technique is also useful to predict software bug through a different technique. Machine Learning is having different techniques which can be classified as supervised and unsupervised learning and it is further subdivision which is shown in Fig. 1 and explains as follows:

3.1 Supervised Learning

Supervise leaning is a process of taking a sample from the data source with already assigned classification. This technique uses multilayer perception (MLP) and feed forward techniques. Some characteristics of MLP are:

(a) A higher degree of connectivity exhibits through interconnection among the models in the networks.
(b) Neuronal activities are easily differentiable through nonlinearity features. Through these characteristics, one can easily solve complicated and assorted problems.

3.2 Unsupervised Learning

Machine Learning algorithms can be subdivided into supervised and unsupervised learning. Whereas unsupervised learning tool is used for neither for labeled nor for classified data and hence new algorithm prepared to act on that information without any roadmap this means that only input is given without any specified output.

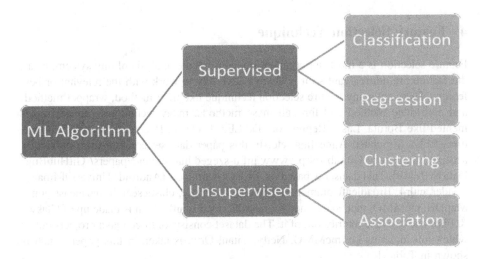

Fig. 1. Types of machine learning algorithm.

3.3   Machine Learning Techniques for Bug Detection

a. Naïve Bayes classifier
  It is a set of different classification algorithm which is based on Bayes Theorem. It is a collection of the algorithm where all of them are having a similar concept and all the features which are being classified are independent of each other. Naïve Bayes classification algorithm used for high dimension input. One can predict and output of some events and observe some evidence. Generally, it is better to have more than one evidence to support the prediction of an event.

b. Decision Tree
  It is a classifier of a root node that generates other branches as a result node. An indecision tree made up of branches and nodes. Where branches represent experiments made on a dataset and notes represents the final results generated class name is there at the leaf node.

c. Random Forest: It is the simple learning techniques used to produce results this technique is used in regression as well as in classification. Machine learning having different types of algorithms and Random Forest comes under the supervised learning algorithms.

d. Linear regression: It is the part of regression and before the linear regression the concept of the regression comes whereas regression always talk about some target values which can be calculated from some independent predictors therefore Linear regression always used for single input variable and when the real variable being evaluated by the user for example if the price of the house then its values always depend on the area of the particular house.

e. Support Vector Machine (SVM): It is a classification technique that is used to find several different hyperplanes that distinctly classify the data point for example data space can be further divided into small segments and then each segment contains only a single kind of data. It is a technique where variables filter a set of data and exact different sets of useful data from different groups.

4   Feature Selection Technique

Feature selection is a most important component for the analysis of any system, as all the feature are not relevant so it is always advisable to work with the relevant or best feature. There are many feature selection technique like filter method, wrapper method, and embedded method and through these methods, many techniques can be implemented like Boruta, Lasso Regression, DALEX Package, Recursive Feature Elimination (RFE), Simulated Annealing, etc. In this paper data set is taken from publically accepted repository Github (http://www.inf.u-szeged.hu/~ferenc/papers/ GitHubBug-Data Set/) [19]. This dataset is based on 15 JAVA projects (Android- Universal-Image-Loader,antlr4, BroadleafCommerce, Ceylon-ide eclipse, elasticsearch, hazelcast, junit, MapDB, mcMMO, mct, neo4j, netty, orientdb, oryx, titan) which is made up of Classes & Files and produce metrics out of it. The dataset consists of fifteen java projects out of which four datasets i.e. mcMMO, Netty, Titan, Oryx is taken in this paper which is shown in Table 1.

Table 1. Data set of Java projects

Java projects	No. of observation	No. of variables
mcMMO	85	8
Netty	586	6
Titan	348	100
Oryx	533	107

As shown in the Table 1, the feature selection technique Boruta is applied to each java project. When Boruta is applied to these java projects, some variables were rejected and some were accepted [18]. The total accepted variables in each java projects are been shown in Table 2.

Table 2. Table explaining about the accepted & rejected variables

Dataset	Variables	Important variables
mcMMO	8	2
Netty	6	2
Titan	100	31
Oryx	107	59

When wrapper algorithm Boruta [11] is applied as shown in Fig. 2, A graph is created where important variables are accepted and rejects the least important variables Boruta show the Z-Scores boxplot where Green boxplot indicates accepted or important variables Blue boxplot indicates average variables which can be accepted and Red boxplot indicates rejected variables for Java Projects Data set.

Each dataset is having several variables some is selected and some are rejected as shown in Table 2 [17]. In this paper, 5 datasets being used and in every dataset, different feature selection technique used in the dataset through which some variables are accepted which are important variable and some are rejected which are not so important whereas some are average variables which user can either accept or reject the variable as per the user consent these are shown in Figs. 2, 3, 4, 5.

Imp.Variables for oryx

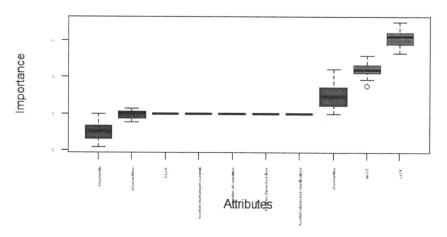

Fig. 2. Depicting feature selection in oryx dataset (Color figure online)

Imp.Variables for netty4

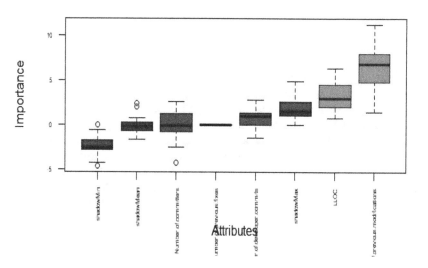

Fig. 3. Depicting feature selection in netty4 dataset (Color figure online)

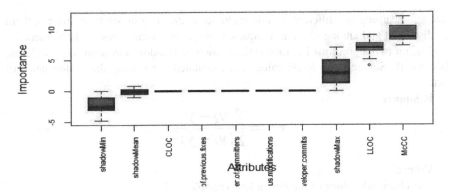

Fig. 4. Depicting feature selection in McMMo dataset (Color figure online)

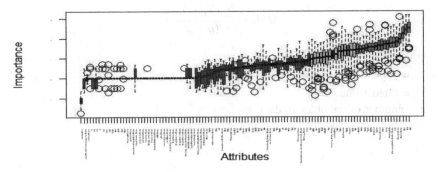

Fig. 5. Depicting feature selection in titan dataset (Color figure online)

The feature selection technique Boruta is applied on the data set Oxy, Netty, McMMO and Titan to get the important variable (accepted) which is in green colour, average variable which can be accepted or rejected which is in yellow colour, least significant variable (rejected) in red colour as shown in Figs. 2, 3, 4 and 5 respectively. The process of feature selection helps in finding the best feature in the data which will further help in finding the accuracy of the model. Table 2 shows the detailed accepted and rejected variable.

5 Mathematical Model

Machine Learning has different techniques to detect the error in software, some of them are discussed and among many techniques, in paper two techniques are implement R2 & MSE on two algorithms i.e. Linear Regression & Random forest on using different datasets. R- Squared and MSE values are calculated for finding the performance of metrics [16].

R-Square

$$r^2 = \frac{\sum(\dot{y}_i - \bar{y})^2}{\sum(y_i - \hat{y})^2}$$

Where

y_i = observed values of the dependent variable

$\bar{y}$ = mean

$\hat{y}_i$ = fitted value

MSE (Mean Square Error)

$$MSE = \frac{\sum(Y_i - \hat{Y}_i)^2}{(n - p)}$$

Where

Yi = dependent variable

$\hat{Y}_i$ = fitted value

n = number of variables in data set

p = observed values of the explanatory variable

Table 3. Calculating R2 & MSE on a different dataset

S No.	Dataset used	Linear regression		Random forest	
		R^2	MSE	R^2	MSE
1	mcMMO	0.22	0.47	0.90	0.081
2	Netty	0.16	0.03	0.79	0.007
3	Titan	0.82	0.011	0.64	0.009
4	Oryx	0.027	0.165	0.81	0.011

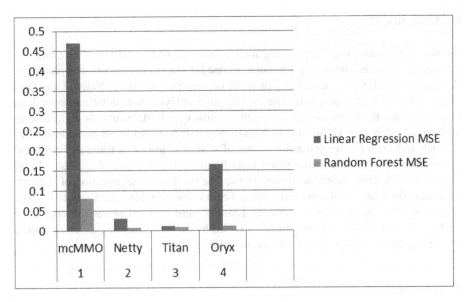

Fig. 6. Comparative study of LR & Random Forest with MSE

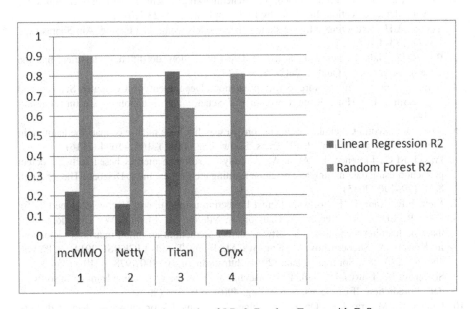

Fig. 7. Comparative study of LR & Random Forest with R Square

6   Conclusion

As discussed various machine learning models can be used to predict software bugs. In this paper, Linear Regression and Random Forest are used. The performance parameter R square and MSE was calculated on five datasets i.e. mcMMO, Netty, Titan, and Oryx, out of 15 java program. The comparative analysis was done on these Java modules using R square and MSE which is shown in Table 3 and throught this an analysis are drawn which are shown in Figs. 6 and 7. Random forest outperformed as compare to Linear Regression as the values of MSE was lowest in Random Forest and the value of R square was better than Linear Regression as it depicted in Tables 1 and 2. Feature Selection technique Boruta is used before the implementation of the performance parameter i.e. R square and MSE. Feature selection is the best way to find out the useful variables from the dataset as in a dataset there were lots of variables but some of them are not useful and this can be extracted by the implementing different feature selection techniques it is also explained in Table 1.

References

1. Aleem, S., Capretz, L.F., Ahmed, F.: Benchmarking machine learning techniques for software defect detection. Int. J. Softw Eng. Appl. **6**(3), 11–23 (2015)
2. Yousef, A.H.: Extracting software static defect models using data mining. Ain Shams Eng. J. **6**(1), 133–144 (2015)
3. Bowes, D., Hall, T., Petrić, J.: Software defect prediction: do different classifiers find the same defects? Softw. Qual. J. **26**(2), 525–552 (2018)
4. Nam, J.: Survey on software defect prediction. Department of Computer Science and Engineering, The Hong Kong University of Science and Technology, Technical report (2014)
5. Tantithamthavorn, C., et al.: Comments on "Researcher bias: the use of machine learning in software defect prediction". IEEE Trans. Softw. Eng. **42**(11), 1092–1094 (2016)
6. Prasad, M.C., Florence, L., Arya, A.: A study on software metrics based software defect prediction using data mining and machine learning techniques. Int. J. Database Theory Appl. **8**(3), 179–190 (2015)
7. Kaur, E.R., Kaur, E.H.: Software Defect Prediction using Support Vector Machine (2016)
8. Rana, R., Staron, M., Berger, C., Hansson, J., Nilsson, M., Meding, W.: The adoption of machine learning techniques for software defect prediction: an initial industrial validation. In: Kravets, A., Shcherbakov, M., Kultsova, M., Iijima, T. (eds.) JCKBSE 2014. CCIS, vol. 466, pp. 270–285. Springer, Cham (2014). https://doi.org/10.1007/978-3-319-11854-3_23
9. Shepperd, M., Bowes, D., Hall, T.: Researcher bias: the use of machine learning in software defect prediction. IEEE Trans. Softw. Eng. **40**(6), 603–616 (2014)
10. Lamba, K., Mishra, A.K.: Optimal machine learning model for software defect prediction. Int. J. Intell. Syst. Appl. **11**(2), 36 (2019)
11. Lamba, T., Mishra, A.K.: Optimal metrics selection for software defect prediction. Int. J. Data Min. Emerg. Technol. **7**(2), 82–91 (2017)
12. Khanna, A., Goyal, R., Verma, M., Joshi, D.: Intelligent traffic management system for smart cities. In: Singh, P.K., Paprzycki, M., Bhargava, B., Chhabra, J.K., Kaushal, N.C., Kumar, Y. (eds.) FTNCT 2018. CCIS, vol. 958, pp. 152–164. Springer, Singapore (2019). https://doi.org/10.1007/978-981-13-3804-5_12

13. Garg, D., Goel, P., Kandaswamy, G., Ganatra, A., Kotecha, K.: A roadmap to deep learning: a state-of-the-art step towards machine learning. In: Luhach, A.K., Singh, D., Hsiung, P.-A., Hawari, K.B.G., Lingras, P., Singh, P.K. (eds.) ICAICR 2018. CCIS, vol. 955, pp. 160–170. Springer, Singapore (2019). https://doi.org/10.1007/978-981-13-3140-4_15

14. Sharma, N., Singh, A.: Diabetes detection and prediction using machine learning/IoT: a survey. In: Luhach, A.K., Singh, D., Hsiung, P.-A., Hawari, K.B.G., Lingras, P., Singh, P.K. (eds.) ICAICR 2018. CCIS, vol. 955, pp. 471–479. Springer, Singapore (2019). https://doi.org/10.1007/978-981-13-3140-4_42

15. Kumar, Y., Pradeep, K.S.: Improved cat swarm optimization algorithm for solving global optimization problems and its application to clustering. Appl. Intell. **48**(9), 2681–2697 (2018). https://doi.org/10.1007/s10489-017-1096-8

16. Suresh, Y., Pati, J., Rath, S.K.: Effectiveness of software metrics for object-oriented system **6**, 420–427 (2012). www.sciencedirect.com

17. Kursa, M.B.: Feature Selection with the Boruta Package. In: Narayana, P., (ed.) 2010 Software Defect Prevention – in a Nutshell, vol. 36, no. 11 (2016). https://www.isixsigma.com/industries/software-it/software-defect-prevention-nutshell/. Accessed 22 Oct 2016

18. Aggarwal, K., Singh, Y., Kaur, A., Malhotra, R.: Empirical study of object-oriented metrics. Softw. Q. J. **5**(8), 149–173 (2006). Kluwer Academic Publishers

Book References

19. Canadian Bioinformatics Workshops! pp. 1–26 (2016)

Suicidal Tendency on Social Media by Using Text Mining

Priyanka Gupta, Baijnath Kaushik, and Sunanda$^{(\boxtimes)}$

School of Computer Science and Engineering,
Shri Mata Vaishno Devi University, Kakryal, Katra 182320, J&K, India
sunanda.gupta@smvdu.ac.in

Abstract. With a growth in the use of the social media, we have witnessed a positive connection between the demonstration of Suicidal ideation on social networking sites (such as Twitter) and the suicidal cases. One of the most admired and extensively used online social network sites is Twitter. Twitter becomes the mean where every individual can share their emotions whether the emotions are positive negative or neutral. The aim of this study is to design a model for individuals that run the higher risk of committing suicide. By studying different predictors of suicide such as depression, anxiety, hopelessness, hypersomnia, Insomnia and stress the model will be created. Techniques such as that of text mining will be utilized for the prediction purposes. The research uses text mining process for the analysis of data, and on the basis of this analysis, a model is developed that will help predicting suicidal behaviours present in the individual. Then, the Machine Learning algorithms such as Decision Tree (DT) and Naïve Bayes (NB) are used for classification. Which are then compared for the prediction purposes. Data used in such models requires unceasing monitoring; in addition to monitoring, to elevate the prediction's accuracy, data needs to be updated periodically too.

Keywords: Suicidal ideation · Risk factor · Machine learning classifier · Naive Bayesian · Decision Tree

1 Introduction

The process of performing analyzes on amount of unstructured textual data using software that can recognize concepts, patterns, and themes is known as text mining. The procedure of passing an exam into large collections of written resources is known as text analysis, also known as text mining. This grants you to give rise to new information and change unstructured text into structured data to deploy in the interpretation later. To identify facts, relationships, and statements that generally would not have been found in the bunch of large textual data [4]. In today's world, a large amount of data is created daily, whether through any source: media, blogs or social networks such as Twitter, Facebook, Tumblr, Instagram, etc. [5, 23]. This huge amount of data, comprising with feelings, can be linked to some crucial information. It is very difficult and almost impossible to manually follow such a range of data and extract some crucial information. These facts are taken out and transformed into structured data for investigation and visualization, integrated into structured data in databases or warehouses, and refined

P. K. Singh et al. (Eds.): FTNCT 2019, CCIS 1206, pp. 256–263, 2020.
https://doi.org/10.1007/978-981-15-4451-4_20

using machine learning (ML) systems [3]. Nowadays, Twitter is one of the most admired and used online social networking sites. Twitter authorize its users to do many activities - create profiles, post status and share messages with others. Content on Twitter can be published via a web interface, even an SMS or mobile broadcast. It is a free streaming social media site that allows its registered users to interact with others, using 140 character statuses [8].About 23% of online users use Twitter. It has become a medium where all users can express their thoughts, behaviors, feelings or intentions, which can range from positive to neutral to negative. Most people express suicidality in their tweets and one of the prime reasons of death is suicide [11]. According to a WHO survey, one death occurs every 20 s or 3000 per data. It is projected that by 2020, about 1.53 million people will die from suicide [1, 6]. Mental illness is not the only cause that induce suicide, but several other reasons, such as depression, bipolar disorder, anxiety or schizophrenia, can also stimulate it [2].

In fact, many suicide deaths are preventable and, therefore, it is important to understand how people communicate their depression and thoughts to prevent such deaths [7]. With the help of sentimental analysis, we can help classify and understand a user's feelings about a topic of interest.

2   Objective

The main objective of this paper is to design a model for individuals that run the higher risk of committing suicide by designing and implementation of an automated machine learning classifier. This system will comprise of two different machine learning classifier such as Naive Bayes and Decision Tree [22]. In this proposal we use dataset of around thousands twitter dataset, and a classification algorithm (Naive Bayes and Decision Tree) were applied on these dataset to identify the risk of committing suicide [9]. The effectiveness of the propose system for the automated prediction is being done with the use of following recall, precision and F1score and comparing their workability.

The remainder of this paper is structured as follows. First, we give an overview of paper Sect. 2 describes the objective of study Sect. 3 provides an method used in study and discuss about it. Section 4 describe the result of the classifiers of Machine Learning applied on twitter dataset. In Sect. 5 we discuss and compare the results.

3   Methods and Materials

These are some of the briefly explained steps used for predicting Suicidal ideation is given as follows (Fig. 1):

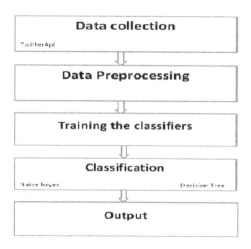

Fig. 1. Steps used in our proposed work

3.1   Collection of Data

Data is collected from the Twitter Streaming API. Continuously monitoring over the tweets is necessary for collection of data. There are some of the examples that we used in our database that are for e.g.:- my life comes to an end, struggling through depression for about a year now and my mom died suffering from a stage four brain cancer and it's been hard [10]. These data are manually annotated and for every tweet t1 it indicates the suicidal ideation and belongs to data-set. We set polarity for them as 1 and polarity 0 for the tweets in which the suicidal content is not present.

3.2   Data Preprocessing

It is observed that the data contained in the Tweets had many duplicate entries. Hence it was necessary to remove repeated data in order to get unbiased results for the analysis of the data [13]. For this, firstly we need to perform Data Cleansing. It is defined as the process of changing data in the storage source to make it accurate and correct. Now that we have finished removing duplication our data requires some preprocessing before we further perform analysis and prepare the prediction model [12]. Hence in the Preprocessing phase we do the following in the same order as mentioned: First step is to remove all the HTML tags followed by the removal of any punctuation marks or limited set of special characters, for instance ',', '.' '#' etc. Secondly, we need to check if the word is made up using English letters and not alpha-numeric ones. Then, analyze whether the length of the word is greater than 2 (as a research shows that there are no 2 - lettered adjectives). Post analyzing the words, convert them in lowercase and remove Stopwords. We apply Snowball Stemming on words (which is observed to be better than Porter Stemming). In the final step, we collect words that describes positive and negative tweets.

3.3   Machine Learning Classifier

A text classifier is developed in which tweets can be classified automatically, Machine learning (ML) classifiers were applied. To learn various ML methods a tool named ScikitLearn toolkit was brought in use. Using this toolkit each tweet was made to represent a vector of features for use along with each machine learning method. As the aim was to study the automatic classification feasibility, basic features such as unigrams and bigrams were used in the first instance with the help of **Bag of Words** [15]. In such representation, the words presented in the observed data set, became features; which resulted as the representational feature of a high dimension. For learning this concept, the classifiers must learn if any sentence in it possesses a defined structure or a keyword that suggests the existence of any sort of suicidal thoughts. Even a slight inclination towards suicidal thoughts needs to be captured. We also used weighting Term **Frequency weighted by Inverse Document Frequency (TFIDF)** [14]. Such weighting groups the amount of inherited information present in the word, linguistic observation as its basis. For example, in English language, the occurring words in many statements represent littlee or no meaning, e.g. The words like 'the' and 'is' frequently occur in sentences of the tweets, but have invaluable semantic content. Whereas, in comparison, parts of speech like the 'nouns' and 'verbs', have greater and relevant meaning, but their frequency of occurrence is less as compared to the functional words. In such feature space variant, weighing on document frequency basis gets multiplied with the word's frequency in the tweet.

$$W_{ab} = tf_{a,b} \times \log(N/df_a)$$

$tf_{a,b}$ = number of occurrences of a in b

df_a = number of documents containing a

N = total number of documents

In this case, 't' is the word feature, 'N' represents the total number of document data items and 'df_a' stands for a document in the document set D containing a. The weighted variant is represented as "tfidf". In order to determine the derived classifiers, without random shuffling have been performed, a division of data sets is done in randomly selected portions of testing and training. Without shuffling randomly, initial 90% of data points were brought to use as training set, while remaining 10% data points were kept as for the testing set. Two algorithms of machine learning text classification were tested i.e. **Naïve Bayes and Decision Tree** enables us to show dependencies among features and classes [16].

The main objective of the decision tree is to create a training model that can make use of the forecast class or the value of the target variables by learning the decision rules concluded from the previous data whereas Naïve Bayes assign a class to a document and it depends on the posterior probability of the class which in turn depends on how the distribution of words is done in the document. Such methods are tested using individual variant of feature space. Experiments are conducted using the algorithm which delivers best performance by determining the k-fold cross-validation results or TimeSeriesCV [17]. The data sets that are held out are used to perform these experiments. Performance as in terms of total accuracy along with recall, precision and

F1 metric for every category is examined. Precision is classified as the items correctly classified (in percentages) in any category particularly by the algorithm. Percentage of the successfully classified category is indicated by Recall. The harmonic mean of the two and the balance between the same is represented by F1. The F1 metric, recall and range of precision all are bounded between 0 and 1, where better performance is indicated by a higher value (Figs. 2, 3 and 4).

$$F1(c) = 2 \text{ X } Precision(c)/Recall(c)$$

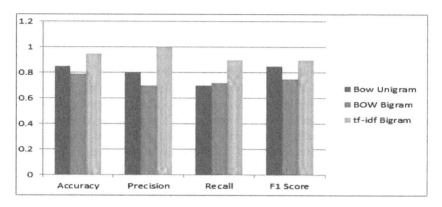

Fig. 2. Performance parameters of Decision Tree

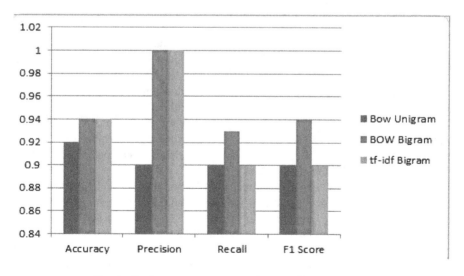

Fig. 3. Performance parameters of Bernoulli Naive Bayes

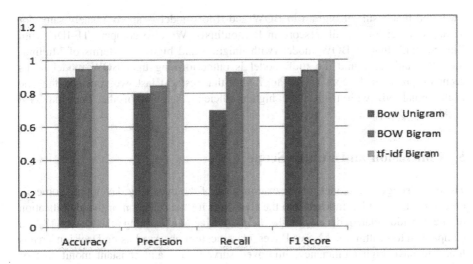

Fig. 4. Performance parameters of multinomial Naive Bayes

4   Experiment and Results

Table 1. Classification results in terms of evaluation metrics

Machine learning algorithm	BOW								TFIDF			
Decision Tree	Unigram				Bigram				Bigram			
	Accuracy	Precision	Recall	F1	Accuracy	Precision	Recall	F1	Accuracy	Precision	Recall	F1
	Training 36.9	0.8	0.8	0.8	Training 37.2	0.7	0.7	0.7	Training 39	0.7	0.7	0.7
	Testing 85				Testing 79				Testing 80			
Bernoulli NB	Training 66.9	0.9	0.9	0.9	Training 65.40	1.0	0.9	0.9	Training 65.4	1.0	0.9	0.9
	Testing 92.4				Testing 94				Testing 94.6			
Multinominal NM	Training 72	1.0	0.7	0.9	Training 73.9	1.0	0.9	0.9	Training 73.9	1.0	0.9	1.0
	Testing 90				Testing 94.6				Testing 96.7			

The comparison table above shows the text classification by using the two machine learning algorithms i.e. Decision Tree and the Naïve Bayes. In our proposed Work we have used the two methods of the Naïve Bayes (Bernoulli Naïve Bayes and the Multinomial Naïve Bayes). The hyper parameter used in decision tree is the max depth of 10 and min split of 50 and we found that the accuracy is approx. 64% and formax depth of 8 and min split of 10, the accuracy gets increased by 71%. In unigram the testing accuracy of decision tree is 85% which is greater than of the Bag of Words model (with bigram) and tf-idf. In the same way, the accuracy of the tf-idf model (with bigram features) is higher than that of BOW model (with unigram and bigram) in Bernoulli NB. When we compare the results of BOW model (with bigram) and tf-idf we found that result of bigram in BOW and tf-idf model is approximately same for accuracy, precision, recall, f1score in BernoulliNB. We also compare TF-IDF (with Bigram) with that of BOW model (with unigram and bigram) in terms of Multino-mial NB and we found the tfidf model is outperforming than BOW model as its accuracy precision f1score values are higher that rest. At last, we conclude that the Multinomial NB with tf-idf have higher efficiency as that of the Decision Tree (Table 1).

5   Conclusion and Future Scope

The paper suggests a model for the examination of the tweets by developing some set of features that can be imposed into the classifiers for the selection or the identification of the suicide related data with the help of Machine learning classifiers [18]. In comparison to Multinomial Naïve Bayes, classification observed using Decision Tree is found to have higher efficiency. Improved surveillance, and constant monitoring of suicide and suicide attempts, are the primary and imperative measures for applying effective suicide avoidance strategies [19, 21]. Identify suicidal ideation among different dataset analysis such as video, blogging on different social media platform with the advent of deep learning and different algorithm such as swarm intelligence and nature inspired algorithm. It is possible to identify the risk factor associated among different section of people [20]. With ease in availability of proper data, prediction accuracy will increase, which, ultimately, will lead to development of more effective suicide prevention strategies.

References

1. Kušen, E., Strembeck, M.: Politics, sentiments, and misinformation: an analysis of the Twitter discussion on the 2016 Austrian Presidential elections. Online Soc. Netw. Media **5**, 37–50 (2018)
2. Colombo, G.B., Burnap, P., Hodorog, A., Scourfield, J.: Analysing the connectivity and communication of suicidal users on twitter. Comput. Commun. **73**(PB), 291–300 (2016)
3. Zhang, J., Liu, B., Tang, J., Chen, T., Li, J.: Social influence locality for modeling retweeting behaviors. In: Proceedings of the Twenty-Third International Joint Conference on Artificial Intelligence, pp. 2761–2767. AAAI Press (2013)
4. Comarela, G., Crovella, M., Almeida, V., Benevenuto, F.: Understanding factors that affect response rates in Twitter. In: Proceedings of the Twenty-Third ACM Conference on Hypertext and Social Media, pp. 123–132. ACM (2012)
5. Karamshuk, D., Shaw, F., Brownlie, J., Sastry, N.: Bridging big data and qualitative methods in the social sciences: a case study of Twitter responses to high profile deaths by suicide. Online Soc. Netw. Media **1**, 33–43 (2017)
6. O'Dea, B., Wan, S., Batterham, P.J., Calear, A.L., Paris, C., Christensen, H.: Detecting suicidality on Twitter. Internet Interv. **2**(2), 183–188 (2015)
7. Firdaus, S.N., Ding, C., Sadeghian, A.: Retweet: a popular information diffusion mechanism–a survey paper. Online Soc. Netw. Media **6**, 26–40 (2018)

8. Graham, T., Jackson, D., Broersma, M.: New platform, old habits? Candidates use of Twitter during the 2010 British and Dutch general election campaigns. New Media Soc. **18**(5), 765–783 (2016)

9. Zdanow, C., Wright, B.: The representation of self injury and suicide on emo social networking groups. Afr. Sociol. Rev. **16**, 81–101 (2012)

10. Abdullah, N.A., Nishioka, D., Tanaka, Y., Murayama, Y.: User's action and decision making of retweet messages towards reducing misinformation spread during disaster. J. Inf. Process. **23**(1), 31–40 (2015)

11. Bermingham, A., Conway, M., McInerney, L., O'Hare, N., Smeaton, A.F.: Combining social network analysis and sentiment analysis to explore the potential for online radicalisation. In: Proceedings of the IEEE International Conference on Advances in Social Network Analysis and Mining (ASONAM), pp. 231–236. IEEE Computer Society (2009). https://doi.org/10.1109/asonam

12. Baldwin, B., Carpenter, B.: (2003). Lingpipe. http://alias-i.com/lingpipe

13. Blei, D.M., Ng, A.Y., Jordan, M.I.: Latent Dirichlet allocation. J. Mach. Learn. Res. **3**, 993–1022 (2003)

14. Cerel, J., Jordan, J.R., Duberstein, P.R.: The impact of suicide on the family. Crisis **29**(1), 38–44 (2008)

15. Chan, K., Fang, W.: Use of the internet and traditional media among young people. Young Consum. **8**(4), 244–256 (2007)

16. Chen, T., Guestrin, C.: XGBoost: a scalable tree boosting system. In: Proceedings of the 22nd ACM SIGKDD International Conference on Knowledge Discovery and Data Mining, pp. 785–794. ACM (2016)

17. Coppersmith, G., Ngo, K., Leary, R., Wood, A.: Exploratory analysis of social media prior to a suicide attempt. In: Proceedings of the Third Workshop on Computational Linguistics and Clinical Psychology, pp. 106–117 (2016)

18. Costello, E.J., et al.: Development and natural history of mood disorders. Biol. Psychiatry **52**(6), 529–542 (2002)

19. Daine, K., Hawton, K., Singaravelu, V., Stewart, A., Simkin, S., Montgomery, P.: The power of the web: a systematic review of studies of the influence of the internet on self-harm and suicide in young people. PLoS ONE **8**(10), e77555 (2013)

20. De Choudhury, M., Gamon, M., Counts, S., Horvitz, E.: Predicting depression via social media. ICWSM **13**, 1–10 (2013)

21. De Choudhury, M., Kiciman, E., Dredze, M., Coppersmith, G., Kumar, M.: Discovering shifts to suicidal ideation from mental health content in social media. In: Proceedings of the 2016 CHI Conference on Human Factors in Computing Systems, pp. 2098–2110. ACM (2016)

22. Chadha, A., Kaushik, B.: A Survey on prediction of suicidal ideation using machine and ensemble learning. Comput. J. (2019)

23. Chadha, A., Kaushik, B.: Suicidal ideation from the perspective of social and opinion mining. In: Singh, P.K., Kar, A.K., Singh, Y., Kolekar, M.H., Tanwar, S. (eds.) Proceedings of ICRIC 2019. LNEE, vol. 597, pp. 659–670. Springer, Cham (2020). https://doi.org/10.1007/978-3-030-29407-6_47

Classification of Imbalanced Data: Addressing Data Intrinsic Characteristics

Armaan Garg[(⊠)], Vishali Aggarwal, and Neeti Taneja

Department of Apex Institute of Technology - Computer Science
and Engineering (AIT-CSE), Chandigarh University, Mohali, India
armaangarg7@gmail.com, vishalisingla30@gmail.com,
neeti.ibmcse@cumail.in

Abstract. Misclassification of skewed datasets is one of the major problems in data mining. In the case of skewness, the number of instances presenting an important class are very short as compared to other classes. Many real world applications suffer from this skewed distribution. Depending on application to application, misclassification of the minority class instances could lead to huge losses. Some of the recent investigations have suggested that there are some issues related to data intrinsic characteristics which heavily affects the performance of the classifier. The major issues are: presence of small disjuncts, lack of density, overlap between classes, presence of noise, borderline instances and the problem of data shift. Through this study, we have discussed an insight into these issues and proposed potential algorithmic solutions that helped us in minimising these problems. For this study we have considered a binary classification model, one being the minority class and other being the majority class. The results induced by the study shows that, this can be use as a basis for future algorithms in addressing the issues of data intrinsic characteristics. The paper is divided into following sections- 1. Introduction 2. Related Work 3. Nature of the problem 4. Proposed Solutions 5. Experiments & Results 6. Conclusion

Keywords: Data intrinsic · Imbalance · Data mining · Classification

1 Introduction

In current times, various studies has been undertaken where large amount of data streams can be classified into different classes. In most real world applications the skewness of the data stream is high and there is varying degree of class imbalance which can complicate the task of accurate classification. In scenarios like these, class imbalance is particularly difficult to overcome and has not been as thoroughly studied. Most of the past studies assumed every particular data is in right format and balanced [1, 3]. But when classifiers act out results in biasing towards the majority class which results in misclassification of minority class examples. As minority class examples are too less than the majority class, the classifiers are not able to study the minority class instances and in testing phase misclassify them [7].

Data stream is the data generated continuously by the applications. Applications such as network traffic monitoring, credit card fraud detection, and web click stream.

© Springer Nature Singapore Pte Ltd. 2020
P. K. Singh et al. (Eds.): FTNCT 2019, CCIS 1206, pp. 264–277, 2020.
https://doi.org/10.1007/978-981-15-4451-4_21

The high risk factor involved in misclassifying the minority instances have highlighted the need of precise classification. As classification is an important step in decision making, predicting the classes of unknown data based on past analysis, data stream classification has become one of the most important field of research in recent years. When relating to real world applications, many a times we have seen a distribution where almost all of the cases belong to one category and a few of the cases belong to the other category. This skewness in distribution of data makes it difficult for the classifier to properly classify the instances of minority class.

In few investigations, it was observed that they are few other factors that lead to the poor performance of the classifier. The goal of this study was to look into these factors. There are few issues related to intrinsic characteristics of data which have a major impact on classification of the skewed datasets [1, 4, 12, 13]. In previous investigations, the issues have been discussed but lacked in a throughout solution. This study focuses on six major underlying issues. Based on mathematical algorithms each issue was addressed individually and later on integrated. The significant increase in the performance of classifiers shows the need of such measures to reduce the effects of data intrinsic characteristics issues. In the first section of this paper, we have discussed six major issues related to these data intrinsic characteristics and in the later section we have put up the potential mathematical algorithms to solve these issues.

2 Related Work

There has been work done on the identification of the problems related to class imbalances and the data intrinsic characteristics [1] (Victoria López et al.). This study presented a detailed discussion on the data intrinsic characteristics. The study was aimed on the broad spectrum of the issues [12] that arise due to data intrinsic characteristics. Most of the issues were similar to previous studies. A more detailed understanding was explored. Błaszczyński et al. (2018) proposed a similar study, working on few similar characteristics and proposed a tuned model to address these issues [13].

3 Nature of the Problem

Skewed class distributions do not hinder the learning task by itself, but usually a series of difficulties related with this problem turn up. Related to this issue, in this section we have discussed on the nature of the problem itself, emphasising several data intrinsic characteristics that do have a strong influence on degraded classification, in order to be able to address this problem in a more feasible way.

3.1 Small Disjuncts

One of the major cause of class imbalance is the presence of small disjuncts. This situation arises when we have small groups of instances belonging to one category present in a huge space of instances belonging to other class [1, 3]. The classifier is unable to understand whether to consider these groups as another class or its simply the mere presence of noise. This dilemma leads to the misclassification of the positive instances. (Wherever used, positive instances represent the data points belonging to minority class and negative instances are the data points representing the majority class).

3.2 Lack of Density

The second issue that arise due to the intrinsic characteristics of data is having a small sample size [9]. It is related to the 'lack of data' where we do not have enough instances to make generalisations about these instances. The positive class instances are so limited that the classifier is not properly able to study them which leads to the misclassification of these instances, hence resulting in the poor performance of the classifier. Having such kind of issue in a dataset, it would be very had to develop a model which can properly classify the positive class instances. Most of the classifiers will simply ignore these instances by declaring them as instances of noise.

3.3 Overlapping or Class Separability

Sometimes, a situation arises where we have similar type of instances representing different classes. When we use these instances to train our classifier, the classifier is not properly able to generalise these instances into different classes due to the similarity between the data. In training phase the classifier is able to learn about the minor dissimilarities between instances belonging to different classes because of the supervised learning but in the testing phase when unknown data is presented to the classifier, it gets completely confused resulting in misclassification of the data [2]. Higher the region of overlap (meaning, higher the similarity between instances belonging to different categories) lower is the accuracy of the classifier in properly categorising the instances.

3.4 Noisy Data

Noise is present in every system upto some extent. Presence of noise in the dataset hinders the process of proper classification of the data. It has even adverse effect on the classification process if we have a skewed distribution of data. In skewed dataset, we already have a few numbers of positive instances, so even if the noise is present in small amount it has a huge impact on the classification of the positive instances [6, 11]. The classifier easily mistakes the positive class instances with noise, as both are present in small amount. So, the classifier ignores many of the positive instances, considering then as noise. This leads in the degraded performance of the classifier. We could use some of the pruning techniques to remove the noise but this will also lead to the removal of some of the positive instances. So, pruning wouldn't help us in this case.

3.5 Borderline Examples

The instances of both the majority and minority class tend to overlap at the borderline region. It becomes difficult for the classifier to accurately distinguish between the positive and negative instances at the borderline [6]. At the boundary, the positive instances are sometime closer to the cluster of negative instances instead of their own class cluster and same is true for the negative instances also which are present at the borderline. So, the need is to get the borderline instances closer to their own cluster, so that they could be properly classified.

3.6 Dataset Shift

It may so happen that the instances follow a very distinct pattern of distribution in two different datasets. The classifier learns through the training dataset, but the test dataset could contain a very different pattern of distribution as compared to all the training datasets. Sometimes, the instances belonging to one class are closer to the cluster of another class as compared to their own cluster, if the classifier is unknown of such pattern it may lead to very poor results. This issue is known as data shift [1, 8, 10]. What happens is that the classifier thinks that the instance (which is shifted to the cluster of another class) belongs to the class to whom its closer. So, that particular instance gets misclassified. Data shift problem is more dominant in the case of skewed distributions the classifier is not properly able to study the minority class and it's very easy to misclassify the instances of minority class [4].

4 Proposed Solutions

In this section, we had proposed algorithmic solutions addressing each problem one-by-one. These solutions have the potential to resolve the issues related to the data intrinsic characteristics.

4.1 Algorithm for Solving the Issue of Small Disjuncts

Input: I = Dataset containing Small chunks of minority class data.

Output: O = Balanced dataset (i.e., having enough amount of data for each class, so that they can be classified properly) by enhancing the dataset.

Step 1: Partition the dataset into disjunct sets (similar data assigned the same set, positive instances represent the minority class and the negative instances represent the majority class). say S1 and S2, one representing the minority class and the other representing the majority class.

Step 2: Compare the size of sets (S1 and S2) to find out the type of data which are present in small chunks (to find out the minority class).

Step 3: Collect the data corresponding to the positive instances (minority class data elements) from the other similar domains representing the same type of data as our input dataset (in this case, we may consider other NASA or Promise Metrics Data Program defect dataset, for example pc5). Let the data collected be represented by set S3.

Step 4: Embed the data collected (set S3) into the current dataset to decrease the imbalance in the classes, which will help us in eliminating the problem of small disjuncts.

4.2   Algorithm for Solving the Issue of Lack of Density

Input: I = Dataset containing non-uniformly distributed data.

Output: O = Relatively balanced frequency for each class in the dataset (i.e., having equivalent distributed amount of data within a range, representing different classes) by mathematically producing synthesised data for the minority class.

Step 1: Partition the dataset into categories (i.e., similar data in the same class and dissimilar data in different classes). Let's say class C1 and C2.

Step 2: Applying averaging within the class (only for minority class chunks) to gain synthesised data elements (say G1) that are well distributed over the data space, to balance the skewness between classes. Distribution is done in such a way, so as not to reintroduce the problem of small disjuncts (distance is calculated between two points and the new point is added at that distance on the either side of that two points to make a spread out distribution).

Step 3: Repeat the above procedure recursively to generate data (Gi) that will balance the minority chunks in proportion to the majority class chunks, as well as keeping in mind to form the synthesised data points in a uniformly distributed manner so as to remove the lack of density problem.

Step 4: Embed the new data elements (Gi) into the initial dataset, and we will have an equally distributed type of data within a given range.

4.3   Algorithm for Solving the Issue of Overlapping

Input: I = Dataset containing different classes of data with overlap between the elements of these classes.

Output: O = Each class well defined within its own space without any overlapping.

Step 1: Partition the dataset into categories (i.e., similar data in same class and dissimilar data in different classes). Let's say class C1 and C2.

Step 2: Applying addition/subtraction of fixed value for each element in the set class which is relatively overlapping the other class (choose a relatively big number and apply to over each element in the set) to push back the overlapping data elements into their own chunks. These will form a well defined between different classes which will make it easier for classifier to distinguish between them.

Step 3: Repeat the above procedure recursively (for each overlapping region) to restrict the data elements to their own clusters, so as to remove the overlapping problem.

4.4   Algorithm for Solving the Issue of Noise

Input: I = Dataset which contains redundant data along with the useful information.

Output: O = The reduction in noise by degrading the value of the complete noise prone regions.

Step 1: Partition the dataset into categories (i.e., similar data in same class and dissimilar data in different classes). Let's say class C1 and C2. We will also see a different set of elements having slightly dissimilar properties to both the above classes i.e., the noise. As it will be hard to distinguish between the noise elements and the elements of the minority class (as they both are present in small amount sand it will be hard of us to study them and classify them properly), we will consider the complete set of those elements (elements that are under the impression of consisting the noise) for the removal of the noise.

Step 2: Distribute the region into k clusters (k is a numerical value and depends upon the dataset), after this, synthetically over- sample each cluster and find which has the minimum noise. Keep the one with the minimum noise and remove other clusters. This is done to keep the uniqueness of the original data elements present in the noise region.

Step 3: Repeat the above step in a recursive manner until the average of all the elements of the set elements in which noisy data exists is under the acceptable threshold value.

4.5   Algorithm for Solving the Issue of Borderline

Input: I = Dataset with different classes of data that are not cleanly defined over their cluster boundaries.

Output: O = Dissimilar class elements far separated from each other (means that there will be large borderline margins between different classes).

Step 1: Partition the dataset into categories (i.e., similar data in the same class and dissimilar data in different classes). Let's say class C1 and C2. Now consider the dissimilar elements that are overlapped at the borderlines.

Step 2: Subtract a common value from each value of border line so that the set value can be fetched back into the set lies into the border.

Step 3: Repeat the above procedure recursively until we have attained a minimum borderline margin between different classes.

Step 4: Check for the elements whose values have been subtracted in step 2, and be sure that these values are grouped together with the right set of clusters (i.e., checking for the class to which they belong).

4.6   Algorithm for Solving the Issue of Data Shift

Input: I = Dataset consisting of data elements that are not well defined within their space.

Output: O = Set of similar clusters with on outliers.

Step 1: Analyse each class for the presence of outliers.

Step 2: Compare each value of the set. If certain value is found to be the outlier of the set then shift that data from containing set to other set where that value will be considered to be the real value. We have to be careful as this could also be the noise. Compare the outlier will all the other sets one-by-one for resemblance.

Step 3: Perform the above operation for each outlier for all the sets recursively till all the outliers are shifted to their appropriate sets.

5   Experiment and Results

5.1   Experimental Setup

A synthesised dataset is formed by collecting data from an online repository named MOA (Massive online analysis) [2]. We have considered the Airlines Dataset. The code is written in java language. To implement it, we have used the NetBeans 8.1 Software and the operating system used is MAC OS Sierra version 10.13.4.

5.2   Dataset Preparation

Original Dataset: In the dataset 5th and 6th attribute are the most important, as using them, we performed all the algorithmic calculations. First four attributes are for keeping track of which data belong to which flight. The last attribute is the class attribute which tells us which instance belong to which class.

Transformed Dataset: Analysing the dataset we have considered two classes that are formed depending on the difference between actual time and the expected time of flight to calculate the delay. The ratio between the minority class instances and the majority class instances is considered to be better than or equal to 0.5, to remove the problem of imbalance. Separate other regions are formed to address the issues like overlapping and borderline to process the instances in that region and separate them depending on which class they belong to. External noise is also introduced using the WEKA tool to make the calculations more realistic.

Different classifiers have been used to showcase the difference in the performance of the classifiers with the unprocessed dataset (Original dataset) and then the transformed dataset. Table 1 highlights the correctness achieved in predicting the right outcome by applying the proposed algorithmic solutions and how they perform if there is no prepossessing done.

Below is the list of the various classifiers that have been considered:

(1)   Naïve Bayesian Model
(2)   Nearest Neighbors Model (K-NN)
(3)   Support Vector Machine Model (Sequential Minimal Optimization SMO in WEKA)
(4)   Random Forest Model
(5)   Logistic Model

5.3   Results and Discussion

Table 1. The correctly and incorrectly classified instances by various classifiers in different datasets

Classifier	Unprocessed dataset (Original)		Processed dataset (Algorithmically transformed)	
	Correctly classified instances	Incorrectly classified instances	Correctly classified instances	Incorrectly classified instances
Naive Bayes	61	39	75	10
K-NN	60	40	71	14
SMO	62	38	70	15
Random Forest	64	36	64	21
Logistic Model	56	44	57	28

Table 1 shows that every classifier performs better with the processed dataset that has been processed using our proposed algorithms. The incorrectly classified instances have decreased drastically, thus helping us with our problem.

Table 2. The Precision and recall obtained by various classifiers by processing different datasets

Classifier	Unprocessed dataset (Original)		Processed dataset (Algorithmically transformed)	
	Precision	Recall	Precision	Recall
Naive Bayes	0.582	0.610	0.882	0.882
K-NN	0.584	0.60	0.834	0.835
SMO	0.570	0.620	0.823	0.824
Random Forest	0.56	0.64	0.750	0.753
Logistic Model	0.599	0.56	0.684	0.671

To analyse the impact and deviation in the results different performance metrics were applied. The following performance measures were used - Precision, Recall, F-measure and ROC area as shown in Tables 2 and 3. These are most widely used classification performance measures. Tables 2 and 3 shows highlights the deviation between different performance measure on applying the proposed solutions.

Table 3. The F-measure and ROC area obtained by various classifiers by processing different datasets

Classifier	Unprocessed dataset (Original)		Processed dataset (Algorithmically transformed)	
	F-measure	ROC area	F-measure	ROC area
Naive Bayes	0.594	0.425	0.882	0.866
K-NN	0.591	0.505	0.834	0.841
SMO	0.588	0.490	0.820	0.80
Random Forest	0.583	0.488	0.746	0.834
Logistic Model	0.575	0.501	0.674	0.703

Observations: The study aimed at achieving applicable algorithms to address the issues that arise due to data intrinsic characteristics. As we can see from Tables 1, 2 and 3, the classifiers perform way superior on with the processed dataset as compared to when with unprocessed dataset. There has been about 15% increase in the number of correctly classified instances and a drop of about 50% in the number of incorrectly classified instances. The precision shows about 18% improvement, recall has an improving of about 15%, and in case of F-measure there is improving of about 25% and the ROC curve area shows an increase of about 30%. All the classifiers perform well, and the Naive Bayes and K-NN stands-out with the best performance results as compared to other dataset. Naive Bayes sees to perform with the highest Precision, Recall, F-Measure and ROC Area. This clearly shows that the data characteristic have critical impact on how the classifier processes it. These results show that if we use such kind of data preprocessing techniques it could help us in achieving better performances from eh classifiers. For better understanding and visualisation bar graph of table results were developed. Each figure numbered Figs. 1, 2, 3, 4, 5 and 6 highlights a significant improvement in the performance of the classifier when it works on the pre-processed data formed from applying the algorithms. Each performance measure showered some change that tells us that these intrinsic characteristics have a crucial impact on the classification process and could hinder the classifiers in achieving high classification accuracy.

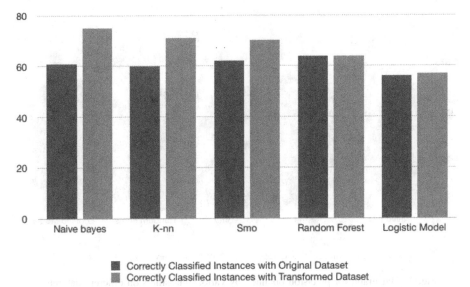

Fig. 1. Bar graph for correctly classified instances by various classifiers

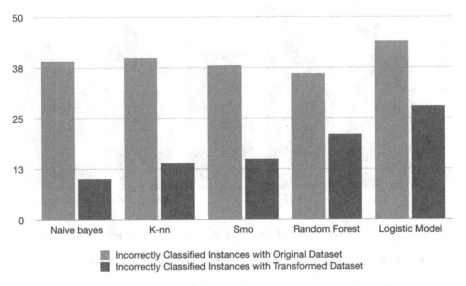

Fig. 2. Bar graph for incorrectly classified instances by various classifiers

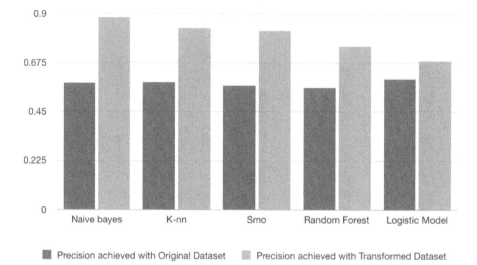

Fig. 3. Bar graph for precision obtained by various classifiers on different datasets

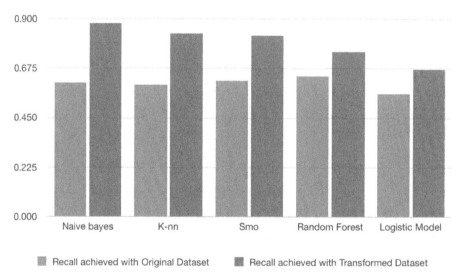

Fig. 4. Bar graph for recall obtained by various classifiers on different datasets

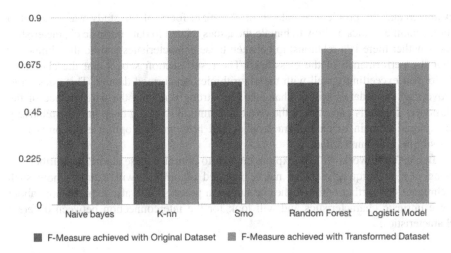

Fig. 5. Bar graph for F-measure obtained by various classifiers on different datasets

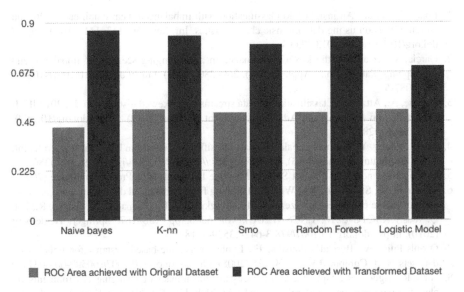

Fig. 6. Bar graph for ROC area obtained by various classifiers on different datasets

6 Conclusion

The intrinsic characteristics has its own crucial role on how the data is studied. This paper presented a clear insight into few of the major issues that arise due to these characteristics and provided the mathematical means on how to overcome those issues. The work highlighted six major characteristics, that are: problem of small disjuncts, noisy data, lack of density, overlapping between the classes, region of borderline examples and the problem of data shift. The main focus of the study was to develop some quantitate rules on how to handle the issues related to data intrinsic characteristics and whether there is a relationship between these characteristics and do they hinder or alter the performance of the classifiers. The result section shows that the classifiers performed exceedingly well with the algorithmic transformed dataset. This goes on to prove that these data intrinsic characteristics strongly impact the performance of the classifier. Thus this paper gives the research community to dig deep into the relatively unexplored domain of data characteristics and how we can optimise the process of classifying imbalanced data.

In our future work, we will explore on how to optimise these algorithms further and using new techniques such as, nature inspired algorithms will examine how such techniques can further optimise the classification process. Will also explore more about these intrinsic characteristics and will look for the interconnection between different characteristics.

References

1. López, V., et al.: An insight into classification with imbalanced data: empirical results and current trends on us ing data intrinsic characteristics. Inf. Sci. **250**, 113–141 (2013). https://doi.org/10.1016/j.ins.2013.07.007
2. García, V., et al.: On the k-NN performance in a challenging scenario of imbalance and overlapping. Pattern Anal. Appl. **11**(3–4), 269–280 (2007). https://doi.org/10.1007/s10044-007-0087-5
3. Godase, A., Attar, V.: Classification of data streams with skewed distribution. In: 2012 IEEE Conference on Evolving and Adaptive Intelligent Systems (2012). https://doi.org/10.1109/eais.2012.6232821
4. Xu, Z., Zhang, Y.: A novel imbalanced data classification algorithm based on fuzzy rule. Int. J. Inf. Commun. Technol. **14**(3), 1 (2019). https://doi.org/10.1504/ijict.2019.10015386
5. Quiñonero-Candela, J.: Dataset Shift in Machine Learning. MIT Press, Cambridge (2009)
6. Napierała, K., Stefanowski, J., Wilk, S.: Learning from imbalanced data in presence of noisy and borderline examples. In: Szczuka, M., Kryszkiewicz, M., Ramanna, S., Jensen, R., Hu, Q. (eds.) RSCTC 2010. LNCS (LNAI), vol. 6086, pp. 158–167. Springer, Heidelberg (2010). https://doi.org/10.1007/978-3-642-13529-3_18
7. Orriols-Puig, A., Bernadó-Mansilla, E.: Evolutionary rule-based systems for imbalanced data sets. Soft. Comput. **13**(3), 213–225 (2008). https://doi.org/10.1007/s00500-008-0319-7
8. Alaiz-Rodríguez, R., Japkowicz, N.: Assessing the impact of changing environments on classifier performance. In: Bergler, S. (ed.) AI 2008. LNCS (LNAI), vol. 5032, pp. 13–24. Springer, Heidelberg (2008). https://doi.org/10.1007/978-3-540-68825-9_2
9. Raudys, S.J., Jain, A.K.: Small sample size effects in statistical pattern recognition: recommendations for practitioners and open problems. In: 1990 Proceedings 10th International Conference on Pattern Recognition (1990). https://doi.org/10.1109/icpr.1990.118138
10. Shimodaira, H.: Improving predictive inference under covariate shift by weighting the log-likelihood function. J. Stat. Plann. Infer. **90**(2), 227–244 (2000). https://doi.org/10.1016/s0378-3758(00)00115-4
11. Weiss, G.M.: Mining with rarity. In: ACM SIGKDD Explorations Newsletter, vol. 6, no. 1, p. 7 (2004). https://doi.org/10.1145/1007730.1007734

12. Fernández, A., García, S., Galar, M., Prati, R.C., Krawczyk, B., Herrera, F.: Data Intrinsic Characteristics. Learning from Imbalanced Data Sets, pp. 253–277. Springer, Cham (2018). https://doi.org/10.1007/978-3-319-98074-4_10
13. Błaszczyński, J., Stefanowski, J.: Local data characteristics in learning classifiers from imbalanced data. In: Gaweda, A.E., Kacprzyk, J., Rutkowski, L., Yen, G.G. (eds.) Advances in Data Analysis with Computational Intelligence Methods. SCI, vol. 738, pp. 51–85. Springer, Cham (2018). https://doi.org/10.1007/978-3-319-67946-4_2

Heterogeneous Cross Project Defect Prediction – A Survey

Rohit Vashisht[(✉)] and Syed Afzal Murtaza Rizvi

CSE Department, Jamia Millia Islamia, Delhi, India
vashishtrohit@akgec.ac.in, sarizvi@jmi.ac.in

Abstract. In the testing phase of Software Development Life Cycle (SDLC), Software Defect Prediction (SDP) is one of the pivotal task which finds the modules that are more vulnerable to defects and therefore need substantial testing for the early identification of these defects. A lot of work has been done on Cross - Project Defect Prediction (CPDP) that aims to predict defects in the target project lacking in historical defect prediction data or having limited defect data to build an effective generalized defect prediction model. Mostly, CPDP approaches predict the defects in target project on the basis of similar metrics found between source and target project. This paper focuses on the prediction of defects using a Heterogeneous metric set such that no common metrics exist between the source and the target projects. In this paper, a systematic literature study has been done to quote the main findings about CPDP from year 2002 to 2019. The main purpose of this survey is to put forward the adequate content in front of computer science researchers for exploring the specific area and to provide various future directions in this field.

Keywords: Quality Assurance · Cross project · Heterogeneous metrics · Defect prediction

1 Introduction

The endurance of desired level of quality in the final software product or service, called as a Software Quality Assurance (SQA), is the main objective of any software quality model. Or it can be said that Software Defect Prediction (SDP) and Software Quality Assurance (SQA) are two complementary activities that emphasize on maximum defect predictions at the right time leading to the production of qualitative software product at the end. Testing phase of SDLC is the most crucial one as it eats up a major part of the aggregate project cost. So, it is essential part to be primed in every project development process. Therefore, a question arises: "How to lessen the testing phase's cost so that the overall project's cost can be minimized?" The SDP is the only way to this problem which predicts defects from the historical database. Various data mining techniques are applied to build SDP models using data from historical databases [1]. Such data usually consist of two components: - Software metrics that are the criteria for evaluating the degree to which a certain software characteristic possesses some property [2] and the labels that are used for binary classification of given instances into defective or non-defective categories using defect models [3]. Mostly defect prediction (DP) models have been designed to find

© Springer Nature Singapore Pte Ltd. 2020
P. K. Singh et al. (Eds.): FTNCT 2019, CCIS 1206, pp. 278–288, 2020.
https://doi.org/10.1007/978-981-15-4451-4_22

defects "within-project" by partitioning the available project dataset into two parts, in such a manner that using one part of dataset (referred as labeled instances dataset) the software defect prediction model is trained and using the another part we can test the built DP model. Testing the built DP model implies to find the labels for unlabelled instances [4] which is either defective or non- defective. But, in the current era, software application development (commonly known as web applications) is done generally through the mash-up approach that combines the existing and useful legacy software models in a novel manner to build new models [5]. When one is doing defect prediction in newly built software model using mash-up approach, one requires to transform or to form some sort of alignment between the old and the new model defect datasets.

In this paper, the whole content has been structured under the following sections: Sect. 2 explains defect prediction, classification of defect prediction, and basic Heterogeneous defect prediction (HDP) model, in Sect. 3, the whole work done related to HDP is explored with some initial survey on CPDP, Sect. 4 explains the various evaluation parameters used by authors for interpreting experimental results and Sect. 4 concludes some research gaps in field of HDP that also provides various future directions in the same field.

2   Heterogeneous Cross Project Defect Prediction (HCPDP)

2.1   Basic Terminologies

The defect can be defined as any deviation of actual outcome from the expected outcome in terms of end-user requirements for a specified environmental setting. The classification of SDP is well described in Fig. 1. Mainly, defect prediction can be categorized into two main categories that are Within-Project Defect prediction (WPDP) and Cross Project Defect Prediction (CPDP). The basic difference between WPDP and CPDP is that WPDP deals with only one project dataset means instances of the same project are used to train and to test the designed defect prediction model but CPDP modeling generally uses more than one project dataset instances. Under CPDP category, there are further two subcategories- CPDP using same metric set (called Homogeneous CPDP) and CPDP using different metric set (called Heterogeneous CPDP or HDP). In homogeneous CPDP, a prediction model is trained on the basis of a common metric set extracted out from the source project and the target project and it predicts defects for the unlabelled instances of the target project having an inadequate historical defect dataset. But, in heterogeneous CPDP, there is a challenge in collection of exactly common metric set between the source and the target dataset. For e.g., it is difficult to match metrics that are language specific if the projects are written in different languages [6]. Some CPDP models use only common metrics, but, this raises a matter of discussion on the accuracy of defect prediction model designed on basis of common metric set because it may be possible that common metric set may not include some factual metric needed to build a good prediction model [7]. CPDP technique creates a model by classifying the given source project data to forecast defects for target project. Source cross-project detects the suitable training data in order to signify the similar defect matrix with the target project to make comprehensible CPDP result [28]. HDP approach predicts the

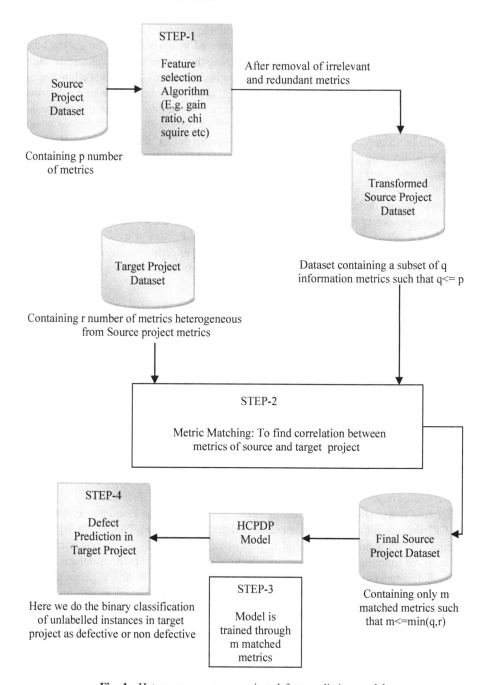

Fig. 1. Heterogeneous cross project defect prediction model

defects across projects consist of only heterogeneous metrics which are showing some kind of similar distribution in their values. For e.g., the number of methods called by a class (RFC) and the number of unique operands can be considered as two heterogeneous metrics which show same alignment in their value distribution for any two project datasets.

2.2 Basic HCPDP Model

The basic model of HDP is described in Fig. 1. HDP modeling initiates with source dataset and target dataset in which each tuple and each column represents dataset's instance and metric respectively.

The very first step in HDP modeling is to eliminate irrelevant, redundant and useless features/metrics by using appropriate feature selection methods [13]. This step aims at reducing the complexity of defect prediction model, to upgrade the accuracy of defect prediction and to build a generalized defect prediction model if the right subset of highly discriminate metrics is selected. The second step is the most important and challenging step in HDP modeling i.e. metric Matching. Metric matching finds some kind of similar distribution in every possible combination of metrics between the source and the target datasets in order to identify matched metric set. Thus, to identify the correlation between metrics, one can use several existing techniques such as KS test, method of least squares, scatter diagram method and Spearman's rank correlation coefficient method [14, 15]. The last step is to train the model using the matched metric set (final processed source dataset) and then to use this model for predicting defects in the target project.

3 Related Work

In 2002, Melo et al. [20] gave the very first identified work on CPDP. Here, the author proposed a novel method of assessment named Multivariate Adaptive Regression Spline (MARS) by gathering fault and design data of two medium sized Java based systems (Xpose & Jwriter). The built model MARS ranked the classes in second system according to the degree of their inclination towards fault using the model built on the basis of first system. MARS performed better than linear regression model and also economically viable. But, the predicted fault probabilities of the classes did not provide any idea about system being predicted.

In 2009, Menzies et al. [21] filtered out the cross project defect data for removing the redundant and irrelevant data and similar data for training was selected using the nearest neighbor (NN) approach. To conduct experiments, authors used 10 projects from two different data sources. The findings of the experiment showed that the performance of CPDP was improved, but still lower than WPDP.

In the same year 2009, Zimmermann et al. [24] applied the classification approach to the projects. The author classified the projects on the basis of their domain, coding standards and process parameters. Using proposed model, the author tried to predict defects in Internet Explorer (IE) using a model trained on Mozilla Firefox defect dataset and vice-versa. The result depicted that for a vice-versa condition, the model gave a poor defect prediction performance. Again, in 2009, Camargo et al. [23] used design complexity metrics for defect prediction, but this data varies from project to project. So, to avoid this variation, the author applied log transformation to achieve similar distribution in training and testing samples. But, the proposed kind of transformation was only applicable to projects whose data was not spread as the data available for defect prediction model designing.

In 2011, Menzies et al. [24] argued that what seems to be relevant from the perspective of global view is sometimes not useful from the perspective of local view. This occurs due to heterogeneity of defect data. The paper concluded that the local treatments were different as well as superior in comparison to global treatments. Rather than emphasizing on majority part in a generic way (that may be pointless to any singular project), one should converge more on condition-based rules.

In 2012, Bettenburg et al. [25] gave a better analogy between local and global analysis. The authors concluded that the local models were more suitable for specific subset of dataset but global models focused more on generality. In the same year 2012, Rahman et al. [26] emphasized that standard evaluation parameters like precision, recall and F- Score were considered over a certain value of threshold and not appropriate for quality control assurance during defect prediction modeling. The proposed work concluded that CPDP models gave a comparable performance to WPDP models in terms of Area under Operating Curve (AUC).

In 2013, Canfora et al. [19] presented a novel multi- objective approach based on a logistic regression model trained by Non- Dominated Sorting Genetic algorithm (NSGA-II). The proposed approach overcame the limitation of single objective model [26] that gave a compromise between precision and recall. It facilitated the defect predictor with a flexibility to attain various trade-offs between the cost of code inspections, estimated in terms of Kilo Lines of Code (KLOC) of source code and the number of artifacts prone to defect predicted by the model.

In 2014, Zhang et al. [16] proposed a universal defect prediction model using 1398 projects from the source forge and Google code. But, this model could only predict defects in target project if there are at least 26 matched metrics between the source and the target dataset. In the same year 2014, Li et al. [17] won over the limitation of previous work [16] using distribution characteristic vectors of an instance as metric. The results were comparable and also improved from the basic CPDP model results. But, here the results of Cross project defect prediction with the imbalance feature set (CPDP-IFS) were not compared with WPDP. Also the experimental results of this model were conducted on only 11 projects in 3 dataset groups.

In 2015, Jing et al. [18] proposed the very first work related to HDP. The proposed model was used to predict the defects based on canonical correlation analysis (CCA). To achieve the similarity in metric value distribution, the proposed model integrated dummy metrics with null values for metrics which didn't exist during metric matching between the source and the target datasets. The experiments were conducted comparatively using smaller number of projects (14 projects in four dataset groups).

In 2015 and 2016, Nam et al. [7] introduced transfer learning approach for HDP modeling. The results were much comparable to WPDP. Moreover, the experiments were conducted on 34 projects in 5 dataset groups. The major advantage of this model was that it didn't change the original source and target project datasets like in CCA [18].

The proposed model didn't possess any such limitation but performance of proposed approach can further be upgraded by various future directions listed in Sect. 4.

In 2017, Li et al. [28] stated that filtering of defect data before using it for training the defect prediction model highly impacts the accuracy of defect prediction. He gave a detailed comparison of existing four filters that are Target Project data guided filter (TGF), Source Project data guided filter (SGF), Data characteristics based filter (DCBF) and local cluster based filter (LCBF). These filters lacked in two aspects. Firstly, because of their exponential time complexity & secondly, these filters weren't scalable with huge datasets. To overcome these two deficiencies, the author proposed a novel filter—Hierarchical selection based filter (HSBF). The software project data was selected by HSBF in a hierarchical fashion, i.e. from the lowest module level to the highest project level. The designed novel filter HSBF gave a better performance in comparison to the existing four filters.

In 2018, Zhou et al. [27] introduced a domain adaptation technique to infix higher dimensional feature spaces of two different domains into an equivalent lower dimensional feature space and then evaluated the difference between two feature spaces using dictionary learning technique. The author generated the experimental results using 94 cross-project combinations of 12 projects from three open source project datasets consisting of NetGene, NASA, AEEEM. He used three performance parameters—F-Measure, recall and Balance for comparing the results of three baselines that were heterogeneous defect adaptation (HDA) [27], HDP [7] and CCA+ [18]. He found that HDP [7] could work only on few cross project pairs, but HDA was accessible to any possible matched metric pair. Also, HDA gave comparable results to WPDP and was much superior to other two heterogeneous defect prediction techniques (HDP & CCA).

In 2018, Porte et al. [28] compared the four well known CPDP models [2008 Watanabe [8], 2009 Cruz [23], 2009 Turhan [21], 2014 He [17]. He proposed meta-learning rule which learned from the past knowledge and experiences and then dynamically explained which method of CPDP would be most suitable for the target project. The four methods gave minor difference in their results when compared on the basis of parameter AUC.

In 2019, Gong et al. [30] suggested that there are more instances of software data than errors that can lead to serious violations in poor conditions. To eliminate these errors, he proposed unsupervised deep domain adaption method to built HDP model. To overcome the heterogeneous problems, Maximum Mean Discrepancy (MMD) is used for calculating the distance between source and target data.

In 2019, Li et al. [31] focused on two essential characteristics of defect data i.e. linear inseparability and class imbalance. He proposed Two- Stage Ensemble Learning (TSEL) approach for HDP, which are: Ensemble Multi-Kernel Domain Adaptation (EMDA) stage and Ensemble Data Sampling (EDS) stage. The proposed technique Two- Stage Ensemble Learning (TSEL) gave better performance in comparison to baseline methods WPDP, CPDP and HDP [7] (Table 1).

Table 1. Year wise summarized work related to HCPDP

Year	Author	Major findings	Strength	Weakness
2002	Melo et al. [20]	The paper concluded that even though the two systems originate from same implementing environments, the system characteristics like design techniques, experience must influence the usage of fault prediction probabilities	The proposed methodology MARS was economically feasible and gave better performance than the linear regression mode	Predicted fault probabilities did not provide any clue about system being predicted
2009	Menzies et al. [21]	The author used analogy based method (NN) to eliminate irrelevancies from cross-company data and proposed a two-phase defect prediction model	The false alarm ratio had been reduced due to application of NN filtering approach in Cross- Company dataset	The proposed model didn't outperform WPDP results
2009	Zimmermann et al. [24]	It was observed that defect prediction (DP) model built using project data of similar domain would not always give accurate results. Other parameters like code data and process must be first interpreted and understood before formulating DP model	Using the proposed method, one could easily predict the various factors that could influence the success of CPDP model	More research was needed to automatically identify a software project's domain
2009	Camargo et al. [22]	The author proposed three univariate linear regression models built on design-complexity metrics	After applying log transformation on training samples, defect prediction results were significantly improved	We couldn't apply these kind of transformation on scattered data samples
2011	Menzies et al. [24]	The author thoroughly investigated whether general conclusions made over the whole dataset were truly applicable to local subset of same dataset or not	The paper explained WHERE and WHICH part of software project should be upgraded in order to increase the overall results of defect prediction model	The proposed analysis didn't give any idea about WHAT should be done locally or globally to improve defect prediction accuracy
2012	Rahman et al. [26]	CPDP models gave a comparable performance than WPDP model in terms of Area Under Operating Curve (AUC)	Unlike previous analysis done on various CPDP models which gave a worse performance in terms of precision and recall, the proposed experiments depicted that same model gave a comparable performance in terms of AUC when compared to WPDP model	The proposed analysis lacked in the validity and diversity of projects being tested

(*continued*)

Table 1. (*continued*)

Year	Author	Major findings	Strength	Weakness
2013	Canfora et al. [19]	The author proposed Multi-objective DP model based on genetic algorithm and compared its performance with previous CPDP models [23, 24]	When compared to other two models, the proposed technique gave the same level of recall with higher precision and lower cost value for same training and testing instances	The built model was tested on only specific product metrics. The results for other process and product metrics were yet to be explored
2014	Zhang et al. [16]	The author tried to eliminate the need to build a unique DP model for an individual project. Rather than he focused on the universality to utilize a defect prediction model in a generic way	The universal model gave higher recall value and higher AUC value when compared to WPDP results	The proposed method could only work if there were at least 26 matched metrics between source and target project data
2014	Li et al. [17]	A hybrid model was proposed to overcome imbalance feature set (IFS) problem using object class mapping approach	The results showed a significant improvement over basic CPDP model results	The experiment was done on a small number of projects. (11 projects in 3 dataset groups)
2015	Jing et al. [18]	The author uses Canonical Correlation Analysis (CCA) technique to do metric matching.	The very first identified work related to HCPDP which shows comparable results to WPDP and other CPDP techniques.	The proposed method requires modifications in source and target dataset samples to perform correlation analysis
2015 & 2016	Nam et al. [7]	The author built a HDP model by using transfer learning approach	The proposed method didn't alter the source dataset like in CCA+.	The proposed method didn't possess any such limitation
2017	Yong Li et al. [28]	The author proposed a novel filter HSBF based on hierarchical selection and compared its performance with existing four filters	The proposed filter HSBF performed best when compared to existing four filters	The designed novel filter used only object-oriented metrics that raises issue on design validity of proposed filter
2018	Zhou et al. [27]	The proposed method used domain adaptation method to embed two domains higher dimensional data into low dimensional and comparable feature space	The proposed technique HDA outperformed other two existing HCPDP techniques- HDP and CCA+	The author didn't consider the class imbalance problem while interpreting experimental results
2018	Porto et al. [29]	The author predicted dynamically the best CPDP model among four traditional CPDP models for a given project using met-learning technique	The performance of all four CPDP models didn't show any significant difference. One could easily find which CPDP model would be suitable for a given project	The training data was comprised of only Java Open Source project data which raised the issue of external validity on the experimental results

(*continued*)

Table 1. (*continued*)

Year	Author	Major findings	Strength	Weakness
2019	Gong et al. [30]	The author developed a Simple Neural Network model (SNN) to solve the problems of heterogeneous and unbalanced software defect prediction (SDP)	It solved class imbalance problem by using class-entropy loss function as classification error	Historical data can't be directly used, as different indicators have been identified among the projects
2019	Li et al. [31]	The author introduced a Two-Stage Ensemble Learning (TSEL) approach to predict software defect for heterogeneous feature sets	The proposed Ensemble Multiple Kernel Correlation Alignment (EMKCA) predictor performed better metric matching	Domain Adaptation Technique (DAT) gave better results only when two dataset have two common features

4   Conclusion and Future Work

HCPDP is very likely-looking research area in the field of software defect prediction which implicitly uses the heterogeneous metric sets to build defect prediction model for the target project depriving of past defect data. This technique is not only bounded to defect prediction, but can be significantly used for decision based approaches related to software engineering. A detailed literature survey of HCPDP leads to the following conclusive findings and future works in the same field:

- The main challenge in HDP modeling is the metric matching. Let us consider metric M is the matched metric between the source and the target projects. And if, presence of more number as well as less number of metric M in the target project leads to higher defect probability, then this type of matching is called noisy metric matching. Designing a novel filter to resolve noisy metric matching is another promising future work for the researchers.
- For further optimization of results, one can use one of the various known data pre-processing techniques (e.g. log transformation) or data sampling techniques to resolve problems like class imbalance problem or imbalance feature set (IFS) problem, i.e. surplus presence of one type of data in comparison to other type of data in a training sample dataset which leads to biased classification results [12].
- In [7], the author has used the concept of transfer learning and its various techniques to model HDP. After the detailed survey, it is found that there is no identified work on attribute characterization transfer learning (a type of transfer learning) till date, which also leads to another future direction that is yet to be explored.
- As future work, one can use deep learning [10] to find out the most informative features to do metric matching between the source and the target projects and then can use a better combination of machine learning classifiers termed as ensemble approach to predict the defects in target project [11].
- In the survey, it is observed that mostly defect prediction models [8] have been evaluated based on parameter AUC, i.e. a plot versus sensitivity and specificity. But, for a better validation of defect prediction model, the model should be analyzed on the basis of the other two parameters- precision and recall [9]. And for this

interpretation, one should identify the proper cut- off threshold to eliminate the poor matched metrics whose matching score is less than the selected cutoff threshold. So, the selection of a threshold is another future direction in HCPDP modeling.

- In order to further optimize the result of heterogeneous defect adaptation (HDA) method [27], the important entities can be selected for dictionary creation by using any appropriate clustering methods instead of random selection. Thus, this is another future scope in eliminating the randomness currently existing in HDA method [27].

- In [31], the proposed technique is specific to the homogeneous data only. Therefore, by using other ways, a universal defect prediction framework can be applied to the HDP problem. Besides this, another future work is to use deep learning and dictionary learning to address the HDP problem.

References

1. J. Adv. Res. Comput. Sci. Softw. Eng. **3**(8) (2013). ISSN: 2277128X
2. https://en.wikipedia.org/wiki/Software_metric
3. Han, D., Hoh, I. P., Kim, S., Lee, T., Nam, J.: Micro interaction metrics for defect prediction. In: Proceedings of the 16th ACM SIGSOFT International Symposium on Foundations of software engineering, New York, USA. ACM (2011)
4. D'Ambros, M., Lanza, M., Robbes, R.: Evaluating defect prediction approaches: a benchmark and an extensive comparison. Empirical Softw. Eng. **17**(4–5), 531–577 (2012)
5. Latih, R., Mulla, R., Na, L., Ahmed, P., Zarina, S., Christopher, W.: A study of mashup as a software application development technique with examples from an end-user programming perspective. J. Comput. Sci. **12**, 1406–1415 (2010)
6. Bener, A.B., Menzies, T., Di Stefano, J., Turhan, B.: On the relative value of cross-company and within-company data for defect prediction. Empirical Softw. Eng. **14**, 540–578 (2009)
7. Fu, W., Kim, S., Menzies, T., Nam, J., Tan, L.: Heterogeneous defect prediction. In: Proceedings of the 2015 10th Joint Meeting on Foundations of Software Engineering, ser. ESEC/FSE, pp. 508–519, New York, NY, USA. ACM (2015)
8. Baesens, B., Lessmann, S., Mues, C., Pietsch, S.: Benchmarking classification models for software defect prediction: a proposed framework and novel findings. IEEE Trans. Softw. Eng. **34**(4), 485–496 (2008)
9. Devanbu, P., Posnett, D., Rahman, F.: Recalling the imprecision of cross-project defect prediction. In: Proceedings of the ACM SIGSOFT 20th International Symposium on the Foundations of Software Engineering, New York, NY, USA. ACM (2018)
10. Mosavi, A., Ruiz, L., Vargas, R.: Deep learning- a review, Adv. Intell. Syst. Comput. (2017). Series Ed.: Kacprzyk, Janusz, Springer
11. http://www.cs.put.poznan.pl/jstefanowski/aed/DMmultipleclassifiers.pdf
12. Kanellopoulos, D., Kotsiantis, S.B., Pintelas, P.E.: Data preprocessing for supervised leaning. Int. J. Comput. Electr. Autom. Control Inf. Eng. **1**(12), 234–245 (2007)
13. Mwadulo, M.W.: A review on feature selection methods for classification tasks. Int. J. Comput. Appl. Technol. Res. **5**(6), 395–402 (2015)
14. Massey, F.J.: The Kolmogorov-Smirnov test for goodness of fit. J. Am. Stat. Assoc. **46**(253), 68–78 (1951)
15. Spearman, C.: The proof and measurement of association between two things. Int. J. Epidemiol. **39**(5), 1137–1150 (2010)

16. Keivanloo, I., Mockus, A., Zhang, F., Zou, Y.: Towards building a universal defect prediction model. In: Proceedings of the 11th Working Conference on Mining Software Repositories, ser. MSR, New York, NY, USA, pp. 182–191. ACM (2014)
17. He, P., Li, B., Ma, Y.: Towards cross-project defect prediction with imbalanced feature sets, CoRR, vol.abs/1411.4228 (2014)
18. Dong, X., Jing, X., Qi, F., Wu, F., Xu, B.: Heterogeneous cross company defect prediction by unified metric representation and CCA-based transfer learning. In: Proceedings of the 2015 10th Joint Meeting on Foundations of Software Engineering, ser. ESEC/FSE 2015, New York, NY, USA, pp. 496–507. ACM (2015)
19. Canfora, G., De Lucia, A., Oliveto, R., Panichella, A., Di Penta, M., Panichella, S.: Multi-objective cross-project defect prediction. In: IEEE Sixth International Conference on Verification and Validation in Software Testing, Luxembourg, Luxembourg. IEEE(2013). ISSN 2159-4848
20. Briand, L.C., Melo, W.L., Wurst, J.: Assessing the applicability of fault-proneness models across object-oriented software projects. IEEE Trans. Softw. Eng. **28**, 706–720 (2002)
21. Bener, A.B., Menzies, T., Di Stefano, J.S., Turhan, B.: On the relative value of cross-company and within-company data for defect prediction. Empirical Softw. Eng. **14**(5), 540–578 (2009)
22. Gall, H., Giger, E., Murphy, B., Nagappan, N., Zimmermann, K.: Cross- project defect prediction: a large scale experiment on data vs. domain vs. process. In: Proceedings of the 7th Joint Meeting of the European Software Engineering Conference and the ACM SIGSOFT International Symposium on Foundations of Software Engineering. ACM, pp. 91–100 (2009)
23. Camargo Cruz, A.E., Ochimizu, K.: Towards logistic regression models for predicting fault-prone code across software projects. In: Proceedings of the Third International Symposium on Empirical Software Engineering and Measurement (ESEM), Lake Buena Vista, Florida, USA, pp. 460– 463 (2009)
24. Butcher, A., Cok, D.R., Marcus, A., Menzies, T., Zimmermann, T.: Local vs. global models for effort estimation and defect prediction. In: 26th IEEE/ACM International Conference on Automated Software Engineering (ASE 2011), Lawrence, KS, USA, pp. 343–351. IEEE (2011)
25. Bettenburg, N., Hassan, A. E., Nagappan, M.: Think locally, act globally: improving defect and effort prediction models. In: 9th IEEE Working Conference on Mining Software Repositories, MSR 2012, Zurich, Switzerland pp. 60–69. IEEE (2012)
26. Devanbu, P., Posnett, D., Rahman, F.: Recalling the imprecision of cross- project defect prediction. In: Proceedings of the ACM-Sigsoft 20th International Symposium on the Foundations of Software Engineering (FSE - 20), Research Triangle Park, NC, USA, pp. 61–65. ACM (2012)
27. Xu, Z., Yuan, P., Zhang, T., Tang, Y., Li, S., Xia, Z.: HDA: cross project defect prediction via heterogeneous domain adaptation with dictionary learning. IEEE Access **6**, 57597–57613 (2018)
28. Li, Y., Huang, Z., Wang, Y., Fang, B.: Evaluating data filter on cross-project defect prediction: comparison and improvements. IEEE Access **5**, 25646–25656 (2017)
29. Porto, F., Minku, L., Mendes, E., Simao, A.: A Systematic study of cross-project defect prediction with meta- learning, IEEE Trans. Softw. Eng. (2018)
30. Gong, L., Jiang, S., Yu, Q., Jiang, L.: Unsupervised deep domain adaptation for heterogeneous defect prediction. IEICE Trans. Info. Syst. **102**(3), 537–549 (2019)
31. Li, Z., Jing, X., Zhiu, X., Zhang, H., Xu, B., Ying, S.: Heterogeneous defect prediction with two-stages ensemble learning. Autom. Softw. Eng. **26**(2), 187–201 (2019)

Deep Learning for Textual Emotion Mining

Shivangi Chawla$^{(\boxtimes)}$ (iD) and Monica Mehrotra

Department of Computer Science, Jamia Millia Islamia, New Delhi, Delhi, India

Abstract. Textual Emotion Mining (TEM) is extensively a widespread and established research problem. It has got a substantial amount of research attention in the previous decade. Over the parallel period, deep learning approaches have demonstrated remarkable success in the area of natural language processing. As a result, deep learning based TEM has attracted the eyes of people from both academia and industry in recent years. This manuscript surveys the current emerging research on the impact of deep learning techniques in TEM domain and contributes in a two-fold manner. Firstly, it provides a summary of the relevant research results concentrated on the application of deep learning approaches for different tasks under the umbrella of TEM. Secondly, it evaluates the viability of deep learning based emotion mining research, examines existing challenges, opportunities and provides future directions in the field. After a thorough survey of the available literature in the relevant domain, to the best of the found understanding, it is the first paper that surveys deep learning efforts in the TEM area.

Keywords: Emotion mining · Emotion intensity detection · Emotion classification · Deep learning

1 Introduction

Technology is constantly advancing in order to amplify human ingenuity, to anticipate, comprehend and address our unrealized needs. However, to completely understand and to cater to human desires, machines must possess an understanding of human behavior including emotion. Emotions are studied as complex psychological reactions to various internal and external events happening in our environment. On parallel grounds, the advent of the digital age has marked an infection in the acceptance of social media worldwide by people of all age groups. The social media are presently inundated with textual data expressing and evoking multiple categories of emotions. This has resulted in the origin, initiation and fast development of the field of Textual Emotion Mining (TEM) [1].

TEM alludes to an umbrella of techniques for detecting, distinguishing, analyzing, recognizing, perceiving and predicting human emotions (namely happiness, shock, wrath, etc.) expressed or evoked from the text; with an objective of making computational systems adapt according to these states. While the elucidation and recognition of these fine-grained emotion states frequently fall into place without any issues for people, these tasks present extreme difficulties and challenges to machines [2]. In the course of the most recent decade, there has been much work on the design of automated systems for emotion recognition. Various lexical, learning based and hybrid approaches have been designed for efficient detection of textual emotions [3–6].

© Springer Nature Singapore Pte Ltd. 2020
P. K. Singh et al. (Eds.): FTNCT 2019, CCIS 1206, pp. 289–303, 2020.
https://doi.org/10.1007/978-981-15-4451-4_23

The parallel evolution of Deep Learning as a most stupefying class of machine learning algorithms that involves cascading multiple layers of processing units to approximate highly nonlinear functions, has achieved monumental research interest in past years [7–10]. Yet the application of these techniques in the field of TEM is in its infancy. Most of the TEM literature is focused on the use of simple machine learning classifiers along with the employment of various emotion lexicons [11–15]. Only in recent five years, researchers started exploring the huge potential of deep neural networks and their inherent ability of automatically learning the internal representations of raw data to mine the textual expressions of emotion [16].

Before diving into the details of this survey, it is always better to present a brief discussion about the reasons and motivations behind it. As both deep learning and TEM are progressing hot research areas in the past few years, a mammoth of new techniques and emerging models have come up for deep learning based TEM. In light of these significantly expanding number of research studies, it is important to make a comprehensive summarization of the existing literature studies.

In a nutshell, this survey aims to:

- Clearly, demonstrate how deep learning techniques have permeated the entire field of TEM by thoroughly reviewing the literature on the advances of deep neural models in TEM domain. It provides an overview with which readers can rapidly comprehend and venture into the field of deep learning based TEM.
- Recognize the challenges for effective application of deep learning methods to TEM tasks.
- Highlight specific contributions which fathom and circumvent these challenges.

The remaining paper is further structurally organized in the following manner. Section 2 presents the methodology used to collect the literature focused on the application of deep learning techniques on TEM. Section 3 presents a brief introduction of TEM and various tasks, approaches, and challenges. Section 4 presents a detailed account of TEM research works focused on the use of deep learning. It also puts a light on understanding the impact of powerful approaches under deep learning as a significant contribution to the TEM area. The conclusion of the manuscript is given in Sect. 5 with pointers to future research.

2 Search Strategy and Selection Criteria

The current section depicts the search methodology and selection procedure utilized to collect the literature on the application of deep learning techniques for TEM. We used "Google Scholar" as a web search engine to search for terms like deep learning for emotion mining, deep neural networks for emotion detection, deep belief networks for emotion classification and so on. Further, search was made for different combinations of these terms on other online resources like IEEE Xplore digital library, Web of Science database, ACM digital library, Elsevier Science Direct, Research Gate network, Springer Open etc. and found some additional count of papers. After careful study of the collected literature, only those articles which are concentrated on emotion mining from text were kept in set.

As already mentioned, deep learning based emotion mining efforts are still in its nascent stage; we could constitute the set of few papers. The collected amount of papers are of high quality in terms of indexing and depicts the growth of deep learning based emotion mining systems.

3 Emotion Mining from Text: Related Work

Emotion Mining has been a trend in the last few decades as it became an attractive topic of study for computer scientists as well as computational linguists. There has been a vast body of literature focused on investigating different aspects of emotion recognition. This section describes the process of TEM in light of different tasks, approaches, and challenges encountered in the literature.

3.1 Tasks

The process of TEM spans across three different tasks to which attention has been paid in the past decade. They are Emotion Classification, Emotion Intensity Detection and Emotion Cause Detection. Although a few other tasks have also been reported in the literature [17, 18] like Emotion Detection, Emotion Polarity Detection, Sarcasm Detection etc. but research focus especially from the application of deep leaning learning was not gained by these tasks.

3.1.1 Emotion Classification
It is a fine-grained study where a text containing emotion(s) is categorized into one (or more) emotion labels. This task is well studied in literature as a single-label or multi-label classification problem. It is also regarded as a bi-perspectival task hence, can be done with two entirely different perspectives (reader and writer):

(a) **Writer Emotion Classification:** The Fine-grained study of recognizing emotions of the user writing the text.
(b) **Reader Emotion Classification:** The Fine-Grained task of recognizing emotions of the user reading the text.

Automatic classification of emotions from both types (perspectives) is a separate field of study. Works targeting Writer Emotion Classification can be found in abundance as compared to Reader emotion classification research which has recently got a significant attraction [19].

3.1.2 Emotion Intensity Detection
Intensity conveys the degree or amount of an emotion carried by a text segment. Determining the emotional intensity felt by the writer or a reader of a text is beneficial for a number of applications such as tracking public health, monitoring brand perception, disaster management intelligence and so on. Very recently, this task has been touched by researchers [20–22].

3.1.3 Emotion Cause Detection

It refers to the task of mining causes (events) responsible for eliciting different categories of emotions. This study is very less explored by researchers. Initial works in this direction include Lee et al. [23]. Further, Li et al. [24] contributed to it by finding out the factors which lead to the invocation of a different set of emotions and Gao et al. [25] presented an approach for emotion cause detection in Chinese micro-blogs using ECOCC model.

3.2 Approaches

In the literature of TEM, broadly three different classes of approaches have been reported: lexicon-based, machine learning based and hybrid (lexicon and machine learning). Earlier the class of machine learning methods used to rely on a machine learning method and a set of features to build a classifier for emotion recognition. Some of the most frequently used classifiers include Support Vector Machines (SVM), Naïve Bayes (NB), Logistic Regression (LR), Random Forest (RF), Conditional Random Field (CRF), Multinomial Naïve Bayes (MNB) and Maximum Entropy (MaxEnt). Learning can be done in a supervised or unsupervised manner. Neural networks were also used but the true strength of deep architectures has attained luminance very recently. The following Fig. 1 represents the different tasks and approaches under the umbrella of TEM.

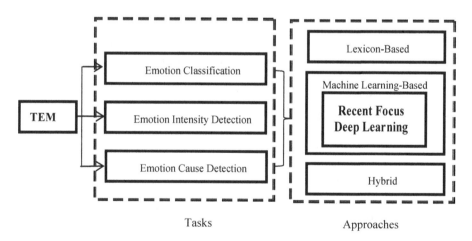

Fig. 1. TEM-tasks and approaches

3.3 Current Challenges

This section exposits some of the dominant challenges that are currently investigated by deep learning approaches for the design of more efficient and accurate emotion mining systems.

- Unavailability of large emotion-annotated datasets for training machine learning models.
- Sparse feature vectors obtained by traditional approaches like Bag-of-words and Term Frequency and Inverse Document Frequency.
- Difficulty in understanding different internal language representations captured in the text.
- Social Media Big Data

The end-to-end learning framework and automatic representation learning ability of deep neural networks made them capable of handling huge amount of social network data, automatically learn internal representations of raw data and tackle other challenges faced by current machine learning as well as lexical approaches developed till date.

4 Application of Deep Learning for Emotion Mining

Abdul-Mageed and Ungar [15] utilized distant supervision technique to acquire a large dataset of tweets on 24 fine-grained categories of emotions as represented in Plutchik Emotion Wheel (except emotion present in blank spaces). Three concentric circles represent emotions in plutchik-1, plutchik-2 and putchik-3 starting from innermost to outermost circle. For each type of emotion category, they prepared a hashtag seed set, followed by the expansion of the original seed set with Google synonyms and other online dictionaries. In this way, a list comprising of total 665 hashtags was prepared for 24 emotion labels. Preprocessing steps include removal of duplicates, retweets, URL, user mentions and normalization of character repetitions. For experimentation, Gated Recurrent Neural Networks (GRNNs), a special class of recurrent neural networks were used. For comparing the performance of GRNNs, four classifiers capable of handling the data size were used viz. Stochastic Gradient Descent (SGD), Multinomial Naïve Bayes (MNB), Perceptron and the Passive-Aggressive Classifier (PAC) which were tested on mini-batches of 10,000 tweet instances. Among online classifiers, PAC performed best with F-score of 64.86%, 53.30% and 68.14% on plutchik-1, plutchik-2, and plutchik-3 respectively. GRRNs gave significant performance improvement over PAC by giving overall F-score of 91.21%, 82.32% and 87.47% over plutchik-1, plutchik-2, and plutchik-3 datasets respectively.

Zhang et al. [26] addressed two challenging tasks of multi-label emotion classification and emotion distribution prediction to determine multiple emotions associated with texts along with the intensity values associated with each label. Two optimization functions were employed namely, cross entropy loss for classification and Kullback-Leibler (KL) loss for distribution learning. In this way, the proposed convolutional neural network (CNN) learns and performs both tasks at the same time. Experimentation was done on five datasets viz. ISEAR, Fairy Tales, TEC, CBET, and SemEval-2007. Except SemEval-2007, remaining four datasets are single-label datasets. In order to enable multi-label classification, the authors also proposed a strategy for transforming the ground truth label to distributions. Comparison studies were done with several baselines including non-negative matrix factorization. Results reveal that the suggested multi-task CNN surmounts all the baselines.

Krebs et al. [27] crawled user posts with reactions on Facebook public pages of various supermarket chains and evaluated Convolutional and Recurrent Neural network architectures (CNN and RNN) with word embeddings for predicting the distribution of these reactions on a new post. They developed a complete emotion prediction system consisting of three components: emotion miner (using SVM) for classifying emotions in user posts and its comments, neural networks with pre-trained word embeddings for reaction distribution prediction and finally a combination of the two methods to create an ensemble providing promising results on emotion reaction prediction. Another work in the same direction is given by Moers et al. [28].

He and Xia in their paper [29] came up with a joint binary neural network (JBNN) for multi-label emotion classification, which extirpated the limitations of both binary relevance neural networks (BRNNs) and threshold dependent neural networks (TDNNs) for multi-label classification. Performance evaluation was done on the widely adopted Ren-CECps dataset [30] and it was confirmed that the proposed neural network model outperformed all the state-of-the-art methods suggested for the task of multi-label classification of emotions, in terms of both classification performance and computational efficiency.

Colneric and Demsar [31] utilized emotion-hashtag based tweet crawling procedure for collecting three large datasets corresponding to three different emotion models viz. Ekman model of emotion, plutchik emotion model and POMS adjectives. They presented a comparative performance evaluation of several word and character-based recurrent and convolutional neural networks using bag-of-words and latent semantic based indexing (LSI) models. Investigation of transfer learning to understand and interoperate between different hidden state representations of different emotion classifications was the agenda behind the further analysis. Furthermore, they built a unison model using shared representations of emotions to predict all emotion labels present in different datasets in a generalized manner.

Naderi et al. [32] worked on the task of emotion intensity detection by proposing a deep learning framework. They worked on the datasets proposed under Task 1 competition held for SemEval-2018 and developed a multi-aspect feature learning mechanism which extracted the most discriminative features of tweets along with the emotion information carried by words in a tweet. Feature set included an ensemble of ngrams, lexicon-based features, word embeddings, a tweet word representation automatically learned by a Long Short Term Memory (LSTM) deep neural network on corpus dedicated to training as well as on a huge tweet corpus containing emotion words and many other handcrafted features. Evaluation studies indicate that the proposed support vector regressor achieved a Pearson Correlation Coefficient of 72% on emotion intensity detection task. Lakomkin et al. [22] also targeted the same task of emotion intensity prediction on twitter messages. Their work proposed an ensemble of the word and character-based recurrent neural networks on WASSA-2017 task. Both Pearson and Spearman correlation coefficients got improved by 18.5%.

Alhuzali et al. [13] followed the approach used by Abdul-Mageed and Ungar [15] for automatic acquisition of Arabic-tweet dataset on the basis of a seed set consisting of 8 emotions defined by Plutchik model. They extended the work presented in manuscript [15] by increasing the number of emotions from 6 to 8 to capture almost twice the number of tweets i.e., 2,984 to 7,268 tweets. The further extension includes the expansion of seeds from 23 to 48 expressions, on account of the complete agreement between two native speakers of the language. For core modeling, they opt for utilization of Gated Recurrent Neural Networks and some base classifiers (Multinomial Naïve Bayes, Passive-Aggressive classifier, Perceptron and linear SVM trained with SGD) for comparison. Experiments were conducted on two crawled datasets viz. LAMA and LAMA-DIST and some other datasets namely DINA, LAMA-DINA, MT-DIST, SE-18. Proposed approach achieved a promising outcome. Best results were achieved on LAMA-DINA dataset with the highest F-score of 70 percent, an absolute gain of 40 percent over baselines. In their another research publication [33], authors worked on IEST-2018 dataset to learn 'implicit emotion' expressed in tweets. They developed a series of deep neural network based models like RNN, Fwd, Bwd and bidirectional LSTMs. Fwd model gave 69.4 percent results whereas further gain in performance was achieved with Bwd and BiLM models to a F-score of 70.7 percent.

Khanpour and Caragea [34] dedicated their research efforts towards detection of fine-grained emotional states in online health communities. They built two health-related datasets and invented a novel computational model named ConvLexLSTM. This model coherently combined the outcome of a CNN capable of exploiting textual semantic information with various lexicon-based and surface-level (abstract) features. The conjoined output was given to LSTM network to uncover the emotions of patients. Moreover, the trained model was utilized in a bigger experiment for studying the correlation between moods of the user and US holidays with an aim to aid the development of smarter techniques to improve patients' moods. ConvLexLSTM showed improvements over the best models available in the literature for F1-score. The statistical significance of improvement was for p-value < 0.05.

Kratzwald and Ili in their paper [16] also utilized deep learning architectures for the targeted task of emotion recognition from various publicly available datasets. Novelness of their approach lies in various modifications proposed by them viz. bidirectional preprocessing by traditional LSTM architecture, enabling dropout layer regularization, and weighted loss function to minimize the data imbalance problem. Both dimensional, as well as categorical emotion models, were taken into account. Results indicate that proposed modified LSTMs consistently outperformed various machine learning baseline models. The enhancements in performance range from 23.2 percent in F1-score for classification and 11.6 percent in MSE for regression. Additionally, authors devised a customized strategy based on transfer learning namely sent2affect to further improve the results of emotion classification.

Chatterjee et al. [12] harnessed the huge potential of deep learning to detect human emotions. They devised a novel method using deep learning namely "Sentiment and Semantic-Based Emotion Detector (SS-BED)". The suggested approach utilized the feature set comprising of both semantic as well as sentiment knowledge to predict user emotions in real-world textual dialogue dataset. Evaluation outcomes were quite promising as compared to off-the-shelf deep learning as well as machine learning models. Training was done on a large dataset comprising of 17.62 million tweet question-answer pairs. Other datasets like ISEAR, Affective Text and WASSA'17 were also used for evaluation. Lee et al. [35] also worked on dialog-based systems by utilizing a LSTM-based emotion classification model for unraveling emotions in dialogue on the EmotionLines dataset (a dialog dataset with emotion annotation at utterance level).

Baziotis et al. [36] participated in the SemEval-2018 Task 1 "Affect in Tweets and suggested a deep learning system based on a Bi-LSTM architecture prepared with a multi-layer self-attention component. This attention component improved model execution by enabling it to recognize salient and notable words in tweets, just as to increase knowledge into the models making them increasingly interpretable. Transfer learning was also utilized to overcome the challenge of a lack of training data.

Toshevska and Gievska [37] introduced a few deep neural models, in view of a blend of CNN and Bidirectional LSTM. Two datasets were used one from SemEval-2018 Task 1 and another one was crowd flower twitter emotion. Three models were investigated in their study: the baseline model following CNN-LSTM architecture; second model utilized emoji2vec embedding as an extension to standard baseline model and the last model took into account both lexicon and emoji2vec embedding. Out of the above-discussed models, the best results were obtained by the third model on both datasets. Yu et al. [38] also worked on SemEval-2018 Task 1 dataset to improve multi-label emotion classification performance with the aid of sentiment classification. Their approach used transfer learning and a dual-attention mechanism (DATN).

Samy et al. [11] devised a technique to capture the context information in which a tweet is made, and supply this information as an additional layer to Gated Recurrent Units by naming this model as C-GRU (Context-Aware GRU). Proposed modified architecture gave excellent results by outperforming the highest ranker reported on SemEval-2018 Arabic tweets dataset for multi-label emotion classification. Zhou et al. [39] devised a novel emotional chatting device with Gated Recurrent Units (GRUs) to determine the influence of emotions expressed in Chinese Weibo dataset.

While the majority of the TEM literature is centered around investigating emotional content in monolingual texts (text written in only one language), Wang et al. [40] worked on code-switching text comprising of a mix of English and Chinese language. Their approach used Bilingual Attention Network (BAN) in order to understand emotion representation captured in bilingual text. A LSTM model was also utilized for construction of document-level representation for each post. Alongside, the attention mechanism captured the context information by means of various informative English and Chinese words.

Bostan et al. [8] targeted emotion classification problem by giving special treatment to intensifiers by enriching word representation of such phrases. Furthermore, they used a post processing pipeline having steps with A La carte and bag of substrings extensions based on pretrained Glove, Word2Vec and FastText embeddings. Experimentation was done on a crowd-sourced intensity-annotated tweet corpus consisting of targeted phrases, by feeding a CNN-LSTM model with their embedding sentence vectors.

Task 3-EmoContext: Contextual Emotion detection in Text of SemEval 2019 invited an overwhelming number of participants from across the globe [41–54]. Understanding the brevity of this manuscript and the huge number of participant TEM systems, only top few systems are described here. SymantoResearch by Basile et al. [55] ensembled BERT and USE models, to distinguish sad, happy and angry emotions from text and separated them from rest (Others category). Huang et al. [56] created another ensemble model of BERT and hierarchical LSTM and achieved promising results, where they encoded the emotional and semantic context of text via Glove, ELMo and DeepMoji embedding. A lot of other end to end neural models were experimented for this task [42, 51, 52]. Liang et al. [57] competed with CNN based models for the task of angry-happy-sad classification and others-or-not classification and finally used multiple levels of voting ensembles of base classifiers to generate accurate predictions. FigureEight [41] utilized ensemble of transfer learning based deep neural models with sophisticated fine tuning techniques described in ULMFiT. After studying the experimental description of top 15 papers concentrated on this task, it is observed that LSTMs or BiLSTMs were among the majorly chosen deep neural models. CNN and GRU based models were also utilized by some to achieve competing performances. Apart from this, Transfer learning using BERT, ULMFiT and ELMo also account among the popular choices but almost all the top teams used ensembled versions of their best models to create a final prediction model.

Table 1 summarizes the existing work done on deep learning based TEM by presenting a short description of the data source under study, their data statistics, methods employed and prominent results.

Table 1. Systematic synthesis of literature cases using deep learning methods for TEM

Ref	Data Source	Data Statistics		Method	Results		
[15]	Twitter	Dataset	#Tweets	GRNN	-PAC performed best with F-score of 64.86% on plutchik-1, 53.30% on plutchik-2 and 68.14% on plutchik-3		
		plutchik-1	2,05,125				
		plutchik-2	7,90,059		-With GRNNs, overall F-score of 91.21% on plutchik-1, 82.32% on plutchik-2 and 87.47% on plutchik-3.		
		plutchik-3	6,13,049				
		Total	16,08,23 3		-GRNN performed better than all other used classifiers		
[22]	Twitter	Dataset	#Tweets	RNN	-Both Pearson and Spearman Correlation Coefficients got Improved by 18.5%		
		WASSA-2017	7,097				
[16]	Hetero-geneous	Dataset	#sen-tences	Bidirectional LSTM	DS	BiLSTM	TLS2A
		ET	1,646		ET	70.0	69.8
		GT	7,902		GT	70.3	69.9
		SE-2007	1,250				
		FB	2,894		*DS=Dataset, TLS2A=Transfer Learning Based Sent2Affect		
		ISEAR	7,666				
		FT	1,207				

(Continued)

Table 1. *(Continued)*

[34]	Online Health Communities	Dataset	#sentences	Modified LSTMs		B-DS F1score	L-DS F1score
		B-DS	1,066		Joy	93.2	89.8
		L-DS	1,041		Sad	92.3	89.4
		Total	2,107				
[13]	Twitter	Dataset	#Tweets	GRNN	-Best results were achieved on lAMA-DINA dataset with the highest F1-Score of 70%, an absolute gain of 40% over baselines.		
		DINA	2,984				
		LAMA	7,268				
		L-DINA	10,252				
		L-DIST	1,82,689				
		MT-DIST	7,56,663				
		SE-2018	4,037				
[33]	Twitter	Dataset	#Tweets	RNN, LSTM, Bidirectional LSTMs	NN		F1-score
		IEST-2018	1,91,731		Fwd LM		0.693
					Bwd LM		0.693
					BiLM		0.707
[12]	Twitter	Dataset	#Tweets	CNN and LSTM	-SS-BED gave higher F1-score(nearly 72%) in comparison to various CNN and LSTM based architectures.		
		Q-A	17.62 million				
[26]	Heterogeneous	Dataset	Size	MutliTask CNNs	-Multi-task CNN outperformed all the baselines		
		ISEAR	7666 sentences		Dataset		F1-Score
		Fairy Tales	185 stories		ISEAR		66.80
		TEC	21,051 tweets		Fairy Tales		78.72
		CBET	76,860 tweets		TEC		56.94
		SemEval-2007			CBET		61.39
					Sem Eval-2007		41.41
[27] [28]	Facebook	Dataset	#Posts	RNN and CNN	-RNN performed better than CNN		
		FB Reactions	25,969		NN		MSE*
					CNN		0.186
					RNN		0.159
					*MSE=Mean square Error		
[11]	Twitter	Dataset	#tweets	GRU	NN		F1-score
		SE-2018	10,983		GRU		0.642
		SE-2017	3,355		C-GRU		0.648
		*SE= SemEval					
[32]	Twitter	Dataset	#tweets	LSTMs	-achieved a Pearson Correlation Coefficient of 72% on emotion intensity detection task.		
		SE-2018	10,983				
		*SE=SemEval					

(Continued)

Table 1. *(Continued)*

[31]	Twitter	Dataset	#tweets	RNN and CNN	-character based RNN performed best.
		Ekman	5,35,788		
		Plutchk	7,98,389		
		POMS	6536,280		

			RNN	CNN
E	W	70.0	69,8
	C	70.3	69,9
Pl	W	67.7	67,0
	C	68.6	66,8
P	W	70.4	68,8
	C	70.6	69,0

*E=Ekman, P=POMS, Pl=Plutchik, W=word, C=char

[37]	Twitter	Dataset	#tweets	CNN and Bidirectional LSTM	Model3	F1-score
		SE-2018	10,983		Glove Emb.	0.327
		SE-2017	40,000		Word2vec	0.321
		*SE=SemEval				

[38]	Twitter	Dataset	#tweets	Dual Attention Network with Transfer Learning (DATN)	NN	F1-score
		SE-2018	10,983		DATN-1	0.410
		*SE=SemEval			DATN-2	0.444

[36]	Twitter	Dataset	#tweets	Bidirectional LSTMs	NN	Jaccard Sim
		Crawled	550		LSTM-RD	0.5788
		Data	million		LSTM-TLFR	0.5243
					LSTM-TLFT	0.5788

[40]	Weibo	Dataset	#posts	BAN And LSTM	NN	F1-score
		Weibo	3530		LSTM	0.656
		posts			BAN	0.672

[29]	Weibo	Dataset	#posts	JBNN	NN	F1-score
		Ren-CECps	3530		JBNN	0.7171
					JBNN-No-Bi	0.7085
					JBNN-No-Att	0.7105

[39]	Weibo	Dataset	#posts	RNN, LSTM And GRU	-designed emotional chatting machine outperformed all baselines.
		NLPCC	23,105		

[8]	Twitter	Dataset	#tweets	CNN-LSTM	-Glove and Word2Vec embedding based models show improvement of 7pp over baseline. FastText embedding based models underperformed the baseline.
		Crawled	32		
		Data	million		

[41] [55] [56]	Dialog	Dataset	#tweets	CNN,LSTM, Transfer Learning	Team	F1
		SE-2019	30,160		SymantoResearch	0.7731
		*SE=SemEval			ANA	0.7709
					FigureEight	0.7608

5 Discussion and Conclusion

The recent ecstasy of the popularization of social media and the textual communication over these social media sites came with the huge challenge of mining these texts for the human emotions expressed in or evoked by reading their content. Activated by that call, the machine learning research community has explored the potential of deep learning approaches for the development of automated emotion detection systems. The success stories of artificial neural networks, deep architectures, transfer, and reinforcement learning in making machines intelligent are well known. Furthermore, additional factors like a decrease in computational costs, an increase in computing power and availability of quasi-unlimited storage for relatively reasonable cost has contributed a lot towards this trend. The above factors have surged researchers to join these learning methods to reshape the machine's capacities to comprehend and unravel hidden emotions from social media texts. To encourage the more extensive organization of such systems and to fill in as a source of perspective point the future, this article provides a comprehensive review of the most recent studies on the subject of the application of deep learning techniques in TEM.

Deep Learning has achieved good success in the field of TEM, which will enable multiple application domains (e.g. ecommerce, economics, biomedicine, healthcare and policies etc.) to benefit from the knowledge learned from TEM. Although deep learning promises to act as a key for stepping forward in the development of TEM, still deep learning based methods encounter a few challenges documented as follows:

- TEM greatly suffer with the challenge of poorly annotated large data resources which hamper the performance of deep learning models, as these methods rely on large amounts of labeled data.
- Different literature studies pertain to different data source domains e.g. Twitter, Facebook, online news etc. This makes it difficult for researchers to generate a comparative analysis the performance of proposed models. Also, very few studies touch the problem of cross domain TEM which is required to bring generalization in TEM research.
- The biggest limitation faced is that most of the neural models fail to provide reasonable performance while learning implicit expressions of emotions such as humor, irony, sarcasm, deep reasoning etc.

Thus, there is still a long way to proceed in TEM domain with deep learning. Hence, this area is still fresh and has great potential for further research and investigation as it has been scantily studied yet.

References

1. Hakak, N.M.: Emotion Analysis: A Survey, pp. 397–402 (2017)
2. Shaheen, S., El-Hajj, W., Hajj, H., Elbassuoni, S.: Emotion recognition from text based on automatically generated rules. In: IEEE International Conference on Data Mining Workshop, ICDMW, vol. 2015, pp. 383–392 (2015)
3. Suet, J., Liew, Y.: Fine-Grained Emotion Detection in Microblog Text, May 2016

4. Mac Kim, S.: Recognising Emotions and Sentiments in Text, p. 128, April 2011
5. Binali, H., Wu, C., Potdar, V.: Text, pp. 172–177 (2010)
6. Binali, H., Potdar, V.: Emotion detection state of the art. In: Proceedings of the CUBE International Information Technology Conference, CUBE 2012, p. 501 (2012)
7. Kamal, R., Shah, M.A., Maple, C., Masood, M., Wahid, A., Mehmood, A.: Emotion classification and crowd source sensing; a lexicon based approach. IEEE Access **7**, 27124–27134 (2019)
8. Bostan, L., Klinger, R.: Exploring Fine-Tuned Embeddings that Model Intensifiers for Emotion Analysis (2019)
9. Gaind, B., Syal, V., Padgalwar, S.: Emotion Detection and Analysis on Social Media (2019)
10. Jabreel, M., Moreno, A.: A deep learning-based approach for multi-label emotion classification in tweets. Appl. Sci. **9**(6), 1123 (2019)
11. Samy, A.E., El-Beltagy, S.R., Hassanien, E.: A context integrated model for multi-label emotion detection. Procedia Comput. Sci. **142**, 61–71 (2018)
12. Chatterjee, A., Gupta, U., Chinnakotla, M.K., Srikanth, R., Galley, M., Agrawal, P.: Understanding emotions in text using deep learning and big data. Comput. Hum. Behav. **93**, 309–317 (2018)
13. Alhuzali, H., Abdul-Mageed, M., Ungar, L.: Enabling Deep Learning of Emotion with First-Person Seed Expressions, no. 2, pp. 25–35 (2018)
14. Goyal, P., Pandey, S., Jain, K.: Deep learning for natural language processing, 人工知能学会論文誌, vol. 27, pp. 1–277 (2018)
15. Abdul-Mageed, M., Ungar, L.: EmoNet: fine-grained emotion detection with gated recurrent neural networks. In: Proceedings of the 55th annual meeting of the association for computational linguistics (Volume 1 Long Papers), pp. 718–728 (2017)
16. Kratzwald, B., Ili, S.: Deep learning for affective computing : text-based emotion recognition in decision support (2018)
17. Yadollahi, A., Shahraki, A.G., Zaiane, O.R.: Current state of text sentiment analysis from opinion to emotion mining. ACM Comput. Surv. **50**(2), 1–33 (2017)
18. Sailunaz, K., Dhaliwal, M., Rokne, J., Alhajj, R.: Emotion detection from text and speech: a survey. Soc. Netw. Anal. Min. **8**(1), 1–26 (2018)
19. Li, X., Rao, Y., Xie, H., Liu, X., Wong, T.L., Wang, F.L.: Social emotion classification based on noise-aware training. Data Knowl. Eng. **123**, 101605 (2017)
20. Mohammad, S.M., Bravo-Marquez, F.: WASSA-2017 Shared Task on Emotion Intensity (2017)
21. Mohammad, S.M.,, Bravo-Marquez, F.: Emotion Intensities in Tweets (2017)
22. Lakomkin, E., Bothe, C., Wermter, S.: GradAscent at emoint-2017: character and word level recurrent neural network models for tweet emotion intensity detection. In: Proceedings of the 8th Workshop on Computational Approaches to Subjectivity, Sentiment and Social Media Analysis, pp. 169–174 (2017)
23. Lee, S.Y.M., Ying, C., Huang, C.-R.: Emotion cause events: corpus construction and analysis. In: Proceedings of the Seventh International Conference on Language Resources and Evaluation, (LREC 2010), pp. 19–21 (2010)
24. Li, W., Xu, H.: Text-based emotion classification using emotion cause extraction. Expert Syst. Appl. **41**(4), 1742–1749 (2014). PART 2
25. Gao, K., Xu, H., Wang, J.: Emotion cause detection for chinese micro-blogs based on ECOCC model. In: Cao, T., Lim, E.-P., Zhou, Z.-H., Ho, T.-B., Cheung, D., Motoda, H. (eds.) PAKDD 2015, Part II. LNCS (LNAI), vol. 9078, pp. 3–14. Springer, Cham (2015). https://doi.org/10.1007/978-3-319-18032-8_1
26. Zhang, Y., Fu, J., She, D., Zhang, Y., Wang, S., Yang, J.: Text Emotion Distribution Learning via Multi-Task Convolutional Neural Network (2017)

27. Krebs, F., Lubascher, B., Moers, T., Schaap P., Spanakis, G.: Social Emotion Mining Techniques for Facebook Posts Reaction Prediction (2017)

28. Moers, T., Krebs, F., Spanakis, G.: SEMTec: social emotion mining techniques for analysis and prediction of facebook post reactions. In: van den Herik, J., Rocha, A.P. (eds.) ICAART 2018. LNCS (LNAI), vol. 11352, pp. 361–382. Springer, Cham (2019). https://doi.org/10.1007/978-3-030-05453-3_17

29. He, H., Xia, R.: Joint binary neural network for multi-label learning with applications to emotion classification. In: Zhang, M., Ng, V., Zhao, D., Li, S., Zan, H. (eds.) NLPCC 2018, Part I. LNCS (LNAI), vol. 11108, pp. 250–259. Springer, Cham (2018). https://doi.org/10.1007/978-3-319-99495-6_21

30. Quan, C., Ren, F.: Sentence emotion analysis and recognition based on emotion words using ren-CECps. Int. J. Adv. Intell. **2**(1), 105–117 (2010)

31. Colneric, N., Demsar, J.: Emotion recognition on twitter: comparative study and training a unison model. IEEE Trans. Affect. Comput. **3045**(1), 1 (2018)

32. Naderi, H., Haji Soleimani, B., Mohammad, S., Kiritchenko, S., Matwin, S.: DeepMiner at SemEval-2018 task 1: emotion intensity recognition using deep representation learning. In: Proceedings of The 12th International Workshop on Semantic Evaluation, no. 2016, pp. 305–312 (2018)

33. Alhuzali, H., Elaraby, M., Abdul-Mageed, M.: UBC-NLP at IEST 2018: Learning Implicit Emotion With an Ensemble of Language Models, pp. 342–347 (2018)

34. Khanpour, H., Caragea, C.: Fine-Grained Emotion Detection in Health-Related Online Posts, pp. 1160–1166 (2018)

35. Lee, Y.J., Park, C.Y., Choi, H.J.: Word-level emotion embedding based on semi-supervised learning for emotional classification in dialogue. In: 2019 IEEE International Conference on Big Data and Smart Computing, BigComp 2019, pp. 1–4 (2019)

36. Baziotis, C., et al.: NTUA-SLP at SemEval-2018 Task 1: Predicting Affective Content in Tweets with Deep Attentive RNNs and Transfer Learning, (2018)

37. Kalajdziski, S., Ackovska, N. (eds.): ICT 2018. CCIS, vol. 940. Springer, Cham (2018). https://doi.org/10.1007/978-3-030-00825-3

38. Yu, J.: Improving multi-label emotion classification via sentiment classification with dual attention transfer network. In: Proceedings of the 2018 Conference on Empirical Methods in Natural Language Processing, pp. 1097–1102 (2018)

39. Zhou, H., Huang, M.,, Zhang, T., Zhu, X., Liu, B.: Emotional Chatting Machine: Emotional Conversation Generation with Internal and External Memory, pp. 730–738 (2017)

40. Wang, Z., Zhang, Y., Yat, S., Lee, M., Li, S., Zhou, G.: A bilingual attention network for code-switched emotion prediction. In: Proceedings of COLING 2016, the 26th International Conference on Computational Linguistics: Technical Papers, pp. 1624–1634 (2016)

41. Xiao, J., Bert, F.: Figure Eight at SemEval-2019 Task 3: Ensemble of Transfer Learning Methods for Contextual Emotion Detection, pp. 220–224 (2019)

42. Bouchekif, A.: EPITA-ADAPT at SemEval-2019 Task 3: Using Deep Sentiment Analysis Models and Transfer Learning for Emotion Detection in Textual Conversations, pp. 215–219 (2019)

43. Smetanin, S.: EmoSense at SemEval-2019 Task 3: Bidirectional LSTM Network for Contextual Emotion Detection in Textual Conversations, pp. 210–214 (2019)

44. Chakravartula, N.: EMOMINER at SemEval-2019 Task 3: A Stacked BiLSTM Architecture for Contextual Emotion Detection in Text, pp. 205–209 (2019)

45. Vera, D.: ELiRF-UPV at SemEval-2019 Task 3: Snapshot Ensemble of Hierarchical Convolutional Neural Networks for Contextual Emotion Detection, pp. 195–199 (2019)

46. Patel, H.: E-LSTM at SemEval-2019 Task 3: Semantic and Sentimental Features Retention for Emotion Detection in Text, pp. 190–194 (2019)

47. Jain, A., Aggarwal, I., Singh, A.N.: ParallelDots at SemEval-2019 Task 3: Domain Adaptation with feature embeddings for Contextual Emotion Analysis, pp. 185–189 (2019)
48. Perełkiewicz, M.: CX-ST-RNM at SemEval-2019 Task 3: Fusion of Recurrent Neural Networks Based on Contextualized and Static Word Representations for Contextual Emotion Detection, pp. 180–184 (2019)
49. Po, R.: ConSSED at SemEval-2019 Task 3: Configurable Semantic and Sentiment Emotion Detector, pp. 175–179 (2019)
50. Li, C.: CLP at SemEval-2019 Task 3: Multi-Encoder in Hierarchical Attention Networks for Contextual Emotion Detection, pp. 164–168 (2019)
51. Cummings, J.R., Wilson, J.R.: CLARK at SemEval-2019 Task 3: Exploring the Role of Context to Identify Emotion in a Short Conversation, pp. 159–163 (2019)
52. Mohammadi, E., Amini, H., Kosseim, L.: CLaC Lab at SemEval-2019 Task 3: Contextual Emotion Detection Using a Combination of Neural Networks and SVM, pp. 153–158 (2019)
53. Gratian, V.: BrainEE at SemEval-2019 Task 3: Ensembling Linear Classifiers for Emotion Prediction, pp. 137–141 (2019)
54. Chatterjee, A., Narahari, K.N., Joshi, M., Agrawal, P.: SemEval-2019 Task 3: EmoContext Contextual Emotion Detection in Text, pp. 39–48 (2019)
55. Basile, A., Franco-salvador, M., Pawar, N., Stajner, S.: SymantoResearch at SemEval-2019 Task 3: Combined Neural Models for Emotion Classification in Human-Chatbot Conversations, pp. 330–334 (2019)
56. Huang, C., Trabelsi, A., Zaïane, O.R.: ANA at SemEval-2019 Task 3: Contextual Emotion detection in Conversations through hierarchical LSTMs and BERT (2019)
57. Liang, X., Ma, Y., Xu, M.: THU-HCSI at SemEval-2019 Task 3: Hierarchical Ensemble Classification of Contextual Emotion in Conversation, pp. 345–349 (2019)

The Cascade Generation Nature of Compartmental Models - A Comparative Study

Syed Shafat Ali$^{(\boxtimes)}$ and Syed Afzal Murtaza Rizvi

Department of Computer Science, Jamia Millia Islamia, New Delhi, India
shafat159074@st.jmi.ac.in, sarizvi@jmi.ac.in

Abstract. Since researchers started analyzing online social networks, under-standing the characteristics of information propagation has been of immense interest. For the same, information diffusion models have been proposed which either explain or predict the diffusion of information as it propagates through a network. In this paper, three such models, viz., SIR, SIS and SIRS, have been used to generate information cascades over a given network. Besides these models, an intuitive mixture of SIS and SIR, called SIR/S has been proposed, also serving as a cascade-generation model. The main aim of this study is to understand the nature of cascades found in various propagation mechanisms. To this end, the cascade generation capacities of these models, intuitively having the tendencies to explain the same, have been explored. The cascades thus generated have been extensively analyzed and compared with each other. Our results show that the cascade size distributions are generally the same across all the models, following power-law and heavy-tailed distributions. In addition to this, the most frequently generated cascades predominantly have the same shapes for all the models. It was also found that the cascades generated by all the models are depth oriented, with breadth-oriented cascades having the least probability to occur. Besides these similarities, the differences among the models are also found. Interestingly, in a number of different aspects, SIS and SIR/S have the tendencies to behave in one way, while SIR and SIRS take a course different from the former two, showing a contrasting behavior. With the help of these findings, this study sheds light over the information diffusion process found in different application areas of these models.

Keywords: Compartmental models · Information diffusion · Infection source · Information cascades · Power-law distribution · Online Social Networks

1 Introduction

Online Social Networks (OSNs) drive this age. With billions of people online, socializing on various social networks like Facebook and Twitter, OSNs play an important role in influencing how people think, produce or consume information. As a result, analyzing the way people interact with each other on these networks has become an important computer science research focus. One of the domains of OSNs analysis is information diffusion which deals with questions like (a) how a piece of information

© Springer Nature Singapore Pte Ltd. 2020
P. K. Singh et al. (Eds.): FTNCT 2019, CCIS 1206, pp. 304–318, 2020.
https://doi.org/10.1007/978-981-15-4451-4_24

propagates through a network, (b) how the information propagation can be modeled and (c) how a piece of information influences people.

In order to model information diffusion, researchers have proposed models explaining or predicting information flow [1–5], and much work has been dedicated towards extending these models [6]. Three such well-known models are SIR, SIS and SIRS, also known as compartmental models. These models classify nodes into several states, viz., S for *Susceptible*, I for *Infected*, R for *Recovered*. In SIS, a node u is initially susceptible to infection from a directed neighbor v, then gets infected with some probability due to initial susceptibility and finally after some time becomes susceptible again. By contrast, in SIR model, the infected node u does not become susceptible but instead gets recovered. To elaborate, in SIS, whenever a piece of information is made available by a node u, a set of its directed neighbors V becomes susceptible to share that information. When a node from V shares that information with some probability, it changes its state from susceptible to infected. After some time, it transitions from infected to susceptible state. However, in case of SIR, rather than becoming susceptible, a node from V recovers instead, moving from infected to recovered state. In SIRS, after an infected node u from V recovers, its recovery wanes over time, thereby, becoming susceptible again. This process of nodes being suscep- tible, getting infected and recovering, keeps on going over a network, giving rise to a concept called information cascade. In addition to the above-mentioned models, there are other compartmental models. Two of such commonly used models are SI (*Sus- ceptible-Infected*) [7], SEIR (*Susceptible-Exposed-Infectious-Recovered*) [8]. In SI model, once a node u gets infected, it stays infected forever unlike SIR and SIS, where a node may get recovered or become susceptible again, respectively. As for SEIR, after a node u becomes susceptible, it may enter a new state called *Exposed* state before becoming infectious. The *Exposed* state may be thought as an incubation period of u before u becomes infectious.

As information propagates through a network, it goes from node to node at various time-steps generating a graph called information cascade. An information cascade explains the information adoption behavior of a person in a social network based on the fact that a person generally follows the actions of earlier people [9].

In this paper, the above explained models, viz., SIS, SIR and SIRS have been used to generate cascades over a given network. Besides these models, a mixture of SIS and SIR models, called SIR/S has been proposed, which also serves as a cascade-generation model. In this model, a node u after becoming infected, instead of recovering (SIR) or becoming susceptible (SIS), it either recovers or becomes susceptible with equal probability of 50%. Since, the main aim of this study is to understand the nature of cascades found in various propagation mechanisms, the generative capacities of these models, intuitively having the tendencies to explain the same, have been explored. The cascades thus generated by all the four models have been analyzed with respect to the following properties: shape, size distribution, breadth cover (nodes produced at levels), depth cover (levels reached by cascades), total cover (total nodes produced by all cascades) and frequency. It was found that for some properties, all the models generally have the same behavior and for others, some models tend to behave differently than the others. For example, the cascade size distributions are generally the same across all the models, following power-law and heavy-tailed distributions. Also, the most frequently generated cascades generally have the same shapes for all the models. The differences, although rare, are found only in the order of the frequency of these cascades. It was also found that the cascades generated by all the models are depth oriented, with breadth-oriented cascades having the least probability to occur. The significant differences among models were found with respect to properties like breadth cover, depth cover and total cover, where SIS and SIR/S have the tendencies to behave in one way, while SIR and SIRS show a contrasting behavior.

The major contributions of this paper are as follows:

- Extensive analysis of different compartmental models has been performed under social network perspective.
- Comparative study of the cascade generation capacities of compartmental models has been performed.
- The results show that while all the models follow power-law distribution as far as the cascade size is concerned and generally produce similar frequent cascades, SIR and SIRS tend to behave in one way from certain analytical standpoints when contrasted against SIS and SIR/S.

2   Related Work

Compartmental models, viz., SIR [2], SIS [3] and SIRS [5], have originally been used to model epidemiological processes in biology, i.e., how a disease spreads over a population. However, these models, in modified or intuitively extended ways, have been used to understand information propagation on online social networks. For example, [10] proposes a generative SIS model in which a node gets infected with probability β and then becomes susceptible at next time step with probability $\gamma = 1$. Furthermore, [11] proposes LIM (Linear Influence Model), another model inspired by compartmental models, in which for each node u, an influence function is estimated that measures the number of subsequent infections which can be attributed to the influence of u over time.

In addition to this, compartmental models have extensively been used in the field of source identification in complex network. Information source identification [12] is a very important problem with effective real-world applications. Various studies have used SIR model to generate infection graphs (cascades) over a network for the purpose of detecting the source of infection [13–16]. Besides SIR model, SI and SEIR models [17–20] have also been used to mimic information diffusion in general networks, again for the purpose of finding information sources.

As for information cascades properties, [10] and [21] found that generally cascades have small depth, with a central node connected to many nodes around it (star-shaped). Studies have also found that only a small number of information cascades are viral in nature [22].

3 Motivation

The motivation for this study could be understood by discussing the above-mentioned models under the light of their respective propagation mechanisms or, in other words, their application areas.

SIR: As described above, in this model a node u is initially susceptible to infection at time t. At time $t + 1$, it becomes infected with probability β and at time $t + 2$, it recovers from infection with probability δ. We can relate the working of this model with the general retweet mechanism on Twitter. On Twitter, a user u is initially susceptible to a tweet made available by one of its directed neighbors. Later u retweets the tweet, i.e., shares the tweet, and afterwards becomes immune to sharing this tweet again. For this type of information sharing or propagation mechanism, SIR model intuitively could be seen as an option.

SIS: In this model, after a node u gets infected, instead of recovering, it becomes susceptible to infection again at time $t + 2$ with probability δ. The application of this model has been discussed in [10] in which an intuitive SIS model is proposed. This model has been used to generate cascades on a blog network. The properties of these cascades are found similar to the real-world cascades on the same network.

SIR/S: In this model, at time $t + 2$, a node u either recovers with probability δ or becomes susceptible again with the same probability. This type of scenario could again be linked with Twitter, albeit, in the light of a different propagation mechanism. Consider a user u who generally follows a convention where she shares a piece of information i from node v and then decides not to share it again from the same node. This can happen because generally when a piece of information i is shared by a user u, i's relevancy for u is considerably dropped. Or in other words, user u is said to recover. However, there are situations when people are promoting an advert or a petition, a user u might look to share same piece of information again from v, making user u susceptible to sharing that information again. Therefore, SIR/S could be intuitively seen as an option to model diffusion in such a propagation scenario.

SIRS: In SIR model, after a node u recovers from infection, its immunity is permanent. However, in SIRS, u's immunity wanes over time, thereby making it susceptible to infection again. As discussed above, there are cases, where a post after being shared loses its relevancy to be shared again. However, there might be cases where a post regains its relevancy over time. For example, a post i on a periodic event might become relevant as the event approaches. As the relevancy of such a post increases over time, the immunity of u decreases, eventually making u susceptible to infection again. Mathematically,

$$I_u(t) \propto \frac{1}{R_i(t)} \tag{1}$$

where, $\mathbf{I_u(t)}$ is the immunity of u from being susceptible at time t and $\mathbf{R_i(t)}$ is the relevancy of post i at time t. This type of propagation scheme could be best linked with

Facebook's "On This Day" feature[1]. Therefore, SIRS could theoretically be seen as an option to model diffusion in such a propagation scenario. Another application could be found in cases where there are chances of recurring themes as studied in [23].

While we have laid out the motivation for this study, it is important to understand the limitations of the above-described models. One critical limitation of these models is neither of them is a generalized model which could be applied or used to mimic information dissipation in any situation. For example, SIS model has been used to mimic the sharing behavior in blog networks [10], whereas, for microblogging networks like Twitter, SIR model is best suited. Also, these models generally are over-simplified in that they assume each node in a network behaves similar to every other node with respect to the different model states (*Susceptible, Infected, Recovered, Exposed*).

4 Definitions

In this paper, information cascades have been classified in three types of shapes, viz., chain, star and chain-star, defined as follows:

Chain: A chain cascade occurs when the root node is linked with a single node and/or which in turn is linked with another, and so on. The in-degree of each node in a chain is one.

Star: A star cascade occurs when a root node is linked with n number of its directed neighbors with $n \geq 2$.

Chain-Star: A chain-star cascade is a mixture of chain and star cascades.

5 Model and Dataset Description

5.1 Model Description

There are two main parameters involved: β and δ, infection rate, and recovery or susceptibility rate, respectively. A node u infects its directed neighbor v with probability β at time-step t. Several values of β parameter were tried and at the end the decision was made to use $\beta = 0.02$, that is the probability with which u infects v is 2%.

Now, at time-step $t + 1$, in:

SIR: v recovers with probability $\delta = 1$, that is with 100% probability.

SIS: v becomes susceptible with $\delta = 1$, that is with 100% probability.

SIR/S: v either recovers or becomes susceptible with $\delta = 0.5$, that is with equal probability of 50%.

SIRS: v recovers with probability $\delta = 1$. Then at time-step $t + 2$, v stays in recovered state, before becoming susceptible again at next time-step.

---

[1] https://newsroom.fb.com/news/2015/03/introducing-on-this-day-a-new-way-to-look-back-at-photos-and-memories-on-facebook/.

5.2   Dataset Description

For this study, we use a network which has been used in [24] and is available at *GitHub*². The network is a directed graph with 1,899 nodes and 20,296 edges. We filtered out 6 nodes and the related edges so that we have only one weakly connected component. This results in a graph $G = (V, E)$, where V is the set of nodes and E is the set of edges with $|V| = 1,893$ and $|E| = 20,292$. The different properties of the network are shown in Table 1 and its degree distribution is shown in Fig. 1. It is clear from the Fig. 1 that the degree distribution of this network follows power-law and heavy-tailed distributions, two of the important properties of a typical social network.

Table 1. Network properties.

No. of nodes	No. of edges	Avg. degree	Avg. path length	Strongly connected components	Avg. clustering coefficient
1,893	20,292	10.72	3.20	596	0.085

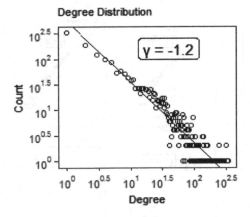

Fig. 1. Degree distribution of the network. (scales are logarithmic, base 10)

6   Results, Discussion and Outcomes

6.1   Cascade Generation

Each model produces 94, 650 cascades. As can be seen from Table 2, chains are the most generated cascade shapes across all the models, followed by chain-star and star. This means that depth-oriented cascades (chain-shaped) are the most frequent. Then those cascades which cross first level are highly likely to show the combined effects of depth orientation as well as breadth (chain-star-shaped). The least likely cascades to

---

² https://github.com/gephi/gephi/wiki/Datasets.

Table 2. Number of different shapes across all the models.

Models shapes	SIR	SIS	SIR/S	SIRS
Chain	9,218	9,160	9,098	9,342
Star	981	1,030	975	957
Chain-star	5,342	5,489	5,610	5,357
Empty (1-node)	79,109	78,971	78,967	78,994
Total cascades	94,650	94,650	94,650	94,650

form are those which only end up at first level exhibiting breadth orientation (star-shaped). It is worth mentioning that an empty cascade contains a node which wasn't able to infect any node in the network.

6.2   Cascade Size Distribution

Figure 2 shows the distribution of cascade size (previously used as analysis metric in [10]) for different cascade shapes as generated by all the models.

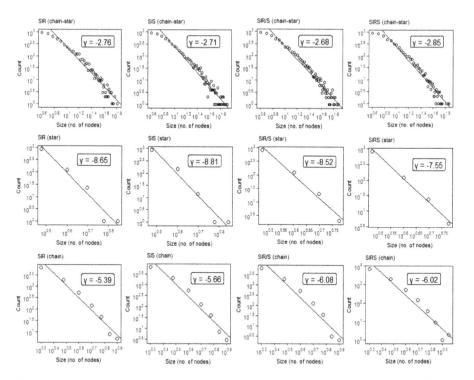

Fig. 2. Cascade size distribution of various shapes for all the models. (scales are logarithmic, base 10)

- *Chain-star:* It can be seen that chain-star-shaped cascades follow power law and heavy-tailed distributions for all the models. SIS has heaviest tail followed by SIR/S, SIRS and SIR. The slopes vary between $\gamma = -2.68$ to $\gamma = -2.85$, with SIR/S having the steepest slope.
- *Chain:* Chain-shaped cascades follow power law distribution across all the models, but, interestingly, they don't follow heavy-tailed distributions however, no model exhibits a heavy-tailed. The slopes are steeper than found in chain-star with SIR/S again having the steepest slope ($\gamma = -6.08$).
- *Star:* Star-shaped cascades also follow power law distribution, with heavy tails occurring in SIR and SIS only. The slopes are even steeper here with SIS having the steepest slope ($\gamma = -8.81$).

Figure 3 shows the overall cascade size distribution (all shaped cascades + empty cascades). Again, all the models follow heavy-tailed and power-law distributions with the slopes ranging between $\gamma = -2.60$ to $\gamma = -2.73$. Notably, SIRS model has the highest slope with $\gamma = -2.73$.

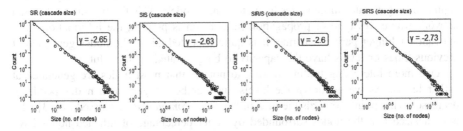

Fig. 3. Overall cascade size distribution for all the models. (scales are logarithmic, base 10)

6.3 Breadth Cover (Nodes Produced Per Level)

To get a better contrast among models, instead of analyzing the nodes at individual levels, we analyze them collectively by combining the levels as shown in Fig. 4. From Fig. 4(a), it can be seen that from levels 0 to 5, the SIR/S and SIS generate the most number of nodes, showing one behavior, whereas SIR and SIRS generate the least number of nodes, exhibiting a different behavior. The same pattern continues up to level 15 as clear from Fig. 4(b) and (c). The reason for SIS and SIR/S behaving the same way is because of the fact that SIR/S is implicitly half-SIS.

As for SIR and SIRS behaving the same way, the properties of the network used in this study need to be considered. In SIRS, a node u recovers for two time-steps, before becoming susceptible again. But, given the number of strongly connected components (SCC) in as small a network as of 1,893 nodes (596 SCC) and power-law degree distribution of the network, it is quite possible that by the time node u becomes susceptible again, the information has propagated beyond its reach. Therefore, there is a very small probability for u to get infected again. However, if node u does have a long reach (the network in question has lesser number of SCC), SIRS could behave more

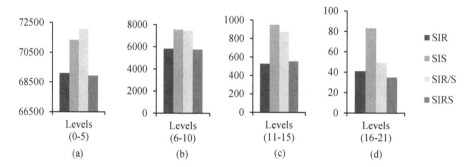

Fig. 4. Number of nodes produced at different levels.

like SIS. It would be worth investigating whether SIRS behaves exactly like SIS if the network in question is strongly connected digraph. (comparatively lesser no. of SCC).

The above mentioned trend, however, breaks from levels greater than 15 as shown in Fig. 4(d), showing the expected power of SIS. As evident from this figure, SIS significantly generates more nodes than any other models. This finding shows that in a network where SIS type of propagation mechanism is present, the information stays relevant for longer periods of time. It is quite expected, since the nodes generated at previous times or levels have the capacity to be generated again in future.

One more interesting finding worthy to note is that most nodes are generated at earlier levels. As we go down the levels, the number of generated nodes per level decreases. This points towards the idea of "*source prominence*" discussed in [13] who hypothesized that the nodes surrounded by larger percentage of infected nodes have more probability to be the sources of information.

6.4   Depth Cover (Levels Reached by Cascades)

Generally, cascades generated by all the four models reach the same maximum depth as shown in Fig. 5 (left). The number of cascades of different depths as generated by all the four models follows heavy-tailed power-law distribution as shown in Fig. 5 (right).

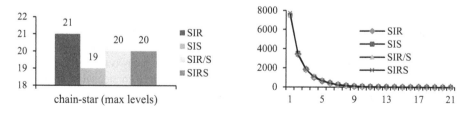

Fig. 5. Maximum depth reached by cascades (left), number of cascades of different depths (right) for all the models.

Importantly, as shown in Fig. 5 (right), there isn't any significant difference in the number of cascades reaching any particular depth across all the models. However, to get a better contrast among models, we split the depths into two parts, viz., depths 1–10 and 11–21. Then, for each part, we count the number of times each model generated the most number of cascades. The results thus produced are shown in Fig. 6.

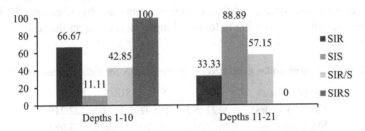

Fig. 6. Percentage of cascades of different depths generated by all the models.

It is clear from Fig. 6 that from depths 1 to 10, 100% of SIRS cascades are greater in number than the rest, followed by SIR, SIR/S and SIS. This shows that of shallower depths, SIS generates least number of cascades whereas SIRS generates the most than rest of the models. As, we go deeper from depths 11 to 21, SIS is a clear winner. Here, SIS generates the most number of cascades (88.89%) followed by SIR/S (57.15%), SIR (33.33%) and SIRS (0%).

It is important to note that both SIR and SIRS experience a drop when moving from 1–10 to 11–21 depths, while SIS and SIR/S experience an increase. This finding again shows that SIR and SIRS follow one trend, whereas SIS and SIR/S follow another trend. The reason of this has been explained in Sect. 6.3.

To further highlight the influence of SIS at deeper depths, we analyze chain-star-shaped cascades generated by all the models. As shown in Fig. 7, SIS generates the most number of cascades of higher depths, significantly beating rest of the models.

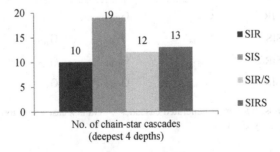

Fig. 7. Number of chain-star cascades of higher depths for all the models.

6.5   Total Cover (Total Nodes Produced by All Cascades)

From Table 3, it can be seen that SIR/S model generates the most number of nodes, followed by SIS, SIR and SIRS. However, there isn't much difference in the number of nodes generated by SIR/S and SIS, and the same pattern can be seen with SIR and SIRS. This type of trend was also seen in Sects. 6.3 and 6.4 and was explained in Sect. 6.3. This further shows that SIR/S and SIS have the tendency to generate cascades which stay relevant for longer periods of time than those generated by other models. In other words, these models are more likely to have longer cascades than the rest.

Table 3. Number of nodes generated by all the models for different cascade shapes.

Models shapes	SIR	SIS	SIR/S	SIRS
Chain (# nodes)	22,095	21,987	21,663	22,219
Star (# nodes)	3,117	3,270	3,095	3,051
Chain-star (# nodes)	50,286	54,682	55,711	50,023
Empty (# nodes)	79,109	78,971	78,967	78,994
Total node count	154,607	158,910	159,436	154,287

6.6   Frequently Generated Cascades

Figure 8 shows 3 most frequently generated cascades, ordered by decreasing frequency. Interestingly, it can be seen that across all the models, top three frequently generated cascades are similar in shape as well as order.

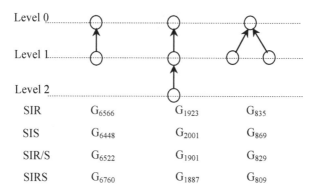

Fig. 8.   Three top most frequently generated cascades*. *Gn is a cascade graph where n denotes the occurrence frequency of G.

This pattern changes to an extent when we explore more cascades (next three most frequent) in decreasing frequencies as shown in Fig. 9. It is clear from this figure that SIS and SIRS generate cascades of same shapes and in the same order, whereas SIR differs in order alone. A special exception is found in SIR/S where a single cascade

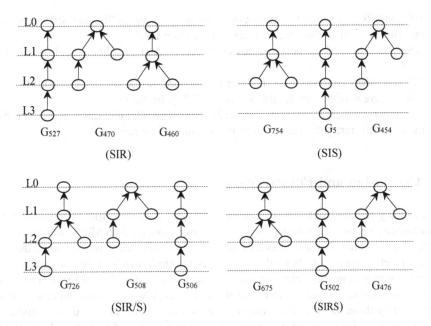

Fig. 9. Next three top most frequently generated cascades*. *G_n is a cascade graph where n denotes the occurrence frequency of G.

shape G_{726} is not generated in any other models. Interestingly, this cascade is also the largest in terms of size among all the cascades generated across all the models.

Furthermore, collectively from Figs. 8 and 9, it can be seen that smaller cascades are more frequent than larger ones which was also found by [10] analyzing real-world datasets. This further shows how model generated cascades could be used to analyze the properties of real-world cascades.

From the above discussion, it can be understood that all the four models used in this study generally produce same shapes of cascades with variations in the order of frequency of cascades.

6.7 Outcomes of the Study

We sum up the above discussions in the form of the following findings:

- All the cascade size distributions follow power-law.
- Chain-star-shaped cascade sizes follow heavy-tailed distributions for all the models.
- Smaller cascades are more likely to occur than the large ones across all the models [22].
- The probability for depth-oriented cascades to occur is the highest, whereas breadth-oriented cascades is the least across all the models.
- The majority of the nodes are generated at shallower levels indicating "*source prominence*" [13].

- SIS and SIR/S generate the most number of nodes whereas SIR and SIRS generate the least at most of the levels except at very deep levels.
- SIS shows its node generation power in comparison to other models at deeper levels.
- SIS and SIR/S generate lesser number of cascades of shallow depths than SIR and SIRS whereas of deeper depths SIS and SIR/S generate more.
- The most frequently generated cascades are generally the same across all the models, with rare differences found in the order of frequency.

7   Conclusion and Future Scope

In this study we used well-known compartmental models, viz., SIR, SIS and SIRS to generate cascades over a network. Another intuitive model, called SIR/S, was proposed in this paper, which also served as a cascade generation model. It is understood that all these models theoretically have the tendencies to mimic the behavior of cascades in various propagation scenarios or real-world applications. Therefore in order to understand cascade properties found in those scenarios, we analyzed the cascades as generated by these models. The cascades thus generated were analyzed and compared with each other. It was found that there are certain properties of cascades where all the models behave in a similar way, while for other properties some models behave differently than the rest. For cascade size distribution, generally all the models generate cascades which follow power-law and heavy-tailed distributions. Also, the most frequently generated cascades were predominantly found to have the same shapes for all the models. It was also found that the cascades generated by all the models were depth oriented, with breadth oriented cascades having the least probability to occur. Having found all these similarities among all the models, some interesting differences were also found. For example, for nodes generated at most of the levels, it was found that SIS and SIR/S have the tendencies to behave in one way, while SIR and SIRS follow a different trend, showing a contrasting behavior. This was also found in depth cover and total cover. With the help of these findings, this study is able to shed light over the nature of cascades as found in different propagation mechanisms.

In future, we look to conduct a similar type of study using multiple networks with different properties. It will be interesting to know how much the network properties affect the behavior of cascades generated by these models. Furthermore, as discussed in Sect. 6.3, it will be interesting to investigate whether SIRS starts behaving more like SIS as the number of strongly connected components of the network in question decrease with time (dynamic network analysis).

References

1. Goldenberg, J., Libai, B., Muller, E.: Talk of the network: a complex systems look at the underlying process of word-of-mouth. Mark. Lett. **12**(3), 211–223 (2001). https://doi.org/10.1023/A:1011122126881
2. Hethcote, H.W.: The mathematics of infectious diseases. SIAM Rev. **42**(4), 599–653 (2000)

3. Newman, M.E.J.: The structure and function of complex networks. SIAM Rev. **45**(2), 167–256 (2003)
4. Granovetter, M.: Threshold models of collective behavior. Am. J. Sociol. **83**(6), 1420–1443 (1978)
5. Song, L.P., Jin, Z., Sun, G.Q.: Modeling and analyzing of botnet interactions. Phys. A: Statist. Mech. Appl. **390**(2), 347–358 (2011)
6. Barbieri, N., Bonchi, F., Manco, G.: Topic-aware social influence propagation models. In: Proceedings of the 12th IEEE ICDM International Conference on Data Mining, pp. 81–90. IEEE, Brussels, Belgium (2012)
7. Allen, L.: Some discrete-time SI, SIR, and SIS epidemic models. Math. Biosci. **124**(1), 83–105 (1994)
8. Yao, Y., Luo, X., Gao, F., Ai., S.: Research of a potential worm propagation model based on pure P2P principle. In: Proceedings of the International Conference on Communication Technology (ICCT), pp. 1–4, Guilin, China (2006)
9. Guille, A., Hacid, H., Favre, C., Zighed, D.: Information diffusion in online social networks: a survey. ACM SIGMOD Rec. **42**(2), 17–28 (2013)
10. Leskovec, J., McGlohon, M., Faloutsos, C., Glance N., Hurst, M.: Patterns of cascading behavior in large blog graphs. In: Proceedings of the 2007 SIAM International Conference on Data Mining, pp. 551–556. SIAM, Minnesota, USA (2007)
11. Yang, J., Leskovec, J.: Modeling information diffusion in implicit networks. In: Proceedings of the 10th IEEE International Conference on Data Mining, pp. 599–608. IEEE, Sydney, Australia (2010)
12. Shah, D., Zaman, T.: Detecting sources of computer viruses in networks: theory and experiment. In: Proceedings of the ACM SIGMETRICS, pp. 203–214, New York, USA, December 2010
13. Wang, Z., Wang, C., Pei, J., Ye, X.: Multiple source detection without knowing the underlying propagation model. In: Proceedings of 31st AAAI Conference on Artificial Intelligence, pp. 217–223. AAAI, California, USA (2017)
14. Zhu, K., Ying, L.: Information Source detection in the SIR model: a sample-path-based approach. IEEE/ACM Trans. Netw. **24**(1), 408–421 (2016)
15. Luo, W.: Identifying infection sources in a network. Ph.D. Dissertation, Nanyang Technological University, Singapore (2015)
16. Zhu, K., Ying, L.: A robust information source estimator with sparse observations. Comput. Soc. Netw. **1**(1), 1–21 (2014). https://doi.org/10.1186/s40649-014-0003-2
17. Pan, J., Zhang, W.: Identifying rumor sources using dominant eigenvalue of nonbacktracking matrix. In: Proceedings of the IEEE Global Conference on Signal and Information Processing (GlobalSIP), pp. 748–752, CA, USA, November 2018
18. Fan, T. H., Wang, I. H.: Rumor source detection: a probabilistic perspective. In: Proceedings of the IEEE International Conference on Acoustics, Speech and Signal Processing (ICASSP), pp. 4159–4163, Calgary, AB, Canada, April 2018
19. Ali, S.S., Rizvi, S.A.M.: Factors influencing infection source identification in complex networks: an empirical study. Int. J. Comput. Sci. Eng. **7**(5), 1791–1804 (2019)
20. Zhou, Y., Wu, C., Zhu, Q., Xiang, Y., Loke, S.: Rumor source detection in networks based on the SEIR model. IEEE Access **7**, 45240–45258 (2019)
21. Goel, S., Watts, D., Goldstein, D.: The structure of online diffusion networks. In: Proceedings of the 13th ACM Conference on Electronic Commerce, pp. 623–638. ACM, Valencia, Spain (2012)

22. Dow, P., Adamic, L., Friggeri, A.: The anatomy of large Facebook cascades. In: Proceedings of the 7th AAAI International Conference on Weblogs and Social Media, vol. 1, issue no 2, p. 12. AAAI, MA, USA (2013)
23. Cheng, J., Adamic, L., Kleinberg, J., Leskovec, J.: Do Cascades Recur? In: Proceedings of the 25th International Conference on World Wide Web, pp. 671–681. International World Wide Web Conferences Steering Committee, Montreal, Canada (2016)
24. Opsahl, T., Panzarasa, P.: Clustering in weighted networks. Soc. Netw. **31**(2), 155–163 (2009)

Data Mining Technologies for Identifying Brand-Switching Patterns of Customers in Telecom Domain

Ritu Punhani[1]($\boxtimes$), V. P. S. Arora[2], A. Sai Sabitha[1], and Nikhil Vazirani[3]

[1] Department of Information Technology, ASET, Amity University, Sector – 125, Noida, Uttar Pradesh, India
ritupunhani@gmail.com
[2] School of Agricultural Economics and Agribusiness, Haramaya University, Haramaya, Ethiopia
[3] Tata Consultancy Services Ltd., Gurugram, Haryana, India

Abstract. Indian Telecom Domain is growing very fast and presently it has the world's second largest Internet user-base. As there are many service providers in this domain, inspiring customers for brand switching, there are many factors that impact customer behavior due to emerging competitive environment. The concern of the study is to identify the factors behind brand switching in Telecom domain. Questionnaires were prepared for data collection and processing on a sample of 350 respondents. Simple clustering technique like K-mean, DBScan is used to find the valuable clusters. These clusters are mapped to other customer evaluation parameters like customer loyalty, customer retention and customer needs. Statistical measures are used to evaluate factors influencing brand switching in telecom domain.

Keywords: Customer behaviour · Price · Customer loyalty · Customer requirement · Customer retention

1 Introduction

Consumer behaviour is a confluence of different features derived from domains like psychology, social anthropology, marketing, economics, sociology, and especially behavioural economics. In this era of fast changing technologies, keeping in pace with the growing aspiration/desires of the society, the telecom services have come a long way. Characteristics of individual consumer such as usage rates, loyalty, and brand advocacy are an attempt to understand people's consumption and are used to study the consumer behaviour. Customer relationship management data enables detailed examination of behavioural factors that influences customer retention, loyalty, requirements and customer citizenship activities.

The telecom sector had grown manifold over the years and with the advent of wireless access to the internet, the telecom services now include web surfing, video calling, social networking etc. These services are growing in faster pace. The market strategies also have changed over a period of time for each telecom operator as they are

© Springer Nature Singapore Pte Ltd. 2020
P. K. Singh et al. (Eds.): FTNCT 2019, CCIS 1206, pp. 319–333, 2020.
https://doi.org/10.1007/978-981-15-4451-4_25

now more consumer-driven than supply driven or just for making profits. The industry wants to retain their consumers forever as now Telecom Regulatory Authority of India (TRAI) has regulated the Mobile number Portability (MNP) option so that the consumer can switch between the telecom operators. Consumers choose a particular service of a telecom operator because it provides best network quality with a reasonable price, quick customer support and resolves issues easily and spontaneously. Most consumers change their telecom operator because they are either not satisfied with the services or if the problem occurs persistently in their services which cause the consumer to lose valuable time, money and consumers complaints are not easily resolved. Some of the known factors of switching the telecom operator by consumers are Network Quality, Price of calls/package, Consumer Service and Promotion.

This research aims to find out the factors that influence customer behaviour to switch telecom operator in the industry and is mapped to the consumer type is clustered using fuzzy clustering technique and further the clusters are analyzed and mapped to different categories like student, government employee, businessman etc. thereby understanding the influential factors in brand switching. This paper is divided into sections like Literature Survey, Methodology, Analysis, Results and Conclusion.

2   Literature Survey

Consumers' attention is a vital parameter to gain consumers. The companies have to adapt and change their market strategies so as to gain market share and retain consumers forever. They attract consumer by offering them with more attractive options in their services and through adopting promotional strategies to create awareness among consumers that they can connect.

Consumer Retention				
Year	Author	Factors	Subject	Technique
2007	M._ Ehalifa et V. Liu[11]	After sale Service, transaction efficency, security, convenience, cost saving	Online consumer retention	Review Paper
2010	J.F. Ali et al[12]	User friendliness, price responsibility, call clarity	Consumer retention in cellular industry (Pakistan)	Review Paper
2001	N. Nguyen et G. LeBlanc[13]	Corporate reputation, corporate image	Customers retention decisions in services	Review Paper

Fig. 1. Customer retention literature survey

Consumer Attention				
Year	Author	Factors	Subject	Technique
2004	H.Y. Ha[9]	Security, privacy, brand name, word of mouth, good online experience, quality of information	Factors influencing consumer perceptions of brand trust (online)	Review Paper
2005	B. Jin et Y.G. Sub[10]	Price, value consciousness, perceived price, consumer innovativeness	Preception factors in predicting private brand purchase	Review Paper

Fig. 2. Customer attention literature survey

Consumer Behaviour				
Year	Author	Factors	Subject	Technique
2011	M.Satish et al[2]	Call rates, network coverage, VAS, customer Care, advertisement	Consumer switching behaviour in cellular service provider(Chennai)	Cluster sampling SS-112
2003	C.H. Park et Y.G. Kim[3]	Information quality, user interface quality, security perceptions	Key factors affecting consumer purchase behaviour: online shopping	Review Paper
2007	C. Mazzoni et al[4]	Consumer/user lifestyles, use motivations, product/service attributes	Consumer behaviour in the Italian mobile telecom market	Cluster analysis SS-1067
2005	H. Katjaluoto et al[5]	Price, brand, interface, properties	Factors affecting consumer choice of mobile phones	Review Paper
2013	M.F Diallo et al[6]	Store image perception, SB price Image, value consciousness, SB attitude	Factors influencing consumer behaviour	Review Paper

Fig. 3. Customer behaviour literature survey

The table represented in Figs. 1 and 2 shows the various reviews that had been conducted based on customer retention and attention. The screenshot of the table represented in Fig. 3 shows the factors that influence and techniques/tools used to understand the customer behaviour. The other factors that are essential in consumer brand switching are privacy of our data, upgradation of services with futuristic vision, educating low end consumer about the services and resolving their problems with ease.

A. *Clustering: Data Mining Technique*

Data mining is computing process of discovering patterns in large data sets. It's main aim is to extract information from a dataset and transform it into an understandable structure. Clustering is an unsupervised learning problem. It structures a set of data or its objects into a set of substantial subclasses, called clusters.

Clustering helps us to identify objects similar and dissimilar to the objects in a cluster [1]. Clusters are classified as Hard Cluster (K-Means and K-Modes) and Soft Cluster (Fuzzy c-Means and Fuzzy k-Modes). The hard cluster methods are formed on the traditional set idea and need an object belonging or not belonging to a cluster. It then divides the data into a definite amount of mutually exclusive subsets, whereas in soft clustering methods, the same object can belong to dissimilar clusters depending upon the membership value. Fuzzy C-mean clustering is also an unsupervised, soft clustering method and fuzziness is defined by membership function that gives the degree of belongingness of an object to a specific cluster [1].

B. *Validation Measures*

There are many validation techniques. For instance the Average Silhouette Clustering Technique is a method of interpretation and validation of consistency within clusters of data. It measures how similar the objects are within the clusters as compared to other clusters. The value ranges from −1 to +1, where +1 denotes that the object is well matched with its own cluster and −1 denotes that the object is poorly matched within its own cluster.

$$S_i = (b_i - a_i)/\max(a_i, \ b_i) \tag{1}$$

where a_i = average distance from the ith point to the other points in the same cluster as i, b_i = minimum average distance from the ith point to points in a different cluster.

C. *Statistical Techniques*

One Sample t-test: It is an inferential statistic technique, used to find whether number of objects could have been created by a technique with a specific mean. A null hypothesis is to be defined so as to compare the mean in the test to tell if there is significant difference between the null hypothesis mean and the mean calculated. The calculated mean gives the probability of observing the test results under the null hypothesis [21].

$$t = \underline{x} - \mu/\sqrt{s^2/n} \tag{2}$$

Where $\bar{x}$ = sample mean, μ = specified population mean, s^2 = sample variance and n = sample size.

Correlation Bivariate: It is a technique for comparing whether two metric variables are linearly related in some sample. In the correlation bivariate table, the row has three parameters,

1. Pearson Correlation: it shows if there is a positive or negative linear relationship between the selected row and column.
2. The p-value (Sig. 2-tailed): shows the percentage of chance of discovering the correlation in the sample. The null hypothesis is often excluded if p < 0.05.
3. Sample Size (N): Sample size [19].

Crosstabs with Chi-Square test: It determines whether there is a relation between categorical variables. It can compare only categorical variables. By comparing the Pearson Chi-square value and Pearson Chi-Square p-value to find if there is a significant relation between the factors or not [20].

$$x_c^2 = \sum \frac{(O_i - E_i)^2}{E_i} \qquad (3)$$

Where c = degree of freedom, O = observed value and E = expected value.

3 Methodology

The main aim of this research work aims to identify factors that influence brand switching. These factors that affect cannot be grouped in as crisp classes as an amount of fuzziness is involved. Fuzzy C-mean clustering is used in the first step, data is collected for the analysis and the attributes Network Quality, Price of Calls/Package, Customer Service, Information about services/prices, Upgradation of service, Privacy

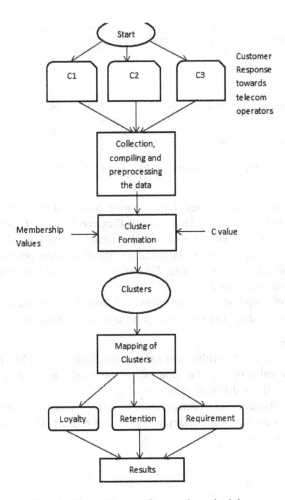

Fig. 4. Flow diagram of research methodology

of Data, Education of low end consumer and promotion are selected for clustering in the data and stored in the data file. Then fuzzy classes are defined and cluster with membership data is formed using Fuzzy Clustering. Then mapping of objects is done using the membership value to find a pattern in the data set. Trends are extracted from the clusters to understand influential parameters as per the objective of the paper mentioned above (Fig. 4).

4   Experimental Setup

The Fig. 5 shows the data correlated from questionnaire [21] (link of questionnaire for Telecom Operator Survey).

Primary Operator	You use Primary Operator for?	Secondary Operator	You use Secondary Operator for?	Does it have 4G?
Airtel	Calls	Jio	Data Services	Yes
Vodafone	Data Services	Jio	None	Yes
Airtel	Calls	Jio	None	Yes
Jio	Data Services	Airtel	Calls	Yes
Jio	Calls	Aircel	Calls	Yes

Fig. 5. Screenshot of data set with parameters

The parameters include Current/Latest phone name, Single/Dual Sim, Date of purchase of current phone, Date of purchase of Previous Phone, 4G Services Availed, whether number ported or not. It also includes rating of Network Quality, Price of Calls/Package, Customer Service, Information about services/prices, Upgradation/ Technology advanced, Privacy of data, Education of low end consumer, Promotion/ advertisement, Consumer input.

The number of responses collected was 350 from the customers. The data was cleaned and approximately 134 responses were considered for analysis.

D. *Silhouette Index*

In this, fuzzy c-mean algorithm was used to get clusters using MATLAB tool and to identify the value of 'c', silhouette means was used. The code of silhouette was run in MATLAB for different values of 'c'.

The highest silhouette value corresponds to 0.6827 with C = 6 shown in Fig. 6 with 6 clusters the silhouette index is higher and has a positive relation with the neighboring clusters.

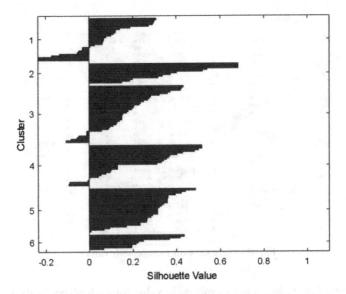

Fig. 6. Silhouette index value = 0.6827 when K = 6

E. Clusters Obtained

Figure 7 shows the clusters observed and indicates O = cluster 1, X = cluster 2, Square = cluster 3, diamond = cluster 4, and * = cluster 5, + = cluster 6.

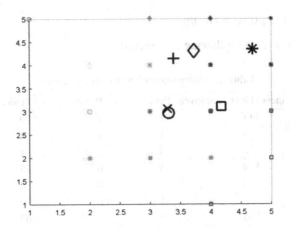

Fig. 7. 6 clusters defined from dataset

1	id	index1	index2	index3	index4	index5	index6	Total
2	1	0	0	0.0001	0	0.9999	0	1
3	2	0.0001	0	0.0002	0.9855	0	0.0142	1
4	3	0.0011	0	0.9969	0.0008	0.0012	0	1
5	4	0	0	0	0.0001	0	0.9999	1
6	5	0.0005	0	0.0003	0.9992	0	0	1
7	6	0.0028	0	0.0047	0.9917	0.0007	0.0001	1
8	7	0.9969	0	0.0002	0.0028	0	0.0001	1
9	8	0.9962	0.0036	0	0.0002	0	0	1
10	9	0	0	0	1	0	0	1
11	10	0	0	0	1	0	0	1
12	11	0	0	0.022	0.9732	0.0047	0	0.9999
13	12	0.9995	0	0.0005	0	0	0	1
14	13	1	0	0	0	0	0	1
15	14	0	1	0	0	0	0	1
16	15	0	1	0	0	0	0	1
17	16	0.9985	0.0009	0.0002	0	0	0.0003	0.9999
18	17	0.9962	0	0.0015	0.0014	0	0.001	1.0001
19	18	0	0	0.0007	0.9992	0	0	0.9999
20	19	0.1276	0	0.8721	0.0004	0	0	1.0001
21	20	0	0	0	0	0	1	1
22	21	0	0	0.9999	0.0001	0	0	1
23	22	0	0	0.9999	0.0001	0	0	1
24	23	0	0	0	0	1	0	1
25	24	0.9415	0.0385	0.001	0.0008	0	0.0182	1
26	25	0.0001	0	0.9808	0.0019	0.0172	0	1
27	26	0.0001	0	0.9808	0.0019	0.0172	0	1
28	27	0.022	0.9349	0.0001	0.0006	0	0.0424	1
29	28	0.9641	0	0.0009	0.0346	0	0.0004	1
30	29	0	0	0	0	0	1	1

Fig. 8. Data set with membership values

The above Fig. 8 shows the membership value for each object in the 6 clusters. For analysis, the memberships with 80% and above are considered. The findings are observed and analyzed. Out of 134 responses, 127 responses were defined with more than 80% of the membership value.

5 Analysis

F. *Case Study 1: Customer Loyalty*

From the Table 1, the following is observed:

Table 1. Distribution of people in categories

Cluster no.	Business	Govt. employee	Public sector	Private sector	Student	Nil	Total
1	1	11	2	1	20	3	38
2	0	8	1	1	4	0	14
3	0	8	3	2	11	1	25
4	0	4	3	0	15	5	27
5	2	3	1	0	8	0	14
6	0	3	1	0	5	0	9
Total	3	37	11	4	63	9	127

- In cluster number 1, 3, 4, 5, and 6 the percentage of "Students" is high under the category user type
- In cluster number 2, the percentage of "Government Employees" is high

In the Table 2, cluster number 2 has the lowest rating and cluster number 5 has the highest rating of Quality, Average Service and Privacy.

Table 2. Loyalty cluster table

Cluster no.	Quality	Avg. service	Privacy
1	2–4	3–4	1–5
2	2–5	1.5–2.75	1–3
3	3–5	3.25–4.5	3–4
4	2–5	3.25–4.25	3–5
5	4–5	4.25–5	4–5
6	3–5	2.5–3.25	2–4

It defines that the cluster number 2 has less loyal consumer to their brand and 5 is more loyal to their brand. It also shows that in cluster 2 there are more government employees and is not much loyal.

From the data set, we can see that the frequency of purchasing a new phone is more when the option is >12 months as the government gives more offers to their employees after a certain period of time and have strict policies over the cellphone usage in the offices.

Hence, they are only loyal to a brand because of the incentive given by government even if the brand does not provide good services.

G. *Case Study 2: Customer Retention*

From the Table 3, cluster 1 and 2 are found to have less values with high frequencies of the data and hence 1 got the low rating which implies that 1 and 2 cluster consumers' may not retain the same brand after some period of time.

Table 3. Retention cluster table

Cluster no.	Promotion	Avg. service	Price	Quality
1	1–5	3–4	2–4	2–4
2	2–4	1.5–2.75	2–5	2–5
3	1–4	3.25–4.5	3–5	3–5
4	4–5	3.25–4.25	3–5	2–5
5	3–5	4.25–5	3–5	4–5
6	3–5	2.5–3.25	3–5	2–4

Cluster 4 and 5 have high value with high frequency in the data set hence is more retained in the same brand because of the factors influencing their behaviour.

H. *Case Study 3: Customer Requirement*

From the Table 4, cluster 2 has the lowest rating and hence consumer requirements of the members of the cluster 2 are not met to the consumers' requirement. Cluster 5 has the highest rating and hence consumer requirements of the members are met to the consumer satisfaction level.

Table 4. Requirement cluster table

Cluster no.	Privacy	Avg. service
1	1–5	3–4
2	1–3	1.5–2.75
3	3–4	3.25–4.5
4	3–5	3.25–4.25
5	4–5	4.25–5
6	2–4	2.5–3.25

The tables presented above show that cluster 2 has low loyalty, requirement and retention rating and has more government sector employees because they are entitled to a restricted allowance for mobile handset and telecom services. On the other hand the cluster 5 consumers have high loyalty, requirement and retention rating because they are more satisfied with their requirement and are retained by the telecom operators and hence are more loyal.

I. *Case Study 4: Sample t-test*

Figure 9 shows that the null hypothesis is accepted for cluster 4 for Loyalty factors. The Sample Mean calculated is 3.73, 3.69 and 3.5690 for Network Quality, Privacy of data and Average Service respectively. Hence, we find that there is not significant difference (≥ 3.7) between the calculated mean and the null hypothesis of Network Quality and Privacy of data but Average Service has a significant difference (< 3.7). Thus if the telecom operator improves his services, the rating would improve and consumer loyalty would also improve.

One-Sample Statistics

	N	Mean	Std. Deviation	Std. Error Mean
Network Quality	134	3.73	.806	.070
Privacy of your data	134	3.69	.896	.077
Avg Service	134	3.5690	.72053	.06224

One-Sample Test

				Test Value = 4		95% Confidence Interval of the Difference	
	t	df	Sig. (2-tailed)	Mean Difference		Lower	Upper
Network Quality	-3.860	133	.000	-.269		-.41	-.13
Privacy of your data	-4.048	133	.000	-.313		-.47	-.16
Avg Service	-6.924	133	.000	-.43097		-.5541	-.3079

Fig. 9. Loyalty sample t-test

Retention Factors: Fig. 10 shows that the null hypothesis is acceptable for cluster 4 for Retention factors. The Sample Mean calculated is 3.73, 3.54, 3.82, and 3.5690 for Network Quality, Price of calls/package, Promotion and Average Service respectively. Hence, we find that there is not significant difference (≥ 3.7) between the calculated

One-Sample Statistics

	N	Mean	Std. Deviation	Std. Error Mean
Network Quality	134	3.73	.806	.070
Price of Calls/Package	134	3.54	.907	.078
Promotion/Advertisement	134	3.82	.848	.073
Avg Service	134	3.5690	.72053	.06224

One-Sample Test

	Test Value = 4					
	t	df	Sig. (2-tailed)	Mean Difference	95% Confidence Interval of the Difference	
					Lower	Upper
Network Quality	-3.860	133	.000	-.269	-.41	-.13
Price of Calls/Package	-5.908	133	.000	-.463	-.62	-.31
Promotion/Advertisement	-2.444	133	.016	-.179	-.32	-.03
Avg Service	-6.924	133	.000	-.43097	-.5541	-.3079

Fig. 10. Retention sample t-test

One-Sample Statistics

	N	Mean	Std. Deviation	Std. Error Mean
Avg Service	134	3.5690	.72053	.06224
Privacy of your data	134	3.69	.896	.077

One-Sample Test

	Test Value = 4					
	t	df	Sig. (2-tailed)	Mean Difference	95% Confidence Interval of the Difference	
					Lower	Upper
Avg Service	-6.924	133	.000	-.43097	-.5541	-.3079
Privacy of your data	-4.048	133	.000	-.313	-.47	-.16

Fig. 11. Requirement sample t-test

		Network Quality	Privacy of your data	Avg Service	Price of Calls/Package	Promotion/Advertisement
Network Quality	Pearson Correlation	1	.330**	.502**	.148	.270**
	Sig. (2-tailed)		.000	.000	.089	.002
	N	134	134	134	134	134
Privacy of your data	Pearson Correlation	.330**	1	.610**	.292**	.331**
	Sig. (2-tailed)	.000		.000	.001	.000
	N	134	134	134	134	134
Avg Service	Pearson Correlation	.502**	.610**	1	.305**	.291**
	Sig. (2-tailed)	.000	.000		.000	.001
	N	134	134	134	134	134
Price of Calls/Package	Pearson Correlation	.148	.292**	.305**	1	.195*
	Sig. (2-tailed)	.089	.001	.000		.024
	N	134	134	134	134	134
Promotion/Advertisement	Pearson Correlation	.270**	.331**	.291**	.195*	1
	Sig. (2-tailed)	.002	.000	.001	.024	
	N	134	134	134	134	134

**. Correlation is significant at the 0.01 level (2-tailed).

*. Correlation is significant at the 0.05 level (2-tailed).

Fig. 12. Correlation bivariate test

mean and the null hypothesis of Network Quality and Promotion but Price of calls/package and Average Service has a significant difference (<3.7). Thus if the telecom operator improves his services and offers competitive price for calls/package the rating would improve and consumer will be retained.

Requirement Factors: Fig. 11 shows that the null hypothesis is acceptable for cluster 4 for Requirement Factors. The Sample Mean calculated is 3.5690 and 3.69 for Average Service and Privacy of data respectively. Hence, we find that there is not significant difference ($\geq$3.7) between the calculated mean and null hypothesis of Privacy of data but Average Service has a significant difference (<3.7), thus, the telecom operators should improve their service for consumer satisfaction of requirement.

Following are important implications from the results shown in Fig. 12:

- Network Quality has a strong correlation with Customer Service, Information about services and upgradation of technology whereas it has low correlation with price of package, privacy of data, education of low end consumer and promotion.
- Price of Calls/Package has a strong correlation with information about prices and has low correlation with network quality, customer service, upgradation, privacy of data, education of low end consumer and promotion.
- Customer Service has a strong correlation with Network quality, information about prices, upgradation, privacy of data, education of low end consumer and has low correlation with price of calls/package and promotion.
- Information about services has a strong correlation with network quality, price of calls/package, customer service, upgradation, privacy of data and education of low end consumer but has low correlation with promotion.
- Upgradation has a strong correlation with network quality, customer service, information about services, privacy of data and education of low end consumer and has a low correlation with price of calls/package and promotion.
- Privacy of data has strong correlation with customer service, information about services, upgradation and education of low end consumer has a low correlation with network quality, price of calls/package and promotion.
- Education of low end consumer has strong correlation with customer service, upgradation, privacy of data and has low correlation between network quality, price of calls/package and promotion.
- Promotion has low correlation with network quality, price of calls/package, customer service, information about services, upgradation and privacy of data and education of low end consumer.

Hence, promotion has no strong correlation with any of the factors hence it is not our major factor of brand switching.

J. *Case Study 5: Chi-Square Test*

The Table 5 below shows that there is a statistically significant relation between the Primary Operator and factors including Network Quality, Privacy of data, Average Service, Price of calls/package and Promotion. Hence all these factors contribute to the factors of Customer Loyalty, Customer Retention and Customer Requirement.

Table 5. Crosstabs with Chi-Square test.

Primary Operator * Network Quality	**Chi-Square Tests**		
		Value	df	Asymptotic Significance (2-sided)
	Pearson Chi-Square	28.040[a]	28	.462
	Likelihood Ratio	31.911	28	.278
	N of Valid Cases	134		
	a. 33 cells (82.5%) have expected count less than 5. The minimum expected count is .01.			

Primary Operator * Privacy of data	**Chi-Square Tests**		
		Value	df	Asymptotic Significance (2-sided)
	Pearson Chi-Square	31.761[a]	28	.284
	Likelihood Ratio	34.579	28	.182
	N of Valid Cases	134		
	a. 33 cells (82.5%) have expected count less than 5. The minimum expected count is .04.			

Primary Operator * Average Service	**Chi-Square Tests**		
		Value	df	Asymptotic Significance (2-sided)
	Pearson Chi-Square	77.787[a]	91	.837
	Likelihood Ratio	70.036	91	.950
	N of Valid Cases	134		
	a. 103 cells (92.0%) have expected count less than 5. The minimum expected count is .01.			

Primary Operator * Price of calls/package	**Chi-Square Tests**		
		Value	df	Asymptotic Significance (2-sided)
	Pearson Chi-Square	62.289[a]	28	.000
	Likelihood Ratio	56.401	28	.001
	N of Valid Cases	134		
	a. 32 cells (80.0%) have expected count less than 5. The minimum expected count is .01.			

Primary Operator * Promotion	**Chi-Square Tests**		
		Value	df	Asymptotic Significance (2-sided)
	Pearson Chi-Square	17.071[a]	28	.947
	Likelihood Ratio	17.368	28	.941
	N of Valid Cases	134		
	a. 33 cells (82.5%) have expected count less than 5. The minimum expected count is .01.			

Chi-Square Test: The above studies show that cluster 2 has less rating and cluster 5 has high rating in customer loyalty, retention and requirement. The tests show that the promotion/advertisement factor is not an important factor for the consumer to choose a specific telecom brand but instead all the other factors like network quality, privacy of data, average service and price of calls/package. We also find that the primary operator has a significant relationship with the following in the Pearson Chi-Square Test: Network Quality, Privacy of data, Average Services, Price of calls/package and promotion.

Hence, the above results imply that all the factors i.e. Network quality, Privacy of Data and Promotion are related and satisfies the null hypothesis but average service and price of calls/package are not related and does not satisfy the null hypothesis.

6 Conclusion and Future Scope

The case studies were discussed and statistical analysis in this research paper is done to understand the relation between the factors/parameters, which are necessary for brand switching. In this work, the Fuzzy c mean clustering technique was used for analyzing the customer requirements, customer loyalty and customer retention factors. By using this analysis, it is found that telecom domain should improve its services and give a competitive price or offers of their services to their customer to improve customer loyalty and retention.

In telecom domain, further analysis can focus on new and improved market strategies to increase market share and to earn good profits. Advance study can be carried out to identify potential customers and help them to make personalized plan according to their requirements and needs, so it will lead them to make different segments of customers in telecom domain.

References

1. Sabitha, A.S., Mehrotra, D., Bansal, A.: Delivery of learning knowledge objects using fuzzy clustering. Educ. Inf. Technol. **21**(5), 1329–1349 (2016)
2. Sathish, M., Kumar, K.S., Naveen, K.J., Jeevanantham, V.: A study on consumer switching behaviour in cellular service provider: a study with reference to Chennai. Far East J. Psychol. Bus. **2**(2), 71–81 (2011)
3. Park, C.H., Kim, Y.G.: Identifying key factors affecting consumer purchase behaviour in an online shopping context. Int. J. Retail Distrib. Manag. **31**(1), 16–29 (2003)
4. Mazzoni, C., Castaldi, L., Addeo, F.: Consumer behaviour in the Italian mobile telecommunication market. Telecommun. Policy **31**(10), 632–647 (2007)
5. Karjaluoto, H., et al.: Factors affecting consumer choice of mobile phones: two studies from Finland. J. Euromarketing **14**(3), 59–82 (2005)
6. Fall Diallo, M., Chandon, J.L., Cliquet, G., Philippe, J.: Factors influencing consumer behaviour towards store brands: evidence from the French market. Int. J. Retail Distrib. Manag. **41**(6), 422–441 (2013)
7. Orth, U.: Consumer personality and other factors in situational brand choice variation. J. Brand Manag. **13**(2), 115–133 (2005)
8. Arya, H.: Brand switching in telecom industry. J. Exclusive Manag. Sci. **5**(10) (2016)
9. Ha, H.Y.: Factors influencing consumer perceptions of brand trust online. J. Product Brand Manag. **13**(5), 329–342 (2004)
10. Jin, B., Gu Suh, Y.: Integrating effect of consumer perception factors in predicting private brand purchase in a Korean discount store context. J. Consumer Market. **22**(2), 62–71 (2005)
11. Khalifa, M., Liu, V.: Online consumer retention: contingent effects of online shopping habit and online shopping experience. Eur. J. Inf. Syst. **16**(6), 780–792 (2007)
12. Ali, J.F., Ali, I., ur Rehman, K., Yilmaz, A.K., Safwan, N., Afzal, H.: Determinants of consumer retention in cellular industry of Pakistan. Afr. J. Bus. Manag. **4**(12), 2402 (2004)

13. Nguyen, N., Leblanc, G.: Corporate image and corporate reputation in customers' retention decisions in services. J. Retail. Consumer Serv. **8**(4), 227–236 (2001)
14. Aydin, S., Özer, G.: The analysis of antecedents of customer loyalty in the Turkish mobile telecommunication market. Eur. J. Market. **39**(7/8), 910–925 (2005)
15. Amin, S.M., Ahmad, U.N.U., Hui, L.S.: Factors contributing to customer loyalty towards telecommunication service provider. Procedia-Soc. Behav. Sci. **40**, 282–286 (2012)
16. John, J.: An analysis on the customer loyalty in telecom sector: special reference to Bharath Sanchar Nigam limited, India. Afr. J. Market. Manag. **3**(1), 1–5 (2011)
17. Khizindar, T.M., AI-Azzam, A.F.M., Khanfar, I.A.: An empirical study of factors affecting customer loyalty of telecommunication industry in the Kingdom of Saudi Arabia. Br. J. Market. Stud. **3**(5), 98–115 (2015)
18. Adjei, K., Denanyoh, R.: Determinants of customer loyalty among mobile telecom subscribers in the Brong Ahafo region of Ghana. Int. J. Bus. Soc. Res. **4**(1), 82–95 (2014)
19. https://www.spss-tutorials.com/spss-correlation-test/
20. https://statistics.laerd.com/spss-tutorials/chi-square-test-for-association-using-spss-statistics.php
21. https://statistics.laerd.com/spss-tutorials/one-sample-t-test-using-spss-statistics.php
22. https://docs.google.com/forms/d/e/1FAIpQLSeJDmZ9a1dq-vRJA0EL6GjhOBivvUK-ldgnuoexePxtKARB1g/viewform?vc=0&c=0&w=1

Feature Selection Optimization Using Genetic Algorithm for Spambot Detection in an OSN

Arjun Singh[(✉)] and Manu Sood

Himachal Pradesh University, Shimla, India
arjunbisht22may@gmail.com, soodm_67@yahoo.com

Abstract. The process of Feature Selection (FS) in Machine Learning (ML) techniques is significant in reference to any the ML based prediction model. Use of significant features for model building elevates the overall performance of the ML model manifolds. In this paper, we have found out and analyzed the best feature sets in the available datasets to build two models for spambot detection in Online Social Networks (OSNs) with a specific reference to Twitter. We have used the Genetic Algorithm (GA) and Support Vector Machine-Recursive Feature Elimination (SVM-RFE) techniques for Feature Selection. To compare the results of both FS techniques, we have again built two models using Random Forest (RF) and K-Nearest Neighbor (KNN) algorithms. This study also includes the experimentation to study the effects of biasing in genuine accounts with spambot accounts. The results show that the performance of classifiers is better for Genetic Algorithm based optimized feature set. The accuracy of the models has been found to be better for the biasing cases within the ranges of 0% to 30% spambot accounts.

Keywords: Online Social Networks (OSNs) · Feature Selection (FS) · Genetic Algorithm (GA) · Recursive Feature Elimination (RFE) · Support Vector Machine-Recursive Feature Elimination (SVM-RFE) · Random Forest (RF) classifier · K-Nearest Neighbor (KNN) classifier · Logistic Regression (LR)

1 Introduction

In today's world, due to its rich features, the use of Internet is spreading so vastly that it is becoming difficult to provide any ICT based solution without the Internet being an integral part of this solution. In addition, with the immense growth of this Internet phenomenon, the OSNs such as Facebook, Twitter, Instagram etc. have revolutionized the ways by which people interact and conduct the day-to-day business. Many people connect to social networks to stay connected with family and friends. These networks are the best places to locate old friends and to stay connected with them. On the other hand, the professionals use it as a professional tool for online business meetings, conferences, promotion campaigns, sharing of ideas etc. Two of the largest OSN's, Facebook and Twitter are used by users such as politicians, celebrities, administrators, activists and others to share their generic or subject/topic specific likes, dislikes, views etc. with one another. An OSN has been described as a social website to provide a

© Springer Nature Singapore Pte Ltd. 2020
P. K. Singh et al. (Eds.): FTNCT 2019, CCIS 1206, pp. 334–345, 2020.
https://doi.org/10.1007/978-981-15-4451-4_26

venue for users to connect with each other, friends, and family [1]. The profiles of users on OSNs describe the social information of user like name, sex, age, location, interests among many other pieces of suitable information depending upon the OSN and/or the purpose of connection. A user can share pictures, videos, thoughts and much more information on these platforms.

Machine Learning (ML) is a concept drawn from Artificial Intelligence. It is a technique for autonomously acquiring and integrating knowledge obtained from experience, analytical observations etc. [1]. Its significant role is to train and test the models with the help of various techniques and Artificial Intelligence concepts. Basically, any ML method can be categorized as one of four methods namely Supervised Learning methods, Semi-supervised learning methods, Unsupervised Learning methods, and Reinforcement Learning methods. In Supervised Learning method, the user feeds the data to the machine or trains the machines using the data which is already labeled. In this method, two techniques, classification and regression are used frequently. In unsupervised learning, the data is not labeled and iterations are performed till the final acceptable results are achieved. Clustering is a technique commonly used by the unsupervised learning method. In semi-supervised learning method, the algorithms are made to learn from data (labeled and unlabeled both) but usually unlabeled data is in abundance. In reinforcement learning method, decisions are made sequentially. The output of first iteration depends on the present state of the input and the output of further iterations will depend upon the output of the immediately preceding iteration. Reinforcement learning method is a reward-based learning and feedback-oriented learning method [1].

Normally, ML process involves five steps respectively: (a) collection of data (b) preparing the input data (c) analyzing the input data (d) training the model and (e) testing [2]. The first step includes the collection of data from the various online sources or creating own data or buying data from original sources or a combination of these three. In the second step, suitable input data is prepared from this data by converting the data into the desired format e.g. converting the file into a '.csv' format. The third step involves analyzing input data, the patterns in the data, outliers (scope and boundaries) of the data and specification of the data. The fourth step includes the training of the model with the help of the processed data. Training of the model is done with the help of different classifiers. The fifth and the last step includes testing of the model whether the model is producing the optimal results or not.

With a steep rise in the number of internet users on a day-to-day basis, malicious activities are also increasing at a very high rate. The main weapon used for these malicious activities is bot, which is a software agent in the form of a computer programs that automatically perform repetitive tasks with ill intentions on large scales. Bot enables one or more self-program(s) on a network which can interact with system or users without being detected as a malicious activity. It is a remote-controlled software program used primarily for malicious activities and disrupting attacks on Internet world. It holds infected attachments too at times. It can also be in the form of a computer application created to propagate spam or unsolicited emails spontaneously in large quantities to any number of gullible users on the Internet. It automatically collects email address from various sources on the Internet [3].

Spambot, a special purpose bot, generally creates a fake account which can be used for spreading spam or unsolicited messages. Spambot sends irrelevant data or message indiscriminately to a large number of Internet users. They always make user insecure with a real threat of maximum chances of data loss. Generally, there are many techniques to detect the spambots in the OSNs such as (a) Completely Automated Public Turing test to tell Computers and Human Apart (CAPTCHA) (b) Detection of unseen and camouflaged web robots (c) user web access logs techniques, (d) survey spam filtering techniques and (e) web spam detection using link based ant colony optimization etc. [4]. The OSNs may either define certain set of rules or may use some software programs to detect and remove spambots which otherwise go undetected and may be successful in their malicious designs. Spambots cannot be removed completely but their number can be reduced or minimized. In this case, insecurity related to individual's account increases very frequently [5–8].

This paper proposes two types of prediction models for the identification of spambot accounts on an OSN and compares their performances. For this purpose, we have first employed two FS techniques namely: GA and SVM-RFE on the available datasets. These two techniques fall under the category of wrapper methods in Feature Selection. First, we have implemented the GA to find the optimum number of features for all the given datasets. After getting optimum number of features, we have selected the same number of features using RFE. SVM-RFE has been deployed for getting the second set of optimum features. To compare the performance of these two FS techniques, we have built two ML models based upon RF and KNN classifier algorithms to detect the spambot accounts in all the datasets under consideration.

The goals of this study are as given below in the form of four objectives:

1. To preprocess the datasets under consideration and select optimum feature sets for them using two different wrapper method FS techniques: GA and SVM-RFE.
2. To compare the performance of these two FS techniques with the help of two classifiers: KNN and RF.
3. To analyze the performances of these two classifiers on all the datasets under consideration.
4. To study and analyze the effect of biasing on genuine accounts with the spambot accounts for all the datasets under consideration.

Rest of the paper consists of the following. Description of datasets used for the conduct of this study is provided in Sect. 2. Steps involved to carry out the study are presented in Sect. 3. Section 4 highlights the results and analyses of experimentation and the conclusion and future work are presented in Sect. 5.

2   Datasets

To achieve the objectives of this paper based upon the above-mentioned research questions, a number of datasets containing genuine accounts and social spambot accounts of Twitter have been used. These datasets have been first used in [9] in which Cresci et al. have presented an extensive study on the social spambots on Twitter. We have also utilized these datasets with due permission from the authors of [9] and we acknowledge their support to our endeavor to find answers to our research questions. The details of all the datasets used have been provided in Table 1.

Total of four datasets have been used, one with data on genuine accounts and three with data on social spambots. The genuine accounts have been manually verified [9]. Spambot 1 contains the data about 991 social bots particularly active during the Mayoral elections in Rome in 2014. Spambot 2 contains the data about the 3457 accounts of paid spammers for mobile devices. The third dataset, Spambot 3 is the group of social bots, 464 in numbers, specifically advertising the products of Amazon on sale via URLs. These datasets contained the profile data of the accounts and the same is used in our study.

Table 1. Datasets details

Name	Datasets	Number of features	Number of accounts
1	Genuine accounts	42	3474
A	Spambot 1	41	991
B	Spambot 2	40	3457
C	Spambot 3	41	464

3 Experimental Setup

3.1 Pre-processing

The numbers of features in these four datasets differ from each other as shown in Table 1. It has also been found that there are many problems with the data itself like missing values, features with no values, etc. Pre-processing helped in dealing with these problems. The process of dealing with the NaN (Not-a-Number), missing values, infinity values, zero values, and scaling problems is known as pre-processing of data [10] (Fig. 1).

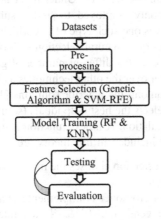

Fig. 1. Process of experimentation

Firstly, the features with no values were eliminated. Since this study uses the concept of classification, we need the data in numeric form and thus the missing values in samples were replaced with '0'. Next step which has been taken is to select the common features in all datasets. Therefore, the number of features in each dataset is reduced to 32 after dropping the uncommon ones. After preparing the datasets with 32 features, the next step is to select the common features in all data sets using Feature Selection techniques.

3.2   The Proposed Models

We have proposed the following models for the prediction of spambot accounts in the datasets. Firstly, GA and SVM-RFE techniques have been applied separately on datasets under consideration to produce two different sets of features. Then the dataset of genuine accounts containing only these feature sets have been biased with the data of spambot accounts to create nine datasets. These different datasets have been further classified using two different classifiers, KNN and RF and the performances of our proposed models have been analyzed based upon the results of these models.

3.3   Feature Selection

The process of selecting a subset of significant/relevant features from the available set of features in any given datasets is known as Feature Selection (FS) process. Among the set of all primary features, a few features contribute more to the output variable than other features. To select these more contributing features and in order to reduce the overhead during model building for classification and prediction as well, Feature Selection process is used. It also helps in simplifying the model interpretation process and reduces the process of overfitting during the process of model training [11, 12].

Two Feature Selection techniques that we have used to find out the optimum set of significant features are GA and SVM-RFE.

Genetic Algorithm. Metaheuristic approach is used to find the optimal number of features set from a set of available features. Under this category too, the Evolutionary Algorithms (EA) are commonly employed to find a subset of significant features amongst a set of features. GA is one such type of EA which has been influenced by the famous Charles Darwin's theory of natural selection or biological evolution. Only the fittest features are preserved over the different number of generations. GA in Machine Learning (ML) performs better over the other techniques as it helps to preserve or in the emergence of best solution among the anterior solutions [10, 11].

For every generation it selects the best individuals (solution/chromosome) from the available set of solutions/population. A fitness function is used for the selection of best individuals. The major steps included in this theory are:

Selection. The process of selection chooses the most fit individual from a generation using an objective function.
Crossover. The process of crossover is implemented on two selected individuals.
Mutation. The values of genes i.e. '0' & '1' are interchanged to create a new individual.

Normally, GA performs better than other feature selection techniques. After applying GA on our datasets, we got an optimal subset of 15 features.

Recursive Feature Elimination. RFE is a term used for selecting the best features from a set of features of a dataset. It recursively keeps on dropping the features with least importance known as the weakest till the desired number of features are reached. The rank wise results are obtained in terms of 'True' and 'False' outputs. This method selects features with the help of classifiers. Hence, we have used a combination of SVM-RFE techniques to get the best features [13] for our datasets.

SVM-RFE. Using Support Vector Machine – Recursive Feature Selection i.e. SVM-RFE, we have got a selection of the best 15 features for all the datasets. In Table 2, the features selected by GA and SVM-RFE [14, 15] are listed.

Table 2. Selected features through GA and SVM-RFE

S. No.	GA	SVM-RFE
1.	Name	url
2.	screen_name	Lang
3.	friends_count	geo_enabled
4.	Lang	profile_image_url
5.	default_profile	profile_banner_url
6.	default_profile_image	profile_use_background_image
7.	geo_enabled	profile_text_color
8.	profile_image_url	profile_sidebar_border_color
9.	profile_use_background_image	profile_sidebar_fill_color
10.	profile_sidebar_border_color	profile_background_image_url
11.	profile_background_tile	profile_background_color
12.	profile_background_image_url	profile_link_color
13.	profile_link_color	utc_offset
14.	Description	description
15.	created at	created_at

Validation. To validate the results of Feature Selection techniques we have used the Logistic Regression (LR) technique. We have measured the accuracy of Logistic Regression for all the 32 features we acquired after pre-processing that came out to be 0.772 and can be considered as 'not significant'. After the Feature Selection process, the accuracy of both feature subsets of GA and SVM-RFE have been validated using LR. The accuracy for feature set selected by GA is 0.86 and for the feature set selected by the SVM-RFE, it is 0.959. We have also employed the LR-RFE to carry out the feature selection process, but the validation result for this feature set produced by this process was found to be 0.776 which obviously is not very promising and is again 'non-significant'. Therefore, this process of FS was not considered further.

3.4   Datasets Biasing

In this dataset, we have four primary sets of data files containing data pertaining to the profiles of accounts of various genuine users and spambots on Twitter. Three files contain the data about spambot accounts namely, Spambot 1, Spambot 2 and Spambot 3. One file contains data about genuine accounts on Twitter in which details of genuine human accounts are present. Biasing has been carried out on this genuine dataset. The biasing of data on all the genuine accounts is carried out with three variations of 30%, 60% and 100% of spambot accounts in each of the three spambot accounts files respectively. This combination of genuine accounts with spambot accounts through biasing resulted in the nine cases of different datasets. The description to these cases is provided in Table 3.

Table 3. Details of biased dataset

Datasets	Biased datasets	Spambot accounts	Genuine accounts	Total accounts	Spam accounts (%)
DS – 1A	1A30	297	3474	4466	6.65
	1A60	595	3474	6932	8.58
	1A100	991	3474	3939	25.15
DS – 1B	1B30	1038	3474	4466	23.24
	1B60	2074	3474	6932	29.92
	1B100	3457	3474	3939	87.76
DS – 1C	1C30	139	3474	4466	3.11
	1C60	279	3474	6932	4.02
	0 1C100	464	3474	3939	11.78

3.5   Classifiers Used in Our Models

Two classifiers have been used to train the models on the selected feature sets namely, K-Nearest Neighbor (KNN) and Random Forest (RF).

Random Forest. It is a supervised learning algorithm. This classifier in ML provides good results most of the times since its default hyper-parameters produce better prediction results on their default values. As the name Random Forest suggests, it creates different decision trees and then merges all of them together in the form of a forest to get a more accurate prediction. The most important advantage of Random Forest is that it can be used for both classification and regression [16].

KNN. It is known as non-parametric and lazy learning algorithm. It is called the lazy learning algorithm because it does use a discriminative function from the training data to learn but instead memorizes the training dataset. It is also used for both classification and regression. KNN is used in a variety of applications such as health, Political Science, detection of handwriting, and video recognition [17].

3.6   Evaluation

Confusion Matrix. This matrix is also known as error matrix. It consists of two rows and columns i.e. 2×2 matrix. It can compare the actual class and predicted class which can be positive and negative. The elements of confusion matrix are True Negative (TN), True Positive (TP), False Negative (FN) and False Positive (FP) [18]. To arrive at the final outcome of these experiments, we have used the following four standard indicators proposed in [18]:

True Positive (TP). No. of actual spambot followers predicted as spambot account.
True Negative (TN). No. of genuine followers identified as genuine account.
False Positive (FP). No. of genuine followers identified as spambot account.
False Negative (FN). No. of actual spambot followers identified as genuine account.

Five Metrics. To evaluate the final results, we have considered the five standard evaluation metrics. These metrics are [18]:

Accuracy. Ratio of predicted true results in the data, $\frac{TP+TN}{TP+TN+FP+FN}$
Precision. Ratio of identified positive cases which were indeed positive, $\frac{TP}{TP+FP}$
Recall. Ratio of real positive cases that are indeed identified positive, $\frac{TP}{TP+FN}$
F-Measure. It is harmonic mean of recall and precision, $\frac{2 \bullet precision \bullet recall}{precision + recall}$
Matthew Correlation Coefficient (MCC). Estimates the correlation between two classes i.e. identified class and real class of samples, given as $\frac{TP \bullet TN - FP \bullet FN}{\sqrt{(TP+FN)(TP+FP)(TN+FP)(TN+FN)}}$

ROC-AUC. Receiver Operating Characteristics – Area Under Curve (ROC-AUC). It is a visualization technique used to demonstrate the outcomes of classification problems. This curve is used to highlight the performance of one or more classification models. It is plotted for the values of True Positive Rate (TPR) and False Positive Rate (FPR). TPR and FPR are referred to as sensitivity and specificity. It is also known as AUROC (Area Under Recursive Operating Characteristics). It states that higher the AUC better the performance of model. To check the FPR and TPR the given formulas are used [19].

- $TPR = TP/(TP + FN)$
- $FPR = FP/(TN + FP)$

4   Results and Analysis

Results for the experimentation are provided in the Tables 4 and 5. Table 4 shows the results for the KNN algorithm for the datasets created on the basis of features selected through both GA and SVM-RFE. The results show that the accuracy for the cases where ratio of biasing with spam accounts varies from 0%–30% was higher. There are a few definite divergent trends while comparing the outcomes of KNN classifier for the datasets processed through GA and SVM-RFE techniques. But overall, the results of KNN for the features set given by the GA are better than the results for SVM-RFE features set.

The values of other metrics, Precision, Recall, F measure and MCC were found the best for almost all the cases having a higher accuracy rate. Overall results follow this trend except in case $1A_{30}$ for SVM-RFE features set in Tables 4 and 5.

Table 4. Results of KNN classifier for features sets obtained through GA and SVM-RFE

Datasets	K-Nearest Neighbor									
	Genetic Algorithm					Support Vector Machine-Recursive Feature Elimination				
	Accuracy	Precision	Recall	F Measure	MCC	Accuracy	Precision	Recall	F Measure	MCC
$1A_{30}$	**0.9982**	0.9802	1.0000	0.9900	0.9891	**0.9647**	0.7849	0.7849	0.7849	0.7657
$1A_{60}$	0.9492	0.8760	0.6928	0.7737	0.7521	0.9640	0.8529	0.8841	0.8683	0.8476
$1A_{100}$	0.9075	0.8491	0.7282	0.7840	0.7290	0.9537	0.9140	0.8703	0.8916	0.8626
$1B_{30}$	**1.0000**	1.0000	1.0000	1.0000	1.0000	0.9335	0.8086	0.9404	0.8696	0.8295
$1B_{60}$	**1.0000**	1.0000	1.0000	1.0000	1.0000	0.9387	0.8707	0.9731	0.9190	0.8735
$1B_{100}$	0.9462	0.9048	1.0000	0.9500	0.8972	**0.9553**	0.9330	0.9853	0.9584	0.9117
$1C_{30}$	**1.0000**	1.0000	1.0000	1.0000	1.0000	0.9576	0.4625	0.9250	0.6167	0.6373
$1C_{60}$	**1.0000**	1.0000	1.0000	1.0000	1.0000	**0.9991**	1.0000	0.9894	0.9947	0.9942
$1C_{100}$	0.9956	0.9606	1.0000	0.9799	0.777	0.9899	1.0000	0.9800	0.9899	0.9800

Table 5. Results of RF classifier for features sets obtained through GA and SVM-RFE

Datasets	Random Forest									
	Genetic Algorithm					Support Vector Machine-Recursive Feature Elimination				
	Accuracy	Precision	Recall	F Measure	MCC	Accuracy	Precision	Recall	F Measure	MCC
$1A_{30}$	**0.9982**	0.9773	1.0000	0.9885	0.9876	**0.9682**	0.7660	0.8372	0.8000	0.7837
$1A_{60}$	0.9419	0.8118	0.8075	0.8097	0.7753	0.9509	0.8360	0.8449	0.8404	0.8114
$1A_{100}$	0.9037	0.7928	0.8148	0.8037	0.7400	0.9582	0.9161	0.9105	0.9133	0.8858
$1B_{30}$	**1.0000**	1.0000	1.0000	1.0000	1.0000	0.9175	0.7679	0.9497	0.8492	0.8017
$1B_{60}$	**1.0000**	1.0000	1.0000	1.0000	1.0000	0.9453	0.8819	0.9837	0.9301	0.8890
$1B_{100}$	0.9495	0.9093	1.0000	0.9525	0.9035	**0.9524**	0.9274	0.9829	0.9544	0.9064
$1C_{30}$	**1.0000**	1.0000	1.0000	1.0000	1.0000	0.9686	0.5694	0.9318	0.7069	0.7148
$1C_{60}$	**1.0000**	1.0000	1.0000	1.0000	1.0000	**0.9982**	0.9875	0.9875	0.9875	0.9865
$1C_{100}$	0.9822	1.0000	0.8467	0.9170	0.9111	0.9822	1.0000	0.8467	0.9170	0.9111

The results of RF classifier for the features sets of both feature selection techniques, GA and SVM-RFE are given in Table 5. These results for RF are almost similar to what have been obtained through KNN. Both classifiers provide the maximum accuracy for same cases of biasing. It is pertinent to note here that the precision of models is also found to be the best for the cases where the accuracy was maximum.

The visualization of results has been presented with the help of ROC and AUC curves. ROC curve in the Fig. 2 provides the visualization of results for Table 4. It also depicts that the performance of classifier i.e. KNN was better for the feature set of Genetic Algorithm. The results for Random Forest was also better for the genetic algorithm feature set as shown in Table 5 and Fig. 3.

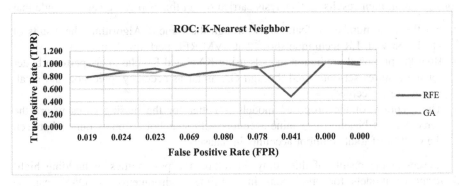

Fig. 2. Performance of KNN classifier for GA and SVM-RFE

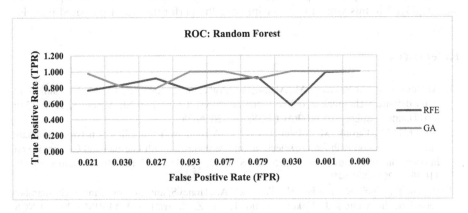

Fig. 3. Performance of RF classifier for GA and SVM-RFE

Results also show that the performances of both the RF and KNN classifiers for the features set optimized by the GA algorithm were better than for the features set obtained from SVM-RFE technique.

5   Conclusion

A study is carried out to compare the two feature selection techniques namely, Genetic Algorithm optimization and Recursive Feature Elimination. A special RFE technique SVM-RFE has been used as a second alternative to the GA optimization technique for the feature's selection. On the basis of experiments conducted on the datasets under consideration, their results and analysis carried out in this paper, we can conclude that

- For the same number of features as through the Genetic Algorithm, the results of validation with LR technique show that SVM-RFE performs better.
- Both the proposed prediction models using KNN and RF classifiers perform better for the features set optimized through GA as far as accuracy, precision and recall values are concerned.
- The accuracy of the proposed models is better for the biasing cases where the percentage of biasing of genuine accounts with spambot accounts ranges between the 0–30% of total spambot accounts in datasets.

Based on the results of this study, in future, the possibilities of building high-performance models for predictions in real-time environments for OSNs can be explored to measure the real-time performances of these proposed prediction models. The authors of this paper at present, are also working on various FS techniques other than deployed in this work to further improve the performances of proposed models.

References

1. Al-Qurishi, M., Al-Rakhami, M., Alamri, A., Alrubaian, M., Rahman, S.M.M., Hossain, M.S.: Sybil defense techniques in online social networks: a survey. IEEE Access **5**, 1200–1219 (2017). https://doi.org/10.1109/ACCESS.2017.2656635
2. Anwer, H.M., Farouk, M., Abdel-Hamid, A.: A framework for efficient network anomaly intrusion detection with feature selection. In: Proceedings of 9th International Conference on Information and Communication Systems, Irbid, pp. 157–162 (2018). https://doi.org/10.1109/iacs.2018.8355459
3. Hayati, P., Chai, K., Potdar, V., Talevski, A.: HoneySpam 2.0: profiling web spambot behaviour. In: Yang, J.-J., Yokoo, M., Ito, T., Jin, Z., Scerri, P. (eds.) PRIMA 2009. LNCS (LNAI), vol. 5925, pp. 335–344. Springer, Heidelberg (2009). https://doi.org/10.1007/978-3-642-11161-7_23
4. Adegbola, I., Jimoh, R.: Spambot detection: a review of techniques and trends. Network **6**(9), 7–10 (2014)
5. Vasudeva, A., Sood, M.: Survey on Sybil attack defense mechanisms in wireless ad hoc networks. J. Network Comput. Appl. **120**, 78–118 (2018)
6. Vasudeva, A., Sood, M.: A vampire act of Sybil attack on the highest node degree clustering in mobile ad hoc networks. Indian J. Sci. Technol. **9** (2016)
7. Vasudeva, A., Sood, M.: Perspectives of Sybil attack in routing protocols of mobile ad hoc network. In: Chaki, N., Meghanathan, N., Nagamalai, D. (eds.) Computer Networks & Communications (NetCom), pp. 3–13. Springer, New York (2013). https://doi.org/10.1007/978-1-4614-6154-8_1

8. Vasudeva, A., Sood, M.: Sybil attack on lowest ID clustering algorithm in the mobile ad hoc network. Int. J. Network Secur. Appl. **4**(5), 135–147 (2012)
9. Cresci, S., Di Pietro, R., Petrocchi, M., Spognardi, A., Tesconi, M.: The paradigm-shift of social spambots: evidence, theories, and tools for the arms race. In: Proceedings of the 26th International Conference on World Wide Web Companion, pp. 963–972 (2017)
10. Bindra, N., Sood, M.: Detecting DDoS attacks using machine learning techniques and contemporary intrusion detection dataset. Autom. Control Comput. Sci. **53**(5), 419–428 (2019). https://doi.org/10.3103/S0146411619050043
11. James, G., Witten, D., Hastie, T., Tibshirani, R.: An Introduction to Statistical Learning. STS, vol. 103, p. 204. Springer, New York (2013). https://doi.org/10.1007/978-1-4614-7138-7
12. Bermingham, M.L., et al.: Application of high-dimensional feature selection: evaluation for genomic prediction in man. Sci. Rep. **5**, 10312 (2015)
13. Granitto, P.M., Furlanello, C., Biasioli, F., Gasperi, F.: Recursive feature elimination with random forest for PTR-MS analysis of agro industrial products. Chemometr. Intell. Lab. Syst. **83**(2), 83–90 (2006)
14. Gysels, E., Renevey, P., Celka, P.: SVM-based recursive feature elimination to compare phase synchronization computed from broadband and narrowband EEG signals in brain–computer interfaces. Sig. Process. **85**(11), 2178–2189 (2005)
15. Rakotomamonjy, A.: Variable selection using SVM based criteria. J. Mach. Learn. Res. **3**, 1357–1370 (2003)
16. Liaw, A., Wiener, M.: Classification and regression by randomForest. R News **2**(3), 18–22 (2002)
17. Cunningham, P., Delany, S.J.: k-nearest neighbor classifiers. Multiple Classifier Syst. **34**(8), 1–17 (2007)
18. Cresci, S., Di Pietro, R., Petrocchi, M., Spognardi, A., Tesconi, M.: Fame for sale: efficient detection of fake Twitter followers. Decis. Support Syst. **80**, 56–71 (2015)
19. Fawcett, T.: An introduction to ROC analysis. Pattern Recogn. Lett. **27**(8), 861–874 (2006)

Exhibiting the Barricades to Academic Research in Computer Science Domain: An Indian Perspective

Anshul Chhabra, Shradha Sapra, Nitasha Hasteer,
and Madhurima Hooda(✉)

Amity University, Noida, India
10madhurima@gmail.com

Abstract. The key to any successful research work depends on overcoming the barriers in the path of the researchers. The upcoming researchers are often being dissuaded in their domain area from the physiological, mental and physical impacts of the research barriers which are being faced by them. The research being carried out gets impacted by the barriers. The cases of young researchers not been able to produce the desired outcome and hence being stressed out are numerous. It is therefore imperative to identify, analyze and categorize the research barriers, so as to adequately address them. This study brings to light the major barriers that hinder the efforts to undertake research endeavors by young computer science enthusiasts. Interpretive structural modeling has been used to rank the barriers accordingly to their driving and dependent power. The study reveals that 'Lack of time for research due to other commitments' and 'Difficulty in accessing the paid research Papers' are the major driving barriers to research. The research is an attempt to help the researchers by giving them a detailed insight of what they must prepare on for fruitful results.

Keywords: Barriers · ISM - Interpretive Structural Modeling · SSIM - Structural Self-Interaction Matrix · Research barriers · Academic research · MICMAC analysis

1 Introduction

The previous years have witnessed an increase in the research paper publications in the field of CS with due acknowledgment to the increase in number of journals and conference. For any organization to grow and flourish, research is an integral area to strength and thus the last three decades have seen an advancement in the R&D activities of the Indian academics. Research is an inquiry conducted by a person that makes an intellectual or creative contribution to the discipline. In this fast growing and emerging technical world, research is becoming a tremendous focus area. Using the data from Google scholar, it was observed that the number of publications in India have increased tremendously from 14,900 to 41,800 between the years of 2004 to 2016. As depicted in Fig. 1, year 2017 saw a dip in the pattern since the numbers dropped to 38,100 and the probable reason can be increasing research barriers in Indian academics. A research barrier can be simply defined as a factor that will affect and hinder the

© Springer Nature Singapore Pte Ltd. 2020
P. K. Singh et al. (Eds.): FTNCT 2019, CCIS 1206, pp. 346–357, 2020.
https://doi.org/10.1007/978-981-15-4451-4_27

success of the research and these act as obstacles lowering the levels of productivity. These factors can be categorized under various domains like personal factors, funding factors, lack of resources, etc. Thus, to tackle the increasing problem of reduced quality research publications, we must counter the research barrier and aim to find ways to identify them, analyze them and eliminate them. The domain of CS-IT is so chosen because it covers a very broad group of researchers. The research aims in identifying, analyzing and categorizing the research barriers to formulate a relational model and effectively provide the researchers knowledge about the research barrier so they can effectively work on their research. The paper is divided into various sections; Sect. 2 talks about literature review while Sect. 3 highlights the barrier identification and the methodology so adopted to formalize the relational model and Sect. 4 are the results of the structural model so designed.

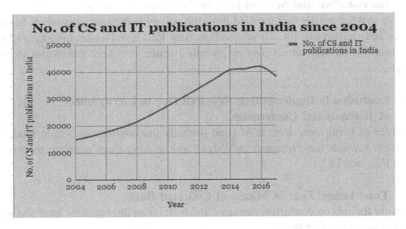

Fig. 1. Number of CS and IT publications in India

2 Literature Review

Many researchers have contributed and worked in the area of identifying and formalizing the research barriers and some of their noteworthy outcomes are listed in this section. A prominent study in the year 2016 [1] has stated research barriers like – Lack of theoretical contribution, poor writing skills (bad grammar, lack of use of technical terms, etc.), specific structure failure, etc. A qualitative study [5] of African American students focuses on research barriers focused on racism and colored discrimination, lack of confidence and lack of confidence which hence takes our focus on personal barriers and issues which are caused at a personal level. Universities around the globe have been keen on focusing and encouraging students and researchers to publish more research and any university can be judged by its research. The government should also have policies to encourage research work and provide them with funding benefits. A study conducted in 2015 by Michael and Soria [7] examines factors like completing family responsibilities, having imbalance in life and similar barriers. We constructed a sample size of 110 respondents for the research and focused specifically on CS-IT disciplines.

3 Methodology

3.1 Barriers to Research

An attempt to have an insight about the most affecting barriers of research a survey was conducted in which the real-time responses of 110 researchers from the CS and IT domain were recorded. Using personal knowledge related work - literature, 29 factors were found out which were the possible barriers of research were rated from a scale of 1 to 5 as 1 being Strongly Disagree, 2 as Disagree, 3 as Neutral, 4 as Agree and 5 as Strongly Agree. The responses were recorded and by analyzing the results of the open survey; the top 12 barriers to research were eliminated and are below listed and elaborated.

3.1.1 Inter-student and Student-Faculty Conflicts
The most striking barrier that resulted from the survey is the raising conflicts between students and student-faculty. These conflicts may lead to misunderstanding and trust issues between the two which may result into disinterest of both the parties in doing research.

3.1.2 Confusion in Implementing Research Due to Unawareness of Journals and Conferences
The barrier of being unawareness of good journals and conferences acts to hinder the researchers towards their research publishing and making them unaware to correctly publish their works.

3.1.3 Trust Issues: Fear of Misuse of Collected Data
The barrier focuses on conflicting interests and trust on an inter-student level and might as well at student-guide level.

3.1.4 Lack of Adequate Time for Research Due to Other Commitments
Lack of time is one of the most important obstruction to researchers and scholars being committed to any other job in the organization failing to always place the research work as their priority.

3.1.5 No External Funding for Travelling or Publication of Research
The funding barrier has been prominently seen hindering researchers to achieve the desired goals. The funding factor is quite helpful in making the research either a success or a failure.

3.1.6 Improper Monitoring by Guide, Lack of Effort and Insufficient Time, Feedback by Guide
The role of the guide is undoubtedly a major contributing factor towards the result of a research which not only helps steering the researchers to new ideas, make research plan for them, etc. Thus, Improper monitoring by the guide being an important barrier is self-explanatory.

3.1.7 Lack of Interest
For any research to flourish or even to continue with some success is very dependent on the skill set and the interest of the students and even if they are interested to carry on with the research and thus the disinterest of disciplines towards research acts as a negative contributor in their research.

3.1.8 Lack of Personal Research Traits
The personal traits may include – lack of focus, lack of self-confidence, lack of motivation to do the research, lack of objective to achieve goal, etc. and all these skills largely effects the research work being carried out.

3.1.9 Irrelevant/Too Little Data Acquired
Data is an inseparable aspect of the research; acquiring and collection of data in a research is very important and any careless behavior shown towards it would produce a faulty dataset and thus an undesired result.

3.1.10 Lack of New Ideas for Research
To be innovative and contribute to literature with newer and better techniques is the need of the hour and a very basic thing expected by the researchers and to fail to do so would fail them in their research work.

3.1.11 Difficulty in Accessing Paid Research Papers
To have an insight to the problem and analyzing the problem it is very important to get enough literature knowledge regarding the same; and so, it is important to have a deep knowledge about similar research works and any difficulty in doing so can have a bad effect to a research.

3.1.12 Lack of Domain Knowledge
For performing any research work the researcher must have the required domain knowledge to carry out and perform the research and complete it. Lack of domain knowledge is a factor that greatly influence the person and also the research he carries out.

3.2 Technique Implemented

ISM stands for interpretive structural modelling, is an interactive learning process. In this a set of different and directly related variables affecting the system under consideration is structured into a comprehensive systemic model. The methodology of ISM is to establish relationship between the different barriers or factors of research and finds their association. It is a multi-step process involving formation of different matrices at different levels and thus drawing a hierarchal table to represent the different barrier at different levels using iterations. It is thus an overall structure is extracted from the complex set of variables. The ISM technique graphically represents the result that explores the driving and the determined factor in the research. The factors that are examined can be classified in the form of a graph used. The various steps involved in the ISM methodology are as per listed below:

Step 1: Creating the Structural Self Interaction Matrix – which involves the inter-linking the different factors listed/eliminated from the survey.

Step 2: After the Structural Self Interaction Matrix, the Reachability matrix is formed which includes giving binary weight to the factors and giving a numerical assumption of the inter relation to each other.

Step 3: Creation of transitive matrix is the next step followed the reachability matrix which include creation of a matrix based upon the transitive property and hence redefining the reachable matrix.

Step 4: The matrix so obtained can be divided into different levels by the process of partitioning which is done by intersection method.

Step 5: The factors that are drawn in the same iteration set or which are explored in the same level are said to be in the same layer in the hierarchy.

Step 6: A graph can be obtained based on the reachability matrix and the relations so formed after transitivity is developed.

Step 7: The graph so formed can be used to explore the driving factors, the dependent factors and the linkage factors which becomes the result of the research. The research highlights the factors which affect to the cause of research barrier and which ones are the dependent factors on it. Also, the ISM model can bring about the linkage factors and the ones which have no importance in the research as these do not fall in any of the three groups.

3.2.1   Structural Self-Interaction Matrix (SSIM)

ISM methodology includes the involvement of experts and expertise suggestions through the process of brainstorming sessions which includes the ranking of different factors with each other. The brain storming session comprised of two or more skilled individuals who were well informed about all the research barriers and for analyzing the most affecting research barrier, a discourse relationship between all the variables is formed. During the creation of the Structural Self Interaction Matrix (SSIM) let us consider any two factors (i and j). The existing directions are considered as follows (Fig. 2) and (Table 1):

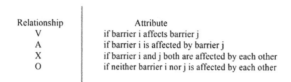

Relationship	Attribute
V	if barrier i affects barrier j
A	if barrier i is affected by barrier j
X	if barrier i and j both are affected by each other
O	if neither barrier i nor j is affected by each other

Fig. 2.   Relationships and their attributes

Table 1. Structural Self-Interaction Matrix (SSIM)

Barriers	12	11	10	9	8	7	6	5	4	3	2
1. Inter-student and student-faculty conflicts	O	O	O	O	A	X	X	O	A	X	O
2. Confusion in implementing research due to unawareness of journals and conferences	A	O	O	O	A	A	A	O	A	O	
3. Trust issues: fear of misuse of collected data	O	O	O	O	A	V	X	O	O		
4. Lack of adequate time for research due to other commitments	O	O	O	V	O	O	V	O			
5. No external funding for travelling or publication of research	O	V	O	V	A	O	O				
6. Improper monitoring by guide, Lack of effort and insufficient time, feedback by guide	A	O	X	V	X	X					
7. Lack of interest	X	O	V	O	X						
8. Lack of personal research traits	A	O	X	O							
9. Irrelevant/Too little data acquired	X	A	O								
10. Lack of new ideas for research	A	A									
11. Difficulty in accessing paid research papers	V										
12. Lack of domain knowledge											

3.2.2 Reachability Matrix
Initial Reachability matrix is formed by transforming the SSIM into a matrix containing 1 s and 0 s (Fig. 3).

Relationship	Transformation
V	(i,j) unit becomes 1 and (j,i) unit becomes 0
A	(i,j) unit becomes 0 and (j,i) unit becomes 1
X	Both (i,j) and (j,i) unit becomes 1
O	Both (i,j) and (j,i) unit becomes 0

Fig. 3. Relationship and their Transformations

The inter relation of the factors in binary form is what is called as the initial reachability matrix which inter relates the 12 factors and thus relates them by weights rather than just reviewing the inter relation like SSIM. The following is shown in Table 2.

Table 2. Initial Reachability Matrix

Barriers	1	2	3	4	5	6	7	8	9	10	11	12
1. Inter-student and student-faculty conflicts	1	0	1	0	0	1	1	0	0	0	0	0
2. Confusion in implementing research due to unawareness of journals and conferences	0	1	0	0	0	0	0	0	0	0	0	0
3. Trust Issues: Fear of misuse of collected data	1	0	1	0	0	1	1	0	0	0	0	0
4. Lack of adequate time for Research due to other commitments	1	1	0	1	0	1	0	0	1	0	0	0
5. No external funding for travelling or publication of research	0	0	0	0	1	0	0	0	1	0	1	0
6. Improper monitoring by guide, lack of effort and insufficient time, feedback by guide	1	1	1	0	0	1	1	1	1	1	0	0
7. Lack of interest	1	1	0	0	0	1	1	1	0	1	0	1
8. Lack of pesonal research traits	1	1	1	0	1	1	1	1	0	1	0	0
9. Irrlevant/Too little data acquired	0	0	0	0	0	0	0	0	1	0	0	1
10. Lack of new ideas for research	0	0	0	0	0	1	0	1	0	1	0	0
11. Difficulty in accessing paid research papers	0	0	0	0	0	0	0	0	1	1	1	1
12. Lack of domain knowledge	0	1	0	0	0	1	1	1	1	1	0	1

As per the ISM methodology, the Final Reachability matrix incorporates the Transitive Closure which states that if variable A is associated with variable B and variable B is associated with variable C in some form then, variable A must be associated with the variable C. The Final Reachability matrix formed after applying the transitive property on the variables is depicted in Table 3. The table of final reachability matrix highlights to the changed inter – factor relation after transitive closure and evaluates the driving power and dependence of the factor as:

Driving Power: The driving power of a barrier can be defined as the total number of barriers which it may help achieve or the total number of 1 s in the row of that barrier.

Dependence: The dependence is defined as the total number of barriers which may help achieving it or the total number of 1 s in the column of that barrier.

Table 3. Final Reachability Matrix

Barriers	1	2	3	4	5	6	7	8	9	10	11	12
1. Inter-student and student-faculty conflicts	1	0	1	0	0	1	1	0	0	0	0	0
2. Confusion in implementing research due to unawareness of journals and conferences	0	1	0	0	0	0	0	0	0	0	0	0
3. Trust issues: fear of misuse of collected data	1	0	1	0	0	1	1	0	0	0	0	0
4. Lack of adequate time for research due to other commitments	1	1	0	1	0	1	0	0	1	0	0	0
5. No external funding for travelling or publication of research	0	0	0	0	1	0	0	0	1	0	1	0
6. Improper monitoring by guide, lack of effort and insufficient time, feedback by guide	1	1	1	0	0	1	1	1	1	1	0	0
7. Lack of interest	1	1	0	0	0	1	1	1	0	1	0	1
8. Lack of personal research traits	1	1	1	0	1	1	1	1	0	1	0	0
9. Irrelevant/Too little data acquired	0	0	0	0	0	0	0	0	1	0	0	1
10. Lack of new ideas for research	0	0	0	0	0	1	0	1	0	1	0	0
11. Difficulty in accessing paid research papers	0	0	0	0	0	0	0	0	1	1	1	1
12. Lack of domain knowledge	0	1	0	0	0	1	1	1	1	1	0	1

The dependencies and driving powers are further utilized in the MICMAC analysis. The analysis classifies the various barriers as autonomous, dependent, linkage and driven or independent.

3.2.3 Level Partitions

The final reachability matrix not only describes driving factor or the dependence but also helps in the formation of Reachability set and the Antecedent set. The reachability set can be explained as a list of factors which are affected by a variable or the list of variables which provide support in achieving the variable. The antecedent set represents the list of factors which effect a factor. The antecedent set can be defined as a list of those variables, which may help in achieving them. Subsequently, the intersection of these sets is derived for all variables. The intersection set helps in eliminating factors or attributes at different levels and those which are eliminated in the same iteration are at the same level at the hierarchy tree. The factors eliminated in the first iteration are said to be present at the first level and the ones at the second level are the ones who were eliminated during second iteration and so on till the all the factors are eliminated at different levels. The working or the elimination of factors at different levels are below described (Tables 4, 5 and 6):

Table 4. Iteration 2

Barrier	Reachability set	Antecedent set	Intersection set	Level
1	1,3,4,5	1,3,4,5	1,3,4,5	II
3	1,3,5	1,3,4,5	1,3,5	
4	1,3,4	1,4,5	1,4	
5	1,3,4,5,11	1,3,5	1,3,5	
11	11	5,11	11	

Table 5. Iteration 3

Barrier	Reachability set	Antecedent set	Intersection set	Level
4	4	4,5	4	III
5	4,5	5	5	

Table 6. Iteration 4

Barrier	Reachability set	Antecedent set	Intersection set	Level
5	5	5	5	IV

3.2.4   MICMAC Analysis

The objective of the MICMAC analysis is to analyse the driving and the dependence power of a factor and also depicts the factors that have weak power of dependence and also those depict weak dependence. The value of dependence and driving power is found out by the column sum and row sums of the final reachability matrix respectively. The different graph quadrants give different results based on the driving power and the dependence of the factors (Fig. 4).

Quadrants	Results
Quadrant I	Autonomous factors
Quadrant II	Dependent factors
Quadrant III	Linkage factors
Quadrant IV	Driving factors

Fig. 4. Quadrants and their results

The first quadrant as stated gives the autonomous factors which does not have any influence on the research and these factors are neither the driving factors nor the factors which are dependent on the driving ones.

The factors which are dependent on the driving factors are graphically represented in the II quadrant and may be called as the affected factors which get affected due to other factors. These factors have weak driver power but strong dependence.

The third quadrant depicts the linkage factors in the research which do not only have a high dependence but also have a high driving power hence they not only affect the other factors but also get affected themselves thus these can be the causing and the affected factors.

Fourth cluster includes the independent barriers having strong driving power but weak dependence. The quadrant thus shows us the driving factors of the research which can be called the cause factor which drive the other factors.

4   Results and Discussions

The barriers hindering the research in the domain of CS-IT pose challenges not only in front of the researches but also in front of the organization and the research guides. Some of the major barriers have been highlighted here and put into an ISM model, to

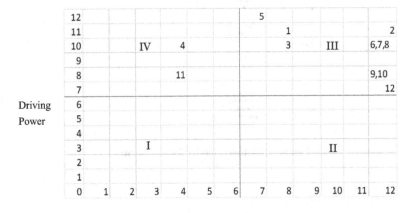

Dependence Power

Fig. 5. Driving Power and Dependence Power diagram

analyze the interaction between the barriers. These barriers need to be overcome for the success of the research programs and are a solution to the increasing problems faced by researchers in their path of successful research (Fig. 5).

The driver-dependence diagram gives some valuable insights about the relative importance and the interdependencies among the barriers. This can give better insights to the researcher and the organizations so that they can proactively deal with these barriers and know what is coming their way to desired results. Some of the observations from the ISM model, which give important managerial implications, are discussed as – Inter student and student conflicts and trust issues are some of the factors that have a high value of dependence and high driving power; thus, not only do these factors effects the other factors but also get themselves affected by them. Also, the factors like lack of adequate time and less data acquired are the factors having high driving power but low dependence power; thus, these factors are mainly responsible to drive the research and thus effect the other factors. The quadrant graph is a clear result of the model and is self-explanatory about the factors, their nature and the traits they carry out. ISM, hence has the capability to develop an initial model through managerial techniques such as brain storming, nominal group techniques, etc. In this sense, ISM is a supportive analytic tool for the discussed situation (Fig. 6).

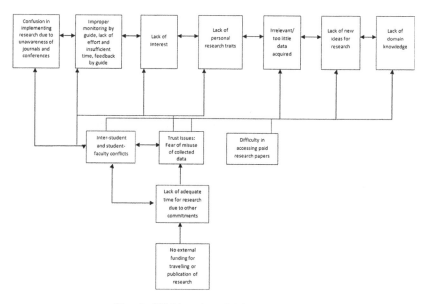

Fig. 6. ISM-based model for the barriers

References

1. Hazen, B.T.: Overcoming basic barriers to publishing research. Int. J. Logistics Manage. **27**(1) (2016)
2. Brew, A., Mantai, L.: Academics' perceptions of the challenges and barriers to implementing research-based experiences for undergraduates. Teach. High. Educ. **22**(5), 551–568 (2017)
3. Altbach, P.G.: What counts for academic productivity in research universities? Int. High. Educ. **79**, 6–7 (2015)
4. Fan, T.-K., Chang, C.-H.: Exploring evolutionary technical trends from academic research papers. In: 2008 The Eighth IAPR International Workshop on Document Analysis Systems. IEEE (2008)
5. Wong, C.A., Eccles, J.S., Sameroff, A.: The influence of ethnic discrimination and ethnic identification on African American adolescents' school and socioemotional adjustment. J. Pers. **71**(6), 1197–1232 (2003)
6. Stebleton, M., Soria, K.: Breaking down barriers: academic obstacles of first-generation students at research universities (2013)
7. Zalevski, A., Tobbell, R., Butcher, J.: Female attrition, retention and barriers to careers in SET academic research. The UKRC Report, vol. 8 (2009)
8. Healey, M., et al.: The research–teaching nexus: a case study of students' awareness, experiences and perceptions of research. Innovations Educ. Teach. Int. **47**(2), 235–246 (2010)
9. Wilson, A., Howitt, S., Higgins, D.: Assessing the unassessable: making learning visible in undergraduates' experiences of scientific research. Assess. Eval. High. Educ. **41**(6), 901–916 (2016)
10. Sørensen, C., Landau, J.S.: Academic agility in digital innovation research: the case of mobile ICT publications within information systems 2000–2014. J. Strateg. Inf. Syst. **24**(3), 158–170 (2015)
11. Brew, A., et al.: Research productivity and academics' conceptions of research. High. Educ. **71**(5), 681–697 (2016)
12. Vanderford, N.L., Weiss, L.T., Weiss, H.L.: A survey of the barriers associated with academic-based cancer research commercialization. PLoS ONE **8**(8), e72268 (2013)
13. Noosrikong, C., Ngamsuriyaroj, S., Na Ayudhya, S.P.: Identifying focus research areas of computer science researchers from publications. In: TENCON 2017–2017 IEEE Region 10 Conference. IEEE (2017)

Answering Questions in Natural Language About Images Using Deep Learning

Vedant Singh[(✉)], Vatsal Doshi, Mitali Dave, Ankit Desai,
Smith Agrawal, Jash Shah, and Pratik Kanani

Dwarkadas J. Sanghvi College of Engineering, University of Mumbai,
Mumbai, India
vedantsingh500@gmail.com, doshivatsal7@gmail.com,
mdave.1197@gmail.com, ankit.desai24@gmail.com,
agrawalsmith14@gmail.com, jashshah1056@gmail.com,
pratikkanani123@gmail.com

Abstract. Visual Question Answering is a perfect mix of issues enveloping different spaces including Natural Language Processing, Computer Vision and knowledge portrayal. The problem involves giving an image and a natural language question as an input to the computer, process them together and give an accurate answer to the question in the context of the image as the output. The answer can be a single word answer, phrase or sentence depending on the question and the image. We explore the various approaches used by global teams to deal with this problem and the specifications of the publicly available dataset in order to analyze the feasibility and scope of this domain. This technology finds its use in helping blind people in object recognition using voice commands. It may also be used by physicians and medical practitioners to confirm or validate their diagnosis about medical imagery. Since this field is relatively new the possibilities are endless when it comes to datasets, algorithms and accuracy achieved. We aim at understanding this expanse of possibilities at hand and develop conclusive ideas about its further growth.

Keywords: Visual Question Answering · Computer Vision · Natural Language Processing · Convolutional neural network · Machine Learning

1 Introduction

The past few years have seen some considerable advancements in a lot of problems in Computer Vision such as classification of images, detection of objects, and action determination. Some recent Convolutional Neural Networks are so accurate, that they can challenge human minds in image classification [1]. Publicly available datasets with a lot of metadata about the images are at an all-time high and it is only expected to increase making Computer Vision tasks more accurate. The human mind is so powerful, that as we see an object, we reference it to some context in our mind, understand object position and establish some relationships with the objects around it to deduce information about it.

© Springer Nature Singapore Pte Ltd. 2020
P. K. Singh et al. (Eds.): FTNCT 2019, CCIS 1206, pp. 358–370, 2020.
https://doi.org/10.1007/978-981-15-4451-4_28

As of not long ago, the improvement of a Computer Vision framework that can respond to self-assertive natural language inquiries regarding pictures was believed to be an over-aspiring objective. Be that as it may, with these abilities, gigantic advancement has been made in creating frameworks since 2014. Visual Question Answering (VQA) is a Computer Vision task in which the framework gets content-based picture question and the appropriate response is required to be derived [5]. There are a lot progressively intricate questions that can be queried past these, for example, inquiries concerning the spatial connections between articles (What drink is the person holding?) and inquiries regarding sound judgment thinking (Is it day or night?). A powerful VQA framework should most likely comprehend a wide scope of established Computer Vision undertakings and need the capacity to reason about pictures (Fig. 1).

Q: What is this? **Q:** What color is this? **Q:** What animal is this?
Ans: Apple   **Ans:** Yellow   **Ans:** Cat

Fig. 1. VQA: an example

VQA is task in Computer Vision wherein a text-based question concerning a picture is given to the framework along with the image, and the objective is to get a response to the inquiry [6]. Abstraction in questions is permitted and they may wrap various sub-zones in Computer Vision, for instance,

- Object Recognition: What is it?
- Object Detection: Is it a dog?
- Attribute Classification: What is the colour of the umbrella?
- Scene Classification: Is it rainy?
- Counting: How many pens are there?

2 Problem Definition and Motivation

VQA is a research problem that grew interest in the most recent couple of years and has been getting a great deal of consideration from the Machine Learning Community. Here we endeavour to utilize profound Figuring out how to understand semantic details of images. The info to the framework is a picture and an inquiry in natural language identified with that picture. VQA is when for some given content based inquiries concerning a picture, the framework needs to induce the appropriate response for each inquiry, where we expect to pick an answer from different decisions or propose an answer straightforwardly as a solitary word without the arrangement of choices [8].

VQA is a vital, engaging problem since it joins the fields of Natural Language Processing and Computer Vision. Vision systems have to be utilized to comprehend the picture and NLP systems have to be utilized to comprehend the inquiry. Besides, both must be joined to successfully respond to the inquiry in setting of the picture. This is testing in light of the fact that truly both these fields have utilized particular strategies and models to illuminate their separate assignments.

While a large portion of the ebb and flow explore in the Computer Vision space occurs in the Image Classification circle, this task is a stage forward, managing understanding the setting of the objects in the images and their connection. Issues at the crossing point of vision and language are progressively drawing more consideration. We are seeing a move past the established "bucketed" recognition worldview (for example mark every image with classes) to rich compositional assignments including natural language.

A portion of these issues concerning vision and language have demonstrated shockingly simple to take on with generally straightforward strategies. Consider image captioning, which includes creating a sentence portraying a given picture. it is conceivable to get cutting edge results with a generally coarse comprehension of the picture by misusing the measurable inclinations (characteristic on the planet and specifically datasets) that are caught in standard language models. Not at all like picture subtitling, addressing questions requires the capacity to distinguish explicit subtleties in the image (for example shade of an item, or movement of an individual). There are a few as of late proposed VQA datasets on genuine images just as on unique scenes. the last permits look into on semantic thinking without first requiring the advancement of exceedingly exact detectors.

Table 1. VQA datasets [1]

	No. of images	No. of questions	Avg. questions per image	Avg. question length	Avg. answer length	Q/A generation
DAQUAR	1449	12468	8.6	11.5	1.2	Human
Visual7W	47300	327939	6.93	6.9	2	Human
Visual Madlibs	10738	360001	33.52	4.9	2.8	Human
COCO-QA	117684	117684	1	9.65	1	Automatic
FM-IQA	158392	316193	1.99	7.38 (Chinese)	3.82 (Chinese)	Human
VQA (COCO)	204721	614163	3	6.2	1.1	Human
VQA (Abstract)	50000	150000	3	6.2	1.1	Human

3   Literature Review

3.1   Datasets for VQA

In the previous 2–3 years, several large-scale public datasets were discharged for the VQA task. A brief description of the datasets is given below. A synopsis of these datasets is presented in Table 1.

DAQUAR: The first public dataset discharged for the VQA task was the DAtaset for QUestion Answering on Real World Images (or DAQUAR), published in 2015. All pictures are indoor scenes. A total of 1449 images are available (795 training, 654 test). [5] The creators produced pairs of questions answering questions in two different ways:

(a) Using question templates to generate the pairs automatically.
(b) Using comments from humans.

VizWiz. The VizWiz dataset was generated using a VQA arrangement where visually impaired or purblind people were to give an image and asked to record a question based on that image. The dataset contains 20,000 training image/QA pairs and 8000 testing image/QA pairs [5] (Fig. 2).

Q: Does this foundation have any sunscreen?   Q: What is this?   Q: Please can you tell me what this item is?   Q: Is it sunny outsid   Q: What color is this?   Q: Is this air conditioner on fan, dehumidifier, or air conditioning?
A: yes   A: 10 euros   A: butternut squash red pepper soup   A: yes   A: green   A: air conditioning

Fig. 2. Examples from VizWiz dataset

Visual7W. The Visual 7 W dataset was created using images for captioning, segmentation and recognition from the MS-COCO dataset [6]. Visual7W gets its name from the 7W questions i.e. who, what, where, when, why, how and what. Questions were generated by experts from Amazon Mechanical Turk (AMT).

Visual Madlibs. The Visual Madlib dataset is a fill-inthe-blanks dataset. MS-COCO is used in collecting photos [7]. Clear blank questions using formats and item data are created naturally.

COCO-QA Dataset. DAQUAR was a smaller dataset than COCO-QA. Containing 123,287 pictures originating from the dataset COCO, it includes ~78,000 training QA pairs and ~40000 testing QA pairs. To make such a lot of QA sets, the creators automatically generated QA sets from COCO picture descriptions using an NLP algorithm. For example, for a given caption, for example, "Professor and student discussing in the room", they would generate an inquiry like "How many people are present in the room?"

FM-IQA. The Freestyle Multilingual Image Question Answering dataset (FM-IQA) takes pictures from the MS-COCO dataset and utilizes the Baidu crowdsourcing server to obtain questions and answers from workers. Answers may be words, phrases, or full phrases. As their English translations, Question/Answer sets are available in Chinese. There are 316,193 questions and 158,392 images in the dataset. They propose human evaluation through a Visual Turing Test, which can be one of the reasons why this dataset did not increase in prevalence [5].

VQA. The dataset Visual Question Answering (VQA) is the commonly used dataset for this task. It has been discharged as a major aspect of the VQA challenge. It is partitioned into two sections: one part contains true MS-COCO pictures, and another part contains abstract clip scenarios made from human and animal models to evacuate the requirement to process noisy pictures and perform high-level reasoning. Questions answer pairs are generated from crowd sourced workers, and workers receive 10 answers for each inquiry. Answers are a word or a brief expression on a regular basis. Approximately 40% of the questions are answered yes or no.

3.2   Models and Approaches/Algorithms

Countless algorithms have been mooted in the previous three years. Every current method comprises of

1. Harvesting image characteristics (image featurization),
2. Harvesting question characteristics (question featurization),
3. An algorithm that consolidates these features to deliver an answer.

Most calculations use pre-trained CNNs on ImageNet for image features, with common examples being VGGNet, ResNET, and GoogleNet. A wider range of question featurization has been investigated, including long-term memory encoder (LSTM), bag-of-words (BOW), gated recurrent units (GRU), and skip vectors of thought. VQA is treated as a classification problem to generate a response. The image-question features are given as input to the classification system in this framework, and each new answer is called a separate category.

Due to their decent results on distinct vision and NLP projects the VQA job was suggested after deep learning methods had already grown broad popularity. As a consequence, virtually all written research on VQA involves deep learning methods rather than classical methods such as graphical models. There are some models that use a non-neural strategy. Furthermore, some easy baselines used by designers include non-neural approaches that are also depicted. There are a few deep learning models that do not include the use of methods based on attention. And then there are a few VQA-based deep learning models [8].

Subsequently, the fundamental contrast between a few methodologies is the manner by which they join the literary and picture highlights. For instance, they can just join them utilizing connection and after that feed a Linear Classifier. Or on the other hand they can utilize Bayesian models to induce the basic connections between the component dispersion of the question, the picture and the answer. Aftereffects of the considerable number of models depicted are condensed in Tables 2 and 3.

Table 2. Implementation of models on the COCO and DAQUAR datasets [1]

	DAQUAR (Reduced)			DAQUAR (All)			COCO-QA		
	Accuracy (%)	WUPS @ 0.9 (%)	WUPS @ 0 (%)	Accuracy (%)	WUPS @ 0.9 (%)	WUPS @ 0 (%)	Accuracy (%)	WUPS @ 0.9 (%)	WUPS @ 0 (%)
SWQA	9.69	14.73	48.57	7.86	11.86	38.79	–	–	–
MWQA	12.73	18.1	51.47	–	–	–	–	–	–
Vis+LSTM	34.41	46.05	82.23	–	–	–	53.31	63.91	88.25
AYN	34.68	40.76	79.54	21.67	27.99	65.11	–	–	–
2Vis+ BLSTM	35.78	46.83	82.15	–	–	–	55.09	65.34	88.64
Full-CNN	42.76	47.58	82.60	23.4	29.59	62.95	54.95	65.36	88.58
DPPnet	44.48	49.56	83.95	28.98	34.80	67.81	61.19	70.84	90.61
ATP	45.17	49.74	**85.13**	28.96	34.74	67.33	63.18	73.14	91.32
SAN	**45.50**	**50.2**	83.60	**29.3**	**35.10**	**68.60**	61.60	71.60	90.90
CoAtt	–	–	–	–	–	–	65.40	75.10	92
AMA	–	–	–	–	–	–	**69.73**	**77.14**	**92.5**

Baselines. In terms of numerous classification issues, a baseline includes providing the most repetitive answer to any question on an ongoing basis. To get an arbitrary reply is another baseline. For example, the work by Antol et al. (2016) shows that continuously choosing the most well-known responses from the VQA dataset's best 1000 answers (the appropriate response is "yes") prompts an accuracy of 29.7%. Leaving aside, this presumably has to do with an unwanted predisposition of the dataset, such an outcome delineates the meaning of having great baselines: they decide worthy of the negligible dimension of execution, and can also give an indication of the inherent intricacy of the undertaking and, in addition, of the dataset.

A progressively modern gauge, generally utilized in VQA, comprises on preparing a Linear Classifier or a Multilayer Perceptron utilizing vectors speaking to a blend of the highlights as information. This mix can be a straightforward join or a element wise addition or multiplication of the highlights [9].

For instance, the past referred to work explores different avenues regarding two models:

- a multi-layer neural system classifier Perceptron (MLP) with two hidden layers and 1000 hidden units (dropout 0.5) in each non-linear *tanh* layer.
- a LSTM model pursued by a soft max layer to create the appropriate response.

In the primary case, they use a BOW approach for the text-based features, using the queries' main 1,000 words and the subtitles' 1,000 most mainstream words to figure them. The last hidden layer of VGGNet is used for the picture highlights. As far as the LSTM model is concerned, they use a one-hot encoding for the questions, and a similar picture includes a straight change to change the picture highlights to 1024 dimensions to coordinate the question's LSTM encoding. question and image encoding is consolidated by the product of the each element [10].

These baselines' exhibitions are extremely intriguing. For example, if the models are prepared only on text-based highlights, the accuracy is 47.1%, while the odds that they are prepared on ocular highlights are reduced to 29.3%. Their best model, an LSTM prepared on both highlights, is 54.8% accurate. The creators affirm that outcomes are superior to open-answer on different decisions and, obviously, all strategies are more regrettable than human execution [11].

Numerous varieties in this structure can be actualized to acquire diverse approaches.

Table 3. Implementation of several models on the VQA dataset [1]

	Test development open ended				MCCC	Test standard open ended				MCCC
	Y/N	Number	Other	All	All	Y/N	Number	Other	All	All
iBOWMIG	76.5	35	42.6	55.7	–	76.8	35	42.6	55.9	–
DPPnet	80.7	37.2	41.7	57.2	–	80.3	36.9	42.2	57.4	–
WTL	–	–	–	–	62.4	–	–	–	–	62.4
AYN	78.4	36.4	46.3	58.4	–	78.2	36.3	46.3	58.4	–
SAN	79.3	36.6	46.1	58.7	–	–	–	–	58.9	–
ATP	80.5	37.5	46.7	59.6	–	80.3	**37.8**	**47.6**	60.1	–
NMN	**81.2**	38	44	58.6	–	**81.2**	37.7	44	58.7	–
CoAtt	79.7	**38.7**	**51.7**	**61.8**	65.8	–	–	–	62.1	**66.1**
AMA	81.01	38.42	45.23	59.17	–	81.07	37.12	45.83	59.44	–

Attention-Based Approaches. The objective of the attention-based methodologies is to set the focal point of the calculation on the most applicable pieces of the information. For instance, if the query is "What is the cat eating", the picture part where the cat has higher importance over the rest. Similarly, "cat" and "eating" are increasingly educational that the remainder of the words.

The most well-known VQA decision is to use spatial attention to create explicit local highlights for the preparation of CNNs. There are two regular techniques for purchasing a picture's spatial areas. First of all, by projecting a grid across the picture. After connecting the network, the particular question dictates the importance of each region.

The other way is to create boundary boxes. In view of the prominent areas, we use the question in determining the importance of the highlights for each, and to select only those that are important to answer the query. These are just two strategies to fuse regard for VQA frameworks, and a lot more can be found in the writing.

There are a ton of approaches for VQA frameworks and this just the tip of the iceberg [12].

Bayesian Approaches. (Kafle et al. in 2016) [20] suggest a Bayesian VQA framework in which they anticipate and use the suitable answer type for a query. The kinds of conceivable responses change over the various kinds of datasets. For instance, they consider four kinds of responses for COCO dataset: count, object, location, and color In this model, the likelihood and type t of a response given the picture x and question q, pursuing the standard of Bayes.

4   Proposed Architecture

Overall, the approach in VQA can be outlined as follows:

- Extract characteristics from the question.
- Extract characteristics from the picture.
- To generate a response, combine the features.

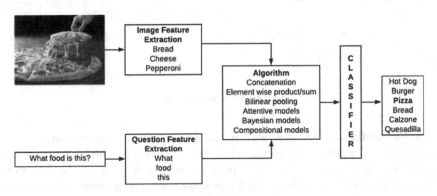

Fig. 3. VQA process

We model the VQA problem as a problem of classification, where each response from the training set is a class. The center of our technique is the stacked attention module, which takes a question embedding as its info, and a set of objects with congruous attributes of an image from the image embedding module. The attention module learns a picture graph portrayal that is adapted on the question and models the significant item connections in the scene. We utilize this graph portrayal to learn picture characteristics impacted by their separate neighbors utilizing graph convolutions, trailed by max-pooling, element wise multiplication and fully connected softmax layers [13] (Fig. 3).

The architecture used consists of the following phases:

- Image Embedding
- Question Embedding
- Stacked Attention
- Classifier
- Image Embedding:

In this step, we have used a convolutional neural network that uses ResNet-152 architecture's pretrained model. This gives us a higher-level view of the input image. ResNets can have very deep networks such as the 152-layer network used since they learn from the residual representation function instead of the signal representation directly. ResNet-152 pretrained model has been used since the ResNet architecture can be scaled to even 100 or 1000 layers successfully. Additionally, it has been found that ResNet network converges faster leading better performance of the used architecture [14] (Fig. 4).

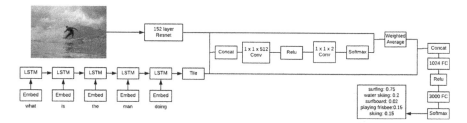

Fig. 4. VQA architecture

Image Embedding. In this step, we have used a convolutional neural network that uses ResNet-152 architecture's pretrained model. This gives us a higher-level view of the input image. ResNets can have very deep networks such as the 152-layer network used since they learn from the residual representation function instead of the signal representation directly. ResNet-152 pretrained model has been used since the ResNet architecture can be scaled to even 100 or 1000 layers successfully. Additionally, it has been found that ResNet network converges faster leading better performance of the used architecture [15] (Fig. 5).

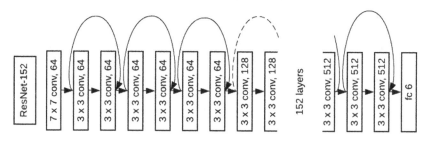

Fig. 5. Resnet 152 layers

Question Embedding. In this step, we firstly break the questions into tokens and then encode them into word embeddings with each embedding corresponding to a single word in the given question. The tokenizer basically splits the given question string into its component words. These embeddings are then provided to an LSTM (Long Short-Term Memory) network. Recurrent Neural Networks (RNNs) help in keeping the information persistent and LSTM networks are a special type of these RNNs that have the capability to learn long term dependencies. They help in the use of previously acquired information for the current task [16] (Fig. 6).

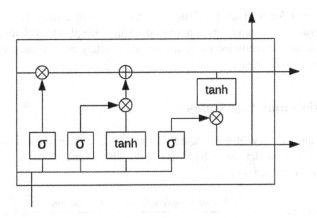

Fig. 6. LSTM network cells

Stacked Attention. The different attention-based dispersion in dimensions of space are computed for image features. For every glimpse of image feature we consider the weighted average for locations in space. Then the normalized weights of attention are taken. The final structure is modelled with twin convolution arrangement [17]. For varied attention distributed alignments, we use various initializing parameters.

Classifier. The image glimpses derived in previous step are concatenated together along with the corresponding states of LSTM based on the textual input or query. Non-linear models are applied to generate probabilities across the classes that represent results.

5 Outcome

The input to the framework is a picture and a question in Natural Language identified with that picture (Fig. 7).

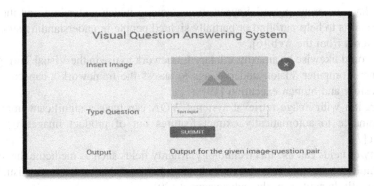

Fig. 7. UI design for proposed system

VQA is when for a given text-based question around a picture, the framework needs to construe the response for each question, where we plan to pick an answer from numerous decisions or recommend an answer legitimately as a solitary word without the arrangement of choices.

6   Evaluation and Test Cases

We achieved an accuracy of 66% based on the above architecture consisting of pre-trained ResNet-152 model and LSTM network. The accuracy for the answers was calculated using the formula [18]

$$accuracy = min\left(\frac{No.\ of\ people\ who\ provided\ that\ answer}{3}, 1\right)$$

Here we consider the achieved answer as correct only if the answer has also been provided by 3 individual human testers (Fig. 8).

Q: What is this?
A: Food

Q: What color is this?
A: Green

Q: What is this?
A: Beer

Q: What is written in the logo?
A: Unanswerable

Fig. 8.   Test cases

7   Applications

- VQA has numerous potential applications, among which a standout and the most important is to help purblind or partially sighted people in understanding substance of pictures from the web [6].
- VQA could likewise be an extraordinary framework to use in the Visual Turing Test or other Computer Vision undertakings to assess the framework's capacity when contrasting and human execution [19].
- Integration with image retrieval systems, VQA can have a significant impact on e-commerce to automatically extract features out of product images or social media [7].
- Variety of fields can use this technology. Mainly fields such as medicine that earlier was limited to textual data due to lack of technology that understands visual data will greatly benefit from this advancement [20].

- In medicine specifically, other than TB detection, this project could also be trained to identify bone fractures or brain imagery or any application that requires an understanding of various objects in the image.
- The ability to ask questions in natural language can be leveraged by many other fields like in Education where it could be used by students of rudimentary age to ask questions about the objects they identify in images.

8   Conclusion and Future Scope

All in all, the Visual Question Answering (VQA) task is presented. The errand is to give an answer given a picture and a question about the picture. We give more than 250K pictures, 760K questions, and 10M answers to a dataset. In our dataset, we show the wide assortment of questions and answers, just as the various arrangement of AI abilities required to react precisely to these inquiries in computer vision, natural language preparing, and sound judgment thinking. The questions we asked were open-ended and not task-explicit from our human subjects. It is valuable to gather task-explicit inquiries for some application spaces. For instance, questions can be gathered from various subjects, or questions could concentrate on one specific area (state politics).

Bigham et al. [18] made an application empowering visually disabled individuals to catch pictures and ask open-ended questions that human subjects answer. Curiously, with conventional subtitles, these questions can infrequently be replied. Preparing on undertaking explicit datasets can help with empowering handy VQA applications. We trust that VQA has the particular favourable position of driving the limits on computer-based intelligence issues while being appropriate for programmed evaluation. Given the network's ongoing advancement, we trust now is the ideal opportunity for such an exertion.

As has been the pattern as of late, Deep Learning models outflank prior graphical methodologies over all the datasets for VQA. Notwithstanding, it is intriguing to take note of that the Answer Type Prediction demonstration performs superior to the non-attention models, which demonstrates that just presenting CNNs or potentially RNNs is insufficient: recognizing portions of the picture that are applicable in a principled way is imperative. The field of VQA has developed significantly in spite of being presented only a scarcely any years back

Deep learning approaches for VQA remain to be the most considered models with the most accurate results. We looked at the most of these models and documented their implementation over numerous extensive datasets. Notable upgrades in implementation continue to be seen on countless datasets, which means that there is still plenty of room in this venture for potential progress.

References

1. arXiv:1705.03865v2 [cs.CL]
2. Antol, S., et al.: VQA: visual question answering. In: 2015 IEEE International Conference on Computer Vision (ICCV), Santiago, pp. 2425–2433 (2015). https://doi.org/10.1109/iccv.2015.279
3. Simonyan, K., Zisserman, A.: Very deep convolutional networks for large-scale image recognition. In: International Conference on Learning Representations (ICLR) (2015)
4. Xu, K., et al.: Show, attend and tell: Neural image caption generation with visual attention. In: International Conference on Machine Learning (ICML) (2015)
5. arXiv:1610.01465 [cs.CV]
6. CloudCV: CloudCV (2018). https://VQA.cloudcv.org/. Accessed 28 Oct 2018
7. Couto, J.: Introduction to visual question answering|Tryolabs Blog, Tryolabs.com (2018). https://tryolabs.com/blog/2018/03/01/introduction-to-visual-question-answering/. Accessed 28 Oct 2018
8. Redmon, J., Divvala, S., Girshick, R., Farhadi, A.: You only look once: unified, real-time object detection. In: The IEEE Conference on Computer Vision and Pattern Recognition (CVPR) (2016)
9. Zhang, Z., Schwing, A.G., Fidler, S., Urtasun, R.: Monocular object instance segmentation and depth ordering with CNNs. In: The IEEE Conference on Computer Vision and Pattern Recognition (CVPR) (2015)
10. Das, A., Agrawal, H., Zitnick, C.L., Parikh, D., Batra, D.: Human attention in visual question answering: do humans and deep networks look at the same regions? In: Conference on Empirical Methods on Natural Language Processing (EMNLP) (2016)
11. Boscaini, D., Masci, J., Rodolà, E., Bronstein, M.: Learning shape correspondence with anisotropic convolutional neural networks. In: NIPS, pp. 3189–3197 (2015)
12. Goyal, Y., Khot, T., Summers-Stay, D., Batra, D., Parikh, D.: Making the Vin VQA matter: Elevating the role of image understanding in visual question answering. In: CVPR (2017)
13. Xu, D., Zhu, Y., Choy, C.B., Fei-Fei, L.: Scene graph generation by iterative message passing. In: CVPR, vol. 2 (2017)
14. Lu, J., Yang, J., Batra, D., Parikh, D.: Hierarchical question-image co-attention for visual question answering. In: NIPS, pp. 289–297 (2016)
15. Kafle, Kushal, Kanan, Christopher: Visual question answering: datasets, algorithms, and future challenges. Comput. Vis. Image Underst. **163**, 3–20 (2017)
16. Schwartz, I., Schwing, A.G., Hazan, T.: High-order attention models forvisual question answering. In: NIPS, pp. 3667–3677 (2017)
17. Kipf, T.N., Welling, M.: Semi-supervised classification with graph convolutional networks. CoRR, abs/1609.02907 (2016)
18. Bigham, J.P., et al.: VizWiz: nearly real-time answers to visual questions. In: ACM User Interface Software and Technology Symposium (UIST) (2010)
19. Szegedy, C., Toshev, A., Erhan, D.: Deep neural networks for object detection. In: Advances in Neural Information Processing Systems (NIPS) (2013)
20. Kafle, K., Kanan, C.: Answer-type prediction for visual question answering. In: The IEEE Conference on Computer Vision and Pattern Recognition (CVPR) (2016)

Information Credibility on Twitter
Using Machine Learning Techniques

Faraz Ahmad[(⊠)] and Syed Afzal Murtaza Rizvi

Department of Computer Science, Jamia Millia Islamia University,
New Delhi, India
faraz159020@st.jmi.ac.in, sarizvi@jmi.ac.in

Abstract. In today's world, people are highly inclined towards social networking sites like Twitter, which provides a platform where users can have easy
access to the high impact occasions/events rising worldwide. Users can share
views and retweet the contents posted by other users with respect to such high
impact event. However, users have diverse interests and hold strong opinions
pertaining to any political party, caste, culture, religion, etc. So, while sharing
any information, it is very essential for the social media users that they do not
post any abusive or absurd content which might hurt the emotions of others and
can end up into dreadful situations. So, there is a dire need of some filtering
techniques to build a credibility analysis model which can filter out all such
uncredible and questionable contents from social media. In this paper, a machine
learning model has been developed to detect the credibility of tweets over four
distinct credibility classes. Approximately 5k tweets were crawled from Twitter
and preprocessed, which helped in developing a model. Initially, the K-Means
clustering algorithm was applied on the dataset to find which tweet falls in
which cluster, based on its similarity measures of feature set. The total variance
in the dataset explained by K Mean Clustering Algorithm is found to be 86.6%.
Furthermore, the Support Vector Machine algorithm is applied to build a classification model and classify the tweets into their respective credibility classes. It
provides 96.53% accuracy with 99.51% area under the curve.

Keywords: Tweet · Credibility · Clustering · Classification · Machine learning

1 Introduction

In this digital era, where social networking platforms are moving far ahead of traditional television news and print media, the authenticity of the information shared is still
debatable. Millions of people from all over the world shared their view w.r.t. any
occasion or events. These events were related to social activist moments, political
issues, or any general occasion. Mostly, people used hashtag features just to refer the
event for which they were talking about. These hashtags will also help others to share
their views about the same event. Some people were in favor while others are against.
However, sometimes while sharing their views people started criticizing each other just
because their views are different from others on any given event. This criticism further
turns into hatred and people started using hate speeches for any person, caste, religion

© Springer Nature Singapore Pte Ltd. 2020
P. K. Singh et al. (Eds.): FTNCT 2019, CCIS 1206, pp. 371–381, 2020.
https://doi.org/10.1007/978-981-15-4451-4_29

or political party, which will end up to a disastrous situation and can spread lots of chaos. This study is to filter out all those contents which is responsible for spreading such abusive content within the society to avoid the chaos.

In this paper, we have crawled more than 5000 tweets using Twitter Rest API on trending political hashtags and mentions such as #Demonetization, #GST, #PulwamAttack #WhyTheyHateModi, @NarendraModi, etc. where people were sharing their views. Further, we preprocessed the tweets and omit all the duplicate ones, tweets which were less than 10 words, tweets which contain only hashtags or emoticons and narrowed down it to finest 2000 tweets. Additionally, we have calculated the emotions (JOY. ANGER, FEAR, SADNESS & DISGUST), sentiments (−1 to +1) using IBM Watson, polarity (P+, P, NONE, N, N+) using Meaning cloud. We also performed topic extraction using Meaning Cloud platform for analyzing the tweet better and to extract in-depth information.

Our approach is better than traditional features-based approach as we have developed a model which is strictly discarding all the tweets which are suspected to create any kind of chaos within the society. If any user is posting or retweeting some others content which contains negative sentiment and emotions like abusive or any kind of disturbing words related to any cast, culture, religion or political party is considered as uncredible and we are suggesting those content to discard right away. The novelty of our suggested model is that it can discard the tweets of those users as well who have a high reputation within society or verified by twitter but still somehow engaged in spreading the rumored and unauthentic content knowingly or unknowingly. These users have a high number of followers and friend count, and they have fulfilled all the condition w.r.t. their associated user and content level features to become credible but still our model find tweets which need to discard and assigned uncredible score to the tweets of these users as well.

For analyzing the credibility of the tweets, we performed both unsupervised and supervised machine learning approach and compared the results. K Mean clustering algorithm is applied based on the given features as an unsupervised approach, where we assumed the tweets fall into one of the four major clusters (Acceptable, Slightly Acceptable, Slightly Unacceptable, and Unacceptable). K Means clustering is an unsupervised machine learning algorithm with huge real-time applications. It can be applied over continuous and numeric data. Some of its applications are, documents-based clustering, to identify crime-prone areas, fraud detection, data analysis for public transport, IT alerts clustering, etc.

Further tweets were annotated with the help of three different human annotators who have in-depth knowledge about the event into the four-level of credibility scale (Credible, Somewhat Credible, Somewhat Uncredible, and Uncredible). Support Vector Machine (SVM) is applied for classifying the tweets into these four-level and we get 96% classification accuracy with 99% precision and 99.2% recall. And finds classification by SVM performed slightly better than K Mean clustering algorithm for the given data. Furthermore, through Sect. 2 we discuss the background study, the work that various authors had performed for analyzing the credibility of tweets on Twitter. Section 3; discuss the processes of data extraction, followed by preprocessing and annotation of tweets by human annotators. Section 4 provides the details of features which are used in clustering and classification techniques.

2 Background Study

In the current scenario, social media has been the major platform of accessing information and collecting news from all over the world however, their credibility is still questionable. We reviewed some articles which help us understand the cause of spreading fake content and suitable measures to overcome these issues.

In this paper Xia et al. [1] developed a model to detect the credibility of the posted content on twitter. Their work is twofold, firstly they developed a model to monitor the outburst of tweets for detecting emergency situation using unsupervised machine learning algorithm. In the next step, they manually annotate tweets with the help of experts and assign credibility score as either credible or incredible. Lastly, the authors tried to find the credibility of tweets using the Bayesian Network model with the help of various features set like user-based, content-based, etc. which are associated with the tweet.

Gupta et al. [2] developed a browser plugin named TweetCred which incorporate with the browser for finding out the credibility of tweets posted on twitter in real-time. The author used semi-supervised machine learning, SVM ranking model to rank the tweet over seven pointer credibility scale. They used a set of 45 features which broadly divided into six major categories like content features, user features, network features, tweet syntactic features, etc.

Zhang et al. [3] proposed an automatic method for detecting rumor on Sina Weibo Social Networks. They extracted 3229 rumored and 12534 non-rumored messages from community management center of Sina Weibo. The author proposed two bread set of features namely shallow and implicit. Shallow features basic elements of user and content, whereas implicit features consist of user polarity, sentiment score, and meta-features associated with the user. For developing a machine learning model author used the random forest and support vector machine algorithms.

Westerman et al. [4] described the psychological perspective of humans related to the judgment of the credibility of the user who had posted content on Twitter. Authors developed six Twitter mock pages which were randomly assigned to 289 students. In these pages, user's followers count and the ratio of followers to follows was different for identifying the credibility of the source. The curvilinear effects were indicated by the data, as too many and too less number of followers will results in lower trustworthiness for users.

Morris et al. [5] presented a survey in which 256 participants were participated in perceiving the credibility of the tweets regarding the user's perception. The author found a significant difference between the features which users consider while judging the credibility of the tweet and the features which were provided by the search engine. While leading the experiments they systematically manipulate various features and found the users are poor in judging the credibility and mostly influence by the heuristics of other users.

Cha et al. [6] described the user's influence on Twitter using three distinctive features such as, in-degree which is a number of followers a user have, re-tweet and mentions. Author crawled approximately around 1.755 Trillion tweets of different users which were further narrowed down to 6 million. The user influence was computed and compared separately. They illustrated three major findings; firstly, the users who have larger in-degree are not essentially an influencer. Secondly, influence users can hold the influence over most of the topics and lastly, for gaining influence a person's active participation is required, influence can't be gained overnight.

O'Donovan et al. [7] focused on finding the credibility of tweets crawled on 8 diverse occasions, from which three major sets of features were extracted namely, Behavioral, Content-based and Social features. Further, tweets were outsourced to 236 Amazon Mechanical Turk employees to annotate the tweets on 5 pointers Likert scale for manually evaluating the credibility of the tweets. Lastly, feature distribution analysis through re-tweet chains of different length and dyadic pair of tweets is explained. The author claims that re-tweet, mentions, tweet-length and URL were the most influential factors for explaining the credibility.

Lorek et al. [8] proposed a study of finding tweet credibility which is based on three major steps. Author crawled 7000 tweets from twitter using Twitter Streaming API; they also extracted user level and content level features. Further, tweets were given to human annotators who evaluate the tweet manually and assigned different credibility score. Moreover, credibility calculation is broadly divided into three steps, in the first step the author used Twitter only features, second is the reconcile features classification and third is a combination of both. Lastly, the authors were in the process of building a credibility analysis tool named Twitterbot.

Resnik et al. [9] proposed an interactive tool for assessing the tweet is a rumor and require further assistance or not. For the experimental purpose, they have extracted 616 tweets related to Jay-Z incident; nearly 900K people were exposed to this news as they were following someone who has reposted this news. This tool requires rigorous human assistance that any particular rumored content was interesting enough to process further. In background automated learning and calculations strengthen the efficacy of human labor which helps the general public and journalist to a great extent.

Thakur et al. [10] extracted around 10K tweets using Twitter Rest API for the purpose of detecting rumor in online social networks. Their approach is two-fold, initially, they differentiate between personal and non-personal content and labeled all personal tweets as non-rumored. Tweets having first and second person pronoun measured as a personal tweet. Further, text classification had performed and authors choose top 3000 keywords from the document term matrix and mapped with the tweet text. It marked true if features are present in the tweets otherwise false. These features helped in classifying the tweets using SVM and Naive Bayes classifiers as rumored or non-rumored to a great extent.

Sicilia et al. [11] developed a novel rumor detection approach on health-related issues which was not only based on features that are available in previous literature but also newly developed features inspired by graph theory. Novel features are influence potential of the users and measure of network characteristics. Furthermore, the author detects rumors with 90% of accuracy with acceptable precision percentage.

3 Data Extraction, Preprocessing, and Annotation

Building a dataset for fulfilling the objective of finding credible information on Twitter we made a crawler in Java using Twitter Rest API. We extracted data by two different ways, either by trending using hashtags or user handle, viz. #Demonetization, #GST, #Corruption, #iamwithmodi, #WhyTheyHateModi, @NarendraModi, @Arvindkejri-wal, @OfficeOfRG and many more. Approximately 5K tweets were crawled from twitter over a different time span w.r.t. the happening of these high impact events, and further conceded for the preprocessing. In data preprocessing step, all the duplicate tweets, tweets which contain less than 10 words, the tweet which contains only hash-tag and emoticons, any other language tweet except English were omitted. And we narrowed down to the 1930 Tweets.

For annotating tweets into the four-level of credibility scale (Credible, Somewhat Credible, Somewhat Uncredible, and Uncredible), three different individuals were assigned who have in-depth knowledge about these above-mentioned events. Tweets which were directly related to the event and do not contain any abusive word or hate speech for any religion, culture or political party should be annotated as Credible. Whereas, the tweets which is somehow related to the event and it was someone's opinion related to the event and do not contains any negative sentiments like abusive words will be annotated as somewhat credible. However, tweets which were not directly related to the event and contain sarcastic and criticizing words for others were labeled as somewhat uncredible. Lastly, all the tweets that contain absurd or abusive words for any person or political party, and propagating hate speeches either it was written them self or re-tweeting other person tweets was considered as Uncredible. The distributions of tweets are shown in Table 1.

Table 1. Tweets distribution for annotation class

Credibility level	Distribution
Uncredible	763
Somewhat Uncredible	228
Somewhat Credible	556
Credible	383

4 Features Extraction and Machine Learning Techniques

Figure 1 explains the overall flow of the paper including, data crawling, feature extraction, data annotation, and applications of K-Means clustering and Support Vector classification algorithms. In this paper, our main concern is to omit all the tweets which were propagating any kind of nuisance or hate speech within the society. Any person no matter how reputed he/she is, if they were involved in propagating any such content, we labeled the tweets as Uncredible. Our aim is to omit out all such tweets and give users a valid message that does not believe, react or further propagate such tweets. All the preprocessed tweets are further analyzed through two different tools provided by IBM. Natural Language Understanding used to calculate the emotions and sentiment whereas;

tweet polarity was calculated by Meaning Cloud. Emotions consist of five categories like Fear, Sadness, Joy, Anger, and Disgust on a scale of (0 to 1). However, sentiment scale is divided into two parts, first is negative sentiment scores range from 0 to −1 and positive sentiment score ranges from 0 to +1 respectively. Lastly, Polarity scale consists of six classes such as N+, N, NONE, NEU, P, and P+. For simplification, we combined NEU and NONE categories. Table 2 describes the set of extracted features and its description which are used for performing credibility analysis of the tweets.

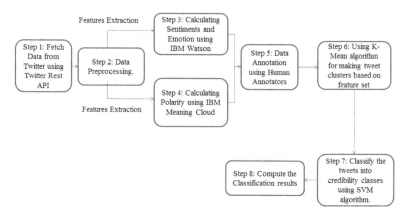

Fig. 1. The overall flow of features extraction and machine learning process

Table 2. Extracted features and its details

Extracted features	Details
Sentiment_Tweet	Sentiment of the tweet 0 to −1 (Negative Sentiment) & 0 to +1 (Positive Sentiment)
Emotion_Tweet (JOY)	Joy Score of the tweet 0 to +1
Emotion_Tweet (FEAR)	FEAR Score of the tweet 0 to +1
Emotion_Tweet (ANGER)	ANGER Score of the tweet 0 to +1
Emotion_Tweet (DISGUST)	DISGUST Score of the tweet 0 to +1
Emotion_Tweet (SADNESS)	SADNESS Score of the tweet 0 to +1
Polarity_Tweet	Tweet Polarity (P+, P, NONE, N, N+)

By using these features, we applied K Means clustering algorithm for finding which tweet will fall in which cluster. In this algorithm we need to specify the number of clusters which we want to make beforehand, however, as we have four credibility classes so we would make 4 distinct clusters and find which tweet will fall in which cluster based on features and annotation provided by the annotators.

Table 3. Features used and its description

	Cluster1	Cluster2	Cluster3	Cluster4
Credible	140	40	202	1
Somewhat Credible	54	391	69	42
Somewhat Uncredible	0	17	0	211
Uncredible	0	15	0	748

Within cluster sum of squares by cluster: 48.89407, 180.40616, 55.90574, 461.56694 (between_SS/total_SS = 86.6%)

Table 3 is illustrating the K Mean clustering results for all four clusters. Here we have found that most of the credible and somewhat credible tweets were either falls in cluster 1, 2 or 3, however, all the uncredible and somewhat uncredible tweets fall in 4th cluster. It clearly defines the efficiency of our features set that we have used for distributing the tweets in one of the four major clusters. Furthermore, 86.6% is the total variance in the data that is explained by K Mean Clustering Algorithm. K Mean reduced by the dispersion of within-group and increases the dispersion of between groups.

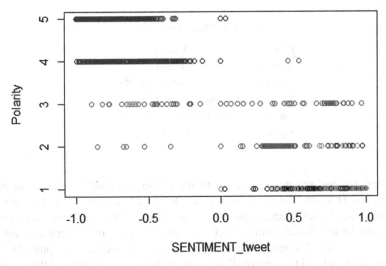

Fig. 2. K-Mean clustering plot between sentiment and polarity

Figure 2 describes the K Mean clustering plot between Sentiment-score which ranges from −1 to +1, we have found that tweets having positive sentiment-score fall into the category of 1 and 2 polarity, however, tweets having negative emotions fall into the polarity of 4 and 5. Lastly, tweets with polarity score 3 contain both kinds of sentiments.

The features used in this paper are easily able to differentiate the tweets into two broad categories of classes which is credible and uncredible tweets, however, clustering techniques are unable to differentiate tweets in all four given credibility classes.

For classifying the tweets into all given credibility classes; we further applied supervised machine learning algorithm classifier i.e. Support Vector Machine. The entire data gets partitioned into 70/30 ratio for training/testing purpose and after running the classification algorithm we get the following testing results.

Table 4 is the contingency table generated by Support Vector Machine Classifier; here we find the equal classification of the tweets in all four major credibility classes which is credible, somewhat credible, somewhat uncredible and uncredible. Furthermore, the classification accuracy of the classifier is 96.53% with kappa statistics of 95.11% shown in Table 5.

Table 4. Contingency table for SVM classifier

	Credible	Somewhat Credible	Somewhat Uncredible	Uncredible
Credible	110	1	0	0
Somewhat Credible	3	164	2	0
Somewhat Uncredible	1	1	63	9
Uncredible	0	0	3	219

Table 5. Overall statistics

Label	Values
Accuracy	0.9653
95% CI	(0.9469, 0.9787)
No information rate	0.3958
P-value [Acc > NIR]	<2.2e−16
Kappa	0.9511

Further, for performance evaluation of the model, we have calculated the recall, precision, and f1 score. The recall is an ability to identify all relevant instances within the classification model, whereas, precision is an ability to find only those instances that are relevant for the classification model and lastly, f1 score is the harmonic mean of precision and recall. The results have shown in Table 6, with an acceptable level of precision and recall and f1 score of 97.77% for credible class, 97.91% of the somewhat credible class, 88.73% of somewhat uncredible class and 97.33% of uncredible class respectively.

Moreover, we plot ROC curve between true positive and false positive rate, it is used to measure the performance of the classification model at different thresholds, whereas, AUC curve tells us how efficiently model will distinguish between credibility classes. Figure 3 shows the roc curve with 99.51% Area under the curve (AUC).

Table 6. Recall, Precision and F1 score

	Credible	Somewhat Credible	Somewhat Uncredible	Uncredible
Recall	0.964912281	0.987951807	0.926470588	0.960526316
Precision	0.990990991	0.970414201	0.851351351	0.986486486
F1 score	0.977777778	0.979104478	0.887323944	0.973333333

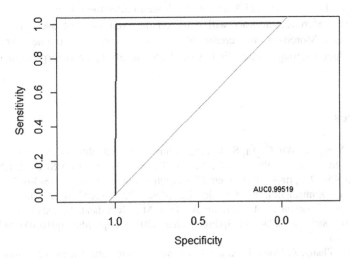

Fig. 3. ROC curve with 99.51% AUC

5 Conclusion and Future Work

Twitter is one of the most popular advancements in the domain of online social networks where people from all over the world can interact with each other and can share views and information over any topic/event without applying much effort. This makes it more popular over traditional news channel or print media. However, sometimes fake or uncredible content is also disseminated with the real news, which can arise chaos among people and can ultimately led to an unstable society. This could be forwarded by any person having different social, political or religious interest. In this paper, a machine learning model is trained and developed using seven different features set incorporating sentiment, emotions, and polarity. It has been observed that there exists a pattern within tweets and its emotions categories which enables us in filtering the credible content from uncredible ones.

Furthermore, K Mean clustering algorithm is applied to find which tweet would fall under which category among the four given clusters. It has been found that majorly tweets with negative sentiment and emotions fell in same cluster, however, the tweets positive sentiment and emotions fell in the other one. Furthermore, we annotated the data over four credibility scale with the help of scholars who had in-depth knowledge of the events on which tweets had been crawled. It was found that most of the tweets with negative emotions and hate speech fell in the category of uncredible tweets, while tweets with positive emotions and sentiments fell in the credible ones.

Lastly, Support Vector Machine classifier is applied for classifying the tweets in one of the four credible classes, and we found that classifier provides 96.53% accuracy with average f1 score as 95.43% and 99.51% area under the curve.

For future reference, authors will work on the credibility of users, based on its posted content. Moreover, the credibility of videos, pictures (memes) and tweets written in other languages like Hindi would also needs to be incorporated in future works.

References

1. Xia, X., Yang, X., Wu, C., Li, S., Bao, L.: Information credibility on Twitter in emergency situation. In: Chau, M., Wang, G.A., Yue, W.T., Chen, H. (eds.) PAISI 2012. LNCS, vol. 7299, pp. 45–59. Springer, Heidelberg (2012). https://doi.org/10.1007/978-3-642-30428-6_4
2. Gupta, A., Kumaraguru, P., Castillo, C., Meier, P.: TweetCred: real-time credibility assessment of content on Twitter. In: Aiello, L.M., McFarland, D. (eds.) SocInfo 2014. LNCS, vol. 8851, pp. 228–243. Springer, Cham (2014). https://doi.org/10.1007/978-3-319-13734-6_16
3. Zhang, Q., Zhang, S., Dong, J., Xiong, J., Cheng, X.: Automatic detection of rumor on social network. In: Li, J., Ji, H., Zhao, D., Feng, Y. (eds.) NLPCC 2015. LNCS (LNAI), vol. 9362, pp. 113–122. Springer, Cham (2015). https://doi.org/10.1007/978-3-319-25207-0_10
4. Westerman, D., Spence, P.R., Van Der Heide, B.: A social network as information: the effect of system generated reports of connectedness on credibility on Twitter. Comput. Hum. Behav. 28(1), 199–206 (2012). https://doi.org/10.1016/j.chb.2011.09.001
5. Morris, M.R., Counts, S., Roseway, A., Hoff, A., Schwarz, J.: Tweeting is believing?: understanding microblog credibility perceptions. In: Proceedings of the ACM Conference on Computer Supported Cooperative Work, pp. 441–450. ACM (2012). https://doi.org/10.1145/2145204.2145274
6. Cha, M., Haddadi, H., Benevenuto, F., Gummadi, P.K.: Measuring user influence in Twitter: the million follower fallacy. In: ICWSM, 10(10–17), 30. (PASSAT), 2012 International Conference on and 2012 International Conference on Social Computing (SocialCom), pp. 91–100. IEEE (2010)
7. O'Donovan, J., Kang, B., Meyer, G., Hollerer, T., Adalii, S.: Credibility in context: an analysis of feature distributions in Twitter. In: Proceedings of the 12th ASE/IEEE International Conference on Privacy, Security, Risk and Trust (PASSAT) and ASE/IEEE International Conference on Social Computing (SocialCom), pp. 293–301. IEEE (2012). https://doi.org/10.1109/socialcom-passat.2012.128
8. Lorek, K., Suehiro-Wiciński, J., Jankowski-Lorek, M., Gupta, A.: Automated credibility assessment on Twitter. Comput. Sci. 16(2), 157–168 (2015). https://doi.org/10.7494/csci.2015.16.2.157
9. Resnick, P., Carton, S., Park, S., Shen, Y., Zeffer, N.: RumorLens: a system for analyzing the impact of rumors and corrections in social media. In: Proceedings of the Computational Journalism Conference, p. 10121-0701 (2014)

10. Thakur, H.K., Gupta, A., Bhardwaj, A., Verma, D.: Rumor detection on Twitter using a supervised machine learning framework. Int. J. Inf. Retrieval Res. (IJIRR) **8**(3), 1–13 (2018). https://doi.org/10.4018/IJIRR.2018070101

11. Sicilia, R., Giudice, S.L., Pei, Y., Pechenizkiy, M., Soda, P.: Twitter rumour detection in the health domain. Expert Syst. Appl. **110**, 33–40 (2018). https://doi.org/10.1016/j.eswa.2018.05.019

Transformation Caused in the Consistency of Landcover Due to Stubble Burning in the Northern India State of Punjab from Suomi NPP Satellite Data

Amit Kumar Shakya[1]([✉]), Ayushman Ramola[1], Ayushi Johri[2], and Anurag Vidyarthi[2]

[1] Department of Electronics and Communication Engineering,
Sant Longowal Institute of Engineering and Technology, Sangrur, Punjab, India
xlamitshakya.gate2014@ieee.org
[2] Department of Electronics and Communication Engineering,
Graphic Era (Deemed to be University), Dehardun, Uttarakhand, India

Abstract. The Indian state of Punjab is known as India's breadbasket. The size is Punjab is relatively small as compared to other Indian states like Uttar Pradesh, Madhya Pradesh, Maharashtra. It ranks among the nation's top wheat and rice producers. The dark part of this achievement is for a few weeks in October and November, Punjab also becomes a major producer of air pollution. The main reason for the air pollution during this period is uncontrolled Stubble burning. Stubble burning is among one of the major problems caused by the farmers of Punjab and Haryana which is affecting entire Northern India. Punjab is having two crops growing season i.e. May to September for rice production and November to April for wheat production. Since rice leave behind a significant amount of plant debris which is not even consumed by cattle's so for quickly preparing the agricultural fields for the next crop, the fields are burnt intentionally. This situation becomes extremely hazardous for the nearby states and even for the people of Punjab. The deadly combination of smoke and fog gets converted in smog which is very dangerous for babies, elder peoples and for patients suffering from Asthma. Since the fires are active only for a short period of time and burnt at relatively at low temperatures but the smoke generally stays in the atmosphere. On November 2, 2016, winds carried over smoke, soil particles, dust residue and partially burnt plants towards the National Capital New Delhi. The smoke from the Punjab field combined from industrial pollutants of NCR region and heavy vehicle pollutants of the New Delhi push levels of particulate matter to an extremely high level. Here we are making an investigation in the change that occurred in the texture features of the landcover due to the burning of the crop fields. We have computed the changes in the texture features for different orientations and distances through the Grey level co-occurrence matrix (GLCM). Texture visual features which are the combination of contrast, correlation, energy, and homogeneity are computed. Finally, through the GLCM technique, we are able to identify the number of areas under fire and thus an estimate is performed for the total number of the area under fire. During this research work, three objectives have been achieved firstly change in the texture features is computed secondly the visual representation of the

© Springer Nature Singapore Pte Ltd. 2020
P. K. Singh et al. (Eds.): FTNCT 2019, CCIS 1206, pp. 382–394, 2020.
https://doi.org/10.1007/978-981-15-4451-4_30

changes along with identification of the areas under fire and finally, a comparison of the original and subset image is presented. We have also developed a theoretical approach for texture quantification through GLCM. This approach can be further extended to study various other natural disasters like a landslide, flood, droughts, etc.

Keywords: Stubble burning · Smog · Grey Level Co-occurrence Matrix (GLCM) · Contrast · Correlation · Energy · Homogeneity

1 Introduction

Our country India is an agriculture-based country, the backbone of our country is mainly the farming sector. This sector provides employment opportunities to nearly 50% of the Indian population [1]. Most of the peoples from rural areas are directly or indirectly dependent on agricultural products. We all are aware of the conditions of farmers in our country, they have to work in limited resources. They do not have even proper agricultural tools and machinery and have to adopt old agricultural techniques. Among these techniques, they follow an old method to re-prepare there agriculture land i.e. burning the field so as to destroy the remains and residue of the old crops and prepare their fields for the new crops [2]. In the region of Punjab stubble burning has become a serious problem as in spite of Government restrictions and Supreme Court order during winters farmers keep on following the traditional methods to re-prepare their fields [3]. The outcome of this practice is the dangerous mixing of air pollutants and hazardous gases resulting in the creation of severe health issues mostly for older peoples and younger children [4, 5]. In this research work, we have investigated the changes occurred in the landcover caused due to the stubble burning at a very large scale. Initially texture visual parameters over the entire region are compared with the small region (region of interest) under fire.

The change in the texture visual features results in the development of the novel pattern of texture features for the classification of the land use/land cover. Change estimation is an important area of investigation in the field of remote sensing, several scientists have developed numerous change detection techniques based on application and features [1, 6]. Change detection techniques are classified as pre and post-classification. Similarly, image classification techniques are classified as supervised [7] and unsupervised classification techniques [8, 9]. Here we have used post-classification, unsupervised texture-based change detection techniques [10]. Post classification change detection [11] includes object-based change detection (OBCD) technique in which pre and post images are compared on the basis of classification objects, these objects are classes categorized as water, urban, bare soil, desert, vegetation, hills, mountains, etc., geographical based change detection (GIS) though these technique change maps are created and compared to detect the amount of change occurred in the land use/land cover [12, 13]. Here we have identified the problem of smoke and haze developed due to the stable burning we have monitored the areas and finally applied GLCM based post-classification change detection technique on our study areas. The changes developed in the area are later on quantified and presented.

2 Mathematical Background of Texture Visual Features

Texture based investigation is performed with the assistance of the GLCM based approach [14, 15]. Here texture features are divided into four different categories we are making an investigation based on texture visual features which are a set of four different features. Let an image contains a total of $m \times n$ pixels and the distance between the individual pixel and the pixel of interest is denoted by 'd', then the texture features are defined as gray tone 'i' followed by gray tone 'j' with distance having a relative frequency $p(i,j)$ [16]. Here $p(i,j)$ represents pixel on interest. Mathematical notation for the texture visual features are expressed as follows.

1. Angular second moment (ASM) or Energy

$$fr_1 = \sum_i \sum_j \{p(i,j)\}^2 \tag{1}$$

The range of energy lies in the interval [0–1]. Energy signifies the amount of light re-radiated by the satellite sensor.

2. Contrast

$$fr_2 = \sum_0^{K_g-1} n^2 \left\{ \sum_{i=1}^{K_g} \sum_{J=1}^{K_g} p(i,j) \right\} \tag{2}$$

Where $|i - j| = n$ (difference of gray level pair)
K_g = Number of distinct gray levels in the quantized image.

3. Correlation

$$fr_3 = \sum_i \sum_j \frac{(i,j)p(i,j) - \mu_x \mu_y}{\sigma_x \sigma_y} \tag{3}$$

Here μ_x, σ_x and μ_y, σ_y are the mean and standard deviation of rows and columns respectively.

4. Inverse difference moment (IDM) or Homogeneity

$$fr_5 = \sum_i \sum_j \frac{1}{1 + (i - j)^2} p(i,j) \tag{4}$$

The range for the texture feature homogeneity is [0–1].

3 Study Area

The Indian state of Punjab is a state bordering Pakistan, it is the heart of India's Sikh community. The name Punjab is given to the state because it contains water of five different rivers i.e. Jhelum, Chenab, Ravi, Sutlej, and Beas. It covers a total of

355,591 km² (137,294 sq mi). The geographical location of Punjab is 31.1471°N, 75.3412°E [17]. Punjab experiences three main seasons. Hot Season (mid-April to the end of June), Rainy Season (early July to the end of September) and Cold Season (early December to the end of February [18].

The main variety of crops, vegetables, and fruits grown in the state of Punjab which includes wheat, rice, barley, maize, etc., beside numbers of fruits grown includes oranges, apples, figs, quinces, almonds, pomegranates, peaches, mulberries, apricots and plums [19] (Fig. 1).

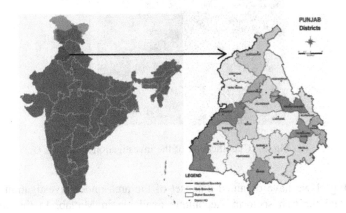

Fig. 1. Geographical location of Punjab in India

4   Experimental Result

In this investigation, we have obtained a Visible Infrared Imaging Radiometer Suite (VIIRS) by the Suomi NPP Satellite. The images obtained are multispectral images providing information about the bands combined together. Figure 2 provides us information about the geographical condition of the study area in the RGB (Red-Green-Blue) format.

Fig. 2. Satellite image of Punjab acquired from Visible Infrared Imaging Radiometer Suite (VIIRS) on the Suomi NPP satellite November 2, 2016 (Color figure online)

In Fig. 3 we can identify the range of the mountainous peak of Himalaya represented in white color. The lower Himalaya peaks are covered with dense forest visible in dark gray color. The area under investigation is represented in an elliptical format. Here we can observe a white patch of smoke, which is actually the dense smoke and dust particles spread over the land cover of Punjab.

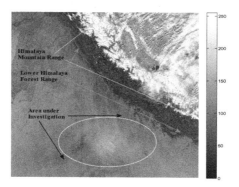

Fig. 3. Classification of the investigation areas

In the Fig. 4 we have obtained a subset of the area under investigation from the original image through sectoring technique available in Matlab. In the area under investigation, we may observe that several areas are under fire are represented through variable red color dots.

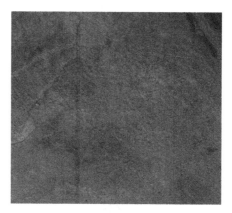

Fig. 4. Subset area under investigation (Color figure online)

Now the greyscale version of the original image is created shown in the Fig. 5(a) which represents several areas in different color compositions. The area under investigation is highlighted with the dotted square.

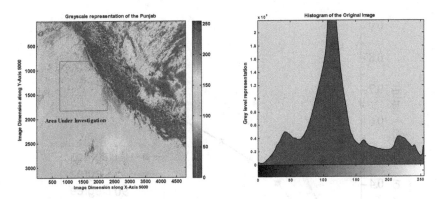

Fig. 5. (a) Greyscale image of the original image (b) Histogram plot of the original image (Color figure online)

Now the histogram of the greyscale image of the original image is plotted shown in Fig. 5(b), the variations in the color and the extent of the plot suggest that several colors are present in the original image which are the result of uniformity in the pixel values. Similarly, it is also concluded that the histogram has obtained the mean value for all the pixels as the graph is centered Now the area under investigation is shown in the Fig. 6(a). The fields which have caught under fire are represented with red squares. The investigation area suggests that around 55–60 areas are under fire. The spread of the yellow color represents the spread of smoke in the investigation area.

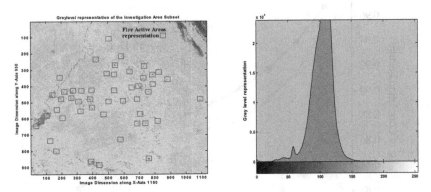

Fig. 6. (a) Greyscale version of the investigation area (b) Histogram of the investigation area (Color figure online)

Now the histogram of the greyscale version of the investigation area is plotted which is shown in Fig. 6(b). Here we can observe that the histogram is unevenly distributed, as the histogram is mostly distributed around the right side of the mean value. The histogram shows that the variation of the color is zero as suggested by the histogram plot. The left side of the histogram shows a slight version in the mean lobe. The overall outcome from the histogram plot is concentrated towards the center only, this happens because of the smoke content in the investigation area. Now the texture

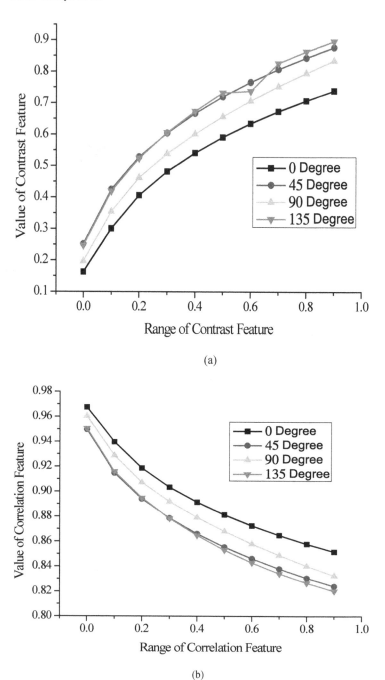

Fig. 7. Variation plot for different orientation angle (a) Contrast (b) Correlation (c) Energy (d) Homogeneity

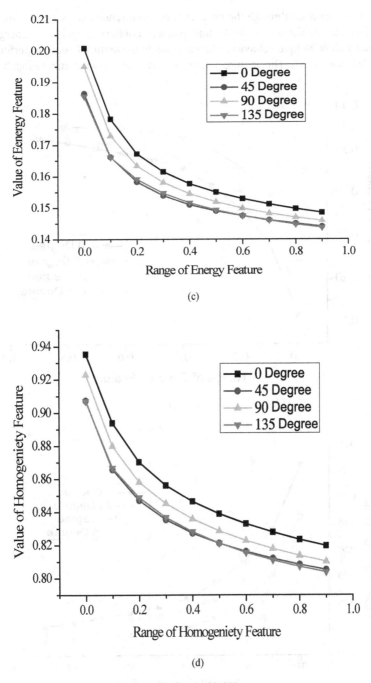

(c)

(d)

Fig. 7. (*continued*)

visual features obtained through the grey level co-occurrence matrix are computed and plotted. Here the variation in the texture features contrast, correlation, energy, and homogeneity show unique behavior. The variation in the texture feature is performed at 0°, 45°, 90° and 135°. The texture feature contrast is showing increasing behavior

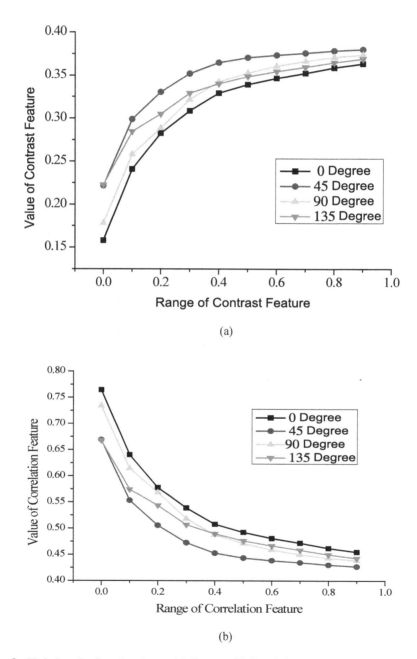

(a)

(b)

Fig. 8. Variation plot for subset image (a) Contrast (b) Correlation (c) Energy (d) Homogeneity

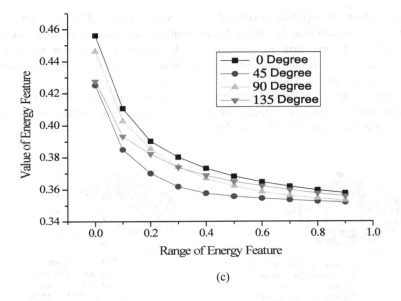

(c)

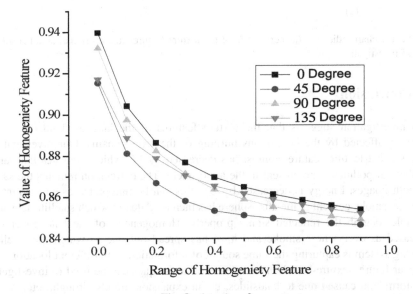

Fig. 8. (*continued*)

towards all the orientation angles shown in Fig. 7(a), whereas correlation, energy, and homogeneity are showing a decrement in their values with every increasing orientation angle shown in Fig. 7(b), 7(c) and 7(d) respectively.

Now the texture features are computed for the subset image under investigation. Texture visual features contrast, correlation, energy, and homogeneity are computed for the subset image. Here the variations in the texture features provide us information about the pattern of variation developed in the subset image. The variation plots provide us information that the texture feature contrast is increasing whereas energy, homogeneity, and correlation are decreasing with increasing orientation angle. The variation plots for increasing contrast and decreasing correlation, energy and homogeneity are shown in Fig. 8(a), 8(b), 8(c) and 8(d) respectively.

Now the average of the GLCM features is obtained so as to make GLCM free from orientation angles, which is followed by the comparison of the individual features between the original and the subset image.

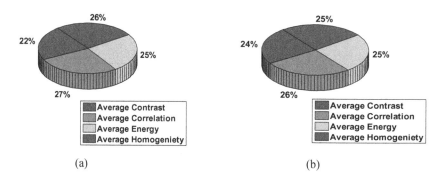

(a)   (b)

Fig. 9. Pie chart indicating (a) percentage of the texture features in the original area (b) subset area of investigation

5   Conclusion

This investigation suggests that the texture features of the land use/land cover are seriously affected by the continuous burning of the crop remains. Our investigation suggests that texture feature contrast has decreased by 1% which indicates that large numbers of pollutants are present in the atmosphere. The correlation remains the same for both images. Energy is decreased by 1%, this can be interpreted as an amount of haze and smoke content in the atmosphere has increased due to which satellite sensor is not able to grab the reflected signal properly. Homogeneity of the land cover has increased as everywhere smoke and haze has spread out due to which the satellite imaging system is capturing the same sought of information from different locations. In the near future, texture-based change detection techniques can be used to investigates transformation caused due to landslides, urban expansion, floods, drought, etc.

Acknowledgment. The authors are thankful to the United States Geological Survey (USGS) and the National Aeronautics and Space Administration (NASA) NASA Earth Observatory for their continuous support in the form of multispectral satellite data.

References

1. Madhusudhan, L.: Agriculture role on indian economy. Bus Eco J. **6**(4), 176 (2015)
2. Singh, J., Singhal, N., Singhal, S., Sharma, M., Agarwal, S., Arora, S.: Environmental implications of rice and wheat stubble burning in North-Western States of India. In: Siddiqui, N.A., Tauseef, S.M., Bansal, K. (eds.) Advances in Health and Environment Safety. STCEE, pp. 47–55. Springer, Singapore (2018). https://doi.org/10.1007/978-981-10-7122-5_6
3. Koshy, J., Vasudeva, V.: Punjab's burning problem. In: Punjab's burning problem. https://www.thehindu.com/news/national/other-states/punjabs-burning-problem/article25339426.ece. Accessed October 2018
4. Poole, J.A., Barnes, C.S., Demain, J.G., Bernstein, J.A.: Impact of weather and climate change with indoor and outdoor air quality in asthma. Journal of Allergy and Clinical Immunology **143**(5), 1702–1710 (2019)
5. Hoang, T., Chu, N., Tran, T.: The environmental pollution in Vietnam: source, impact, and remedies. International Journal of Scientific and Technology Research **6**(2), 249–253 (2017)
6. Shakya, A., Prakash, R., Ramola, A., Pandey, D.: Change detection from pre and post urbanisation LANDSAT 5 ™ multispectral images. In: IEEE, International Conference on Innovations in Control, Communication and Information Systems (ICICCI), Noida NCR India, pp. 1–6 (2017)
7. Shakya, A., Ramola, A., Kandwal, A., Prakash, R.: Comparision of supervised classification techniques with ALOS PALSAR for Roorkee region of Uttarakhand India. In: International Archives of the Photogrammetry, Remote Sensing and Spatial Information Sciences XLII-5(1), pp. 693–701, November 2018
8. Yang, G., Li, H.-C., Wang, W.-Y., Yang, W., Emer, W.: Unsupervised Change Detection Based on a Unified Framework for Weighted Collaborative Representation With RDDL and Fuzzy Clustering, pp. 1–14 (2019)
9. Zhang, F., Du, B., Zhang, L.: Saliency-guided unsupervised feature learning for scene classification. IEEE Trans. Geosci. Remote Sens. **53**(4), 2175–2184 (2015)
10. Shakya, A., Ramola, A., Kandwal, A., Mittal, P., Prakash, R.: Morphological change detection in terror camps of area 1 and 2 by pre and post strike-through MOAB: A. In: Bera R., Sarkar S., Singh O., Saikia H. (eds.) Advances in Communication, Devices and Networking. Lecture Notes in Electrical Engineering, vol 537, pp. 253–263. Springer Nature Singapore, Sikkim, India (2018). https://doi.org/10.1007/978-981-13-3450-4_29
11. Kurt, M.N., Wang, X.: multisensor sequential change detection with unknown change propagation pattern. IEEE Trans. Aerosp. Electron. Syst. **55**(3), 1498–1518 (2019)
12. Ma, L., Jia, Z., Yu, Y., Yang, J., Kasabov, N.: Multi-spectral image change detection based on band selection and single-band iterative weighting, pp. 27948–27956 (2019)
13. Zhang, Y., Peng, D., Huang, X.: Object-based change detection for VHR images based on multiscale uncertainty analysis. IEEE Geosci. Remote Sens. Lett. **15**(1), 13–17 (2018)
14. Park, S., Kim, B., Lee, J., Goo, J., Shin, Y.-G.: GGO nodule volume-preserving nonrigid lung registration using GLCM texture analysis. IEEE Trans. Biomed. Eng. **58**(10), 2885–2894 (2011)
15. Blaschke, T., Feizizadeh, B., Hölbling, D.: Object-based image analysis and digital terrain analysis for locating landslides in the Urmia Lake Basin, Iran. IEEE J. Sel. Top. Appl. Earth Obs. Remote Sens. **7**(12), 4806–4817 (2014)

16. Shakya, A., Ramola, A., Kandwal, A., Mittal, P., Prakash, R.: Morphological change detection in terror camps of area 3 and 4 by pre- and post-strike through MOAB: B. In: Bera, R., Sarkar, S., Singh, O., Saikia, H. (eds.) Advances in Communication, Devices and Networking. Lecture Notes in Electrical Engineering, vol. 537, pp. 265–275. Springer, Singapore (2019). https://doi.org/10.1007/978-981-13-3450-4_30
17. Government, P.: Punjab fin_budget_speech_e_2017_18. Government of Punjab (2018)
18. Punjab, G. In: Government of Punjab (Official). http://www.punjab.gov.in/. Accessed March 2019
19. Singh, J.: Overview of the electric power potential of surplus agricultural biomass from economic, social, environmental and technical perspective—a case study of Punjab. Renew. Sustain. Energy Rev. **42**(1), 286–297 (2015)

Storytelling Data Visualization for Grievances Management System

Anurag Singh Chaudhary[(✉)] and Anuja Arora

Computer Science Department, Jaypee Institute of Information Technology,
Noida, India
Anuragchaudhary004@gmail.com, Anuja.arora29@gmail.com

Abstract. The City Grievance Management system is all about collecting complaints from citizen and presenting it to the authorities responsible for decision making. Grievances/complaints have to be visualized in an explanatory manner to understand it in an effective manner. Visualization plays a big role in any dashboard and also to know insights of content from a broad perspective. Some visualization fails to be informative and does not explain the context of problems. Even, all problems need different representations and couldn't be projected in terms of bar charts and pie charts. The wrong direction of projection may mislead the user. In the current scenario, companies are becoming data driven which has raised the need to extract valuable insights from the humongous amount of data. In this paper, the Gestalt principle is used to design the visualizations for the grievances. The principles are based on human perception of similarity, the law of closure, proximity, connectedness and law of continuity. The study also deals with choosing the right type of visualization over specific objectives of complaints and how to tell a story out of grievances.

Keywords: Gestalt principle · Visualization · Storytelling · Grievances

1 Introduction

The world is moving towards the smart cities and undoubtedly, one of the prime factors of smart cities is its citizens. These citizens voice out their concerns, problems [6], and interact with the government through grievances. Varied amount of open data related to these interactions is available by the government authorities at various repositories such as Data.gov.in. Out of all available government data, Citizens' grievances should be analyzed in a better way by understanding the exhaustive details of the process. Analysis of the complaints data is itself a task in order to get insights of this data and present a clear depiction of work. Samonte et al. has designed a framework to develop a web application to support National Advisory committee of Philippines. Their proposed visualization tool will help government to making useful decisions for poor Filipino families [10]. Indian population is so much that it makes it really hard to look at each complaint with human intervention. The Data Visualization plays a key role in any dashboard and inside that storytelling visualizations are required to understand the problem quickly without too much brainstorming effort. Even, social media sites contain enormous amount of public grievances data which can be used in order to form

© Springer Nature Singapore Pte Ltd. 2020
P. K. Singh et al. (Eds.): FTNCT 2019, CCIS 1206, pp. 395–405, 2020.
https://doi.org/10.1007/978-981-15-4451-4_31

government policies. In 2019, Hossain et al. mined Kolkata Traffic Police Facebook page data which contains traffic alerts and public grievances. This mined data is in form of unstructured data, so efforts in this paper have been made to transform it to structured data. Further, visualization of data and summarization is presented in an effective manner [11]. The work presented in this paper is an extension of Hussain et al. work and methods have been proposed to visualize data efficiently to exhibit knowledge from data. This study presented in this research paper revolves around three points:

- An interactive Selecting and understanding the dataset;
- Finding the right state-of-art approach to draw visualization and use cases of apps and packages of information visual illustrations.
- This study also derives how to use statistics in an engaging manner so that the user interacts with the charts and infographics.

The study illustrates which type of visual works is suitable for what type of dataset. Even, different types of visualization techniques and charts are also discussed in order to get familiar with storytelling context. Open data is easy to access, especially the ones provided by the government. It is good to analyze the future aspects of the open data and the possibilities of it. In this piece of work, Authors have taken in account the four models of open data to showcase the dynamic bond between the government and the residents. It basically involves the government data publish, data objector, tracker for issues and participatory open data. The open data has been analyzed keeping in mind the motivations of open data, the dynamic image of government as providing service, the vulnerable nature of open data. Even, future of open data between government body, residents and users using private sector data is also predicted and explored [5]. Even, Public agencies use twitter to share information and to announce information through post. Researchers have used NLP technique for text enrichment process and further ensemble classifiers have been used to formulate the solution of complaints identification [12]. In 2017, Swati et al. focused on two aspects: awareness among public and bring government attention towards issues; and categorization of complains those needed immediate action/response from the authorities [13]. This work is also a combination of Natural language processing and machine learning platform.

This study illustrates the narration via visualizations and further the techniques used in this process is classified in to four categories, first communicating narrative and explaining the data via Textual narratives, audio narration, labeling, flowchart arrows, text annotations, tooltips & element highlighting. Second technique linking separated story elements via linking element through interaction, color and animation. The Third technique deals in enhancing structure and the navigation with adding next and previous buttons, scrolling, section header buttons, menu selection, geographic maps and timeline and the last fourth technique providing controlled exploration with the help of dynamic queries and embedded exploratory visualizations [6, 7]. This research illustrates about the flow visualizations the research revolves around the color maps/perception and the uncertain visualizations. The author discusses the vector visualizations and the techniques to improve the visualizations with verification and validation in general to understand the cognitive process behind data visualization [1]. The study describes the importance of graphs in in scientific research and to focus on two principles clear vision and clear understanding while designing visualizations that easily removes the flows. The study also focuses on matrix graphs, visualization publishing formats and printing resolutions. The authors take a dig how peer review of visualization adds to innovation in design [2].

Visualization and Analysis of data has become challenging due to every second data post on social media and even in enormous volume. So, researchers worked on the visualization of social media data in form of network. Even structural patterns have been infused with the help of visualization and analysis of social media content [8]. Influence indexing of developers and coding repositories on coding portal github has also been identified using visualization and data analysis [9]. Effective visualization of content can help to resolve problems accurately. The author developed a new data visualization literacy DVL framework that is used to define, teach and assess Data visualization [3]. The framework explains how to understand and construct visualization also to pair reading and writing literacy with mathematical equations, this framework defines the steps to extract insights from data visualization. This piece of work elaborates the emotional engagement of visualization, the components that make sense of data and people first try to relate the data through mathematical equations. This study explains rather than statistically how emotional relation with data is being observed as emotions plays a vital role in making interactive data visualization [4]. The interactive data visualization has the power to directly pass the information and affects the decision making. The contribution of this research paper is as follows:

- Visualization of Geolocation based problem location mapping is depicted
- Effective presentation of Complaints and Employee Analytics
- Efficiently present category wise complain frequency and complex complain.
- Showcase the best visualization to present severity of complains.

The paper is structured in the following manner – This same section discussed about introduction and literature studied to perform the experiments. Section 2 discusses the methodology and tools used in this work which is followed by Sect. 3. This section discusses the analysis and visualization work done to provide a storytelling grievances management system. Finally, concluding remark is discussed in Sect. 4.

2 Methodology and Tools Used

The visualization methodology which is constructed in this work is designed by keeping few steps in mind. These steps are as follows:

2.1 Data Understanding

Understanding the context of data and situation before implementing and designing visualization is important. First of all understand the audience to which you have to communicate the information visualization.

2.2   Visualization Selection

Choose your visualization, there are various ways to showcase data rather than bar, pie and donut. Select the effective visuals that fulfill the requirement of audience.

2.3   Data Importance Using Gestalt Principle

Everything that you add in your graphs and charts takes space whether it is text or shape, identify the details that are taking too much brain power to understand. Therefore, choose carefully what you have to show in your visuals, remove the unnecessary details using Gestalt principles. Gestalt gave 6 laws of visual perception also known as gestalt principles. Principle of Proximity: It states that objects and shapes that are close to one another appear to form groups even if shapes, sizes, and objects are radically different, they will appear as a single group. Elements that are grouped together creates illusion of shapes. Grouping can be done with size, color, shape & value. Principle of Similarity: Our brain uses similarity to distinguish between objects which might lie adjacent to or overlap with each other based upon their visual texture. Principle of Closure: It states Human mind's tendency to see complete figures even if it is incomplete. The reaction stems from our human mind's natural tendency to recognize patterns that are missing. Principle of Good Continuation: When there is an intersection between two or more objects we tend to perceive each object as a single uninterrupted object. This allows differentiation of stimuli even when they come in visual overlap. Human mind have a tendency to group and organize shapes and curves. Principle of common fate: It states that when visual objects are moving in same direction with same rate it is perceived that each object is a part of the whole movement. It is used in user-interface design. Principle of good form: The principle states that the tendency to group together the similar pattern, similar color and shape. used in Olympic rings.

2.4   Designing Strategies

Focus on shapes, color, position and size of visuals on the page because these things have direct impact on audience. Learn to use the color as a strategic tool.

2.5   Label Generation

Effectively use the labels and titles and annotate as possible. Use legends only where necessary do not hamper user with unnecessary details in the visualization. Although the process described in this paper is independent of the tools but in our designing process followings have been explored-Google MyMaps for maps visualization and JavaScript framework D3.js popularly known as Data Driven Documents for plots. To process the raw data, we have used python programming language to preprocess the data with the help of packages such as numpy, pandas, Geopandas, etc.

3 Grievances Management System Analysis and Visualization Outcome

Two different datasets were used in this paper. First dataset contains complaints related to poor voice quality reported to the TRAI in the year 2018 of the months may, June, July and august[1]. The second dataset is of complaints of city grievances management system[2].

3.1 Geo-Coordinates Based Complaints Visualization

This visualization deals with plotting the Geo Coordinates on Maps using the latitude and longitude values. The purpose of this Geo-mapping is to map the complaints on the map that gives insights that which region is facing same type of complaints.

Figures 1 and 2 shows the complaints of poor voice quality for the Month of May and June respectively. An interactive interface is required for authorities to map out the various locations facing complaints. For visualization of same complaints for different month we have used different symbol so that if we plot all the complaints on a single map, audience can directly identify the difference between complaints. Hence, the user interaction won't be hampered to distinguish between complaints

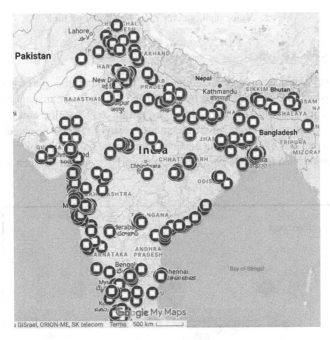

Fig. 1. Voice quality complaints for MAY month

---

[1] Voice call quality customer experience 2018 https://data.gov.in/catalog/voice-call-quality-customer-experience.

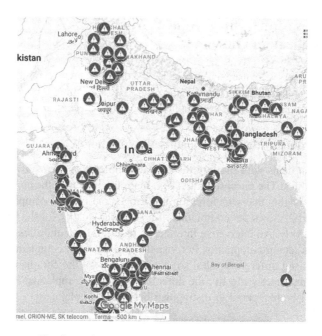

Fig. 2. Voice quality complaints for month of June

3.2   Employees Analytics

The Objective behind this visualization is to understand the performance of an employee to which the grievances has been assigned. In grievance management system, grievances are assigned to employees based on employee's specific area and category of complaint. The visualization depicts and maps the no of open & resolved complaints of each employee. It is clearly visible that every employee has been projected as a circle of equal shape but inside circles depends upon the no of complaints open and resolved (See Fig. 3).

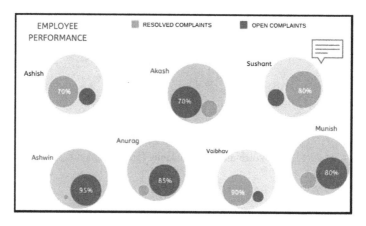

Fig. 3. Employee performance (Color figure online)

The employees who have maximum no of complaints opened there circles are overall red colored. Here, the color gives the indication that these employees are underperforming. So out of this visualization, performance can be inferred easily without too much brainstorming.

3.3 Complaint Analytics

The objective behind complaint visualization is to showcase the number of complaints across various categories and their status. In this three separate parameters need to map out and portray in a single visualization (See Fig. 4). These three parameters are complaint count, complaint category, and status of the complaint. Henceforth, the category vs. status graph shows the exact no of complaints with category and status. Also complaints are mapped based on weekly, Monthly and Yearly schedule.

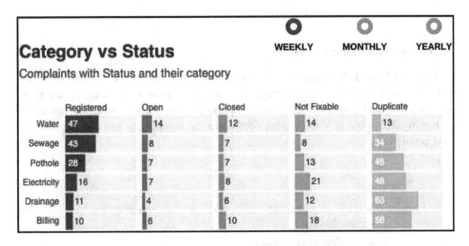

Fig. 4. Complaints category vs. status

3.4 Complaints Frequency

The objective behind this visualization is to analyze the days and time of the week when maximum complaints are registered. For that, we first started with scattered plot with the size of bubble dependent on no of complaints, bigger the size shows increase in no of complaints (see Fig. 5). The axis scales are drawn in terms of days of the week and time of the day. Labels are also placed to show the most active time of the day and most active day of the week.

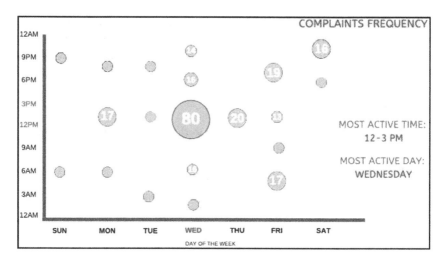

Fig. 5. Complaints frequency: day and Time

3.5   Complaints Remained Open

The intention behind this visualization is to analyze the category of complaint which remained open for maximum no of days. So context is to show the category and no of days the complaint remained open in comparison with other complaints categories (see Fig. 6). This kind of visualization showcases the complexity and solving scenario of the problem.

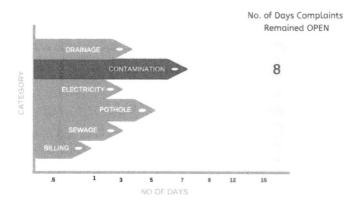

Fig. 6. Complaints open with category

3.6   Complaint Remained Open Inside Category

This is basically the sub part of the visualization to extract the exact no. of complaints remained open inside a particular category. Here, the axis labels changed to number of date vs. complaint id. Focus is towards the red color which is used as a strategic tool to map out maximum open complaints detail (Fig. 7).

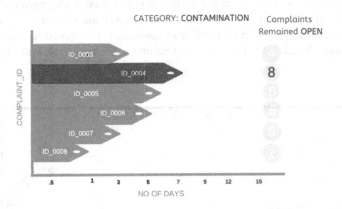

Fig. 7. Complaints Open inside category (Color figure online)

3.7 Re-opened Complaint

The intention behind this visualization is to demonstrate the number of complaints which are reopened across various categories. So, the thought process to construct this visualization was to understand that how to show the number in comparison with total complaints. Percentage of reopened complaints is used to showcase this where category wise reopened complaints are depicted with respect to total number of complaints. The reopened complaints with reference to total number of complaints are showcased so that short term memory of brain directly calculates the difference between the total complaints and reopened complaints. And we have used the inverted pyramid to describe the percentage of reopened complaints with category, higher the no of complaints directly proportional to the size of block as shown in Fig. 8.

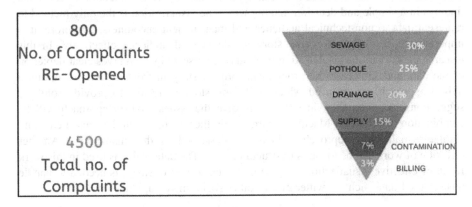

Fig. 8. Number of re-opened complaints with category

3.8   Complaints with Severity

This objective of this information visualization is to find out the no of complaints which have high severity. The same principle which is used in reopened complaints is used here for visualization. To showcase the sever companies is not enough. Severity of complain with respect to total number of complaints is required to present a clear picture. Donut chart is used to show the percentage of complaints with high severity (Fig. 9).

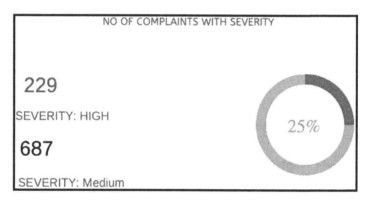

Fig. 9. Complaints with severity ratio

4   Concluding Remark

Undoubtedly, Number of tools are available which makes designing charts and showcasing data an easy task. Whereas conveying your story with right type of visuals, numbers required iterations, and some brainstorming is challenging issue. In this Empirical process, we have understood the fact that we cannot use same chart in each and every visualization to convey our message to audience. The visualizations should be explanatory rather than exploratory. In the process of data science people pay too much attention to the data and algorithms but forgot to give the attention to show the findings in a simple and decision making way. The visualization is the only method to represent data to non-technical audience and management encounters. Therefore, it is important process to convey the story to the general audience effectively. In this research paper, various visualization methods are presented which gives clear depiction of the data and showcase the problem in form of story in front of user. In future, a hybrid approach can be used which will form story of results to provide solution/ suggestions to government in order to resolve the issues. Hybrid approach will be combination of NLP and Machine Learning. Further, solution can be presented using similar visualization approaches those are described in this manuscript. Another direction of work can be towards unstructured data. The data which is used in this work for draw effective visualization is structured data, so improvement is needed to handle unstructured data such as twitter or any other social media application.

References

1. Etiene, T., Nguyen, H., Kirby, R.M., Silva, C.T.: Flow visualization juxtaposed with "visualization of flow": synergistic opportunities between two communities. In: Proceedings of 51st AIAA Aerospace Science Meeting, New Horizon Forum Aerospace Exp, pp. 1–13 (2013)
2. Boers, M.: Designing effective graphs to get your message across. Ann. Rheum. Dis. **77**(6), 833–839 (2018)
3. Börner, K., Bueckle, A., Ginda, M.: Data visualization literacy: definitions, conceptual frameworks, exercises, and assessments. Proc. Natl. Acad. Sci. **116**(6), 1857–1864 (2019)
4. Kennedy, H., Hill, R.L.: The feeling of numbers: emotions in everyday engagements with data and their visualisation. Sociology **52**(4), 830–848 (2018)
5. Sieber, R.E., Johnson, P.A.: Civic open data at a crossroads: dominant models and current challenges. Government information quarterly **32**(3), 308–315 (2015)
6. Saxena, S.: Significance of open government data in the GCC countries. Digital Policy Regul. Governance **19**(3), 251–263 (2017)
7. Stolper, C.D., Lee, B., Riche, N.H., Stasko, J.: Data-driven storytelling techniques: analysis of a curated collection of visual stories. In: Data-Driven Storytelling, pp. 85–105. AK Peters/CRC Press, Natick (2018)
8. Aggrawal, N., Arora, A.: Visualization, analysis and structural pattern infusion of DBLP co-authorship network using Gephi. In: 2016 2nd International Conference on Next Generation Computing Technologies (NGCT), pp. 494–500. IEEE, October 2016
9. Bana, R., Arora, A.: Influence indexing of developers, repositories, technologies and programming languages on social coding community GitHub. In: 2018 Eleventh International Conference on Contemporary Computing (IC3), pp. 1–6. IEEE, August 2018
10. Samonte, M.J., Bal, T.G., Recio, Z.N., San Jose, R.M.: Conditional cash transfer data analysis of the Philippines: an e-government data visualization tool. In: 2018 International Conference on Information and Communication Technology Convergence (ICTC), pp. 783–788. IEEE, October 2018
11. Hossain, M.A., Daga, R., Goswami, S., Chakrabarti, S.: Study of social media activity of local traffic police department: their posting nature, interaction, and reviews of the public. In: Mandal, J.K., Sinha, D., Bandopadhyay, J.P. (eds.) Contemporary Advances in Innovative and Applicable Information Technology. AISC, vol. 812, pp. 221–235. Springer, Singapore (2019). https://doi.org/10.1007/978-981-13-1540-4_22
12. Mittal, N., Agarwal, S., Sureka, A.: Got a complaint?- Keep calm and tweet it! In: Li, J., Li, X., Wang, S., Li, J., Sheng, Quan Z. (eds.) ADMA 2016. LNCS (LNAI), vol. 10086, pp. 619–635. Springer, Cham (2016). https://doi.org/10.1007/978-3-319-49586-6_44
13. Agarwal, S., Sureka, A.: Investigating the role of twitter in e-Governance by extracting information on citizen complaints and grievances reports. In: Reddy, P.K., Sureka, A., Chakravarthy, S., Bhalla, S. (eds.) BDA 2017. LNCS, vol. 10721, pp. 300–310. Springer, Cham (2017). https://doi.org/10.1007/978-3-319-72413-3_21

Susceptibility Assesment of Changes Developed in the Landcover Caused Due to the Landslide Disaster of Nepal from Multispectral LANDSAT Data

Amit Kumar Shakya[1]([⊠]), Ayushman Ramola[1], Anchal Kashyap[2],
Dai Van Pham[3], and Anurag Vidyarthi[2]

[1] Department of Electronics and Communication Engineering, Sant Longowal
Institute of Engineering and Technology, Sangrur, Punjab, India
xlamitshakya.gate2014@ieee.org
[2] Department of Electronics and Communication Engineering,
Graphic Era (Deemed to be University), Dehradun, Uttarakhand, India
[3] Department of Electronics and Communication Engineering,
Institute of Materials Sciences, Vietnam Academy of Science and Technology,
Hanoi, Vietnam

Abstract. In this research work the number of changes developed in the land
use/land cover is investigated that got developed in the mountainous region of
Nepal due to the Landslide disasters that occurred in the month of June 2013.
The multispectral satellite data is obtained from the United States Geological
Survey (USGS) through the Landsat 8 satellite. The data represents the multispectral images before and after the landslide disasters. Here we have used a
post-classification change detection texture-based technique to quantify the
number of changes that got developed in the value of the feature. The pre
landslide and post landslide images are converted into gray-level images. The
features value is computed and quantified through a grey level co-occurrence
matrix-based technique. The pre landslide and post landslide images are compared for the texture features varying from 0° to 135° having a step size of 45°.
This research work showcases the possibility of using a texture-based change
detection technique for quantifying natural disasters like landslides. The process
can be further extended to identify and quantify events other than landslides like
flood, drought, soil moisture retrieval.

Keywords: Landslide · Multispectral images · Grey level co-occurrence
matrix · Texture features

1 Introduction

21st Century is the era of rapid industrial development and urbanization. These
objectives are very dangerous from the point of view of environmental stability as rapid
changes in the surrounding area affecting our nature in an adverse manner. Disasters are
classified into two broad category natural disasters and manmade disasters. Volcanic
eruption, landslide, floods, earthquakes are natural disasters but they are somehow

© Springer Nature Singapore Pte Ltd. 2020
P. K. Singh et al. (Eds.): FTNCT 2019, CCIS 1206, pp. 406–418, 2020.
https://doi.org/10.1007/978-981-15-4451-4_32

influenced by human activities like deforestation for urban expansion and for agriculture purposes. Field burning for the cause of rapid agriculture production. These selfish motives are increasing the content of carbon dioxide and carbon monoxide which are constantly increasing global warming. Landslides occur due to the loss of binding force between trees and ground and this occurs due to uncontrolled deforestation in the mountainous regions. Due to this human activity trees lost their control over the soil and get uprooted due to heavy rainfall and during another natural calamity. Pradhan et al. [1] use data acquired from the Quickbird satellite images for the landslide detection Bukit Antarabangsa, Ulu Klang, Malaysia they have obtained the overall accuracy of 90.06% for data classification and 0.84 as kappa coefficient. Dou et al. [2] developed an automatic approach for landside detection using an object-based image analysis method and genetic algorithm approach. Their result shows good accuracy when compared with the traditional maximum likelihood classification technique. Plank et al. [3] investigated the change developed in the vegetation area through optical and polarimetric SAR data. They applied their developed methodology in Charleston, West Virginia, USA and Bolshaya Tilda, Russia. Gorsevski et al. [4] investigated the cause of the landslide in the Ohio State of USA. They used LiDAR data and artificial neural network-based approach in their investigation. He et al. [5] developed a landslide detection model based on the weakly supervised autoregressive model. They have obtained a finding where their method shows more promising results as compared with the traditional methods. Bo et al. [6] developed a landslide detection method based on image saliency their investigation area includes valley region of Kathmandu Nepal and Guangzhou Province, China. Geertsema et al. [7] developed a landslide detection method for the sensitive clay present in Lakelse lake Canada. So in the field of Landslide detection through remote sensing images, a lot of research works are going on. Reichenbach et al. [8] reviewed various statistical methods for texture classification they have used various landslide events that occurred in various parts of the world especially in countries like Italy, China, India, Turkey, and few in Africa, and South America. There study provided that various methods for texture classification of diasters include neural network analysis, logistic regression, data-overlay, index-based and weight of evidence analyses. Braun et al. [9] developed landslide detection techniques using data mining methods to monitor changes developed in landslide-prone areas of Honduras. Huang et al. [10] used optical satellite images of different time intervals to monitor the changes developed in the landslide-prone areas. They used the NDVI technique to monitor the changes in the green landcover and later used spatiotemporal context (STC) model to predict the change in the landcover caused due to landslides. Mondini et al. [11] used Sentinel 1 satellite data for detecting landslide caused in the mountainous regions. The rapid snow melting result in the development of the landslide which is predicted by the Mondini approach. Konishi et al. [12] studied the case of Kii Peninsula Japan using COSMO Skymed images. There investigated landslide images using polarization backscattering and intensity difference occurred in the satellite images. Uemoto [13] used pre and post landslide X band SAR data to compute the number of differences developed in the landslide area under investigation using satellite data. They compared pre and post landslide images on the basis of their kappa values and classification accuracy. Lu et al. [14] used object-based change detection techniques for the mapping of landslide-prone areas using multitemporal image analysis. Wang [15] used dual-receiver and phase difference measurement techniques for landslide detection they did not perform any field visit but implemented their developed algorithm to illustrate this technique. Lei et al. [16] used a novel technique for landslide area mapping named "fully convolutional network within pyramid pooling (FCN-PP)" over conventional mapping techniques.

2   Mathematical Representation of the Texture Features

Here we have obtain first-order statistical parameters like mean, standard deviation, entropy for the original image and its grey version, for the texture classification purpose we have used second-order statistical parameters like contrast, energy, homogeneity, and correlation features and on the basis of these we have obtained changes that got developed in the features before and after the landslide. Now first-order statistical features include meaning, variance, and standard deviation but first-order features do not provide any sufficient information about the values of the features thus second-order statistical features come into existence which is the combination of energy, contrast, correlation, and homogeneity.

The mathematical representation of the feature is represented with the assistance of Eq. (1) to Eq. (7). Let an image contain pixels $p(i, j)$ ranging from $0 \leq i \leq N - 1$ and $0 \leq j \leq N - 1$. Where N represents the total numbers of pixels

1. **Mean:** It is defined as the ratio of the individual image pixel to the total number of pixels contained in an image.

$$\mu = \frac{1}{N} \sum_{i=0}^{N-1} x_i = \frac{(x_0 + x_1 \pm - - - + x_{N-1})}{N} \tag{1}$$

2. **Standard deviation:** It is a measure of the depressiveness of the image pixel value with respect to the mean value.

$$\sigma^2 = \frac{1}{N-1} \sum_{i=0}^{N-1} (x_i - \mu)^2 \tag{2}$$

3. **Entropy:** It is the measure of the intensity value of the image pixels, through this feature image details can also be obtained.

$$H(x) = - \sum_{x \in X} p(x).\log p(x) \tag{3}$$

4. **Contrast:** It is the measure of the difference between the image pixels so that it is easy to get distinguished. The range of contrast is always greater than zero. A zero contrast value represents a constant image.

$$\sum_{i,j=0}^{N-1} P(i,j)(i-j)^2 \tag{4}$$

5. **Correlation:** It is the representation of how well image pixels are related to each other. The value of the correlation is $[-1, 1]$.

$$\sum_{i,j=0}^{N-1} P(i,j) \frac{(i-\mu)(j-\mu)}{\sigma^2} \tag{5}$$

6. **Energy:** It can be expressed as "brightness" and "intensity". The range of energy is always greater than zero.

$$\sum_{i,j=0}^{N-1} P(i,j)^2 \tag{6}$$

7. **Homogeneity:** It is the measure of how well image pixels are arranged along with each other. The range of homogeneity is always is $[0, 1]$.

$$\sum_{i,j=0}^{N-1} \frac{p(i,j)}{1+(i-j)^2} \tag{7}$$

3   Study Area

Nepal is a Himalayan country which included parts in Indo-Gangetic Plain. It is having a total area of 147,181 km^2 and holds 2.8% of the world's total water share. The geographical coordinates of the Kathmandu Nepal are 27°46′N 85°16′E. The total area of the country is 51 km^2 (20 sq mi). Due to its mountainous location, the Kingdom of Nepal is very prone to landslides, avalanche, winter storms, etc. So we have obtained two multispectral satellite images of landslides from Kathmandu region of Nepal acquired from United States Geological Survey (USGS). The multispectral images are acquired from the operational land imager sensor installed on Landsat 8 which is currently operational.

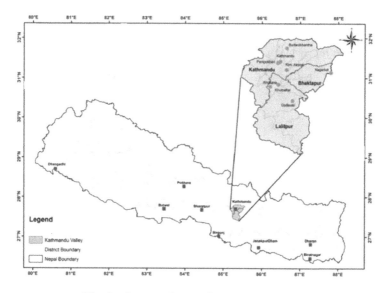

Fig. 1. Geotagged map of the study area [23]

Figure 2 represents the various optical images of the real-time Landslides disasters that occurred in Nepal during different time intervals.

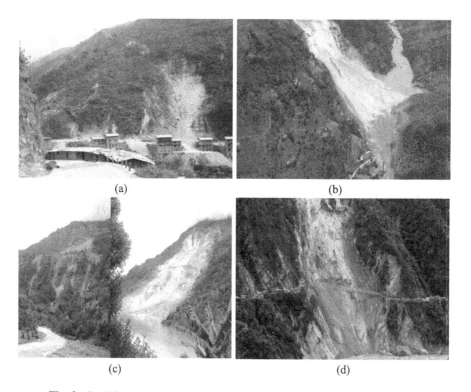

Fig. 2. Real time landslide diasters in Nepal (a) [17] (b) [18] (c) [19] (d) [20]

4   Experimental Results

Change quantification is important from the point of mathematical analysis. If quantification is available then it can be easily identified what amount of change has developed in which visual features. This can be set as standard for e.g. If contrast has increased and energy, homogeneity, and correlation get decreased then this can be considered as a standard for landslide events, we have identified several landslide cases and mathematically applied this technique on several cases and obtain the same sought pattern. Here we are presenting a single case of landslide disaster occurred in Nepal, change quantification is performed and later a pattern is established in the visual features.

The multispectral pre landslide Landsat data and post landslide data are represented in terms of images shown in the Fig. 3(a) and (b) respectively.

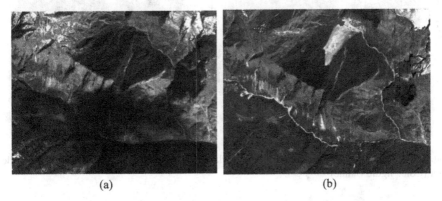

(a)   (b)

Fig. 3. Landsat data of the investigation area (a) Pre Landslide (b) Post Landslide

The pre landslide image is converted to a greyscale image and the value of the feature is obtained for the image shown in Fig. 4(a). Figure 4(b) represents the area under investigation which is the place where landslide occurs.

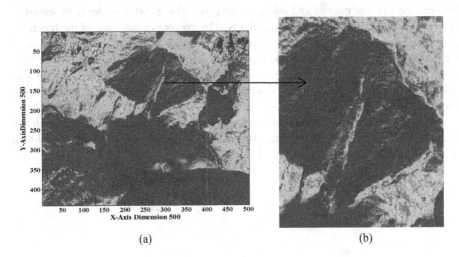

(a)   (b)

Fig. 4. (a) Grey level representation of the pre landslide area (b) Subset image of the area under investigation

The post landslide image is similarly converted to a greyscale image shown in Fig. 5(a). Figure 5(b) represents the area where landslide occurs the landslide area is detected in intense red color.

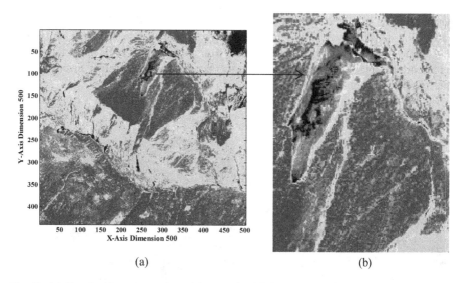

(a)   (b)

Fig. 5. (a) Grey level representation of the post landslide area (b) Subset image of the landslide area (Color figure online)

The texture features are computed for the pre and post landslide images through the grey level co-occurrence matrix (GLCM) technique. In this technique, the GLCM features are computed for four different directions i.e. 0, 45, 90 and 135°. The detailed information about the GLCM can be obtained from [21, 22]. While calculating features value through GLCM it is also recommended to choose the best possible distance between the pixel of interest and initial image pixel. These distances are represented as D = 1, D = 2, D = 3, and D = 4 respectively. The average of the value of the feature is performed so as to make the GLCM direction independent. Firstly we have calculated the GLCM for pre and post landslide image and afterward, we have calculated the first-order statistical parameter for the pre and post landslide images. Tables 1 and 3 represents the values of the features whereas Tables 2 and 4 represents the first-order statistical features value.

Now the average of the GLCM features are obtained and pre and post landslide features values are compared with each other to obtain the amount of change developed in the texture features shown in Fig. 8.

Table 1. Change in the second-order parameter value for pre landslide

S. No	Distance	0°	45°	90°	135°	Total
1	D = 1	0.5132	0.8282	1.0210	1.1720	3.5344
2		0.9239	0.8772	0.8487	0.8263	3.4761
3		0.1375	0.1229	0.1168	0.1125	0.4897
4		0.8362	0.7936	0.7734	0.7585	3.1617
5	D = 2	0.6167	0.9134	1.1146	1.2717	3.9164
6		0.9085	0.8637	0.8346	0.8112	3.4180
7		0.1308	0.1192	0.1128	0.1085	0.4713
8		0.8176	0.7807	0.7602	0.7457	3.1042
9	D = 3	0.4453	0.7693	0.9897	1.1697	3.3740
10		0.9340	0.8858	0.8531	0.8263	3.4992
11		0.1380	0.1217	0.1147	0.1096	0.4840
12		0.8422	0.7948	0.7717	0.7550	3.1637
13	D = 4	0.6584	1.0481	1.3107	1.5228	4.5400
14		0.9024	0.8445	0.8054	0.7738	3.3261
15		0.1282	0.1151	0.1079	0.1027	0.4539
16		0.8126	0.7706	0.7470	0.7298	3.0600

Table 2. Change in the first-order parameter for Original and Grey pre landslide image

S. No	Parameters	Original image	Grey image	Difference
1	Mean	69.9457	71.0536	1.1079
2	Standard deviation	57.7694	58.0331	0.2637
3	Entropy	7.4120	7.3463	−0.0657

Table 3. Change in the second-order parameter value for post landslide

S. No	Distance	0°	45°	90°	135°	Total
1	D = 1	0.5214	0.8818	1.1062	1.2688	3.7782
2		0.8773	0.7922	0.7392	0.7006	3.1093
3		0.1372	0.1188	0.1120	0.1070	0.4750
4		0.8238	0.7751	0.7531	0.7367	3.0887
5	D = 2	0.6435	1.0198	1.2477	1.4080	4.3190
6		0.8484	0.7594	0.7052	0.6670	2.9800
7		0.1289	0.1146	0.1079	0.1038	0.4552
8		0.8634	0.7608	0.7388	0.7239	3.0869
9	D = 3	0.4942	0.8282	1.0517	1.2177	3.5918
10		0.8837	0.8049	0.7521	0.7127	3.1534
11		0.1352	0.1186	0.1112	0.1062	0.4712
12		0.8232	0.7770	0.7540	0.7378	3.0920

(*continued*)

Table 3. (*continued*)

S. No	Distance	0°	45°	90°	135°	Total
13	D = 4	0.6435	1.0198	1.2477	1.4080	4.3190
14		0.8484	0.7594	0.7052	0.6670	2.9800
15		0.1289	0.1146	0.1079	0.1038	0.4552
16		0.8034	0.7608	0.7388	0.7239	3.0269

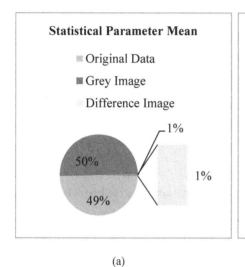

(a)

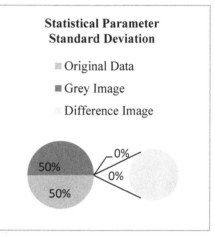

(b)

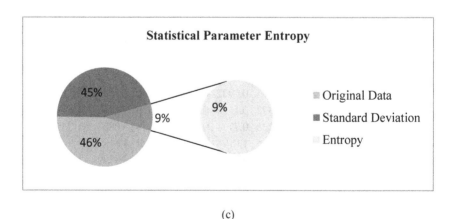

(c)

Fig. 6. Pie chart indicating percentage change in pre landslide statistical features (a) Mean (b) Standard deviation (c) Entropy

Table 4. Change in the first-order parameter for Original and Grey post landslide image

S. No	Parameters	Original image	Grey image	Difference
1	Mean	82.5647	85.7988	3.2341
2	Standard deviation	46.2749	47.6246	1.3497
3	Entropy	7.3151	7.2457	−0.00694

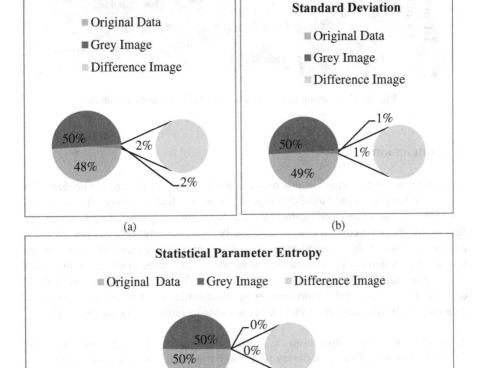

(a)   (b)

(c)

Fig. 7. Pie chart indicating percentage change in post landslide statistical features (a) Mean (b) Standard deviation (c) Entropy

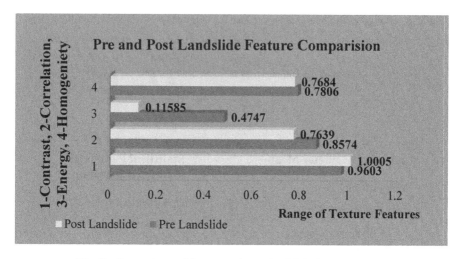

Fig. 8. Comparison of the pre and post landslide features values

5   Conclusion

The investigation performed in this research work represents the change developed in the texture features of the landslide images. The texture feature contrast has developed a 4.18% positive change, the correlation has a 10.90% negative change, energy has developed 75.73% negative change and finally, homogeneity has developed 1.562% negative change. This changing pattern can be identified as a standard pattern for the texture classification of the landslides. The important advantage of this technique is that it can be applied to various other cases of remote sensing field like urbanization, flood, drought studies. One of the shortcomings of this technique is it is applicable to optical data only with SAR data the technique is not able to produce convincing results.

Acknowledgment. The author wishes to express sincere thanks to NASA Earth Observatory and the United States Geological Survey (U.S.G.S) for the multispectral Landsat images of the landslide in the Himalayan region of Nepal.

References

1. Pradhan, B., Jebur, M., Shafir, H., Tehrany, M.: Data fusion technique using wavelet transform and taguchi methods for automatic landslide detection from airborne laser scanning data and quickbird satellite imagery. IEEE Trans. Geosci. Remote Sens. **54**(3), 1610–1622 (2016)
2. Dou, J., et al.: Automatic case-based reasoning approach for landslide detection: integration of object-oriented image analysis and a genetic algorithm. MDPI Remote Sens. **7**, 4318–4342 (2015)

3. Plank, S., Twelve, A., Martinis, S.: Landslide mapping in vegetated areas using change detection based on optical and polarimetric SAR data. MDPI Remote Sens. 8(4), 1–20 (2016)

4. Gorsevski, P.V., Brown, M.K., Panter, K., Onasch, C.M., Simic, A., Snyder, J.: Landslide detection and susceptibility mapping using LiDAR and an artificial neural network approach: a case study in the Cuyahoga Valley National Park, Ohio. Landslides 13(3), 467–484 (2015). https://doi.org/10.1007/s10346-015-0587-0

5. He, S., Tang, H., Jin, H., Lei, T., Chang, J.: Weakly supervised landslide detection using media regression mode. In: IEEE International Geoscience and Remote Sensing Symposium (IGARSS), Fort Worth, TX, USA (2017)

6. Yu, B., Chen, F., Muhammad, S., Li, B., Wang, L., Wu, M.: A simple but effective landslide detection method based on image saliency. Photogramm. Eng. Remote Sensing 83(5), 351–363 (2017)

7. Geertsema, M., et al.: Sensitive clay landslide detection and characterization in and around Lakelse Lake, British Columbia, Canada. Elsevier Sediment. Geol. 364, 217–227 (2018)

8. Reichenbach, P., Rossi, M., Malamudb, B., Mihir, M., Guzzetti, F.: A review of statistically-based landslide susceptibility models. Earth Sci. Rev. 180, 60–91 (2018)

9. Braun, A., Leonardo, E., Urquia, G., Lopez, R., Yamagishi, H.: Landslide susceptibility mapping in Tegucigalpa, Honduras, using data mining methods. In: IAEG/AEG Annual Meeting Proceedings, San Francisco, California, vol. 1 (2019)

10. Huang, Q., Wang, C., Meng, Y., Chen, J., Yue, A.: Landslide monitoring using change detection in multitemporal optical imagery. IEEE Geosci. Remote Sens. Lett. 17(2), 312–316 (2020). https://doi.org/10.1109/LGRS.2019.2918254

11. Mondini, A.C., Santangelo, M., Rocchetti, M., Rossetto, E., Manconi, A., Monserrat, O.: Sentinel-1 SAR amplitude imagery for rapid landslide detection. Remote Sens. 11, 760 (2019). https://doi.org/10.3390/rs11070760

12. Konishi, T., Suga, Y.: Landslide detection using COSMO-SkyMed images: a case study of a landslide event on Kii Peninsula, Japan. Eur. J. Remote Sens. 51(1), 205–221 (2018). https://doi.org/10.1080/22797254.2017.1418185

13. Uemoto, J., Moriyama, T., Nadai, A., Kojima, S., Umehara, T.: Landslide detection based on height and amplitude differences using pre- and post-event airborne X-band SAR data. Nat. Hazards 95(3), 485–503 (2018)

14. Lu, P., Stumpf, A., Kerle, N., Casagli, N.: Object-Oriented Change Detection for Landslide Rapid Mapping. IEEE Geosci. Remote Sens. Lett. 8(4), 701–705 (2011)

15. Wang, B.-C.: A landslide monitoring technique based on dual-receiver and phase difference measurements. IEEE Geosci. Remote Sens. Lett. 10(5), 1209–1213 (2013)

16. Lei, T., Zhang, Y., Lv, Z., Li, S., Liu, S., Nandi, A.: Landslide inventory mapping from bitemporal images using deep convolutional neural networks. IEEE Geosci. Remote Sens. Lett. 16(6), 982–986 (2019)

17. Petley, D.: Landslides in Nepal. In: AGU 100 Advanced Earth and Space Science. https://blogs.agu.org/landslideblog/2011/03/10/landslides-in-nepal/

18. Network, A.: Nepal landslide victims 'will never be found'. In: NEWS/ASIA. https://www.aljazeera.com/news/asia/2014/08/nepal-landslide-victims-will-never-be-found-201483112811321721.html

19. Gupta, A.: Nepal landslide was a disaster waiting to happen, say experts. In: Down To Earth. https://www.downtoearth.org.in/news/nepal-landslide-was-a-disaster-waiting-to-happen-say-experts-45839

20. Network, T.: Landslide in Nepal leads to 8 death. In: Telesur. https://www.telesurenglish.net/news/Landslide-in-Nepal-Leaves-at-Least-8-Dead-20140802-0020.html

21. Shakya, A.K., Ramola, A., Kandwal, A., Prakash, R.: Change over time in grey levels of multispectral landsat $5^{TM}/8^{OLI}$ satellite images. In: Nath, V., Mandal, J.K. (eds.) Proceedings of the Third International Conference on Microelectronics, Computing and Communication Systems. LNEE, vol. 556, pp. 309–356. Springer, Singapore (2019). https://doi.org/10.1007/978-981-13-7091-5_29

22. Shakya, A., Ramola, A., Kandwal, A., Mittal, P., Prakash, R.: Morphological change detection in terror camps of area 1 and 2 by pre- and post-strike through MOAB: A. In: Bera, R., Sarkar, S., Singh, O., Saikia, H. (eds.) Advances in Communication, Devices and Networking. Lecture Notes in Electrical Engineering, vol 537, pp. 253–263. Springer, Singapore, Febraury 2019. https://doi.org/10.1007/978-981-13-3450-4_29

23. Baniya, B., Techato, K., Ghimire, S.K., Chhipi-Shrestha, G.: A review of green roofs to mitigate urban heat Island and Kathmandu Valley in Nepal. Appl. Ecol. Environ. Sci. 6(4), 137–152 (2018). https://doi.org/10.12691/aees-6-4-5

A Hybrid Model for Detecting Anomalous Ozone Values

P. Raghu Vamsi[1] and Anjali Chauhan[2(✉)]

[1] Computer Science and Engineering Department,
Jaypee Institute of Information Technology, Noida, India
prvonline@yahoo.co.in
[2] Computer Science and Engineering Department,
Inderprastha Engineering College, Ghaziabad, India
anjisingh.chauhan@gmail.com

Abstract. One class Support Vector Machine (OCSVM) is remarkably an efficient semi-supervised learning method for classifying one class anomaly in the applications such as fault detection in hardware, document classification, novelty detection, etc. However, many studies showed that due to the presence of anomalies in the training data the boundary measured by OCSVM is biased towards anomalies and thereby results in to low classification accuracy. Classifying ozone measurements obtained from the environment is one such application where the dataset composes huge number of anomalies due to irregularities in the deployed sensors. To this end, this paper presents a technique to improve the anomaly classification accuracy of OCSVM using Deep Belief Networks (DBN). First, the data are pre-processed and then DBN is used for extracting linearly separable data. This outcome is then given to the OCSVM for classification of anomalous ozone measurements in the next step. It is observed from the simulation results that the proposed method shows better classification and achieved high accuracy of 92.71%.

Keywords: Anomaly detection · Deep Belief Networks · One Class SVM · Ozone measurements · Restricted Boltzmann Machines

1 Introduction

Air Quality Monitoring (AQM) systems are widely deployed nowadays in many cities and places due to rapidly growing industries and vehicular traffic on the roads. AQM systems composed of various sensing and communication devices to sense and report the levels of green house gasses present in the air. Ground level ozone is one of the most air pollutants which create irritation in human eyes and breathing problems. In recent years, the capital region of our country (India) witnessed the rise in pollution level which led to shutting of schools and colleges for a few days. Hence, continuous tracking of air quality is vital for preparing the necessary action plan by the government authorities. Generally, sensing devices in AQM systems are openly deployed in the monitoring areas which will lead to various irregularities such as sensor malfunctioning, sensor faults, physical tampering, etc. In such irregularities, the collected

© Springer Nature Singapore Pte Ltd. 2020
P. K. Singh et al. (Eds.): FTNCT 2019, CCIS 1206, pp. 419–430, 2020.
https://doi.org/10.1007/978-981-15-4451-4_33

sensor data compose of huge number of anomalies. To this end, accurate identification of anomalies in the sensor data is of paramount importance for taking subsequent actions.

Machine learning and deep learning are the emerging fields helping the academic and research communities to classify and predict the results from the datasets with or without supervision. In the supervised learning, the required model is trained first and then the anomalous ozone data is analyzed to determine which ozone measurement is anomalous. On the other hand, under unsupervised learning, the model learning will happen automatically for anomaly detection depending on the given data. Later, any ozone measurement falls within the boundary region is considered as correct otherwise the measurement is considered as anomalous. There are various unsupervised classification algorithms present in the literature such as isolation forest, decision trees, Bayesian network, Support Vector Machine, and others [19].

In recent years, along with the ML methods the research community focusing on the Deep Learning (DL) based methods. DL methods found best for the feature extraction and thereby the extracted features are used for classification. Deep Belief Network (DBN) is a DL method to classify the given data set into linearly separable data. DBNs have been widely used in applications such as object identification, speech recognition, spatial and temporal feature extraction from various sensors, and others.

The classification problem can be either one class or multi class. In multi class classification, two or more classes data will be available and the decision boundary is decided based on the samples from these classes. On the other hand, in single class classification, the decision will be made using one class. One Class Support Vector Machine (OCSVM) [20–22] is one class classification method which works fine when there are very few anomalies in the data. It means that the boundary for negative values will not present in the OCSVM and hence only one boundary can be determined using the available data. The performance of OCSVM depends on the hyper parameter setting. However, limited studies are available in this direction.

To this end, the objective of the paper is to process one class data into linearly separable before providing it to the OCSVM. For this, DBN a DL technique is used to process the ozone measurements into linearly separable measurements. Once separable data are available the OCSVM can effectively form the positive boundary to hold the positive ozone measurements.

The rest of the paper is organized as follows. Section 2 presents the literature survey; Sect. 3 presents the assumptions and dataset description. Section 4 illustrates the proposed method. Section 5 discusses the results followed by conclusion and future work in Sect. 6.

2 Anomaly Detection Previous Work

Anomaly detection has become a major field of research on academic front. This can be applied to various fields. The works in [6, 12] have generalized anomaly detection in many fields and gave an idea over the possible fields that can be referred further for the same. Anomaly detection being fundamentally based on classification problem focuses on machine learning approaches. Researches in [1, 4] compares the various prevailing machine learning models. The comparison is based on various supervised and unsupervised learning models of classification. These models were CART (Classification and regression trees) [1], RF (Random Forests) [1], Isolation Forests [3], SVM (support vector machines) [4], LDA (linear discriminant analysis) [4], Decision Trees [5] etc.

Based on the analysis of these models, the proposed hybrid models use the unsupervised models for further research as these are most effective in giving significant outcomes [7]. Various performance metrics have been compared in [7] and summarized the best models for performing anomaly detection. The proposed hybrid model inspires from [6, 7]. These researches used OSVM for anomaly detection over different fields. Live data anomaly detection also plays an important role to detect runtime anomalies. A big networked system collects data continuously with the help of live feeds. This live data requires treatment for anomaly as soon as an anomaly is found. Researches in [2, 5] deal with the live data and propose progressive models in which the entry of a certain data runs for the race of finding anomaly. Further based on the degree of anomaly, it is treated further for the particular dataset. IOT devices and app data have been covered in [4]. This way, the variations in this field were also referred, showing that anomaly detection is diverse and applied to various fields. The research in [16] tells about the methodology of DBN and its functionalities. These functionalities were refereed further such that could be applied to proposed hybrid model.

Researches in [10, 11] were surveys that gave an overview of all the aspects of anomaly detection. They helped in getting familiar with all the challenges and concepts that fall under anomaly detection.

In all the researches above, we have come across various accuracy metrics. But when unsupervised methods of learning are taken into account, the already applied methods might not be sufficient. Hence, research in [8], uses mass and volume as metrics to find the accuracy of the models applied.

Research in [15] proposes labeling the dataset using Z-Score and Mahalobonis Distance. This labeling not only gives us accurate labels for the data, but also help us in knowing the trends and patterns in the data for predicting labels. Mahalobonis Distance signifies the distance between the data points on a plane.

The Restricted Boltzmann Machine that is stacked to form a DBN has given many satisfying results in [13] and [14]. The properties and use cases of RBM have been well utilized in the proposed work in order to get desired results. Also, as a summary of various comparison made in [1, 4, 6, 17] gave a major finding that OSVM has the best visual method to showcase anomalies as compared to other methods of classification. OSVM takes more time in training and predicting but gives out deterministic results which can be easily analyzed visually with the help of Scatter Plots etc. Also OSVM performs best when the number of outliers is very less as compared to the normal data. Air Quality Monitoring (AQM) systems are widely deployed nowadays in many cities and places due to rapidly growing industries and vehicular traffic on the roads. AQM systems composed of various sensing and communication devices to sense and report the levels of green house gasses present in the air. Ground level ozone is one of the most air pollutants which create irritation in human eyes and breathing problems. In recent years, the capital region of our country (India) witnessed the rise in pollution level which led to shutting of schools and colleges for a few days. Hence, continuous tracking of air quality is vital for preparing the necessary action plan by the government authorities. Generally, sensing devices in AQM systems are openly deployed in the monitoring areas which will lead to various irregularities such as sensor malfunctioning, sensor faults, physical tampering, etc. In such irregularities, the collected sensor data compose of huge number of anomalies. To this end, accurate identification of anomalies in the sensor data is of paramount importance for taking subsequent actions.

Machine learning and deep learning are the emerging fields helping the academic and research communities to classify and predict the results from the datasets with or without supervision. In the supervised learning, the required model is trained first and then the anomalous ozone data is analyzed to determine which ozone measurement is anomalous. On the other hand, under unsupervised learning, the model learning will happen automatically for anomaly detection depending on the given data. Later, any ozone measurement falls within the boundary region is considered as correct otherwise the measurement is considered as anomalous. There are various unsupervised classification algorithms present in the literature such as isolation forest, decision trees, Bayesian network, Support Vector Machine, and others [19].

In recent years, along with the ML methods the research community focusing on the Deep Learning (DL) based methods. DL methods found best for the feature extraction and thereby the extracted features are used for classification. Deep Belief Network (DBN) is a DL method to classify the given data set into linearly separable data. DBNs have been widely used in applications such as object identification, speech recognition, spatial and temporal feature extraction from various sensors, and others.

The classification problem can be either one class or multi class. In multi class classification, two or more classes data will be available and the decision boundary is decided based on the samples from these classes. On the other hand, in single class classification, the decision will be made using one class. One Class Support Vector Machine (OCSVM) [20–22] is one class classification method which works fine when there are very few anomalies in the data. It means that the boundary for negative values will not present in the OCSVM and hence only one boundary can be determined using the available data. The performance of OCSVM depends on the hyper parameter setting. However, limited studies are available in this direction.

To this end, the objective of the paper is to process one class data into linearly separable before providing it to the OCSVM. For this, DBN a DL technique is used to process the ozone measurements into linearly separable measurements. Once separable data are available the OCSVM can effectively form the positive boundary to hold the positive ozone measurements.

The rest of the paper is organized as follows. Section 2 presents the literature survey; Sect. 3 presents the assumptions and dataset description. Section 4 illustrates the proposed method. Section 5 discusses the results followed by conclusion and future work in Sect. 6.

The proposed methodology works on the data best suitable for OSVM and merged with deep learning concepts. Later, it is computed and analyzed for the purpose of outlier detection.

3 Model Assumptions

The structure of sensor data and the assumed correlation within the data, for implementation of the proposed model, are described in this section. AQ data used is collected from sensor networks placed in an area logging down several components of the environmental particles. Ozone is formed with collaboration of other particles in the environment. Vehicular effluents also form a part of the composition of ozone. This way, findings in form of anomaly in Ozone depicted the degraded AQ. While having abnormal values of ozone, it was observed that even other particles or pollutants had high values. These high values were recorded and a trend within this data was referred for checking AQ. But since, the data are collected from sensors, there is a high probability that some sensors might not function properly and stand as faulty. This faulty sensor might give a high value for a pollutant and for the other pollutant the value may be normal. Null values may also be encountered by a faulty sensor. Thus abnormal ozone values with a normal value of other pollutant helped in detecting faults within the sensor networks. The proposed hybrid model is implemented using python, giving a user- friendly environment to work.

3.1 Dataset Description

This paper considered the AQ data logged in Aarhus University, Denmark. This data is collected from AQ detection sensors [18] that continuously logged data for 40 days in University campus. Total 12,997 data entries were taken that had attributes such as Ozone, Particulate matter, nitrogen dioxide, sulfur dioxide, carbon monoxide, timestamp and category. The description of the dataset is provided in Table 1.

Table 1. Dataset description.

Attribute	Value
Ozone	Numeric values 0, 1, 2, 3 ... n
Particulate matter	Numeric values 0, 1, 2, 3 ... n
Carbon monoxide	Numeric values 0, 1, 2, 3 ... n
Sulphur dioxide	Numeric values 0, 1, 2, 3 ... n
Nitrogen dioxide	Numeric values 0, 1, 2, 3 ... n

4 Proposed Methodology

Figure 1 shows the flow of the proposed method. From the dataset, the data are pre processed first to normalize the data. The normalized data are given to the RBMs to extract the linearly separable data. This data is then given to the OCSVM for better classification. The rest of the section explains the steps in detail.

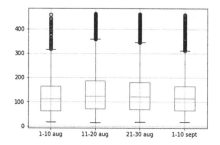

Fig. 1. Trends in Ozone per 10 days in Aarhus, Denmark.

4.1   Data Preprocessing

Anomalies in a dataset depict that few values fall out of the general trend of the data and therefore are abnormal. Abnormality can be treated as erroneous data or a novel data, depending upon the approach to classify these anomalies. In case of AQ data, an abnormal data entry will be a novelty, which will be considered as an event to notify the changes in AQ to the people around. However, in case of data coming from a faulty sensor, either the sensor needs to be changed or the data are neglected. The data are categorized in the ratio of 80:20 as train data and test data. Attribute 'Ozone' is the main feature for classification. General trends in the Ozone values per ten days are shown in Fig. 2.

The preprocessing of the data collected is done in order to assign labels to each entry. Because the learning technique is based on unsupervised learning, therefore, the labels were only used to check the accuracy with the help of the predicted data. Hence, this way the efficiency of the model could be found. The labeling was done on the basis of normal distribution of the ozone values. The labels were assigned to a column as 'Category'. This column 'Category' contained all the labels that were found on the basis of Normal distribution. As shown in Fig. 3, the values on the extreme points of

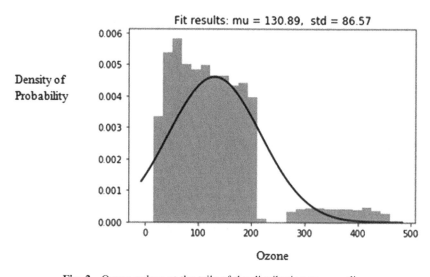

Fig. 2. Ozone values at the tails of the distribution were outliers

the Normal Distribution are labeled as outliers. The value 1 was assigned to the entries containing the normal ozone measurements and 1 was assigned to those containing abnormal ozone values.

4.2 Input the Dataset into the Hybrid Model

- **Deep Belief Network Formation Using Stacked RBM's.** DBNs are designed to form a network, based on stacking process of Restricted Boltzmann Machines, as shown in Fig. 3, which are defined as a stochastic neural network. Boltzmann machines (BM) are undirected graphical models, which are also considered as Markov Random Fields. They are a powerful tool for estimating a probability distribution of input datasets. The formula for probability distribution is:

$$p(x) = (a|x; w) \tag{1}$$

Here, p(x) is the probability function of the weighted x with respect to activation function. With the help of these distributions, the network grows further. DBNs are structures, trained in an unsupervised way with unlabeled data as shown in Fig. 4. They are applied to extract and discover a complex hierarchical representation of the training data through multiple transformations of inputs over layers. In a DBN, the visible units of the top layer include not only the input but also the labels. Then the top layer RBM learns the distribution of p(v, label, h). The input v is still provided from the bottom of the network. Here, h stands for hidden layers and v is the node from the trained data earlier. Thus with the help of RBM's, we form a deep belief network from the dataset mentioned. Total three layers were there in the Deep Belief Network formed and further processing was done using these layers only. Generally, DBN's are used for feature extraction, but, since, the used data has limited features. The properties of DBN were efficiently used to pick up only that data that is linearly separable, in order to get improved efficiency in anomaly detection. This linearly separable data is further used as an input to One-Class SVM.

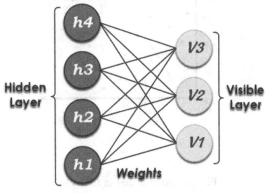

Fig. 3. Structure of RBM

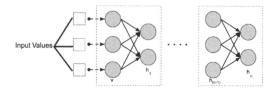

Fig. 4. DBN network formed with the help of stacked RBM

- **Using Output of DBN as an Input to OSVM.** SVM is a special case of unsupervised classification, which is applied to solve one class classification problem. It deals with the scenarios of high dimensionality case. OSVM is trained in unsupervised manner with the help of unlabeled normal data in order to construct boundaries or the hyper-planes. These hyper-planes are used to evaluate new testing observations. If the new observation shares similar features as the normal class in features space F, it is classified as normal. However, in the other case, the entry is termed as abnormal. Setting up OSVM boundaries helps in analyzing the membership of newly observed data to the same features space of training dataset defined by the hyper-planes. The assigning of classes to newly observed data is done with the help of a decision function. The decision function response is -1 for outliers and $+1$ for inliers. The decision function f(x) maximizes the distance between the hyper plane H separating the training dataset in features space and the origin (Fig. 5).

The One-Class SVM machine is fed with the DBN network data and then analyzed to find anomalies. The output of DBN network, i.e. the linearly separable data is used to find the boundaries between the normal and abnormal data using OCSVM. In this phase, data is separated on the basis of hyper planes and further modifications were done. Both the OCSVM and DBN have been trained completely in an unsupervised manner.

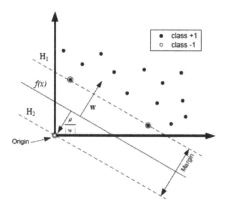

Fig. 5. Hyper-planes in OCSVM

The algorithm in form of the flow diagram in Fig. 6 depicts a more clear view of the methodology.

To show the efficiency of the proposed algorithm performance metrics will be checked using the hybrid model i.e. using the DBN as well as without using the DBN model. These models are checked to test if the hybrid model outperforms than the standalone OSVM. The better performance metrics will signify the purpose of DBN, which enhances the OSVM capability to define outliers.

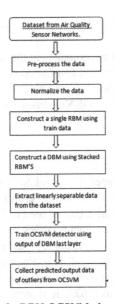

Fig. 6. DBN-OCSVM algorithm

5 Simulation Study

The algorithm proposed has detected 3,200 anomalies from the test dataset. The OCSVM detector hence, predicts the labels for the data and hence, accuracy with Test data is evaluated. Decision function of OCSVM detector was used to plot a Scatter Plot.

5.1 Simulation Setup

- **Hyper-Parameters for the Model**
  The best parameters have been chosen to make an efficient model and hence, combining their properties for most efficient anomaly detection. The various parameters that are essential to run the models with respect to the distribution of the dataset are described below.

Model	Parameter	Value
DBN	No. of epochs	1000
	Learning rate	0.001
	Layers	3
OCSVM	Kernal	Rbf linear
	Nu-value	0.1
	Gamma-value	0.001

5.2   Simulation Results

The scatter plot in Fig. 7, shows the anomalies in the dataset, in the form of data plots outside the learner frontier. The learned frontier comes from the Decision Function of the proposed OSCVM detector. These all are values that were outliers and also linearly separable on the hyper plane. The DBN extracted only the data that was linearly separable.

5.3   Accuracy Estimation

The accuracy metrics were evaluated for standalone OCSVM model as well DBN-OCSVM model. Standalone OCSVM model didn't use any DBN network. The comparison of the performance metrics can be seen in Table 2. It can be observed from the table that standalone OCSVM have an accuracy of 80.20, while DBN-OCSVM has an accuracy of 92.71%. F1 score is an accuracy metric generally used to evaluate the test accuracy of the classification method. It is observed that OCSVM have 0.674 F1 score whereas use of DBN improved the accuracy of OCSVM to 0.857. As 0.857 is near the value to 1 as compare to 0.674, it signifies that the proposed method has achieved good test accuracy. Further, the measure of degree of separation, AUC score also shows that DBN-OCSVM has achieved a high degree of separation of anomalous and correct ozone measures of 0.756 as compare to the standalone OCSVM of 0.459.

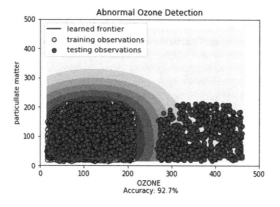

Fig. 7. Scatter plot of OCSVM detector

Table 2. Comparative accuracy estimations

Models	F1 score	AUC score	Accuracy
Standalone OCSVM	0.674	0.459	80.20
DBN-OCSVM	0.857	0.756	92.71

6 Conclusion

This paper used DBN for processing linearly separable ozone measurements and the output has been given to the OCSVM to improve classification accuracy. The performance metrics found from the comparison clearly shows the significant increase in classification accuracy when OCSVM detector was used with a Deep Belief Network. Hence, it is necessary to find the linearly separable data in order to perform the classification accurately, else there will be a lot of misclassification error while prediction thereby decreasing the efficiency of any model to find the outliers. The outliers found with the proposed method have found anomalous ozone values which have to be logged such that these high ozone values display a dangerous situation in the context of AQ.

7 Future Works

After effectively going through the techniques that can be used to find anomalies, this algorithm can be applied on Time–series data and non-stationary data collected on computer Networks. Social networks can also be a vast field to work with outliers and hence, can give quite significant results.

References

1. Nesa, N., Ghosh, T., Banerjee, I.: Outlier detection in sensed data using statistical learning models for IoT. In: 2018 IEEE Wireless Communications and Networking Conference (WCNC), Barcelona, pp. 1–6 (2018)
2. Souza, A.M.C., Amazonas, J.R.A.: An outlier detect algorithm using Big Data processing and Internet of Things architecture. In: ANT/SEIT (2015)
3. Hofmockel, J., Sax, E.: Isolation forest for anomaly detection in raw vehicle sensor data. In: Proceedings of the 4th International Conference on Vehicle Technology and Intelligent Transport Systems, vol. 1, pp. 411–416. In: VEHITS (2018). ISBN 978-989-758-293-6
4. Wang, W., Li, Y., Wang, X., Liu, J., Zhang, X.: Detecting Android malicious apps and categorizing benign apps with ensemble of classifiers. Future Gen. Comput. Syst. **789**(P3), 987–994 (2018). https://doi.org/10.1016/j.future.2017.01.019
5. Das, S., Wong, W.K., Fern, A., Dietterich, T.G., Siddiqui, M.A.: Incorporating feedback into tree-based anomaly detection (2017). arXiv preprint arXiv:1708.09441
6. Harrou, F., Dairi, A., Sun, Y., Senouci, M.: Reliable detection of abnormal ozone measurements using an air quality sensors network. In: 2018 IEEE International Conference on Environmental Engineering (EE), pp. 1–5. IEEE (2018)

7. Perera, P., Patel, V.M.: Learning deep features for one-class classification (2018). arXiv preprint arXiv:1801.05365

8. Ngai, E.W.T., Hu, Y., Wong, Y.H., Chen, Y., Sun, X.: The application of data mining techniques in financial fraud detection: a classification framework and an academic review of literature. Decis. Support Syst. **50**(3), 559–569 (2011)

9. Goix, N.: How to evaluate the quality of unsupervised anomaly detection algorithms? (2016). arXiv preprint arXiv:1607.01152

10. Mahdavinejad, M.S., Rezvan, M., Barekatain, M., Adibi, P., Barnaghi, P., Sheth, A.P.: Machine learning for Internet of Things data analysis: a survey. Digit. Commun. Netw. **4**, 161–175 (2017)

11. Chandola, V., Banerjee, A., Kumar, V.: Anomaly detection: a survey. ACM Comput. Surv. (CSUR) **41**(3), 15 (2009)

12. Ryan, P.J., Watson, R.B.: Research challenges for the Internet of Things: what role can OR play? Systems **5**(1), 24 (2017)

13. Nair, V., Hinton, G.E.: Rectified linear units improve restricted Boltzmann machines. In: Proceedings of the 27th International Conference on Machine Learning (ICML-2010), pp. 807–814 (2010)

14. Salakhutdinov, R., Mnih, A., Hinton, G.: Restricted Boltzmann machines for collaborative filtering. In: Proceedings of the 24th International Conference on Machine Learning, pp. 791–798. ACM (2007)

15. Killourhy, K.S., Maxion, R.A.: Comparing anomaly-detection algorithms for keystroke dynamics. In: IEEE/IFIP International Conference on Dependable Systems and Networks, DSN 2009, pp. 125–134. IEEE (2009)

16. Lee, H., et al.: Convolutional deep belief networks for scalable unsupervised learning of hierarchical representations. In: Proceedings of the 26th Annual International Conference on Machine Learning. ACM (2009)

17. Manevitz, L.M., Yousef, M.: One-class SVMs for document classification. J. Mach. Learn. Res. **2**, 139–154 (2001)

18. http://iot.ee.surrey.ac.uk:8080/datasets.html

19. Khan, S.S., Madden, M.G.: A survey of recent trends in one class classification. In: Coyle, L., Freyne, J. (eds.) AICS 2009. LNCS (LNAI), vol. 6206, pp. 188–197. Springer, Heidelberg (2010). https://doi.org/10.1007/978-3-642-17080-5_21

20. Ghafoori, Z., et al.: Efficient unsupervised parameter estimation for one-class support vector machines. IEEE Trans. Neural Netw. Learn. Syst. **29**, 5057–5070 (2018)

21. Harrou, F., Dairi, A., Taghezouit, B., Sun, Y.: An unsupervised monitoring procedure for detecting anomalies in photovoltaic systems using a one-class Support Vector Machine. Sol. Energy **179**, 48–58 (2019)

22. Saari, J., Strömbergsson, D., Lundberg, J., Thomson, A.: Detection and identification of windmill bearing faults using a one-class support vector machine (SVM). Measurement **137**, 287–301 (2019)

23. Singh, P.K., Paprzycki, M., Bhargava, B., Chhabra, J.K., Kaushal, N.C., Kumar, Y. (eds.): FTNCT 2018. CCIS, vol. 958. Springer, Singapore (2019). https://doi.org/10.1007/978-981-13-3804-5

Evaluating the Performance of Navigation Prediction Model Based on Varied Session Length

Honey Jindal$^{(\boxtimes)}$ and Neetu Sardana

Computer Science and Engineering, Jaypee Institute of Information Technology,
Noida, India
honey.cs0990@gmail.com, neetu.sardana@jiit.com

Abstract. Web navigation prediction plays a vital role in web, due to its broad research applications. It can be used for personalization, improvise website design, and business intelligence. Main aim of these applications is to enhance user's satisfaction levels who are visiting the website. Web navigation prediction model tries to predict the future set of the webpage from their historical navigations. The past navigations are collected in the web server log file. Navigations form the sessions of varied length which are used for building the navigation model. Selecting very long sessions or very small sessions degrades the model performance. Thus, selecting an optimal session length is mandate as it would impact the model performance positively. This paper presents pre-investigation measures like page loss, branching factor and session length. We investigate the performance of prediction model based on two different ranges of session length. First range that has been considered is three to seven (3 to 7) and second range is two to ten (2 to 10). The Model has been evaluated on three real datasets. The experimental results show that selecting session of length ranging from 2 to 10 gives better learning hence intensifies accuracy of navigation prediction model. The model accuracy of Set B showed improvement from 0.27 to 8.73% in MSWEB, 0.62 to 2.8% in BMS and 10.81 to 14.23% in Wikispeedia dataset.

Keywords: Prediction · Session length · N-gram · Navigation · Web · Markov

1 Introduction

The continuous growth of web is resulting in enormous websites. The structure of websites is also becoming complex. Often users face difficulty in locating the desired information while navigating through the website. With the website designer perspective, the main challenge is to analyze the user behavior and personalize them. This will not only help them in locating required information but also improve user's satisfaction level.

Web Navigation Prediction (WNP) is an emerging research area to address these issues. In WNP, a model is trained such that it predicts the next web page(s) from the visited web pages. WNP can be generalized and applied on different applications [14] like search engines [16], caching systems and latency reduction [17], anomaly detection

© Springer Nature Singapore Pte Ltd. 2020
P. K. Singh et al. (Eds.): FTNCT 2019, CCIS 1206, pp. 431–443, 2020.
https://doi.org/10.1007/978-981-15-4451-4_34

[8], personalization [5], website design [18], detecting malicious web pages [26, 27], recommendation systems [1], event detection [32] and location prediction [9, 28]. User navigation history is captured in the log file through cookies or web servers. A snapshot of weblog file shown in Fig. 1. The fields of web logs are user IP address, user authentication, date/time, action, return code, size, referral, browser/platform. Each row in the log file [10] represents single web page request. It consist important information about the client and the requested web page. The information is recorded by the server to understand user behavior.

```
02:49:12 127.0.0.1 GET / 200
02:49:35 127.0.0.1 GET /index.html 200
03:01:06 127.0.0.1 GET /images/sponsered.gif 304
03:52:36 127.0.0.1 GET /search.php 200
04:17:03 127.0.0.1 GET /admin/style.css 200
05:04:54 127.0.0.1 GET /favicon.ico 404
05:38:07 127.0.0.1 GET /js/ads.js 200
```

Fig. 1. Web log file [10]

Web logs are preprocessed and sessions are constructed from the log file which is used for making prediction model. Session consisting set of pages can be of varied length. Longer sessions often have noise as they may be repetition of pages or user is following longer path to reach desired page. This results in poor browsing experience of the user and may harm the popularity of the website. According to Janrain [15], about 74% of the online users get frustrated with website when they do not get their required web content. According to Forrester research [11], a good website design can attract more user's and vice versa. Half of the sales will get negative impact, if user is unable to locate his desired information. Due to the negative experience faced by the users on their first visit, 40% users may not return to the website. In 2013, a Monetate/eConsultancy study [15] found that in-house marketers who are personalizing their browsing experience observed 19% uplift in their sales. Smaller sessions will dilute the learning of prediction model so it is important to use the session length that can help in building the prediction model optimally.

This paper analyses the performance of prediction model based on two different ranges of session length. The two set of ranges are Set A (3 to 7) and Set B (2 to 10). Generally Set A has been used in past studies [4]. We will compare this range with longer session length range two to ten (2–10) to find suitable session length for model building. This study analyzes the impact of varied session length on prediction model.

1.1 Research Objectives

1. This paper highlights pre-investigations measures which are required to inject good quality inputs to the training model.

2. Web navigations have been analysed and detail summary of how pre-investigations will affect the model is discussed.
3. We have evaluated model performance using varied session length on three real datasets(MSWEB, BMS and Wikispeedia)

The rest of the paper is organized as follows. Section 2 gives preliminaries and model representation. Related work is presented in the Sect. 3. Experimental details are described in Sect. 4 and conclude the paper in Sect. 5.

2 Preliminaries

This section describes the basic terminology, representation and modeling of a session.

- *Sessions:* A Session represents the web page(s) visit order of the user during the website navigation. A session, S is represented as {P1, P2, ..., Pn} where n denotes the number of pages. Each user browsing history is stored in a session.
- *N-grams:* In WNP, N-gram is prominently used to represent the training model. The N-gram can be represented as $<p_1, p_2, ...,p_N>$. This depicts sequences of web page(s) navigation of the user's. Each web page is represented with unique page id. For example, if we consider session consisting six pages having session length as six, S = <P11, P22, P5, P13, P20, P8>. In the given example, 1-gram will contain five sessions <P11, P22>, <P22, P5>, <P5, P13>, <P13, P20>, <P20, P8> and 2-gram will contain four sessions <P11, P22, P5>, <P22, P5, P13>, <P5, P13, P20>, <P13, P20, P8>. N-gram is a fixed length representation of sessions. Due to the fixed length representation of the training set, the model complexity, state-space complexity, computational complexity required to build the model can be easily determined.
- *Markov Model (MM):* Markov model [2, 3, 12, 13] is the well known representation used for the WNP. User navigation behavior is captured in the log file and analyzed to predict the next desired information. The log file is pre-processed to find the sessions. These sessions are used as the input for modeling the Markov model. MM is the graphical representation of sessions. Each node is represented by the pages and links between them represents the transition probability to move from one state to another. Markov models can be formed in varied order. In first-order MM, each state is represented with single page. For instance, a link between state A and B is formed using the transition probability. The transition probability is defined as the ratio of number of times <A, B> occurs to the number of times <A> occurs.

Transition probability to move from A to B is given by,

$$P(A \rightarrow B) = \frac{\mu(A, B)}{\mu(A)} \quad \text{where, } \mu \text{ denotes frequency}$$

In the second-order MM, each state is represented with two pages. For instance, a link between state <A, B> and <C> is formed using the transition probability.

The transition probability is defined as the ratio of number of times <A, B, C> occurs to the number of times <A, B> occurs.
Transition probability to move from <A, B> to C is given by,

$$P((A, B) \rightarrow C) = \frac{\mu(A, B, C)}{\mu(A, B)} \quad \text{where } \mu \text{ denotes frequency}$$

Similarly, higher order MM can be formed. In a Kth-order MM, each state is represented by K web pages. Since, the accuracy of Kth-order MM is low, All-Kth Markov model (KMM) comes into existence. In KMM, all lower order models are nested inside the higher order model. If a higher order KMM fail to predict then the search begins in the next subsequent lower order model.

- **All-Kth Modified Markov Model (KMMM):** The accuracy of MM is very low. Therefore, Modified Markov model (MMM) is proposed by Mamoun et al. [2]. In this model order of the pages does not matter. For example, if the sessions have same set of pages then they are represented in the same state. In order to further enhance the performance of MMM, all-Kth model are embedded with it. This model is known as All-Kth Modified Markov Model (KMMM). Jindal et al. [7] and Mamoun et al. [2] analyzed that All-Kth Modified Markov Model (KMMM) is proved to the compressed and effective prediction model. Therefore, in this work we choose KMMM as a prediction model to evaluate the performance over varied session length.

3   Related Work

During website browsing, user navigation history is captured in the web log file. The web log file cannot be used directly for analysis sand prediction as it consists of lot of noisy information like image, video, audio and robotics files. Thus, these log files are cleaned and pre-processed. During this phase the noisy information is filtered and user's as well as sessions are identified. Sessions are the sequence of the navigation trails of the users. Users' are identified using their IP address.

In past several sessions generation techniques were found which attempts to obtain relevant patterns from the web log file. Broadly, three session generation techniques have been used in the past namely, time-based, navigation-based and integer programming.

- Time-based: Catledge et al. [19] and Cooley et al. [21] have used page-stay time and session duration thresholds. Zhang et al. [20] proposed dynamic time-oriented method. The sub sessions are formed from the session when their time exceeds from the respective thresholds. Time-oriented heuristics do not consider website structure, thus most of the useful navigation patterns are missed in the session generation. Session generated may have duplicate web pages in the same session. For example {P2, P1, P1, P7, P3} or {P2, P1, P7, P1, P3} are allowed in the time-based heuristics. Here, {P1, P1} or {P1, P7, P1} causes unnecessary duplication of web page P1 that makes sessions longer. Moreover, these heuristics are not reliable as user(s) might get involved in some other activities during web page navigation. Other factors like web page content, content size, web page components, busy communication line may impact the session formation.

- Navigation-based: Cooley et al. [22, 23] have proposed navigation-based graphical structure of web sessions. In this network, nodes are represented by the web pages and edges are represented by the direct link between the web pages. For each navigated session, if there is no connection found between the two consecutive web pages then backward browsed webpage is inserted. This artificial insertion generates longer sessions.
- Integer programming: Dell et al. [24, 25] proposed integer programming based session generation techniques. Herein, web sessions are partitioned into the chunks using IP and agent information through logarithmic objective function. This objective function assigns the each web page to the chunk of the particular session such that there is no duplicate web page found in the session. For example, the given session is {P1, P3, P6, P3, P6, P8, P7, P6, P6, P8, P10} there is actually no link present between page P7 and P10. In this approach the session will split into two subsessions as {P1, P3, P6, P8, P7} and {P10}. However, according to website topology, the correct subsessions should consist of {P1, P3, P6, P8, P7} and {P1, P3, P6, P8, P10}. In addition, the obtained subsession with web page P10 have no correlation with other web pages which is not correct.

Session generation techniques presented varied session identification methods but they do not focused on deriving optimal session length. West et al. [29] observed that session length defines the user navigation behavior. Shorter path means user step towards the right direction and longer path means user did not get the right path. He might be circling around the desired page. In addition, longer path requires more state-space complexity and high computational cost [30]. It makes the prediction model development cumbersome [30] and degrades model performance. Since, the success of pattern discovery depends on the quality of input session injected to it [31], we have evaluated the impact of varied session lengths on web navigation prediction model. The paper discusses the pre-investigation measures that required to be performed before generating a prediction model. The pre-investigations are required mainly to choose the optimal session length for web navigation prediction as the quality of prediction accuracy depends upon the input sessions. To the best of our knowledge, no work has been done in past that inquires the optimal session length for web navigation prediction. Although logs are generated, cleaned and later used for prediction in so many application areas that we have mentioned in the paper but none of them have discussed the session length to be important component which need attention.

4 Experimental Details

Selecting an optimal Session length is a major concern before developing the prediction model. This is because the accuracy of the model depends on the sessions taken as an input. This study main focus is to analyze the effect of session length over prediction model. This section presents the experimental details like the dataset used, pre-investigation measures, evaluative parameters and the results obtained. Therefore, we analyses the performance of prediction model based on two different ranges of session length. We perform experiment on two sets. Set A consists sessions whose length lies in between 3 to 7. Set B consists sessions whose length lies in between 2 to 10. Generally Set A has been used in past studies [4]. We will compare this range with Set B. The training and testing for both sets is divided in the ratio of 0.7 and 0.3.

4.1 Dataset Description

We have conducted experiments on three datasets: MSWEB, BMS and Wikispeedia. The detail characteristics of each dataset have been presented in Table 1.

Table 1. Dataset summary

Dataset & Year	Source	Application	#Sessions	#Unique pages	Avg. session length
MSWEB (1999)	www.microsoft.com	Microsoft website	38000	294	3.01
BMS (2000)	www.gazelle.com	E-Commerce	59601	497	2.42
Wikispeedia (2009)	www.snap.stanford.edu	Wiki Pages	51000	3326	5.5

- *Dataset 1: MSWEB*

This dataset was collected from the Microsoft logs. The data consists of 38000 sessions from random users in February, 1998. Each row represents sequence of areas of the website that the user visits in a period of one week.

- *Dataset 2: BMS*

This dataset was collected from e-commerce web server logs (Gazelle.com) and used as a part of the KDD Cup 2000 competition. It contains 59,601 web sessions of items and 497 distinct items. The average length of the sessions is 2.42 items.

- *Dataset 3: Wikispeedia*

This is a popular online web page game. In this, each player has given a task to find a shortest path from source to destination web page. The player navigates from source web page to destination web page using the hyperlinks. The player has no knowledge of the global network structure. Therefore, he uses local information provided on the webpages. The player's navigations were collected in the web log file which consists 4606 articles and 3326 distinct articles. It comprises 51 K navigations collected over 2009.

The details of training and testing sessions are summarized in Table 2. After 0.7 (training) and 0.3 (testing) split, sessions are further divided categorized into N-gram using sliding window concept. It has been clearly observed that training and testing sessions of Set B is more as compared to Set A sessions. This is because Set B is a superset of Set A.

Table 2. Training and testing dataset

N-Gram	MSWEB (Set A)		MSWEB (Set B)		BMS (Set A)		BMS (Set B)		Wikispeedia (Set A)		Wikispeedia (Set B)	
	Train	Test	Train	Test	Train	Test	Train	Test	Train	Test	Train	Test
1	22670	1918	58278	3351	19211	4046	43114	7592	92388	14612	152104	13818
2	27670	1918	36172	2111	19211	4046	25402	4503	69468	14612	119879	13584
3	15258	1167	22499	1360	10187	2423	15462	2880	47152	13277	88218	12590
4	7585	680	13565	873	4919	1268	9278	1725	26925	9895	58988	10009
5	3176	362	7895	555	2087	667	5530	1124	11874	5615	35735	6675
6	896	154	4089	347	626	282	2946	739	3484	2384	20089	4254

4.2 Pre-investigation Measures

Pre-investigation measures are the metrics which is used to measure the effectiveness of input data. Measuring quality of data is very important before developing a model. A good quality input data injected to the model will produce better results. This section presents two pre-investigation measures: Page Loss and Branching Factor.

(a) Page Loss

Page loss determines the missing percentage of the pages in the training model. It defines as the ratio of number of web pages missing in the dataset to the total number of web pages of the website. The page loss would yield unseen pages and will not generate predictions for such pages. It also impacts models negatively. For example, if a web page P9 occurs in a test dataset which was not available in the training model; then training model will fail to generate predictions for web page 9. This measure is important to understand model incapability before model development phase. Table 3 depicts page loss of set A and set B training model. While investigating the datasets, we have found that some web pages were lost while dividing the dataset into training and testing. It has been observed that page loss is less in set B as compared to set A. Since, Set B has long session range; it produces more subset of sessions in the dataset with large combination of pages. Addressing this page loss is important, because it will give rise to more cold-start pages and cold-start sessions.

Table 3. Training page loss

Page loss	MSWEB	BMS	Wikispeedia
Set A	37 (12.58%)	112 (22.53%)	1057 (22.94%)
Set B	16 (5.44%)	110 (22.13%)	438 (9.50%)

(b) **Branching Factor**

Branching factor measures the network characteristics of the model. It is defined as the average number of outlinks present in the model corresponding to each state. Branching factor determines model prediction capability. It gives network structure insights which is helpful to understand "how much predictions a model may generate corresponding to its current state". This pre-investigation measure is important to compute average outlink percentage of the network states. Table 4 presents branching factor of Set A and B on varied N-grams. It has been found that branching factor of Set B is higher in all the datasets. This is because Set B injects more sessions in the training model which will have more outlinks corresponding to each state.

Table 4. Branching factor

N-Gram	MSWEB (Set A)	MSWEB (Set B)	BMS (Set A)	BMS (Set B)	Wikispeedia (Set A)	Wikispeedia (Set B)
1	17.23	19.99	16.36	26.57	9.40	10.05
2	3.76	4.205	2.93	3.549	3.25	3.47
3	2.32	2.430	2.02	2.221	2.01	2.04
4	1.92	1.927	1.78	1.858	1.73	1.79
5	1.79	1.731	1.70	1.716	1.64	1.67
6	1.76	1.655	1.68	1.658	1.62	1.51

4.3   Evaluation Parameters

In this section, we will define some prediction parameters used to evaluate model performance [6, 7]. The definitions of the predicting parameters are given below:

Definition 1: Prediction Accuracy
Prediction accuracy is defined as the ratio of correct predictions to the total number of test cases.

$$Prediction\ Accuracy = \frac{Correctly\ predicted\ test\ cases}{Total\ test\ cases}$$

Definition 2: Model Accuracy
Model accuracy is defined as the ratio of correct predictions to the total predictions.

$$Model\ Accuracy = \frac{Correctly\ predicted\ test\ cases}{Total\ test\ cases\ matched\ with\ the\ training\ model}$$

Definition 3: Coverage
Coverage is defined as the ratio of total number of predictions to the number of total test cases.

$$Coverage = \frac{Total\ Predictions}{Total\ test\ cases}$$

4.4   Experimental Results

(1) *Coverage*
Coverage is the evaluative measure which defines percentage of outlinks (prediction paths) covered by the test state. The value of coverage is depended on network structure. Table 5 presents coverage of the Set A and B over varied N-grams. It has been found that coverage of set B is more in all the datasets. Since, the branching factor of training models of Set B is higher; the model with Set B covers more outlinks during prediction as compared to model with Set A.

Table 5. Coverage

N-Gram	MSWEB (Set A)	MSWEB (Set B)	BMS (Set A)	BMS (Set B)	Wikispeedia (Set A)	Wikispeedia (Set B)
1	5.40	5.46	7.04	7.04	7.32	7.33
2	6.15	6.37	5.24	5.68	8.32	12.87
3	4.62	5.11	3.72	4.12	6.50	9.21
4	3.70	4.06	3.34	3.87	5.54	8.29
5	3.29	3.55	3.26	3.70	5.06	6.88
6	3.23	3.51	3.07	3.57	4.94	6.58

(2) *Prediction Accuracy*
Table 6 presents the effect of varying the session length on the prediction accuracy of the model. It has been seen clearly that the prediction accuracy decreases as N-gram increases. This is because the number of training examples becomes less as session length increases (N) (see Table 2). We have observed that the prediction accuracy of set B is higher as compared to set A on both datasets. This is because set B has less page loss while having high coverage corresponding to each test example session. Due to more availability of sessions, Set B has more chances to make correct predictions than Set A.

Table 6. Prediction accuracy of Set A and B

N-Gram	MSWEB (Set A)	MSWEB (Set B)	BMS (Set A)	BMS (Set B)	Wikispeedia (Set A)	Wikispeedia (Set B)
1	65.01	73.85	51.26	54.06	43.96	55.93
2	74.03	74.56	41.89	44.60	38.57	52.80
3	63.00	63.09	38.05	40.16	33.54	46.42
4	54.35	54.98	37.77	39.45	33.54	45.98
5	49.10	49.87	38.23	39.73	34.60	45.41
6	47.40	47.83	35.46	36.08	33.97	45.79

(3) Model Accuracy

The difference between model and prediction accuracy is that during the evaluation phase, model accuracy removes unseen test sessions from the total test set. Unseen sessions are those which are not known to the training model.

Model accuracy with respect to varied session length is presented in Table 7. It shows model prediction ability with respect to the test sessions which are available in the training model. It has been observed that Set B has more correct prediction ability than Set A on all datasets. Since, Set B has more outlinks for each state as compared to Set A. It generates more predictions and has more chances to make correct predictions.

Table 7. Model accuracy of Set A and B

N-Gram	MSWEB (Set A)	MSWEB (Set B)	BMS (Set A)	BMS (Set B)	Wikispeedia (Set A)	Wikispeedia (Set B)
1	65.15	73.88	53.31	57.02	44.24	55.93
2	74.28	74.60	44.88	48.08	38.82	52.80
3	62.56	63.13	41.16	43.94	33.76	46.42
4	54.77	55.04	41.87	44.57	33.79	45.98
5	49.67	50.00	42.85	45.94	34.91	45.41
6	47.34	47.98	40.48	42.93	34.35	45.80

4.5 Discussion

From the experiment results, we have inferred that early investigation of the input would yield better predictions. Before making predictions, the optimal split of training and testing dataset and optimal session length should be consider. To investigate the performance of prediction model, two investigation parameters have been used. Page loss indicates the amount of page loss in the training and testing dataset. It is important to consider because it provide insight of cold-start web pages and cold-start sessions or unseen sessions. Presence of unseen sessions makes model difficult to learn and causes prediction failure. Second investigation parameter is the branching factor. This measure is important as it provides insight of the number of predictions possible from the training state. The Set B has less page loss and high branching factor as compared to

Set A which indicates Set B is more preferable. Our experimental results revealed that model trained with Set B attains better coverage, prediction and model accuracies. The experimental results confirm the inference drawn from the pre-investigations measures.

5 Conclusion and Future Work

In this paper, we conduct experiments to evaluate the performance of prediction model over varied session length. For this, we select two set of session length. In set A, session with length 3 to 7 are selected and in Set B sessions with length 2 to 10 are selected. We evaluate the effectiveness of the input sessions injected to the model using two pre-investigation measures: page loss and branching factor. A set which has less page loss and high branching factor should be considered for the predictions.

In addition, we evaluate the performance of the model using evaluative measures over varied N-grams. The measures used in the study are: coverage, prediction accuracy and model accuracy. More crucially, it has been observed that set B has high coverage and high accuracy as compared to set A. It has been found that the session length do impacts the coverage and accuracy of the prediction model. Session length ranging from 2 to 10 is found to be best for development of prediction model. The model accuracy of Set B showed improvement from 0.27 to 8.73% in MSWEB, 0.62 to 2.8% in BMS and 10.81 to 14.23% in Wikispeedia dataset.

In the near future, we plan to do focus domain-centric session evaluation as user browsing behaviour varies with domains. Moreover, other pre-investigations measures can be explored which are required to develop high quality sessions.

References

1. Abrishami, S., Naghibzadeh, M., Jalali, M.: Web page recommendation based on semantic web usage mining. In: Aberer, K., et al. (eds.) SocInfo 2012. LNCS, vol. 7710, pp. 393–405. Springer, Heidelberg (2012). https://doi.org/10.1007/978-3-642-35386-4_29
2. Awad, M.A., Khalil, I.: Prediction of user's web browsing behavior: application of markov model. IEEE Trans. Syst. Man Cybern. - Part B: Syst. Hum. 42(4), 1131–1142 (2012)
3. Awad, M.A., Khan, L.R.: Web navigation prediction using multiple evidence combination and domain knowledge. IEEE Trans. Syst. Man Cybern. - Part B: Syst. Hum. 37(6), 1054–1062 (2007)
4. Madhurai, B.C., Anand, C.J., Ramya, K., Phanidra, M.: Analysis of users' web navigation behaviour using GRPA with variable length Markov chains. Int. J. Data Min. Knowl. Manag. Process 1(2), 1–20 (2011)
5. Pierrakos, D., Paliouras, G.: Personalizing web directories with the aid of web usage data. IEEE Trans. Knowl. Data Eng. 22(9), 1331–1344 (2010)
6. Pirolli, P.L.T., Pitkow, J.E.: Distributions of surfers' paths through the World Wide Web: empirical characterizations. World Wide Web 1(2), 29–34 (1999). https://doi.org/10.1023/A:1019288403823
7. Jindal, H., Sardana, N.: Web navigation prediction using Markov based models: an experimental study. Int. J. Web Eng. Technol. 11(4), 310–334 (2016)

8. Xie, Y., Tang, S.: Online anomaly detection based on web usage mining. In: 26th IEEE International Parallel and Distributed Processing Symposium Workshops & PhD Forum, pp. 1177–1182 (2012)
9. Xue, A.Y., et al.: Solving the data sparsity problem in destination prediction. The VLDB Journal 24(2), 219–243 (2015)
10. Web Server Log File Samples - IIS and Apache. http://www.herongyang.com/Windows/Web-Log-File-IIS-Apache-Sample.html. Accessed 18 May 2019
11. Usability. http://www.usability.gov. Accessed Nov 2015
12. Sunil, K., Sanjeev, G., Abhinav, G.: A survey on Markov model. MIT Int. J. Comput. Sci. Inf. Technol. 4(1), 29–33 (2014)
13. Borges, J., Levene, M.: Evaluating variable-length Markov chain models for analysis of user web navigation sessions. IEEE Trans. Knowl. Data Eng. 19(4), 441–452 (2007)
14. Facca, F.M., Lanzi, P.L.: Mining interesting knowledge from weblogs: a survey. Data Knowl. Eng. 53(3), 225–241 (2005)
15. 94% of businesses say personalisation is critical to their success. https://econsultancy.com/94-of-businesses-say-personalisation-is-critical-to-their-success/. Accessed 25 May 2019
16. Daxin, J., et al.: Mining search and browse logs for web search: a survey. ACM Trans. Comput. Logic 4(4), 1–42 (2013)
17. Praveen, K., et al.: Pre fetching web pages for improving user access latency using integrated web usage mining. In: International Conference on Communication, Control and Intelligent Systems. IEEE (2015)
18. Ketukumar, B., Patel, A.R: Web data mining in e-commerce. Study, analysis, issues and improving business decision making. Ph.D. thesis, Hemchandracharya North Gujarat University, Patan, India (2014)
19. Catledge, L.D., Pitkow, J.E.: Characterizing browsing strategies in the World-Wide Web. Comput. Netw. ISDN Syst. 27(6), 1065–1073 (1995)
20. Zhang, J., Ghorbani, A.A.: The reconstruction of user sessions from a server log using improved time-oriented heuristics. In: Second Annual Conference on Communication Networks and Services Research Proceedings, pp. 315–322. IEEE (2004)
21. Cooley, R., et al.: Data preparation for mining World Wide Web browsing patterns. Knowl. Inf. Syst. 1(1), 5–32 (1999)
22. Cooley, R., et al.: Web usage mining: discovery and application of interesting patterns from web data. Ph.D. thesis, Dept. of Computer Science, University of Minnesota (2000)
23. Cooley, R., Tan, P.-N., Srivastava, J.: Discovery of interesting usage patterns from web data. In: Masand, B., Spiliopoulou, M. (eds.) WebKDD 1999. LNCS (LNAI), vol. 1836, pp. 163–182. Springer, Heidelberg (2000). https://doi.org/10.1007/3-540-44934-5_10
24. Dell, R.F., et al.: Web user session reconstruction using integer programming. In: Proceedings of the IEEE/WIC/ACM International Conference on Web Intelligence and Intelligent Agent Technology, vol. 1, pp. 385–388. IEEE Computer Society (2008)
25. Dell, R.F., Román, P.E., Velasquez, J.D.: Fast combinatorial algorithm for web user session reconstruction. In: Proceedings of 24th IFIP TC7 Conference, Buenos Aires, Argentina (2009)
26. Lui, J., et al.: A Markov detection tree-based centralized scheme to automatically identify malicious webpages on cloud platforms. IEEE Access 6, 74025–74038 (2018)
27. Kazemian, H.B., Ahmed, S.: Comparisons of machine learning techniques for detecting malicious webpages. Expert Syst. Appl. 42(3), 1166–1177 (2015)

28. Ahmad, S., et al.: A stochastic approach towards travel route optimization and recommendation based on users constraints using Markov chain. IEEE Access **7**, 90760–90776 (2019)
29. West, R., Leskovec, J.: Human way finding in information networks. In: Proceedings of the 21st International Conference on World Wide Web, pp. 619–628. ACM (2012)
30. Jindal, H., et al.: Elimination of backward browsing using decomposition and compression for efficient navigation prediction. Int. J. Web Based Commun. **14**(2), 196–223 (2018)
31. Bayir, M.A., Toroslu, I.H., Demirbas, M., Cosar, A.: Discovering better navigation sequences for the session construction problem. Data Knowl. Eng. **73**, 58–72 (2012)
32. Xu, J., et al.: Automatic generation of social event storyboard from image click-through data. IEEE Trans. Circuits Syst. Video Technol. 1–12 (2015, accepted)

Geo-Spatial Analysis of Information Outreach in Twitter Social Network

Muskan Banthia[1](✉), Shipra Goel[1](✉), Deepanshi[2](✉),
and Adwitiya Sinha[1](✉)

[1] Department of Computer Science and Engineering,
Jaypee Institute of Information Technology, Noida, Uttar Pradesh, India
muskan.banthia2l@gmail.com, goelshipra23@gmail.com,
mailtoadwitiy@gmail.com
[2] Department of Computer Science, ABES Engineering College,
Ghaziabad, India
deepanshi.jiit.cse@gmail.com

Abstract. With the expansion of social media at a very degree, analysis of user interest, influence, popularity etc. has become essential using the available data. A large amount of information about the twitter user can be extracted using twitter API according to the requirement for the analysis. Millions of users spread their opinions around the world by posting tweets on daily basis. This model aims to develop an application that creates the network of any particular twitter user using mention-based anomaly and state the most active users and influencers based on two different criteria in the network. It also aims at geospatial analysis to study the virality of the trend spread by the user throughout the world. This model extracts the top mentioned usernames from the user tweets and custom them to create the network. The projected model assist user in finding influencers in their network so that the information can be made to spread through them and also depicts their reach and connections. The model also proposes a formula for finding the most active users in the network. Diverse visualization methods are used to demonstrate the analysis of mentioned usernames, network model and for geospatial analysis using various python packages.

Keywords: Social media · Twitter · Social Network Analysis · Geospatial analysis · Information diffusion

1 Introduction

Social Network Analysis has been a trend in past few years. It inspects the relationship that exists on social media platform [11, 12]. The network is represented in terms of nodes and ties. Nodes are the actors (users) and ties are the relationship between the actors. Not only it visualizes and analyzes the connections between people but also determine the important influencers in the network [13–15]. In this model, we aimed to build a network analysis program that takes a user's twitter handle as input, and on the basis of his tweets find the top N most mentioned usernames visualizing it using word cloud which ultimately results into the formation of a network model based on the most

© Springer Nature Singapore Pte Ltd. 2020
P. K. Singh et al. (Eds.): FTNCT 2019, CCIS 1206, pp. 444–455, 2020.
https://doi.org/10.1007/978-981-15-4451-4_35

mentioned users. Having all the inter-connection details about the user in the network can be very beneficial in analyzing the most influential node(s) in the network through which if the information is passed could have a large outreach. We did our research work on 2 aspects: Topology Centric (using centrality measures on mention-based network). Profile Centric (using our proposed algorithm to find the top active users of the network).

- The network is analyzed, offering several degree measures, betweenness, centrality, communities, density, diameter, eccentricity and some other measures by which the progression of communication is reckoned on account of specified concepts.
- Twitter mention key ensures that the necessary information reaches to the full extent of your network.
- Identifying the key influencer of the network created on basis of top mentioned user (based on centrality measure).
- Finding the recent and popular trend (based on hashtags) by the user and its most influential node in network and visualizing it on the world map. The key influencer can be used as a main source of information diffusion from future perspective.
- Finding the set of active users based on our proposed algorithm which can be used as seed set for future analysis.

2   Related Work

Social connections analysis over the complex web network of twitter has gained extensive interest in the research community [16–20]. Some of the research are highlighted in this section. In paper [1] prediction is done using regression method. Efficiency in ranking and prediction methods are shown by experimenting it on two real world data set.

According to the authors, precise results of both user vitality ranking and prediction can profit many people in various social networking services, e.g., a user vitality ranking list can help people to better display their advertisement to active users and reach out to more potential customers. The authors of [2] depicted the use of mentions to spread an information far beyond the neighborhood and improves its visibility by making it available to the appropriate set of users. In this model, mentions from the tweets for a hashtag are extracted and the influence is compared with other strategies. The model in [3] shows very good scale-up properties, which lead to an almost linear decrease of the execution time needed to update the betweenness centrality on parallel systems. As a result, the method is able to keep up with the incoming rate of updates in large real-world graphs and in an online fashion. The authors of [4] devised theory of optimal control to devise strategies for jointly identifying good seeds and allocating campaign resources over time, to groups of nodes, such that a net reward function is maximized.

The model in [5] aimed to find different roles user play in social media, used Indegree (popularity), retweets (content value of one's tweets) and mentions (name value of a user). Used the concept of "active users". Used Spearman's rank correlation coefficient which gives strength of correlation between 2 rank set. According to their study the top Twitter users had a disproportionate amount of influence, which was indicated by a power-law distribution and they even concluded that Influence is not gained spontaneously or accidentally, but through concerted effort.

The author of paper in [6] aimed to recognize new trends and identifying the users starting these new trends. How the brands and influential user change i.e. increase or decrease in their popularity is measured using TF-IDF. The analysis in [7] even work on uncertainty of high dimension and unstructured data. In urban context how the different features and analyzing human activity can help in finding out hidden patters and society for social interaction sharing same geographical features and language. In the article in [8], the authors proposed a method which is a data driven approach to provide benefit to the users by using social media information and making use of friendship in locality, social closeness and content closeness for finding geographical nearby users. The authors of [9] applied the methodology to a suite of synthetic datasets and demonstrated the model's strength in detecting individual documents describing novel events, and moved on to process raw Twitter data to detect trending topics and proposed algorithms to detect the novel topics, calculate the degree of change, or measure between the word distribution of each topic before and after an update, and classify a topic as being novel if the measure exceeds a threshold. The model in [10] gives a technique for ranking the twitter users on the basis of their influence in the network. The ranking is the combination of the position of the user, user opinion polarity score and the quality of the tweet text.

3   Model Assumptions and Algorithmic Framework

This section illustrates the network model generation of the twitter data based on mentions of a particular user and find the key node of the network on basis of the requirements of user. Various measures like centrality, degree distribution, average path length, diameter, eccentricity of the mention-based network is calculated. The activity of the user is also calculated which gives us the seed set for information diffusion model.

3.1   Data Sources

Data is extracted using Twitter API with respect to user handle, and multiple features are extracted from the twitter regarding the user handle. Data is processed only on English language tweet discarding all other language tweets.

3.2   Languages and Libraries Used

We have used Python in our research. Libraries applied for designing our Twitter mention-based influencer detection system are:

Tweepy is an open source twitter API developed in Python that provide access to twitter data and extract tweets, retweets, hashtags, user handle, number of likes, retweets and many more.

NetworkX is used to generate model using tweets. Tweets are scrapped and pre-processing is done. It is a tool for the study of structure, dynamics and functions of complex social networks. It also provides us the standard programming interface and Graph implementation, suitable for many applications.

Geopy is used to locate the coordinates of tweets location across the globe. It is a client for several popular geo-coding web services. It uses Nominatim, an open street map to find the geo location of tweets.

Gmplot is a package for drawing geo-locations on the Google maps. It is for development purpose only. It generates a Java script-based HTML file that extract all geo-location statistics on Google maps.

3.3   Model Selection and Generation

Twitter has been one of the most powerful emerging social media platforms in recent years. Not only it serves as a medium of personal communication but can also cater mass communication. Twitter not only contains information in form of text but also depicts sentiments and emotions. While mentioning other users has become a convention inside Twitter, participants mentions for diverse reasons.

Analyzing the trend of top mentions of a user handle can not only give us the idea of genre, the user is interested in but also can help us to trace the spread of the tweet message. Taking a master handle from the user as our input we find their top mentions which are subsequently added to a queue and iteratively top mentions are figured out from their recent tweets. A network is formed which can be further analyzed to find how people are inter-connected, their social interaction, and all the top influencers in any given network. The graph allows us to represent the formation of the network's, interconnection between the nodes and extract the list of users whose reachability, connectivity and positioning is the highest. The key influencer of the network can be obtained using betweenness and closeness centrality.

Betweenness centrality is the count of any node that lies in the shortest path of any two nodes. When a node act as bridge between the nodes in a network its measure is called betweenness of that node. It is calculated by recognizing all the shortest paths and then calculating number of times any node falls on one. It is used for finding the users who stimulate, effect and impact the flow around a system.

Closeness centrality of a user is a degree of its centrality in any network, which is computed as the inverse of the sum of the distance of the shortest path between any two node and all other nodes in the given network. It is used for extracting the users who are closest to all other users.

In this case we are using betweenness and closeness centrality instead of degree centrality as degree centrality is basically concerned with the immediate neighbor in our network. A person with elevated degree centrality needs not to be the most influencing person. Analyzing the recent tweets of the master user and the key influencer and finding its recent popular hashtags so as to geographically locate its trend and compare. The model focuses on two different aspects:

A. **Topology-based:** This module focuses on the topology of the network and its structure. Various metrics like betweenness and closeness centrality are used to find the key influencer of the network based on what kind of property the influencer should hold.

Connectivity and Bridging. For finding the key influencer of the network which has highest connectivity and bridging property (i.e. the node that acts as the bridge/connection between most of other pairs of nodes through which most of the information travel and that help to transfer information of most of the nodes) we used the betweenness centrality measure. The node with highest betweenness centrality is said to be the key influencer.

Reachability and Positioning. For finding the key influencer of the network which has highest reachability and positioning property (i.e. the node that lies in the core/center of the network and that can reach every other node easier than others so that it could spread the information easily to other nodes) we used the closeness centrality measure. The node with highest closeness centrality is said to be the key influencer.

Further, most used hashtag of main profile, key influencer through connectivity and bridging and key influencer through reachability and positioning are analyzed. Then location of tweets on these recent hashtags issued worldwide is extracted using geopy library and their spread of trend is compared on Google maps using a python's library gmplot.

B. **Profile centric:** In this module we focused on finding the most active user of the network being that it may not lie in core of the network or it may not act as a bridge to others. The basic idea of this module is to find a user that is much more active than other users on twitter platform. Activity of a user is a combined effect of many user profile centric metrics. The parameters used for our experimentation are enlisted as following:

- followers count, fc: no. of followers a user has
- statuses, s: no of tweets issued by the user till date
- retweets count, rc: no of retweets of the user's recently issued tweets
- likes, l: no of likes user has got on his recent tweets
- favorites, f: no. of tweets liked by the user till date

Hence, we used the normalized value of each metric to give each factor equal weightage and then calculated the score of each user.

$$score = \frac{fc + s + rc + l + f}{5} \tag{1}$$

Every parameter is normalized using the standard normalization

$$\bar{z} = \frac{z - mean}{max - min} \tag{2}$$

Hence, higher the activity score highly active the user is. These active users now could act as the seed set in the diffusion of information.

3.4   Algorithm for the Model

In this section, the proposed algorithm is highlighted, that explains the formation of csv containing tweets of entered user, word cloud of mentioned users, csv containing nodes and edges of network, network statistics table, network model, most influential node in the network, map containing comparison of spread of trend of key influencers and the master profile and the list of top active users in the network. (Algorithm 1). The proposed algorithm generates file containing tweets of entered user, word cloud of mentioned users, csv containing nodes and edges of network, network statistics table, network model, most influential node in the network, map containing comparison of spread of trend of key influencers and the master profile and the list of top active users in the network. Table 1 illustrates the list of symbols used in the algorithm.

Algorithm 1: Mention-based Network Generation

Input: User Handle from Twitter
Procedure:
 1:    Begin
 2:    Authenticate Twitter developer's account
 3:    $X \leftarrow$ User Handle from Twitter
 4:    Most Mentions Queue, $Q(M) := [\,]$
 5:    Temporary Queue, $C(M) := [\,]$
 6:    while $\big((C.\text{Size} \leq M)\&\&(Q \neq \text{NULL})\big)$
 7:        $Q(M).\text{insert}(1) := X$
 8:        $Y \leftarrow Q(M).\text{delete}(1)$
 9:        $F_{\text{timeline}}(Y) \leftarrow$ Extract tweets from user profile Y & store in file
10:        $\bar{F}_{\text{timeline}}(Y) \leftarrow \text{Pre} - \text{process } F_{\text{timeline}}(Y)$ to clean file
11:        $\text{Data} - \text{frame } d(Y) \leftarrow$ filtered mentioned user handles from $\bar{F}_{\text{timeline}}(Y)$
12:        if $(Y == X)$
13:            print word cloud of mentioned users, $d(Y)$
14:        List $L \leftarrow$ Top N mentioned users from $d(Y)$
15:        Network. csv $\leftarrow \text{source}(X), \text{destination}(L)$
16:    Trend $H_X \leftarrow$ most used hashtag of X
17:    Location vector $L_x \leftarrow$ location of tweets of H_X
18:    Model $N_X \leftarrow$ Network. csv
19:    Stats Table$(N_X) \leftarrow N_X$
20:    influential node B $\leftarrow$ Node with max Betweenness Centrality
21:    Trend $H_B \leftarrow$ most used hashtag of B
22:    Location vector $L_B \leftarrow$ location of tweets of H_B
23:    Map plot of $L_B \& L_X$
24:    influential node C $\leftarrow$ Node with max Closeness Centrality
25:    Trend $H_C \leftarrow$ most used hashtag of C
26:    Location vector $L_C \leftarrow$ location of tweets of H_C
27:    Map plot of $L_C \& L_X$
28:    $\text{Score}_{\text{Activity}} \forall$ nodes in N_X
29:    List A $\leftarrow$ top 20 active users
30:    End

Table 1. List of symbols used

S. no.	Symbol	Description
1.	X	User handle from twitter
2.	$Q(M)$	Mention Queue of top 20 mention
3.	$C(M)$	Temporary Queue for processing
4.	A	List of top 20 Active users
5.	Y	Temporary Variable for processing
6.	$F_{timeline}(Y)$	Tweets from user profile
7.	$\overline{F}_{timeline}(Y)$	Cleaned Tweet data for user profile
8.	$d(Y)$	Data frame of Cleaned tweet data from user profile
9.	L	List of top mention
10.	H_X	Most used hashtag in user profile
11.	N_X	Network CSV file for creating network
12.	L_X	Location of tweet
13.	L_B	Location of Tweets on basis of H_B
14.	H_B	Most used hashtag using betweenness centrality
15.	L_C	Location of Tweets on basis of H_C
16.	H_C	Most used hashtag using Closeness centrality
17.	B	Node with maximum Betweenness Centrality
18.	C	Node with maximum Closeness Centrality

4   Experimental Outcome

The proposed model generates the dynamic output as the data is extracted from twitter dynamically which is updated at every instance with every new tweet (Fig. 1). Updating the timeline by every tweet or retweet is completely dependent on the target user for whom we are analyzing the data therefore giving different results which are dynamic in nature. For the evaluation of functioning of our model we have targeted the user handle of the @PMOIndia and fed it as an input to our proposed model which scraps tweets and store it in csv file which on further processing gives the list of most mentioned usernames by the input user handle. Figure 2 represents a word cloud which shows the top mentioned usernames and the size of the username depends upon its frequency the bigger the name the higher the occurring frequency and vice versa. The network generated by the most mentions is illustrated in Fig. 3. Along with this, the network statistics are calculated as illustrated in Fig. 4.

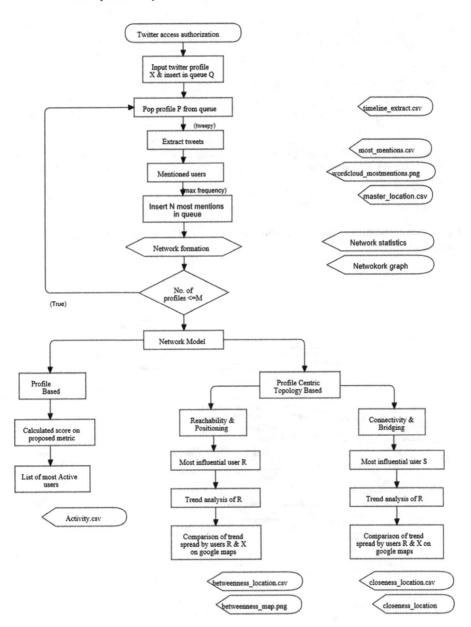

Fig. 1. Control flow diagram of proposed model

Fig. 2. Most mentioned user of profile as word cloud

Metrics	Values
Average Path Length	3.625
Average Degree	{10: 11.3333333333334, 11: 4.8454545454546, 10: 4.66666666666667, 12: 4.8333333333333, 14: 7.392857142857143, 1: 11.160377358490566, 2: 11.75, 3: 12.0}
Density	0.019
No of Nodes	140
No of Edges	186
diameter	5
Average Eccentricity	4.721

Fig. 4. Network statistics

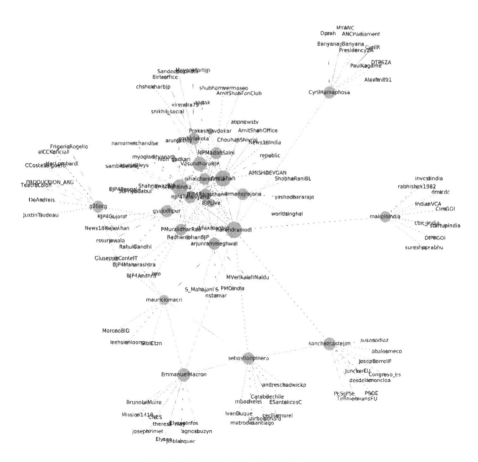

Fig. 3. Mention-based Social Network

The proposed model finds the key influencer using centrality measures and then finds their subsequent most used hashtags. The most used hashtag of both the key influencer and the master handle is plotted on Google map and the trend is compared. It was found that the most used hashtag of the master handle is *#Mannkibaat50* and, key influencer based on reachability and positioning is *@BJP4India* (Case 1) and the most used hashtag by this handle is *#MamtaFearsBJP*. The key influencer based on connectivity and bridging is *@EmmanuelMacron* (Case 2) and hashtag by this user is *#ChooseFrance*. These trends are illustrated in Figs. 5 and 6 (Black color is for master handle and red for the key influencer).

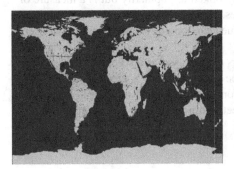 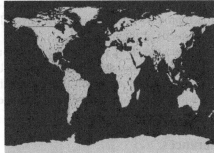

Fig. 5. Trend comparison of key Influencer and master handle (Case 1) (Color figure online)

Fig. 6. Trend comparison of key Influencer and master handle (Case 2) (Color figure online)

Further we calculated the activity score of every node in our network using some user centric parameters and then return top 20 active users. Retweet count and likes are calculated with last 50 tweets of ever user (Fig. 7).

Node	followers_count	favourite_count	statuses	retweets_count	likes	Score
0 narendramodi	0.950274439	-0.082442876	-0.01166748	0.504221423	0.85951584	0.443980269
1 RahulGandhi	0.129703602	-0.070740625	-0.06190789	0.837196172	0.95814406	0.358479065
2 aajtak	0.120669542	0.559514732	0.762658973	-0.076338663	-0.0378962	0.265721675
3 POTUS	0.502524165	-0.078412962	-0.06025472	0.921741175	-0.0418559	0.248748345
4 Oprah	0.885224599	-0.076398005	-0.03747865	0.113086561	0.29274246	0.235435393
5 virendra79	-0.049422684	0.917557124	-0.04056799	0.275675773	-0.0414195	0.212364535
6 BJP4India	0.180401716	-0.082442876	0.427133784	0.250771492	0.02224365	0.159621553
7 News18Rajasthan	-0.043681295	-0.071205615	0.926608424	-0.078108451	-0.0414947	0.138423681
8 mauriciomacri	0.055692067	-0.078529209	-0.04735199	0.199343516	0.38561889	0.102954655
9 VasundharaBJP	0.029094153	0.316906138	-0.03015502	0.164121251	0.01631658	0.099256622
10 AmitShah	0.219573208	-0.076320506	-0.05172333	0.16202758	0.23835797	0.098382984
11 WhiteHouse	0.346149881	-0.082094134	-0.05569779	0.121276171	0.11681915	0.089290655
12 News18India	-0.029204646	-0.070159387	0.659357199	-0.07781927	-0.0406612	0.088302535
13 BJP4Maharashtra	-0.047004793	0.532622804	0.03839876	-0.073250208	-0.0385687	0.082439575
14 BJPLive	-0.041341706	-0.079536688	0.338810482	0.233779208	-0.0408615	0.082169953
15 PIB_India	-0.017610699	0.041399492	0.492521123	-0.075841271	-0.0405933	0.079975077
16 abpnewstv	0.129479922	-0.082326629	0.4529164	-0.075945376	-0.0367766	0.07746954
17 arunjaitley	0.254311896	-0.080970407	-0.06486875	0.046875644	0.15072182	0.06121404
18 RadhamohanBJP	-0.043128054	0.30973754	-0.03743868	0.072740006	-0.0397741	0.052427337
19 sambitswaraj	0.007347052	0.05515545	0.038575783	0.135064329	0.00735623	0.04869977

Fig. 7. Activity score of top Active users of Mention-based Social Network

5 Conclusion

Social Network Analysis with Twitter science is wide research area which has greater scopes towards scientific exploration. In our research, we performed analysis of the mention-based network of Twitter data and identified the key influencers. The activity of a user is not only based on its popularity but also the number of various other parameters which tells us about the users' actions. A trend comparison of the key influencer and master user has been conducted based on the most used hashtag in his recent tweets. Further, the activity of nodes in the network is calculated to provide with the list of top active users. Activity is not only linked to popularity but is a measure of total participation of user on social media sites. Hence, we conclude that our proposed approach provides the user with the key influencer (topology-based) and active users (profile-based) of the network.

As future direction, the list of active users can be used as a seed set to a diffusion model and the information spreading can be observed with a great accuracy. This model works only for English tweets, therefore a multi lingual model can be shaped which will be language independent and tweets from worldwide can be analyzed.

References

1. Hong, R., He, C., Ge, Y., Wang, M., Wu, X.: User vitality ranking and prediction in social networking services: a dynamic network perspective. IEEE Trans. Knowl. Data Eng. 29(6), 1343–1356 (2017)
2. Pramanik, S., Wang, Q.: On the role of mentions on tweet virality. In: IEEE International Conference on Data Science and Advanced Analytics (DSAA), 17–19 October 2016, pp. 204–213 (2016)
3. Kourtellis, N., De Francisci Morales, G., Bonchi, F.: Scalable online betweenness centrality in evolving graphs. IEEE Trans. Knowl. Data Eng. 27(9), 2494–2506 (2015)
4. Kandhway, K., Kuri, J.: Using node centrality and optimal control to maximize information diffusion in social networks. IEEE Trans. Syst. Man Cybern.: Syst. 47(7), 1099–1110 (2017)
5. Cha, M., Haddadi, H.: Measuring user influence in Twitter: the million follower fallacy. In: Proceedings of the Fourth International AAAI Conference on Weblogs and Social Media (2010)
6. Gloor, P.A., Krauss, J.: Web science 2.0: identifying trends through semantic social network analysis. In: 2009 International Conference on Computational Science and Engineering, 29–31 August 2009, pp. 215–222 (2009)
7. Psyllidis, A., Yang, J., Bozzon, A.: Regionalization of social interactions and points-of-interest location prediction with geosocial data. IEEE Access 6, 34334–34353 (2018)
8. Xu, D., Cui, P., Zhu, W., Yang, S.: Graph-based residence location inference for social media users. IEEE Multimed. 21(4), 76–83 (2014)
9. Lau, J.H., Collier, N.: Online trend analysis with topic models: #Twitter trends detection topic model online. In: Proceedings of COLING 2012: Technical Papers, COLING 2012, pp. 1519–1534, December 2012
10. Bigonha, C., Cardoso, T.N.C., Moro, M.M., Gonçalves, M.A., Almeida, V.A.: Sentiment-based influence detection on Twitter. J. Braz. Comput. Soc. 18(3), 169–183 (2012). https://doi.org/10.1007/s13173-011-0051-5

11. Shi, L.-L., Liu, L., Wu, Y., Jiang, L., Hardy, J.: Event detection and user interest discovering in social media data streams. IEEE Access **5**, 20953–20964 (2017)
12. Roy, S.D., Lotan, G., Zeng, W.K.: The attention automaton: sensing collective user interests in social network communities. IEEE Trans. Netw. Sci. Eng. **2**(1), 40–52 (2015)
13. Phad, P.V., Chavan, M.K.: Detecting compromised high-profile accounts on social networks. In: 2018 9th IEEE International Conference on Computing, Communication and Networking Technologies (ICCCNT), 10–12 July 2018, pp. 1–4 (2018)
14. Aiello, L.M., Petkos, G., Martin, C., Corney, D., Papadopoulos, S.: Sensing trending topics in Twitter. IEEE Trans. Multimed. **15**(6), 1268–1282(2013)
15. Zhan, Q., Zhang, J., Philip, S.Y., Emery, S., Xie, J.: Inferring social influence of anti-tobacco mass media campaign. IEEE Trans. NanoBiosci. **16**(5), 356–366 (2017)
16. Srinivas, A., Velusamy, R.L.: Identification of influential nodes from social networks based on Enhanced Degree Centrality Measure. In: 2015 IEEE International Advance Computing Conference (IACC), 12–13 June 2015, pp. 1179–1184. IEEE (2015)
17. Guille, A., Favre, C.: Mention-anomaly-based event detection and tracking in Twitter. In: 2014 IEEE/ACM International Conference on Advances in Social Networks Analysis and Mining, ASONAM 2014, 17–20 August 2014 (2014)
18. Bakshy, E., Hofman, J.M.: Everyone's an influencer: quantifying influence on Twitter. In: WDSM 2011 Proceedings of the Fourth ACM International Conference on Web Search and Data Mining, 09–12 February 2011, pp. 65–74 (2011)
19. Wolny, W.: Knowledge gained from Twitter data. In: 2016 Federated Conference on Computer Science and Information Systems (FedCSIS), Date of Conference 11–14 September 2016 (2016)
20. Abascal-Mena, R., Lema, R.: From tweet to graph: social network analysis for semantic information extraction. In: 2014 IEEE Eighth International Conference on Research Challenges in Information Science (RCIS), 28–30 May 2014, pp. 1–10 (2014)

Sustainable Approach for Forest Fire Prediction

Paras Chaudhary[(✉)], Somya Jain[(✉)], and Adwitiya Sinha[(✉)]

Department of Computer Science and Engineering,
Jaypee Institute of Information Technology, Noida-62, UP, India
paras.vc18@gmail.com, somya.jain@jiit.ac.in,
mailtoadwitiya@gmail.com

Abstract. With the rising global temperatures and already depleting forest cover there is one phenomenon which gets fiercer due to the first issue and worsens the second issue, respectively, and it is called forest fire. With already rapidly decreasing forests it is very important to curb, predict and mitigate the cases of forest fire which 90% of the times occurs due to a human error. Forests are of prime importance to the sustainability of the planet and hence desperately need to be conserved. The paper demonstrates the successful usage of various Data Mining models to predict the burned area in case of a forest fire by considering four low cost meteorological variables, temperature, rain, relative humidity and wind. A rigorous comparative study is presented of the performance of each Data Mining model for the given task and its reviewal reveals that Gene Expression Programming is the best at predicting forest fire area with four weather variables.

Keywords: Forest fire prediction · Data mining · Regression model · Sustainability

1 Introduction

Humans depend on forests for their survival from the air they breathe to the wood they use. Forests are the source of livelihood to human settlements of 300 million people including 60 million native people. Besides providing for humans, forests provide habitats to 80% of the world's terrene biodiversity and offer watershed protection, prevent soil from eroding, provide fuel security and mitigate climate change. Between 1990 and 2015 planet earth lost about 129 million ha of forest (which is roughly area size of Africa) and losing forests does not mean simply the removal of trees, rather it is the beginning of the whole eco-system falling apart. This rate of loss is only increasing and one of its biggest cause is the increasing number of forest fires, which too is only likely to increase with the increasing global temperatures.

Forest fires are not unnatural and have existed on the earth for millions of years and earth's forest ecosystem has developed and sustained with fire. But it is only controlled and naturally occurring fires that are useful to the forest ecosystem and anything caused

© Springer Nature Singapore Pte Ltd. 2020
P. K. Singh et al. (Eds.): FTNCT 2019, CCIS 1206, pp. 456–469, 2020.
https://doi.org/10.1007/978-981-15-4451-4_36

anthropogenically (by humans) are a harm to the sustainability of ecology and it has been recorded that more than 90% of forest fires today are caused by human beings, by their active acts or their passive negligence [19]. Highest regional estimates of human caused forest fires were observed in Mediterranean and South Asian countries with 95% and 90% cases respectively [9]. It is evident that the acreage of forest area burnt is rapidly increasing with time, in the United States of America it has increased from 1.62 million ha to 4.05 million ha in 2006, and by 2100 might be the cause of 40,000 human deaths in the USA due to chronic inhalation of wildfire smoke [11]. In India the percentage of area prone to forest fires ranges between 33 and 90% in a few states annually, and the number of fire incidents shot up by 49.32% in the years 2016 to 2018 according to Forest Survey of India (FSI). It is estimated that globally the Landscape Fire Smoke (LFS) causes 339,000 deaths annually [16].

Hence to maintain a sustainable environment and to mitigate the dire effects of wild fires on environment the early detection of these incidents is of prime importance. Early detection should be followed by a prediction of the expanse or severity of a fire that erupted to ensure quick and efficient allotment of resources to the firefighting authorities and help in decision making. The scope of humans in providing a continuous and effective surveillance is limited and hence there is a need for the development of automatic solutions. Such solutions can be of three type [1] satellite, smoke/infra-red scanners or meteorological sensors. Satellites are an overkill solution, with high costs of acquisition, low resolution and localization delays, making them least favourable solution kind. Smoke and infrared sensors have high installation and maintenance costs associated with them but real time meteorological data is often readily available from meteorological stations (e.g. India has 32 stations) for low costs [15].

In this paper we present Data Mining techniques (DM) to utilise this meteorological data to predict the expanse of a forest fire that has erupted. The paper also strives to choose minimal yet the most effective weather variables for the prediction. The proposed method in the paper predicts the burned area from small wild fires by applying multiple DM models on only four weather features, rain, wind, temperature and humidity from the elaborate meteorological data. A comparative study of the efficiency of each model in predicting the area is presented from which the best can be chosen and applied, to strive towards a more sustainable earth. The information predicted from the proposed model is very useful for implementing better forest fire alerting and mitigation systems which in turn will result in saving human and natural resources to make the affected ecology more sustainable.

The paper is organised as follows: Sect. 2 describes all the literature related to the paper's field of study. Section 3 elaborates on the dataset that was collected and then operated upon by the chosen DM techniques. In the next part of the paper, Sect. 4, the error metric formulas are provided and the 9 DM models which are used for the regression task to predict the burned area are described individually. Section 5 is broken down into two parts, of which the first gives the visualization of the actual and predicted values from the chosen DM model along with the respective parameter settings and the second part tabulates all the models with all the errors calculated for each one of them.

2 Related Works

Forest Survey of India (FSI) is working in close collaboration with the forestry professionals of the country to solve the problems with forest fires by using remote sensing and communication technology. The currently active Forest fire management initiatives include Near Real Time (NRT) Forest Fire alerts (FFA) and Forest Fire Pre-warning alerts (FFPWA). NRT forest fire alerts work on a model proposed in the paper [4], in its functioning FSI alerts State Forest Departments (SFD) of locations of forest fire by the Moderate Resolution Imaging Spectro-radiometer (MODIS) sensor on the Aqua and Terra Satellites both of which have two passes over the country daily and capture all thermal anomalies in 1 km × 1 km resolution which are then filtered out by FSI if they lie outside forest boundaries, this data is then enriched by adding attributes like State, District Division and sent to State Nodal Officer, registered users and updated on FSI website. FFA 2.0 is a sensor-based improvement of NRT FFA which is inspired from the paper [25] and utilizes Suomi National Polar-orbiting Partnership (S-NPP) Visible and Infrared Imager/Radiometer Suite (VIIRS) to automate the night-time fire alerts. The inclusion of SNPP-VIIRS Sensor with higher resolution of 375 m × 375 m to the existing MODIS sensor has improved the identification of smaller fires and detecting their boundary. Several famous contemporary Wireless Sensor Network (WSN) technologies like those that use MODIS and Unmanned Aerial Vehicles, for their application in the wild fire detection, have been juxtaposed to bring out their relative pros and cons in a study conducted by Singh and Sharma [21]. The data from these WSNs can be used to prepare PHP and MySQL based analytics and supervision dashboards, to be used by Forest Officials, using integrated Decision Support System (DSS) [5]. The systems developed on WSN data has also been used to make whole even more wholesome systems that apart from prediction also help in mitigation of the same using drones to constrict the expanse of wild fires [12].

FFPWA strives to do what the proposed method in the paper does efficiently, that is predict forest fire on the basis of limited meteorological variables. Currently FFPWA employs 6 parameters Forest Cover Density Classes, Forest Type Groups, Daily Relative Humidity, Daily Maximum Temperature, Rainfall (past and forecasts) and Fire Alert database (2004–2016), three parameters of which are non-meteorological, forest cover and type and fire alert database.

In the past, meteorological data has been tried to be transformed into numerical indices. The Canadian forest fire index (FWI) considers four meteorological parameters, temperature, relative humidity, rain and wind. To accurately indicate fuel characteristics and fire behavior FSI integrated a suitable drought index called Keetch-Byran Drought Index (KBDI) in their predictive model.

Multiple Data Mining (DM) or Knowledge Discovery in Databases (KDD) techniques are being used to find out complex trends and patterns in raw data. Therefore, a lot of DM techniques have also been used in the field of wild fires, like the application of Neural Networks (NN) to predict the occurrences human caused forest fires [22]. Infrared Sensors were used along with NN to reduce the number of false alarms while alerting for forest fires with a 90% success rate [1]. Fully connected feed forward NN has been used on data collected from Raspberry Pi microcontroller based IOT devices

[6]. FASTCiD a spatial clustering was used to spot forest fires in satellite images [20]. Support Vector Machine (SVM) on being applied to satellite images of North American forest fires and obtained 75% accuracy at finding smoke at a 1.1 km pixel [14]. SVM has also been used to detect fire from non-fire on a region of interest that is extracted from video data by applying special wavelet analysis on background subtracted CIELAB colour space data [18]. Logistic Regression, Random Forest and Decision Trees were applied on satellite based and meteorological data of the Slovenian forests, maximum accuracy of 80% was achieved on using a bagging Decision Tree [17].

3 Dataset

The Canadian system for rating fire danger called the Fire Weather Index (FWI) includes 5 subcomponents that are used to compute the final FWI [23]. The first three codes Fine Fuel Moisture Code (FFMC), Duff Moisture Code (DMC) and Drought Code (DC) are fuel codes where FFMC describes the factors that influence the ignition and spread of fire like moisture content surface litter, DMC and DC both represent factors that affect fire intensity like the content of moisture in deep and shallow organic layers. ISI considers fire velocity spread and BUI represents the availability of fuel. FWI is computed from the last two components and indicates the intensity of fire. A high value of FWI suggests severe burning conditions.

The paper uses wild fire data from the Trás-os-Montes northeast region of Portugal's Montesinho Natural Park which contains a lot of diverse flora and fauna. With an average temperature between 8–12 °C it comes in a Supra-Mediterranean climate. The data used in the study was collected from two sources in the course of 3 years between 2000 and 2003. The first source being the inspector of fire occurrences at Montensinho who whenever a wildfire event occurred recorded several features like the date, time, x and y coordinates (in a 9 × 9 grid) of the spot of occurrence, the kinds of vegetation involved and the 5 components of FWI along with the computed FWI along with the total burned area. The second database was made using data from the Bragnça Polytechnic Institute which records weather observations at every 30 min from a meteorological station in Montesinho. The obtained two datasets were combined into a single data set that has 517 entries [3]. The data can be viewed at: http://www.dsi.uminho.pt/ ~ pcortez/forestfires.

12 data features were selected out of which the first four being the spatial and temporal variables, only the x and y coordinates are used to locate the geographic location of fire and features like vegetation etc. were ignored because of 80% of entries in that field were missing. On consulting the fire inspector month and day of the week were decided as the two temporal factors because the average monthly weather conditions are very unique and since majority of the times forest fires occur due to human interaction that attribute can be studied by keeping the day of the week in focus. Four mutually exclusive features of FWI were included, which are FFMC, DMC, DC and ISI. BUI and FWI were discarded as they were derivatives of the other ones and hence would be redundant. The meteorological station provided for the weather variables used to compute FWI which are outside temperature (temp), relative humidity (RH),

wind speed (wind) and rain (rain). But FWI uses time lags to be computed but the dataset denotes instant records except in the case of rain variable which denotes total rain in the past 30 min.

Burned area shows a positive skew with most fires erupting being small in size with 247 entries with 0 values which means they had an area less than 100 m². To improve the regression results $y = ln(x + 1)$ was applied which reduced skewness to increase symmetry. This transformed variable is the output target of the proposed method.

4 Data Mining Models Discussions

A dataset, for regression, D has k ∈ {1, ... , N} entries, and each input vector $(x_1^k, \ldots, x_A^k)$ is associated with a, provided, target y_k. The error in prediction is given by $c_k = y_k - \hat{y}_k$ where $\hat{y}_k$ is the predicted value for all the k input patterns. The performance of these regression model applications can be calculated by many global metrics. This paper utilizes most of the major performance metrics to rate all the data mining models employed during the course of the study to give a thorough comparative study which can finally be used to choose the most suitable model in the end for the chosen problem statement. The metrics employed are correlation coefficient (R), Normalized Mean Squared Error (NMSE), Maximum Error (ME), Root Mean Squared Error (RMSE), Mean Squared Error (MSE), Mean Absolute Error (MAE) and Mean Absolute Percentage Error (MAPE), which can be computed in using Eqs. (1–6) as:

$$NMSE = \left(1/N \times \sum\nolimits_i |y_i - \hat{y}_i|^2\right) / \left(\left(1/N \times \sum\nolimits_i y_i\right) \times \left(1/N \times \sum\nolimits_i \hat{y}_i\right)\right) \quad (1)$$

$$ME = Max_i(|y_i - \hat{y}_i|) \quad (2)$$

$$RMSE = \sqrt{\left(1/N \times \sum\nolimits_i |y_i - \hat{y}_i|^2\right)} \quad (3)$$

$$MSE = 1/N \times \sum\nolimits_i |y_i - \hat{y}_i|^2 \quad (4)$$

$$MAE = 1/N \times \sum\nolimits_i |y_i - \hat{y}_i| \quad (5)$$

$$MAPE = 100\%/N \times \sum\nolimits_i |(y_i - \hat{y}_i)/y_i| \quad (6)$$

In all of the above metrics the lower the values of the error the better is the prediction by the model.

A lot of DM algorithms have been proposed and used for regression tasks, each of which has its own properties and capabilities. This study compares 9 such DM models on the basis of above described error metrics for predicting the burned area using the given meteorological inputs. The 9 models used are namely Cascade Correlation (CC),

Decision Tree Forest (DTF), Gene Expression Programming (GEP), Group Method of Data Handling Polynomial Network (GMDH-PN), Linear Regression (LR), Multilayer Perceptron Neural Network (MLP), Radial Basis Function Neural Network (RBF), Epsilon Support Vector Regressor (ε-SVR) and Nu Support Vector Regressor (Nu-SVR).

CC works by combining two key ideas, one is its cascaded architecture in which one by one hidden units are added and once added do not change and the second is its learning algorithm which creates new hidden units and then installs them. For every new hidden unit, the aim is to maximize the correlation between the new unit's residual error signal (that we are trying to eliminate) and output [8].

DTF is a model that gives a single prediction after combining the results of multiple individual Decision Trees (DT), in DTs the predictions are based on a series of IF-THEN rules [24].

GEP is very similar to genetic algorithms (GA) or genetic programming (GP), since it utilizes populations of individuals, chooses them on the basis of their respective fitness to introduce a genetic variation using some kind of genetic operator, the only main difference between these three is that in GA individuals are represented as strings which are linear and of a fixed length whereas in GP they are not linear and are of varied shapes and sizes but in GEP first they are encoded as linear fixed length strings and later as non-linear entities of different sizes [10].

GMDH has been used to create a function inside a feed-forward network which uses a second-degree transfer function to do so, the number of neurons, the layers formed by them (hidden layers), their structure and effective input variables are determined by the algorithm itself, the output and input variables are mapped to one another by Volterra series and GMDH is aimed at finding its unknown coefficients [7].

LR tries to find a linear relationship between the input and the output and make predictions based on that.

A MLP is made up of more than one perceptron (that produces a one output based on multiple inputs after making a linear combination using the input weights along with the passing output through a non-linear activation function), arranged in input, output and hidden layers, the training of a MLP adjusts the weights and biases via back-propagation to reduce the error between the predicted and actual values, and it then can make predictions [13].

A RBFN does classification by measuring the similarity of an input to the examples in the training set, and stores it as a prototype and to classify a new input it then finds the Euclidean distance between the prototype and input, and classifies it to whichever prototype class it is the closest to [13].

Support vector machines use such learning machines which implement a inductive principle of reducing structural risk to achieve good generalization on a limited number of learning models. Structural risk reduction involves an effort to reduce empirical risk and Vapnik Chervonenkis dimensions. In regression, different loss functions can be chosen depending upon the distribution of the noise in the measurement [2]. The paper implements epsilon and nu SVR.

5   Results and Visualizations

5.1   Model Parameters Settings and Predictions

Cascade Correlation. The parameters settings chosen for CC include setting the minimum and maximum number of neurons in the hidden layer as 0 and 50 respectively with the hidden neuron kernel function as Sigmoid and Gaussian while the output neuron kernel function was set to linear. Cross-validation with 10 folds was used to validate the predictions. The actual values are plotted against the predictions made by the model with the described parameter settings in Fig. 1.

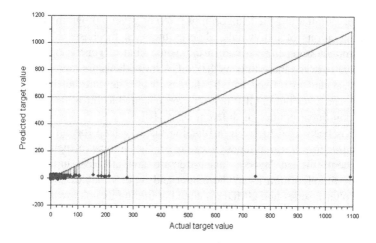

Fig. 1.   Actual vs predicted values of area from CC

Decision Tree Forest. The parameters settings chosen for DTF include setting the number of maximum trees in forest to 200 with a maximum 50 splitting levels and equal variable weights. The minimum size of node split was chosen to be 2 and max 1000 categories for continuous predictors. Surrogate splitters were used but not necessarily for all cases. Out of bag method was employed for validation. Actual values are plotted against the predictions made by the model with described parameter settings in Fig. 2.

Gene Expression Programming. The parameters settings chosen for GEP include setting the number of generations required to train the model to 1528, with complexity of model before and after simplification to 31 and 22 respectively. 110,150 evaluations of the fitness function were done and 12 execution threads were used in the process. It was observed that a non-linear regression did not improve the model. GEP resulted in the formation of the following Eq. (7) for the target variable, area.

$$area = (temp - 4.0679895) + (((((2 * temp) - 8.7223582) - (76.079532/wind))/RH) + (wind - Sqrt(RH - 7.1408537)))$$

$$(7)$$

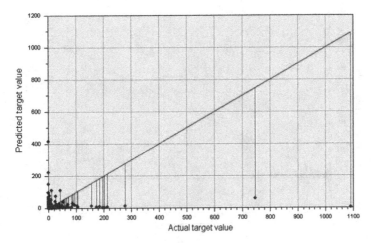

Fig. 2. Actual vs predicted values of area from DTF

The actual values are plotted against the predictions made by the model with the described parameter settings in Fig. 3.

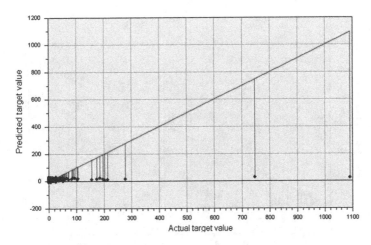

Fig. 3. Actual vs predicted values of area from GEP

GMDH Polynomial Network. The parameters settings chosen for GMDH polynomial network include setting the maximum network layers to 20 with 20 neurons each and maximum polynomial order of 16. Previous layer along with the original input variables were connected to each network layer. A 10-fold setting cross-validation was used to validate the predictions. The actual values are plotted against the predictions made by the model with the described parameter settings in Fig. 4.

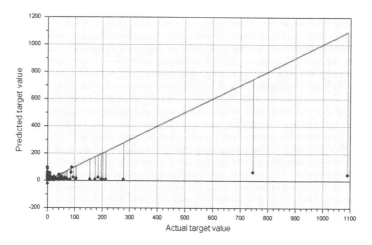

Fig. 4. Actual vs predicted values of area from GMDH polynomial network

Linear Regression. Default settings were used in LR, with a 10-fold setting cross-validation to validate the predictions. The actual values are plotted against the predictions made by the model with the described parameter settings in Fig. 5.

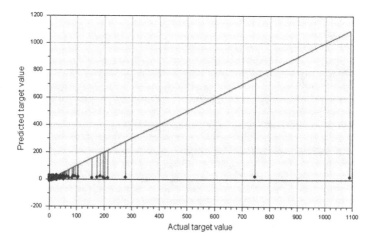

Fig. 5. Actual vs predicted values of area from LR

Multilayer Perceptron Neural Network. The parameters settings chosen for MLP neural network include setting the number of layers to 3 (including 1 hidden). The hidden layer uses a Logistic activation function and search from 2 to 20. The output layer has a linear activation. A 10-fold setting cross-validation was employed to validate the predictions. The actual values are plotted against the predictions made by the model with the described parameter settings in Fig. 6.

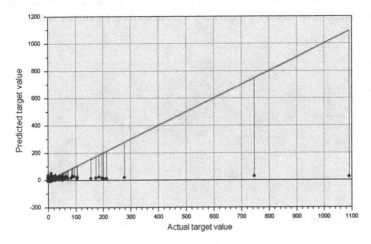

Fig. 6. Actual vs predicted values of area from MLP Neural Networks

Radial Basis Function Network. The parameters settings chosen for RBF neural network include setting the number of maximum neurons to 100, a minimum and maximum radius of 0.01 and 400 respectively with a minimum and maximum lambda values of 0.001 and 10 respectively. The neuron tuning parameters included population area of 200, maximum number of generations as 20, max. gen. flat of 5 and 50 max. boost iterations. A 10-fold setting cross-validation was employed for validation. The actual values are plotted against the predictions made by the model with the described parameter settings in Fig. 7.

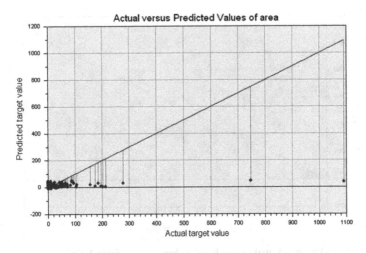

Fig. 7. Actual vs predicted values of area from RBF network

Epsilon SVR. The parameters settings chosen for SVM include setting the type of model to epsilon-SVM and used an RBF kernel function. The range for C is set from 0.1 to 5000, of gamma from 0.001 to 50 and P is in 0.0001 and 100. A 10-fold setting cross-validation was employed to validate the predictions. The actual values are plotted against the predictions made by the model with described parameter settings in Fig. 8.

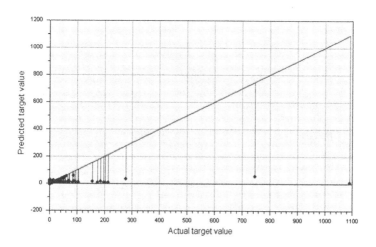

Fig. 8. Actual vs predicted values of area from ε-SVR

Nu SVR. The parameters settings chosen for SVM include setting the type of model to nu-SVM and used a RBF kernel function. The range for C is set from 0.1 to 5000, of gamma from 0.001 to 50 and Nu is in 0.0001 and 0.6. A 10-fold setting cross-validation was employed for validation. The actual values are plotted against the predictions made by the model with the described parameter settings in Fig. 9.

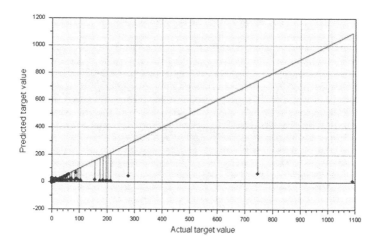

Fig. 9. Actual vs predicted values of area from Nu-SVR

5.2   Evaluation

Computed values for all correlation coefficient and the error metrics defined in Sect. 4 have been tabulated in Table 1 for all the 9 models applied in the paper.

Table 1. Performance comparison of distinct models

Models	R	NMSE	ME	RMSE	MSE	MAE	MAPE
CC	0.03	1	1074.7	63.7	4069.2	19.9	556.5
DTF	0.01	1.14	1088.3	68.0	4630.3	20.3	620.9
GEP	0.10	0.98	1069.4	63.2	3995.5	19.2	617.7
GMDH	0.03	1.12	1075.8	67.5	4562.5	19.6	522.4
LR	0.05	1	1073.9	63.7	4059.4	19.4	616.5
MLP	0.05	1	1073.9	63.6	4050.4	19.5	629.6
RBF	0.04	1.01	1066.3	64.1	4119.9	20.1	723.3
ε-SVR	0.09	0.99	1084.6	63.5	4034.0	16.2	365.8
Nu-SVR	0.10	0.99	1085.3	63.4	4023.4	16.3	376.3

Correlation coefficient's (R) value can be in the range $[-1, 1]$ and is a measure of the strength of the relationship between two variables, a negative value suggests that as one variable increases the other decreases while a highly positive value tells that two variables increase together strongly. None of the models gave a negative correlation coefficient and the most positive value was observed in GEP. The least value of ME was observed in RBF, while ε-SVR had the lowest MAE and MAPE value. From the table it is evident that Gene Expression Programming gave the most promising predictive results in comparison to all other models, it outperformed all the other 8 algorithms in 4 out of the 7 chosen accuracy metrics. The two SVR models (epsilon and nu) separately came close to giving good predictive results too but both were beaten by GEP in error metrics that were more responsive to errors (like NMSE, RMSE and MSE). With the most positive value of R (0.1) and the least values of NMSE (0.98), RMSE (63.2) and MSE (3995.5) scores GEP is the most suitable algorithm to predict the area which was burned using the four meteorological features of temp, relative humidity, wind and rain.

6   Conclusion

Forest fires are a big threat to the sustainability of the earth and every living organism living on it. This threat is increasing with rising global temperatures and increasing world population the carelessness of which is the cause of wildfires in 90% of the cases. Because of these afore mentioned reasons a substantial amount of resources is being put and efforts are being done all over the world, including India, to build automatic detection/prediction tools that can help the Fire Management Systems (FMS) in mitigating the ill effects of large-scale forest fires. The paper proposed a data mining solution to predict the severity of wildfires using real data obtained from low-cost real-time providers like the meteorological stations. The problem of predicting the burned area in forest fires was modeled as a regression task and by applying 9 unique kinds of DM algorithms on four selected features it was concluded that Gene Expression Programming very efficiently and accurately does the task.

The study was based on data that was collected beforehand hence is an example of offline learning hence it opens avenues for larger scale real-time predictive analysis using the models proposed by this paper. Finally, these ways can be incorporated into the usual meteorological forecasts to devise proactive responses to forest fires (that haven't yet occurred).

References

1. Arrue, B.C., Ollero, A., De Dios, J.M.: An intelligent system for false alarm reduction in infrared forest-fire detection. IEEE Intell. Syst. Their Appl. **15**(3), 64–73 (2000)
2. Basak, D., Pal, S., Patranabis, D.C.: Support vector regression. Neural Inf. Process.-Lett. Rev. **11**(10), 203–224 (2007)
3. Cortez, P., Morais, A.D.J.R.: A data mining approach to predict forest fires using meteorological data (2007)
4. Davies, D.K., Ilavajhala, S., Wong, M.M., Justice, C.O.: Fire information for resource management system: archiving and distributing MODIS active fire data. IEEE Trans. Geosci. Remote Sens. **47**(1), 72–79 (2008)
5. Devadevan, V., Sankaranarayanan, S.: Forest fire information system using wireless sensor network. In: Environmental Information Systems: Concepts, Methodologies, Tools, and Applications, pp. 894–911. IGI Global (2019)
6. Dubey, V., Kumar, P., Chauhan, N.: Forest fire detection system using IoT and artificial neural network. In: Bhattacharyya, S., Hassanien, A.E., Gupta, D., Khanna, A., Pan, I. (eds.) International Conference on Innovative Computing and Communications. LNNS, vol. 55, pp. 323–337. Springer, Singapore (2019). https://doi.org/10.1007/978-981-13-2324-9_33
7. Ebtehaj, I., Bonakdari, H., Zaji, A.H., Azimi, H., Khoshbin, F.: GMDH-type neural network approach for modeling the discharge coefficient of rectangular sharp-crested side weirs. Eng. Sci. Technol. Int. J. **18**(4), 746–757 (2015)
8. Fahlman, S.E., Lebiere, C.: The cascade-correlation learning architecture. In: Advances in Neural Information Processing Systems, pp. 524–532 (1990)
9. FAO: Fire management global assessment 2006. FAO Forestry Paper No. 151, Rome (2007)
10. Ferreira, C.: Gene expression programming: a new adaptive algorithm for solving problems. arXiv preprint cs/0102027 (2007)
11. Ford, B., et al.: Future fire impacts on smoke concentrations, visibility, and health in the contiguous United States. GeoHealth **2**(8), 229–247 (2018)
12. Grover, K., Kahali, D., Verma, S., Subramanian, B.: WSN-based system for forest fire detection and mitigation. In: Subramanian, B., Chen, S.S., Reddy, K. (eds.) Emerging Technologies for Agriculture and Environment. LNMIE, pp. 249–260. Springer, Singapore (2020). https://doi.org/10.1007/978-981-13-7968-0_19
13. Haykin, S.: Neural Networks: A Comprehensive Foundation. Prentice Hall PTR, Upper Saddle River (1994)

14. Hsu, W., Lee, M.L., Zhang, J.: Image mining: trends and developments. J. Intell. Inf. Syst. **19**(1), 7–23 (2002). https://doi.org/10.1023/A:1015508302797
15. Jain, S., Bhatia, M.P.S.: Performance investigation of support vector regression using meteorological data. Int. J. Database Theory Appl. **6**(4), 109–118 (2013)
16. Johnston, F.H., et al.: Estimated global mortality attributable to smoke from landscape fires. Environ. Health Perspect. **120**(5), 695–701 (2012)
17. Lee, B.S., Woodard, P.M., Titus, S.J.: Applying neural network technology to human-caused wildfire occurrence prediction. AI Appl. **10**, 9–18 (1996)
18. Mahmoud, M.A.I., Ren, H.: Forest fire detection and identification using image processing and SVM. J. Inf. Process. Syst. **15**(1), 159–168 (2019)
19. Mazzoni, D., Tong, L., Diner, D., Li, Q., Logan, J.: Using MISR and MODIS data for detection and analysis of smoke plume injection heights over North American during Summer 2004 (2005)
20. Satendra, Kaushik, A.D.: Forest Fire Disaster Management. New Delhi: National Institute of Disaster Management, Ministry of Home Affairs, Government of India (2014)
21. Singh, P.K., Sharma, A.: An insight to forest fire detection techniques using wireless sensor networks. In: 2017 4th International Conference on Signal Processing, Computing and Control (ISPCC), pp. 647–653. IEEE (2017)
22. Stojanova, D., Panov, P., Kobler, A., Dzeroski, S., Taskova, K.: Learning to predict forest fires with different data mining techniques. In: Conference on Data Mining and Data Warehouses, SiKDD 2006, Ljubljana, Slovenia, pp. 255–258, October 2006
23. Taylor, S.W., Alexander, M.E.: Science, technology, and human factors in fire danger rating: the Canadian experience. Int. J. Wildland Fire **15**(1), 121–135 (2006)
24. Tong, W., Hong, H., Fang, H., Xie, Q., Perkins, R.: Decision forest: combining the predictions of multiple independent decision tree models. J. Chem. Inf. Comput. Sci. **43**(2), 525–531 (2003)
25. Zhizhin, M., Elvidge, C.D., Hsu, F.C., Baugh, K.E.: Using the short-wave infrared for nocturnal detection of combustion sources in VIIRS data. Proc. Asia-Pac. Adv. Netw. **35**, 49–61 (2013)

Rumour Control Model to Prevent Falsehood Propagation in Social Media

Nayan Garg, Somya Goel, Parinay Prateek, Sanjana Roshan,
Adwitiya Sinha$^{(\boxtimes)}$, and Prantik Biswas

Jaypee Institute of Information Technology, Noida, Uttar Pradesh, India
mailnayan.garg@gmail.com, mailtogoelsomya@gmail.com,
contactparinay@gmail.com, mailtoroshansanjana@gmail.com,
mailtoadwitiya@gmail.com, pranmasterbi@gmail.com

Abstract. Social media has rapidly evolved as a standard of communication that potentially facilitates information sharing and publishing across virtual communities. This online networked community is often victimized of rumours and fake content being diffused in streams of social dialogues. Propagation of rumours is considered as a devastating social phenomena, which results in fatal consequences over social media. With the advent of online social networks, malicious users have started using these platforms for spreading rumours. Most research focuses on analyzing the post impacts of the rumours spread. However, the underlying idea of our research lies in the fact of detecting possibilities of preventing the falsehood propagation, thereby controlling the spread of rumours in the network. This is achieved by designing a directed network graph of the users on the basis of the followers they have. The edges of the graph were assigned weights which is the probability of rumours likely to be diffused by the associated nodes provided that its follower or followee has already been infected. The performance of our proposed Rumour Control Model (RCM) is verified for different parameters as well as with existing Independent Cascade (IC) diffusion model for simulating the spread of rumour.

Keywords: Social media · Rumour propagation · Node influence · Diffusion probability · Twitter · Dominator tree

1 Introduction

Twitter is one of the first places to check for news, gigs, parody, comedy, declarations, announcements and links to fantastic writing, fabulous compositions, photos and videos. Twitter being the most influential social media platform of the modern times, holds the privilege of becoming front page news specially when it comes to public figures. But, like everything else twitter also has a dark side, comprising of all the scandals, meltdowns, incessant trolling and hounding. A major part of the downside of twitter involves people contradicting themselves

© Springer Nature Singapore Pte Ltd. 2020
P. K. Singh et al. (Eds.): FTNCT 2019, CCIS 1206, pp. 470–481, 2020.
https://doi.org/10.1007/978-981-15-4451-4_37

and spreading rumours or gossipy titbits. Twitter is a great place to network and organize but being accountable for each and every action is very important because a wrong action or statement tweeted can lead to a lot of troublesome consequences and doubtfulness in the minds of general public. Hence, it becomes the social responsibility of one to make sure that only authentic data reaches the public. Initially, the identification and detection of the rumour is essential. Once the rumour is known, the work in this paper directs the approach to prevent it from spreading further on the twitter platform. The dataset consisting of 4500 tweets is collected to perform required analysis from Twitter. The users with verified accounts were identified from this dataset referred as verified users. A directed graph is obtained from the network of verified users along with their verified followers. The influence for each user is calculated using a formula obtained by considering the pivotal factors which are number of followers, number of following, number of tweets and retweets the user is involved in and the active time of the user. Since a tweet posted by a user is equally visible to all his followers, the followers have equal chance of getting influenced by the rumour. Hence, it is considered that all followers of a user have equal probability of being influenced by him. The weight of an edge in the directed graph plotted between a user and his follower is calculated using this extend of influence along with the above mentioned factors. Once the nodes infected with the rumour are known, all of these infected nodes are merged into one super-node. The network graph is thereby converted into a dominator tree. The k dominating profiles which have the maximum benefit, i.e., the potential of saving the greatest number of nodes are removed. The benefit is calculated with the weights assigned along with the number of neighbours of the node. The work is further discussed in detail in the methodology section of the paper. Towards the result section a graph is plotted visualizing the difference in the reach of the rumour by using the standard Independent Cascade Diffusion Model and the proposed model, Rumour Control Model (RCM). Independent Cascade Model (IC) is a stochastic data dissemination model where the data streams over the system through Cascade.

2   Related Work

Back in the lane when analysis began in the field of social networks, the utmost priority was to define what is a valid post/blog and what has been posted just to attain attention from other users. In [1] some of the similar kind of issues related to micro-blog social media are addressed. First, the rumour is detected as a type of misinformation propagation and then the task of Rumour Data Classification (RDC) is performed with the help of an algorithm, which was proposed for two distinguished data-sets, one comprising of a single rumour and the other containing a mix of rumours. The results obtained while using the two-step approach show F-measure of 0.82 in RDC (mixed rumours data) and 84% for a data-set involving a single rumour. Once the rumour was detected, the people who promote them need to be recognized. There has been a lot of research in the field of detection of malicious user. The activities performed by a user have been recorded over time, the patterns and behaviour used as metrics to determine the authenticity of any user. The authors in [2] describes about the designing of the detector on the undertaking that extremely automated accounts will manifest certain fixed patterns in their tweet times. While the non-automated accounts will not reveal any specific pattern. In another research contribution conducted in [3] detects the inauthentic users which will safeguard the authentic ones. The basic framework for the paper involves identification of malignant users, non-malignant users and celebrities. This is done by attribute set for user classification based on the characteristics of the user by developing a crawler for twitter. Using Supervised Machine Learning techniques the malicious users have been identified. The algorithms used for the purpose are BayesNet, Naive Bayes, SMO, J48 and Random Forest. The people who have a greater reach are more likely to infect other users with a fake post or blog. These people might not be the actual source of the rumour but will definitely be a huge factor in deciding how far it goes. Hence, determining the influence of a given user was an important task as described in a survey conducted to find the influencers on a social media platform by using the cascade models [4]. The models are the way in which the information is propagated in a social network. The Independent Cascade model is amongst the several diffusion models used in social media networks analysis. Yet another model proposed for the analysis is the Linear Threshold Model [5]. The Social Media analysis is taken up after inferring from the results of both the models separately. The optimization problem for picking up the top influential nodes is shown to be NP hard. According to the analysis framework it shows that using greedy strategy provable results based on sub-modular function are obtained. Further taking these generalised model specifically to Twitter, on the basis of retweet, cascade size and density pattern inside the cascade dispersion of messages and influence of users on each other, the site [6] accumulates the tweets and recovers them when required in future restricted by applying group immunization by both cascade and threshold models. The patterns for studying online diffusion [7] of an information is looked after and the factors determining how rapidly any information is diffused is determined by quality of the post or blog besides the domain of information and time taken. The influence along with tweets, retweets, number of followers and following, the calculation of weights between two nodes of an edge [8] is achieved and a formula is suggested to compute the most influential users in a network. The algorithm for the removal of the infected nodes proposed formerly involved undirected and unweighted graphs [9]. The factor in this case considered for the removal of infected nodes is benefit of that node. Later polynomial-time heuristics Data Aware VAccination (DAVA) and DAVA-fast [10] were proposed where the infected nodes are removed to prevent the spread of epidemics. The benefit along with the graph converted into a dominator tree was taken for better efficiency. The weights allotted to these dominator trees [11] is by considering shortest distance path of the nodes. Further, works in the field are to immunize the network [12] by identifying the entire communities on social media platform which are most likely to be affected by the rumours. The spread of rumours is then restricted by applying group immunization by both cascade and threshold models.

3 Methodology

This section illustrates our novel Rumour Control Model (RCM) for preventing the rumour propagation in the network. Initially, historical tweets were extracted from twitter using Developer API. For this purpose, premium developer account was created on twitter. The searchtweets library of python was used to authenticate and use the 30-day search API from twitter to download tweets in json format. Forty five pages each consisting of hundred tweets were extracted resulting in 4500 tweets (Fig. 1).

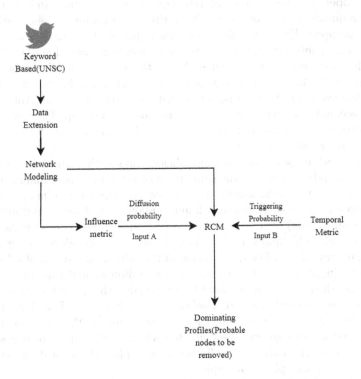

Fig. 1. Working model of proposed approach.

This is followed by extraction of the verified users who posted the tweets on twitter. This had also included all those users who had retweeted the mined tweets. File containing tweet objects comprised of user id, name and number of followers for each user in json format. A class name User was created, having three characteristics, id, handle and follower count. The authenticity of a user was checked and if a user was authentic, a User type object was created and pushed into a list 'users'. In the similar fashion, if the tweet was a retweet, the source user if verified was also pushed into the list. This list was sorted by number of followers each user had using operator library. Finally, csv file was written which had 150 lines, each line representing a user.

Once the users were known, next task was to construct a directed graph connecting the users if one of them followed the other. For this purpose, for each id we had to make requests to the twitter API to check if the rest of the 149 ids were its followers or not by using the tweepy library. After authentication, we read the csv file and created a pandas dataframe from it for listing all user ids. We traversed this list for every user, so as to check if the pair of users were friends or not. We used the show_friendship(a,b) method of the tweepy library. It returned a json carrying the information of the bilateral friendships. Here, the main challenge was that twitter did not allow us to make so many requests. The developer API has a limit of 180 requests in a 15 min window. In total, 150*149 requests were to be made. Every time the rate limit was exceeded, the program stopped. Exception handling was required. Fortunately, tweepy had made arrangements for that and rate limit exceptions were handled. But still after a few rate limit errors, twitter broke the connection with other errors. With the use of try catch, this was resolved and linear backoff was used to prevent the execution from stopping. In order to prevent this, an Amazon Web Services account was created and an EC2 Instance was set up. This instance was used to execute our codes and get all the data. Nohup was used for background processing for rapid execution.

The network is looked up for the malicious nodes, that are the nodes which have been already infected by the rumour. In order to find these malicious nodes we have used a temporal metric, time of tweets, the earliest made tweets in the database and the corresponding handles making the tweets (multiple tweets may have same time) were considered source nodes. These nodes are saved in a separate csv file. The final stage is visualization, which is achieved using an open source platform, Gephi. For the creation of the edges, the csv file of followers is taken as an input in a python code, and a two dimensional list of the csv files is made and then the edges are stored by traversing this list which had the first column as the user and the next n columns as its followers. Therefore, the first column along with next n columns each corresponding to the same row is taken and is stored as an edge in a new csv file which is the input for edges file in Gephi software. The data once collected is now plotted into a directed graph, using an open source platform Gephi.

The edges of the graph have been allotted some weights. These weights are giving the measure of the influence that a node has on its successor(s). The formulation of the weights is done by determining some of the important factors which contribute to the fact that how influential a user is. The factors incorporated in the computation include - tweets of the user, retweets of the user, time for which user is active, followers and followings of the user.

$$Influence = \frac{(tweets + retweets)}{T} * OOM(followers)$$
$$* log10((followers/(following + 1)) + 1) \tag{1}$$

where T is time for which the user is active and OOM: Order of Magnitude of Followers. The steps described now onwards are in the direction of obtaining a graph free of infected nodes. The networkx library is used to input the graph in Python. The csv file of edges is given as input to plot the graph. The file with infected nodes is taken as input so that the infected nodes are recognized and merged into a single super infected node. The connections of the infected nodes are connected to the super infected node with the probability p defined as:

$$p(I, v) = 1 - (\Pi(1 - p(I_i, v))) \tag{2}$$

where, $p(I_i, v)$ is the probability of the ith infected node infecting its follower v and I is super infected node. This super infected node might result in some disconnected nodes in the graph. The removal of these nodes is required, before it is used to create a dominator tree, which is more efficient in recognizing the nodes to be removed as stated in [4]. The weights between two nodes in an edge is updated as:

$$w(u, v) = \Sigma(p(u, k) * p(k, v)) \tag{3}$$

where $w(u, v)$ is an edge of dominator tree and k is the predecessor of v which are connected to u. Once the dominator tree is created, one can figure out the most influential nodes but yet another essential aspect is the benefit gained by removing a particular node which is obtained by multiplying the weights of all the edges of the particular node. The benefit is computed by taking the sum of the products of the probability of node n with all its predecessors. In this way we are able to combine the factors of maximum number nodes saved and most influential node. The fact that infection must have been reached some more nodes by this time, we need to look upon the infection diffusion and the 'n' nodes with maximum benefit are removed. In order to obtain infection free graph the process is repeated until the values are repeated.

4   Design

In the following section, the dataset for the work performed is described followed by the technologies used. Python being the programming platform, the packages used are also defined along with the other softwares used for the completion of the research.

4.1   Dataset

The above derived method has its application on twitter based networks, so in order to obtain the results, 4500 tweets were collected with the help of Tweepy Python package with developer's mode enabled. The keyword 'UNSC' (United

Nations Security Council) was searched. The relevant information of the tweets such as the time, entities, tweetid, text, source, language of tweet, truncated, filter level, location, favourited, retweeted, favourite count retweeted status, retweet count, reply count along with the user object was collected in json format. The user object included userid, profile picture, name, profile image url, location of the user, created at time, statuses count, description, favourites count, listed count, followers count, friends count and verified (to check authenticity of the user). The extracted users were arranged in a csv file in ascending order of there number of followers. From this list it was checked whether these users are following each other or not. The another set of information extracted was the measurement of influence of each of these users taken by the formula derived earlier in the paper.

4.2 Softwares and Packages Used

Following is the list of significant packages that are applied for our experimentation purpose.

- Tweepy: The extraction of the data present on the Twitter API can be easily achieved by a code of few lines with the use of this package as all the functions are predefined. This tool is of great use when one is in need of real time messages from Twitter.
- Networkx: This python package enables one to plot graphs with easy to use functions. The library offers functions for Addition of nodes and edges, find all neighbors (successors and predecessors separately), find immediate dominators, Display all the information of graph and various others.
- Matplotlib: As the name suggests this package offers a plethora of predefined functions to plot graphs. This can also be used with the networkx library to visualize the graphs created. The scatter and bar graphs can also be made.
- Heapq: This package's utility is in the implementation of a priority queue. A python list is given as an input for the heap. The push, pop, merge, heapify, nlargest and nsmallest functions are used for the manipulation of the priority queue.
- Search Tweets: This package comes into picture when one wants to search the Twitter API without getting into the API's details. One can automatically iterate through all the tweets and can even load further pages. Supports the Search Counts endpoint, which can decrease API call use and give quick bits of knowledge whether you just need Tweet volumes and not Tweet payloads.
- JSON: The information obtained from the browser is of the text form and this information can be reformed as javascript objects with no hustle of parsing and translations. While mining the data (tweets) a json file was received from the browser, to handle this file json package of python was used.
- Time: The various time related functions available in this module helps the programmer to handle system time related problems with the help of the C runtime library. The time.sleep(secs) function used in the code of extraction of dataset ensures that the current thread halts its execution for some time.

The time of sleep may be increased or decreased subjected to the scheduling of some other process.

- Operator: The package offers user friendly functions to be used instead of using the arithmetic, sequential, logical or relational (comparisons) operators directly. The functions are named after the operators they support.
- Pandas: Pandas takes data (CSV, TSV file, or a SQL database) and creates dataframes which are Python object with rows and columns and are very similar to table in a statistical software such as Excel Spreadsheets.
- CSV: The python library csv provides access to rte and do other manipulations on tabular data in comma separated values.
- Gephi: Gephi is an open-source network analysis and visualization tool wear, well known for creating Social Networks. A csv file can be visualized in several formats as per the user requirements using Gephi.

In the following section, the resultant outcomes are summarized with brief explanations.

5 Results

The data extracted from the mined tweets is used to create edges file, which is further visualized as directed Twitter social network (Fig. 2). The Fig. 3 displays the graph with central impact of nodes in terms of the number of associations. Further, Fig. 4 highlights the graph with influences of each node as previously computed by our proposed RCM, specified in equation (1). The followers of each user can be affected by the false rumours with a probability and these probability is the weights of the edges of the directed graph. The nodes have been sized in accordance with the influence they carry and similarly the edges are sized with the weights that are being assigned through our model computation.

The subsequent results in Fig. 5 illustrate the outcomes from performance comparison of our novel Rumour Control Model (RCM) framework with the existing benchmark, Independent Cascade (IC) Model. The diffusion of the rumour takes place rapidly within the network, but our proposed RCM approach makes sure that the spread of rumours is limited to a few initial nodes. The graph in Fig. 6 shows the plot between diffusion time steps used for simulation and the number of nodes infected with rumours. The graph shows that our proposed RCM algorithm is efficient in immunization of the nodes as compared to IC diffusion model and with the increase in value of number of nodes to be removed in a single step (k), the nodes infected with rumours decreases. The next experimental trend shown in Fig. 6 highlights the study between the value of k and the extent of the infected nodes. It can be observed from the graph that as the top k influential nodes, when detached from the graph, the extent of the spread of rumour is decreased.

The trend of influence probabilities derived by our RCM approach for each user in the network is represented in Fig. 7. This trend is sorted over the number of associations of the nodes, specified as node degree. Moreover, the degree distribution in the network is represented by the graphs in Fig. 8. The fewer number

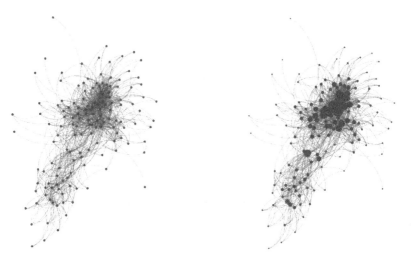

Fig. 2. Twitter extracted social network

Fig. 3. Twitter extracted social network with degree centrality

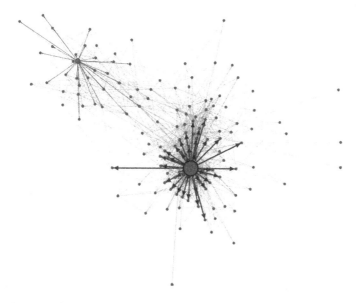

Fig. 4. Twitter social network with influential nodes

of nodes in the graph, have a higher influence while more number of nodes in the graph, have a lesser influence. Moreover, there are more number of nodes with lesser degree, while lesser number of nodes enjoy larger associations. This highlights that our work follows power law distribution, which is considered as a measure of inherent property of real world phenomena.

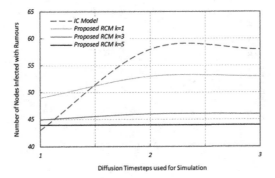

Fig. 5. Comparison of RCM with IC model

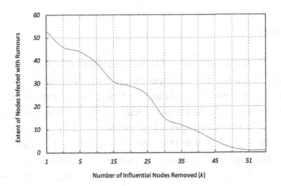

Fig. 6. Number of influential nodes removed vs extent of rumour spread.

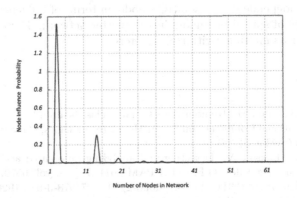

Fig. 7. Influence probability of nodes in Twitter social network

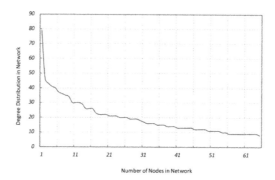

Fig. 8. Degree distribution of nodes in Twitter social network

6 Conclusion

Social media is a powerful platform for information propagation, whose use and misuse can result in social devastation through online networked communities. Hence, it becomes immensely significant to track and prevent the propagation of unauthorized posts through social platforms. The purpose of this research is to create a model which prevents spread of rumours. This is achieved by creating social graph on the basis of Twitter extracted data and identifying the most influential nodes through our proposed Rumour Control Model (RCM). This is followed by removal of the identified node(s) and examine the resultant impact on the restricted flow of rumours. Our generated social network follows power law distribution. The results justify better performance of our innovated RCM over existing Independent Cascade (IC) model in terms of influence probability, extent and rate of spread of rumors in the twitter network. These results have been tested across multiple twitter parameters.

References

1. Hamidian, S., Diab, M.: Rumour detection and classification for Twitter data. In: Fifth International Conference on Social Media Technologies, Communication, and Informatics (SOTICS) (2015)
2. Zhang, C.M., Paxson, V.: Detecting and analyzing automated activity on Twitter. In: Spring, N., Riley, G.F. (eds.) PAM 2011. LNCS, vol. 6579, pp. 102–111. Springer, Heidelberg (2011). https://doi.org/10.1007/978-3-642-19260-9_11
3. Singh, M., Bansal, D., Sofat, S.: Detecting malicious users in Twitter using classifiers. In: 7th International Conference on Security of Information and Networks, p. 247. ACM (2014)
4. Guille, A., Hacid, H., Favre, C., Zighed, D.: Information diffusion in online social networks: a survey. ACM SIGMOD Rec. **42**(2), 17–28 (2013)
5. Kempe, D., Kleinberg, J., Tardos, E.: Maximizing the spread of influence through a social network. In: Ninth ACM SIGKDD International Conference on Knowledge Discovery and Data Mining, pp. 137–146. ACM (2003)

6. Veijalainen, J., Semenov, A., Reinikainen, M.: User influence and follower metrics in a large Twitter dataset. In: WEBIST 2015–11th International Conference on Web Information Systems and Technologies, pp. 487–497. Science and Technology Publications (2015)

7. Matsubara, Y., Sakurai, Y., Prakash, B., et al.: Nonlinear dynamics of information diffusion in social networks. ACM Trans. Web 11, 1–40 (2017). https://doi.org/10.1145/3057741

8. Razis, G., Anagnostopoulos, I.: InfluenceTracker: rating the impact of a Twitter account. In: Iliadis, L., Maglogiannis, I., Papadopoulos, H., Sioutas, S., Makris, C. (eds.) AIAI 2014. IFIP AICT, vol. 437, pp. 184–195. Springer, Heidelberg (2014). https://doi.org/10.1007/978-3-662-44722-2_20

9. Chen, C., Tong, H., Prakash, B., et al.: Node immunization on large graphs: theory and algorithms. IEEE Trans. Knowl. Data Eng. 28, 113–126 (2016). https://doi.org/10.1109/tkde.2015.2465378

10. Zhang, Y., Prakash, B.: DAVA: distributing vaccines over networks under prior information. In: Proceedings of the 2014 SIAM International Conference on Data Mining (2014). https://doi.org/10.1137/1.9781611973440.6

11. Chen, W., Wang, C., Wang, Y.: Scalable influence maximization for prevalent viral marketing in large-scale social networks. In: Proceedings of the 16th ACM SIGKDD International Conference on Knowledge Discovery and Data Mining – KDD 2010 (2010). https://doi.org/10.1145/1835804.1835934

12. Zhang, Y., Adiga, A., Saha, S., et al.: Near-optimal algorithms for controlling propagation at group scale on networks. IEEE Trans. Knowl. Data Eng. 28, 3339–3352 (2016). https://doi.org/10.1109/tkde.2016.2605088

An Inclusive Study of Several Machine Learning Based Non-functional Requirements Prediction Techniques

Naina Handa[1]($\boxtimes$), Anil Sharma[1], and Amardeep Gupta[2]

[1] Lovely Professional University, Phagwara, Punjab, India
{naina.41500146,anil.19656}@lpu.co.in
[2] DAV College, Dasuha, Punjab, India
dramardeepgupta@gmail.com

Abstract. Requirement Engineering is a critical area in the arena of Software Engineering. Non Functional Requirements (NFRs) are very important as Functional Requirements but often ignored. Especially the automated correct prediction and prioritization of Non Functional Requirements (NFRs) is highly needed. Non Functional Requirements can be predicted with the help of machine learning models. The Machine Learning models have shown more promising output than Natural Language Processing. In this paper, the comprehensive review on the recently proposed NFRs prediction techniques has been presented. The output of the review showed that the different authors have used different Clustering and Classification algorithms. But Naïve Bayes algorithm has used by most of the researchers. The most of researchers have used Precision and Recall as their performance metric. Machine learning techniques like Ensembling and Parameter Tuning has neglected by researchers. The overall objective is to evaluate the numerous shortcomings in machine learning based NFRs prediction techniques and to draw suitable future directions.

Keywords: Machine Learning · Non-functional Requirements · Requirement engineering

1 Introduction

Requirement Engineering has a crucial role in software development process. Requirement engineering process can be divided into different phases like Requirement Elicitation, Requirement Analysis, System Modeling, Requirement Specification, Requirement Validation and Requirement Validation [1]. It is the process of establish the services that the stakeholders needed from the system and the constraints imposed on the system. Requirements can be segregated into Functional and Non-Functional Requirements [2].

The Functional Requirements depict the functionality (or statement of services) that a system should provide. It is a high level statement of what the system is supposed to do e.g. User will be able to search the whole database or a subset of it. Functional requirements can be technical details, data processing, manipulations and calculations that a system is supposed to accomplish. It derives the application architecture of the

© Springer Nature Singapore Pte Ltd. 2020
P. K. Singh et al. (Eds.): FTNCT 2019, CCIS 1206, pp. 482–493, 2020.
https://doi.org/10.1007/978-981-15-4451-4_38

system. Functional requirements are the main services that the user expects from the system e.g. in banking system create, update and delete account etc., whereas Non Functional Requirements are not straight forward requirements [3]. The Non Functional requirements are the actually constraints on the functions offered by the system e.g. Timing constraints, constraint on Development process, Performance constraint to name a few [4]. NFRs are often conflicting, difficult to implement during development and usually evaluated for the stakeholders just before the delivery [5].

Non-functional requirements are consider as utilities like usability, modifiability, reliability, portability, scalability, maintainability, adaptability, variability, volatility, customizability to name a few. Non Functional Requirements are implicit requirements or expected from the product. These are expected features so known as quality attributes. Non Functional Requirements derive the technical architecture of the system. It elaborates the performance characteristics of system. NFRs are very important factor for determine the success and failure of any software project. So there is need to give equal importance to Non Functional Requirements as Functional Requirements [6].

Table 1. Comparison between Functional and Non Functional requirements

Functional Requirements (FR)	Non Functional Requirements (NFR)
FR deals with What a system is supposed to do	NFRs depict the constraints on the functionality of a system
FRs explain the behavior of system like technical details, Data processing and manipulation details	NFRs elaborate performance characteristics of the system like Fault tolerance, Accessibility, Capacity, to name a few
FRs are fully specified in System Design. These are detailed requirements	NFRs are generally informally stated, subjective in nature and often contradictory with each other
FRs are user defined requirements. These are detailed by stakeholders themselves	NFRs are usually defined by different technical people e.g. Software developers, Architect and Technical leaders etc.
FRs testing verifies that the software system is executing actions as it should do	The testing of NFRs verify that the stakeholders expectations are met or not
FRs are the function specific requirements	NFRs are defined as metrics. All Quality Requirements are NFRs

The Table 1 has depicted that the FRs are the actual functionality of the system. These are detailed and easy to verifiable requirements. Where as NFRs are the not straightforward requirements. Actually NFRs are subjective, contradictory and difficult to verifiable requirements. The problem of getting proper requirements for software project is a problematic issue. Missing requirement specification often leads to projects failure. Gathering NFRs is a different from FRs (Functional Requirements). People are usually able to tell that what they want from system, but are often neither interested nor aware of a way to get it from them. It is reported in literature that properly considering the NFRs can lead to software crises like software system goes over budget, over time and result in failure of project [7]. But it is very important to elicit the NFRs in complete, consistent and unambiguous form and important to be considered in the early phases of system development life cycle can definitely help the software developers.

In Traditional as well as in Agile software development technique the user and developer spent their major efforts on forming FRs. NFRs are often overshadowed in FRs and ignored or neglected till the end of system development life cycle, Moreover NFRs are taken as second class requirements [7]. NFRs are difficult to model, develop and test and retrofit late in software development can result in lower quality and increase repair cost. The knowledge of NFRs is very important to be implemented in software development process. It is therefore of interest to develop improved methods for eliciting NFRs [8].

2   Importance of NFR

Software requirements are very crucial in software engineering. FRs are use defined requirements and comparatively easy to elicit where as NFRs are usually hidden, contradictory and not directly defined requirements, So difficult to elicit. Revealing the NFRs like Interface requirements, Quality requirements and designing constraints of software system is very important in designing the architectural early design decisions.

The extraction of NFRs is highly needed for the development of quality software and it is quiet beneficiary if the extraction process becomes automatic. The automatic process helps in reducing human efforts, mental fatigue and time. So the efficient elicitation of NFRs plays a vital role in software development process.

NFRs are important to be considered in the early phases of system development life cycle. It identifies the selection of technology, allocation of hardware and standards adopted in the software development. The failure of IT projects is often linked to shortcomings in the requirements phase. For example, IN an investigation of a US Air Force venture, it was discovered that beyond what 40% of found mistakes could be followed back to blunders in the requirements [6]. Moreover, it was evaluated that finding and fixing errors in requirements represent 70 to 85% of rework cost [7].

An especially troublesome piece of requirement engineering is managing and the administration of NFRs. Not properly taking NFRs into account leads to the most expensive and difficult errors which can be corrected only once a system is completed and it is appraised as one of the ten greatest dangers in Requirement Engineering [8].

Researchers have addressed the significance of NFRs in Software projects. Quality attributes, for example, exactness, security and execution, are crucial for the achievement of software systems. In that capacity software become increasingly more focal in our regular day to day existence, so does our anxiety for their quality. For example, A credit card system, it is alluring to have account data kept up precisely, put away safely, and handled rapidly, in an easy to understand way. Neglecting to address NFRs in the plan stage can prompt a product item that may meet all the FRs however neglect to be usable because of an inability to meet the NFRs. Elicitation of NFRs is important in the early stages is very important.

3   Process of Applying Machine Learning to NFR

Machine Learning is the arena of computer science which provides the learning ability to computer without being explicitly programmed [9]. The process of extract, classify and prioritization can be divided into different phases (Fig. 1).

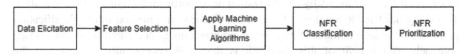

Fig. 1. Process of applying machine learning to NFR

3.1   Elicitation Phase

During this phase the data has gathered from different sources like from SRS, Promise Repository, online reviews etc. [10]. The different elicitation techniques like questionnaires, interview, brainstorming and catalogs to name a few are used [11].

3.2   Feature Selection

It is a process of selection of useful or subset of features from the dataset. FS Algorithm model may return the weights (estimating feature relevance) or subset of selected features [12]. It is an essential preprocessing step and helps to overcome the curse of dimensionality. The high dimension data can leads to increase complexity and reduce accuracy of ML model [13]. The objective of feature selection is to proficiently build up the prediction model and give a superior execution.

3.3   Apply Machine Learning Algorithms

The different machine learning algorithms has been applied on dataset [14, 15]. Supervised [16], Semi-supervised and Unsupervised algorithms [17] as well as different clustering techniques are applied for constructing a model.

3.4   NFR Classification

On the basis of training data the Machine Learning Model can make predict and classify the NFRs into different categories [18]. The different papers have given different NFR classifications.

3.5   NFR Prioritization

It is the process of ranking the requirements [19]. The classified NFRs can be ranked on the basis of their importance, So that important Requirements can be developed in the early cycles. There are different Prioritization algorithms like (AHP) Analytic Hierarchy Process, Wiege method, Cost value approach and genetic algorithms can be applied.

4 Related Work

[21] Casamayor et al. have addressed semi-supervised text categorization technique for identifying NFRs from a textual document using Naïve bayes algorithm. The supervised text categorization technique proposed earlier require a lot of pre categorize requirements to train a classifier before finding an accurate NFRs, with supervised technique it required manually categorization of numerous requirements by the analyst. This study has tried to automate this process. The learning method in the classification process used reduce number of categorize requirements as compared to the supervised approach. The benefit of this approach is that it is successfully used during the requirement analysis process and reduced the effort needed for manual identification and classification. The semi-supervised approach shows accuracy results that are above 70% which is higher than the supervised learning results using the same standards for the collection of documents.

[22] Rahimi et al. addressed a data mining technique for extracting NFRs. The proposed technique captures the quality concerns such as usability, performance and security of the system from the document. A hierarchy is developed which helps the extracted NFRs to model them according to the quality concerns. Sequence of machine learning and data mining techniques are used in the paper to automatically detect different quality concerns from the document. A meaningful hierarchy is proposed to organize these quality concern, some are related to each other so at different stages of the hierarchy some relevant attributes are neglected. The authors have evaluated their approach against two health care related systems.

[23] Ramadhani et al. used FSKNN (Fuzzy similarity based K-nearest neighbor) a requirement sentences-based classification algorithm for the identification of NFRs. In FSKNN algorithm semantic factors and semantic relatedness measurement are not considered. The propose system classify different non-functional requirements from text documents. The system works on labeling of training data, classification of the data, measure the semantic relatedness between different classes and used terms. The Automatic process of labeling training data save the time than labeling the data manually. HSO method is used. The result shows the improved result by making use of Semantic Factor.

[24] Slankas and Williams proposed a tool (NFR Locator) to extract and classify the sentences into 14 predefined categories. This tool is used to identify different NFRs according to their categories from available natural language documents. A k-NN classifier is used to identify the similar types of sentences in documents. Classification of the sentences is made on the basis of different categories of NFRs. It helps the analyst to extract those non-functional requirements that are relevant. Multiple types of classifiers are used in the paper and it is resulted that k-NN classifier achieve the maximum result in identifying non-functional requirements.

[25] Mahmoud and Williams have used unsupervised approach for detecting and classifying the non-functional requirements. The early methods used for classification and detection of non-functional requirements use manually classified data to train the model, classifier needs large training data set but for achieving high accuracy large data is not always available. A technique is used for extracting natural language content of

source code to support NFRs traceability. Words semantic similarity methods are used in context to software requirements. Cluster configuration is used to generate the most logical clusters of requirements words. The proposed approach shows a modest complexity that helps it to scale it on larger systems without wearing issues of time and space requirements. The proposed approach is unsupervised so it cannot require any data set so it can operate with minimum adjustment. The paper highlights long term benefit for software development process.

[26] Riaz et al. have tended to the security requirements by designing total and grouped arrangement of security requirements. The authors utilized the Machine Learning technique for the first time automatically identify security related sentences from natural Language artifacts. The context-specific security requirements templates have been designed for translating the security related sentences into functional security requirements. The authors have grouped 10,963 sentences and effectively foresee and order 82% of the security objectives for all the sentences (precision).

[27] Gazi et al. have proposed a classification scheme of NFRs for Information systems (IS). Many classification schemes are proposed for NFRs but they do not classify requirements for IS, web base system, real time system. A tree like structure is proposed for classifying NFRs. In this classification scheme, similar NFRs are identified for both real systems and web based systems. It is important that the NFRs that are included in classification scheme for IS are included in the software requirements specification document. Reliability and availability are two important NFRs for information system. In the classification scheme reliability requirement is further decomposed into accuracy, maturity, completeness. NFRs that are similar in Information System as well as Real time systems are interoperability and privacy and that are similar in Web base systems and Information system are security, performance and usability requirements.

[28] Sharma et al. proposed a framework for identifying and analyzing different non-functional requirements from the text document. A textual pattern identification technique is propose to identify terms that are related to non-functional requirements attributes from a natural language text and on the basis of applying different set of rules it identify different categories of NFRs. The proposed rule based approach for detecting and classifying different NFRs in natural language uses rules instead of identifying keywords approach like other machine language techniques. Developed approach is analyzed against different manual categorize approaches for identifying non-functional requirements from the sentences.

[29] Sachdeva and Chung addressed the need of NFRs handling early in the software life cycle. It illustrate that the security and performance NFS are become very crucial in projects related to cloud and big data, whose lack of concerns can also severely damage other crucial NFRs. Authors have proposed a novel approach to handle the non-functional requirements such as security and performance individually and in conflicting way for the projects related to cloud and big data using agile approach. The acceptance criteria (AC) and definition of done (DOD) has used to measure the fulfillers of NFRs. The authors also suggested that there is need to to address Process related NFRs and NFRs other than security and performance for Big data projects and Cloud in an Agile environment.

[30] Maiti and Mitropoulos have used the existing αβγ-framework for prioritizing NFR in the early phases of agile. The main focus of the paper is to improve the prioritization of NFR in the early stages of software development. The author suggested that there is further need of methods to prioritize and predicting NFR as functional requirements. The prediction of NFR based on current NFR and FR dataset. The prediction is valuable to software engineers where NFR are overlooked.

[31] Iqbal et al. have demonstrated the use of Machine learning (ML) for automating the various tasks in Software Engineering domain. The researchers have particularly focused on Requirement engineering. The authors concluded that the Machine Learning has good effect on the different phases of Requirement Engineering. The researchers have focused on the datasets, the features and algorithms used in literature and envision the opportunities in the area of ML and NFRs.

[32] Marinho et al. have described the significance of taking NFRs into consideration during early phases of system development and Requirement Elicitation become the most important. The objective of the paper is to show that the Machine Learning is a promising approach for synthesis of dataset by using the NFR framework catalogues. The authors have use the Promise repository for experiment and evaluate their model on the basis of Recall, Precision and F1. In this paper the Usability, Security and Performance is mainly focused.

[33] Baker et al. explored that the use of ML is not well appreciated for decision making during SDLC because of the parameter tuning required by the different models. The authors have developed an efficient approach for classify NFRs. An ANN (Artificial Neural Network) and CNN (Convolutional Neural Network) have used as ML approach. The Maintainability, Operatibility, Performance, Security and Usability have focused in this paper. Recall, Precision and F1 metric have used and concluded that the CNN efficiently classify NFRs.

[34] Taj et al. have focused on classify Requirements into FRs and NFRs. The authors in this paper proposed a model which helps for Requirement Elicitation and Classification process. The requirements are collected using crowdsourcing approach and different stakeholders have participated in elicitation process. The Naïve Bayes and Decision Tree have used for classify data. The case study has performed for showing the efficiency of model.

[35] Bhowmik and Do examined 50 NFRs from the Open Source Software i.e. Firefox, Lucene, and Mylyn. This research explored that how OSS undertaking groups make quality high-lights from basic introductory depictions of JIT requirements and reveal activities progressively specific to JIT requirements engineering. It is a follow-up of the preliminary study which was more focused on implementation rather than requirements. This study is more focused on NFRs.

[36] In numerous software projects, examiners are required to manage the framework's requirements from new areas. Recognition with the area is important so as to get full influence from cooperation with partners and for removing applicable data from the current project documents. Precise and opportune extraction and grouping of requirements is a difficult task for analysts. The methodology used in the paper is to mine ongoing interaction records and documents for the applicable phrasal units about the prerequisites related points being talked about during elicitation. The authors have used SVM (Support Vector Machine) for variable-sized element vectors to effectively

and powerfully extract and classify requirements. The Precision, Recall, and Distance metric has used for measuring the performance.

[37] Portugal et al. focused on the challenge of eliciting NFRs. The authors have developed NFRFinder which is a semi-automatic technique for mining the NFRs from unstructured data. Initially it was applied on structured text and use Recall and Precision as metric. NFRFinder has given promising results in structured and exhibited that NFRs classification be influenced by of the context and the stakeholders involved in classification.

[38] Salman et al. explored that the Requirement elicitation, understanding and classifying is very stimulating task. The requirement classification is very important for allocating the requirements into the set of sub projects. The authors have proposed a technique for clustering requirements into semantic cluster. The technique is based on textual similarity between the Requirement statements. The agglomerative hierarchical clustering algorithm has been used in the framework. The experiment has done using open access software and the proposed work achieved a higher performance. The authors have planned to do comparative analysis of clustering algorithms with respect to clustering FRs and also find the keywords from clusters that define the domain knowledge.

[39] Martino et al. explored that the Requirement specification is very challenging task in the field of cloud computing. In the paper, an automatic technique has been proposed for extracting and classifying which are in Natural Language Form for developing cloud based applications. The different Machine Learning like Maximum Entropy, Naïve Bayes and NLP approaches has been used in paper. The data for experiment has taken from the PROMISE repository.

[40] Tóth and Vidács have providing a comparative study of Machine Learning and NLP techniques with respect to their application and performance in the field of software engineering. The Precision, F1 and Recall metric has used. The dataset has taken from Stack Overflow and Promise repository for experiment purpose. The Naive Bayes, (SVM) Support Vector Machine, Logistic Regression, Decision Tree have used in paper. The implementation of Neural Network and Recurrent network has given as future perspective.

5   Findings of the Review

The output of the review is that the different papers have used different clustering and classification algorithms for Extracting and Classify NFRs. The NFRs are extracted from SRS documents, online reviews, Requirement document, Feature Request, User stories and Web based software requirements of different domains. Many reviewers have taken data from Promise repository for Experiment purpose. The different NFRs are focused by different authors like Performance, Security, Accuracy, Portability, Safety, Legal, Privacy, Reliability, Availability, Interoperability, and Integrity. But most of the research has focused on Performance and Security. It is also find in review that the existing techniques have neglected the use of Ensembling and Parameter tuning. There is also lack of standard dataset concerned NFRs.

6 Challenges of Existing Techniques

After conducting the review on NFRs prediction it has been found that the designing an efficient NFRs prediction model is an ill-posed problem. Following gaps have been formulated after reviewing the existing techniques:

Ensemble learning: Majority of the existing researchers has utilized Ensembling of different machine learning models to achieve higher accuracy rate. However, Ensembling methods are computationally extensive in nature, and also, unable to achieve maximum accuracy.

Table 2. Review of existing techniques

Authors	Algorithm Used	Accuracy Achieved	Model Validation	Source Document	Dataset/ Test Bed	No. of Requirements	Types of NFRs Identified
[21]	Naïve Bayes	75%	Experimental	Text document	Promise	370 NFRs 255 FRs	Performance ,Security
[22]	Incremental diffusive clustering	Yes	Experimental	SRS Document		235 (CCHIT) 1736(WORLD VISA)	Security,Performance, Usability
[23]	FSKNN	Improved Accuracy by 43.7%	Experimental	SRS, System Document	6 dataset like Promise , Itrust, CCHIT, World Vista, Online Project Marking System SRS etc	Requirement sentences (1342)	Performance ,Access control
[24]	KNN,Naïve Bayes	Naïve Bayes F1=0.34 KNN F1=0.54	Experimental	System Related Documents	Promise and Health care	14 categories of NFRs	Maintainability,Performance,Scalability,Security,Usability,Recoverability,Privacy,Access
[25]	Hierarchical clustering, Partition clustering	---------------	Experimental	SRS Documents	Smart Trip,safe drink,blue wallet	-----------	Security,Performance,Accuracy,Portability,Safety,Legal,Privacy,Reliability,Availability,Interoperatibility
[26]	KNN, SMO	Prediction=8 2% Identification =79	Study oracle (set of procedures)	Requirement document ,Feature Request, User stories	Electronic Healthcare(HER)	Requirement sentences=10, 963	Confidentiality, Integrity, Availability
[27]	-----------------	---------------	Case Study	Web based software requirements	Information system	---------------	Availability ,Performance,Security,Usability,Privacy,Access control,Accuracy, Reliability
[29]	Rule based algorithm	Performance 91%	Case Study	Requirements statements	Promise	625 req. statements	Legal,Privacy,Usability,Security, Performance, Availability

Parameter tuning: Existing machine learning models suffer from the parameter tuning issues. It has been observed from the literature that the meta-heuristic techniques can be used to overcome the issue of parameter tuning in an efficient manner. However, majority of existing researchers have neglected the use of meta-heuristic techniques.

Dataset: There is lack of standard dataset available for NFRs. Moreover, there is no standard classification of NFRs. The different authors have given different classifications (Table 2).

7 Conclusion

This paper presents the comprehensive review on NFRs prediction techniques.

After literature survey, it has been found that Neglecting NFRs leads to the most expensive and difficult errors which can be corrected only after the completion of the system. NFRs extraction and classification is very important issue of Requirement engineering. The automation of NFRs extraction using different machine learning algorithms has done by different authors. But most of them have neglected Ensembling which has been utilized to achieve higher accuracy rate. There is need of developing an efficient Machine Learning model for the efficient extraction and classification of NFRs. There is also a lack of standard dataset for NFRs.

References

1. Li, Y., et al.: Automated requirements extraction for scientific software. Procedia Comput. Sci. **51**, 582–591 (2015)
2. Alam, S., Shah, S.A.A., Bhatti, S.N., Jadi, A.M.: Impact and challenges of requirement engineering in agile methodologies: a systematic review (2017)
3. Davis, A.M., Leffingwell, D.A.: Using requirements management to speed delivery of higher quality applications. Ration. Softw. Corp. **20**, 2004 (1996)
4. Martens, N.: The impact of non-functional requirements on project success. Utrecht University, Msc Thesis, Utrecht (2011)
5. Babar, M.I., Ghazali, M., Jawawi, D.N.A.: Systematic reviews in requirements engineering: a systematic review. In: 2014 8th Malaysian Software Engineering Conference (MySEC), pp. 43–48 (2014)
6. Abad, Z.S.H., Karras, O., Ghazi, P., Glinz, M., Ruhe, G., Schneider, K.: What works better? a study of classifying requirements. In: 2017 IEEE 25th International Requirements Engineering Conference (RE), pp. 496–501 (2017)
7. Khan, F., Jan, S.R., Tahir, M., Khan, S., Ullah, F.: Survey: dealing non-functional requirements at architecture level. VFAST Trans. Softw. Eng. **9**(2), 7–13 (2016)
8. Ezami, S.: Extracting non-functional requirements from unstructured text Master's thesis, University of Waterloo (2018)
9. Kotsiantis, S.B., Zaharakis, I., Pintelas, P.: Supervised machine learning: A review of classification techniques. Emerg. Artif. Intell. Appl. Comput. Eng. **160**, 3–24 (2007)
10. Kiran, H.M., Ali, Z.: Requirement elicitation techniques for open source systems: a review. Int. J. Adv. Comput. Sci. Appl. Pak. 330–334 (2018)
11. Tiwari, S., Rathore, S.S.: A methodology for the selection of requirement elicitation techniques. arXiv preprint arXiv:1709.08481 (2017)

12. Asadi, M., Soltani, S., Gasevic, D., Hatala, M., Bagheri, E.: Toward automated feature model configuration with optimizing non-functional requirements. Inf. Softw. Technol. **56**(9), 1144–1165 (2014)

13. Groen, E.C., Sylwia, K., Hauer, M.P., Krafft, T.D., Doerr, J.: Users—the hidden software product quality experts?: a study on how app users report quality aspects in online reviews. In: 2017 IEEE 25th International Requirements Engineering Conference (RE), pp. 80–89 (2017)

14. Pham, B.T., Bui, D.T., Prakash, I., Dholakia, M.B.: Hybrid integration of Multilayer Perceptron Neural Networks and machine learning ensembles for landslide susceptibility assessment at Himalayan area (India) using GIS. CATENA **149**, 52–63 (2017)

15. Barzegar, R., Moghaddam, A.A., Deo, R., Fijani, E., Tziritis, E.: Mapping groundwater contamination risk of multiple aquifers using multi-model ensemble of machine learning algorithms. Sci. Total Environ. **621**, 697–712 (2018)

16. Kurtanović, Z., Maalej, W.: Automatically classifying functional and non-functional requirements using supervised machine learning. In: 2017 IEEE 25th International Requirements Engineering Conference (RE), pp. 490–495, September 2017

17. Luo, M., Nie, F., Chang, X., Yang, Y., Hauptmann, A.G., Zheng, Q.: Adaptive unsupervised feature selection with structure regularization. IEEE Trans. Neural Netw. Learn. Syst. **29**(4), 944–956 (2017)

18. Kopczyńska, S., Nawrocki, J., Ochodek, M.: An empirical study on catalog of non-functional requirement templates: usefulness and maintenance issues. Inf. Softw. Technol. **103**, 75–91 (2018)

19. Maiti, R.R., Mitropoulos, F.J.: Capturing, eliciting, predicting and prioritizing (CEPP) non-functional requirements metadata during the early stages of agile software development. In: SoutheastCon 2015, pp. 1–8, April 2015

20. Aasem, M., Ramzan, M., Jaffar, A.: Analysis and optimization of software requirements prioritization techniques. In: 2010 International Conference on Information and Emerging Technologies, pp. 1–6, June 2010

21. Casamayor, A., Godoy, D., Campo, M.: Identification of non-functional requirements in textual specifications: a semi-supervised learning approach. Inf. Softw. Technol. **52**(4), 436–445 (2010)

22. Rahimi, M., Mirakhorli, M., Cleland-Huang, J.: Automated extraction and visualization of quality concerns from requirements specifications. In: 2014 IEEE 22nd International Requirements Engineering Conference (RE), pp. 253–262, August 2014

23. Ramadhani, D.A., Rochimah, S., Yuhana, U.L.: Classification of non-functional require-ments using semantic-FSKNN based ISO/IEC 9126. Telkomnika **13**(4), 1456 (2015)

24. Slankas, J., Williams, L.: Automated extraction of non-functional requirements in available documentation. In: 2013 1st International Workshop on Natural Language Analysis in Software Engineering (NaturaLiSE), pp. 9–16, May 2013

25. Mahmoud, A., Williams, G.: Detecting, classifying, and tracing non-functional software requirements. Requir. Eng. **21**(3), 357–381 (2016)

26. Riaz, M., King, J., Slankas, J., Williams, L.: Hidden in plain sight: Automatically identifying security requirements from natural language artifacts. In: 2014 IEEE 22nd International Requirements Engineering Conference (RE), pp. 183–192, August 2014

27. Gazi, Y., Umar, M.S., Sadiq, M.: Classification of NFRs for Information System. Int. J. Comput. Appl. **115**(22) (2015)

28. Sharma, V.S., Ramnani, R.R., Sengupta, S.: A framework for identifying and analyzing non-functional requirements from text. In: Proceedings of the 4th International Workshop on Twin Peaks of Requirements and Architecture, pp. 1–8, June 2014

29. Sachdeva, V., Chung, L.: Handling non-functional requirements for big data and IOT projects in scrum. In: 2017 7th International Conference on Cloud Computing, Data Science & Engineering-Confluence, pp. 216–221, January 2017

30. Maiti, R.R., Mitropoulos, F.J.: Prioritizing non-functional requirements in agile software engineering. In: Proceedings of the SouthEast Conference, pp. 212–214, April 2017

31. Iqbal, T., Elahidoost, P., Lúcio, L.: A bird's eye view on requirements engineering and machine learning. In: 2018 25th Asia-Pacific Software Engineering Conference (APSEC), pp. 11–20. IEEE, December 2018

32. Marinho, M., Arruda, D., Wanderley, F., Lins, A.: A systematic approach of dataset definition for a supervised machine learning using NFR framework. In: 2018 11th International Conference on the Quality of Information and Communications Technology (QUATIC), pp. 110–118, September 2018

33. Baker, C., Deng, L., Chakraborty, S., Dehlinger, J.: Automatic multi-class non-functional software requirements classification using neural networks. In: 2019 IEEE 43rd Annual Computer Software and Applications Conference (COMPSAC), vol. 2, pp. 610–615, July 2019

34. Taj, S., Arain, Q., Memon, I., Zubedi, A.: To apply data mining for classification of crowd sourced software requirements. In: Proceedings of the 2019 8th International Conference on Software and Information Engineering, pp. 42–46, April 2019

35. Bhowmik, T., Do, A.Q.: Refinement and resolution of just-in-time requirements in open source software and a closer look into non-functional requirements. J. Ind. Inf. Integr. **14**, 24–33 (2019)

36. Abad, Z.S.H., Gervasi, V., Zowghi, D., Far, B.H.: Supporting analysts by dynamic extraction and classification of requirements-related knowledge. In: Proceedings of the 41st International Conference on Software Engineering, pp. 442–453, May 2019

37. Portugal, R.L.Q., Li, T., da Silva, L.F., Almentero, E., do Prado Leite, J.C.S.: NFRfinder: a knowledge based strategy for mining non-functional requirements. In: SBES, pp. 102–111, September 2018

38. Eyal Salman, H., Hammad, M., Seriai, A.D., Al-Sbou, A.: Semantic clustering of functional requirements using agglomerative hierarchical clustering. Information **9**(9), 222 (2018)

39. Di Martino, B., Pascarella, J., Nacchia, S., Maisto, S.A., Iannucci, P., Cerri, F.: Cloud services categories identification from requirements specifications. In: 2018 32nd International Conference on Advanced Information Networking and Applications Workshops (WAINA), pp. 436–441, May 2018

40. Tóth, L., Vidács, L.: Study of various classifiers for identification and classification of non-functional requirements. In: Gervasi, O., et al. (eds.) ICCSA 2018. LNCS, vol. 10964, pp. 492–503. Springer, Cham (2018). https://doi.org/10.1007/978-3-319-95174-4_39

Heuristics for Minimum Weight Directed Dominating Set Problem

Mallikarjun Rao Nakkala⬤ and Alok Singh$^{(\boxtimes)}$⬤

School of Computer and Information Sciences, University of Hyderabad,
Hyderabad 500 046, Telangana, India
nmrao@uohyd.ac.in, alokcs@uohyd.ernet.in

Abstract. For any node-weighted directed graph (digraph), a directed dominating set S_D is a subset of nodes such that every node of the digraph either belongs to S_D or has an arc directed from a node in S_D to itself. The minimum weight directed dominating set problem (MWDDS) seeks a directed dominating set with minimum sum of weights of its constituent nodes. It is an $\mathcal{NP}$-hard combinatorial optimization problem which finds applications in modelling a wide variety of directed interactions in complex heterogeneous networks like chemical reaction, metabolic regulation, spread of an infectious disease. In this paper, we present five greedy heuristics to solve MWDDS. To our knowledge, these are the first heuristic approaches for MWDDS. We have also proposed a local search based on redundant node removal to improve the solutions obtained by these greedy heuristics. Performance of these five heuristics were evaluated on a wide range of digraph instances. Computational results show the effectiveness of these heuristics.

Keywords: Directed dominating set · Minimum weight directed dominating set · Heuristic · Combinatorial optimization

1 Introduction

Given a directed graph $D = (V, A)$, where V is the set of nodes and A is the set of arcs or directed edges, each arc $(u, v) \in A$ is directed from node u to node v. With respect to the arc (u, v), node u is called the parent or predecessor node and node v is called the child node or successor node. A directed dominating set $S_D \subseteq V$ such that every node $v \notin S_D$ is child of at least one node in S_D. A node that is a member of S_D is termed as a dominating node or dominator. A node that does not belong to S_D is termed as a dominated or dominatee or non-dominating node. The minimum directed dominating set problem (MDDS) seeks a directed dominating set on D with minimum cardinality. In minimum weight directed dominating set problem (MWDDS), each node of V is assigned a weight according to a weight function $w : V \to \Re^+$, and the objective is to

The first author acknowledges the support of the Senior Research Fellowship from the Council of Scientific & Industrial Research (CSIR), Government of India.

© Springer Nature Singapore Pte Ltd. 2020
P. K. Singh et al. (Eds.): FTNCT 2019, CCIS 1206, pp. 494–507, 2020.
https://doi.org/10.1007/978-981-15-4451-4_39

find a directed dominating set that minimizes the sum of the weights of the constituent nodes. MWDDS can be considered as a generalization of MDDS as it is equivalent to MDDS when every node has unit weight, i.e., $w(v) = 1 \; \forall v \in V$. MWDDS is $\mathcal{NP}$-hard as it can be considered as a generalization of minimum weight dominating set problem (MWDS) in undirected graphs which is known to be $\mathcal{NP}$-hard [3]. The number of parent nodes of a node v is termed as in-degree of node v, and the number of child nodes of a node v is termed as out-degree of node v. A node with no parent is termed as a source node. A node with no child is termed as a leaf node. If a node has neither a child nor a parent, then it is termed as an isolated node. Clearly, all source nodes and all isolated nodes (isolated nodes can also be considered as source node with no children) must belong to any directed dominating set.

MDDS and MWDDS find applications in modelling a wide variety of directed interactions in complex networks like spread of infectious diseases [12], genetic regulation [13,15], chemical reaction & metabolic regulation [7] and power generation & transportation [16]. MDDS is used to model networks comprising homogeneous nodes, whereas MWDDS is used when nodes are heterogeneous

In the literature, minimum weight dominating set problem on undirected graphs is a well-known problem, and many heuristic approaches [1,2,5,6,9,11,14] have been proposed for this problem. However, corresponding problem in directed graphs, viz. MWDDS is not studied at all from the heuristic perspective though there are heuristic approaches for MDDS [4,8,10,12].

In this paper, five greedy heuristics are presented for MWDDS. These heuristics appropriately utilize the ideas presented in [2] and [4] for MWDS and MDDS respectively by extending them to MWDDS. The results obtained through these heuristics are improved further by using a redundant node removal procedure. A node v belonging to a directed dominating set S_D is redundant if $S_D \setminus \{v\}$ remains a directed dominating set. Redundant node removal procedure iteratively removes redundant nodes till it is no more possible to remove any node. Performance of our proposed heuristics with and without redundant node removal procedure were evaluated on a wide range of directed graph (digraph) instances.

The remainder of this paper is organized as follows: Sect. 2 describes our proposed greedy heuristics. Computational results and their analysis are presented in Sect. 3. Finally, Sect. 4 outlines some concluding remarks.

2   Heuristics

In this paper, five greedy heuristics are presented to solve the minimum weight directed dominating set (MWDDS) problem on digraphs. These five heuristics will be referred to as H1, H2, H3, H4 & H5. All these five heuristics first constructs a directed dominating set by using greedy methods, then they use the redundant node removal procedure to further improve the solution quality. Starting with an empty solution, these heuristics construct the solution iteratively. In every iteration, a node is added to the solution until the solution becomes a directed dominating set. The node, which is added to the partially constructed solution, is selected by following a greedy policy which differs from one heuristic to another. A common framework of five heuristics has given in Algorithm 1 where *greedy_policy()* is a function which selects a node for addition into the dominating set and which differs from one heuristic to another. Another function, *redundant_node_removal()* removes the redundant nodes to improve the quality of the solution.

Algorithm 1: Framework of presented HEURISTICS

Input: A node-weighted directed graph $D := (V, A)$, $w(v) \in \Re^+ \forall v \in V$.
Output: Best solution found.

$S_D \leftarrow \emptyset$;
while S_D *is not a directed dominating set* **do**
$\quad \mid \quad v \leftarrow$ greedy_policy($V \setminus S_D$);
$\quad \mid \quad S_D \leftarrow S_D \cup \{v\}$;
$S_D \leftarrow$ redundant_node_removal(S_D);
return S_D;

To implement the greedy policy, each of these heuristics uses a score function while determining the next node to be added to the partially constructed solution. The scores of nodes in the graph are updated each time a node is added to the solution. In addition, H2 & H3 use the information about source nodes while determining the next node to be added, whereas H4 & H5 use the information about source nodes as well as a special case pertaining to a child node and its parent. These heuristics are presented in subsequent subsections. Before describing these heuristics, we will introduce the notational conventions used in the description of these heuristics.

Table 1. Notational convention

Symbol	Meaning
$W_s(u)$	Sum of weights of white successors of node u
$CLR(u)$	1 in case node u is white, otherwise 0
$WOUT_{degree}(u)$	Number of white successors of u
$in\text{-}degree(u)$	Number of predecessors (parents) of u

Before starting the dominating set construction, all nodes $v \in V$ are assumed to have white color. Each time a node is added to the partially constructed directed dominating set, it is colored black and each of its white successor node is colored grey. Obviously, as per this coloring strategy, a heuristic iterates until no white node is left. So, at the end, all nodes will have either black color or grey color. The nodes with black color are dominating nodes and those with grey colors are dominated nodes. Our heuristics make use of four quantities, viz. $W_s(u)$, $CLR(u)$, $WOUT_{degree}$, and $in\text{-}degree$, which are defined in the Table 1, while determining the next node to be added. The first three quantities make use of color of nodes and are updated each time a node is added to the partially constructed directed dominating set, whereas the fourth quantity $in\text{-}degree(u)$ does not depend on the color of the node and can be computed a-priori before starting the dominating set construction.

The first heuristic, referred to as H1, can be considered as a direct extension of heuristic presented in [2] for computing minimum weight dominating set in undirected graphs. To select a node for addition into a partially constructed dominating set S_D, this heuristic computes the score of each node in $V \backslash S_D$ by making use of Eqs. 1 and 2 and then it selects the node with maximum score as per Eq. 3. In case, there are more than one node with maximum score as per Eq. 3, then it selects the node with maximum score as per Eq. 6, where T refers to the set of nodes with maximum score as per Eq. 3. If there are more than one node with maximum score as per Eq. 6, then one such node is selected randomly to break the tie. It is to be noted that score computed as per Eq. 2 for a node u is the sum of weights of all those white nodes which will no longer remain white once u is added to S_D divided by its own weight. Clearly, such nodes can either be successor of u or u itself in case it is white. Obviously, this score needs to be maximized for constructing a good solution and that is what Eq. 3 does. Likewise, score computed as per Eq. 5 for a node u is the number of white nodes which will no longer remain white once u is added to S_D divided by its own weight and this score needs to be maximized.

$$W_s(u) \leftarrow \sum_{(u,v) \in A} w(v) \times CLR(v) \tag{1}$$

$$score(u) \leftarrow \frac{W_s(u) + (w(u) \times CLR(u))}{w(u)} \tag{2}$$

$$v \leftarrow arg\ max_{u \in V \backslash S_D} (score(u)) \tag{3}$$

$$WOUT_{degree}(u) \leftarrow \sum_{(u,v) \in A} CLR(v) \tag{4}$$

$$score_{tie}(u) \leftarrow \frac{WOUT_{degree}(u) + CLR(u)}{w(u)} \tag{5}$$

$$v \leftarrow arg\ max_{u \in T} (score_{tie}(u)) \tag{6}$$

2.1   Second Heuristic (H2)

This heuristic, referred to as H2, first adds all source nodes into the partially constructed directed dominating set and then it proceeds exactly like H1. The basic idea behind this heuristic is that the source nodes have to be part of any solution. Therefore, by adding these source nodes at the beginning of the heuristic can lead to a better solution.

Figure 1 illustrates H2 & H3. The digraph given in Fig. 1(a) will be used as input graph. In this figure, the number inside the circle represents the node id. The positive integer number on the top of the circle represents the weight of the respective node. The direction of the arc represents the connection from parent node to child node. Each node is shown in white color in this figure to conform to our coloring strategy before beginning the construction of directed dominating set. In Figs. 1(b) and (c) dominating nodes are represented with black color, and the dominated nodes are represented with grey color. To save space, we have illustrated H2 & H3 only.

Figure 1(b) shows the directed dominating set having the weight 267 computed by H2. The dominating nodes are selected in the order 4, 0, 8, 6. In the first iteration, source node 4 is added to S_D and is colored black, its successors 0 and 7 are colored grey. Now, there are no more source nodes. In the second iteration, nodes 0 & 3 have same highest scores as per Eq. 3, so Eq. 6 is used to break the tie and node 0 which is having highest score as per Eq. 6 is added to S_D and is colored black, it's successors 1, 2, 3 & 5 are colored grey. In the next iteration, nodes 6 & 8 have the same maximum score. There is also a tie in scores as per Eq. 6 also, so randomly node 8 is added to S_D which is not having any white successors in the current graph. In the fourth iteration, the highest score node 6 is added to S_D and is colored black. Now, in the current graph, there is no white node, the heuristic returns $S_D = \{0, 4, 6, 8\}$ as the directed dominating set with weight 267.

2.2   Third Heuristic (H3)

Third heuristic, referred to as H3, like H2, also begins by adding the source nodes and then it proceeds like H1 with one difference. In case of a tie as per Eq. 3, instead of using Eqs. 4, 5 and 6, it uses the following rules to break the tie

1. White nodes are preferred over grey nodes. In case there are more than one white node with maximum score as per Eq. 3, then Eq. 7 is used. If even after using Eq. 7, there are more than one node with minimum value then one such node is chosen randomly. The motivation behind preferring white nodes over grey nodes is that a white node being uncovered is more likely to get selected in latter iterations and therefore its better to select it now. Likewise, the motivation behind using Eq. 7 is that a white node having lesser number of predecessors is more likely to get selected in latter iterations, and, therefore, its better to select it now. Please note that a node is white if none of its predecessors is black, and, therefore, all of its predecessors can be selected

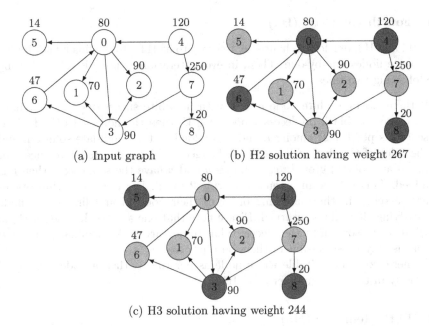

(a) Input graph

(b) H2 solution having weight 267

(c) H3 solution having weight 244

Fig. 1. Illustrating H2 & H3

and that is why we have taken in-degree in Eq. 7 instead of count of only those predecessors which are white (white in-degree). This has saved us from updation of white in-degree of affected nodes every time a node is added to the partially constructed directed dominating set.

2. If there is no white node having maximum score as per Eq. 3, then a grey node having the maximum score is chosen uniformly at random

$$v \leftarrow arg\ min_{(u \in T \wedge CLR(u)=1)}\ (in\text{-}degree(u)) \qquad (7)$$

Figure 1(c) shows the directed dominating set having the weight 244 computed by H3. The dominating nodes are selected in the order 4, 3, 5, 8. In the first iteration, source node 4 is added to S_D and is colored black, its successors 0 and 7 are colored grey. Now, there are no more source nodes. In the second iteration, nodes 0 & 3 have same highest scores as per Eq. 3. However, node 0 is grey and node 3 is white, so node 3 is added to S_D and is colored black, it's successors 1, 2, and 6 are colored grey. In the next iteration, nodes 5 & 8 have the same maximum score as per Eq. 3. There is also a tie in scores as per Eq. 7 also, so randomly node 5 is added to S_D which is not having any white successors in the current graph. In the fourth iteration, the highest score node 8 is added to S_D and is colored black. Now, in the current graph, there is no white node, the heuristic returned $S_D = \{4, 3, 5, 8\}$ as the directed dominating set with weight 244.

2.3   Fourth Heuristic (H4)

Like H2 and H3, our fourth heuristic, referred to as H4, also begins by adding all the source nodes one-by-one. Then, in every iteration, a node is selected using the following two rules:

1. If there exists a white node $u \in V$ with no white successors and that have only one non-black predecessor node $v \in V$, then the node with the highest score (as per Eq. 2) among u and v is added to the candidate solution, and the color of the just added node is changed to black. All its white successor nodes are colored grey. In case, nodes u and v have the same score then v is added. This rule is an extension of rule 2 in [4]. For this rule, white nodes are searched in the increasing order of their node id and first white node satisfying this rule is returned. Please note that one among the node with no white successors and its predecessor has to be part of the dominating set and that is why we select one of them on a priority basis.
2. If there exists no suitable white node as per rule 1, then a node is selected exactly in the same manner as in H1.

2.4   Fifth Heuristic (H5)

H5 is similar to H4 except in rule 2, a node is added exactly in the same manner as in H3 when there is no source node.

2.5   Redundant Node Removal

As explained in introduction section, a node v belonging to a directed dominating set S_D is redundant if $S_D \backslash \{v\}$ remains a directed dominating set. Our redundant node removal procedure works in two stages. During first stage, it iteratively computes the set of redundant nodes and removes all nodes belonging to this set from the solution S_D, thereby making it infeasible and then the same heuristic which obtained S_D is again used to obtain a new solution S_D'. If S_D' is better than S_D, then S_D is replaced with S_D' and next iteration begins. Otherwise, we moves to second stage. If no redundant node remains then redundant node removal procedure exits immediately without going to the second stage.

The second stage is an extension of the redundant node removal procedure used in [2]. It removes redundant nodes one-by-one in an iterative manner. During each iteration, it removes a redundant node having highest ratio of its weight to its out-degree, and then it recomputes the set of redundant nodes. This process is repeated till no redundant node remains.

3   Computational Results

To evaluate the performance of our heuristics, we have derived the benchmark instances for MWDDS from benchmark instances available in the literature for MWDS. There exist three datasets, viz. Type I, Type II and unit disk graphs

Table 2. Results of H1, H2, H3, H4 and H5 heuristics for Type-I directed graph instances

$|V|$	$|A|$	Before redundant node removal					After redundant node removal				
		H1	H2	H3	H4	H5	H1	H2	H3	H4	H5
50	50	754.4	749.6	749.6	**744.7**	**744.7**	750.3	747.5	747.5	**744.7**	**744.7**
50	100	605.9	583.3	583.3	**580.0**	**580.0**	590.1	577.9	577.9	**574.6**	**574.6**
50	250	327.6	327.6	327.6	**325.4**	**325.4**	322.1	322.1	323.2	**318.8**	**318.8**
50	500	195.7	195.7	195.7	195.7	195.7	191.6	191.6	195.7	191.6	195.7
50	750	143.7	143.7	143.7	143.7	143.7	139.5	139.5	139.5	139.5	139.5
50	1000	99.8	99.8	99.8	99.8	99.8	99.8	99.8	99.8	99.8	99.8
100	100	1526.3	**1483.4**	**1483.4**	1488.1	1488.1	1492.7	1481.1	**1478.5**	1485.8	1485.8
100	250	1037.2	**1030.3**	**1030.3**	1041.4	1041.4	1027.2	**1025.5**	**1025.5**	1041.4	1041.4
100	500	681.5	677.2	677.2	**673.6**	**673.6**	674.8	668.4	668.4	**667.0**	**667.0**
100	750	495.3	495.6	495.6	**495.2**	**495.2**	**483.8**	486.4	486.4	488.0	488.0
100	1000	**404.5**	404.5	404.5	404.5	404.5	398.0	**398.0**	**398.0**	**398.0**	398.0
100	2000	**219.3**	219.3	219.3	219.3	219.3	217.1	**217.1**	**217.1**	**217.1**	217.1
150	150	2320.0	2270.5	2270.5	**2270.0**	**2270.0**	2275.8	**2260.5**	2260.7	2262.7	2262.7
150	250	1949.3	1891.5	1887.9	**1886.0**	**1886.0**	1909.8	1880.4	1876.5	**1871.8**	1874.3
150	500	1322.1	1293.2	1293.2	**1291.6**	**1291.6**	1287.8	1278.9	1278.9	**1273.6**	**1273.6**
150	750	1030.3	1022.3	1022.3	**1013.2**	**1013.2**	1023.7	1015.7	1015.7	**998.8**	**998.8**
150	1000	831.7	831.7	843.7	**828.6**	840.6	829.3	829.3	838.3	**826.2**	835.2
150	2000	480.1	480.1	480.1	480.1	**480.1**	476.1	476.1	**476.1**	**476.1**	476.1
150	3000	349.6	349.6	349.6	349.6	349.6	345.3	345.3	345.3	345.3	345.3
200	250	2876.0	2825.8	2825.8	**2814.2**	**2814.2**	2833.8	2808.9	2811.8	**2802.3**	2805.2
200	500	2105.8	2072.2	2072.2	2065.1	**2065.0**	2065.7	2062.8	2062.8	2049.4	**2049.3**
200	750	1683.2	1659.9	1656.5	**1650.4**	1651.3	1646.9	1629.0	1625.3	**1624.4**	1624.8
200	1000	**1354.5**	1355.9	1355.9	1355.5	1355.5	**1336.9**	1340.5	1342.7	1341.1	1341.1
200	2000	812.2	812.2	812.2	812.2	812.2	808.0	808.0	**803.1**	808.0	**803.1**
200	3000	589.4	589.4	589.4	589.4	589.4	587.4	**587.4**	**587.4**	**587.4**	587.4
250	250	3753.2	3687.3	3688.4	3669.4	**3668.0**	3709.2	3678.5	3679.6	3664.7	**3663.3**
250	500	3003.7	2945.5	2947.2	2923.0	**2922.6**	2943.3	2910.5	2909.1	2906.4	**2906.0**
250	750	2409.9	2390.8	**2390.8**	2396.1	2396.1	2369.7	**2365.2**	**2365.2**	2382.1	2382.1
250	1000	1985.1	1998.5	1998.5	**1979.0**	**1979.0**	1956.7	1965.5	1967.5	1942.4	**1939.6**
250	2000	**1216.1**	**1216.1**	1218.3	**1216.1**	1218.3	1197.4	1197.4	**1197.1**	1197.1	**1197.1**
250	3000	892.7	892.7	892.7	892.7	892.7	884.1	884.1	**884.1**	884.1	884.1
250	5000	579.6	**579.6**	580.3	579.6	579.6	577.4	577.4	**577.4**	578.1	578.1
300	300	4650.0	4540.1	4540.1	**4536.1**	**4536.1**	4572.9	**4530.6**	**4530.6**	4534.1	4534.1
300	500	3922.1	3835.2	3831.9	**3823.2**	3826.5	3850.4	3811.0	**3807.7**	3810.4	3813.1
300	750	3312.4	3197.0	3199.3	**3178.2**	**3178.2**	3205.9	3161.3	3168.7	**3152.0**	3154.0
300	1000	2719.2	2675.4	2675.4	**2668.8**	**2668.8**	2667.9	2639.7	2636.1	**2635.4**	**2635.4**
300	2000	1674.6	1670.2	1668.4	1670.1	**1668.3**	1658.5	1658.7	1651.5	1652.8	**1648.8**
300	3000	1208.1	1208.1	**1204.2**	1208.1	**1204.2**	1199.4	1199.4	**1195.5**	1199.4	**1195.5**
300	5000	803.4	803.4	803.4	803.4	803.4	799.0	799.0	799.0	799.0	799.0
500	500	7618.0	7497.7	7496.1	**7489.7**	**7489.7**	7546.1	7485.4	7480.4	7482.4	7482.4
500	1000	5933.6	5833.0	5833.0	**5822.6**	**5822.6**	5833.9	5789.2	**5786.7**	5796.7	5796.7
500	2000	4084.8	4059.0	4059.0	**4031.7**	**4031.7**	4001.9	3985.7	3986.3	**3973.6**	**3973.6**
500	5000	**2032.0**	**2032.0**	**2032.0**	2032.0	2032.0	2012.6	2012.6	2012.6	2012.6	2012.6
500	10000	1204.4	1204.4	1204.4	1204.4	1204.4	1200.2	1200.2	1200.2	1200.2	1200.2
800	1000	11408.0	11132.8	11129.8	11102.0	**11100.8**	11238.7	11088.2	11087.1	**11085.4**	11087.3
800	2000	8616.5	8440.5	8441.0	**8399.5**	**8399.5**	8442.3	8382.7	8378.6	**8350.2**	**8350.2**
800	5000	4740.4	4697.6	**4695.8**	4698.4	4696.4	4664.6	4639.0	**4634.8**	4639.1	4636.8
800	10000	2709.7	2709.7	**2705.4**	2709.7	**2705.4**	2697.9	2697.9	**2691.5**	2697.9	**2691.5**
1000	1000	15138.7	14878.2	14874.9	**14873.8**	**14873.8**	14956.5	14847.4	**14839.8**	14863.6	14863.6
1000	5000	6887.4	6900.4	6898.6	6888.1	**6886.2**	6768.5	6814.3	6816.6	6790.3	**6792.0**
1000	10000	4104.8	4104.8	4108.4	4105.9	4109.5	4050.6	4050.6	4057.7	**4047.0**	4054.1
1000	15000	2966.9	2966.9	2966.9	2966.9	2966.9	2945.7	2945.7	**2943.7**	2945.7	**2943.7**
1000	20000	2344.8	2344.8	2344.8	2344.8	2344.8	2331.0	**2331.0**	2331.0	**2331.0**	2331.0

(UDG) for MWDS in the literature comprising undirected connected node-weighted graphs. First two datasets (Type I & Type II) are due to Jovanovic et al. [5]. The number of nodes in these two datasets ranges from 50 to 1000, whereas the number of edges ranges from 50 to 20000. There are ten instances for each combination of the number of nodes ($|V|$) and the number of edges ($|E|$). For the same $|V|$, there are several different values of $|E|$ so that the variation in the solution with $|E|$ for the same $|V|$ can be observed. Node weights are distributed uniformly at random in [20, 70] for Type I dataset. On the other hand, in case of Type II dataset, node weights are distributed uniformly at random in [1, $degree(v)^2$], where $degree(v)$ is the degree of node v. Each of these two datasets contains 530 instances. UDG dataset is due to Potluri and Singh [11]. The nodes in this dataset are distributed uniformly at random in an area of 1000 × 1000 units and the number of nodes belongs to the set {50, 100, 250, 500, 800, 1000}. There are two values for range (R) of nodes, viz. 150 or 200 units. The weights of the nodes in this dataset are distributed uniformly at random in [1, 100]. Like previous two datasets, this dataset also contains 10 instances for each combination of $|V|$ and R. So this dataset contains 120 instances.

We have converted these datasets for MWDS into datasets for MWDDS by following the process described in [4]. It makes use of the fact that each edge u, v in an undirected graph corresponds to two arcs (u,v) and (v,u) in the corresponding digraph. Therefore, to convert an instance of MWDS to an instance of MWDDS, for each edge in the MWDS instance, we have chosen one of the two corresponding arcs uniformly at random, and, put it into the instance of MWDDS. The weights of nodes in MWDDS instances remain the same as in corresponding MWDS instances. We will also refer to these datasets as Type I, Type II and UDG.

We have implemented our five heuristics in C and executed them on a Linux based 3.1 GHz Core-i5-2400 system with 4 GB of RAM. We have executed each of our heuristic on each instance once. We have reported the results of heuristics before and after redundant node removal procedure to measure the effect of redundant node removal procedure on performance. Further, the relative performance of different heuristics may change after redundant node removal procedure For Type I and Type II instances, we have reported the average solution quality obtained by each heuristic before and after redundant node removal procedure for each group of 10 instances with same $|V|$ and same number of arcs ($|A|$). For UDG instances, we have done the same for each group of 10 instances with same $|V|$ and same range (R). We have not reported the execution times as they are negligible in most cases and in all cases less than 1 s.

Tables 2, 3 and 4 present the results of these five heuristics on Type I, Type II and UDG instances respectively. Tables 5 and 6 are summary tables. Table 5 presents the summary of results before redundant node removal on each of the three instance types, viz. Type I, Type II and UDG, whereas Table 6 presents the summary after redundant node removal. These tables show the number of instance groups on which the average solution quality of heuristic on the left is

Table 3. Results of H1, H2, H3, H4 and H5 heuristics for Type-II directed graph instances

$|V|$	$|A|$	Before redundant node removal					After redundant node removal				
		H1	H2	H3	H4	H5	H1	H2	H3	H4	H5
50	50	102.7	101.6	101.7	103.7	103.6	100.6	101.0	100.8	103.4	103.5
50	100	171.7	170.4	170.1	187.9	184.4	165.9	166.7	165.8	185.6	182.2
50	250	400.5	400.5	400.5	403.6	403.6	379.5	379.5	379.5	382.6	382.6
50	500	532.3	532.3	532.3	532.3	532.3	521.4	521.4	521.4	521.4	521.4
50	750	742.8	742.8	742.8	742.8	742.8	674.3	674.3	674.3	674.3	674.3
50	1000	658.4	658.4	658.4	658.4	658.4	618.6	618.6	618.6	618.6	618.6
100	100	203.6	200.0	200.2	202.8	202.9	198.9	198.6	198.4	202.3	202.3
100	250	410.1	402.3	403.0	422.8	422.8	390.7	386.9	386.9	414.5	414.5
100	500	750.8	748.7	748.7	761.0	761.0	712.3	710.8	711.3	723.5	724.0
100	750	969.9	969.9	969.9	967.7	967.7	932.9	932.9	932.9	930.7	930.7
100	1000	1293.1	1293.1	1293.1	1293.1	1293.1	1233.9	1233.9	1233.9	1233.9	1233.9
100	2000	1861.7	1861.7	1861.7	1861.7	1861.7	1743.8	1743.8	1743.8	1743.8	1743.8
150	150	314.5	307.1	306.8	308.9	308.9	307.9	304.9	305.2	308.2	308.2
150	250	430.8	422.9	422.9	443.7	444.1	419.9	417.7	417.4	439.8	439.4
150	500	773.5	765.0	765.0	784.3	781.9	743.4	744.0	744.0	766.0	765.2
150	750	1119.5	1112.2	1112.2	1111.9	1111.9	1064.2	1062.3	1060.8	1064.9	1063.4
150	1000	1430.3	1430.3	1430.3	1430.3	1430.3	1358.0	1358.0	1358.0	1358.0	1358.0
150	2000	2233.7	2233.7	2233.7	2233.7	2233.7	2066.4	2066.4	2066.4	2066.4	2066.4
150	3000	2742.4	2742.4	2742.4	2742.4	2742.4	2550.3	2550.3	2550.3	2550.3	2550.3
200	250	490.6	474.9	474.7	489.8	489.6	472.7	470.3	470.9	486.8	486.8
200	500	819.8	816.2	816.2	862.7	862.7	795.2	792.5	792.5	846.3	847.4
200	750	1180.5	1177.9	1177.9	1202.8	1202.8	1128.4	1127.5	1127.5	1156.3	1156.3
200	1000	1467.7	1470.0	1470.0	1467.9	1467.9	1404.6	1407.3	1407.3	1402.6	1402.6
200	2000	2493.4	2493.4	2493.4	2493.4	2493.4	2336.1	2336.1	2336.1	2336.1	2336.1
200	3000	3204.8	3204.8	3204.8	3204.8	3204.8	2999.0	2999.0	2999.0	2999.0	2999.0
250	250	509.3	499.1	499.6	503.7	503.5	498.7	496.0	497.4	502.5	502.4
250	500	883.4	873.3	872.5	915.4	914.6	850.7	849.6	849.2	895.3	893.9
250	750	1196.9	1183.1	1182.4	1218.8	1218.8	1138.5	1135.7	1135.3	1181.7	1182.6
250	1000	1592.1	1584.0	1584.0	1618.9	1618.9	1511.1	1510.1	1510.1	1551.8	1551.3
250	2000	2708.4	2708.4	2708.4	2708.4	2708.4	2505.3	2505.3	2505.3	2505.3	2505.3
250	3000	3726.1	3726.1	3726.1	3726.1	3726.1	3568.3	3568.3	3568.3	3568.3	3568.3
250	5000	4978.0	4978.0	4978.0	4978.0	4978.0	4633.5	4633.5	4633.5	4633.5	4633.5
300	300	645.7	629.3	629.0	634.6	634.6	629.1	625.7	626.2	632.8	632.8
300	500	923.5	905.1	905.5	951.8	952.3	891.8	888.0	887.4	941.2	941.7
300	750	1313.8	1292.3	1291.2	1328.5	1328.8	1256.0	1250.7	1249.8	1296.0	1296.5
300	1000	1716.5	1695.2	1694.3	1729.1	1720.0	1630.4	1625.8	1627.9	1665.4	1663.5
300	2000	2825.8	2825.7	2825.7	2840.6	2840.6	2657.2	2657.3	2657.3	2672.2	2672.2
300	3000	3990.5	3990.5	3990.5	3990.5	3990.5	3717.0	3717.0	3719.1	3717.0	3719.1
300	5000	5405.0	5405.0	5405.0	5405.0	5405.0	5115.8	5115.8	5115.8	5115.8	5115.8
500	500	1045.6	1021.9	1021.5	1035.5	1035.3	1022.5	1018.2	1017.0	1034.0	1033.8
500	1000	1777.2	1738.3	1738.6	1831.9	1832.2	1711.4	1699.2	1699.9	1800.7	1802.5
500	2000	3208.2	3191.3	3191.3	3268.8	3269.6	3038.9	3036.9	3036.9	3111.0	3114.9
500	5000	6478.6	6478.6	6478.6	6478.6	6478.6	6116.7	6116.7	6118.6	6116.7	6118.6
500	10000	10404.7	10404.7	10404.7	10404.7	10404.7	9761.6	9761.6	9761.6	9761.6	9761.6
800	1000	1948.7	1900.0	1899.5	1953.4	1954.1	1891.8	1880.4	1879.7	1945.6	1945.2
800	2000	3492.1	3438.6	3437.6	3574.6	3574.4	3342.2	3339.7	3340.4	3493.5	3494.7
800	5000	7313.6	7302.0	7302.0	7311.9	7311.9	6905.2	6909.9	6909.9	6917.3	6917.3
800	10000	12199.4	12199.4	12199.4	12199.4	12199.4	11541.3	11541.3	11541.3	11541.3	11541.3
1000	1000	2067.3	2020.4	2019.5	2044.4	2044.0	2023.7	2012.2	2012.4	2041.1	2040.4
1000	5000	7764.0	7745.4	7744.7	7825.8	7824.7	7365.4	7354.1	7354.6	7449.7	7450.3
1000	10000	13230.3	13230.3	13225.8	13227.0	13222.5	12489.7	12489.7	12485.1	12475.4	12470.8
1000	15000	17699.4	17699.4	17699.4	17699.4	17699.4	16447.3	16447.3	16447.3	16447.3	16447.3
1000	20000	20861.3	20861.3	20861.3	20861.3	20861.3	19694.3	19694.3	19694.3	19694.3	19694.3

Table 4. Results of H1, H2, H3, H4 and H5 heuristics for UDG directed graph instances

$|V|$	R	Before redundant node removal					After redundant node removal				
		H1	H2	H3	H4	H5	H1	H2	H3	H4	H5
50	150	834.0	**823.4**	**823.4**	833.3	833.3	820.0	**818.1**	**818.1**	828.0	828.0
50	200	612.6	**604.2**	**604.2**	615.8	615.8	**588.1**	**588.1**	**588.1**	605.3	605.3
100	150	1141.2	**1126.3**	**1126.3**	1149.9	1149.9	**1089.8**	1091.9	1091.9	1111.3	1111.3
100	200	679.5	**676.6**	**676.6**	677.9	677.9	642.8	**641.0**	**641.0**	644.7	644.7
250	150	1098.3	1092.4	**1092.1**	1092.4	**1092.1**	1025.2	1025.2	**1024.1**	1025.2	**1024.1**
250	200	**552.5**	552.5	552.5	552.5	552.5	517.2	517.2	**517.2**	**517.2**	**517.2**
500	150	**926.0**	**926.0**	926.2	**926.0**	926.2	856.9	856.9	**855.1**	856.9	**855.1**
500	200	**399.9**	**399.9**	**399.9**	**399.9**	**399.9**	375.3	375.3	**374.8**	375.3	**374.8**
800	150	**708.5**	708.5	708.5	**708.5**	**708.5**	659.0	659.0	659.0	659.0	659.0
800	200	**321.3**	321.3	321.3	**321.3**	**321.3**	302.5	302.5	302.5	302.5	302.5
1000	150	**712.2**	712.2	712.2	**712.2**	**712.2**	665.2	665.2	665.7	**665.2**	665.7
1000	200	**318.1**	318.1	318.8	**318.1**	318.8	290.2	290.2	291.0	**290.2**	291.0

Table 5. Summary table (before redundant node removal)

		H1			H2			H3			H4			H5		
		W	E	B	W	E	B	W	E	B	W	E	B	W	E	B
TYPE-I	H1	–	–	–	27	22	4	29	16	8	30	19	4	32	15	6
	H2	4	22	27	–	–	–	11	34	8	29	19	5	31	15	7
	H3	8	16	29	8	34	11	–	–	–	31	15	7	29	19	5
	H4	4	19	30	5	19	29	7	15	31	–	–	–	9	38	6
	H5	6	15	32	7	15	31	5	19	29	6	38	9	–	–	–
TYPE-II	H1	–	–	–	29	23	1	30	22	1	11	20	22	11	20	22
	H2	1	23	29	–	–	–	14	33	6	4	20	29	4	20	29
	H3	1	22	30	6	33	14	–	–	–	3	20	30	4	20	29
	H4	22	20	11	29	20	4	30	20	3	–	–	–	12	34	7
	H5	22	20	11	29	20	4	29	20	4	7	34	12	–	–	–
UDG	H1	–	–	–	5	7	0	5	5	2	3	7	2	3	5	4
	H2	0	7	5	–	–	–	1	9	2	0	8	4	1	5	6
	H3	2	5	5	2	9	1	–	–	–	2	5	5	0	8	4
	H4	2	7	3	4	8	0	5	5	2	–	–	–	1	9	2
	H5	4	5	3	6	5	1	4	8	0	2	9	1	–	–	–

worse (W), equal (E) or better (B) in comparison to the average solution quality of the heuristic at the top.

These tables clearly show that the relative performance of heuristics vary as per instance type. H2 and H3 performed better than other three heuristics on

Table 6. Summary table (after redundant node removal)

		H1		H2			H3			H4			H5		
		W	E	B	W	E	B	W	E	B	W	E	B	W	E	B
TYPE-I	H1	–	–	–	26	22	5	32	12	9	29	19	5	32	12	9
	H2	5	22	26	–	–	–	18	22	13	24	19	10	27	12	14
	H3	9	12	32	13	22	18	–	–	–	24	12	17	22	19	12
	H4	5	19	29	10	19	24	17	12	24	–	–	–	11	31	11
	H5	9	12	32	14	12	27	12	19	22	11	31	11	–	–	–
TYPE-II	H1	–	–	–	24	23	6	26	20	7	3	20	30	4	18	31
	H2	6	23	24	–	–	–	12	29	12	3	20	30	3	18	32
	H3	7	20	26	12	29	12	–	–	–	5	18	30	3	20	30
	H4	30	20	3	30	20	3	30	18	5	–	–	–	12	29	12
	H5	31	18	4	32	18	3	30	20	3	12	29	12	–	–	–
UDG	H1	–	–	–	2	9	1	5	4	3	0	8	4	3	3	6
	H2	1	9	2	–	–	–	3	7	2	0	8	4	3	3	6
	H3	3	4	5	2	7	3	–	–	–	2	3	7	0	8	4
	H4	4	8	0	4	8	0	7	3	2	–	–	–	3	7	2
	H5	6	3	3	6	3	3	4	8	0	2	7	3	–	–	–

Type II and UDG instances, whereas on Type I instances H4 and H5 performed better. Among all the five, H1 performed worse overall, thereby validating the idea of adding all source nodes to the partially constructed directed dominating set at the beginning. H4 and H5 process leaf nodes on a priority basis and this idea works in Type I instances, but not in Type II and UDG instances. This can be attributed to large difference in weights of nodes in Type II and UDG instances. All the heuristics return more or less similar results on instances with relatively large number of arcs in comparison to number of nodes. These conclusions hold in both the cases, i.e., before and after using redundant node removal procedure. Further, the benefits of using redundant node removal procedure can be clearly seen as it is able to improve the results for each instance group and for each heuristic. However, solutions obtained through H1, H2 and H4 after redundant node removal are improved by a larger amount in general than those obtained with H3 and H5 as can be observed by comparing the two summary tables.

4 Conclusions

In this paper, we have proposed five heuristics, viz. H1, H2, H3, H4 and H5 for the minimum weight directed dominating set problem (MWDDS). These five heuristics, which are variants of one another, are the very first heuristic approaches for MWDDS . A redundant node removal procedure is used to further improve the results obtained through these heuristics. H1 extends the ideas presented in [2] for MWDS to MWDDS, whereas H4 & H5 extends the idea presented in [4] for MDDS to MWDDS. The performance of these heuristics have been evaluated on three benchmark datasets, viz. Type I, Type II and UDG which are derived from the standard benchmark datasets for MWDS. The relative performance of these heuristics vary as per instances types. On Type I dataset, H4 & H5 performed the best, whereas for Type II and UDG datasets, H2 and H3 performed the best. These five heuristics, being the first heuristics for MWDDS, will serve as the baseline approaches for evaluating the performance of future heuristic and metaheuristic approaches for this problem.

As a future work, we would like to develop metaheuristics approaches for MWDDS utilizing some of the ideas presented here. We intend to extend our approaches to other variants of the dominating set problem in directed graphs.

References

1. Albuquerque, M., Vidal, T.: An efficient matheuristic for the minimum-weight dominating set problem. Appl. Soft Comput. **72**, 527–538 (2018)
2. Chaurasia, S.N., Singh, A.: A hybrid evolutionary algorithm with guided mutation for minimum weight dominating set. Appl. Intell. **43**(3), 512–529 (2015). https://doi.org/10.1007/s10489-015-0654-1
3. Garey, M.R., Johnson, D.S.: Computers and intractability: A Guide to the Theory of NP-Completeness. W. H. Freeman, San Francisco (1979)
4. Habibulla, Y., Zhao, J.-H., Zhou, H.-J.: The directed dominating set problem: generalized leaf removal and belief propagation. In: Wang, J., Yap, C. (eds.) FAW 2015. LNCS, vol. 9130, pp. 78–88. Springer, Cham (2015). https://doi.org/10.1007/978-3-319-19647-3_8
5. Jovanovic, R., Tuba, M., Simian, D.: Ant colony optimization applied to minimum weight dominating set problem. In: Proceedings of the 12th WSEAS International Conference on Automatic Control, Modelling and Simulation (ACMOS 2010), pp. 322–326. World Scientific and Engineering Academy and Society (WSEAS), Stevens Point (2010)
6. Lin, G., Guan, J.: A binary particle swarm optimization for the minimum weight dominating set problem. J. Comput. Sci. Technol. **33**(2), 305–322 (2018). https://doi.org/10.1007/s11390-017-1781-4
7. Liu, Y., Slotine, J., Barabási, A.: Observability of complex systems. In: Proceedings of the National Academy of Sciences, USA, vol. 110, pp. 2460–2465. National Academy of Sciences, USA (2013)
8. Molnár Jr., F., Sreenivasan, S., Szymanski, B., Korniss, K.: Minimum dominating sets in scale-free network ensembles. Sci. Rep. **3**, 1736 (2013)
9. Nitash, C., Singh, A.: An artificial bee colony algorithm for minimum weight dominating set. In: 2014 IEEE Symposium on Swarm Intelligence, pp. 1–7. IEEE (2014)
10. Pang, C., Zhang, R., Zhang, Q., Wang, J.: Dominating sets in directed graphs. Inf. Sci. **180**, 3647–3652 (2010)
11. Potluri, A., Singh, A.: Hybrid metaheuristic algorithms for minimum weight dominating set. Appl. Soft Comput. **13**(1), 76–88 (2013)
12. Takaguchi, T., Hasegawa, T., Yoshida, Y.: Suppressing epidemics on networks by exploiting observer nodes. Phys. Rev. E **90**, 012807 (2014)

13. Wang, H., Zheng, H., Browne, F., Wang, C.: Minimum dominating sets in cell cycle specific protein interaction networks. In: Proceedings of the International Conference on Bioinformatics and Biomedicine (BIBM 2014), pp. 25–30. IEEE (2014)

14. Wang, Y., Cai, S., Chen, J., Yin, M.: A fast local search algorithm for minimum weight dominating set problem on massive graphs. In: Proceedings of the Twenty-Seventh International Joint Conference on Artificial Intelligence (IJCAI 2018), pp. 1514–1522. IJCAI (2018)

15. Wuchty, S.: Controllability in protein interaction networks. In: Proceedings of the National Academy of Sciences, USA, vol. 111, pp. 7156–7160. National Academy of Sciences, USA (2014)

16. Yang, Y., Wang, J., Motter, A.: Network observability transitions. Phys. Rev. Lett. **90**, 258701 (2012)

A Database for Printed Takri Class
of North-West Indian Regional Scripts

Shikha Magotra[✉], Baijnath Kaushik, and Ajay Kaul

SoCSE, SMVDU, Katra, J&K, India
shikhabhimanyu.bali@gmail.com,
{baijnath.kaushik,ajay.kaul}@smvdu.ac.in

Abstract. The foremost step towards research in natural language processing is the availability of benchmark databases for various scripts or languages used worldwide. It was observed that no benchmark database has been developed so far for Takri class of scripts which is known to have abundant data lying unrecognized in North-west India. Thus, the paper presents a standard database for Printed Takri script collected manually from various sources and pre-processed for binarization, noise removal and skew correction. The database contains 272 text images in single font as no fonts have been developed so far in Takri and the metal fonts developed earlier for this century-old script are also of the same size. The database could be used for segmentation and recognition of Takri characters using various machine learning approaches. We believe that the database developed will encourage more researchers to work in this direction. The database is freely available to all the researchers on demand.

Keywords: Printed Takri · Chambeali · Pre-processing · Dataset

1 Introduction

The baseline of research in the field of script recognition system development is the availability of standard databases for the scripts. Most of the research done in the field has largely been for Latin script due to the free availability of a large number of standard databases in different fonts and forms. Besides, there are standard databases available for other scripts too like Arabic, Chinese, and Indian scripts which includes Devnagari and Bangla scripts [1–3].

As India is a multi-script country with almost 12 scripts in use including one national script and 11 regional scripts, the databases for the various scripts of India are not standardised yet. However, the standard datasets for most of the Indian scripts have been prepared by ISI Kolkata which is made available on-demand only. Still, research needs to be done for standardising the remaining scripts of India to encourage research in the field on large scale.

Moreover, Takri is a class of Indian regional scripts which covers an enormous amount of writings from Northwest India and no work has been done so far for the preservation and recognition of such cultural heritage. This paper is the first attempt to provide a standard database for Printed Takri script which could serve as a benchmark database for further research in the field.

© Springer Nature Singapore Pte Ltd. 2020
P. K. Singh et al. (Eds.): FTNCT 2019, CCIS 1206, pp. 508–520, 2020.
https://doi.org/10.1007/978-981-15-4451-4_40

The rest of the paper is organised as - Sect. 2 gives a brief review of the availability of different Indian script databases with significant contributions of the paper. Section 3 describes the history and characteristics of the Takri class of scripts. Section 4 describes the standardised database for Printed Takri script along with the challenges faced. Lastly, Sect. 5 concludes the paper along with possible future research directions.

2 Available Databases of Indian Scripts

2.1 Related Work

The available work done on Indian scripts has been mostly on small datasets collected in laboratory experiments [4]. However, two large databases for handwritten numerals of the most popular Indian scripts - Devnagari and Bangla, was developed by Bhattacharya et al. in 2009 for the first time [5]. Work done in the field of dataset development for other Indian scripts is described in [6, 7]. After this, ISI Kolkata developed large databases for major Indian scripts which are available to researchers on demand. The various Indian scripts database research centres are tabulated in Table 1.

Table 1. List of Indian scripts database along with their centres [4]

Indian script	Research centre	Availability
Devnagari	ISI Kolkata	On-demand
Bengali	ISI and Jadavpur University, Kolkata	On-demand
Assamese	IIT Guwahati	
Gujarati	M.S. University of Baroda, Vadodara	
Kannada	IISc Banglore and University of Mysore	On-demand
Malayalam	CDAC, Thiruvananthapuram and Kannur University	
Oriya	Utkal University, Bhubaneshwar	
Gurmukhi	Thapar Institute of Engineering and Technology, Patiala	On-demand
Tamil	IIT Madras, Anna University, Chennai and HP lab India	Freely available (by HP lab India)
Telugu	IIIT & University of Hyderabad	
Urdu	CDAC, Pune and CENPARMI, Canada	

Some of these datasets are very large collected from diverse sources while the datasets for Kannada, Tamil, Telugu are small.

Apart from these, a dataset of 11 official Indian scripts in handwritten form has been prepared by Obaidullah et al. [8]. Another cross-language framework was proposed using a dataset of 3 Indian scripts namely Devnagari, Bangla and Gurmukhi by Bhunia et al. [9]. Also, a new multi-column CNN based technique was proposed for recognition of handwritten Indian numerals using publicly available datasets of 5 main Indian scripts [10].

A handwritten dataset of 3 Indian scripts - Devnagari, Bangla and Urdu along with Roman has also been prepared for research in handwritten numerals of these scripts in [11]. One more benchmark database of handwritten Bangla-Roman and Devnagari-Roman has been prepared in [12] for mixed-script research. A newly created handwritten database for multi script identification is used in [13] at the page, block and word levels. The information regarding benchmark Indian script databases is provided in a survey shown in [14].

2.2   Findings and Contributions

From the extensive review of related work done in the field of database development, it is observed that there has been a significant rise of research in the field recently only. Most of the datasets developed for Indian scripts are from Devnagari and Bangla scripts only. However, some of the Indian script databases standardized include Gurmukhi and Urdu scripts also. Only one work has been observed for database development which includes all official 11 Indian scripts [8].

Besides, no work for database development has been done so far for Takri script. Therefore, our work focuses on this direction. The significant contributions of the paper are-

• A novel database for research in Printed Takri has been standardised in the paper.
• Archival data is collected manually and then, pre-processed and divided into 272 blocks of Takri text.
• The database provided will serve as a benchmark database for research in Takri text segmentation and recognition as no work has been observed so far for this north-west Indian regional script.

3   Overview of Takri Class of Scripts

3.1   History

Takri script is a regional script of India used for writing languages of hilly regions of North-west India from 16th to 20th century [15]. It is known to have originated from Sharada family of Brahmi scripts through an intermediate form – Devashesha which is also known as later Sharada (Fig. 1).

Sharada was popular in use in the mountainous regions of pir panjal range comprising today's J&K, Punjab, Himachal Pradesh, Uttarakhand, Haryana until the beginning of 13th century [16]. Later with time, Gurumukhi was developed from Sharada to be used in the plains of Punjab and Takri was developed for use in hilly areas like J&K, H.P., Uttarakhand. Now, as this script was used in the hilly areas of North-western India, due to less communication among people in these areas & as different rulers ruled different parts of this huge area, many variations of Takri were developed. Therefore, it is known to have almost 13 variations in North-west India. These are tabulated in Table 2.

Fig. 1. Origin of Takri Script from Brahmi script

According to George Grierson, in his Linguistic Survey of India, all these variations share inherent characteristics i.e., style of writing is different but the script is one. So, Takri may now be called as a 'class of scripts' rather than a single script with a different script for different hilly state/area. Out of these, Gaddi & Garhi have no specimen for this script [17]. Moreover, due to many variations, it is difficult to decipher by a single person.

Table 2. Variations of Takri with their state of dialect [17]

S.No.	Variation name	State of dialect
1	Chambeali	Chamba, H.P.
2	Dogri	Jammu, J&K
3	Bhatteali	Chamba, H.P.
4	Kangri	Kangra, H.P.
5	Kochi	Bashahr
6	Kulvi	Kullu, H.P.
7	Kashtwari	Kishtwarh, J&K
8	Mandeali	Mandi, H.P.
9	Gaddi	Bharmaur, Uttarakhand
10	Gahri	Garhwal, Uttarakhand
11	Kinnauri	Kanaur
12	Jaunsari	Dehradun, Uttarakhand
13	Sirmauri	Sirmur

Takri was in wide use in North India from 16th to the middle of 20th century A.D., for writing manuscripts, copper plates/pattas, revenue records, royal orders, inscriptions on paintings, stone sculptures & masks. Available Hand-written records in Takri are in the form of agreements by rajas of that time, inscriptions on paintings, temples, pattas/copper plates, sanads/grant deeds, official & political letters [18]. Besides some important machine-printed writings in Takri are –

- Christian Missionary published books, primers, folk tales of Chamba & Holy Scriptures in Takri in 19th century.
- In day to day use in Chamba till 1947. An official patwari was employed by the revenue department in Chamba to decipher/read records & old revenue papers in Takri till 2006. Even now, some Takri knowing person is employed for reading such records in Chamba [19].
- Bilingual grant deeds by Maharaja Ranbir Singh (1857–85) & Pratap Singh (1885–1925).
- Takri books published in J&K are Ranbir Chikitsa, Vyavhar Gita, Lilavati, Qanoon zabta Dewan, Niyam Sena Vibhag, Ranbir Dand Vidhi, Pravesika [20].
- It is in Jammu only that Takri engraved on coins is recorded [21].
- Takri used for writing petitions that are read before Maharaja Ranbir Singh & for this purpose, it replaced Persian. Knowledge of Takri was compulsory. No official not knowing Takri could be recruited. Maharaja himself signed in Takri on local official papers.

Later this script lost usage after independence. Rare manuscripts, documents, records are lying in state of neglect as these cannot be deciphered or read various revival programs of Takri were initiated in Chamba state: in January 2009, the government of H.P. conducted a workshop for teaching Takri in collaboration with IGNOU based on national Manuscript Mission [17].

Finally, the script is not in use today. Only a few people exist who could read the script. No literacy of script is there but piles of material exist.

3.2   Character Set

Knowing Takri as a class of scripts, rather than a script, each class/variation has its own character set. However, these sets of characters of different classes of Takri share common inherent characteristics besides depicting differing writing styles.

Out of the 13 variations mentioned before, characters of only chambeali & new Dogri or Namay Akkhar or Dvigrit Akkhar were standardised & metal fonts were developed for printing various books in Takri. Among these, new Dogri was confined to the printing of Dogri literature only by Maharaja Ranbir Singh in the 19th century while chambeali was used to print other forms of Takri too like kangri along with chambeali itself. Therefore, chambeali form is the most well-defined & refined form of Takri. Standardization of this form was used for printing specimens of the literature of other variations also. George Grierson used chambeali metal fonts for prints alphabets of all variations of Takri in his linguistic survey of India. Also, it was used by a Christian missionary to print gospels of various Saints in Takri. So, we chose chambeali as our baseline script for representing Takri.

Moreover, in the Unicode developed by Anshuman Pandey, Chambeali form was used for a standard form for unified Takri [17]. So, for the remaining part of the paper, we have used chambeali form as unified Takri representation.

The character sets/Takri alphabet for Chambeali form comprise of 11 vowels, 33 consonants & 10 numerals. Different characters/glyphs are shown in Fig. 2.

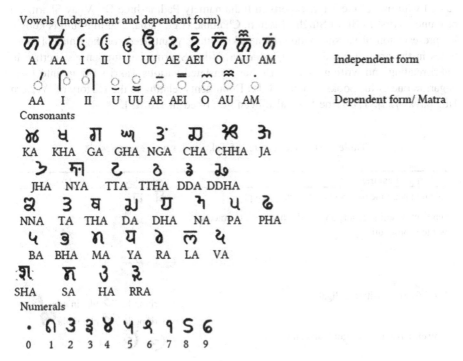

Fig. 2. Character set of Chambeali Takri

3.3 Features

- Takri does not contain headline. However, some characters of the script have an inherent headline in their glyph form like in characters kha ध & tha ष or in pa U & ya प. When two or more such characters are written consecutively, the inherent line over these characters is not joined in Takri.
- Half-forms are used only for writing ha ౩, half form is used like ᠬᠠ mha.
- Ligatures are infrequently written. However, when writing two consonants sequentially if the second character is ya प or ra ᶗ ligatures are used.

  1. For writing ya प, ᶜ᠂ symbol is used as ligature like ᠯᠥ chhya.

  2. For writing ra ᶗ, ᶜᶜ symbol is used as ligature like ৼ tra or प़ pra.

- Geminated consonants like ss, are not used in Takri unlike Gurmukhi in which addak symbol is used to represent geminated consonant.
- Presence of more than one connected component in each character like ᠬ, 3᠂, ᠬᠠ
- Compound characters like ksha क्ष in devnagari, is not present in chambeali form of Takri.

The uniqueness of this script is in its wide range of variations across large geographical area. The unique features of the script which distinguishes it from other Indian scripts are tabulated in Table 3. The script characteristics are thoroughly discussed with one of the Takri experts in India namely Padmashree Dr. Vijay Sharma, a prominent artist in Bhuri Singh Museum, Chamba, H.P., India. The museum is known for preservation of various handwritten Takri letters, grant deeds of the Rajas of those times in the area of North - west India. Dr. Vijay Sharma has immense expertise in Takri reading and writing as well. He has translated various Takri writings into Devnagari in one of his books namely "Takri Documents relating to the History of Western Himalaya" [22]. The same have also been described in [16–19].

Table 3. Unique features of Takri script with examples

Unique Features	Examples
Inherent headline over some character's glyph	ब , य
Inherent headline is left unjoined when such characters written consecutively	४ग३। , ४ली , ल्ऊधळॅ
Half- forms – written as ligatures	For writing ha ꝝ like in mha ꝱ For writing la ꝗ like in lla ꝣ
Vowels have more height than consonants	꒳ , ꒴ , ꒵

3.4   Related Scripts

Takri is most closely related to Sharada, Landa & Gurumukhi scripts as shown in Fig. 3. Gurmukhi can be considered as sister script to Takri as both descended from Sharada family of scripts. Also, Takri shares 12 similar characters with Gurmukhi script and 5 similar characters with Devnagari script. And, both the Devnagari and Gurmukhi scripts contain Headline over characters to form words while Takri is a non-headline script. Among these scripts, no work has been done on recognition of sharada & landa scripts except proposal for Unicode of sharada as well as landa by anshuman pandey [23]. However, various segmentation and recognition algorithms have been developed for Gurmukhi script which can be applied for Takri recognition as Takri is most closely related to Gurmukhi [24–30]. Despite being very close to Gurmukhi script, Takri has various attributes which distinguishes it from Gurmukhi, described in Table 4 and thus, makes recognition of its characters quite challenging.

Fig. 3. Heirarchy showing relationship among related scripts to Takri

Table 4. Features distinguishing between Takri and Gurumukhi scripts

Gurumukhi	Takri
Uses headline for connecting characters to form words	No headline used to connect characters in a word
Half forms joined with respective consonants in lower zone	Half forms are joined on the right side of character or, inside the character form
Geminated consonants are used using addak symbol over the consonant	No geminated consonants are used
Matras with phonation 'i' & 'ii' are joined with the respective consonant	Matras 'i' & 'ii' are left unjoined with the consonant
Presence of horizontally overlapping lines of text	No horizontally overlapping lines of text

Being non-headline script, character segmentation approaches used for Gurumukhi may not give desired accuracy. Also, most of the existing segmentation approaches used for Gurumukhi uses structural features to segment half-forms from characters. This, when applied to Takri, will not work correctly due to the structural dissimilarities between the two scripts. Also, for segmenting horizontally overlapping lines in Gurumukhi text, the approach used is to calculate the number of headlines present in a multi-strip for detecting the actual number of strips. Again, as Takri is a non-headline script, this approach would not be able to segment horizontally overlapping lines in Takri text.

Along with this, various characters in Takri have inherent headline in their glyph formation which is left unjoined to the consecutive characters in a word like kha ੫ & tha ੩; pa ੫ & ya ੫; ma ੧ & sa ੧; cha ੫ & da ੪. So, applying algorithms using headline deletion approaches will lead to loss of character. The feature of Takri having various sets of characters with very high similarity index like jha ੭, ta ੩, ha ੩ makes recognition of individual character quite challenging. Moreover, out of 33 consonant characters of Takri, only 12 are similar to its most closely related script Gurumukhi. So, existing methodologies need not provide sufficient accuracy for character recognition of Takri script.

4   Printed Takri Database

4.1   Issues and Challenges

Takri script served as an official script in the states of North-west India only till 20th century. After this, other scripts like Urdu and Devnagari replaced Takri for these purposes. So, very less printed literature is known. Only one printing press was established in Ludhiana by Britishers to print in Takri script for which no metal fonts exists now. Even the literature printed during Maharaja Ranbir Singh rule in J&K is through the litho press, which can be considered in hand-printed form only.

Also, the Machine-printed forms of Takri data are difficult to find in the Archives of the states of North-west India. Piles of material exist in handwritten form but, our focus is to collect data in printed form as it is the most appropriate & standardised form of data. So, we surveyed various libraries, museums & archival departments of J&K and Himachal Pradesh, and collected some books in machine-printed form. Some specimen of one of the printed book in Takri in 1930 namely 'Mangal Samachar'- translation of gospels of St. John by Biblical Society of India are shown in the Fig. 4.

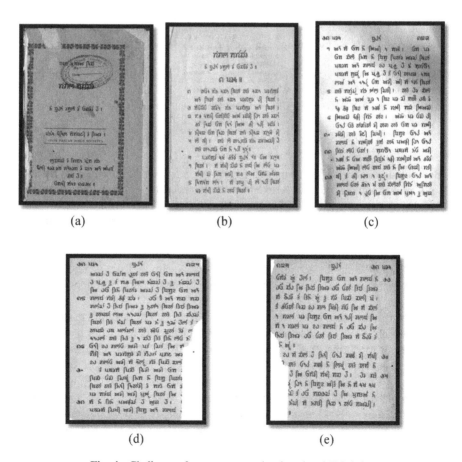

(a)   (b)   (c)

(d)   (e)

Fig. 4. Challenges for pre - processing in printed Takri data

Fig. 5. Pre-processed images of printed Takri text

The data collected in the form of books are digitised by scanning it with horizontal & vertical resolution of 200 & 200 dpi respectively & bit depth 24. Further, the scanned grayscale documents are binarized using standard thresholding techniques. However, the database developed contains 272 pre-processed images of Takri text. More work for dataset development needs to be done for larger datasets, Takri handwritten data as well and also for other variations of Takri. Various stray marks are present in binarized images including library stamp mark on the front page as shown in Fig. 4a. The images are skewed in either direction which needs to be corrected for database development. Also, some broken characters are present in text images, may be because of century - old printing quality used. Some 2–3 pages among the documents were torn from either sides as shown in Fig. 4d and e.

4.2   Preprocessing

For the preparation of Printed Takri data set, about 136 scanned pages are preprocessed using standard techniques for binarization, skew correction and noise removal. The scanned data is divided into 2 blocks for each page of text and pre-processed further. So, the database contains 272 text blocks with about 2,584 lines of Takri text which further contains about 10,880 words. Thus, it contains a total of 83,250 Printed Takri characters. These include characters showing the presence of overlapping bounding boxes, half-forms and touching characters as well. Also, the database developed is in single font only.

The dataset developed can be further used for research in script recognition of Takri script using statistical as well as machine learning approaches (Fig. 5).

5   Conclusion and Future Scope

The standardization of the database is our first step towards research in Takri script. It will encourage the researchers of NLP and AI community to explore deeper into the script and conduct further research in the field. The database could be used for text segmentation and classification using various machine learning, deep learning techniques. It could also be used for development of script identification algorithm for Takri script, as various bilingual documents, letters, grant deeds in Takri- Persian-Devnagari- Sharada scripts available in north- west regions of India.

However, the database developed contains limited pre-processed images of Takri text. More work for dataset development can be done for development of larger datasets of Indian Regional scripts. Along with it, development of Takri handwritten datasets for various variations of Takri class of scripts can be done.

Acknowledgement. We would like to thank Padmashri Dr. Vijay Sharma, Artist & Takri expert, Bhuri Singh Museum, Chamba, H.P. for sharing his valuable expertise on this rare script & authenticating the genuinity of the script.

References

1. Jaiem, F.K., Kanoun, S., Khemakhem, M., El Abed, H., Kardoun, J.: Database for Arabic printed text recognition research. In: Petrosino, A. (ed.) ICIAP 2013. LNCS, vol. 8156, pp. 251–259. Springer, Heidelberg (2013). https://doi.org/10.1007/978-3-642-41181-6_26
2. Al-Ma'adeed, S., Elliman, D., Higgins, C.A.: A database for Arabic handwritten text recognition research. In: Proceedings Eighth International Workshop on Frontiers in Handwriting Recognition. IEEE (2002)
3. Chung, Y.M., Lee, J.Y.: A corpus-based approach to comparative evaluation of statistical term association measures. J. Am. Soc. Inf. Sci. Technol. **52**(4), 283–296 (2001)
4. Pal, U., Jayadevan, R., Sharma, N.: Handwriting recognition in Indian regional scripts: a survey of offline techniques. ACM Trans. Asian Lang. Inf. Process. (TALIP) **11**(1), 1–35 (2012). Article 1

5. Bhattacharya, U., Chaudhuri, B.B.: Handwritten numeral databases of Indian scripts and multistage recognition of mixed numerals. IEEE Trans. Pattern Anal. Mach. Intell. **31**(3), 444–457 (2008)

6. Alaei, A., Pal, U., Nagabhushan, P.: Dataset and ground truth for handwritten text in four different scripts. Int. J. Pattern Recognit. Artif. Intell. **26**(04), 1253001 (2012)

7. Ahmed, S.B., et al.: UCOM offline dataset-an Urdu handwritten dataset generation. Int. Arab J. Inf. Technol. (IAJIT) **14**(2), 2 (2017)

8. Obaidullah, Sk.Md., et al.: PHDIndic_11: page-level handwritten document image dataset of 11 official Indic scripts for script identification. Multimedia Tools Appl. **77**(2), 1643–1678 (2018)

9. Bhunia, A.K., et al.: Cross-language framework for word recognition and spotting of Indic scripts. Pattern Recogn. **79**, 12–31 (2018)

10. Sarkhel, R., et al.: A multi-scale deep quad tree based feature extraction method for the recognition of isolated handwritten characters of popular indic scripts. Pattern Recogn. **71**, 78–93 (2017)

11. Obaidullah, Sk.Md., et al.: A new dataset of word-level offline handwritten numeral images from four official Indic scripts and its benchmarking using image transform fusion. Int. J. Intell. Eng. Inform. **4**(1), 1–20 (2016)

12. Singh, P.K., Sarkar, R., Das, N., Basu, S., Kundu, M., Nasipuri, M.: Benchmark databases of handwritten *Bangla-Roman* and *Devanagari-Roman* mixed-script document images. Multimedia Tools Appl. **77**(7), 8441–8473 (2017). https://doi.org/10.1007/s11042-017-4745-3

13. Obaidullah, Sk.Md., Santosh, K.C., Halder, C., Das, N., Roy, K.: Automatic Indic script identification from handwritten documents: page, block, line and word-level approach. Int. J. Mach. Learn. Cybern. **10**(1), 87–106 (2017). https://doi.org/10.1007/s13042-017-0702-8

14. Obaidullah, Sk.Md., et al.: Handwritten Indic script identification in multi-script document images: a survey. Int. J. Pattern Recognit. Artif. Intell. **32**(10), 1856012 (2018)

15. Mule, G.: akara. к к [The Story of Indian Scripts]. Rajakamala Prakasana, Dilli (1974)

16. Vogel, J.Ph.: Antiquities of Chamba State, I, Calcutta, pi. XXXI: 218 (1911)

17. Pandey, A.: Proposal to Encode the Takri Script in ISO/IEC 10646, vol. 2. L2/09-424 (2009). http://www.Unicode.org

18. Kaul, P.K.: Antiquities of the Chenāb Valley in Jammu: Inscriptions-Copper Plates, Sanads, Grants. Firmāns and Letters in Brāhmi-Shārdā-Tākri-Persian and Devnāgri Scripts. Eastern Book Linkers, Delhi (2001)

19. Chhabra, B.Ch.: Antiquities of Chamba State, Part II, Medieval and Later Inscriptions. Memoirs of the Archaeological Survey of India. Government of India Press, New Delhi (1957)

20. Shivanath: Two Decades of Dogri Literature. Sahitya Akademi (1997)

21. Charak, S.D.S., Singh, M.R.: Life and Times of Maharaja Ranbir Singh, 1830–1885. Jay and Kay Book House (1985)

22. Ohri, V.C., Sharma, V.: Takri Documents relating to the History of Western Himalaya. Chamba Shilpa Parishad (2010)

23. Pandey, A.: A Roadmap for Scripts of the Landa Family. No. 3766. N3766 L2/10-011R, 9 February 2010 (2010). http://std.dkuug.dk/JTC1/SC2/WG2/docs

24. Lehal, G.S.: A complete machine-printed Gurmukhi OCR system. In: Govindaraju, V., Setlur, S. (eds.) Guide to OCR for Indic Scripts. Advances in Pattern Recognition, pp. 43–71. Springer, London (2009). https://doi.org/10.1007/978-1-84800-330-9_3

25. Pal, U., Chaudhuri, B.B.: Indian script character recognition: a survey. Pattern Recogn. **37**(9), 1887–1899 (2004)

26. Lehal, G.S., Singh, C.: A technique for segmentation of Gurmukhi text. In: Skarbek, W. (ed.) CAIP 2001. LNCS, vol. 2124, pp. 191–200. Springer, Heidelberg (2001). https://doi.org/10. 1007/3-540-44692-3_24

27. Lehal, G.S., Singh, C.: Feature extraction and classification for OCR of Gurmukhi script. VIVEK-BOMBAY **12**(2), 2–12 (1999)

28. Kaur, S., Bhatia, R.: Gurmukhi printed character recognition using hierarchical centroid method and SVM. Int. J. Comput. Appl. **149**(3), 24–27 (2016)

29. Jindal, M.K., Lehal, G.S., Sharma, R.K.: Segmentation problems and solutions in printed degraded Gurmukhi script. Int. J. Sig. Process. **2**(4), 258–267 (2005)

30. Jindal, M.K., Sharma, R.K., Lehal, G.S.: Segmentation of touching characters in upper zone in printed Gurmukhi script. In: Proceedings of the 2nd Bangalore Annual Compute Conference. ACM (2009)

A Taxonomy of Methods for Handling Data Streams in Presence of Concepts Drifts

Veena Mittal[1]($\boxtimes$) and Ritesh Srivastava[2]

[1] Department of Information Technology,
Galgotias College of Engineering and Technology, Greater Noida, India
veena.mittal06@gmail.com
[2] Department of Computer Science and Engineering,
Galgotias College of Engineering and Technology, Greater Noida, India
ritesh21july@gmail.com

Abstract. Concept drift is the scenario in online learning in which value of target variable changes with respect to time. The learning algorithms should be adaptive in nature in order to cater the changes imposed due to change in concept. This paper discusses about the adaptive algorithms that are used in learning from the evolving data with different changing patterns. The various applications owing concept drift that are major sources of digital data stream and other real-world problems addresses concept drift are also discussed in this paper.

Keywords: Concept drift · Adapting algorithms · Forgetting data · Incremental learning · Real and virtual drifts

1 Introduction

In stationary (or static) data streams, the underlying data distribution of the data stream remains uniform throughout the stream. Conversely, in non-stationary data stream the underlying data distribution of the data stream changes very frequently with respect to time.

However, since, in the real world, most of the applications are inherently dynamic in nature and produce data streams with non-uniform underlying data distribution, hence, this non-uniformity increases challenge in data stream mining with classical batch learning approaches of data mining and machine learning directly. The data streams whose underlying data distribution changes over time are commonly referred as concept drifting data streams and the change in the underlying data distribution is called concept drift.

The challenges in online learning are generally due to the presence of concept drifts in the data streams. In general, classical data stream mining methods are not able to cater the need of continuously generated rapid data records. It requires data to be processed on its arrival only and insights to be generated at a very fast rate.

The collected data is processed in offline mode in traditional data mining. The models are trained to predict the output of unknown inputs. However, the data in the form of streams is not possible to accommodate in the main memory of machine

© Springer Nature Singapore Pte Ltd. 2020
P. K. Singh et al. (Eds.): FTNCT 2019, CCIS 1206, pp. 521–531, 2020.
https://doi.org/10.1007/978-981-15-4451-4_41

therefore online processing is required for such data streams. The models of prediction for data streams learn incrementally by updating the learner for every recent batch of data. In dynamically changing environment apart from efficiency, the change in data distribution over time is also of major concern, this changing phenomenon is called concept drift, and it depletes the accuracy of current classifier. The real time concept drift refers to the change in the target variable while the distribution of input remains unchanged. Adaptive learning is the updating of predictive models during operation in order to react to concept drifts, which learn incrementally and also need to be processed in limited memory and computational facilities.

2   Concept Drift in Real-World Applications

2.1   Real vs Virtual Drifts

The change in data distribution over time is known to be virtual drift [9, 40] but the corresponding change in assignment of class is called real drift. The Fig. 1 depicts the virtual and real concept-drifting scenario.

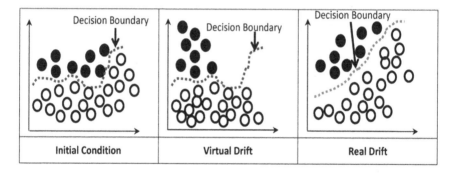

Fig. 1. Virtual and real type concept drifts

The real and virtual concept drifts can be explained with the help of data distribution probability. Let $P(X)$ denotes the data distribution of X and $P((c)/X)$ is the class conditional probability of class label c, and the prior probability of the class c is given by $P(c)$. Therefore, the virtual and real concept drifts can be formally defined as below.

(i)   The change in $P(c/X)$ is called real concept drift [20].
(ii) The unaffected value of $P(c/X)$ when $P(X)$ is changing is called virtual drift [20].

2.2   Real World Applications

In recent years, the abundance of smart digital devices likes smart phones, which are loaded with all kind of sensors as shown in Fig. 2. Additionally, availability of high speed internet and digital data stream sources in the world data are increasing exponentially day-by-day. Moreover, the requirement of efficient and effective tools for concept drifting data stream is also very crucial for online decision making in to cater the adverse effects post facto offline analysis methods.

In the era of information technology, the data can be gathered and shared at anytime and anywhere in the world. It is very challenging task to extract information from the big data streams [19]. It is applicable in many application areas like social networking credit applications, fraud detection, manufacturing, medicine, banking, health care, research, stock market, entertainment, telecommunications, retail, finance banks and credit applications, etc. The example of concept drift applications includes real time sentiment analysis [14, 18], event detection of real world [15, 17] election monitoring through online social network [16].

These applications are the sources of concept drifting data stream in which underlying data distribution changes with time and it depletes the accuracy of current classifier. The machines learning which is a field of computer science gives the ability to machines to learn without being programmed for it and therefore it can be used to make predictions based on the learning of algorithms. A huge amount of data gathered from the storage in computer systems is presented in the form of datasets on which these learning algorithms are implemented. The datasets may contain many useful and interesting hidden patterns which can be extracted as knowledge, therefore the knowledge discovery methods are of great importance in data mining.

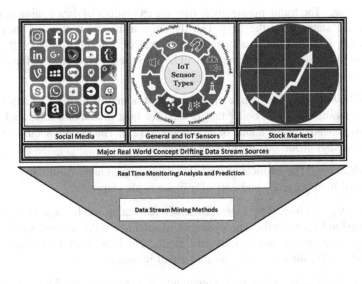

Fig. 2. Major digital data stream sources of real world

Furthermore, the applications can be broadly classified into four categories namely monitoring and control, decision making, personal assistance and AI & Robotics on the various factors such as decision speed, cost of mistakes and accuracy required.

Monitoring and Control. There is huge volume of data, that requires processing in real time. It includes computer security, telecommunications, finance, transportation and industrial monitoring.

Computer Security. It falls under the category of monitoring problems. The adversary actions against the detection of intrusion through internet can be a source of concept drift. Lane and Brodly [34] illustrates about the problem of concept drift in the intrusion detection. It can be dealt with general supervised learning or with help of ensemble techniques given by [36].

Telecommunications. The intrusion detection problem comes under the category of masquerade problem and to prevent from unauthorized access made to private data is the major goal in telecommunication. The action is required in order to cater the changing behavior of legitimate users that results in concept drift. The detection of fraud and to prevent it in the industry of telecommunications [29] is also a source of concept drift.

Finance. The use of learning techniques (supervised and unsupervised) are made [23] for the detection of fraud transactions in financial sector. The unnoticed frauds, mis-interpretations of legitimate transactions, imbalance of classes are the reasons for imprecise data labeling. The changing behavior of users is a source of concept drift and challenging to cater the needs.

Transportation. The traffic management uses the techniques of data mining in order to determine the states of traffic [25]. The dynamic nature of traffic and its patterns, driving ability and change in seasons are the sources of concept drift which the system should able to handle and furthermore it will be used for the prediction of travel time in public transport.

Industrial Monitoring. The source of concept drift is involvement of human factor in production monitoring. The boiler that is used for heat production have fuel feeding that in turn depends on the habits of an individual [21]. The system should be able to handle the change made due to different individuals.

Decision-Making. The applications involve decision making with limited amount of data required high accuracy and cost of mistake is also large.

Document Organization. The Latent Dirichlet Allocation model was equipped with time dimension [22] recently. The dynamics of scientific topic articles were analyzed and incorporated timestamp [11] into static model. The framework for content analysis is provided in [31] for the organization of email messages.

Economics. The change of concept comes into picture in the prediction phases of a business cycle [32] and in making forecasts in microeconomics [27] due to large number of influencing factors. The financial time series is non-stationary in making predictions as it is not feasible to corporate the influencing factors into prediction models. The prediction of project time employs data mining models that are equipped with concept drift handling algorithms.

Personal Assistance and Communication. The organization of flow of information is major component in these applications. It is grouped into two categories (i) individual assistance and (ii) customer profiling for business use. The cost of mistakes made are low.

Personal-Assistance. A rich technical presentation can be found in [26] for user modeling. The user modeling is representation of news, queries, blog entries with respect to user interests. The large part of personal assistance applications are related with textual contents. The news story classification [41] and categorization of document are source of concept drift due to the changing interest of users and it is called as reoccurring contexts [30]. The web personalization and dynamics is also related with drifting user interests. The spam filtering [39] is also highly relevant in this context.

Customer Profiling. The goal is to identify customers according to their interest and that can be changing with time, which in turn required by customer profiling algorithms to take care of this changing pattern into account. The customer segmentation deals with preferences for product [25] or for service usage. The social network analysis has also been performed in customer segmentation [35] and the changes over time can also be addressed via time weighting.

Biomedical Application. The adaptive nature of microorganisms [39] can be a subject of concept drift. The system needs adaptive mechanism to deal with changes that are caused by human demographics [33]. The drift in training and tests can be caused by non-uniform sampling in the incremental drug discovery experiments. The change in concept can also come into picture in biometric authentication [10] that can be caused due to change in physiological factors like growing beard.

AI and Robotics. The applications related with artificial intelligence are also having the problem of concept drift due to its dynamic nature. The learners need to be adaptive according to changing environment.

Robotics and Mobile Systems. The Ubiquitous Knowledge Discovery is used to deal with dynamic, complex and unstable environment. The navigation for DARPA was presented in [42]. A winning entry to classify roads into drivable and not drivable used online methods. In robotics, adaptive nature to changing environments was addressed in [37] for designing a player of robot soccer.

Intelligent Systems. The applications need to be adaptive like smart home systems [38] intelligent household appliances due to changing environment and user needs.

The applications of virtual reality also require concept drift to be taken into account. The adversary actions of the players in computer games [24] might be the source of drift. The skill and strategies differ across different users [28] in flight simulations.

3   Methods for Adaptation of Concept Drifting Data Streams

To understand the problem, Let $X_t \in \mathbb{R}^P$ represents an instance generated at time t by a data source $S_t \in S$, where $S = (S_1, S_2, \ldots, S_{t+1})$ is set of heterogeneous data sources i.e. $S_i \neq S_j$. Also, let that in the ordered pair $\{X_t, c_t\}$, the $c_t \in \mathbb{R}^1$ represents the class label of X_t. The learning under concept drifting data stream is depicted by Fig. 3.

Let $X^{\Delta} = (X_1, X_2, ..., X_t)$ represent a window of size t of already generated t historical instances and L_t is a classifier trained on X^{Δ}. Based on the above assumptions, the problem is to design a classifier L_t such that it can predict class label c_{t+1} of the newly arriving instance X_{t+1} accurately in spite of having heterogeneous data generation source S as given in Eq. (1)

$$L_t : X_{t+1} \to c_{t+1} \tag{1}$$

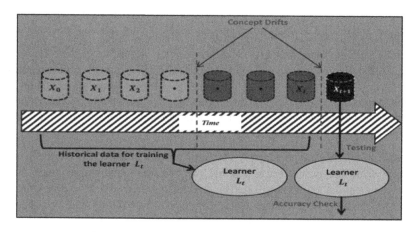

Fig. 3. Learning under concept drifting data stream

Learning of predictive model from evolving data with unknown dynamics depends upon memory and forgetting of data. The memory can be classified as short term and long-term memory that represents data and generalization of data respectively. The short-term memory deals with data management and forgetting mechanism. The adaptive learning algorithms work on the assumption that the data which is most recent is used for the prediction. It can be learnt from both single and multiple examples.

There is no need to store whole dataset in memory in case of single example as its name signifies there is only one example stored in memory. The model is updated based upon the errors. For an instance, the prediction which is made by current hypothesis is different from the true value of prediction then the model is updated based upon the estimation of loss. The Winnow [1] is an example of this category of algorithm. This algorithm is very effective in dealing with irrelevant features.

The online algorithms do not have forgetting mechanisms but they are adaptive to evolving concepts due to continuously updating in the model by current examples. The reason of adaptation is the dilution of old concepts upon the arrival of new data. The Winnow [1] and VFDT [4] react fairly to gradual changes but slow in adapting to sudden changes. The model is required to be set in terms of sensitivity while updating upon the arrival of new examples and stability. The algorithms that explicitly deal with concept drift includes Dynamic Weighted Majority [5, 6], STAGGER [7] and SVM [8].

The multiple example approach maintains a model that is predictive in nature and also having consistency with recent examples. The FLORA [40] falls under the category of incremental algorithm maintaining the order in First-in-First out form. It works by retaining some examples in the training window based upon them a model is built. The size of window needs to be maintained due to the limited memory constraint which is accomplished by discarding the old data known as forgetting mechanism.

The forgetting mechanism is discarding the outdated data which can be done in two ways: abrupt forgetting and gradual forgetting as shown in Fig. 4. The reactivity of system is higher in case of abrupt forgetting but prone to noise that demands for robustness against it.

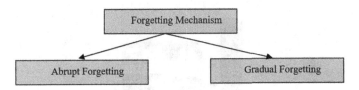

Fig. 4. Forgetting mechanism used in data streams

3.1 Abrupt Forgetting

The various types of windows-based techniques are available in the literature such as sequence based and timestamp based. The observations are present exactly inside or outside the window in abrupt forgetting. The instances which needs to be dropped are moved outside the window. The sequence-based techniques are based upon the fact that only fixed number of instances can be kept inside the window whereas in case of timestamp based the size of window is determined with the interval of duration. Moreover, the size of window is fixed but it can be dynamic as in case of sliding window that keeps the most recent examples. The size of window can be variable also that stores the observations based upon landmark timestamp.

3.2 Gradual Forgetting

The observations are not removed from the memory at once but they have been assigned some weights based upon their aging. The instances having more age is of less importance as compared to that of less aged. The age of examples can be calculated by using the concept of linear and exponential decay techniques. The exponential aging function is given by Eq. 2 to calculate the weight assigned to the instances as per their age. In Eq. 2, the example X appeared j time steps ago and λ controls that how fast the weights decrease.

$$w_\lambda(X) = \exp(-\lambda j) \tag{2}$$

4 Learning Modes

Data Stream is a sequence of instances with very fast speed of arrival rate, which is impossible to store in a memory. It is very large in size, due to which, most of the data mining approaches fail to process it accurately [12, 13].

Learning of these data streams refers to the techniques of predicting the evolving data which is based upon the learning of previous examples and it is accomplished by updating the model when new data points are available. Learning modes include Retraining, Incremental and Streaming as shown in Fig. 5.

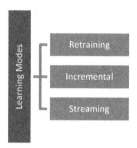

Fig. 5. Learning modes for concept drifting data streams

Retraining is rebuilding of new model using the buffered data stored in memory therefore discarding the current model. The new data points are merged with previous data to build a new model to make a new model learned based upon this data. This approach is utilised by [2, 3].

Incremental learning is one in which examples are trained one by one and updates the existing model by storing the sufficient statistics received after each and every instance. Therefore, the arrival of every new instance is updating the learning of classifier for the prediction of next instance as shown in Fig. 6. The online learning is one in which classifier is updated upon the occurrence of errors and it is used for the streaming of huge amount of data in a single pass which is required characteristic of a classifier. It made the learning of classifier in a limited memory which is constraint in mining of big data streams.

Streaming algorithms are based on online learning that are used to process high speed and continuous streams which are required to be processed in few passes and also able to work on limited memory. Hoeffding Tree is an incremental classifier for data streams proposed by [4]. In this algorithm, there is no need to store examples in memory after update of a tree. It induces a decision tree by modifying the tree incrementally from a data stream.

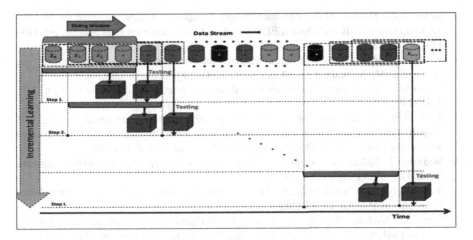

Fig. 6. Process of incremental learning in for concept drifting data stream

5   Conclusion

This paper explained about the various algorithms that are capable of handling concept drifting applications. The concept drifting data streams require more attention while processing as compared to static data. This paper also illustrates about various concept drifting applications and major digital data stream sources of real world. The problem of concept drift is very well known in various application domains such as social media, general and IoT sensors, stock markets that requires real time monitoring analysis and prediction. It also explains about the taxonomy of adaptive algorithms in context of memory requirements and learning methods used for dealing with concept drifting problems. Furthermore, this paper also discussed about the forgetting of data is required in adaptive algorithms in order to maintain the limited memory constraint and incremental learning approach that is best suited for concept drifting data stream mining. The algorithms need to learn continuously from data streams while maintaining its previous learned knowledge as the occurrence of concept drift depletes the accuracy of existing classifier.

References

1. Littlestone, N.: Learning quickly when irrelevant attributes abound: a new linear-threshold algorithm. Mach. Learn. **2**(4), 285–318 (1988)
2. Street, W.N., Kim, Y.S.: A streaming ensemble algorithm (SEA) for large-scale classification. In: Proceedings of the Seventh ACM SIGKDD International Conference on Knowledge Discovery and Data Mining, pp. 377–382. ACM (2001)
3. Klinkenberg, R., Joachims, T.: Detecting concept drift with support vector machines. In: ICML, pp. 487–494 (2000)
4. Domingos, P., Hulten, G.: Mining high-speed data streams. In: KDD, vol. 2, p. 4 (2000)

5. Kolter, J.Z., Maloof, M.A.: Dynamic weighted majority: a new ensemble method for tracking concept drift. In: Third IEEE International Conference on Data Mining, pp. 123–130. IEEE (2003)

6. Kolter, J.Z., Maloof, M.A.: Dynamic weighted majority: an ensemble method for drifting concepts. J. Mach. Learn. Res. **8**(Dec), 2755–2790 (2007)

7. Schlimmer, J.C., Granger, R.H.: Incremental learning from noisy data. Mach. Learn. **1**(3), 317–354 (1986)

8. Syed, N.A., Liu, H., Sung, K.K.: Handling concept drifts in incremental learning with support vector machines. In: Proceedings of the ACM SIGKDD International Conference on Knowledge Discovery and Data Mining (KDD-1999), pp. 317–321 (1999)

9. Widmer, G., Kubat, M.: Learning in the presence of concept drift and hidden contexts. Mach. Learn. **23**(1), 69–101 (1996)

10. Yampolskiy, R.V., Govindaraju, V.: Direct and indirect human computer interaction based biometrics. JCP **2**(10), 76–88 (2007)

11. Yang, Y., Xindong, W., Zhu, X.: Mining in anticipation for concept change: proactive-reactive prediction in data streams. Data Min. Knowl. Discov. **13**(3), 261–289 (2006)

12. Mittal, V., Kashyap, I.: Online methods of learning in occurrence of concept drift. Int. J. Comput. Appl. **117**(13), 18–22 (2015)

13. Mittal, V., Kashyap, I.: Empirical study of impact of various concept drifts in data stream mining methods. Int. J. Intell. Syst. Appl. **8**(12), 65–72 (2016)

14. Srivastava, R., Bhatia, M.P.S.: Offline vs. online sentiment analysis: issues with sentiment analysis of online micro-texts. Int. J. Inf. Retr. Res. (IJIRR) **7**(4), 1–18 (2017)

15. Srivastava, R., Bhatia, M.P.S.: Real-time unspecified major sub-events detection in the twitter data stream that cause the change in the sentiment score of the targeted event. Int. J. Inf. Technol. Web Eng. (IJITWE) **12**(4), 1–21 (2017)

16. Srivastava, R., Kumar, H., Bhatia, M.S., Jain, S.: Analyzing Delhi assembly election 2015 using textual content of social network. In: Proceedings of the Sixth International Conference on Computer and Communication Technology 2015, pp. 78–85. ACM (2015)

17. Srivastava, R., Bhatia, M.P.S., Tayal, V., Verma, J.K.: Framework for real-world event detection through online social networking sites. In: Jain, L.C., Balas, V.E., Johri, P. (eds.) Data and Communication Networks. AISC, vol. 847, pp. 195–203. Springer, Singapore (2019). https://doi.org/10.1007/978-981-13-2254-9_17

18. Srivastava, R., Bhatia, M.P.S.: Challenges with sentiment analysis of on-line micro-texts. Int. J. Intell. Syst. Appl. **9**(7), 31 (2017)

19. Tayal, V., Srivastava, R.: Challenges in mining big data streams. In: Jain, L.C., Balas, V.E., Johri, P. (eds.) Data and Communication Networks. AISC, vol. 847, pp. 173–183. Springer, Singapore (2019). https://doi.org/10.1007/978-981-13-2254-9_15

20. Žliobaitė, I.: Learning under concept drift: an overview. arXiv preprint arXiv:1010.4784 (2010)

21. Bakker, J., Pechenizkiy, M., Žliobaitė, I., Ivannikov, A., Kärkkäinen, T.: Handling outliers and concept drift in online mass flow prediction in CFB boilers. In: Proceedings of the Third International Workshop on Knowledge Discovery from Sensor Data, pp. 13–22. ACM (2009)

22. Blei, D.M., Lafferty, J.D.: Dynamic topic models. In: Proceedings of the 23rd International Conference on Machine Learning, pp. 113–120. ACM (2006)

23. Bolton, R.J., Hand, D.J.: Statistical fraud detection: a review. Stat. Sci. **17**, 235–249 (2002)

24. Charles, D., et al.: Player-centred game design: player modelling and adaptive digital games. In: Proceedings of the Digital Games Research Conference, vol. 285, p. 00100 (2005)

25. Crespo, F., Weber, R.: A methodology for dynamic data mining based on fuzzy clustering. Fuzzy Sets Syst. **150**(2), 267–284 (2005)

26. Gauch, S., Speretta, M., Chandramouli, A., Micarelli, A.: User profiles for personalized information access. In: Brusilovsky, P., Kobsa, A., Nejdl, W. (eds.) The Adaptive Web. LNCS, vol. 4321, pp. 54–89. Springer, Heidelberg (2007). https://doi.org/10.1007/978-3-540-72079-9_2

27. Giacomini, R., Rossi, B.: Detecting and predicting forecast breakdowns. Rev. Econ. Stud. **76**(2), 669–705 (2009)

28. Harries, M.B., Sammut, C., Horn, K.: Extracting hidden context. Mach. Learn. **32**(2), 101–126 (1998)

29. Hilas, C.S.: Designing an expert system for fraud detection in private telecommunications networks. Expert Syst. Appl. **36**(9), 11559–11569 (2009)

30. Katakis, I., Tsoumakas, G., Vlahavas, I.P.: An ensemble of classifiers for coping with recurring contexts in data streams. In: ECAI, pp. 763–764 (2008)

31. Kleinberg, J.: Bursty and hierarchical structure in streams. Data Min. Knowl. Discov. **7**(4), 373–397 (2003)

32. Klinkenberg, R.: Meta-learning, model selection, and example selection in machine learning domains with concept drift. In: LWA, vol. 2005, pp. 164–171 (2005)

33. Kukar, M.: Drifting concepts as hidden factors in clinical studies. In: Dojat, M., Keravnou, E.T., Barahona, P. (eds.) AIME 2003. LNCS (LNAI), vol. 2780, pp. 355–364. Springer, Heidelberg (2003). https://doi.org/10.1007/978-3-540-39907-0_49

34. Lane, T., Brodley, C.E.: Temporal sequence learning and data reduction for anomaly detection. ACM Trans. Inf. Syst. Secur. (TISSEC) **2**(3), 295–331 (1999)

35. Lathia, N., Hailes, S., Capra, L.: kNN CF: a temporal social network. In: Proceedings of the 2008 ACM Conference on Recommender Systems, pp. 227–234. ACM (2008)

36. Masud, M.M., Gao, J., Khan, L., Han, J., Thuraisingham, B.: A multi-partition multi-chunk ensemble technique to classify concept-drifting data streams. In: Theeramunkong, T., Kijsirikul, B., Cercone, N., Ho, T.-B. (eds.) PAKDD 2009. LNCS (LNAI), vol. 5476, pp. 363–375. Springer, Heidelberg (2009). https://doi.org/10.1007/978-3-642-01307-2_34

37. Procopio, M.J., Mulligan, J., Grudic, G.: Learning terrain segmentation with classifier ensembles for autonomous robot navigation in unstructured environments. J. Field Robot. **26**(2), 145–175 (2009)

38. Rashidi, P., Cook, D.J.: Keeping the resident in the loop: adapting the smart home to the user. IEEE Trans. Syst. Man Cybern. Part A **39**(5), 949–959 (2009)

39. Song, X., Jermaine, C., Ranka, S., Gums, J.: A bayesian mixture model with linear regression mixing proportions. In: Proceedings of the 14th ACM SIGKDD International Conference on Knowledge Discovery and Data Mining, pp. 659–667. ACM (2008)

40. Widmer, G., Kubat, M.: Effective learning in dynamic environments by explicit context tracking. In: Brazdil, P.B. (ed.) ECML 1993. LNCS, vol. 667, pp. 227–243. Springer, Heidelberg (1993). https://doi.org/10.1007/3-540-56602-3_139

41. Widyantoro, D.H., Yen, J.: Relevant data expansion for learning concept drift from sparsely labeled data. IEEE Trans. Knowl. Data Eng. **17**(3), 401–412 (2005)

42. Thrun, S.: Winning the DARPA grand challenge. In: Fürnkranz, J., Scheffer, T., Spiliopoulou, M. (eds.) ECML 2006. LNCS (LNAI), vol. 4212, p. 4. Springer, Heidelberg (2006). https://doi.org/10.1007/11871842_4

Copy-Move Image Forgery Detection Using DCT and ORB Feature Set

Vikas Mehta[1], Ankit Kumar Jaiswal[2]([✉]), and Rajeev Srivastava[2]

[1] Institute of Technology, Nirma University, Ahmedabad, India
vikasmehta50@gmail.com
[2] Computing and Vision Lab, Department of Computer Science and
Engineering, Indian Institute of Technology (BHU) Varanasi, Varanasi, India
{ankitkrjaiswal.rs.cse17,rajeev.cse}@iitbhu.ac.in

Abstract. The unprecedented use of digital images and videos for communication, the ease of access and use of graphic editing applications have consequently led to the increased importance of detecting copy-move forgery. The proposed copy-move forgery detection (CMFD) technique relies on DCT and ORB feature extraction and distance-based clustering approach. Extracted DCT features are matched based on Euclidean distance. Extracted key-points using ORB are matched using k-NN procedure based on Hamming distances. To improve accuracy, false matches are removed with the help of a distance-based clustering technique. The proposed technique is applied for testing on CoMo-FoD small dataset. Results on experimentation showcase that the technique is efficient in detecting copy-move forged regions and also robust towards brightness and contrast change, noise addition, geometric transformations like scaling and rotation and several forgeries. The proposed technique is compared with two state-of-the art techniques.

Keywords: Copy-move image forgery · Image forgery detection · DCT · ORB

1 Introduction

There are two primary methods in forgery detection in images. The active method includes images in conjunction with embedded data like digital watermarks or digital signatures. Passive methods are void of such extraneous data. They are based on an analysis of the given image alone and hence provide a more pragmatic approach. There are mainly two types of forgery in image forensics. Image splicing is an act of cropping regions of an image and replacing a different region with that region into the same or a different image to create a new forged picture [10]. A copy move image forgery is a case where a particular part of the same image is copied and applied on another, intentionally, to hide information depicted by that image [8]. It is a fairly common procedure and can be done using basic image editing tools.

The ease of access to image processing software like Adobe's Photoshop or Coral Draw has made digital image forgery a commonplace. Organizations have been using digital image forgeries discussed above to gain political favors. Even governments have been using forged images to claim false achievements in order to gain more votes. The

© Springer Nature Singapore Pte Ltd. 2020
P. K. Singh et al. (Eds.): FTNCT 2019, CCIS 1206, pp. 532–544, 2020.
https://doi.org/10.1007/978-981-15-4451-4_42

accessibility and availability to sophisticated tools to digitally forge images and even video clips increase public skepticism towards the credibility and value of the videos and images. It poses even a greater threat when images are used as forensic evidence in courtrooms or used to do scientific fraud. Thus, tackling this problem of image forgery is necessary to curb such practices (Fig. 1).

Fig. 1. (a) A case depicting a simple copy and paste forgery attack on an image. The frame in the image is copied and applied on a part of that image itself. (b) An example of image splicing attack. A camera lens from the second image is copied and applied onto the desk in the first image

During copy-move forgery, there are several post-processing techniques that act as hurdles towards its detection. Several techniques like contrast adjustment, brightness change, blurring, noise addition, jpeg and other compression and transformation techniques thwart the efficient process of CMFD. Block matching techniques based on discrete cosine transform can handle such post-processing techniques but is not invariant to scaling, rotation and other major geometric transformation [24]. Most CMFD techniques fail to detect multiple image forgeries which have undergone such transformations on a single image.

Geometric transformations mentioned above can be tackled using key-point based matching techniques. Techniques like SIFT which are invariant to rotation and scaling are based on their descriptors and key-points.

In this paper, an approach is presented to detect and locate copy-move forged regions in an altered image. It utilizes a combination of both block-based along with a traditional key-point based method. Invariance to contrast changes, brightness changes, Gaussian noise and some degree of blurring is provided by block-based methods. On the contrary, key-point based methods have an invariance towards geometric altercations like rotation changes and scale changes on image segments. Employing a combination of discrete cosine transform, a block-based method, and ORB [6], a key-point based method, we are able to tackle such aforementioned attacks. Compared to other key-point based methods is computationally faster, equivalently robust. Thus, it is more pragmatically applicable. The technique is also robust towards multiple forgeries in a single image.

The paper is further organized as: The paper is delineated into several sections. The first section presented an overview of the technique, the background surrounding it and the motivation towards the subject and some challenges that need to be tackled. The second section summarizes the important research work that was referred to for understanding and implementing a CMFD technique and their contributions towards the subject. The third section presents the proposed method with various subsections describing the flow of the technique. The fourth section contains information regarding the test set and the system along with the analysis of the results. The report concludes with further challenges.

2 Literature Review

Active image forgery detection technique relies on digital watermarking and signatures. In [1] a survey of different techniques for digital watermarking are provided. [11] provides a recent contribution in the field of active image forgery detection using digital image watermarking techniques and alpha mattes. A detailed review of CMFD techniques that are currently used to detect passive image is as follows.

Fridrich et al. [8] initiated research on CMFD. Their paper proposed a discrete cosine transform (DCT) coefficients-based block matching method to detect simple copy paste forgeries in digital images. Popescu [15] presented an identical approach, which utilized principal component analysis (PCA) and none of the cosine transforms. It used some of the DCT features which increased efficiency. These methods, however, couldn't segregate and detect copy-move forgeries with a degree of rotation changes. In [12], an enhanced DCT-based method was introduced. It increased DCT efficiency by truncation of feature vectors. In [13], local binary patterns (LBP) which had an invariance towards rotation are used along with circular block based feature extraction. The technique is resilient towards various non-geometric altercations and some degree of rotation changes, but it couldn't detect areas which were rotated to extreme angles. In [7] a block based technique to find out the forged regions is employed with the help of Polar Complex Exponential Transform (PCET). In [2] a fusion of LBP and DCT is used to detect copy move image forgeries. In [9] a SIFT-based CMFD technique is used. It is invariant to scale and rotation but doesn't work efficiently in areas of forged smooth regions where key-points can't be extracted using SIFT. In [18] Zernike moments are used to detect forged regions and they are invariant to rotation and usual post-processing operations like blurring, distortion, Gaussian noise and compression. In [22] an end-to-end deep neural architecture based CMFD technique called BusterNet is introduced. It is shown that it is robust against various known attacks and outperforms previously known methods of CMFD. In [23] KAZE and SIFT keypoints were combined to provide a larger pool of keypoints for effective matching and detection of forged regions within an image.

Zhu et al. in [24] proposed a scaled ORB based CMFD where features and keypoints were extracted at every Gaussian scale and then mapped back to the original image. These features were matched using hamming distances to detect geometrically transformed copied regions. In [20] for performing forgery detection a color and scale invariant feature detection technique along with a fast quaternion radial harmonic Fourier moment technique and gradient entropy is used. Delaunay triangles constructed from the keypoints are matched with the help of a hashing technique and local features. In [3, 5, 22] deep learning based architectures to detect such image forgeries have been presented. Wenchang et al. in [21] proposes a CMFD method involving particle swarm optimization techniques for custom image parameters in SIFT framework to detect forged images.

3 Proposed Work

The proposed work is segmented into the four following sub-sections and the overall process is depicted in the framework given in Fig. 2.

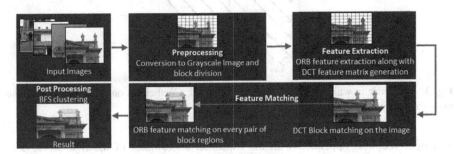

Fig. 2. The framework image for CMFD.

3.1 Preprocessing

The image on which CMFD is required to be done is converted to a grayscale image if it already isn't. Further processes are done on this grayscale image since color doesn't play a significant role in the process. To apply a discrete cosine transform to the image it is required that it be divided into overlapping blocks. 8 × 8 pixel sized blocks were utilized to meet this purpose. Key-points are distributed in several regions within the image. 50 × 50 pixel sized non-overlapping blocks were used to divide the image into regions which housed the key-points in that particular region. Since, discrete cosine transform is applied to all the overlapping blocks in the image, if the size of the image is extremely large, it would take a large amount of time to convert all the blocks to their transform vector representations.

3.2 Feature Extraction

DCT Feature

The blocks are square in dimension. Let the region size be b = 8, if the dimensions of the image are p × q pixels then the number of blocks for DCT will be $(p - b + 1)$ $(q - b + 1)$. Here every block will contain a feature vector the size of feature vector space will then be $(p - b + 1) \times (q - b + 1) \times b^2$ for the image. These features are extracted by sliding over a b × b sized block over the entire image. The feature space is now a 3-dimensional matrix. DCT is now applied to each of the two-dimensional blocks. The feature vector is extracted as shown in Fig. 3.

Features are extracted in this fashion since the lower frequency terms in a DCT are rather more important in determining the true form of an image than the higher frequency terms which can even be avoided. Thus, we take only the coefficients until the diagonal of the square block. (For example, in this case of an 8 × 8 block first 36 features are only extracted). This is done to decrease further computational costs. The

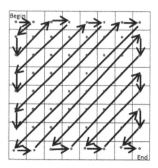

Fig. 3. The order in which a block's features extracted. Coefficients on the diagonal have the same frequency

36-length vector is appended with the Cartesian coordinates of the first block. The vector's length is now 38. Now, we have a two-dimensional feature space. This dimensional feature space is now lexicographically sorted.

ORB Feature

The key-points and their respective descriptors are obtained using Oriented FAST and Rotated BRIEF respectively [6]. The key-points are drawn out using FAST (Features from Accelerated Segment Test) algorithm which is as follows [16].

Oriented FAST

The FAST method focuses on every pixel and a corresponding 16 length feature vector obtained by a radius of 3 from the point of the pixel. This is the Bresenham circle as depicted in Fig. 4. The features are then divided into three different classes based on a fixed threshold (for example 20% of the intensity of the pixel under consideration).

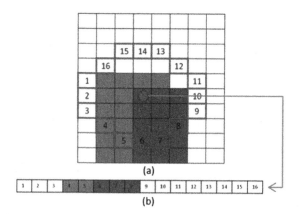

Fig. 4. (a) The red dot depicts the pixel under consideration. The surrounding pixels values that correspond to its feature are depicted with a red border. (b) The extracted feature vector of length 16 (Color figure online)

The 16 values are assigned the three different states using the following equation:

$$S_{pc} := \begin{cases} 1, I_{pc} \leq I_{px} - T_h \\ 2, I_{px} - T_h < I_{pc} < I_{px} + T_h \\ 3, I_{px} + T_h \leq I_{pc} \end{cases} \tag{1}$$

Where S_{pc} is the state of pixel and I_{px} is the intensity of the pixel which is described by the feature vector. I_{pc} is the intensity value of the pixel under consideration. The pixel to be classified as a key-point is determined by a variable Ppx which is true if the point is to be considered as a key-point and false otherwise. Each subset is fed to an ID3 algorithm which classifies the key-point. ID3 algorithm works on entropy minimization. This is applied recursively to all three subsets. The entropy for a set P is given as:

$$H(P) := (c + \bar{c}) \, log_2(c + \bar{c}) - c log_2 c - \bar{c} log_2 \bar{c} \tag{2}$$

Here $H(P)$ is the entropy. c denotes the quantity of components in the positive class and $\bar{c}$ quantifies the others. (The number of corners accounts in the positive class and the number of non-corners are accounted in the other class). To produce multi-scale features, a scale pyramid of the image is used and FAST features which are filtered by the Harris corner filter at each level of the pyramid. A pyramid of scales is utilized along with FAST features refined by Harris corner detection at every level of the pyramid to extract multiple scaled features.

To find the inclination of the FAST key-points [17] the intensity centroid as a measure is used. It is expected that a point's intensity value is not aligned at that point, and this vector can be utilized to find the inclination. The moment of order (r + s) of a key-point P is given below. The neighborhood NB(x, y) is located at the first quadrant with P as origin in a Cartesian coordinate system. The resulting point of interest is called an oFAST point (oriented FAST point).

$$IM_{r,s} = \sum_{x,y} x^r y^s I(x, y) \tag{3}$$

The Centroid of the neighborhood is given by:

$$C = \left(\frac{IM_{10}}{IM_{00}}, \frac{IM_{01}}{IM_{00}} \right) \tag{4}$$

The orientation θ of the keypoint 'P' is the angle formed by $\overrightarrow{OC}$ which is determined by the equation given below where atan2 signifies a variant of arctan that also denotes the quadrant.

$$\theta = atan2(IM_{01}, IM_{10}) \tag{5}$$

rBRIEF Descriptors

These descriptors are a string of binary values that describe a patch of smooth image (*Sim*) from a set of binary intensity tests [4]. These binary tests are described as:

$$T(Sim; x_1, x_2) := \begin{cases} 1, Sim(x_1) < Sim(x_2) \\ 0, Sim(x_1) \geq Sim(x_2) \end{cases} \tag{6}$$

Here Sim(x) represents the intensity of Sim at a point x.
A feature consists of many binary tests. The feature vector is defined as follows:

$$FV_n(Sim) := \sum\nolimits_{i=1}^{n} 2^{i-1} T(Sim; x_{1i}, x_{2i}) \tag{7}$$

A vector of length 256 is chosen and a Gaussian distribution of tests around the centre of the patch was used. To make this invariant to same plane rotation steered BRIEF [4] features are used. An efficient way perform steering of BRIEF is through the orientation of oFAST point x_i. Let S be a two-dimensional matrix given by S and rotation matrix for particular orientation θ_i is given by R_θ and S_θ by $R_\theta.P$:

$$\sum = \begin{pmatrix} x_{11}, \ldots x_{1n} \\ x_{21}, \ldots x_{2n} \end{pmatrix} R_{\theta_i} = \begin{bmatrix} \cos\theta_i & -\sin\theta_i \\ \sin\theta_i & \cos\theta_i \end{bmatrix}$$

$$S_\theta := R_{\theta_i}.S \tag{8}$$

The ORB descriptors of oFAST are given by:

$$ORB(i) = FV_n(Sim)|(x_{1i}, x_{2i}) \in S_\theta \tag{9}$$

ORB (*i*) extraction is implemented on every scale. Each of these features and key-points is assigned in their particular regions based on their positions in the image. Extremely blurred regions and perfectly geometrical shapes like a perfect circle without any detail form a roadblock for feature extraction as they generally do not contain distinctively contrasting areas for identification and extraction of interesting keypoints.

3.3   Feature Matching

Every adjacent pair of rows in the lexicographically sorted feature space is compared. Rows are viewed as indistinguishable if the Euclidean separation between the two is not beyond a defined threshold (D_T). A shift vector is calculated for similar rows and the count of the particular shift vector is incremented. Finally, all the shift vector counts are checked and the ones that exceed a particular count threshold (C_T), the blocks that constitute it are considered as matched blocks.

For matching features of ORB key-points a brute force k-Nearest Neighbors (k-NN) method is used. For every pair of regions in the image as described in Sect. 3.1 that houses the extracted key-points and their descriptors, the above method is applied.

The k-NN matcher returns the best k matches based on Hamming distance between the descriptors. We use hamming distance since we have binary descriptors for the key-points. Here we take k = 2 and apply Lowe's ratio test [14] to gain accurate matches between key-points. The resulting matches are appended to a matched list.

3.4 Post Processing

To reduce false matches and refine the resulting image a breadth-first search-based clustering technique is implemented. The original and the key-point that is matched are clustered separately for every key-point that is included in matches. The clusters are created based on a distance parameter, D_P and a grouping size parameter G_P. When breadth-first search is applied to cluster key-points into a single cluster, key-points that are at a distance less than D_P are only considered to be in that cluster. This process is continued until all the keypoints have been clustered. Now, only those clusters whose membership count exceeds G_P are considered in the final clusters that make up the matches. If both the matched key-points are a part of the final clusters then these matches are included in the resulting final matches.

Finally, the block-based matches along with key-point matches are mapped onto the image for depicting the forged regions.

4 Experiment and Result Analysis

The experiment is performed on Microsoft Windows 10 Home with system type x64-based PC and Intel(R) Core™ i5-8300H CPU of clock speed 2.30 GHz with 4 Core(s) Processor. The system has installed physical memory 8 GB (RAM). The programming language is used for implementation purpose is Python 3.6.7 with Matlab R2017a tool where additional libraries are OpenCV, Matplotlib, Numpy and Matlab Engine API.

The process is tested on the CoMoFoD dataset [19] in the small image category. The image size is 512 × 512. Various transformations like translation, rotation, scaling, and distortion have been applied to the images to obtain the forged images. Every image includes a bunch of an image, a mask with color, a black and white mask for the forged image. Every image set also consists of a blurred image set, a set of images with added noise, a set of images with changed brightness, a color reduced image set and a contrast adjusted image set.

The evaluation metrics used in this paper for performance evaluation include precision (P) given by:

$$P = \frac{TP}{TP + FP} \tag{10}$$

TP includes all those images that are truly forged, and the algorithm detects that it is forged, FP refers to a all those images which are not forged but the algorithm detects them as being forged. Other metrics include recall (R) and accuracy (A) and given by:

$$R = \frac{TP}{TP + FN} \tag{11}$$

$$A = \frac{TP + TN}{TP + FP + FN + TN} \tag{12}$$

TN includes all those images that are not forged, and the algorithm detects that it is original, FN refers to all those images which are truly forged but the algorithm detects them as not forged.

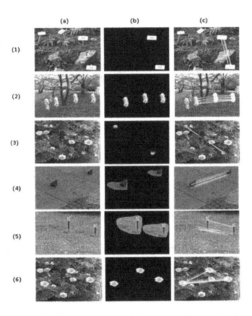

Fig. 5. Image a1 consists of plain copy-move forgery, a2 consists of multiple copy-move forgery attack, a3 consists of copy-rotate-copy-move forgery attack, a6 consists of a combination of all the aforementioned attacks. Images b1 to b6 depict the respective ground truths for figures a1 to a6. These images are taken from the dataset itself. Images c1 to c6 depict the respective delineation of forged regions resulting from the proposed algorithm

The presented technique is assessed on sets of 200 PNG images from the CoMo-FoD small dataset [19]. Images 001_F to 40_F consist of plain copy-move forgery attack, images 041_F to 080_F consist of copy-rotate-move forgery attack, images 081_F to 120_F consists of scaled copy-move forgery attack, images 121_F to 160_F consist of distorted copy-move forgery attack while images from 161_F to 200_F consist of images with a combination of aforementioned attacks. Hence, each group consists of 40 images. For DCT feature matching $D_T = 0.001$ and $C_T = 200$. For ORB the, maximum number of keypoints is set at 30000, the distance parameter D_P is set to 18 while the grouping parameter G_P is set to 6.

Table 1. Performance evaluation on simple copy-move forgery attack

Type of attack	Accuracy	Precision	Recall	F1-score
Translation	92.5	88.63	97.50	92.85
Rotation	90.00	88.09	92.50	90.24
Scaling	82.50	80.95	85.00	82.92
Distortion	85.00	85.00	85.00	85.00
Combination	77.50	78.90	75.00	76.90

The performance metrics on these groups are depicted in Table 1. The method is evaluated along with BusterNet [22] and Zernike [18]. The result of comparison on the base set with no post-processing operations performed on 200 images (001_F to 200_F) is given in Table 2. The robustness towards scaling rotation distortion and multiple copy move forgeries are depicted in Fig. 5.

Table 2. Performance comparison. #Passed represents the quantity of forged images which were successfully detected from a set of 200 forged images

Technique	#Passed	Precision	Recall	F1
Zernike [18]	90	96.27	69.84	79.93
BusterNet [22]	117	83.52	78.75	63.13
Proposed	174	84.31	87	85.58

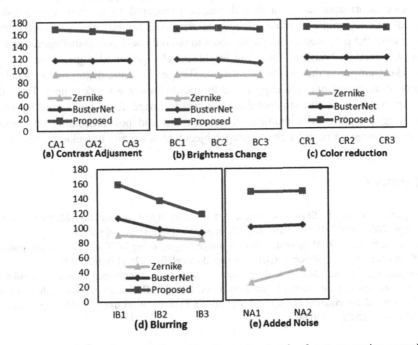

Fig. 6. (a) to (e) depicts the comparison charts for various levels of post-processing operations and the respective number of images passed by the techniques

From performance curves depicted in Fig. 6(a) to (e) it can be concluded that the method outperforms other techniques by a large margin in detecting copy move forged images even when post-processing operations like Brightness change, Color reduction, Contrast Adjustment and added noise. The proposed method is susceptible to blurring as in a blurred image large number of key-points cannot be found and hence the dipping curve. Zernike [18] fails to detect forged images in images with high noise while the proposed technique is effective in detecting forged regions in different types of noisy images. Even though Zernike [18] is algebraically invariant to geometric transformations, quantization and interpolation errors plague the technique hence, it is still underperforms under images forged by copied regions with different scaling and radical rotational angles. BusterNet [22] is limited by training over synthetic data and hence fails to correctly determine copied regions which undergo professional editing that is usually imperceptible to the human eye. From the curves, it can be seen that the proposed technique is quite robust to different post-processing operations applied along with different geometric transformations and is thus effectively better at determining forged images.

5   Conclusion

This paper presented a copy-move image forgery detection method which is based on ORB and DCT features along with a distance-based clustering algorithm and k-NN matching based on Hamming distance. It is able to detect copy-move regions without any prior information about a forged image. Compared to previously established methods our technique is more effective at detecting forged images. Experimental results show the proposed technique is robust to not only post-processing operation like contrast reduction, blurring, noise and brightness change but also geometric altercations like changes in the degree of rotation, changes in scale, distortion, an amalgamation of them and multiple copy move forged regions in a single image. Thus, the paper provides a significant contribution towards image forensics. Detecting copy move forged regions with multiple transformations and post-processing on smooth regions of an image is still a challenging subject which we aim to tackle in the future.

References

1. Agarwal, N., et al.: Survey of robust and imperceptible watermarking. Multimed. Tools Appl. **78**(7), 8603–8633 (2019). https://doi.org/10.1007/s11042-018-7128-5
2. Alahmadi, A., et al.: Passive detection of image forgery using DCT and local binary pattern. Signal Image Video Process. (2017). https://doi.org/10.1007/s11760-016-0899-0
3. Bayar, B., Stamm, M.C.: A deep learning approach to universal image manipulation detection using a new convolutional layer. In: IH and MMSec 2016 - Proceedings of the 2016 ACM Information Hiding and Multimedia Security Workshop (2016). https://doi.org/10.1145/2909827.2930786

4. Calonder, M., Lepetit, V., Strecha, C., Fua, P.: BRIEF: binary robust independent elementary features. In: Daniilidis, K., Maragos, P., Paragios, N. (eds.) ECCV 2010. LNCS, vol. 6314, pp. 778–792. Springer, Heidelberg (2010). https://doi.org/10.1007/978-3-642-15561-1_56

5. Cozzolino, D., et al.: Recasting residual-based local descriptors as convolutional neural networks: an application to image forgery detection. In: IH and MMSec 2017 - Proceedings of the 2017 ACM Workshop on Information Hiding and Multimedia Security (2017). https://doi.org/10.1145/3082031.3083247

6. El-Hallak, M., Lovell, D.: ORB an efficient. Arthritis Rheum. 65(10), 2736 (2013). https://doi.org/10.1002/art.38045

7. Emam, M., et al.: PCET based copy-move forgery detection in images under geometric transforms. Multimed. Tools Appl. (2016). https://doi.org/10.1007/s11042-015-2872-2

8. Fridrich, J., et al.: Detection of copy-move forgery in digital images. In: Digital Forensic Research Workshop (2003). https://doi.org/10.1109/PACIIA.2008.240

9. Hailing, H., et al.: Detection of copy-move forgery in digital images using sift algorithm. In: Proceedings - 2008 Pacific-Asia Workshop on Computational Intelligence and Industrial Application, PACIIA 2008 (2008). https://doi.org/10.1109/PACIIA.2008.240

10. Hakimi, F., et al.: Image splicing forgery detection using local binary pattern and discrete wavelet transform. In: 2015 2nd International Conference on Knowledge-Based Engineering and Innovation, KBEI 2015, pp. 1074–1077 (2016). https://doi.org/10.1109/KBEI.2015.7436195

11. Hu, W.C., et al.: Effective image forgery detection of tampered foreground or background image based on image watermarking and alpha mattes. Multimed. Tools Appl. (2016). https://doi.org/10.1007/s11042-015-2449-0

12. Huang, Y., et al.: Improved DCT-based detection of copy-move forgery in images. Forensic Sci. Int. 206(1–3), 178–184 (2011). https://doi.org/10.1016/j.forsciint.2010.08.001

13. Li, L. et al.: [2013 Li JIHMSP]20 + An efficient scheme for detecting copy-move forged images by local binary patterns. J. Inf. Hiding Multimed. Signal Process. (2013)

14. Lowe, D.G.: Distinctive image features from scale-invariant keypoints. Int. J. Comput. Vis. (2004). https://doi.org/10.1023/B:VISI.0000029664.99615.94

15. Popescu, A.C., Farid, H.: Exposing digital forgeries by detecting duplicated image regions. IEEE Trans. Signal Process. (2004). https://doi.org/10.1109/TSP.2004.839932

16. Rosten, E., Porter, R., Drummond, T.: Faster and better: A machine learning approach to corner detection. IEEE Trans. Pattern Anal. Mach. Intell. 32(1), 105–119 (2010). https://doi.org/10.1109/TPAMI.2008.275

17. Rosten, E., Drummond, T.: Machine learning for high-speed corner detection. In: Leonardis, A., Bischof, H., Pinz, A. (eds.) ECCV 2006. LNCS, vol. 3951, pp. 430–443. Springer, Heidelberg (2006). https://doi.org/10.1007/11744023_34

18. Ryu, S.J., et al.: Detection of copy-rotate-move forgery using Zernike moments. In: Lecture Notes in Computer Science (including subseries Lecture Notes in Artificial Intelligence and Lecture Notes in Bioinformatics) (2010). https://doi.org/10.1007/978-3-642-16435-4_5

19. Tralic, D., et al.: CoMoFoD - new database for copy-move forgery detection. In: 55th International Symposium ELMAR (2013)

20. Wang, X.Y., et al.: Copy-move forgery detection based on compact color content descriptor and Delaunay triangle matching. Multimed. Tools Appl. 78(2), 2311–2344 (2019). https://doi.org/10.1007/s11042-018-6354-1

21. Wenchang, S., et al.: Improving image copy-move forgery detection with particle swarm optimization techniques. China Commun. (2016). https://doi.org/10.1109/CC.2016.7405711

22. Wu, Y., Abd-Almageed, W., Natarajan, P.: BusterNet: detecting copy-move image forgery with source/target localization. In: Ferrari, V., Hebert, M., Sminchisescu, C., Weiss, Y. (eds.) ECCV 2018. LNCS, vol. 11210, pp. 170–186. Springer, Cham (2018). https://doi.org/10. 1007/978-3-030-01231-1_11

23. Yang, F., et al.: Copy-move forgery detection based on hybrid features. Eng. Appl. Artif. Intell. (2017). https://doi.org/10.1016/j.engappai.2016.12.022

24. Zhu, Y., et al.: Copy-move forgery detection based on scaled ORB. Multimed. Tools Appl. (2016). https://doi.org/10.1007/s11042-014-2431-2

A Study of E-Healthcare System for Pregnant Women

Rydhm Beri[1(✉)], Mithilesh Kr. Dubey[1], Anita Gehlot[2],
and Rajesh Singh[2]

[1] School of Computer Applications, Lovely Professional University,
Phagwara, India
rydhmberi@gmail.com, mithilesh.21436@lpu.co.in
[2] School of Electronics and Communication Engineering,
Lovely Professional University, Phagwara, India
eranita5@gmail.com, srajsssece@gmail.com

Abstract. Pregnancy is a phase in women's life where the women give birth to the new life, and that new life gives birth to the mother. In this paper, a model is of the E-health care system for pregnant women is proposed, which will monitor health variations of pregnant women in the real-time environment. Several technologies from the past seven years have been reviewed, and it is evaluated that the features include in the proposed study is not available in the existing studies. According to the survey taken during the study, 88% of doctors reported that there is a need for a pregnancy E-health care system that monitors every activity of the women. The proposed model concerned with measurement of different parameters like a number of steps, blood pressure, heartbeat, the posture of sleeping, the position of baby etc. and after measuring these parameters, the data will be collected at the fog devices so that the data in huge amount will be filtered at fog devices and transferred at cloud servers. The result of this model will be the detailed data of the health variations of pregnant women that can help a doctor to deeper analyze the women in case of high-risk pregnancies.

Keywords: Issues during pregnancy · Pregnancy E-Healthcare system · Smart healthcare

1 Introduction

Pregnancy is the phase of nine months, divided into three trimesters, comes with lots of excitement to meet the little person. With lots of excitement, pregnancy comes with the hormonal changes in the woman's body that mainly impacts on the living manner of the women. In pregnancy, some hormonal changes are casual, but these changes can cause various health issues to the women as well as the child inside the womb. The hormonal changes lead to some significant issues like high BP, change in diabetic level, abnormal heartbeat, abnormal body temperature and so forth. Due to these issues some diseases like Pre-eclampsia, eclampsia, gestational diabetes, cardiac attacks occur in a woman's body.

© Springer Nature Singapore Pte Ltd. 2020
P. K. Singh et al. (Eds.): FTNCT 2019, CCIS 1206, pp. 545–556, 2020.
https://doi.org/10.1007/978-981-15-4451-4_43

These diseases can cause the occurrence of certain complications seizures, heart failure, renal and liver failure, miscarriage, or even leads to the death of the women during pregnancy. Studies have shown that approximately 830 women die every day from diseases that occurred during pregnancy and childbirth [1]. Figure 1 represents the maternal death rate around the world as per the statistics of the World Health Organization (WHO) due to the preventable cause. This occurred due to the different factors includes poverty, distance, lack of information, inadequate services, and cultural practices [2]. As per the statistics in India, approximately 45k deaths occur during pregnancy in the year 2015. Figure 2 represents the maternal mortality ratio of different states in India, as per the statistics of the NITI AYOG Government of India [3]. Maternal Mortality Ratio (MMR) is the ratio of the number of 100000 live births over maternal deaths. As per the survey has shown, in Punjab, MMR is 122 approximately, due to preventable cause, which is very high. So, there is an immediate need for a cost-effective and efficient system that will reduce maternal deaths as some of the complications occurred while pregnancy is preventable and treatable, which can be prevented by evaluation of health conditions of women at regular intervals and by providing health care solutions at their doorstep.

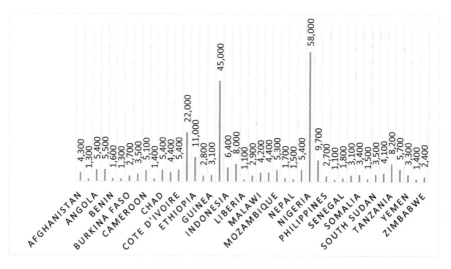

Fig. 1. Maternal death rate as per the World Health Organization

Moreover, today, women indulge in different activities, and due to their busy schedule, sometimes, she may not take the necessary precautions required during pregnancy. So, there should be an E-health care system that monitors health variations occurred in her body and guide her to take appropriate precautions so that specific preventable disease can be cured easily and better health services can be provided to pregnant women regardless of their work type or location.

The health services provided by hospitals are not sufficient. The current century is considered as the technological era, in which the persons are carrying gadgets and like to do their every work with devices. If we provide health solutions to the person by using these gadgets, this leads to the most beneficial thing for the person. E-Health care systems offer different health care services like cardinal health care, maternal health care, or renal health care to the person at his/her doorstep.

This study discusses an E-health care model that will provide health care services to pregnant women. Moreover, this study will discuss the various existing E-health care solution supplied to pregnant women.

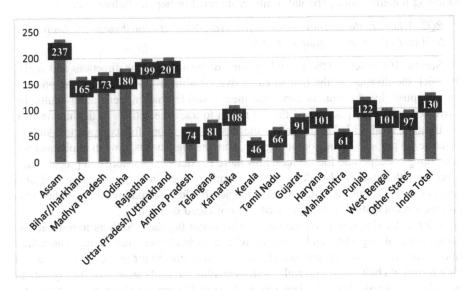

Fig. 2. Maternal mortality ratio

The study organizes in following sections; Sect. 2 is the literature review of the various studies, Sect. 3 compares the multiple systems developed by different authors to measure health parameters, Sect. 4 includes the details about the proposed model and Sect. 5 concludes the study and discussing the future perspective of the proposed system.

2 Literature Review

2.1 Research Questions

The primary aim of this review is to find the answer of the following research questions (RQ). These are

- *RQ1: What are the various problems occurred during pregnancy?*

Tomlinson, et al. [4–7] describes various risk factors that occurred during pregnancy. Authors discussed that women during pregnancy have different risk factors like High BP, High Pulse rate, Gestational Diabetes, seizures, etc. that leads to creation of various dangerous diseases like, Polycystic Ovary Syndrome, Preeclampsia, Eclampsia,

Thyroid, Obesity, etc. which may lead to miscarriage, premature delivery, prodromal labor, week of fetus, low birth weight, etc. Authors also describe the lady can face one or many issues at a time during pregnancy.

Ganguly et al. [8], in their study, describes the impact of high blood pressure on the body of the pregnant lady and her baby. The author specified that high blood pressure could increase the chances of cesarean. They also described that high blood pressure is associated with increased risk of adverse fetal, neonatal, and maternal outcomes, including preterm birth, perinatal death, acute renal or hepatic failure, etc.

- *RQ2: What are the existing technologies available that contribute to the healthcare field and offer various solutions in it?*

Steven [10], describes the possible posture of the arm, and the directions and angles in which the division of the human can move. Shadmehr [11], explains, the postural force applied by the human arm and their possible role in generating multijoint movements. Luis [12] describes, the 3D model to track the actions of the human arm.

Bonomi et al. [13–17], describes the description about fog computing. Authors describe the purpose of fog computing, what are the fog devices, how to implement fog computing concept onto fog devices, how these fog devices can store and process data. Moreover, the studies also describe the security issues in fog computing and also perform comparisons of different technologies by fog computing. The studies also present fog computing as an advanced form of cloud computing.

Chen et al. [18] discussed the information about big data. Authors introduced the background of big data and different related technologies like cloud computing, Internet of Things, data centers and Hadoop. Then discussed the phases of big data and their technical challenges. The authors also examine the application areas of big data to provide brief details about big data. Labrinidis et al. [19] proposed the various technical challenges of big data. Authors described the problems include, lack of structure, error-handling, privacy, timeliness, provenance, visualization at all stages of analysis pipeline from data acquisition to result from interpretation.

Saxena et al. [20, 21], provides the brief description about the cloud computing paradigm. The authors discussed different challenges that occurred in cloud computing and how cloud computing is implemented. Fox et al. [22, 23] describes the information about cloud computing, the reference architecture of cloud computing, the persons involved in cloud computing. Moreover, the authors discussed some obstacles that occurred in cloud computing. Jain et al. [24, 25] describes in their study the role of virtualization how the vitalization is implemented in cloud computing, and challenges occurred in the implementation of virtualization in cloud computing. Singh et al. [31] discussed the latest trends in wireless and communication technologies. They discussed the trends in wireless and IoT networks and also the security aspects of these networks. Paul et al. [30] proposed a three-tier wireless sensor network to capture and differentiate context-sensitive health information. They analyze the security issues that occurred at the fog layer while before and while sending health-related data to the cloud servers.

- *RQ3: What is the existing solutions available?*

Jubadi et al. [9] proposed a model that will capture the heartbeat of the person and send the data to doctors or the patient's near and dears via SMS. They use a PIC circuit connected to the device that measure the heart beat and this device in turn connected with Modem and send SMS. This system senses the heartbeat by placing a figure between LDR and Super-Bright LED at the sensor circuit. Khanum et al. [28] proposed a Pregnancy Care Network to create a connection between hospitals and pregnant women using GPS technology. In their study, the network is designed around pregnant women using smartphones to provide health services to women. They offer only the communication network between women and health officials.

3   Comparison of Various E-Healthcare Systems

Table 1, shows the comparative analysis of different studies.

Table 1. Comparative analysis of different studies

Study	Findings
Adolescent pregnancy [26]	This study includes the various aspects of pregnancy in teenage, such as risk issues, care, post effects on women of adolescent pregnancy
What are the factors that put a pregnancy at risk? [7]	This article describes different elements that make a healthy pregnancy at risk. Authors also states that the risk factors depends upon existing health (high BP, Polycystic Ovary Syndrome, Diabetes, Kidney Disease, Thyroid, Infertility, Obesity, HIV), Age (Teen Age, First Pregnancy at age 35) Lifestyle factors (Drink, Smoke) or gestational factors (Preeclampsia, Eclampsia, Multi gestational, gestational Diabetes)
Maternal mortality [27]	The article discussed the maternal death ratios that occurred across the world. Key facts include in the article are • Every day, approximately 830 women die from preventable causes related to pregnancy and childbirth • 99% of all maternal deaths occur in developing countries • Maternal mortality is higher in women living in rural areas and among more impoverished communities • Young adolescents face a higher risk of complications and death as a result of pregnancy than other women • Skilled care before, during, and after childbirth can save the lives of women and newborn babies • Between 1990 and 2015, maternal mortality worldwide dropped by about 44%
Pregnancy care network [28]	The authors proposed a Pregnancy Care Network that connects women with nearby hospitals using GPS. In their study, the network is created around pregnant women using smartphones to provide health services to women. They offer only the communication network between women and health officials
E-Health care system for pregnant women using the GIS system [25]	The author proposed an algorithm that connects pregnant women with her nearby hospitals by using GPS service provided by her mobile. Moreover, they include a technique in their algorithm that also sends emergency messages to the hospitals
Remote E-Health care system [29]	The author proposed a framework in which health services are provided according to the health conditions of the women. It merely guides the women, not measure the activity of the women

4 Proposed Model Pregnancy E-Healthcare System

The model proposed in this study is named "Tech Preg." Tech Preg is a complete E-health care solution that will monitor health variations of the pregnant women by measuring various parameters like, BP, pulse rate, change in body temperature, number of steps taken, movement of baby, the posture of sleeping, the posture of baby, the swelling ratio in the body of women. By measuring these parameters, the solution will analyze the health variations of the women and categorize the health of the women according to the complications ratio like no complications, minor complications, or significant complications.

In case of no complications noticed in the health of women, it merely stores every captured result generated by sensors to the cloud servers and also will provide the necessary reminders to the women. In the case of minor complications, it sends alerts to the family members and even to the doctors about the health variations of the women and also guides women to take necessary precautions to reduce the impact of the complications. Moreover, in case of high-risk pregnancy, the Tech Preg will monitor the discussed parameters at every second and will store the summarized result to the cloud storage and also will generate the alerts about the health of the women to her family as well as to concerned doctor at regular interval. Tech Preg will also provide the facility to automatic call or message to the family members and nearby hospitals in case of any emergency. Moreover, Tech Preg solution will also measure the chances of occurrence of the particular disease in the body of women due to the significant change in the values of the parameters.

Tech Preg solution will work with the internet connectivity as well as the GPS systems of the gadget. Tech Preg solution measures the discussed parameters by using two devices, and these devices will connect with an app that captures data from devices that will further used for processing. This section discusses the features included in the secondary and app used in the Tech Preg E-health care solutions.

4.1 Tech Preg Wrist Band

Tech Preg Wrist Band is a smart band that captures the health parameters of pregnant women like BP, pulse rate, heartbeat, the sleeping position of women, and posture of the baby in the womb in a real-time environment. Tech Preg wrist band will then analyze the collected data and provide suggestions to the women to take necessary precautions according to the requirement. Moreover, the wrist band will give reminders to the women, and women can also call or message the nearby hospitals or her family members in case of an emergency. In this case, the location of women will immediately send to nearby hospitals or her family members. Table 2 shows the comparative analysis of different prominent wrist bands available in the market.

Different wrist bands available in the market that measures some of the health parameters, but no device is available that monitors every parameter measured by the proposed Tech Preg wrist band. As the table shows, a maximum of 3 features of any gadget matches with a recommended wrist band. So, according to the comparison, the proposed system will work more efficient and can provide better health services when its model converts to the gadget.

Tech Preg wrist band uses different sensors such as temperature sensor, pulse oximetry sensor, LDR module, gyroscope sensor, accelerometer sensor and so forth to provide these features.

Table 2. Comparative analysis of different Smart Wrist Bands

Features	Bellabeat Leaf	Apple iWatch	Samsung Gear fit 2 Pro	Vintage Smart Watch	Tech Preg Wrist Band
Automatic start by wearing	✗	✗	✗	✗	✓
Detect blood pressure	✗	✗	✗	✗	✓
Pulse rate	✗	✗	✗	✗	✓
Heartbeat	✗	✓	✓	✓	✓
Kilometer walked	✓	✓	✓	✓	✓
Sleeping posture of woman	✗	✗	✗	✗	✓
Posture of infant	✗	✗	✗	✗	✓
Labour pain detection	✗	✗	✗	✗	✓
Stable position time	✗	✓	✗	✗	✓
Reminders	✗	✓	✓	✓	✓
Estimated date of delivery	✓	✗	✗	✗	✓
Communication with family	✗	✗	✗	✗	✓
Doctor communication	✗	✗	✗	✗	✓

4.2   Tech Preg Smart Shoes

Tech Preg smart shoes will offer different functionalities to the women and take care of the comfortable walking of the women. During pregnancy, the primary requirement of the women is a convenient walk, and also the major issue occurred during pregnancy is swelling of feet. The swelling ratio of feet describes the specific issues that happened in the body of women and even the types of complications that can face by women during childbirth.

Tech Preg smart shoes will measure different parameters like weight, swelling ratio, wrong style of walking, no. of steps taken, several times movements to upstairs or downstairs, will track the location and also will provide soft a comfortable walk. Tech Preg smart shoes use different sensors such as gyroscope, Flexi sensor, nodeMCU microcontroller to provide features in a single system.

There are different smart shoes available in the market that offers different functionalities. Table 3 shows the comparison between different intelligent shoes with the proposed model.

As the table shows, a maximum of 1 feature of any smart shoes matches with proposed tech preg intelligent shoes. So, according to the comparison, the proposed system will work more efficient and can provide better health services when its model converts to the gadget.

Table 3. Comparative analysis of different smart shoes

Features	Digisole shoe	Xiaomi Mijia smart shoes	Altra IQ smart shoes	Tech Preg smart shoes
Automatic start by wearing	✗	✗	✗	✓
Weighing scale	✗	✗	✗	✓
Detect swelling ratio	✗	✗	✗	✓
Location tracker	✓	✗	✗	✓
Wrong walk detector	✗	✗	✗	✓
Cloud connectivity	✗	✓	✗	✓

4.3   Tech Preg Smart App

Tech Preg smart app will connect to these intelligent devices and gathers data from these devices. Moreover, the app will also connect to the fog devices where it can transfer data after collection from smart devices and also the app will transfer data to cloud storage for further processing. The app can be able to run onto various platforms like android, iPhone, or desktops or PCs, either windows or Mac platform. The smart app will include multiple features:

- This smart app will be run on the fog devices.
- The intelligent app will analyze and measure the real-time data provided by these smart devices and apply filtration onto the data.
- After filtration, the data is sent to the cloud devices from where one can get data quickly.
- This app will also send messages to the devices of the dearest person of the women.
- By connecting this app, doctors can get the summarized report of the day to day activities of the women.
- This app helps to analyze the health variation of the women and provides care to the women even at their job.
- This app will also act as a complete guide to the women about by some videos, or some Do's and Dont's about pregnancy.

- By using this app, women can directly connect with their doctor, husband, near, and dears.
- By this app, women can record all the activities of her pregnancy.

In this manner, Tech Preg can provide better health services to women. According to the survey taken during the study, approximately 85% of women respond that there is a need for such kind of devices during pregnancy, and 88% of doctors respond that such types of machines in the future can become a necessity of the women.

Every smart device includes in Tech Preg solution will connect to the nearby fog devices, and then the filtration process will be applied onto these devices so that significant data issues will not occur at the cloud storage. Then data will be sent to the cloud servers from where we can capture the collected data at any time from any location.

5 The Architecture of the Proposed Model

The architecture of E-health care system work for a pregnant woman is described in Fig. 3. The proposed model consists of two smart devices one is wristband and one is smart shoes. These smart devices are controlled by a smart app and can monitor data of pregnant woman and issues alerts in real time environment. The Smart Wristband starts by wearing and detects the pulse to perform its required functions, and smart shoes will also start by wearing when shoes will capture the feet fit the shoes, it gets connected by smart app automatically. After getting started, both the devices will monitor the health parameters and will perform their required functions. As the whole collected data can be used by doctors to monitor the patient in a deeper way, and also the health messages to be sent to her family members, this will be done only by using cloud storage. Moreover, the gadget will generate a huge amount of data as it will collect data every second, so there is a need to filter the data so that big data issue would not occur at the cloud storage. To perform this filtration process, firstly the collected data from gadgets will be sent to fog devices and then filtration process is done onto these devices and after filtration, the final data will be uploaded to the cloud server. The use of fog devices will reduce the latency issues occurred while uploading data to the cloud servers and also reduce the chances of big data issues may occur at the cloud servers. After collection of data at the cloud storage, the doctors and the family members will get the health information and activities of the woman by the smart app provided to them by their desktops, laptops, smartphone or tablets. Doctors will get the analytical report of every activity of the woman which will help the doctor to deeper analyze the women even with the cases of high-risk pregnancies. Moreover, the family members will get the health information about the women, whether the required activities performed by her on time or not, and also they will get to know the health variations like the start of labor pain etc.

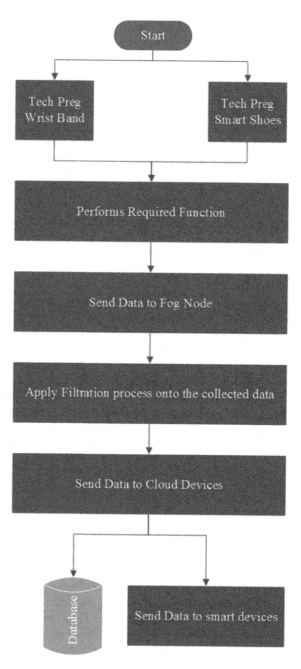

Fig. 3. Architecture of the proposed model

6 Conclusion and Future Perspective

Pregnancy is the crucial period in which there are lots of complications that occur due to carelessness attitude towards health. It may even lead to maternal or infant death. This study focused on the various problems that occur during pregnancy and how the impact of these issues can be reduced to a safe life by using technological gadgets. The study proposed a model that can provide health care solutions to pregnant women and can run on smart devices based on the comparison made with the usage of already existing gadgets. After comparison, it is revealed that one system with all the features is not available in existing systems and the proposed system providing better health options, which will reduce maternal mortality.

The future scope of the study is the implementation of the proposed system, which may be used as a lifesaver gadget available to the women.

References

1. Trends in Maternal Mortality: 1990 to 2015, 28 September 2018. https://www.who.int/reproductivehealth/publications/monitoring/maternal-mortality-2015/en/
2. Maternal Mortality Evidence Brief. World Health Organization (2015)
3. Data: Maternal mortality ratio (per 100,000 live births) (2015). NITI Aayog. https://www.niti.gov.in/content/maternal-mortality-ratio-mmr-100000-live-births
4. Tomlinson, M., et al.: Multiple risk factors during pregnancy in South Africa: the need for a horizontal approach to perinatal care. Prev. Sci. 15(3), 277–282 (2014)
5. Klein, J.D.: Adolescent pregnancy: current trends and issues. Pediatrics 116(1), 281–286 (2005)
6. High-risk pregnancy and high-risk obstetrics. UKHealthCare (2016)
7. Shriver, E.K.: What are some factors that make a high pregnancy risk? National Institute of Child Health and Human Development, pp. 1–8 (2018). https://www.nichd.nih.gov/health/topics/high-risk/conditioninfo/factors
8. Ganguly, S., Begum, A.: Rate of caesarean operation and complications in hypertensive disorders of pregnancy. ORION 27, 463–466 (2007)
9. Jubadi, W.M., Sahak, S.F.A.M.: Heartbeat monitoring alert via SMS. In: 2009 IEEE Symposium on Industrial Electronics & Applications, vol. 1, pp. 1–5, October 2009
10. Wiker, S.F., Langolf, G.D., Chaffin, D.B.: Arm posture and human movement capability. Hum. Factors 31(4), 421–441 (1989)
11. Shadmehr, R., Mussa-Ivaldi, F.A., Bizzi, E.: Postural force fields of the human arm and their role in generating multijoint movements. J. Neurosci. 13(1), 45–62 (1993)
12. Goncalves, L., Di Bernardo, E., Ursella, E., Perona, P.: Monocular tracking of the human arm in 3D. In: Proceedings of IEEE International Conference on Computer Vision, pp. 764–770, June 1995
13. Fog computing and the Internet of Things: extend the cloud to where the things are. Cisco (2015). https://www.cisco.com/c/dam/en_us/solutions/trends/iot/docs/computing-overview.pdf
14. Chatterjee, J.M.: Fog computing: beginning of a new era in cloud computing. Int. Res. J. Eng. Technol. 4(5), 735–739 (2017)

15. Bonomi, F., Milito, R., Zhu, J., Addepalli, S.: Fog computing and its role in the Internet of Things. In: Proceedings of the First Edition of the MCC Workshop on Mobile Cloud Computing, pp. 13–16, August 2012
16. Stojmenovic, I., Wen, S.: The fog computing paradigm: scenarios and security issues. In: 2014 Federated Conference on Computer Science and Information Systems, pp. 1–8, September 2014
17. Satyanarayanan, M.: The emergence of edge computing. Computer **50**(1), 30–39 (2017)
18. Chen, M., Mao, S., Liu, Y.: Big data: a survey. Mob. Netw. Appl. **19**(2), 171–209 (2014)
19. Labrinidis, A., Jagadish, H.V.: Challenges and opportunities with big data. Proc. VLDB Endow. **5**(12), 2032–2033 (2012)
20. Saxena, V.K., Pushkar, S.: Cloud computing challenges and implementations. In: 2016 International Conference on Electrical, Electronics, and Optimization Techniques (ICEEOT), pp. 2583–2588, March 2016
21. Beri, R., Behal, V.: Cloud computing: a survey on cloud computing. Int. J. Comput. Appl. **111**(16), 19–22 (2015)
22. Fox, A., et al.: Above the clouds: a berkeley view of cloud computing. Department of Electrical Engineering and Computer Sciences, University of California, Berkeley, Rep. UCB/EECS 28, no. 13 (2009)
23. Malhotra, L., Agarwal, D., Jaiswal, A.: Virtualization in cloud computing. J. Inform. Tech. Softw. Eng **4**(2), 136 (2014)
24. Jain, N., Choudhary, S.: Overview of virtualization in cloud computing. In: 2016 Symposium on Colossal Data Analysis and Networking (CDAN), pp. 1–4, March 2016
25. Ismaeel, A.G., Jabar, E.K.: Effective system for pregnant women using mobile GIS. arXiv preprint arXiv:1302.3749 (2013)
26. WHO: Adolescent pregnancy: issues in adolescent health and development. WHO (2004)
27. Maternal Mortality. World Health Organization (2018). https://www.who.int/en/news-room/fact-sheets/detail/maternal-mortality
28. Khanum, S., de Souza, M., Sayyed, A., Naz, N.: Designing a pregnancy care network for pregnant women. Technologies **5**(4), 80 (2017)
29. Spaanderman, M., Velikova, M., Lucas, P.: e-MomCare: remote monitoring in pregnancy care background to the research, pp. 1–19 (2011)
30. Paul, A., Pinjari, H., Hong, W.H., Seo, H.C., Rho, S.: Fog computing-based IoT for health monitoring system. J. Sens. **2018**, 7 (2018)
31. Singh, P.K., Paprzycki, M., Bhargava, B., Chhabra, J.K., Kaushal, N.C., Kumar, Y. (eds.): FTNCT 2018. CCIS, vol. 958. Springer, Singapore (2019). https://doi.org/10.1007/978-981-13-3804-5

Multi-modality Medical Image Fusion Using Fuzzy Local Information C-Means Clustering in SWT Domain

Manoj Diwakar[1](✉), Vanshika Rastogi[1], and Prabhishek Singh[2]

[1] CSE Department, Graphic Era Deemed to be University, Dehradun,
Uttarakhand, India
manoj.diwakar@gmail.com, vanshikarastogi869@gmail.com
[2] CSE Department/ASET, Amity University, Noida, India
prabhisheksingh88@gmail.com

Abstract. In medical science, the role of medical images is very crucial to identify the diagnosis. Variety of medical images such as CT (Computed Tomography) images, MRI (magnetic resonance imaging) images are available but many times these different modalities need more informatics images. Therefore, multi-modality medical image fusion technique is one of the solutions which can provide more informatics details by fusing multi-modality medical images. In this paper, a new approach of multi-modality medical image fusion approach is proposed where fuzzy local information based C-means clustering and local entropy fusion approach is performed in SWT (stationary wavelet transform) Domain. To measure the performance of proposed scheme, a comparative study is also performed over the existing methods. The result analysis is performed in both visually and also by performance metrics such as mutual information, edge based similarity and blind image quality. From experimental evaluation, it can be analyzed that proposed scheme gives better outcomes in compare to existing methods.

Keywords: Clustering · Local entropy · Stationary wavelet transform

1 Introduction

Multi-modality image fusion based approach has been prominent research year in the coming years. By applying this we get medical images from various modalities that enhance the robustness and accuracy in the field of the biomedical research and clinical detection of the disease [1]. The main focus of medical based image fusion can be widely described the integration of information through visually hold in whichever quantity of medical image based fusion input converted into only one fusion image in the absence instigated noise or loss in the information [2]. In actual form it is not possible, so the next optimized alternative will take more from the crucial facts through the source predominantly believed like acceptable object [3]. Simplest techniques of range of pixels value in the image based fusion determine the averaging of the source images create fusion variety. The technique deliberately decreases quality of source images. Low resolution color image converted into the hue-saturation. Since intensity

© Springer Nature Singapore Pte Ltd. 2020
P. K. Singh et al. (Eds.): FTNCT 2019, CCIS 1206, pp. 557–564, 2020.
https://doi.org/10.1007/978-981-15-4451-4_44

level identical as multiple resolution, several of the research article resizing the intensity level to identical quality as compare to multiple resolution, supervised before numerous fusion at high quality level to create latest level of intensity.

Consequently, significant development on fusion methods and many set of rules have are elaborated. Image fusion can be accomplished in three types: one is decision-type, pixel-type, and feature-type [4–6]. Fusion for the pixel type is accomplished on the basis of pixel by pixel, developing image fusion on the fact analogous from the set of pixels every pixel is taken from the input images [7]. Medical image fusion of the feature type needs the removal of prominent environment-contingent on attribute, like as textures, edges or pixel intensities [8]. The combination of information in decision-level fusion provide the more abstraction level, joining output through various set of rules to produce the ultimate fused based decision [9, 10]. The acquired information is then joined by related decision rules to strengthen the usual elucidation. The concluding two types are depending on the incorporate between the desired spectral consistency and the spatial enhancement.

Wavelet transform gives the wide platform in which the image disintegrates to a sequence rough-quality of sub-levels, multiple-levels and excellent-quality of sub-levels. Various methods [11–13] in transform domain have been published. However the merits of each method can be enhanced by using better utilization. The conventional DWT image based fusion introduced in Li et al. [14]. Traditional DWT has shortcoming of shift-invariance and utilization shift-invariance transformation in image processing applications [15]. Li et al. [16] approach depends on the redundant wavelet transform to overcome the shift-invariant issue and enhances consistent performance the fused outcome. The identical approach is used in Singh et al. [17] medical images from the distinguished input images. In accordance with particular sequence to attain best fusion outcome, diverse methods for the wavelet fusion has been measure through many scientific research. In the combined contourlet contrast measurements Yang et al. [18] with the further fusion methods, such as local energy, selection and weighted average to enhance the quality of the fusion based images. Similar fusion works also done by using other multi-resolution methods [19] such as multi-scale local extrema method [20]. Various image processing applications such as medical image denoising [21, 22] are also processed using wavelet transform; however image fusion is the only one approach through which, more details can obtained.

With the motivation of multi-resolution based fusion approach, a method is proposed for multimodality image fusion in stationary wavelet domain. This paper is organized as: Sect. 2 describes the clustering of Fuzzy Local Information C-Means (FLICM). The proposed algorithm is discussed in Sect. 3. Experimental evaluation and result analysis is demonstrated in Sect. 4. Lastly, Sect. 5 gives the conclusion of this work.

2 Fuzzy Local Information C-Means Clustering (FLICM)

To overcome the sensitiveness and conserve the quality measurement, fuzzy local similarities [5] have the characteristics which can use for multimodality medical image fusion. Generally, a novel factor fuzzy $Q(ai)$ is presentation to objective fuzzy local information C-Means function to increase the execution of clustering. Factor for Fuzzy membership can be expressed as:

$$Q(ai) = \sum_{\substack{j \in N_i \\ i \neq j}} \frac{1}{d_{ij}+1} (1 + u_{ki})^m \left\| x_j - v_k \right\|^2 \tag{1}$$

Here i^{th} is the local window for the center, j^{th} pixel neighbouring pixels, i^{th} surrounding pixels value and Spatial Euclidean Distance d_{ij} in between i and j. Cluster prototypes v_k, cluster a, and fuzzy membership gray value u_{ki} j wrt to the cluster a^{th}. Through the definition of $Q(ai)$, of the fuzzy local information C-Means objective function is described as:

$$P_m = \sum_{i=1}^{N} \sum_{k=1}^{c} [u_{ki}^m \| x_i - v_k \|^2 + g_{ki}] \tag{2}$$

Here v_k denotes the prototype a^{th} cluster u_{ki} denotes the membership for the fuzzy, N data items and c number of clusters.

3 Proposed Methodology

In the proposed method, multimodality images are fused in the wavelet domain where clustering based image fusion concept is used. In compare to discrete wavelet transform, stationary wavelet transform gives better resolution in decomposition part. Hence in proposed scheme, stationary wavelet transform is utilized to get approximation and detail parts of input images. Both approximation parts are fused on the basis of FLICM. Similarly, both detail parts are fused on the basis of local entropy.

The proposed algorithm is described in the following steps.

Step 1: Apply stationary wavelet transform (SWT) over the both input images (A & B) to get Approximation and detail parts.

Step 2: Perform FLICM on both Approximation parts using Eqs. 1 and 2.

Step 3: Calculate Local entropy (LE) [21] over the both detail parts of multi-modality input images.

Step 4: Perform FLICM based image fusion on approximation parts of both multi-modality input images using below equation:

$$\text{Modified\_Approx} = \begin{cases} A & FLICM_A > FLICM_B \\ \frac{A+B}{2} & FLICM_A = FLICM_B \\ B & FLICM_A < FLICM_B \end{cases} \tag{3}$$

Step 5: Perform local entropy based image fusion on detail parts of both input images using following equation:

$$\text{Modified\_Detail} = \left\{ \begin{array}{ll} A & A_{LE} > B_{LE} \\ \frac{(A+B)}{2} & A_{LE} = B_{LE} \\ B & A_{LE} < B_{LE} \end{array} \right\} \tag{4}$$

Step 6: To get fused outcome of multimodality images, perform inverse stationary wavelet transform.

4 Results and Discussion

The experimental evaluation is performed using MATLAB 2018a tool. The size of all images which are used for experimental results are 512×512. In Figs. 1, 2 and 3, different multi-modality results are indicated. In Fig. 1(a) and (b) are the two input multi-modality images CT and MRI. Both images are fused into Existing methods such as [4], [12], [16], [20] and proposed method also. The results of [4], [12], [16], [20] and proposed method are shown in Figs. 1(c), (d), (e), (f) and (g) respectively. Similarly proposed method is also tested in different modality on MR-T2 image and SPET image. Both MR-T2 image and SPET image are shown in Fig. 2(a) and (b). These both images are fused into existing methods such as [4], [12], [16], [20] and proposed method also. The results of [4], [12], [16], [20] and proposed method are shown in Figs. 2(c), (d), (e), (f) and (g) respectively. One more different modality dataset is also used to test the proposed and existing methods.

The proposed and existing methods also tested on MR-T1 image and MR-T2 image as shown in Fig. 3. Figures 3(a) and (b) are MR-T1 image and MR-T2 image respectively. The results of [4], [12], [16], [20] and proposed method are shown in

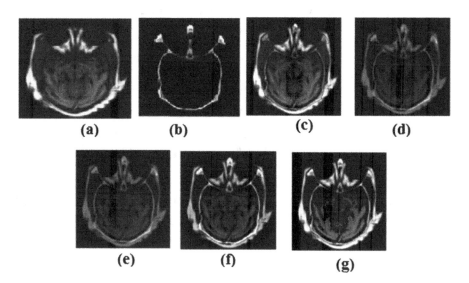

(a)　　**(b)**　　**(c)**　　**(d)**

(e)　　**(f)**　　**(g)**

Fig. 1. (a) Input CT image (b) Input MR image, (c) Outcomes of [4], (d) Outcomes of [12], (e) Outcomes of [16], (f) Outcomes of [20], (g) Outcomes of proposed method

Figs. 3(c), (d), (e), (f) and (g) respectively. From visual analysis, it is analysed that proposed methods visual quality in terms of edges and details of information is better in comparison to existing methods. Due to the clustering concept in fusion technique, the results are contains more visual details.

To measure the quality of proposed method and existing methods some performance metrics are used such as Mutual Information ($mI_{AB,f}$), Edge Based Similarity Measure ($q_{AB,f}$) and blind image quality analysis $BSSIM$.

Mutual Information (MI) is one of the performance metrics which is used to measure the quality of fused images. It can be expressed as:

$$mI_{xf} = \sum\nolimits_{k-1}^{q} \sum\nolimits_{k-1}^{q} H_{xf}(k,l) \log_2 \frac{H_{xf}(k,l)}{H_x(k,l)H_f(k,l)} \tag{5}$$

Here maximum pixel value normalized joint histogram H_{xf}, normalized histogram H_x of image x, *and* normalized histogram H_f of f. Cumulative mutual information $(mI_{AB,f})$ acquired through:

$$mI_{AB,f} = mI_{Af} + mI_{Bf} \tag{6}$$

Edge Based Similarity Measure ($q^{AB/F}$) is one of the performance metrics which is used to calculate the resemblance in the edge relocation from the input images to the fusion based image. The elucidation follows as:

$$q^{AB/F} = \frac{\sum_{i=1}^{mI} \sum_{j=1}^{N} [q^{AF}(i,j)wg^A(i,j) + q^{BF}(i.j)wg^B(i,j)]}{\sum_{i=1}^{mI} \sum_{j=1}^{N} [wg^A(i,j) + wg^B(i,j)]} \tag{7}$$

In which

$$q^{AF}(i,j) = q_\alpha^{AF}(i,j)q_r^{AF}(i,j) \tag{8}$$

$$q^{BF}(i,j) = q_\alpha^{BF}(i,j)q_r^{BF}(i,j) \tag{9}$$

Here in this $wg^A(i,j)$ and $wg^B(i,j)$ the identical strengths of the gradient for images A and B respectively. $q_\alpha^{xF}(i,j)$ and $q_r^{xF}(i,j)$ representation of the strength of the edge and conservation of feature values at position (i,j) for every source image. The values of $q^{AB/F}$ should be close to one, which recommend as best fused image.

We apply the definition of intent image fusion based performance ($q_{AB,f}$) straightly from.

562   M. Diwakar et al.

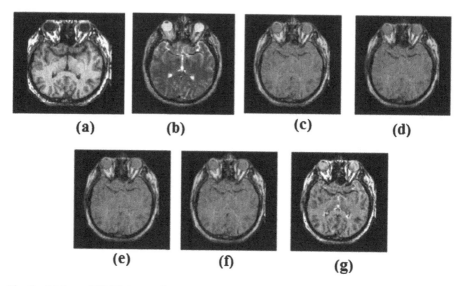

Fig. 2. (a) Input MR-T1 image (b) Input MR-T2 image, (c) Outcomes of [4], (d) Outcomes of [12], (e) Outcomes of [16], (f) Outcomes of [20], (g) Outcomes of proposed method

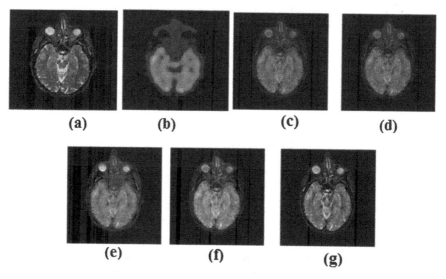

Fig. 3. (a) Input MR-T2 image (b) Input SPET image, (c) Outcomes of [4], (d) Outcomes of [12], (e) Outcomes of [16], (f) Outcomes of [20], (g) Outcomes of proposed method

In the practical approach of medical based image fusion, introduce a new fusion quality measure known BSSIM. The identical between the two images can be computed by the structural similarity (*SSIM*) index. We apply the definition of *SSIM* (*structural similarity*) from to elaborate BSSIM (*blind image quality analysis*) as:

$$BSSIM_{AB,f} = 0.5 \times \left(SSIM_{Af} + SSIM_{Bf} \right) \tag{10}$$

Where, SSIM gives the similarity value in terms of edge preservation which can be measured between input and output images.

Table 1. Objective computation of outcomes applying group images ($\mathcal{N} = 1$).

Approach	$MI_{AB,F}$	$Q_{AB,F}$	$BSSIM$
[4]	3.8704	0.7537	0.9976
[12]	3.8859	0.7763	0.9976
[16]	3.8820	0.7028	0.9965
[20]	3.4520	0.7918	0.9975
Proposed	**3.9738**	**0.8109**	**0.9987**

From Table 1, it can be observed that performance of proposed algorithm gives better outcomes in terms of given performance metrics.

5 Conclusion

This paper describes the multimodality based medical image fusion using clustering based fusion concept in SWT domain. The advanced information about human should be sensitive to the better contrast (high), intensity in the pixel, edge information and depend on the fusion approach are directive to contrast, show dependencies between distinguish scales or orientations, edge and texture detection. Different types of errors in this loss of noise and the increase of information presented in the fused image how much information is extracted from the original image for the measurement. The results are indicating that proposed method is giving better results using other similar schemes. Other than visual results, the performance metrics also indicates that proposed method gives better outcomes in comparison to similar existing methods.

References

1. He, C., Liu, Q., Li, H., Wang, H.: Multimodal medical image fusion based on intensity hue saturation and principal component analysis. Procedia Eng. **7**, 280–285 (2010)
2. Sabalan, D., Hassan, G.: Multi resolution analysis and positron emission tomography image fusion by combining intensity hue saturation and retina-inspired models. Inf. Fusion **11**(2), 114–123 (2010)
3. Escalante-Ramírez, B.: The Hermite transform as an efficient model for local image analysis: an application to medical image fusion. Comput. Electr. Eng. **34**(2), 99–110 (2008)

4. Yang, J., Han, F., Zhao, D.: A block advanced principal component analysis fusion algorithm based on positron emission tomography and computed tomography. In: Proceedings of the Fourth International Conference on Intelligent Computation Technology and Automation ICICTA, vol. 2, pp. 925–928 (2011)

5. Li, T., Wang, Y.: Multiscaled combination of magnetic resonance and single photon emission tomography images in neuroimaging. Comput. Methods Programs Biomed. **105**(1), 31–39 (2010)

6. Wang, L., Li, B., Tian, L.: Multi-modal medical image fusion using the inter-scale and intra-scale dependencies between image shift-invariant shearlet coefficients. Inf. Fusion **19**, 20–28 (2014)

7. Singh, S., Anand, R.S.: Ripplet domain fusion approach for CT and MR medical image information. Biomed. Signal Process. Control **46**, 281–292 (2018)

8. Bhatnagar, G., Wu, Q.J., Liu, Z.: Directive contrast based multimodal medical image fusion in NSCT domain. IEEE Trans. Multimed. **15**(5), 1014–1024 (2013)

9. Aishwarya, N., Bennila Thangammal, C.: Visible and Infrared image fusion using DTCWT and adaptive combined clustered dictionary. Infrared Phys. Technol. **93**, 300–309 (2018)

10. Liu, X., Mei, W., Du, H.: Multi-modality medical image fusion based on image decomposition framework and nonsubsampled shearlet transform. Biomed. Signal Process. Control **40**, 343–350 (2017)

11. Omar, Z., Stathaki, T.: Image fusion: an overview. In: 5th International Conference on Intelligent Systems, Modelling and Simulation (ISMS), pp. 306–310 (2014)

12. Krishn, A., Bhateja, V., Sahu, A.: Medical image fusion using combination of PCA and wavelet analysis. In: International Conference on Advances in Computing, Communications and Informatics (ICACCI), pp. 986–991 (2014)

13. Sroubek, F., Flusser, J.: Registration and fusion of blurred images. In: Campilho, A., Kamel, M. (eds.) ICIAR 2004. LNCS, vol. 3211, pp. 122–129. Springer, Heidelberg (2004). https://doi.org/10.1007/978-3-540-30125-7_16

14. Li, H., Manjunath, B.S., Mitra, S.K.: Multisensor image fusion using the wavelet transform. Graph. Models Image Process. **57**(3), 235–245 (1995)

15. Rockinger, O.: Image sequence fusion using a shift-invariant wavelet transform. In: Proceedings of the International Conference on Image Processing, vol. 3, pp. 288–291 (1997)

16. Li, X., He, M., Roux, M.: Multifocus image fusion based on redundant wavelet transform. IET Image Proc. **4**(4), 283–293 (2010)

17. Singh, R., Vatsa, M., Noore, A.: Multimodal medical image fusion using redundant DWT. In: Proceedings of the ICAPR, pp. 232–235 (2009)

18. Yang, L., Guo, B.L., Ni, W.: Multimodality medical image fusion based on multiscale geometric analysis of contourlet transform. Neurocomputing **72**(1–3), 203–211 (2008)

19. Li, S., Yang, B., Hu, J.: Performance comparison of different multi-resolution transforms for image fusion. Inf. Fusion **12**(2), 74–84 (2011)

20. Du, J., Li, W., Xiao, B., Nawaz, Q.: Medical image fusion by combining parallel features on multi-scale local extrema scheme. Knowl.-Based Syst. **113**, 4–12 (2016)

21. Diwakar, M., Kumar, M.: CT image noise reduction based on adaptive wiener filtering with Wavelet packet thresholding. In: 2014 International Conference on Parallel, Distributed and Grid Computing, pp. 94–98. IEEE (2014)

22. Diwakar, M., Kumar, M.: CT image denoising based on complex wavelet transform using local adaptive thresholding and Bilateral filtering. In: Proceedings of the Third International Symposium on Women in Computing and Informatics, pp. 297–302. ACM (2015)

A Comparative Study on Machine Learning Techniques for Benzene Prediction

Veerawali Behal$^{(\boxtimes)}$ (iD) and Ramandeep Singh (iD)

School of Computer Science and Engineering,
Lovely Professional University, Phagwara, India
behalveerawali@yahoo.in, ramandeep.singh@lpu.co.in

Abstract. Air pollution is one of the major public health issues confronting the world. The toxic levels of air pollutants in and around world are creating quite a menace. Detrimental air pollutants have accelerated the rate of cancer among human beings. Several studies have utilized different machine learning models for predicting air quality. In this paper, various machine learning based air quality monitoring techniques have been studied that can predict the concentration of benzene in air which is considered as one of the carcinogenic air pollutant. It has been observed that machine learning models have been extensively utilized in the various studies to reduce the prediction error rate. The overall objective of this paper is to compare well-known machine learning techniques which have been used to predict concentration of benzene in the atmosphere. Furthermore, the proposed ensemble based model for benzene prediction is also developed. The proposed technique is tested on well-known publicly available air pollution datasets for quantitative analysis. The proposed model achieves 91.56% of coefficient of determination and lower prediction error rate. In addition to these, performance metrics like Mean Absolute error (2%) and Root Mean Square error (3.1%) were estimated to determine the overall effectiveness of the proposed system. The proposed model is compared with the existing system and outcome of proposed model is improved. The comparative analysis of study shows that the proposed ensemble model performed better prediction results than the baseline existing machine learning models. Thus, it is well suitable to build effective benzene prediction model.

Keywords: Air quality monitoring · Benzene · Machine learning techniques · Prediction model

1 Introduction

Today world is moving towards modernization, moving from villages to cities, more civilized than before either in industrial or transportation sector. Although there is advancement in every sector, air pollution is a major threat to society. Air pollution is a worldwide environmental challenge continuously receiving great attention [1]. At present, it has become a crucial issue in today and is becoming major reason of occurrence of numerous diseases such as asthma, Chronic Obstructive Pulmonary Disease (COPD), cancer, reduction of lung functioning, pulmonary cancer, mesothelioma, pneumonia and so forth to individuals. According to World Health Organization

© Springer Nature Singapore Pte Ltd. 2020
P. K. Singh et al. (Eds.): FTNCT 2019, CCIS 1206, pp. 565–578, 2020.
https://doi.org/10.1007/978-981-15-4451-4_45

(WHO) latest report, it reveals that every year around 4.2 million deaths occur due to ambient air pollution, around 3.8 million mortality occurs due to household air pollution [2]. As per the latest survey country wise pollution index in mid-year 2019 [3] is shown in Fig. 1. As indicated by the World Health Organization (WHO), metropolitan urban areas are the foremost critically areas influenced by the barometrical contamination. Therefore, estimating the air quality turn into a noteworthy zone of research. Due to the speedy development, migration of rural population towards urban metropolitan cities and industrial enterprise, cities like Delhi, Mumbai, Chennai, and Bangalore etc. are on high of the Indian map in terms of pollution.

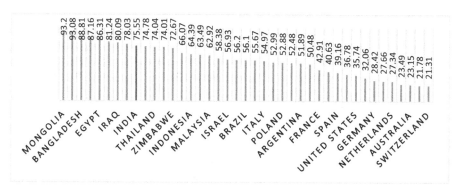

Fig. 1. Pollution Index country wise mid-year 2019 [3]

Volatile organic compounds (VOCs) are substantial gathering of carbon-based chemicals that effortlessly evaporates at room temperature. Various industries normally utilize paints, solvents, varnishes and fuels that create VOCs such as benzene. Detection of VOCs is of vital necessity for an individual wellbeing in hazardous atmosphere.

The contamination could be a noteworthy downside in every country, as locale contaminants have a fantastic outcome on human wellbeing. Several disorders like Leukemia, Lymphoma, (respiratory and cardiovascular disorder) is additionally caused by pollutants in atmosphere which are Ozone (O_3), nitrogen dioxide (NO_2), (CO), toxin (SO_2), Benzene (C_6H_6), PM10 and PM 2.5 [17, 22]. Air Pollutants such as Sulphwhich is being contaminated is a wellbeing risk for individuals around the globe. There exist a few gases noticeable all around, which worsen health of people. Benzene is observed as harmful gas for individuals because it leads to blood malignancy to general public. Benzene is expanding gradually because of hike in cars as an outcome of expanding transportation. This scenario stresses the need for cost effective prediction system with the collaboration of machine learning techniques. Consequently, proper monitoring is required which can be accomplished using various prediction techniques. This study is an attempt in this direction.

Air Pollution Sources

Air Pollution sources are categorized into four classes as shown in Fig. 2. Air pollution can arise through mobile sources like different vehicles used in transportation. However, stationary pollution may arise due to the waste material generated by different sources like, oil refineries, commercial organizations, factories etc. These sources may generate huge amount of air pollutants, while processing raw material or generating of goods. One of the other major reasons of air pollution is due to particular areas like, agriculture areas, metro cities and so forth. Natural sources like, fog, mist, forest fire, etc. can also sometimes significantly consider as the vital elements of air pollution [20].

Fig. 2. Air pollution sources (use color monitor for better visualization) (Color figure online)

The progressions in innovation and quick change in community's necessities prompts industrialization. The advancement of industrialization results in air contamination ends up noticeably. It is of significant worry that needs to be anticipated. Resultingly, few control techniques ought to be attempted to address the detrimental impacts of air pollution. This study reveals a survey of the models carried out in tracking ambient air quality. Several models for anticipating air contamination are basically investigated and examined in this work.

Organization of Paper
The rest of paper is organized into various sections. Section 2 summarizes review of various studies and contributions in the field of machine learning based air quality techniques. Section 3 addresses various air pollution prediction models. Section 4 discusses ensemble based proposed methodology. Section 5 provided a detailed experimental implementation and results. Section 6 shows the comparative study of various existing machine learning based techniques and proposed technique and Sect. 7 concludes the paper.

2 Review of Related Work

Osowski and Siwek [15] shows that pre-selection of the foremost vital attributes, permits broadening accurate prediction in an effective manner. Several data mining techniques for air quality prediction are discussed and natural selection based genetic optimization approach is used. Sharma et al. [4] have employed ANFIS (adaptive network-based fuzzy inference system) for forecasting air pollutants concentration.

Pollutants such as Sulphur dioxide (SO_2) and Ozone (O_3) in Delhi, India are being taken as environmental agents. A new application of Modified Particle Swarm Optimization for training ANFIS for air pollutants forecasting turned into positively inspected. Fu et al. [5] address the prediction of PM2.5 and PM10 by developing and improved Feed Forward Neural Network model. Yu et al. [6] described Random Forest Approach for prediction of quality of air in urban sensing system. Nebot and Mugica [7] address the prediction of concentration of PM2.5 by using fuzzy techniques which are neuro-fuzzy approach hybrid fuzzy-pattern recognition techniques. De Vito et al. [8] used ANFIS to development of a prediction model for estimating concentration of carbon monoxide release in environment which further used the statistics taken from clinical waste incineration plant. Kocadağl et al. [11] have proven that Bayesian regularized ANN are considered well organized than existing techniques. Chen et al. [12] have discussed various machine learning algorithms for forecasting quality of air in urban areas. The discussed machine learning prediction models are used to predict the concentration of benzene in air. An effective machine learning based model is created for estimation of engrossment of Benzene in the air. Liu et al. [13] in their study predict Air Quality Index (AQI) of three China cities viz. Beijing, Tianjin, and Shijiazhuang by using Support Vector Machine (SVM) prediction model. Authors predicted two years AQI values of these cities including several pollutants amalgamation, such as PM2.5, PM10, SO_2, CO, NO_2, and O_3, meteorological factors like temperature, velocity, wind direction, and also weather description like cloudy/sunny, or rainy/snowy, and so forth. The study used 4-cross validation method to split data into testing and training set and then results are compared with other studies for observation. Henceforth, the authors concluded that the performance of the model is going to improve by inclusion of air quality data of surrounding cities.

3 Machine Learning Based Air Quality Prediction Models

3.1 Linear Model

A linear Regression analysis yields a mathematical equation, a linear model that estimates a dependent variable Y from a set of predictor variable or regressor X. Such a linear model is represented as Eq. (1)

$$Y = b_0 + b_1 X_1 + b_2 X_2 + \ldots \ldots + b_k X_k + e \tag{1}$$

Each regressor in a linear model is given a numerical weight, where b is represented as regression coefficient linear modeling is widely used throughout the medical research, air quality prediction business and marketing and countless other fields [9].

3.2 Artificial Neural Network

ANN is most important branch of artificial intelligence which consists of large scaled interconnected nonlinear nodes [14]. However, ANN is self-adaptive and data driven method which means it learn from some examples. It is basically used in multiple phase of biological science [11]. Recent studies have shown that neural network is beneficial in environment forecasting issues as compared to traditional statistical available techniques [25, 27].

3.3 Decision Tree

Decision tree is a supervised learning approach which follows top-down and greedy method to solve problem in recursive manner [16]. It is also termed as Classification & Regression Trees methodology. Initially at the root node all the observations laid under same region then the observation split into sub-regions on the behalf of answers of questions asked at each node.

3.4 Support Vector Machines (SVM)

SVM is modern supervised learning technique used for classification and regression [18, 19]. SVM prediction is used to determine the quantity of the dataset in future based on past data [21, 26]. SVM is a discriminative classifier which classes into hyper plane. In 2-D space the created hyper plane divide plane in 2 sections with every class laid on opposite side.

3.5 K-Nearest Neighbor (K-NN)

K-NN is defined as non-parametric method which is based on classification and regression terminology. It provides the prediction results as classifiers on the basis of similarities between attributes, within lesser time and its output is easier to predict [10].

4   Proposed Methodology

This section discusses the details of the methodology which will be used to implement the proposed technique. This step by step methodology of the proposed technique is shown in Algorithm 1 (Table 1).

4.1   Proposed Ensemble Approach

The performance of machine learning model can be boosted through a robust approach of ensembling. The best three models based on performance evaluation are taken as base learners and further unified to form a proposed ensemble model as depicted in Fig. 3. The ultimate aim of ensemble model is to generate a strong learner by a joint contribution of a set of week learners. Stacking is a special type of ensemble model in which training of a new model is done by combining the predicted results from any number of (at least 2) previous models. The predicted results from the models are fed as inputs for each sequential layer and are further combined to generate predictions as output.

Table 1. Machine learning based Benzene Prediction Mechanism

Algorithm 1: Machine learning based Benzene Prediction Mechanism	
Step 1	Input publicly available dataset
Step 2	The given dataset will be divided into training and testing datasets
Step 3	For training dataset, apply data pre-processing
Step 4	Apply feature selection technique using key performance indicator (KPI) which will be used to extract only those attributes which influences the target class i.e. Benzene (C_6H_6) a lot
Step 5	Evaluate best machine learning model by considering various performance metrics
Step 6	Apply optimization technique (if any) to tune best evaluated machine learning model
Step 7	Train benzene prediction model by considering the best evaluated solution from step 6
Step 8	Target class i.e. benzene (C_6H_6) will be removed from testing dataset
Step 9	Apply trained model (from Step 7) on testing dataset obtained (from Step 8). Return predicted value of testing dataset
Step 10	In this phase, the various performance metrics will be evaluated by comparing the actual values of testing dataset with predicted values

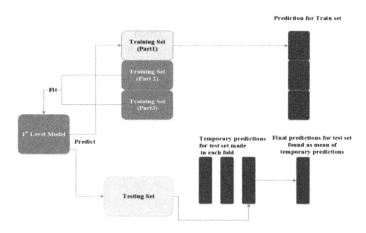

Fig. 3. Proposed ensemble approach for benzene prediction

Working Mechanism of Proposed System

Following is the working mechanism followed for a proposed stacked ensemble technique depicted in Fig. 3.

Step 1: The training set is splitted into ten chunks.

Step 2: One of the model is chosen as a base model on the basis of performance evaluation and is applied on nine chunks and further last chunk is taken for benzene prediction. Each part of training set is utilized as per this scheme.

Step 3: The base model is then applied on the entire train dataset.
Step 4: Employing this model, test set is utilized to predict concentration of benzene.
Step 5: Repetition of step 2 to 4 is performed for another base model. Subsequently; other set of predictions for the training set and testing set is generated.
Step 6: The new model is built by utilizing the predictions as features from the train set.
Step 7: This final model is utilized for building final predictions on the test prediction set.

5 Experimental Implementation

5.1 Dataset Description and Experimental Design

In present investigation, we have taken two different air quality regression based dataset which are downloaded from UCI and Kaggle data repository [28, 29]. First dataset (AQ-IC) comprises total of 9,358 observations. Each observation contributes to the averaged readings of 5 metal oxide chemical sensors which are measured on hourly basis. One of the polluted areas of Italian city was chosen for the deployment of device and readings have been taken for a period of 11 months (March 2004–Feb 2005). Another dataset (AQ-TA) is taken from Environmental Protection Administration, Executive Yuan, R.O.C. (Taiwan). It comprises total of 218641 observations. This data is recorded in polluted areas of northern Taiwan in year 2015.

5.2 Experimental Setting

The implementation is done on Windows10 operating system with Intel core i5 processor consisting of 8 GB RAM. Python programming language is used for further development. For preprocessing of inputted data, Pandas library is used. Scikit learn library, an open source machine learning library is utilized for implementation of machine learning algorithms is used. Graph plotting has been done by importing Matplotlib library whereas evaluation has been done using sklearn metrics. Jupyter Notebook is used as Integrated Development Environment. Ten-fold cross validation technique is used for tuning hyper parameters. Dataset is splitted into training and testing samples. 70% of data is taken as training data which is further fed to activate the regressor and remaining data is used as testing data. This training data is utilized for training the regressor. Regressor is tested on independent new samples of testing data. To test the robustness of the designed framework, the process is iterated. To evaluate the performance of the proposed framework, three different parameters metrics namely, Mean Absolute Error (MAE), Coefficient of Determination (R^2) and Root Mean Square Error (RMSE) are used.

5.3 Performance Analysis

This section discusses the detailed comparative analysis of existing air quality prediction based machine learning techniques with proposed ensemble based technique. Publicly available dataset is being used for benchmark testing. The betterment of the results is proved on the basis of different algorithms viz. K-Nearest Neighbor, Linear Model, Decision Tree, Support Vector Regression and ANN. Performance of these algorithms is measured on the behalf of different parameters like, R^2, RMSE, and MAE. Out of these five models, selection of best models (on basis of performance evaluation metrics) for our dataset is done so that to perform ensembling on these models. The comparison of the proposed ensemble technique has been drawn with existing prediction techniques on both air quality data by considering various metrics.

5.3.1 Performance Evaluation and Results

Mean Absolute Error (MAE) Analysis
Mean absolute error is defined as the average magnitude of the absolute error in the dataset. In a test sample, MAE is the average of the absolute differences between actual and prediction observations. It is calculated as in Eq. (2):

$$MAE = \frac{1}{N} \sum_{i=1}^{N} |F_i - A_i|. \tag{2}$$

Where, N is the number of observations, F_i is the actual value and A_i is the predicted value.

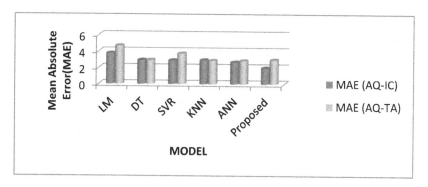

Fig. 4. Testing MAE

Table 2. Comparative analysis of MAE

Models	MAE (AQ-IC)	MAE (AQ-TA)
LM	3.7788	4.7023
DT	2.9521	2.9654
SVR	2.9201	3.7653
KNN	2.9537	2.8965
ANN	2.7221	2.8765
Proposed	2.0041	2.9937

The comparative analysis of MAE value of proposed ensemble based machine learning model as well as existing machine learning models has been depicted in Fig. 4 and Table 2. From this analysis it has been investigated that proposed model has value of MAE in case of AQ-IC as 2.0041 and 2.9937 in case of AQ-TA which is comparatively low as compared to other machine learning models.

Coefficient of Determination (R^2) Analysis

The coefficient of determination (R^2) is defined as the square of correlation between independent and dependent variable. It is given by the variation of variable y explained by the variable x. It is calculated as in Eq. (3):

$$R^2 = \left(\frac{n(\sum xy) - \sum x \sum y}{\sqrt{[n \sum x^2 - (\sum x)^2][n \sum y^2 - (\sum y)^2]}} \right)^2 \tag{3}$$

Where, n is the number of observations, x is the independent variable and y is the dependent variable.

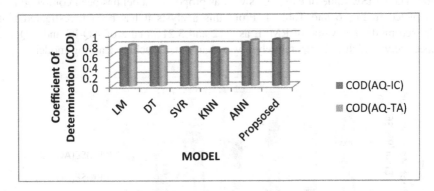

Fig. 5. Testing coefficient of determination

Table 3. Comparative analysis of coefficient of determination

Models	COD (AQ-IC)	COD (AQ-TA)
LM	0.726317	0.8087
DT	0.75421	0.76543
SVR	0.746742	0.75443
KNN	0.736722	0.71076
ANN	0.848321	0.897544
Proposed	0.908041	0.91564

Figure 5 and Table 3 depict the coefficient of determination (R^2) analysis of the existing as well as proposed ensemble-based machine learning technique. The comparison has been done in terms of (R^2) value of the models and accordingly describes which among them is the most desirable. From this analysis it has been investigated that proposed model has value of Coefficient of Determination as 0.908041 and 0.91564 in case of AQ-IC and AQ-TA respectively, which is comparatively higher than other machine learning models. It has been observed that the proposed ensemble technique outperforms others in both cases because it has better R^2 value as compared to other machine learning techniques.

Root Mean Squared Error (RMSE) Analysis

RMSE is defined as the root average of absolute error square. This error summarizes the difference between the observed and the predicted concentrations. It is calculated as in Eq. (4):

$$RMSE = \sqrt{\frac{1}{N} \times \sum_{i=1}^{N} (F_i - A_i)^2}. \tag{4}$$

Where, N is the number of observations, F_i is the actual value and A_i is the predicted value. The RMSE value of existing as well as proposed model has been compared and is depicted in Fig. 6 and Table 4. From this analysis it has been investigated that proposed model has value of RMSE as 3.12 and 3.21 in case of AQ-IC and AQ-TA respectively, which is comparatively lower than other machine learning models.

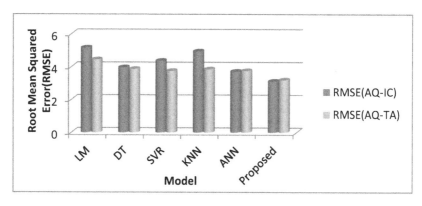

Fig. 6. Testing RMSE

Table 4. Comparative analysis of RMSE

Models	RMSE (AQ-IC)	RMSE (AQ-TA)
LM	5.1625	4.4543
DT	3.9743	3.87654
SVR	4.3771	3.76433
KNN	4.9525	3.86532
ANN	3.7254	3.76543
Proposed	3.1267	3.21456

From this analysis it has been interpreted that the proposed model achieves the lower RMSE value in comparison with existing machine learning models. As our dataset is of regression type, we have used five regressor type models to predict the concentration of benzene. The results of all the models are shown in Tables 2, 3, 4. ANN model gives us minimum RMSE, MAE values for both datasets, followed by Decision tree and then SVR model.

Further proposed ensemble approach is applied on these three models and performance is evaluated. After comparative analysis it is evaluated that the proposed ensemble approach outperforms all baseline machine learning models.

6   Comparative Analysis

Various studies have been proposed by different researchers. This section discusses comparative analysis of proposed technique and some of the existing techniques with environmental agents and some other comparative parameters (Optimization, Ensemble and K Cross Validation) as depicted in Table 5. There are numerous challenges occur while developing efficient machine leaning model that predict the quantity of air pollutants in the environment.

6.1   Ensembling

Ensemble modeling is a commanding for enhancement of model performance. Some of the researchers have ignored the ensemble based techniques for designing benzene prediction model.

6.2   Parameters Tuning

Machine models based on parameter tuning perform very well. Nonetheless, a significant number of the researchers have disregarded the effect of parameters tuning while designing benzene forecasting model.

6.3   Processing Time

While designing benzene perdition model processing time also become challenging issue. Consequently, the removal of above issues is primary inspiration driving this research work.

Table 5. Comparative analysis of machine learning models and proposed model

Ref	Technique used	Environmental agent	Parameters used			Complexity
			Optimization	Ensemble	K-cross validation	Where, (n is the number of training sample, p is the number of features, n_{trees} is the number of trees, n_{sv} is the number of support vectors, n_{Li} the number of neurons at layer 'i' in a neural network.)
[23]	SVM	PM2.5	✓	✗	✓	$O(n_{sv}p)$
[5]	Neural network	PM2.5, PM10	✓	✗	✗	$O\ (p+n_{L1}\ n_{L2}+...)$
[6]	Random forest	CO, NO$_2$, O$_3$, SO$_2$, PM10, PM2.5	✗	✓	✗	$O(pn_{trees})$
[16]	Decision tree	PM2.5, CO	✓	✗	✗	$O(p)$
[24]	Linear regression	PM10	✗	✓	✓	$O(p)$
	Proposed	✓		✓	✓	✓	$O(n^2)$

7   Conclusion and Future Perspective

In this study, the performance of various machine learning models is evaluated based in terms of RMSE, coefficient of determination and mean absolute error. The proposed ensemble based air quality prediction model outperforms other existing machine learning models. Numerous features of the existing machine learning algorithms have been explored to encourage further research. Extensive analysis has shown that the prediction of benzene is still an open area of research. Hence, future research will focus on designing an optimistic machine learning model to predict benzene from air. Also, tuning of designed machine learning model will also be done by using various meta-heuristic techniques.

References

1. Gass, K., Klein, M., Chang, H.H., Flanders, W.D., Strickland, M.J.: Classification and regression trees for epidemiologic research: an air pollution example. Environ. Health **13**(1), F7 (2014)
2. Air pollution. https://www.who.int/airpollution/en/. Accessed 19 June 2019

3. Pollution Index for Country 2019 Mid-Year (2019). https://www.numbeo.com/pollution/rankings_by_country.jsp
4. Sharma, S., Kalra, U., Srivathsan, S., Rana, K.P.S., Kumar, V.: Efficient air pollutants prediction using ANFIS trained by modified PSO algorithm. In: 2015 4th International Conference on Reliability, Infocom Technologies and Optimization (ICRITO) (Trends and Future Directions), pp. 1–6. IEEE, September 2015
5. Fu, M., Wang, W., Le, Z., Khorram, M.S.: Prediction of particular matter concentrations by developed feed-forward neural network with rolling mechanism and gray model. Neural Comput. Appl. **26**(8), 1789–1797 (2015)
6. Yu, R., Yang, Y., Yang, L., Han, G., Move, O.: RAQ–a random forest approach for predicting air quality in urban sensing systems. Sensors **16**(1), 86 (2016)
7. Nebot, À., Mugica, F.: Small-particle pollution modeling using fuzzy approaches. In: Obaidat, Mohammad S., Filipe, J., Kacprzyk, J., Pina, N. (eds.) Simulation and Modeling Methodologies, Technologies and Applications. AISC, vol. 256, pp. 239–252. Springer, Cham (2014). https://doi.org/10.1007/978-3-319-03581-9_17
8. De Vito, S., Massera, E., Piga, M., Martinotto, L., Di Francia, G.: On field calibration of an electronic nose for benzene estimation in an urban pollution monitoring scenario. Sens. Actuators B: Chem. **129**(2), 750–757 (2008)
9. Vlachokostas, C., Achillas, C., Chourdakis, E., Moussiopoulos, N.: Combining regression analysis and air quality modelling to predict benzene concentration levels. Atmos. Environ. **45**(15), 2585–2592 (2011)
10. Qin, Z., Cen, C., Guo, X.: Prediction of air quality based on KNN-LSTM. J. Phys: Conf. Ser. **1237**, 042030 (2019). https://doi.org/10.1088/1742-6596/1237/4/042030
11. Kocadağlı, O.: A novel hybrid learning algorithm for full Bayesian approach of artificial neural networks. Appl. Soft Comput. **35**, 52–65 (2015)
12. Chen, L., Cai, Y., Ding, Y., Lv, M., Yuan, C., Chen, G.: Spatially fine-grained urban air quality estimation using ensemble semi-supervised learning and pruning. In: Proceedings of the 2016 ACM International Joint Conference on Pervasive and Ubiquitous Computing, pp. 1076–1087. ACM, September 2016
13. Liu, B.C., Binaykia, A., Chang, P.C., Tiwari, M.K., Tsao, C.C.: Urban air quality forecasting based on multi-dimensional collaborative support vector regression (SVR): a case study of Beijing-Tianjin-Shijiazhuang. PLoS ONE **12**(7), e0179763 (2017)
14. Feng, X., Li, Q., Zhu, Y., Hou, J., Jin, L., Wang, J.: Artificial neural network forecasting of PM2.5 pollution using air mass trajectory based geographic model and wavelet transformation. Atmos. Environ. **107** (2015). https://doi.org/10.1016/j.atmosenv.2015.02.030
15. Siwek, K., Osowski, S.: Data mining methods for prediction of air pollution. Int. J. Appl. Math. Comput. Sci. **26**(2), 467–478 (2016)
16. Sekar, C., Gurjar, B., Ojha, C., Goyal, M.: Potential assessment of neural network and decision tree algorithms for forecasting ambient PM2.5 and CO concentrations: case study. J. Hazard. Toxic Radioactive Waste **20**, A5015001 (2015). https://doi.org/10.1061/(asce)hz.2153-5515.0000276
17. Hu, H., Ha, S., Roth, J., Kearney, G., Talbott, E.O., Xu, X.: Ambient air pollution and hypertensive disorders of pregnancy: a systematic review and meta-analysis. Atmos. Environ. **97**, 336–345 (2014)
18. Li, S., Ma, K., Jin, Z., Zhu, Y.: A new flood forecasting model based on SVM and boosting learning algorithms. In: Proceedings of the 2016 IEEE Congress on Evolutionary Computation (CEC), Vancouver, BC, Canada, 24–29 July 2016, pp. 1343–1348 (2016)
19. Tehrany, M.S., Pradhan, B., Jebur, M.N.: Flood susceptibility mapping using a novel ensemble weights-of-evidence and support vector machine models in GIS. J. Hydrol. **512**, 332–343 (2014)

20. National park service, sources of air pollution. https://www.nature.nps.gov/air/aqbasics/sources.cfm. Accessed 11 Mar 2017
21. Shmilovici, A.: Support vector machines. In: Maimon, O., Rokach, L. (eds.) Data Mining and Knowledge Discovery Handbook, pp. 257–276. Springer, Boston (2005). https://doi.org/10.1007/0-387-25465-X_12
22. Xi, X., et al.: A comprehensive evaluation of air pollution prediction improvement by a machine learning method. In: 2015 IEEE International Conference on Service Operations and Logistics, and Informatics (SOLI), pp. 176–181. IEEE, November 2015
23. Yeganeh, B., Hewson, M.G., Clifford, S., Knibbs, L.D., Morawska, L.: A satellite-based model for estimating PM2. 5 concentration in a sparsely populated environment using soft computing techniques. Environ. Model Softw. **88**, 84–92 (2017)
24. Karatzas, K., Katsifarakis, N., Orłowski, C., Sarzyński, A.: Revisiting urban air quality forecasting: a regression approach. Vietnam J. Comput. Sci. **5**, 177–184 (2018). https://doi.org/10.1007/s40595-018-0113-0
25. Barai, S.V., Dikshit, A.K., Sharma, S.: Neural network models for air quality prediction: a comparative study. In: Saad, A., Dahal, K., Sarfraz, M., Roy, R. (eds.) Soft Computing in Industrial Applications. Advances in Soft Computing, vol. 39, pp. 290–305. Springer, Heidelberg (2007). https://doi.org/10.1007/978-3-540-70706-6_27
26. Eldakhly, N., Aboul-Ela, M., Abdalla, A.: A novel approach of weighted support vector machine with applied chance theory for forecasting air pollution phenomenon in Egypt. Int. J. Comput. Intell. Appl. **17**, 1850001 (2018). https://doi.org/10.1142/S1469026818500013
27. Daniel, G.G.: Artificial neural network. In: Runehov, A.L.C., Oviedo, L. (eds.) Encyclopedia of Sciences and Religions. Springer, Dordrecht (2013). https://doi.org/10.1007/978-1-4020-8265-8
28. UCI Machine Learning Repository: Air Quality Data Set. In: Archive.ics.uci.edu (2019). https://archive.ics.uci.edu/ml/datasets/Air+Quality. Accessed 30 Sept 2019
29. Air quality in northern Taiwan. In: Kaggle.com (2019). https://www.kaggle.com/nelsonchu/air-quality-in-northern-taiwan/kernels. Accessed 30 Sept 2019

Carcinoma Classification from Breast Histopathology Images Using a Multi Level Spatial Fusion Mechanism of Deep Convolutional Features from Differently Stain Normalized Patches

Ritabrata Sanyal[1](✉), Kunal Chakrabarty[1], Gummi Deepak Reddy[2], and Vinayak Sengupta[3]

[1] Kalyani Government Engineering College, Kalyani, West Bengal, India
sritabrata@gmail.com, kunalchakrabarty@gmail.com
[2] Jawaharlal Nehru Technological University, Hyderabad, India
gummideepak@gmail.com
[3] BITS Pilani, Dubai, UAE
vinayak.sengupta@gmail.com

Abstract. Breast cancer is one of the leading causes behind death of women worldwide. Core needle biopsy of breast tissue, followed by analysis of the breast histopathological image is one of the most widely used breast cancer diagnosis techniques today. Deep learning pipelines involving a single stain normalization of the raw histology images, followed by patch extraction and CNN based patch wise classification methods with integration of patch wise results by majority voting for image wise classification, have already been proposed in literature. This paper presents a novel architecture, based on spatial fusion of features of two different stain normalizations of the an input patch. The underlying mechanism of stain normalization algorithms being different, they bring forth different salient features of a histopathology image. This will aid a CNN network learn better representations, which will not be possible had only one stain normalization method been used like previous methods. The final feature representation of a patch is rich and multilevel, that is it takes both low level (finer features) and high level (coarser features) features into account. Finally, the feature vector extracted from every patch is fed to a Bidirectional Long Short Term Memory (BLSTM) network for image wise classification, to exploit long term and short term contextual information between neighbourhood patches. Experiments reveal that our model achieved a 87.75% and 97.5% for patch and image wise classification respectively on the ICIAR 2018 breast histopathological images dataset, thereby outperforming other state of the art methods to the best of our knowledge.

Keywords: Breast cancer · Histopathology analysis · Deep Learning · Convolutional Neural Network (CNN) · Long Short Term Memory (LSTM)

© Springer Nature Singapore Pte Ltd. 2020
P. K. Singh et al. (Eds.): FTNCT 2019, CCIS 1206, pp. 579–591, 2020.
https://doi.org/10.1007/978-981-15-4451-4_46

1   Introduction

Breast Cancer is a global health problem accounting for the second most cancer deaths in women worldwide. The microscopic analysis of hematoxylin and eosin (H & E) stained histopathological images is the most widely used method for it's diagnosis and early detection. However, manual analysis of these images suffers from various shortcomings including pathologists' bias and diagnostic inconsistencies, thus, necessitating the development of automated breast cancer detection mechanisms.

The recent advancements of Deep Learning methods in various image classification tasks has inspired scholars to use them for classification of medical images. Spanhol et al. [14] released a breast cancer histopathological patches dataset, captured at different magnifications, based on which they used a Convolutional Neural Network trained on Imagenet for classifying breast cancer type from the histopathological images. Araujo et al. [1] first considered the problem of high resolution breast histopathology image classification, and proposed a pipeline comprising of Macenko [9] stain normalization, patch extraction and classifying each patch with a AlexNet CNN. Roy et al. [12] also used Macenko [9] stain normalization and proposed a custom CNN architecture for patch based classification. Vang et al. [17] used both Vahadane [16] and Macenko [9] stain normalized patches to train an Inceptionv3 [15] network for patch wise classification. Then they ensembled the predictions from Vahadane [16] and Macenko [9] stained patches trained CNNs, to obtain the final classification result.

A common trait among the deep learning based methods heretofore is the use of a single stain normalization method on the raw histopathological images, followed by dividing the image into patches, classifying each patch and finally integration of patch wise classification results, to obtain image wise predictions. Stain normalization methods help reduce the undesirable colour variations that may arise from H & E staining on histopathological images. Various such stain normalization procedures have different underlying principles to mitigate such colour variations. However, we observed that various stain normalization methods bring forth different salient features in the histology images. That is, the use of only one stain normalization method therefore is somewhat inimical to the network's ability to learn global features and generalize well. As mentioned earlier, Vang et al. [17] used two stain normalization methods for patch wise classification, but they trained their networks independently and ensembled the predictions. However, this process fails to fuse the features of two stain maps of a patch spatially to output a single representation incorporating features of both the stained patches. This can be only obtained with joint training, so that during a single forward pass through the entire network, features from both the stain normalized patches contribute to the final output. We hypothesize that a rich spatial feature fusion of the feature map generated by two stain normalization methods will give better results than using a single stain normalization method. The two stain normalized patches will bring forth different prominent regions of the input patch.

To that end we propose a novel architecture, that uses two different stain normalization methods on patchwise training of histopathological images as suggested in Macenko et al. [9] and Vahadane et al. [16]. We effectively combine features from different convolutional layers to get an accurate feature representations of these normalization procedures to obtain a richer multilevel representation for the histopathological image patch. We then extract a feature vector representation of the patch. The patches of the image are then input to a bidirectional long short-term memory (LSTM) [6] module and the class label of the image is predicted.

2 Dataset

Our work uses the Breast Cancer Histology Challenge (BACH) 2018 dataset [2] which was hosted as part of the ICIAR 2018 conference, consisting of high resolution H&E stained breast histology images. These RGB images are of size 2048×1536 pixels with each pixel covering $0.42\,\mu m \times 0.42\,\mu m$ of tissue area. Each image is annotated into 4 different classes, namely Benign, Normal, Insitu Carcinoma and Invasive Carcinoma. Figure 1 shows sample images from each category. There are 100 images in each category.

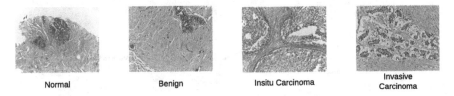

Normal Benign Insitu Carcinoma Invasive Carcinoma

Fig. 1. Sample images with their corresponding classes from the ICIAR 2018 dataset (Color figure online)

3 Methodology

In this section we will describe our model architecture. At first, two stain maps of a breast histology image is computed by the Vahadane [16] and Macenko [9] stain normalization algorithm respectively. Each of the stain normalized images are divided into 35, 512×512 patches with 50% overlap, generating two patch wise datasets—one of Vahadane type and the other Macenko type. Two pretrained VGG19 [13] networks are then fine-tuned on the two patch datasets, for feature extraction of each type of stain images. After this, higher and lower level feature maps, extracted from the 2 VGG19 nets, are fed to the Stain-feature Fusion Network, to compute a rich representation of a patch, and finally classify the patch. For image level classification, the rich patch representations are fed to a BLSTM network, to maintain both long and short term associations between various patches. The methods are elaborated as follows:

3.1 Preprocessing

Accurate preprocessing is of histology images is of paramount importance towards development of a rigorous prediction model. H & E stained images suffer from unwanted color shifts due to the variations in slide scanners and level of stain absorption. Other variations like difference in stain reactivity from different manufacturers may contribute to this as well. These shifts in color may introduce a bias in our model prohibiting it from generalizing well. So to normalize this we use the methods suggested by Vahadane et al. [16] and Macenko et al. [9]. Vahadane et al. [16] uses a sparse non-negative matrix factorization based technique for normalizing stained patches whereas Macenko et al. [9] proposed a method based on normalizing the colors in the input RGB image to optical density (OD). It is then followed by applying Singular Value Decomposition on the optical density vectors, which effectively restores useful features by projecting the image in a 2-D plane and using the vectors with a high degree of variance. In Fig. 2, we can see the results of each stain normalization method on a sample image.

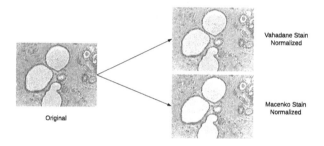

Fig. 2. The two types of stain normalization on an image (Color figure online)

3.2 Patch Extraction

The images in our dataset are of a very high resolution (2048×1536). Deep Learning models trained on such large spatial dimensions tend to suffer from over-fitting and the paucity of images in the dataset exacerbates the problem. To rectify this, we extract patches from the images. This both helps us process these large images and also acts as a data augmentation technique.

Patches of dimensions 512×512 with 50% overlap are extracted from the original images in a sliding window fashion. We have empirically observed these dimensions to be yielding the best results.

3.3 Patch Wise Classification

Our Patch wise classifier consists of two component networks, namely the Stain Feature Extraction Network (SFEN) and the Stain Feature Fusion Network

(SFFN). SFEN deals with finetuning two CNNs on the two stain normalized patch datasets, and thus extracting higher and lower level features. SFFN fuses the high and low level features extracted from each CNN, to effectively combine spatial information of two stain normalized versions of the same input patch. Figure 3 is a visual representation of the same.

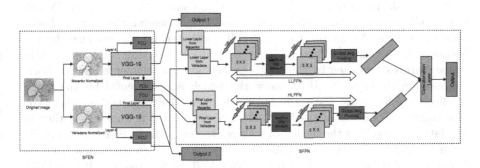

Fig. 3. The patch-wise classification pipeline. Output 1 and 2 represents the softmax outputs of the backbone VGG-19 networks. Output 3 is the softmax output of the SFFN.

Stain Feature Extraction Network (SFEN). SFEN consists of two independent backbone CNN networks, each responsible for learning features from a Vahadane and Macenko stained normalized input patch, respectively, and a novel Feature Control Unit (FCU) as shown in ??, for extracting high and level features from the two backbone CNNs. The backbone networks are two VGG19 networks [13], pretrained on the Imagenet [3] dataset, which we finetune on both of the stain normalized patch datasets. Finetuning strategy is chosen, mainly due to the paucity of our dataset and that fine-tuning helps the CNN to learn target task specific features, yet with considerably less training data than it would be required if the CNNs were trained from scratch. After fine-tuning, we extract both high and low level features from both CNNs. It is essential to make up for the coarser convolutional features with more receptive fields. Retaining fine information like edges, corners, curves, local intensity variations which are extracted by the lower layers, we extract both high and low level features from both the CNNs. It is to be noted that, the rich multilevel features extracted by the backbone nets must spatially correspond to each other, for the SFFN network to construct coherent meaning of the input patch—that is, any spatial location of a low level feature map output of the backbone net trained on Vahadane [16] stained patches must correspond to the same location in the low level feature map output of the backbone net trained on Macenko [9] stained patches. To that end, we propose a novel rich feature extraction mechanism, namely the Feature Control Unit (FCU) (demonstrated in Fig. 4). A FCU takes as input the feature map output (a $3-D$ tensor) of a certain convolutional layer of a backbone CNN, and outputs a single feature map (a $2-D$ matrix). The FCU consists of a stack

of 512, 1×1 [8] convolutional kernels for increasing the non-linearity of the decision function without influencing the receptive fields of the convolutional layer
of the backbone network, which is followed by channel-wise pooling with a single
1×1 kernel for projecting the output from the previous layer into a space of
lower dimensionality $(2 - D$ from $3 - D)$. Rectified Linear Unit (ReLU) [4] non-
linearity is used in every layer of the FCU. The maps are channel wise pooled,
as it would decrease the complexity of feature combination of the SFFN network, while preserving the spatial correspondence between maps extracted from
both the CNNs. An architecture like FCU is chosen mainly because the two
backbone CNNs and the feature fusion net (SFFN) are trained independently,
so the features extracted by the backbone nets are not augmented during back-
propagation through the SFFN network—which is detrimental for the SFFN
to effectively learn the feature fusion mechanism. Hence we add another layer
of non-linearity on top of the backbone CNN extracted feature maps, thereby
regulating/controlling the nature of features to flow into the SFFN network. To
extract lower level features, we take the 256×256 feature map output from the
fourth convolutional layer of each backbone VGG19 net and feed it to a FCU.
The procedure is same for extracting high level features, except we use the last
convolutional layer 32×32 feature map output.

Stain Feature Fusion Network (SFFN). After the high and low level feature
maps are extracted by the FCU of the SFEN network, the high level maps of
both the backbone nets are paired, and same is done with the low level maps,
which are then fed to the SFFN network. The fusion strategy entails in effective
combination of high level features of both stain normalized patches and low level
features of the same. This is done to incorporate high and low level features of
both Vahadane [16] and Macenko [9] stain normalized versions, to generate a
rich, multilevel feature representation of an input patch. SFFN network consists
of two parallel networks, one for combining high level features, namely High Level
Feature Fusion Net (HLFFN), and the other for combining low level features,
namely Low Level Feature Fusion Net (LLFFN), as described below:

– **LLFFN:** This network accepts two 256×256 lower level feature maps, and
  fuses them to obtain a vector representation. This aids in incorporating features of any spatial region, which are accentuated by either or both the
  Vahadane [16] and Macenko [9] stain normalized versions of an input patch.
  LLFFN consists of two convolution layers followed by a Global Average Pooling (GAP) layer [8]. The first convolutional layer has 128, 3×3 kernel filters,
  followed by a Max-Pooling layer to reduce the spatial dimensions of the feature map. The second convolutional layer has 256, 3×3 kernel filters, followed
  by the GAP layer to output a 256 dimensional feature vector. The GAP layer
  carries out feature pooling on the output feature map, hence helps in dimensionality reduction, compared to flattening the map as a vector.

- **HLFFN:** HLFFN accepts two 32×32 feature maps and outputs a 128 dimensional feature vector, representative of the high level features of an input patch. The topology of this network is almost same as LLFFN except for a few differences. The first convolutional layer has 64, 3×3 kernel filters, and the second one has 128, 3×3 kernel filters.

All the convolutional layers of the LLFFN and HLFFN nets have ReLU nonlinearity. The low and high level feature vectors, output by the LLFFN and HLFFN are concatenated and fed as input to a Fully Connected (FC) layer and a softmax layer having 4 output classes. The concatenated high and low level feature vector is the final rich multilevel feature representation of an input patch.

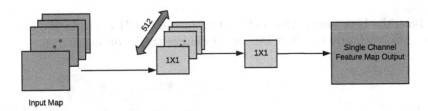

Fig. 4. The Feature Control Unit (FCU)

Training Details. The two pretrained VGG19 backbone nets are fine tuned individually, independent of each other and other networks—one on Vahadane stain normalized patch dataset, and the other on Macenko stain normalized patch dataset. After fine-tuning, the final weights of both the nets are frozen for later use. The FCUs and the SFFN network are trained jointly—the Vahadane and Macenko stain normalized versions of an input patch are fed to the corresponding backbone networks and the information flows via the FCUs to the SFFN, which are trained using an integrated loss function. When these nets are trained with this integrated objective, weights of only the FCUs and the SFFN are updated, and those of the backbone nets are not updated by backpropagation. The integrated loss function, inspired by [7], takes the predictions of the backbone networks, into account. This is done to incorporate predictions by considering only Vahadane [16] or Macenko [9] stain normalized inputs and predictions using a rich feature combination of both, and thereby aiding the feature fusion mechanism of the SFFN. The integrated loss function is formally expressed as,

$$L_{Intg} = \sum_{i=1}^{3} \alpha_i L_i \tag{1}$$

where L_i and α_i are the loss and tuning weight of the ith model respectively. The three models here, are the backbone network trained on Macenko [9] stain normalized patches ($i = 1$), the backbone network trained on Vahadane [16] stain normalized patches ($i = 2$) and $i = 3$ corresponds to the SFFN and FCU trained in parallel. We empirically set the hyperparameters α_1, α_2, α_3 to 1, 1 and 0.5 respectively. Each loss function L_i is a cross entropy loss which is defined as:

$$L_i = -\sum_{j=1}^{k} y_j log(\hat{y}_{i,j}) \tag{2}$$

where k is the number of classes, which in our case is 4 (Benign, Normal, Insitu Carcinoma and Invasive Carcinoma). y_j is the jth value of the ground truth label, $\hat{y}_{i,j}$ is the jth value of softmax output of network i.

$$\hat{y}_{i,j} = g_s(l_{i,j}) \tag{3}$$

where $l_{i,j}$ is the jth logit value of network i and $g_s(.)$ is the softmax activation function.

Both the backbone CNNs and joint SFFN and FCU networks are trained using the Stochastic Gradient Descent Optimizer (SGD) optimizer.

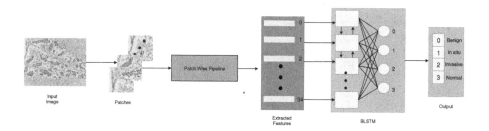

Fig. 5. The image wise pipeline

3.4 Image Wise Classification

After classifying the constituent patches of a high resolution histopathology image, the next problem is to integrate the patch level features or predictions, to obtain the output class of the image. Most previous methods use majority voting or a SVM classifier for that purpose. But the problem that arises by using those methods, is the inability to maintain the long and short term associations between the patches of an image, and the inability to incorporate contextual information of neighbouring patches. Integration of the results of individual patches are thus computed using a bi-directional LSTM. The BLSTM helps retain contextual information by processing from both left-to-right and right-to-left, thereby taking into account past, as well as future context for every patch. We concatenate the multilevel feature vector output from the SFFN, as input to a BLSTM. Thus each timestep of the LSTM corresponds to a patch of the original image. A four node fully connected layer with softmax activation, is connected to the end of the network, to output the class of the entire image. The BLSTM network is trained with Adadelta optimizer. The image-wise pipeline is shown in Fig. 5.

4 Experiments

Following the standard practice, the ICIAR 2018 [2] data set is split into three parts for training, validation and testing purposes. 70%, 10% and 20% of the images are used for training, validation and testing respectively. The classification performance of the entire model is evaluated using metrics like accuracy, precision, sensitivity, specificity. The 4-class patch and image level classification accuracies are 87.75% and 97.5% respectively. The 2-class patch and image level classification accuracies are 96% and 98.75% respectively. 2-class classification entails in classifying a patch as carcinoma (insitu, invasive) or non-carcinoma (benign, normal). To evaluate the effectiveness of hierarchical feature fusion of two stain normalized versions of an input patch over the individual backbone networks, and to evaluate the efficacy of BLSTM over SVM or majority voting for image wise classification, we compare our final model with some baselines. Figure 7 shows the confusion matrices for image and patch wise classifications while Fig. 6 shows the precision recall curves for the same. From Table 1, we can see that the proposed model incorporating high level and low level features of both the stain normalized patches, perform better than the models using a single stain normalized patch. Also it can be seen that, using the BLSTM in the image wise pipeline in Fig. 5 gives better classification performance compared to SVM and Majority Voting. Table 2 provides us with image-wise and patch-wise metrics of 4-class classifications while, from Table 3, we can see that our proposed model outperforms other state of the art methods, both for four-class and two-class classification.

Table 1. Comparison of the 4-class classification accuracy of the proposed model with baseline models. M-VGG19 and V-VGG19 corresponds to the backbone VGG-19 nets finetuned on Macenko and Vahadane stain normalized patch datasets respectively.

Model		Accuracy (%)	
Patch wise	Image wise	Patch wise	Image wise
M-VGG19	SVM	84.50	90
V-VGG19	SVM	85.70	91.25
M-VGG19	Majority Vote	84.50	88.75
V-VGG19	Majority Vote	85.70	90
M-VGG19	BLSTM	84.50	92.50
V-VGG19	BLSTM	85.70	93.75
Proposed		87.75	97.50

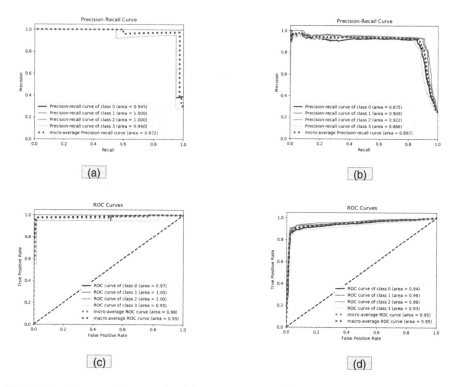

Fig. 6. Precision-recall curves for (a) image wise and (b) patch-wise classification and ROC curves for (c) image wise and (d) patch-wise classification for the four classes. 0: Benign, 1: Insitu, 2: Invasive, 3: Normal

Table 2. Image Wise and Patch Wise metrics of 4 class classification

Metric type	Metrics	Classes				Avg
		Benign	InSitu	Invasive	Normal	
Patch Wise	Precision	87.88	87.37	87.62	88.15	87.75
	Sensitivity	86	90	91	84	87.75
	Specificity	96.04	95.66	95.71	96.23	95.91
	F1 Score	86.93	88.66	89.27	86.02	87.72
Image Wise	Precision	95	100	100	95	97.5
	Sensitivity	95	100	100	95	97.5
	Specificity	98.33	100	100	98.33	99.16
	F1 Score	86.995	100	100	95	97.5

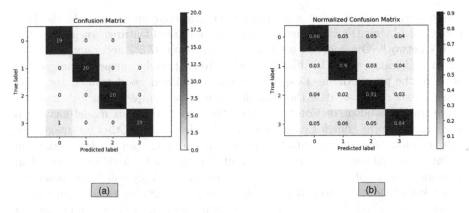

Fig. 7. Confusion Matrix for (a) image wise and (b) patch-wise classification. 0: Benign, 1: Insitu, 2: Invasive, 3: Normal

Table 3. Comparison of proposed method with some state of the art methods

Method	Dataset used	Number of classes	Patch level accuracy (%)	Image level accuracy (%)
Araujo et al. [1]	Bioimaging 2015	4	66.7	77.8
Araujo et al. [1]	Bioimaging 2015	2	77.6	83.3
Rakhlin et al. [11]	ICIAR 2018	4	-	87.5
Rakhlin et al. [11]	ICIAR 2018	2	-	93.8
Vang et al. [17]	ICIAR 2018	4	-	87.5
Golatkar et al. [5]	ICIAR 2018	4	79	85
Golatkar et al. [5]	ICIAR 2018	2	-	93
Roy et al. [12]	ICIAR 2018	4	77.4	90
Roy et al. [12]	ICIAR 2018	2	84.7	92.5
Nazeri et al. [10]	ICIAR 2018	4	-	95
Wang et al. [18]	ICIAR 2018	4	-	91
Proposed method	ICIAR 2018	4	87.75	97.50
Proposed method	ICIAR 2018	2	96	98.75

5   Conclusion

In this study, we proposed a novel architecture based on spatial fusion of features of two different stain normalisations of an input 512×512 patch. To use the long term and short term contextual information between patches for classifying the entire high resolution image, we extract a feature representation from every patch and feed it as input at every time step of a BLSTM network. We demonstrate that, incorporating features of two differently stain normalized patches, give better classification results than CNNs trained on any one of the stain normalized patches. For image level classification, using BLSTM gives better results compared to combining patch wise results with Majority Voting and SVM. In this paper, we also present a novel architectural component, namely the Feature Control Unit (FCU), which regulates the nature of features flowing into the SFFN network. Our method achieved a 87.75% and 97.5% accuracy on 4-class patch and image wise classification respectively, thereby outperforming other state of the art methods. Despite our model achieved good results, the most conspicuous caveat of it is that the design is a bit complex hence demanding more training and prediction time. The other one is that our model has a two stage architecture—one for patch wise classification and the other for image wise classification, thus the output of a high resolution image can not be obtained in a single forward pass. Although these limitations are not critical as our problem statement does not demand a real time performance, they can be overcome by designing efficient end to end model architectures, where an entire high resolution image can be fed to the network. For future work, we will work on designing these end to end models, to overcome the above caveats.

References

1. Araújo, T., et al.: Classification of breast cancer histology images using convolutional neural networks. PloS One **12**(6), e0177544 (2017)
2. Aresta, G., et al.: Bach: grand challenge on breast cancer histology images. Med. Image Anal. **56**, 122–139 (2019)
3. Deng, J., Dong, W., Socher, R., Li, L.J., Li, K., Fei-Fei, L.: ImageNet: a large-scale hierarchical image database. In: 2009 IEEE Conference on Computer Vision and Pattern Recognition, pp. 248–255. IEEE (2009)
4. Glorot, X., Bordes, A., Bengio, Y.: Deep sparse rectifier neural networks. In: Proceedings of the Fourteenth International Conference on Artificial Intelligence and Statistics, pp. 315–323 (2011)
5. Golatkar, A., Anand, D., Sethi, A.: Classification of breast cancer histology using deep learning. In: Campilho, A., Karray, F., ter Haar Romeny, B. (eds.) ICIAR 2018. LNCS, vol. 10882, pp. 837–844. Springer, Cham (2018). https://doi.org/10.1007/978-3-319-93000-8_95
6. Hochreiter, S., Schmidhuber, J.: Long short-term memory. Neural Comput. **9**(8), 1735–1780 (1997)
7. Jung, H., Lee, S., Yim, J., Park, S., Kim, J.: Joint fine-tuning in deep neural networks for facial expression recognition. In: Proceedings of the IEEE International Conference on Computer Vision, pp. 2983–2991 (2015)
8. Lin, M., Chen, Q., Yan, S.: Network in network. arXiv preprint arXiv:1312.4400 (2013)
9. Macenko, M., et al.: A method for normalizing histology slides for quantitative analysis. In: 2009 IEEE International Symposium on Biomedical Imaging: From Nano to Macro, pp. 1107–1110. IEEE (2009)
10. Nazeri, K., Aminpour, A., Ebrahimi, M.: Two-stage convolutional neural network for breast cancer histology image classification. In: Campilho, A., Karray, F., ter Haar Romeny, B. (eds.) ICIAR 2018. LNCS, vol. 10882, pp. 717–726. Springer, Cham (2018). https://doi.org/10.1007/978-3-319-93000-8_81
11. Rakhlin, A., Shvets, A., Iglovikov, V., Kalinin, A.A.: Deep convolutional neural networks for breast cancer histology image analysis. In: Campilho, A., Karray, F., ter Haar Romeny, B. (eds.) ICIAR 2018. LNCS, vol. 10882, pp. 737–744. Springer, Cham (2018). https://doi.org/10.1007/978-3-319-93000-8_83

12. Roy, K., Banik, D., Bhattacharjee, D., Nasipuri, M.: Patch-based system for classification of breast histology images using deep learning. Comput. Med. Imag. Graph. **71**, 90–103 (2019)
13. Simonyan, K., Zisserman, A.: Very deep convolutional networks for large-scale image recognition. arXiv preprint arXiv:1409.1556 (2014)
14. Spanhol, F.A., Oliveira, L.S., Petitjean, C., Heutte, L.: A dataset for breast cancer histopathological image classification. IEEE Trans. Biomed. Eng. **63**(7), 1455–1462 (2015)
15. Szegedy, C., et al.: Going deeper with convolutions. arxiv 2014. arXiv preprint arXiv:1409.4842 1409 (2014)
16. Vahadane, A., et al.: Structure-preserving color normalization and sparse stain separation for histological images. IEEE Trans. Med. Imag. **35**(8), 1962–1971 (2016)
17. Vang, Y.S., Chen, Z., Xie, X.: Deep learning framework for multi-class breast cancer histology image classification. In: Campilho, A., Karray, F., ter Haar Romeny, B. (eds.) ICIAR 2018. LNCS, vol. 10882, pp. 914–922. Springer, Cham (2018). https://doi.org/10.1007/978-3-319-93000-8_104
18. Wang, Y., Sun, L., Ma, K., Fang, J.: Breast cancer microscope image classification based on CNN with image deformation. In: Campilho, A., Karray, F., ter Haar Romeny, B. (eds.) ICIAR 2018. LNCS, vol. 10882, pp. 845–852. Springer, Cham (2018). https://doi.org/10.1007/978-3-319-93000-8_96

Predictive Modeling to Predict the Residency of Teachers Using Machine Learning for the Real-Time

Chaman Verma[1(✉)], Zoltán Illés[1], and Veronika Stoffová[2]

[1] Eötvös Loránd University, Budapest, Hungary
{chaman,illes}@inf.elte.hu
[2] Trnava University, Trnava, Slovakia
NikaStoffova@seznam.cz

Abstract. To support the identification system of demographic features of educators, residential place is an essential feature and the machine learning techniques play a vital role to predict the residential place of educators based on their responses provided. This paper shows the predictive model to predict the residency of Indian university teachers concerning Information and Communication Technology (ICT) awareness with three algorithms Support Vector Machine (SVM), Multilayer Perceptron (MLP), Random Forest (RF). There are four different experiments are conducted on the primary dataset with 344 instances and 35 features. These Machine learning (ML) algorithms used three different testing procedures like training ratio, k-fold Cross-Validation (CV) and Leave one out. A statistical t-test is also applied to compare the time of prediction by each algorithm. The consequences of the first three experiments shown that the RF algorithm outperformed others in the prediction of the residency of teachers. The findings of the fourth experiment revealed that SVM's CPU user time significantly differs from others. The authors recommended the RF model to be positioned as a real-time model cause of the highest accuracy of 72.8% with moderate prediction time 0.12 s.

Keywords: Multilayer Perceptron · Random Forest · Support Vector Machine · Real-time · Residency prediction

1 Introduction and Related Work

Educational data mining is a trending research area using ML techniques. The ML is a part of artificial intelligence and it is the scientific study of statistical models and algorithms to make an exact job without using explicit commands, depending on data patterns and implication instead. These algorithms are so popular to build predictive models for identifying educational data patterns with different prospective. Previously, the statistical analysis was not adequate in the prediction jobs to spot the data patterns [1–5]. The educator's demography feature prediction is also a novel area of research in the educational field. Recently, work has been conducted in this area and to inspect the modern technological impact on educators, there is a requirement to apply various algorithms on educational datasets.

© Springer Nature Singapore Pte Ltd. 2020
P. K. Singh et al. (Eds.): FTNCT 2019, CCIS 1206, pp. 592–601, 2020.
https://doi.org/10.1007/978-981-15-4451-4_47

Using popular ESSIE dataset, the gender of the principal [6], teacher [7] and student [8, 9] was predicted with ML techniques [10]. Other demography features of students such as national identity [11], Locality scope [12, 13], national level status [14] and locality such as rural and urban [15], age group [16]. Further, the residency features such as country were also transformed in predictive models with different algorithms [17]. Also, the level of studies such as postgraduate and graduate towards the technology was predicted [18] for the real-time system [19]. The ML algorithms played a vital role in the identification of the students' university towards ICT [20]. Instead of demography features also few student sociological characteristics like student's attitude [21], level of awareness towards the trending technology [22]. Although, the development and availability of the modern ICT resources were modeled [23]. Also, few major features are suggested to predict the residence location of educators [24].

The present paper used the RF algorithm which is an ensemble learning technique for the identification of residency of teachers and it also constructs multiple decision trees during training and resulting the residency class which means the calculation of the individual trees. Also, the SVM algorithm classifies the Punjab teachers versus Haryana teachers to discover a plane with a maximum margin which provides strengthening the confident classification of future data points. The third algorithm MLP also applied in which is fed forward neural network with three layers. The input layer has 35 features and output layers with a residency class having two values. The learning rate is set as 0.3 and no. of hidden layers are selected with the formula (attribute + classes)/2.

This paper is organized into five major sections. Section 1 describes the problem statement and the basic introduction of the presented work. Section 2 discusses the research methods applied such as dataset preprocessing, dataset training and testing, algorithms and tools, metrics, etc. Section 3 describes the experimental analysis and Sect. 4 discusses the evaluation of the predictive model. Section 5 concludes the crux of the experiments with a momentous endorsement for forthcoming work.

2 Research Methods

2.1 Preprocessing Dataset

To identify the residency of the teacher, a primary data samples has been collected by the first author during the year 2014. The mode of collection was stratified random sampling. The scale of data collection was 5-point Likert. Table 1 shows a total number of participants who taken part in this research. A total of 184 teachers from Punjab state and 160 teachers belongs to Haryana state are shown.

Table 1. Dataset instances.

	Punjab	Haryana
N	184	160
%	53.5	46.5
Total	344	

Table 2 shows the overview of the questionnaire which was separated into five parts: the first one was demographic and the other four belong to ICT parameters like Availability (10 attributes), Usability (08 attributes), Problem (03 attributes) Solution (05 attributes) and Opportunity (09 attributes). A total of 35 attributes were considered to collect the answers of teachers towards ICT awareness in two states.

Table 2. Dataset attributes.

Availability	Usability	Problem	Solution	Opportunity
10	08	03	05	09

The very few missing values were encountered and handled well using *Missing Value filter* and replaced with the mean values of the dataset. Also, to boost the prediction accuracy, normalization is performed with the help of a *Normalize* filter with a scale of 0 to 1. The residency state is the class variable that has two values: Punjab teacher and Haryana teacher and converted into numeric to nominal using with *NumericToNominal* filter.

Table 3. Universities as participants.

GKU	CDLU	GJUST	PU	SGT	CU
50	56	52	48	52	86

Table 3 displays the number of samples gathered from the Indian university in which the Government universities were the Ch. Devi Lal University (CDLU), Guru Jambheshwar University of Science & Tech. (GJUST), and, Punjabi University (PU). The private universities were the Shree Guru Gobind Singh TriCentenary University (SGT), Chandigarh University (CU), and Gurukashi University (GKU).

2.2   Training, Testing, and Validation

There are a few testing methods to test the strength of the ML algorithms. To test and train the dataset, three various approaches were also applied. In the first method, k-fold CV with the dynamic k value is applied and the value of k is considered as 5, 10, 15 and 20. The second method is training ratio with 3 different ratios are applied such as 50:50, 60:40 and 70:30. Afterward, a fully k-fold CV technique named leave one out in which each record gets out from training data to become test set (k) and used this test set with the rest of assumed as train test (k − 1). In a few cases, this method has been found so reliable and provided the highest accuracy [10]. Lastly, to discover a noteworthy variance between the accuracy and training CPU time of algorithms, the T-test at 0.05 level of confidence are applied. For this, 5-fold CV and 70:30 training ratios are selected.

2.3 Algorithms, Tool and Metrics

There are many powerful languages such as Matlab, R, and Python, etc. are trending and a tool like IBM modeler, Weka, MiniTab, etc. are also using by the researchers and data analyst. Due to the ease of the modeling of the ML algorithms, the Weka 3.9.3 tool is chosen to predict the residency of university teachers towards ICT awareness. By keeping in view the strength of SVM, MLP and RF algorithms are modeled and the accuracy with training time is also compared with the statistical T-test.

To judge the performance of each algorithm, the following measures are adopted:

1. Accuracy: It is the total number of correct predictions of residency from overall predictions.
2. Error: It is the total number of incorrect predictions of residency from overall predictions.
3. Area Under Curve (AUC): To show the degree or measure of separability across the thresholds.
4. F-score: It is harmonic mean of precision and recall which also states the significance of the predictive model is calculated by the formula

$$F = 2 * (\text{Recall} * \text{Precision})/(\text{Recall} + \text{Precision}) \tag{1}$$

5. Kappa Static: The Cohen's Kappa is statistical which determines the agreement among instances in the dataset. The formula to calculate Kappa is given below

$$\text{Kappa} = (\text{Calculated accuracy} - \text{Expected accuracy})/(1 - \text{Expected accuracy}) \tag{2}$$

3 Experimental Analysis

3.1 Prediction with K-Fold

The present experiment holds the results of each prediction algorithm using a k-fold CV method on the normalized dataset. Data from Fig. 1 reflects the feasible judgment of three classifiers compared with k-fold with dynamic k values. In k-fold cross validation k is considered as a subset to be divided according to its value. The k value is considered as test subset and k − 1 is considered as train subsets. It is found that the RF algorithm outperformed others in the prediction of teacher's residency towards ICT awareness at each fold. Also, the RF provided the highest prediction accuracy of 72.7% at 5 fold as compared to 10,15 and 20 fold. The second highest accuracy of 67.4% is also provided by the MLP algorithm at 10 and 15 folds. The least accuracy of 61.0% is scored with the SVM algorithm at 5 fold. Therefore, the k-fold testing method preserved k = 5 with the RF algorithm to provide maximum accuracy in prediction of the residency state of teachers towards ICT awareness.

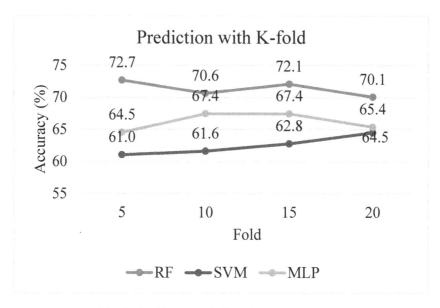

Fig. 1. Residency prediction with varying K-Fold.

3.2   Prediction with Training Ratio

The training ratio is also a reliable method to evaluate the dataset by dividing it into two subsets only whereas one is called a train set and the second is nominated as a test set to authenticate the training data. Here, the three training ratios of 50:50, 60:40 and 70:30 are applied with each algorithm. Figure 2 evident accuracy of each algorithm is directly

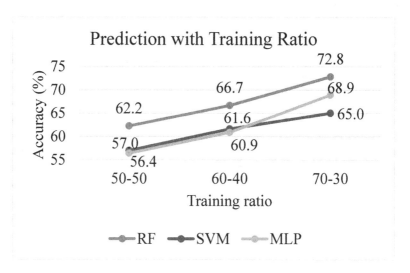

Fig. 2. Residency prediction with varying training ratio.

relative to the increase of train sets by reduction of test sets. It is clearly seen that the RF algorithm also outperformed others in peak accuracy of 72.8% at 70:30 ratios. The second maximum accuracy of 68.9% is provided by the MLP algorithm. The least accuracy of 56.4% is attained by the SVM algorithm at 50:50 ratios. Hence, it is revealed that the training ratio of 70:30 enhanced the accuracy of the RF algorithm by 0.1.

3.3 Prediction with Leave One Out

In this method, the value of k is considered as entire number of records. It is also called a fully k-fold CV method in which base dataset is divided into 344 subsets and the same rule applied as like of k-fold previously in Sect. 3.1.

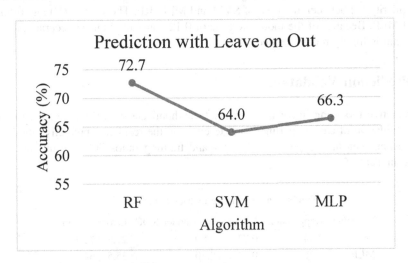

Fig. 3. Residency prediction with leave one out.

Figure 3 shows the results provided by leave one out testing on each algorithm. The uppermost accuracy of 72.7% is gained by the RF algorithm as compared to others. The MLP and SVM algorithms have an accuracy of 66.3 and 64% respectively.

3.4 Prediction in Real-Time

Every online system is affected by the specific time constraint which is called deadline. The residency of teachers can be online by developing an online website based on the client-server model. The real-time tasks are formed due to the occurrence of either internal or external events. In the nay real-time systems, the absolute deadline for task begins with time zero and the relative deadline concerning the task released time [19]. To make it online, we need to define prediction time by each algorithm. The prediction time can be CPU USER training time and CPU USER testing time. The experiment application is used to compute both times. The statistical T-test at 0.05 significant level is used to find the dissimilarity between the CPU training time of each algorithm. In the Weka experiment environment, the time measurement unit is second. The iteration control variable is set to 10 by testing the algorithm's first option.

Table 4. Real-time difference with T-test at 0.05 significant level.

Test-method	RF-time	MLP-time	SVM-time
5-fold	0.11	2.26 v	0.02*
70:30	0.12	1.90 v	0.01*

(V/ /*)

Table 4 shows that at 5-fold and training ratio 70:30, maximum prediction time is consumed by MLP and minimum prediction time is taken by the SVM algorithm. The moderate time is taken by the RF algorithm and the statistical t-test found a significant dissimilarity (*) between the time of SVM and MLP, RF. The winner (V) algorithm is found MLP. Because of the moderate time of 0.12 s and the highest accuracy, the RF algorithm is highly recommended.

4   Prediction Validation

In predictive modeling, there is necessary to authenticate the results. Hence, to carefully validation of each experiment and to evaluate the residency predictive model, 5-fold testing measures exposed in Table 4 and training ratios 70:30 results are mentioned in Table 5.

Table 5. Performance metrics at the 05-Fold.

Classifier	Kappa static	F-score	Area under ROC	Error	Accuracy
RF	0.44	0.72	0.80	27.3	72.7
MLP	0.28	0.64	0.70	35.5	64.5
SVM	0.21	0.60	0.60	38.9	61.1

Table 6. Performance metrics at the 70-30 training ratio.

Classifier	Kappa static	F-score	Area under ROC	Error	Accuracy
RF	0.44	0.73	0.80	27.2	72.8
MLP	0.36	0.72	0.80	31.1	68.9
SVM	0.28	0.65	0.64	35	65

Tables 5 and 6 displays the highest accuracy is attained by the RF algorithm as compared to others. Also, kappa static is found very good to reflect the significant bonding among instances to predict the residency of teachers. The f- score is also found more than 70% which sensing the prediction power of the RF algorithm. The maximum AUC is calculated by 0.80 with the RF at 5-fold and the same by MLP at 70:30 ratios. The highest prediction error is found by 38.9% with the SVM algorithm at 5-fold. It is also found the accuracy of the RF algorithm is increased by 0.1 with a training ratio of 70:30 as compared to cross-validation.

5 Conclusion

This paper presented a residency predictive model of Indian university teachers towards ICT awareness. During the training ratio method, the prediction accuracy is increasingly sharply. by each algorithm. On one hand, with the CV method, the RF algorithm is found top algorithm in prediction task with a maximum accuracy of 72.7% at 5-fold and another hand 70:30 ratios, the accuracy is improved with 0.1% and goes up to 72.8%. Also, a full CV method proved an optimistic approach to the RF algorithm as well. Although, it is concluded that the RF algorithm outperformed others to right identification of residency of teachers based on their answers towards ICT awareness survey. Further, the statistical T-test at 0.05 significant level also found that the SVM accuracy significantly differs from the MLP and the RF algorithms. The maximum prediction time (2.26 s) has been taken by the MLP and the least prediction time (0.01 s) is elapsed by SVM. Finally, the authors recommended the RF algorithm for the prediction of residency of teachers in real-time due to the highest accuracy with moderate CPU user training time (0.12 s). The future work is endorsed to apply more feature filter approaches to enhance the prediction accuracy and to be modeled extreme gradient boosting tree.

Acknowledgment. The Hungarian Government and European Social Funds have supported this work under the project "Talent Management in Autonomous Vehicle Control Technologies (EFOP-3.6.3-VEKOP-16-2017-00001)".

References

1. Verma, C., Dahiya, S., Mehta, D.: An analytical approach to investigate state diversity towards ICT: a study of six universities of Punjab and Haryana. Indian J. Sci. Technol. **9**, 1–5 (2016)
2. Verma, C.: Educational data mining to examine mindset of educators towards ICT knowledge. Int. J. Data Mining Emerging Technol. **7**(1), 53–60 (2017)
3. Verma, C., Dahiya, S.: Gender difference towards information and communication technology awareness in Indian universities. SpringerPlus **5**(1), 1–7 (2016). https://doi.org/10.1186/s40064-016-2003-1
4. Verma, C., Stoffová, V., Illés, Z.: Analysis of situation of integrating information and communication technology in Indian higher education. Int. J. Inf. Commun. Technol. in Edu. **7**(1), 24–29 (2018)
5. Verma, C., Stoffová, V., Illés, Z.: Perception difference of Indian students towards information and communication technology in context of university affiliation. Asian J. Contemporary Edu. **2**(1), 36–42 (2018)
6. Bathla, Y., Verma, C., Kumar, N.: Smart approach for real-time gender prediction of European school's principal using machine learning. In: Singh, P., Kar, A., Singh, Y., Kolekar, M., Tanwar, S. (eds.) Proceedings of ICRIC 2019. LNEE, vol. 597, pp. 159–175. Springer, Cham (2020). https://doi.org/10.1007/978-3-030-29407-6_14
7. Verma, C., Tarawneh, A.S., Stoffová, V., Illés, Z., Dahiya, S.: Gender prediction of the European school's teachers using machine learning: Preliminary results. In: Proceeding of 8th IEEE International Advance Computing Conference, pp. 213–220 (2018)

8. Verma, C., Stoffová, V., Illés, Z., Dahiya, S.: Binary logistic regression classifying the gender of student towards computer learning in European schools. In: The 11th conference of Ph.D. students in computer science, p. 45 (2018)

9. Verma, C., Stoffová, V., Illés, Z.: An ensemble approach to identifying the student gender towards information and communication technology awareness in European schools using machine learning. Int. J. Eng. Technol. 7(4), 3392–3396 (2018)

10. Verma, C., Illés, Z., Stoffová, V.: Gender prediction of Indian and Hungarian students towards ICT and mobile technology for the real-time. Int. J. Innovative Technol. Exploring Eng. 8(9S3), 1260–1264 (2019)

11. Verma, C., Tarawneh, A.S., Illés, Z., Stoffová, V., Singh, M.: National identity predictive models for the real time prediction of european school's students: preliminary results. In: IEEE International Conference on Automation, Computational and Technology Management, pp. 418–423 (2019)

12. Verma, C., Stoffová, V., Illés, Z.: Ensemble methods to predict the locality scope of Indian and Hungarian students for the real time. 4th International Conference on Advanced Computing and Intelligent Engineering. Advances in Intelligent Systems and Computing, pp. 1–13. Springer, In Press (2019)

13. Verma, C., Stoffová, V., Illés, Z.: Prediction of locality status of the student based on gender and country towards ICT and Mobile Technology for the real time. In: XXXII International Scientific Conference, DIDMATTECH 2019, pp. 1–10 (2019, in press)

14. Verma, C., Illés, Z., Stoffová, V.: Real-Time Classification of National and International students for ICT and Mobile Technology: An experimental study on Indian and Hungarian University. In: The First International Conference on Emerging Electrical Energy, Electronics and Computing Technologies, pp. 1–8, Journal of Physics, IOP Science, UK. In Press (2019)

15. Verma, C., Stoffová, V., Illés, Z.: Real-time prediction of student's locality towards information communication and mobile technology: preliminary results. Int. J. Recent Technol. Eng. 8(1), 580–585 (2018)

16. Verma, C., Stoffová, V., Illés, Z.: Age group predictive models for the real time prediction of the university students using machine learning: Preliminary results. In: 2019 IEEE Third International Conference on Electrical, Computer and Communication, pp. 1–7 (2019)

17. Verma, C., Stoffová, V., Illés, Z.: Prediction of residence country of student towards information, communication and mobile technology for real-time: preliminary results. In: International Conference on Computational Intelligence and Data Science, pp. 1–12 (2019, in press). Procedia Computer Science. Elsevier

18. Verma, C., Illés, Z., Stoffová, V.: Study level prediction of Indian and Hungarian students towards ICT and Mobile Technology for the real-time. In: IEEE International Conference on Computation, Automation and Knowledge Management, UAE, pp. 1–6 (2019)

19. Verma, C., Stoffová, V., Illés, Z.: Rate-monotonic vs early deadline first scheduling: a review. In: Proceeding of Education Technology-Computer science in building better future, pp. 188–193 (2018)

20. Verma, C., Illés, Z., Stoffová, V., Singh, M.: ICT and Mobile Technology features predicting the university of Indian and Hungarian student for the real-time. In: IEEE System Modeling & Advancement in Research Trends, pp. 1–7 (2019, in press)

21. Verma, C., Illés, Z.: Attitude prediction towards ICT and mobile technology for the real-time: an experimental study using machine learning. In: The 15th International Scientific Conference eLearning and Software for Education, Romania, pp. 247–254 (2019)

22. Verma, C., Stoffová, V., Illés, Z.: Prediction of students' awareness level towards ICT and mobile technology in Indian and Hungarian University for the real-time: preliminary results. Heliyon 5(6), 1–7 (2019)

23. Verma, C., Illés, Z., Stoffová, V.: Real-Time prediction of development and availability of ICT and mobile technology in Indian and Hungarian university. In: Singh, P., Kar, A., Singh, Y., Kolekar, M., Tanwar, S. (eds.) Proceedings of ICRIC 2019. LNEE, vol. 597, pp. 605–615. Springer, Cham (2020). https://doi.org/10.1007/978-3-030-29407-6_43
24. Verma, C., Stoffová, V., Illés, Z.: Feature selection to identify the residence state of teachers for the real-time. In: IEEE International Conference on Intelligent Engineering and Management, London, pp. 1–6 (2019)

Communication Technologies, Security and Privacy

Sybil Account Detection in Online Social Networks Using Statistical Feature Selection Techniques

Amit Chauhan[(⊠)] and Manu Sood

Himachal Pradesh University, Shimla, India
chauhanamit37@gmail.com, soodm_67@yahoo.com

Abstract. Online Social Networks (OSNs) are fast becoming an essential media for social interactions among its users. With the rapid growth of these OSNs, the malicious and illegal activities are also on the rise posing potential threats such as disruption of communication, influencing decision making process of the gullible users, unauthorized control of resources etc. Sybil accounts pose such kind of potential threats in the OSNs in addition to wireless ad-hoc networks. Twitter is an OSN which we have used in this research work to identify such Sybil accounts with the help of Machine Learning (ML). ML helps in building models which are capable of learning from the existing datasets so as to be able to then apply it to solve Real-time or futuristic problems. The supervised ML techniques train the model with the labelled data which can be used to predict the discrete values based on its learning. In this paper, a classification model is trained using two classifiers namely, Random Forest (RF) and Support Vector Machine (SVM). To make the classification model more effective, Univariate and Correlation Matrix with Heatmap, these two Feature Selection (FS) techniques have also been used. The ML model then used the selected features to identify Sybil accounts. This study also explores the effect of biasing of data of real accounts with that of illegitimate Sybil accounts during the process of classification and Feature Selection. The results of this study show that the RF outperforms SVM by shade as far as the accuracy of prediction models is concerned under the given experimental setup.

Keywords: Online Social Networks · Feature selection · Univariate feature selection method · Correlation with heatmap feature selection method · Support Vector Machine classifier · Random Forest classifier

1 Introduction

With the speedy proliferation in Online Social Network (OSNs) such as Twitter and Facebook, the data is growing at a rapid rate across the length and breadth of this globe. The number of users actively getting associated with these OSNs is growing by leaps and bounds. According to the statistics shown in [1], (a) the average of google monthly searches on the Internet is more than 100 billion, (b) more than 50 billion web pages are indexed on Google, (c) the number of users of YouTube has already crossed the 1 billion mark, and (d) amongst one third of total users of the Internet, each one of them

© Springer Nature Singapore Pte Ltd. 2020
P. K. Singh et al. (Eds.): FTNCT 2019, CCIS 1206, pp. 605–618, 2020.
https://doi.org/10.1007/978-981-15-4451-4_48

uploads 100 h of video every minute. The data is so produced and stored across the cloud servers has plenty of information, knowledge and/or intelligence embedded into it. Special techniques along with supporting tools are being proposed to dig these out so as to use these outputs for the overall betterment of society at large.

Machine Learning (ML) has come out as one of the most significant contributors to this purpose. It can be described as the competency of the software to perform a single or series of tasks intelligently without being programmed for those activities. Normally, a software behaves in the way the programmer programs it, but the ML facilitates the software of being capable of accomplishing intended tasks by using statistical analysis and predictive analytics techniques. This apparent learning of the machines has been divided into four categories: supervised learning, unsupervised learning, semi-supervised learning and reinforcement learning. Supervised learning consists of classification and regression. Unsupervised learning is self-learning process where a model tries to find the hidden structures between data. The semi-supervised learning techniques use a combination of both supervised learning and unsupervised learning techniques. Reinforcement learning trains the model based on responses from the surrounding environment. We have used two separate classification techniques in this paper for the detection of Sybil accounts on social media.

Nowadays, it is very common to either buy Facebook likes, YouTube comments, views or to create these using fakery in order to influence various processes on the OSNs. The Sybil attack takes place in an OSN when one creates multiple fake or forged accounts of users. In this type of an attack, a malicious user or users can create multiple fake accounts intentionally circumventing their easy detection by the social media providers [2]. There are several studies available in the literature on the development of defence mechanisms against the Sybil attack [3–6]. These methods are categorized into these three categories: Prevention mechanism, graph-based and machine learning techniques. In this paper, we have used machine learning techniques for the detection of the Sybil accounts in the Twitter database.

One of the most popular OSNs, Twitter was started as a micro-blogging social website combination of blogging and instant messaging. It can be used as broadcast and receiver. Twitter message handling is done by the software written in programming language SCALA. But with the growth in the users now it became a kind of information publishing website. In the beginning, the tweets were text only. Now tweets can include pictures as well as six seconds of the video clips. Tweets were originally restricted to 140 characters but know it has been doubled to 280 characters except for three languages: Chinese, Japanese and Korean.

Rapid increment in the number of users results in the increase of a number of Sybil accounts in OSNs. Online social networks (OSNs) are designed to offer a platform for users to connect with other users, family members, and friends [1]. OSNs allow the users to share videos, photos and other personal information with friends and worldwide.

In this paper, a classification model is developed to identify the Twitter accounts whether they are a genuine or fake account. If a genuine user can check in advance whether an account is real or fake it can help in avoiding the unwanted, harmful and spam [7] contents. The fake account also acts as a genuine account. The main purpose of this research is to detect the fake account of twitter using machine learning techniques. In this study, the machine learning classification techniques are used to detect fake twitter accounts with the use of some significant features. Here we have used the Support Vector Machine (SVM) and Random Forest (RF) classification techniques.

Objectives. The main objectives of this research work are as follows:

1. To analyze the importance of feature selection process.
2. To select the rightest features by using statistical techniques i.e. Correlation Matrix with Heatmap and Univariate Feature Selection.
3. To analyze the effect of biasing of fake accounts with human accounts on feature selection.
4. To analyze the results of classification with the selected features on a predictive model using Support Vector Machine (SVM) and Random Forest (RF). The biasing on classification is also analysed.

Paper Structure. This paper is partitioned into five sections. Section 2 explains a brief description of the dataset used for this study. Section 3 explains the methodology used to carry out in this research work. Section 4 provides the results of the experiments of the work done in this research paper. The conclusion of this study is given in Sect. 5 and suggest the way in which this study can be useful for future work.

2 Dataset

In this section, the description of the datasets is provided which are used to carry out this research work. Table 1 describes the details of the datasets used in our study. Study-related to these datasets done by the authors of [8] and we have used the same set of datasets. The requisite permission to use these datasets for this research work has been obtained from the authors and we thankfully acknowledge it. The primary dataset consisted of the total of five datasets which includes two humans (numbered as 1 & 2) and 3 fake account datasets (numbered as 1, 2 & 3). The dataset we have used in our study has five different datasets two are genuine account details and rest three are fake account details. Genuine account datasets are collected by Twitter and fake account details are purchased from twitter online market [8]. The total number of accounts in each dataset are described in Table 1. Number of features in each of these dataset files was 34. But there were some missing and redundant values in some features. To deal with these, we have used pre-processing techniques as explained in a subsequent subsection. The resulting feature set after pre-processing of datasets contained 28 features. NaN (Not a number) values are filled with 0.

Table 1. Details of primary datasets.

Type	S. no	Dataset	Number of accounts
Real	1	E13 (Elezioni 2013)	1481
	2	TFP (The Fake Project)	469
Fake	1	FSF (Fast Followerz)	1169
	2	INT (Inter Twitter)	1337
	3	TWT (Twitter Technology)	845

3 Experimental Setup

Datasets we have used in our study for the purpose of experimentation are described in Table 2 with the total number of accounts each of these contain along with their respective names. E13 and TFP are the datasets which contain genuine accounts having human account details and rest INT, TWT & FSF are fake user accounts. As shown in the table, six combinations of datasets shown below (C-11, C-12, C-13, C-21, C-22 & C-23) were generated by merging each of the real datasets with one of the fake datasets and then applying to sort on each of these aggregated datasets.

Table 2. Description of datasets used during experiments.

S. no	Dataset	Case	Number of accounts
1	E13 - FSF	C-11	1481 + 1169 = 2650
2	E13 - INT	C-12	1481 + 1337 = 2818
3	E13 - TWT	C-13	1481 + 845 = 2326
4	TFP - FSF	C-21	469 + 1169 = 1638
5	TFP - INT	C-22	469 + 1337 = 1806
6	TFP - TWT	C-23	469 + 845 = 1314

Further, in order to realize the effect of biasing on the data, the fake datasets were merged with the real datasets in the ratios of 100:25, 100:50, 100:75 and 100:100 so as to create cases $C-11_{25}$, $C-11_{50}$, $C-11_{75}$, $C-11_{100}$, $C-12_{25}$, $C-12_{50}$ and so on up to $C-23_{100}$ as shown in Tables 6, 7 and 8 later. For the sake of clarity, we can say that $C-11_{25}$ contains a sorted set of the merger of 25% records of the fake dataset FSF with all the records of datasets E13.

3.1 Data Pre-processing

Data pre-processing involves the techniques used to clean and transform the target datasets. It also includes the process of scaling of data. Data scaling is also known as normalization [9]. Data scaling usually includes the standardization of feature ranges available in the dataset. When the NaN (Not-a-Number), inconsistent values, missing values, infinity values are dealt with appropriately, it is known as data cleaning [9].

The datasets used in this study contained many missing values which represented the absence of the specific values of data. So these missing data values are filled with zero (0). There were few more cases where whole feature values were missing and features with redundant data values were also available. To solve this problem, the respective features were dropped from all the datasets. After the data pre-processing was over, we were left with a set of 28 features from the original set of 34 features.

3.2   Feature Selection

In this section, the following research question is answered.

RQ1. *What is feature selection role and its significance in the accuracy of the prediction model used?*

With the growth of hugely high data, feature selection algorithms have become all important components of the learning process [10]. The main reason for the big size of datasets is a number of features. The general thinking is that more no. of the features better the performance of the predictive model will be. But there are irrelevant, noisy, and redundant features involved in the feature set [10]. The resulting effect of these features is that they decrease the efficiency of the model. Common troubles caused by these features are: they generally contain the noisy data which causes the ML model to perform poorly; more features increase the training time of the model.

Feature selection technique removes the noisy and redundant features. It also selects the significant features which contribute most to the prediction of target variable [11]. The algorithms of feature selection based on the relation with the classifiers can be divided into three different classes: filters, wrappers and embedded. The data cleaning process requires a huge amount of human efforts, which is time-consuming and expensive [11]. While the prediction model deals with datasets containing redundant and irrelevant features result in the slow training and testing process with higher resource usage as well as very poor detection rate [12].

In general, there are two reasons why the feature selection technique is necessary:

1. To understand better use of features and their respective relationship to the response variables.
2. Feature selection is used to reduce the number of features. Feature selection is also used to reduce overfitting and also enhance the generalization of models.

Correlation Matrix with Heatmap. It is a feature selection technique of machine learning. This technique is a graphical representation of data. Here, the single values contained in a matrix and are represented as different colours. It gives the visualization of the 2D in a data matrix. Large values are represented in a small dark grey or the black pixels and smaller values represented by the lighter squares [13, 14].

The correlation matrix with heatmap is a statistical term where common usage tends to how close the two variables are to having a linear relationship with each other. The feature selection using a correlation matrix with heatmap is done on the dataset with four different cases. Each case includes a distinct number of fake accounts samples. As follows in Table 3.

Table 3. Feature selection: correlation matrix with heatmap.

S. no	Features	Correlation with %age bias			
		25%	50%	75%	100%
1	time_zone	0.61	0.71	0.75	0.78
2	profile_banner_url	0.53	0.63	0.68	0.7
3	geo_enabled	0.43	0.52	0.57	0.6
4	url	0.31	0.38	0.42	0.45
5	profile_background_tile	0.3	0.38	0.42	0.45
6	Description	0.29	0.3	0.29	0.28
7	statuses_count	0.23	0.29	0.33	0.35
8	friends_count	0.14	0.18	0.21	0.22
9	favourites_count	0.11	0.14	0.16	0.18
10	listed_count	0.074	0.096	0.11	0.12
11	followers_count	0.026	0.033	0.037	0.04
12	default_profile_image	0.013	0.017	0.02	0.021
13	name	0	0	0	0
14	screen_name	0	0	0	0
15	created_at	0	0	0	0

Univariate. This is a feature selection technique in machine learning which uses the machine Statistical tests. These tests are used to select those features that have the strongest relationship with the output variable. Univariate FS selects each feature individually to check the strength of the relationship of the features with the response variable [13, 14]. These methods are much simpler to run and understand and particularly good for gaining a better understanding of data. The features selected with the help of univariate FS technique are shown below in Table 4.

Table 4. Feature selection: Univariate selection.

S. no	Features	Scores with bias (In %age)			
		25%	50%	75%	100%
1	Id	352587000000	470292800000	530196000000	565552900000
2	statuses_count	872018	1740955	2607455	3468007
3	followers_count	190967	380400	568729	754794
4	favourites_count	98261	196493	294714	392577
5	friends_count	23941	42234	57508	70182
6	listed_count	1685	3370	5055	6734
7	default_profile	312	416	620	825
8	time_zone	207	413	548	729
9	profile_banner_url	183	365	467	581
10	geo_enabled	146	291	437	498
11	url	93	187	280	373
12	profile_background_tile	91	183	274	365
13	Location	19	31	40	45
14	Description	5	10	13	15
15	profile_sidebar_border_color	2	3	4	5

Tables 3 and 4 show the features selected by using both the FS techniques. These both FS techniques show score values for features by using mathematical functions. After analysing the score values we selected the top 11 features from both techniques since the later values were too small.

Table 5. Common features.

Common features
time_zone
profile_banner_url
geo_enabled
url
profile_background_tile
Description
statuses_count
friends_count
favourites_count
listed_count
followers_count

In this study, the features selection is done with the help of Correlation matrix with Heatmap and Univariate FS techniques. The above Table 5 shows the features taken in our study these features are the common features of univariate and correlation matrix with heatmap.

To analyse the significance of FS we have first checked the accuracy of the linear regression model on 28 features and then on selected 11 features. The accuracy of the model before the process of FS was 0.498 and for selected features 0.954. these results show the importance of feature selection.

While selecting the feature we have 3 main feature selection techniques univariate, correlation matrix with heatmap and feature importance from which we have selected two feature selection univariate and correlation matrix with heatmap. The reason behind selecting these two because univariate FS checks each feature one by one to discover the strength of their relationship, correlation matrix heat map creates a table-like structure with interlinked features to each other with the help of different shades of colour.

3.3 Models

Here, Random Forest and Support Vector Machine (SVM) are ML algorithms used for the training and testing of the classification models in our study. The ratio of testing and training was (70%–30%) is used respectively. Random Forest and support vector machine both are machine learning supervised learning classifier used in classification.

Random Forest is a method of ensemble learning by constructing a multitude of decision trees at the time of training [15]. An SVM model is a set of training examples each resembles one of the two classes. SVM training algorithm creates a model that denotes to one category or other [16].

3.4   Prediction and Evaluation Criteria

3.4.1   Confusion Metrics

While considering the two classes fake and human, the experiment was conducted for each case mentioned above [8]. To evaluate the final outcomes of these experiments some metrics were considered based on standard indicators, namely [8]:

(a)   **True Positive (TP).** A number of fake followers identified as a fake account.
(b)   **True Negative (TN).** A number of human followers identified as human account.
(c)   **False Positive (FP).** A number of human followers identified as a fake account.
(d)   **False Negative (FN).** A number of fake followers identified as a human account.

3.4.2   Evaluation Metrics

To evaluate the final results, we considered the five standard evaluation metrics. These metrics are:

(a)   *Accuracy.* The ratio of predicted true results in the population is $\frac{TP+TN}{TP+TN+FP+FN}$
(b)   *Precision.* The ratio of identified positive cases which were indeed positive is $\frac{TP}{TP+FP}$
(c)   *Recall.* The ratio of real positive cases that are indeed identified positive, is $\frac{TP}{TP+FN}$
(d)   *F-Measure.* It is harmonic mean of recall and precision, is $\frac{2 \cdot precision \cdot recall}{precision + recall}$
(e)   *Matthew Correlation Coefficient (MCC).* Estimates the correlation between the identified class and the real class of samples, given as $\frac{TP \cdot TN - FP \cdot FN}{\sqrt{(TP+FN)(TP+FP)(TN+FP)(TN+FN)}}$

4   Results and Analysis

These cases refer to check the possible effects of biasing in the FS process. This process of biasing is done with 100% of human dataset and then merged one by one 25%, 50%, 75% and 100% respectively of fake human datasets. The process of biasing is done with the number of fake accounts in the dataset and keeping the number of human accounts remain the same for all cases. The biasing is done in four different sets like C-$1X_{25}$, C-$1X_{50}$, C-$1X_{75}$ and C-$1X_{100}$. We have five datasets 2 human and 3 fake. The first human dataset is merged with three fake account dataset and the second human with the dataset is with the same three fake account datasets. After this, now we have a total of 6 datasets ready. Now we had applied biasing on it (25%, 50%, 75% and 100%) as shown in Table 6.

Table 6. Cases details.

Case	Biasing (%age) with fake accounts	Fake	Human	Total samples
C-11$_{25}$	25	275	1100	1375
C-11$_{50}$	50	550	1100	1650
C-11$_{75}$	75	825	1100	1925
C-11$_{100}$	100	1099	1100	2199
C-12$_{25}$	25	334	1100	1434
C-12$_{50}$	50	668	1100	1768
C-12$_{75}$	75	1002	1100	2102
C-12$_{100}$	100	1337	1100	2437
C-13$_{25}$	25	211	1100	1311
C-13$_{50}$	50	422	1100	1522
C-13$_{75}$	75	633	1100	1733
C-13$_{100}$	100	845	1100	1945
C-21$_{25}$	25	275	469	744
C-21$_{50}$	50	550	469	1019
C-21$_{75}$	75	825	469	1294
C-21$_{100}$	100	1099	469	1568
C-22$_{25}$	25	334	469	803
C-22$_{50}$	50	668	469	1137
C-22$_{75}$	75	1002	469	1471
C-22$_{100}$	100	1337	469	1806
C-23$_{25}$	25	211	469	680
C-23$_{50}$	50	422	469	891
C-23$_{75}$	75	633	469	1102
C-23$_{100}$	100	845	469	1314

Cases of biasing the human accounts with fake accounts in the datasets with respect to 25%, 50%, 75% and 100% respectively were created e.g. for C-11$_{25}$, 100% of the human account details were merged with 25% of fake user account details with a common set of selected features as shown in the first row of Table 6. Similarly, further 23 cases were also created.

RQ 2. *Does the biasing with Sybil accounts of the real datasets affect the classification process?*

We tested the model with the help of ML classifiers i.e. Random Forest and SVM algorithms. The model was tested on total 6 datasets of with 24 subsets. The subsets were created to test the biasing effect of fake accounts on the performance of the ML model. The results of the tests are given in Tables 7 and 8. It includes the values of evaluation metrics for all cases of biasing. Each model is run for all cases of biasing and results were collected.

Table 7 represents results of Random Forest classifier. In the dataset 1 the best accuracy is in 25% biasing (C-11$_{25}$), in dataset 2 the best accuracy is in 50% biasing

(C-12$_{50}$), in dataset 3 the best accuracy is in 25% biasing (C-13$_{25}$), in dataset 4 the best accuracy is in 50% biasing (C-21$_{50}$), in dataset 5 the best accuracy is in 75% biasing (C-22$_{75}$) and in dataset 6 the best accuracy is in 100% biasing (C-23$_{100}$).

Table 7. Results of Random Forest for 24 cases of datasets.

Datasets	Cases	Random Forest technique				
		Accuracy	Precision	Recall	F Measure	MCC
Dataset 1	C-11$_{25}$	**0.99779736**	0.98850575	1	0.99421965	0.99288448
	C-11$_{50}$	0.9959596	0.98809524	1	0.99401198	0.991003824
	C-11$_{75}$	0.99653979	0.99152542	1	0.99574468	0.992854844
	C-11$_{100}$	0.99393939	0.9884058	1	0.9941691	0.987933193
Dataset 2	C-12$_{25}$	0.9942029	0.97959184	1	0.989690722	0.98576
	C-12$_{50}$	0.99689922	0.99009901	1	0.995024876	0.992799
	C-12$_{75}$	**0.99871134**	1	0.99695122	0.998473282	0.997362
	C-12$_{100}$	0.9929078	1	0.98561151	0.992753623	0.985909
Dataset 3	C-13$_{25}$	0.9980315	0.98550725	1	0.99270073	0.991598435
	C-13$_{50}$	**0.99825175**	0.9921875	1	0.99607843	0.994966263
	C-13$_{75}$	0.99370079	0.99438202	0.98333333	0.98882682	0.984470832
	C-13$_{100}$	0.96561605	0.95652174	0.94901961	0.95275591	0.925747268
Dataset 4	C-21$_{25}$	0.98689956	0.98823529	0.97674419	0.98245614	0.972046
	C-21$_{50}$	0.99683544	1	0.99465241	0.997319035	0.993479
	C-21$_{75}$	0.99752475	0.99606299	1	0.998027613	0.994719
	C-21$_{100}$	**0.99796748**	0.99706745	1	0.998531571	0.995243
Dataset 5	C-22$_{25}$	0.98340249	1	0.96039604	0.97979798	0.966291039
	C-22$_{50}$	**0.99415205**	1	0.99047619	0.99521531	0.987771716
	C-22$_{75}$	0.98868778	0.996633	0.98666667	0.99162479	0.974321247
	C-22$_{100}$	0.98708487	0.98979592	0.99232737	0.99106003	0.967814585
Dataset 6	C-23$_{25}$	**0.9902439**	0.96923077	1	0.984375	0.977537535
	C-23$_{50}$	0.98880597	0.99166667	0.98347107	0.98755187	0.977410471
	C-23$_{75}$	0.97289157	0.98387097	0.96825397	0.976	0.945022334
	C-23$_{100}$	0.9443038	0.95951417	0.95180723	0.95564516	0.880870203

Table 8 represents the results of Support vector machine classifier. In the dataset 1 the best accuracy is in 100% biasing (C-11$_{100}$), in dataset 2 the best accuracy is in 50% biasing (C-12$_{50}$), in dataset 3 the best accuracy is in 50% biasing (C-13$_{50}$), in dataset 4 the best accuracy is in 25% biasing (C-21$_{25}$), in dataset 5 the best accuracy is in 25% biasing (C-22$_{25}$) and in dataset 6 the best accuracy is in both 75% and 100% biasing (C-23$_{100}$).

Table 8. Results of SVM for 24 cases of datasets.

Datasets	Cases	SVM technique				
		Accuracy	Precision	Recall	F Measure	MCC
Dataset 1	$C-11_{25}$	0.990315	0.9625	0.987179	0.974684	0.968815
	$C-11_{50}$	**0.99798**	0.993976	1	0.996979	0.995472
	$C-11_{75}$	0.99654	0.991701	1	0.995833	0.9929
	$C-11_{100}$	0.99697	0.994118	1	0.99705	0.993953
Dataset 2	$C-12_{25}$	0.992661	0.990476	0.971963	0.981132	0.976644
	$C-12_{50}$	**0.995349**	0.985366	1	0.992629	0.989289
	$C-12_{75}$	0.990979	0.982456	0.997033	0.989691	0.981757
	$C-12_{100}$	0.99409	0.989848	0.997442	0.993631	0.988143
Dataset 3	$C-13_{25}$	0.998031	1	0.984375	0.992126	0.991041
	$C-13_{50}$	**0.998252**	0.992188	1	0.996078	0.994966
	$C-13_{75}$	0.995276	1	0.983333	0.991597	0.988379
	$C-13_{100}$	0.968481	0.964143	0.94902	0.956522	0.931877
Dataset 4	$C-21_{25}$	0.9869	0.974684	0.987179	0.980892	0.970971
	$C-21_{50}$	0.993691	0.99422	0.99422	0.99422	0.987275
	$C-21_{75}$	**0.997967**	0.997167	1	0.998582	0.99501
	$C-21_{100}$	**0.997967**	1	0.997167	0.998582	0.99501
Dataset 5	$C-22_{25}$	**0.995851**	1	0.99	0.994975	0.991478
	$C-22_{50}$	0.98827	0.985915	0.995261	0.990566	0.975139
	$C-22_{75}$	0.988688	0.983607	1	0.991736	0.974152
	$C-22_{100}$	0.987085	0.98263	1	0.991239	0.967222
Dataset 6	$C-23_{25}$	**0.990244**	0.964912	1	0.982143	0.975729
	$C-23_{50}$	0.988806	0.983607	0.991736	0.987654	0.977443
	$C-23_{75}$	0.978852	0.994382	0.967213	0.980609	0.957808
	$C-23_{100}$	0.954315	0.97479	0.95082	0.962656	0.90432

From the results of Table 7 and Table 8, we can easily compare the performance of both the Machine Learning Classifiers. As can be judged from these tables, the results of Random Forest classifier are a shade better than those of SVM classifier as far as the accuracy of prediction of Sybil accounts is concerned. On perusal of the results in Tables 7 and 8, it can be concluded that the biasing of the datasets in these classifiers does not produce any significant conclusion. The authors are in the process of dealing with the issue of biasing separately to arrive at some definite conclusive analysis in future. While performing the experiments using Jupyter which is an open-source web-based application, we have found that the time taken by SVM classifier for the training of the model is higher than that of the Random Forest.

AUC – ROC is termed as Area Under Curve – Receiver Operating Characteristics as it is used to visualize and compare the performance of classification models. Higher the value of AUC i.e. closer to the '1', better the model is at predicting 0's as 0's and 1's as 1's. On the y-axis, it depicts the value of TPR (True Positive Rate) and on the x-axis, it depicts the value of FPR (False Positive Rate). To calculate the TPR and FPR, the formulas given below were used:

(1) $FPR = FP/(TN + FP)$

(2) $TPR = TP/(TP + FN)$

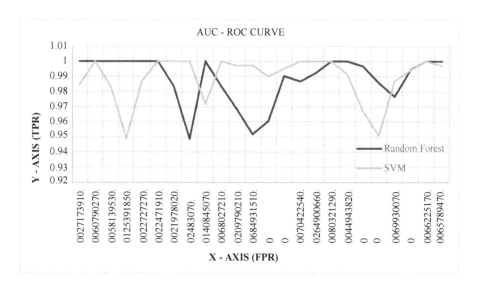

Fig. 1. AUC-ROC curve for Random Forest and SVM

Figure 1 also highlights the comparison of the performance of two Machine Learning classifiers which are Random Forest and SVM classifiers. It compares the results of both the classifiers. The orange line shows the SVM statistics and the blue line shows the Random Forest statistics. In reference to this AUC-ROC, RF technique has produced better results in our experiments as shown in this figure.

5   Conclusion and Future Work

In this paper, we have highlighted the significance of pre-processing and feature selection techniques on the datasets and the prediction models. Data pre-processing helps in taking care of the redundant and null values from the data. Feature selection techniques help in increasing the performance of a prediction model by eliminating the unnecessary or insignificant features from the datasets. The five datasets (two human and three fake) used in this paper have been taken from the authors of another research paper after the due permission for their use was granted by them. Two classifiers namely RF and SVM have been used for the building of the prediction models. Through rigorous experimentation, we have found that the accuracy of prediction/identification of Sybil accounts in an OSN (Twitter in our case) in case of Random Forest classifier is almost similar to that of SVM classifier. But the time taken for the classification by the SVM classifier has been found to be on the higher side. Hence, it can be concluded that RF classifier is more efficient in this case.

We also conducted experimentation on the same datasets to analyse the effect of biasing but achieved results with varying degrees of accuracy and precision, hence no concrete conclusion could be drawn from these results. The authors intend to use the set of features selected in this paper along with same classifiers for the training of a model which will run on the real-time datasets so as to predict the presence of Sybil accounts in real-time. In order to further analyse the effect of biasing on the datasets, the authors are currently working in three different directions using the biasing process proposed in this paper: (a) fine-tuning the FS process for any possible modifications in the set of features selected, (b) using different classifiers on same datasets with same FS techniques, and (c) using different datasets with different suitable combination of Feature Selection techniques and classifiers.

References

1. Al-Qurishi, M., Al-Rakhami, M., Alamri, A., Alrubaian, M., Rahman, S.M.M., Hossain, M. S.: Sybil defense techniques in online social networks: a survey. IEEE Access **5**, 1200–1219 (2017). https://doi.org/10.1109/ACCESS.2017.2656635
2. Al-Qurishi, M., Alrubaian, M., Rahman, S.M.M., Alamri, A., Hassan, M.M.: A prediction system of Sybil attack in social network using deep-regression model. Fut. Gener. Comput. Syst. **87**, 743–753 (2018). https://doi.org/10.1016/j.future.2017.08.030
3. Vasudeva, A., Sood, M.: Survey on Sybil attack defense mechanisms in wireless ad hoc networks. J. Netw. Comput. Appl. **120**, 78–118 (2018)
4. Vasudeva, A., Sood, M.: A vampire act of Sybil attack on the highest node degree clustering in mobile ad hoc networks. Indian J. Sci. Technol. **9** (2016)
5. Vasudeva, A., Sood, M.: Perspectives of Sybil attack in routing protocols of mobile ad hoc network. In: Computer Networks & Communications (NetCom), vol. 131, pp. 3–13. Springer, New York (2013). https://doi.org/10.1007/978-1-4614-6154-8_1
6. Vasudeva, A., Sood, M.: Sybil attack on lowest id clustering algorithm in the mobile ad hoc network. Int. J. Netw. Secur. Appl. **4**(5), 135 (2012)
7. Cresci, S., Di Pietro, R., Petrocchi, M., Spognardi, A., Tesconi, M.: The paradigm-shift of social spambots: evidence, theories, and tools for the arms race. In Proceedings of the 26th International Conference on World Wide Web Companion, pp. 963–972 (2017)
8. Cresci, S., Di Pietro, R., Petrocchi, M., Spognardi, A., Tesconi, M.: Fame for sale: efficient detection of fake Twitter followers. Decis. Support Syst. **80**, 56–71 (2015)
9. Bindra, N., Sood, M.: Detecting DDoS attacks using machine learning techniques and contemporary intrusion detection dataset. Autom. Control. Comput. Sci. **53**(5), 419–428 (2019). https://doi.org/10.3103/S0146411619050043
10. Kalousis, A., Prados, J., Hilario, M.: Stability of feature selection algorithms: a study on high-dimensional spaces. Knowl. Inf. Syst. **12**(1), 95–116 (2007)
11. Nkiama, H., Said, S.Z.M., Saidu, M.: A subset feature elimination mechanism for intrusion detection system. Int. J. Adv. Comput. Sci. Appl. **7**(4), 148–157 (2016)

12. Chen, Y., Li, Y., Cheng, X.-Q., Guo, L.: Survey and taxonomy of feature selection algorithms in intrusion detection system. In: Lipmaa, H., Yung, M., Lin, D. (eds.) Inscrypt 2006. LNCS, vol. 4318, pp. 153–167. Springer, Heidelberg (2006). https://doi.org/10.1007/11937807_13

13. Zhao, S., Guo, Y., Sheng, Q., Shyr, Y.: Advanced heat map and clustering analysis using heatmap3. BioMed Res. Int. **2014**, 1–6 (2014). https://doi.org/10.1155/2014/986048

14. Saeys, Y., Inza, I., Larrañaga, P.: A review of feature selection techniques in bioinformatics. Bioinformatics **23**(19), 2507–2517 (2007)

15. Liaw, A., Wiener, M.: Classification and regression by randomForest. R News **2**(3), 18–22 (2002)

16. Joachims, T.: Text categorization with support vector machines: learning with many relevant features. In: European conference on machine learning, pp. 137–142 (1998)

Performance Evaluation of Lung Segmentation Techniques in Computer Aided Lung Nodule Detection System

Shabana R. Ziyad[1]([⊠]), V. Radha[2], and V. Thavavel[1]

[1] CCES, Prince Sattam Bin Abdulaziz University, Al-Kharj,
Kingdom of Saudi Arabia
ziyadshabana@gmail.com, t.thangam@psau.edu.sa
[2] Avinashilingam Institute for Home Science and Higher Education for Women,
Coimbatore, India
radhasrimail@gmail.com

Abstract. Cancer related deaths are on a steady increase in India according to the latest statistics. Early diagnosis of cancer will improve the prognosis in the cancer patients. Identification of lung nodules at early stages can enhance the survival rate and prognosis of the lung cancer patients. As a boon to the radiologist the computer aided detection system and computer aided diagnosis system for malignant nodule detection have been proposed and designed by several eminent researchers. This technical support available to the radiologist has proven to improve the survival rate in lung cancer patients. However the identification of malignant lung nodules in a CT image is a challenging task for any radiologist. With the advent of computer aided diagnosis tools it has turned out to be an achievable task. The high accuracy of lung nodule delineation is highly dependent on accurate segmentation of the lung region. Lung segmentation is one of the important phases in achieving high specificity and sensitivity for a computer aided detection or computer aided diagnosis system. This paper attempts to analyze the lung segmentation techniques and compare the performance of various segmentation techniques using standard metrics of overlap rate and mean absolute distance. The experimental results depict that the Fuzzy C-means method has the highest overlap rate of 82.91% and mean absolute distance of 59.4 mm compared to the other techniques. This paper also proposes a method based on genetic algorithm to improve the lung segmentation method.

Keywords: Lung segmentation · Thresholding · Region growing · K-means · Fuzzy c means · Overlap rate · Mean absolute distance · Genetic algorithms

1 Introduction

In India the latest statistics presented by National Institute of Cancer Prevention and Research (NICPR) depicts that there are around 2.5 million people suffering from cancer and there is an increase in this rate by 7 lakhs every year. The cancer related deaths have risen to around 5,56,400 in a year. Men are especially under high risk of lung cancer due to excess tobacco usage and exposure to smoke as well as air pollution.

© Springer Nature Singapore Pte Ltd. 2020
P. K. Singh et al. (Eds.): FTNCT 2019, CCIS 1206, pp. 619–633, 2020.
https://doi.org/10.1007/978-981-15-4451-4_49

Lung cancer is the second most common type of cancer found in men [1]. Repeated screening for cancer is fruitful in early detection of lung cancer. The radiologists recognize the computer aided diagnosis (CAD) and computer aided design (CADx) systems as highly competent systems for detecting the malignant lung nodules. It assists radiologists in reducing the chances of missing the malignant lung nodules in lung CT images. The increased use of such detection tools has led to versatile research in the field of development of CAD or CADx for lung nodule detection. This inspired the authors to analyze the lung segmentation techniques in a CAD or CADx. This paper also analyses the popular lung segmentation techniques namely thresholding, Sobel operator, K-means and fuzzy c-means techniques for computed tomography (CT) lung images. The performance of these above mentioned techniques are compared using the metrics of overlap rate (OR) and mean absolute distance (MAD) of the reference lung and the segmented lung. To the best of the knowledge of the authors this paper is a unique attempt to analyze the performance of four lung segmentation techniques in terms of above said metrics. Section 2 describes the importance of lung segmentation process. Section 3 throws light on the various lung segmentation techniques for lung nodule detection. Section 4 proposes a novel algorithm for lung segmentation based on the concepts of genetic algorithm. Section 5 shows experimental results from comparison of performance of the lung segmentation techniques.

2 Lung Segmentation

Segmentation is a technique to identify objects in any image. Sharma specifies that "Segmentation is majorly used in video surveillance system, in human activity recognition, in shadow detection which includes both static and moving objects" [2]. Segmentation of lung extracts the lung region from the adjoining regions of trachea, heart and diaphragm. Segmentation of the lung is a preliminary step in the architecture of the CAD as the identification and delineation of the organ [3] under study is an important task before the identification and classification of the nodules in it. Lung segmentation refers to the identification of boundaries or margins of the lungs with lesion present within it. Some factors that affect the segmentation process are partial volume effect, presence of artifacts and closeness in gray level of different soft tissues in the lung. Different approaches adopted for lung segmentation are discussed in the next section.

3 Lung Segmentation Techniques

The lung segmentation techniques can be broadly classified as threshold based segmentation approach, edge based segmentation approach, region based approach, supervised approach, unsupervised approach, Bayesian approach and graph cut approach as shown in Fig. 1.

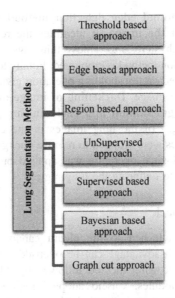

Fig. 1. Lung segmentation techniques.

3.1 Thresholding Approach

Thresholding method for CT images is one of the simplest methods that converts the image into a binary image with only pixel intensity value 0 or 255. The pixels in the image are segmented based on a threshold value. Thresholding can be classified as global thresholding methods, adaptive thresholding methods [4], connected thresholding method and optimal thresholding [5]. This study includes global thresholding method using Otsu algorithm and multithresholding algorithm for comparison. These methods are inefficient in segmenting medical images that have multimodal histograms and noise in it. The attenuation values are constant for lung and air hence this method can segment the lung with minimum pathological conditions. The thresholding methods fail when there are attenuation variations in the image [6]. In connected thresholding method the threshold value is a set of two set limit values and the pixel value beyond this range is considered as background [7]. Gulistan Raja adopted the method of optimal thresholding to segment the lung followed by rolling ball technique [8].

3.2 Edge Based Segmentation Approach

Edges depict the regions of sharp intensity changes in images. These sharp intensity changes can identify the boundaries of the objects in the image. The edges are detected by first derivative, second derivative, and Laplacian derivative filters to identify the discontinuities in images. Gradient edge based detectors such as Sobel, Prewitt employ the first derivative operation. Applying the Laplacian operator which is isotropic second order differential operator can identify the intensity variation and detect the edges

[9]. **Canny method or optimal edge detection method uses Gaussian filter to remove noise and smooth the image.** It identifies the regions image gradient to highest regions and applies hysteresis to remove thin edges. To generate a thin sharp edge non maximal suppression method is employed. Finally to preserve the edges from noise a tracking process based on thresholding operation gives the exact boundaries of the object and segments the image. **Darkening of image on one side is the disadvantage of edge based segmentation approach.** In this paper we use the **Sobel operator** to detect the edges of the lung images in the edge based segmentation approach. Initially the images were cropped to remove background followed by image binarization. Later morphological operation was applied on the images. Finally the Sobel operator was applied to delineate the lung region.

3.3   Region Based Approach

The juxta-pleural nodules attached to the pleura cannot be delineated with the thresholding method. This disadvantage can be overridden by a method which is a combination of 3D region growing method followed by dilation process applied to include the juxta-pleural nodules. Cascio adopted region growing algorithm for selection of volume of interest and morphological process includes high intensity structures like juxta-pleural nodules [10]. As the voxel intensity of the lung volume is less compared to the surrounding regions a region growing algorithm may be sufficient to segment the regions of lungs. The region based approach is efficient for identifying homogenous regions in the CT image. The method can be improved by automatic seed generation algorithm. The automatic seed generation based region growing algorithm is adopted in this paper. As the region growing method is computationally expensive the results of few images are recorded. The algorithm uses the seed point which is automatically generated as the initial pixel and considers the neighboring pixel values proximity to the initial pixel for concatenating to the growing region. The seed point in the region growing algorithm has been generated automatically by calculating the regional maxima. In gray scale images the top of spherical objects is represented by high intensity. Morphological processing can identify the regional maxima which is a region of high intensity connected pixels with low intensity of surrounding pixels. 3D region growing algorithm is used for lung segmentation in the research work of Jing [11]. Rahman in his paper performed the lung segmentation by employing a multimodal image retrieval method which involves automatic region segmentation [12].

3.4   Unsupervised Approach

When a member of a set does not crisply belong to the set and has a certain degree of membership towards the specified set the concept of fuzzy set emerges. Fuzzy C-means clustering is a method which allows the image pixels to become a member of two or more clusters based on a minimization function. Fuzzy C-means clustering is efficient for segmentation of images without noise but for segmentation of lung CT images corrupted with Gaussian noise a novel approach was introduced by Gomathi using the fuzzy possibilistic c-means algorithm [13]. A weak-supervised method based on a modified self-adaptive FCM algorithm is adopted for lung nodule segmentation [14].

Nizami has attempted to use the wavelet packet frames and K-means clustering for automatic segmentation of lung [15]. In this paper the most commonly used fuzzy-c-means algorithm is used for comparison. This approach is based on the following minimization function [16].

$$J_m = \sum_{i=1}^{n} 1 \sum_{i=1}^{n} u_{ij}^m \|x_i - c_j\|^2 \quad 1 \le m \le n \tag{1}$$

where u_{ij}^m is the membership degree of x_i in cluster j where x_i is the image pixel intensity data and c_j is the cluster center. The cluster center c_j and membership function u_{ij}^m are updated using the following objective function.

$$u_{ij} = \frac{1}{\sum_1^c \left[\frac{\|x_i - c_j\|}{\|x_i - c_k\|}\right]^{\frac{2}{m-1}}} \tag{2}$$

3.5   Supervised Approach

If there is a prior knowledge about the features of the lung and other surrounding tissues being eliminated then supervised learning algorithms are employed for segmentation of the lung images. The features of the lung are extracted from the images and then used to identify the lung boundaries. The factors like accuracy of classification, processing capabilities and powerful workstations has made the classification based algorithms quite powerful. Shiloath et al. proposed a segmentation approach which is a combination of thresholding followed by feature extraction of the lung shape. The multilayer feed forward neural network crosschecks the segmentation process [17]. Ferreira proposed a fully automatic method of lung lobe segmentation using Fuzzy regularized V-net [18]. Deep Convolutional Neural Network has been applied to segment pulmonary lobe in CT and MRI images [19]. Lung Segmentation is done using a fully convolutional neural network with weak supervision [20].

3.6   Bayesian Approach

It is inevitable step to segment the lung region from the CT image for effective delineation of the lung nodules. This hierarchical Bayesian approach employs hierarchical non parametric Dirichlet process based on a mathematical model with assumption that all the CT images share the same structure [21]. In the research article by Heewon Chung et al. a novel method to segment lung parenchyma taking into consideration the juxta-pleural nodule issue has been proposed. The author adopts the Chan-Vese model and the results of this model formed the base for the Bayesian approach [22].

3.7   Graph Cut Approach

The graph cut approach is one of the efficient segmentation techniques for images. Dai et al. developed a novel algorithm for lung segmentation with graph cut method. Every pixel in the CT image is considered as a node in the adjacency graph which has a weight corresponding to the probability that it is a set of background or foreground. Then the segmentation is done by min-cut/max-flow type of graph cut algorithm [23].

4   Proposed Algorithm

Medical image segmentation is challenging in many cases due to poor contrast of the images. Preprocessing of the medical images is an inevitable phase of every CAD and CADx. Preprocessing comprises of two stages – noise removal and contrast enhancement. Noise in images is eliminated with filters like Gaussian filter, Median filter, and Wiener filters [24]. Signals that arise in medical images are not ideally suited for analysis with traditional frequency domain, the Fourier techniques. This is because, in general, such signals are non-stationary, and therefore do not exhibit global periodic behavior. Instead, relevant signal features are localized in both space and frequency. Wavelet transform (WT) possesses such a capability, leading to efficient solution in time and space frequency analysis problems. Wavelets were first introduced to medical imaging research in 1991 describing the application of WT for noise reduction in MRI images [25]. Ever since, WT have many applications including tomographic reconstruction, image compression, noised reduction, image enhancement, texture analysis, segmentation and multi-scale registration. Two review papers in 1996 [26] and 2000 [27] provide a summary and overview of research works related to wavelets in medical image processing from the past few years. Many multiresolution features such as wavelet entropy features based on WT [28] have found widespread use. While WT are suitable for objects that could be represented as point singularities, they are not-suitable for line and surface singularities because of their lack of directionality [28]. As medical images are composed of bones, tissues, blood vessels and tumors which are curves as well, there came the idea of analyzing the curves of the images and it resulted in the discovery of a new transform named as Curvelet Transform as proposed in [29].

Challenges for lung segmentations arises in every method discussed in Sect. 3. To put in a nutshell thresholding is inefficient for noisy images, edge based has the disadvantage of darkening of images, Region growing is a computationally expensive method and supervised approach needs prior knowledge of features. Hence this paper proposes an algorithm which basically on applying DWT on images retrieves the sub bands, extracting 3D texture features vector from sub bands and finally applying the genetic algorithm will lead to clustering the feature space. Genetic algorithms are found to provide optimal solution to complex problems in medical field. Genetic algorithms find its application in edge detection, detect microcalcification and segmentation and feature selection [30]. In this paper extracting the texture feature vector of the pixels is done by multilevel local ternary patterns. The optimal cluster center is calculated using the genetic algorithm through the process of initialization, fitness evaluation, selection, crossover, mutation and replacement. The proposed algorithm overrides the disadvantages pointed out in the literature review section. The proposed algorithm is specified in the following section can be adopted for segmentation of lung in CT images for more accurate delineation of the lung region.

1. Apply DWF on image to get approximation and detail sub bands.
2. Define feature vector for each image pixel by extracting the texture feature from approximation sub band and texture feature from HL and LH sub band.
3. Initialize population size, crossover probability, mutation and termination criterion.
4. Generate a population with randomly generated cluster centers

```
While ((TWCSE))
   for i = 1 to popSize do
    for each individual
  Calculate the fitness value using
```

$$Objective\ function(\delta) = \min(TWCSE(\delta))$$

Where

$$TWCSE(\delta) = \sum_{k=1}^{K} \sum_{X_i \in C_k} \|X_i - Z_k\|^2$$

$$Z_k = \frac{\sum_{X_i \in C_k} X_i}{|C_k|}$$

Here $|C_k|$ denotes the number of pixels in C_k, $(Z_1, Z_2, ..., Z_K)$ denote the target cluster centers
   Calculate the selection probability then select parents
   E is not optimized // test for termination criterion
   Apply crossover & create offspring and Mutate offspring
   end // for loop

5. Replace the old population by the new one
6. Cluster the feature space using the GA optimized centers
7. Find the edge map for the clustered image and superimpose on the original image to determine the accuracy of the proposed system.

5   Experimental Results

This section demonstrates the performance of the five techniques namely thresholding, Sobel edge, region growing, k-means and fuzzy c-means techniques by two metrics that are commonly used to assess the performance of the lung segmentation, overlap rate and mean absolute distance. The other techniques will be compared with the proposed algorithm as future work. These metrics of OR and MAD were adopted by

Jiahui Wang in segmentation of lungs with severe interstitial lung disease [31]. A comparative analysis of lung segmentation techniques like thresholding, marker controlled watershed and edge detection is performed by Priyanshu Tripathi [32]. ur Rehman et al. in their paper performed a critical analysis of lung segmentation techniques published in reputed journals and summarized the techniques and challenges. The issue of high sensitivity with high false positive rate has been identified in these techniques [33]. The reference lung area in the lung CT image is delineated by expert pulmonologist. Twenty five samples of the lung CT images are acquired from the LIDC dataset. The metrics mean absolute distance is calculated which is the distance between the boundaries of the lung segmented image and reference image. If IR is the reference lung CT image and IS the segmented lung CT image then overlap rate OR is given by the following formula [31].

$$OR = IR \cap IS : IR \cup IS \tag{3}$$

The overlap rate is represented as percentage in the tables given below. The mean absolute distance is defined as the mean of all distance between the points on the boundary of reference lung region and segmented lung region in CT images measured in mm. The metrics of OR and MAD calculated for lung segmentation techniques of thresholding, edge detection, region growing, k-means and fuzzy c-means are tabulated in Tables 1, 2, 3, 4 and 5 respectively. The software used for this calculation is Matlab R2015a. Table 1 records the results of OR with an average of 82.88% and MAD with an average of 61.94 mm on applying the thresholding method for the lung CT images. The Table 2 records the results of OR with an average of 75.1% and MAD with an average of 46.76 mm for Sobel operator method. The Table 3 records the results of region growing technique with automatic seed generation. The Table 4 records the results of OR with an average of 81.63% and MAD with an average of 59.00 mm on applying the K-means method for the lung CT images. The Table 5 records the results of OR with an average of 82.91% and MAD with an average of 59.45 mm on applying the Fuzzy C-means method for the lung CT images. The Figs. 2, 3, 4, 5, 6, and 7 show the experimental results of applying the different lung segmentation techniques. The graph representing the comparison of four lung segmentation techniques of thresholding, edge detection, K-means and Fuzzy C-means are depicted by two graphs Figs. 6 and 7 below. In the Fig. 7 the x-axis represents the CT image sequence number and the y-axis represents the overlap rate which is depicted in percentage. In the Fig. 8 the x-axis represents the CT image sequence number and the y-axis represents the mean absolute distance (Fig. 9).

Table 1. Comparison of OR and MAD for Thresholding and K-means segmentation technique for LIDC dataset of 25 lung CT images.

Img SNo	IR ∩ IS	IR ∪ IS	OR	MAD
1	3.43	4.21	81	62.76
2	2.45	2.64	93	38.78
3	3.44	4.24	81	67.3
4	3.59	4.48	80	70.46
5	3.3	4.14	80	73.42
6	3.57	4.54	79	70.39
7	4.04	5.28	77	58.41
8	3.35	4.08	82	69.24
9	3.32	4.16	80	71.78
10	3.56	4.26	84	65.12
11	3.48	4.21	83	66.22
12	2.53	2.99	85	41.97
13	3.54	4.27	83	66.27
14	3.52	4.31	82	67.46
15	2.62	3.07	85	43.73
16	4.49	5.39	83	65.24
17	2.27	2.45	93	37.06
18	3.37	4.19	80	70.32
19	3.59	4.31	83	65.04
20	3.32	3.99	83	60.85
21	3.3	3.96	83	62.08
22	2.94	3.6	84	64.75
23	1.74	2	87	44.22
24	3.27	4.07	80	74.61
25	3.35	4.12	81	71.25
Ave	3.25	3.9	82.88	61.94

Table 2. Comparison of OR and MAD applying Sobel Edge Detection Operator for LIDC dataset of 25 lung CT images.

Img SNo	IR ∩ IS	IR ∪ IS	OR	MAD
1	3.44	4.17	82	55.94
2	2.49	2.74	91	40.6
3	3.44	4.3	80	67.62
4	3.25	3.81	85	61.29
5	3.65	4.63	79	73.39
6	3.55	4.44	80	64.45
7	3.89	5.26	74	58.48
8	3.39	4.04	84	62.54
9	3.35	4.16	81	67.23
10	3.6	4.29	83	65.9
11	4.37	5.79	75	74.41

(continued)

Table 2. (*continued*)

Img SNo	IR ∩ IS	IR ∪ IS	OR	MAD
12	2.5	3	83	39.61
13	3.59	4.27	84	65.14
14	3.54	4.38	81	67.31
15	2.65	3.1	85	38.03
16	4.57	5.39	85	65.93
17	2.32	2.53	92	41.18
18	3.4	4.15	82	68.37
19	4.03	5.12	78	35.19
20	3.32	3.99	83.2	60.85
21	3.3	3.96	83.33	62.08
22	2.94	3.6	84.05	64.75
23	1.74	2	87	44.22
24	3.27	4.07	80.34	74.61
25	3.35	4.12	81.31	71.25
Ave	2.64	3.48	75.1	46.76

Table 3. Comparison of OR and MAD for Region growing Segmentation Technique for LIDC dataset of 2 lung CT images.

Img SNo	IR ∩ IS	IR ∪ IS	OR	MAD
1	2.36	2.54	93	34.04
2	3.21	3.65	88	50.49
Ave	2.78	3.09	88	42.26

Table 4. Comparison of OR and MAD by applying K-means segmentation technique for LIDC dataset of 25 lung CT images.

Img SNo	IR ∩ IS	IR ∪ IS	OR	MAD
1	3.44	4.17	82	55.94
2	2.49	2.74	91	40.6
3	3.44	4.3	80	67.62
4	3.25	3.81	85	61.29
5	3.65	4.63	79	73.39
6	3.55	4.44	80	64.45
7	3.89	5.26	74	58.48
8	3.39	4.04	84	62.54
9	3.35	4.16	81	67.23
10	3.6	4.29	83	65.9
11	4.37	5.79	75	74.41
12	2.5	3	83	39.61
13	3.59	4.27	84	65.14
14	3.54	4.38	81	67.31
15	2.65	3.1	85	38.03

(*continued*)

Table 4. (*continued*)

Img SNo	IR ∩ IS	IR ∪ IS	OR	MAD
16	4.57	5.39	85	65.93
17	2.32	2.53	92	41.18
18	3.4	4.15	82	68.37
19	4.03	5.12	78	35.19
20	3.32	3.99	83	60.85
21	3.35	4.03	83	56.98
22	3.32	3.95	84	59.5
23	2.98	3.67	81	65.18
24	1.76	2.11	83	43.17
25	3.28	4.03	81	71.38
Ave	3.33	4.12	81.63	59.00

Table 5. Comparison of OR and MAD Fuzzy C-means Segmentation Technique for LIDC dataset of 25 lung CT images.

Img SNo	IR ∩ IS	IR ∪ IS	OR	MAD
1	3.43	4.13	83	56.33
2	2.49	2.72	92	39.23
3	3.41	4.24	80	64.86
4	3.23	3.76	86	59.38
5	3.6	4.25	85	66.06
6	3.51	4.38	80	61.25
7	3.56	4.32	82	52.49
8	4.87	6.33	77	68.62
9	3.34	4.09	82	65.28
10	4.97	6.54	76	73
11	4.9	6.57	75	74.32
12	2.56	3.05	84	39.02
13	3.57	4.2	85	62.98
14	3.49	4.26	82	68.49
15	2.67	3.09	86	38.13
16	4.34	5.34	81	64.96
17	2.31	2.52	92	40.47
18	3.37	4.09	82	66.27
19	3.63	4.31	84	63.56
20	3.15	3.7	85	62.38
21	3.3	3.9	85	57.28
22	2.97	3.61	82	63.19
23	3.99	4.88	81	50.51
24	2.81	3.39	83	65.06
25	3.36	3.99	84	63.19
Ave	3.47	4.23	82.91	59.45

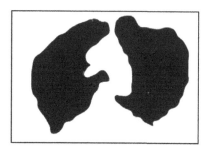

Fig. 2. Sample reference CT lung image.

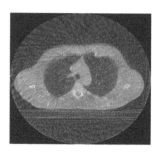

Fig. 3. CT lung image to be segmented.

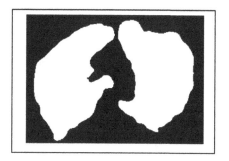

Fig. 4. Results of thresholding method

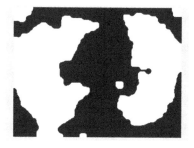

Fig. 5. Results of Sobel method

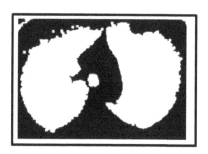

Fig. 6. Results of Fuzzy C-means method.

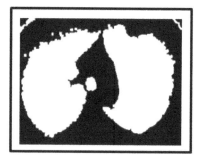

Fig. 7. Results of edge detector Sobel operator.

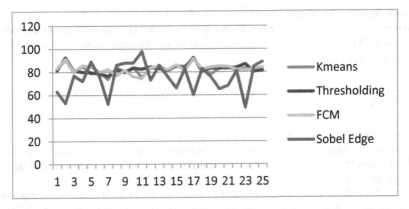

Fig. 8. The measure of overlap rate of the reference lung CT image with lung CT images delineated with, Thresholding, Sobel, FCM and K means segmentation techniques.

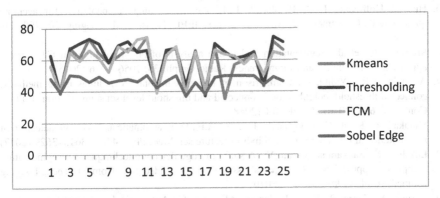

Fig. 9. The measure of mean absolute distance of the reference lung CT image with lung CT images delineated with, Thresholding, Sobel, FCM and K means segmentation techniques.

6   Conclusion

This paper compares the performance of different lung segmentation techniques namely thresholding, Sobel edge detection, region growing, K-means segmentation, and Fuzzy C-means techniques. The experimental results depict that Fuzzy C-means and K means are suitable techniques for lung segmentation in CT images. Future work is to implement the proposed algorithm for lung segmentation of CT images and to compare the performance of the proposed algorithm with previously mentioned segmentation methods. Future research work also includes comparison of all the techniques including the one proposed in this paper using the all relevant metrics such as OR, MAD, speficity, sensitivity and accuracy.

Acknowledgment. We would like to thank Dr. Jayamohan Unnithan, Pulmonologist, Kovai Respiratory Care and Research Center, Coimbatore, India for his valuable support towards the research work. He is the lung expert who performed the manual segmentation of the lung for the reference lung CT images.

References

1. Cancer India. http://cancerindia.org.in/statistics
2. Sharma, A., Singh, P.K., Khurana, P.: Analytical review on object segmentation and recognition. In: Proceedings of 6th International Conference on Cloud System and Big Data Engineering, pp. 524–530 (2016)
3. Chen, X., Udupa, J.K., Bagci, U., Zhuge, Y., Yao, J.: Medical image segmentation by combining graph cuts and oriented active appearance model. IEEE Trans. Image Process. **21**(4), 2035–2046 (2012)
4. Lavanya, M., Muthu Kannan, P.: Lung lesion detection in CT scan images using the fuzzy local information cluster means (FLICM) automatic segmentation algorithm and back propagation network classification. Asian Pac. J. Cancer Prev. **18**(12), 3395–3399 (2017)
5. Hu, S., Hoffmann, E.A., Reinhardt, J.M.: Automatic lung segmentation for accurate quantitation of volumetric X-Ray CT images. IEEE Trans. Med. Imaging **20**, 490–498 (2001)
6. Mansoor, A., et al.: Segmentation and image analysis of abnormal lungs at CT: current approaches, challenges, and future trends. Radio Graph. **35**, 1056–1076 (2015)
7. Amanda, A.R., Widita, R.: Comparison of image segmentation of lungs using methods: connected threshold, neighborhood connected and threshold level set segmentation. J. Phys. Conf. Ser. **694** (2016). Article id 012048
8. Shaukata, F., Rajab, G., Gooyaa, A., Frangia, A.F.: Fully automatic and accurate detection of lung nodules in CT images using a hybrid feature set. Med. Phys. **44**(7), 3615–3629 (2017)
9. Lakshmi, S., Sankaranarayanan, V.: A study of edge detection techniques for segmentation computing approaches. IJCA Special Issue Comput. Aided Soft Comput. Tech. Imaging Biomed. Appl. **149**(9), 42–47 (2010)
10. Cascio, D., Magro, R., Fauci, F., Iacomi, M., Raso, G.: Automatic detection of lung nodules in CT datasets based on stable 3D mass- spring models. Comput. Biol. Med. **42**, 1098–1109 (2012)
11. Gong, J., Liu, J.Y., Wang, L.J., Zheng, B., Nie, S.D.: Computer-aided detection of pulmonary nodules using dynamic self-adaptive template matching and a FLDA classifier. Eur. J. Med. Phys. **32**(12), 1502–1509 (2016)
12. Rahman, M.M., You, D., Simpson, M.S., Antani, S.K., Demner-Fushman, D., Thoma, G.R.: Interactive cross and multimodal biomedical image retrieval based on automatic region-of-interest (ROI) identification and classification. Int. J. Multimed. Inf. Retr. **3**, 131–146 (2014)
13. Gomathi, M., Thangara, P.: A new approach to lung image segmentation using fuzzy possibilistic C-Means algorithm. Int. J. Comput. Sci. Inf. Secur. **7**(3), 222–228 (2010)
14. Liu, H., Geng, F., Guo, Q., Zhang, C., Zhang, C.: A fast weak-supervised pulmonary nodule segmentation method based on modified self-adaptive FCM algorithm. Methodol. Appl. **22** (12), 3983–3995 (2017). https://doi.org/10.1007/s00500-017-2608-5
15. Nizami, I.F., Hasan, S.U., Javed, I.T.: A wavelet frames + K-means based automatic method for lung area segmentation in multiple slices of CT scan. In: 17th IEEE International Multi Topic Conference, Pakistan (2014)
16. https://home.deib.polimi.it/matteucc/Clustering/tutorial_html/cmeans.html

17. Darmanayagam, S.E., Harichandran, K.N., Cyril, S.R.R., Arputharaj, K.: A novel supervised approach for segmentation of lung parenchyma from chest CT for computer-aided diagnosis. J. Digit. Imaging **26**(3), 496–509 (2013)

18. Ferreira, F.T., Sousa, P., Galdran, A., et al.: End-to-end supervised lung lobe segmentation. In: 2018 International Joint Conference on Neural Networks (2018)

19. Tang, H., Zhang, C., Xie, X.: Automatic pulmonary lobe segmentation using deep learning. In: 2019 IEEE 16th International Symposium on Biomedical Imaging (2019). arXiv:1903.09879

20. Huang, Y., Zhou, F.: Lung segmentation using a fully convolutional neural network with weekly supervision. In: Proceedings of the 2018 3rd International Conference on Biomedical Imaging, Signal Processing, pp. 80–85. ACM. Italy (2018)

21. Cheng, W., Ma, L., Yang, T., Liang, J., Zhang, Y.: Joint lung CT image segmentation: a hierarchical bayesian approach. PLoS ONE **11**(9), e016221 (2016)

22. Chung, H., Ko, H., Jeon, S.J., Yoon, K.H., Lee, J.: Automatic lung segmentation with juxtapleural nodule identification using active contour model and bayesian approach. IEEE J. Trans. Eng. Health Med. **6**, 1800513 (2018)

23. Dai, S., Lu, K., Dong, J., Zhang, Y., Chen, Y.: A novel approach of lung segmentation on chest CT images using graph cuts. Neurocomputing **168**, 799–807 (2015)

24. Shabana, R., Ziyad, V., Radha, T.V.: Critical review of computer aided detection and computer aided diagnosis systems for lung nodule detection in computed tomography. Curr. Med. Imaging **15**, 1 (2019)

25. Weaver, J.B., Yansun, X., Healy, D.M., Cromwell, L.D.: Filtering noise from images with wavelet transforms. Magn. Reson. Med. **21**(2), 288–295 (1991)

26. Unser, M., Aldroubi, A.: A review of wavelets in biomedical applications. Proc. IEEE **84**(4), 626–638 (1996)

27. Laine, A.: Wavelets in spatial processing of biomedical images. Ann. Rev. Biomed. Eng. **2**, 511–550 (2000)

28. Al AlZubi, S., Islam, N., Abbod, M.: Multiresolution analysis using wavelet, ridgelet, and curvelet transforms for medical image segmentation. J. Biomed. Imaging **2011**(4), 136034 (2011)

29. Candes, E.: Fast discrete curvelet transforms. Multiscale Model. Simul. **5**(3), 861–899 (2006)

30. Ghaheri, A., Shoar, S., Naderan, M., Hoseini, S.S.: The applications of genetic algorithms in medicine. Oman Med. J. **30**(6), 406–416 (2015)

31. Wang, J., Li, F., Li, Q.: Automated segmentation of lungs with severe interstitial lung disease in CT. Med. Phys. **36**(10), 4592–4599 (2009)

32. Tripathi, P., Tyagi, S., Nath, M.: A comparative analysis of segmentation techniques for lung cancer detection. Pattern Recogn. Image Anal. **29**(1), 167–173 (2019)

33. ur Rehman, M.Z., Javaid, M., Shah, S.I.A., Gilani, S.O., Jamil, M., Butt, S.I.: An appraisal of nodules detection techniques for lung cancer in CT images. Biomed. Signal Process. Control **14**, 140–151 (2018)

Survey on Domain Name System Security Problems - DNS and Blockchain Solutions

Mukesh Kumar Bansal$^{(\boxtimes)}$ and M. Sethumadhavan

TIFAC CORE in Cyber Security, Amrita School of Engineering,
Amrita Vishwa Vidyapeetham, Coimbatore, India
mukesh.k.bansal@gmail.com, m_sethu@cb.amrita.edu

Abstract. Domain Name System constitutes the major part in the
Internet services. The machine or computers identify a website through
an IP address, but the users can remember the names. The translation from name to IP address can be achieved easily through DNS. DNS
includes root severs, which are operated by govt organizations. Although
DNS system is implemented, there are threats within them. Also, these
root servers have risks of censorship, data tracking, privatization and
commercial use etc. To overcome these threats and issues, various solutions have been provided by research community and various organizations. This paper surveys on the security problems of DNS and the
solutions proposed by various authors including Blockchain based solutions. Blockchain based solution bring immutability of data, which avoid
issue like DNS Cache poisoning or corrupting DNS data. Blockchain also
helps in removing censorship of govt or any specific private agencies on
DNS servers ownership.

Keywords: Blockchain · DNS · Namecoin · Blockstack · BNS ·
ConsortiumDNS · Dnssec · DNSCurve

1 Introduction to DNS

The Domain Name System (DNS) is an Internet service, which helps in translating domain name to Internet Protocol (IP) address. All the devices/systems
on internet are identified with unique IP address that helps the internet users
to access that device or system. The DNS service for easier access eliminates
the need for users to remember IP addresses (IPv4) or complex alphanumeric
IP addresses (IPV6). The DNS resolution converts a hostname into a computer
understandable IP address format. When an internet user try to access any webpage, a translation occurs from the DNS name to the machine understandable
address [4].

1.1 DNS Components

DNS components form the fundamental core elements of the DNS Service; mainly
it contains names and corresponding IP addresses information like it is captured

© Springer Nature Singapore Pte Ltd. 2020
P. K. Singh et al. (Eds.): FTNCT 2019, CCIS 1206, pp. 634–647, 2020.
https://doi.org/10.1007/978-981-15-4451-4_50

in host file, but there is significant difference in accessing, modifying or adding these names compare to host file. The key component of DNS are as mentioned in below sections:

DNS Namespace: DNS namespace has a hierarchical inverted tree structure and each branch of the tree is a called domain, each subbranch is a subdomain. Each domain consists the list of records, which includes host names, corresponding IP addresses, and other key information. This DNS namespace tree can be queried to access a specific records from a specific branch (domain).

Recursive Server: The initial query from the client interacts with the Recursive Server, which is the server that responds to client for their recursive request; it takes sometime to find the expected DNS record by making a series of recursive requests until it gets access to an authoritative DNS nameserver for the required record and if the record is not found it returns an error. Recursive servers contain local cache too, which may contains few of DNS Name and IP Address information, this local cache can also serve some of the DNS requests. Cache is maintains persistent data, if specific requested data is available in local cache, it enable short-circuit of that specific requests by responding to client with desired information. The DNS record request process is captured in Fig. 1 below.

Fig. 1. DNS record request

Authoritative Server (Name Servers): The Authoritative server keep the domain information for which it is authority, hence it is able to respond DNS queries of client and for these domain and forward other domain queries for which it is not authority, to other servers. It provides original and definitive answers to the DNS queries for any domain in the tree. The cached answers are not directly fetched from other name servers, hence, it only responds to queries about domain names that are stored in its configuration system. The Authoritative Name Servers are of two types: 1. Master Server and 2. Slave Server.

Master Server (Primary Name Server): This type of master server maintains the master copies (originals) of all zone records. The records in master server zone can only be updated by a host master.

Slave Server (Secondary Name Server): It is duplicate of master server, it maintain an identical copy of the master records. Updates to slave server happens automatically using special mechanism of the DNS protocol. Slave servers share

DNS server load, which improves DNS zone availability by acting as secondary server in case there is any failure in master server.

Domain availability is very crucial, it is requited 24×7 access to support DNS queries from across globe. To avoid any unforeseen failure situation of any DNS name server due to security, hardware failure or to support peaks of load, a network of multiple Name Servers is made, which make sure domain access is active. On the internet each domain name is assigned with a set of authoritative name servers. Authoritative servers can be located or verified by using this shell prompt command host -t ns dnsknowledge.com.

Thus, the authoritative name server and the recursive name server plays a major role in DNS resolution. The authoritative server and the recursive server are registered with the DNS using unique identification. So, that the genuine servers can be identified.

1.2 DNS Message Format

This section describes about DNS message format basic DNS message format, which is used for all DNS related operations like following, which is also illustrated in the Fig. 2.

- Host name queries/requests
- Responses
- Notifications
- Zone Transfers
- various Dynamic updates.

The DNS message format information is taken here from various RFCs (including RFC 2136, 2535, 2929). Few key fields are described in below figure.

It contains fixed and variable length sections where fixed is 12-byte header followed by the variable-length sections. They are Queries, Answers, Authority records and Additional records.

The four fields in the subsequent section are 16 bits in size and require the entries in the question, authority, answer, and additional information sections that completes the DNS message (Fig. 3).

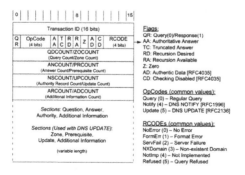

Fig. 2. DNS message format

Field Name	Length (bits)	Details
Transaction ID	16	It is set by the client and returned by the server, which lets the client match responses to requests
QR	1	0 - indicated message as query and 1 as response
OpCode	4	The value of field is described as: '0' - Query (request / response), '2' - Status, '4' - Notify, '5' - Update, '1', '3', '6 to 15' - Unassigned or OBSOLETE
AA	1	Presents answer is "authoritative" or from cache
TC	1	It means total response size exceeded 512 bytes and now "truncated".
RD	1	It means "recursion desired". If set, a recursive query is performed.
RA	1	It means "recursion available". Root servers generally do not support recursion.
Z	1	This field is reserved for future use.
AD	1	Value is set to 1 if data is authenticated.
CD	1	Value is set to 1 if security checking is disabled.
RCODE	4	The details of RCODE value is given in Figure below "Response Code (RCODE).

Fig. 3. DNS fields details

- In the query section, the number of questions is usually 1 and the remaining three counts are 0.
- In the reply section, the number of answers is at least 1. Questions contains name, type, and class whereas the other sections contains zero or more RRs. RRs contains the fields such as name, type, and class information, it also contains the Time to Live field to represent the time of the cached information.

1.3   DNS Communication

This section talks about various communications, which take place while resolving hostname with IP address. All these communications may take few seconds in resolving hostname, the process use the existing DNS resolver to forward the required query message to the targeted DNS server, which maintains the names, which are required to be resolved.

Below are various steps taken for Internet name resolution process (Fig. 4).

Value	Name	Reference	Description and Purpose
0	NoError	[RFC1035]	No error
1	FormErr	[RFC1035]	Format error; query cannot be interpreted
2	ServFail	[RFC1035]	Server failure; error in processing at server
3	NXDomain	[RFC1035]	Nonexistent domain; unknown domain referenced
4	NotImp	[RFC1035]	Not implemented; request not supported in server
5	Refused	[RFC1035]	Refused; server unwilling to provide answer
6	YXDomain	[RFC2136]	Name exists but should not (used with updates)
7	YXRRSet	[RFC2136]	RRSet exists but should not (used with updates)
8	NXRRSet	[RFC2136]	RRSet does not exist but should (used with updates)
9	NotAuth	[RFC2136]	Server not authorized for zone (used with updates)
10	NotZone	[RFC2136]	Name not contained in zone (used with updates)

Fig. 4. Response codes (RCODE)

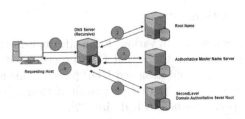

Fig. 5. Name resolution process

1. User specify the URL (DNS name) of target server in web browser of user's machine. The API call is invoked from browser application to the local DNS server that is also called the recursive server of user. This server generates a query message (comprises the server name to be resolved) and sends it destined DNS server, which is listed in the its TCP/IP configuration.
2. After receiving the name resolution query, the DNS server look into its resource records (RR) to verifies its authoritativeness for the zone of queried server. If it is not authoritative for requested server, its creates an iterative query and sends to one of the root name servers. Then the server inspects the name requested by client's DNS server and checks its RRs to find-out the required authoritative servers of the top-level domain (also called TLD). The root name server sends the response (containing top-level domain server IP addresses) to user's local DNS server.
3. The local DNS server, now creates new iterative query using the master server address and sends to the top-level domain server.
4. The local DNS server creates one more iterative DNS query and sends it to the second level domain server. If this server is the respective server for that zone then the RRs are compared to obtain the IP address and responds to the local DNS sever.
5. The local DNS server obtains the reply from the authoritative server and sends it to the resolver present in the client system as shown in Fig. 5. The resolver in turn transmits the address to the application which then initiates the IP communication for the respective user [3,5].

The paper is organized as follows, Sect. 2 gives a comprehensive explanation about the threats associated with the DNS. Section 3 is the survey of the various secure protocols using cryptographic methods proposed by other authors. Section 4 deals with Blockchain based solution to overcome the DNS flaws. Final section concludes as well as describes the future work.

2   DNS Threats

The existing DNS procedure has few vulnerabilities, which can be exploited by the adversaries. Few of the key DNS threats are discussed in this section [11].

2.1   Packet Interception

DNS Packet interception occurs in various forms like man-in-the-middle attacks (MITM), eavesdropping etc. In the actual DNS procedure, it sends a query or response as an un-encrypted and unsigned UDP packet. This makes the packet-interception attack easier on a shared or transit network. The attackers can simply modify DNS packet as per their desire [12].

2.2   Name Chaining

These attacks come under cache poisoning attacks and most of these attacks have a partial mitigation. The mitigation provides established defence of checking the RR's in the response messages with respect to the actual query but this method is not useful to identify the name-chaining attacks. In these attacks the attacker introduces an arbitrary DNS name of his choice and further information associated with these names are also provided. The victim will not be able to recognize unless he has a better knowledge of the data with the names. So this kind of attack is very difficult to be mitigated [11].

2.3   Denial of Service (DoS) and Distributed Denial of Service (DDoS)

DNS is vulnerable to both DoS and DDoS attacks. In these attacks, the attacker generates bogus DNS requests that seems be from the target network and sends them directly to weakly configured DNS servers. The strengthening occurs as the intermediate DNS servers respond to the faked DNS requests. The responses contain large volume of data than ordinary DNS responses, which may require more computational resources to process, that in turn leads to the access denial for the genuine user.

2.4   Cache Poisoning

If the answer to a query within its cache is unavailable in the DNS server, it passed the query onto another DNS server on behalf of the client. But, if that another DNS server has incorrect information, whether placed there intentionally (by some malicious attacker) or unintentionally, then cache poisoning can occur. Malicious cache poisoning is commonly referred to as DNS spoofing [10].

2.5   Dynamic DNS Update Vulnerabilities

Dynamic DNS Updates is a modification to RFC 1035 that allows dynamic updating of DNS information contained within a zone. Protocols such as Dynamic Host Configuration Protocol (DHCP) make use of Dynamic DNS (DDNS) protocol to add and delete RR on demand. These dynamic RR updates are take place on the primary server for the zone. As part of this update, RR records are added or deleted. The DDNS protocol has provisions to update a primary server dynamically based on required controls and perquisites. Even if DDNS is deployed, system is still vulnerable to threats such as IP spoofing due to its weak form of access control, which makes system compromised.

A malicious attacker, can perform a variety of dynamic updating attacks against the primary server of the zone. These attacks may include like denial of service attack, deletion of records or malicious redirection by changing the IP address information of RR which is being sent in an update.

3   Survey of DNS Security Solutions

This section talks about various DNS Security protocol available to overcome the DNS threats mentioned in above section using crypto methods and other privacy and data protection solutions [14]. We also will discuss the limitation of these DNS Security protocols in this section.

3.1   Overview of DNSSEC

DNSSEC is a security layer on top of the DNS Protocol. It provides origin of authentication, data integrity and authenticated denial of existence to DNS provided by the name server. Signature checking mechanism is performed by the resolver of DNSSEC to determine the legitimate user by verifying with the authoritative name server. Fours records type are added by DNSSEC to original DNS, these are:

- Resource Record Signature (RRSIG) - The validation and expiry time of the signature is captured in this field
- DNS Public Key (DNSKEY)
- Delegation Signer (DS) - It verifies the public keys of zones
- Next Secure (NSEC) - Each distinctive name in the secured zone is aligned with respective NSEC RR, which target to the next entry (name) present in the zone.

It also enhance the capability to find-out MITM attacks on DNS via the new features: data origin authentication, transaction and request authentications. DNSSEC must be used by both servers and resolvers for maintaining data origin authenticity and integrity [7].

Secured zone consists of following key pair:

- Zone private key - All RRs in a secured zone are signed by the zone's private key.
- Public key - Stored as a RR (type KEY) as DNSKEY in the secured zone. It is utilized by DNS servers and Resolver to validate the zone's digital signature.
- Key Signing Keys (KSKs) - In a zone, Top-level KEY RRs are signed using KSKs.
- Zone Signing Keys (ZSKs) - RRSets in a zone are sined using ZSKs.

DNSSEC - Flaws

1. Security Issue: DNSSEC does not protect from poor configuration or bad information in the authoritative name server, it also does not help in protecting buffer overruns and DDoS attacks.
2. Operations Issue: The asymmetric key algorithm used is RSA, because of which the key length is more due to which key rollover is not possible.
   - Computational load on the servers and resolvers also become high.
   - Cryptographic key management issues which includes initial key configuration and key rollover, key authentication and verification also add-up further in deploying DNSSEC on a global scale.

3. Deployment Issues: Servers requires better time synchronization and management tools during deployment, which is lacking. Also the hierarchical model of trust further make deployment difficult.
4. Another issue is the storage of Zone Private key and also the overall architecture is complex to implement.

3.2 DNSCURVE - Overview

The alternate Public key cryptography method for the DNS protocol is inclusive in the DNSCurve. In this they use Elliptic Curve Cryptography (ECC), which has a shorter key-length and relatively the encryption and decryption speed is much higher than the DNSSEC mechanism. This provides a secure communication between the Name Server (NS) and client.

The Authoritative name server will contain the public key of every name server and the RR of the servers are located in the parents zone file. During the recursive DNS resolver process, the initial check determines if the DNSCurve public key is a valid one or not from the authoritative' s domain name. Then, a shared key k is generated from the server's public key and its secret key. In server end, the secret key and the client's public key produces the shared key. The shared key can be used for following transactions between these two entities and to increase the performance it could be stored locally.

Encryption-Procedure in DNSCURVE. The nonce of length 12-byte is selected by the client and it is assigned to the packet. Then the shared key is used for the expansion of nonce to long key via using function of Salsa20 (stream cipher). Stream cipher's input nonce size is 24-bytes, which is made of the 12 byte from client and the remaining 12 bytes are zeros. This 24 bytes stream is utilized for authentication as well as encryption of packets.

Now the client makes use of the previously computed key stream to create message authenticator. The authentication function used in this scenario is Poly1305-AES. The initial query is encrypted by XORing the remaining key stream. The updated encipherment contains the information of authenticator and the ciphertext. The client creates query packet and sends to the NS. This packet contains DNSCurve public key, the 12-byte nonce specific to the packet and the cryptographic box used for encoding the packet (query packet). The purpose of this box is to prove the authenticity and confidentiality of the actual packet.

At the receiving end, the NS obtains the senders public key and the nonce for that packet. At this side, shared stream keys are generated. Afterwards the calculation and validation of the code takes place to check if the private key is valid for that public key or not. Then, the box is decrypted for extracting the query. If this process fails at any point, then the packet is handled as unprotected by server. Else proper response is created and send to the client in the encrypted format.

After the query is processed and send to the client, the response has to be constructed in the similar procedure as followed above with only one exception:

Salsa20 function input, which is 24-byte string contains 12 bytes nonce from client side and the remaining 12 bytes chosen by the server. So the response packet includes 12 bytes nonce in clear text of the server, and the other part contains the original response in the cryptographic box.

The combination of the (a) server's private key, (b) the client's public key and (c) 24-bytes nonce are used to form the cryptographic box. To get the desired response, this box is verified and decrypted by client. But if any chance, process fails, then the packet is not valid. Therefore, the client rejects the packet and continues to wait for a legitimate one. There is cryptographically crucial requirement that different nonce must be generated and used by client and server for each DNSCurve packet encrypted with the same shared key.

Flaws in DNSCURVE

1. The structure of the DNS protocol has to modified drastically to implement DNSCURVE.
2. If the DNSCURVE packet size is greater than 512 bytes, it needs to shift to TCP connection. As the record format and computation capability is high; most of the time it exceeds 512 bytes where there is a delay in shifting from UDP to TCP.
3. The key storage takes place online, if the key is lost the attacker will be able to launch attacks like cache poisoning, zone attack and so on.
4. Quantum computers existence can break this architecture.

4   Blockchain Based DNS Security Solutions

There are few blockchain based DNS solutions [13] that have emerged in recent times, they are discussed in the below subsections.

4.1   Blockchain Naming Service (BNS)

The Blockchain Naming Service (BNS) simplifies the access of hash values. It replaces the complicated hash values with the human-readable names to interact with the decentralized network. The other functions include enabling the users to send cryptocurrencies, interact with smart contacts, and visit dApp [6].

BNS is composed of three unique smart contracts, they are registry, registrar, and resolver. Registry is an uncompounded contract mapping registered names to owners and resolvers. Registrar owns the domains in the registry and allocates subdomains. Resolver maps a name to the corresponding resource such as multi-hash, wallet address, and so on. This BNS service solves the identity problem in this new internet that involves many meaningless hash. By empowering users to have human readable names, BNS plays an important role that closes the gap between users and the technology, therefore, it is considered as the solution that will foster the rise of dApps, wallets, platforms and cryptocurrency.

4.2 Namecoin

Namecoin works with the same code as Bitcoin and it is considered the first fork, both operate independently as separate blockchains. This gives an additional feature to store the identity of the users within blocks. The information that is kept can be any personal or digital identity and is stored as a key/value pair. Namecoin is an opensource technology that can be used to improve the speed, security, privacy of the internet setup for DNS and identities [2].

Namecoin is resistant to any attack as they are tamper-proof and every user in the Namecoin platform must be altered to perform attacks. As mentioned, it is decentralized and transactions takes place in a peer-peer network. This platform works in a .bit extension and all the websites are published in this domain. For the creation of .bit domain, only the private key has to be stored physically and they do not require any personal information. There are few Namecoin based applications such as nmcontrol and ncdns which can be used to create our own public or private DNS. This DNS can be shared privately or utilized by other Namecoin users. Another advantage of Namecoin is that any information published by the users can be audited by at any time to check the integrity.

Bitcoin addressed are randomly generated characters and it is very difficult to remember the name, instead of using random-characters .bit addresses can be used to create the bitcoin address that is more accessible and easy to remember. The wallet has to be compatible for transaction of bitcoin to .bit address. The Netki Wallet is one of the compatible source for this kind of transactions. Namecoin generally has a .bit domain address system and it can be purchased through the wallet for .01 NMC. This amount is used only for creation and maintenance of the services. Also, the domain name chosen to represent the Namecoin should be unique as well as renewed after 35,999 blocks which usually takes 200 to 250 days.

Namecoin - Working. NameID and the Dot-bit DNS are the two main assets of Namecoin where the NameID provides security and decentralized properties of the bitcoin and as an additional layer it also provides meaningful-names for the network which was not implemented in Bitcoin addressing system. The NameID is the combination of the identities on Namecoin along with OpenID, an authentication protocol. This NameID, can be used to login to any OpenID-enabled website with the Namecoin identity.

The Namecoin used the Dot-bit domain, where Dot-Bit operates DNS and issues it to all the participants on the network. By doing this, no single entity can control the website without owning it. This dot bit domain is more advantageous than the DNS system. One of the major advantage is that it is censorship-resistance. Dot-Bit has an inbuilt free HTTPS, which is an additional security feature. The Network traffic is not generated by the DNS so it is fast and easier to access. Generally the computer stores a copy of the Dot-Bit DNS, so websites take less than three milliseconds to load that is significantly quicker than the 100 ms for regular sites.

Drawbacks of Namecoin. The disadvantage of the .bit DNS system is that many systems are not compatible to access .bit domains, as it can be used only by altering the system requirements. The reason behind the incompatibility is that the dot bit domain are not listed under the main of the Internet Corporation for Assigned Names and Numbers (ICANN). To overcome this issue an proxy domain name system can be added as an extension. There are few resources such as okTurtles Foundation and zeroNET which helps in accessing .bit domains in a secure way.

The next drawback of Namecoin is that scalability, as the blocksize varies from 500 KB to 1 MB, this size can be accepted only for the deployment of smaller applications. So it is not practical to implement this platform for large-scale applications or as a de-centralized file storage platform.

This uses virtual .bit top-level domain name which is not formally registered in existing DNS system. This inturn refers that Namecoin is secluded from the DNS system and users cannot resolve .bit domain names without installing additional software for resolving the .bit domain. Due to this additional software implementation on DNS servers is not a viable implementation solution worldwide, hence not a feasible solution witch can be accepted across organizations or research scholars.

4.3 Blockstack

Blockstack is one of the blockchain based DNS solution, that preserves a naming system that acts as an independent logical layer on top of the underlying blockchain platform. The blockchain platform provides their consensus for the blockstack to achieve the naming system and binding names to the data records. The operations such as name registrations, updates and the transfers are all taken care by the blockstack, it basically provides the ordering and the consensus helps in adding them to the blockchain platform [1].

Blockstack uses control and data planes to separate out the security of name registration and ownership from the availability of data associated with names.

The control plane describes the procedure for recording human-readable names, it creates the bindings for name-hash, and also creates bindings to own the cryptographic keypairs. The control plane contains a blockchain and a logically isolated layer on top, known as a "virtual-chain". The data plane is accountable for data storage and data availability. It consists of

– zone files to discovering data by hash or URL, and
– External storage systems for storage of data.

The values of the data's are generally signed by the public key of the name owners and the clients can read the data's from the data-plane layer. The authenticity can be verified by validating the hash of the data in the zone file or by checking the signature in comparison with the public key of the owner.

A virtualchain introduced in blockstack consist of new kind of state machines compatible to the underlying blockchain. Blockstack has introduces a globally available naming system that addresses name and its associated data. This virtual chain concept can be extended to define other types of state machines.

Four sections are present in Blockstack, first one is the blockchain layer where consensus mechanism takes place and the area where the blockstack operations are stored. Second layer is the virtual layer where any changes are implemented and later it is added as an additional metadata to the blockchain layer, the rules are also incorporated in this layer. The third layer is the routing layer, where in the control plane the zone files hash can be added and integrity can be verified. Most of the production servers stores the entire zone files. Finally, the topmost layer is the storage layer where the name-value pairs are accommodated. The storage system is of two types they are mutable and immutable, where mutable storage can be used to update any data's without the involvement of blockchain as zone files cannot be altered whereas the immutable storage allows the update as separate transactions in the ledger.

There is implementation limitation in blockstack as it acts as a separate layer to the blockchain, and the flaws in the underlying blockchain can impact the blockstack, additional layers. For instance if the bitcoin is used as an underlying blockchain the network delay, the time delay all these delays can affect the entire architecture of blockstack. Thus various proposed solutions for DNS security and their advantages and disadvantages were discussed in the above section. Next section concludes the paper as well as define the future work of DNS security.

4.4 ConsortiumDNS

The ConsortiumDNS is a distributed domain name Service, which is based on Consortium Chain [8] and underpinned by P2P network.

A hierarchical architecture is used by ConsortiumDNS to overcome the performance issue of bitcoin blockchain. This architecture separates out the actual DNS data and operations performed for any DNS related transactions. ConsortiumDNS architecture consists of 3 layers namely;

- Blockchain Layer
- Consensus Layer
- Block Storage

ConsortiumDNS uses gossip protocol [9] for synchronizing blocks among various nodes. But this solution still suffers with low throughput in DNS transactions.

5 Future Work

These DNS security solutions, mentioned above are still not giving complete solution, hence further work is required for have DNS security solution. Authors of this paper are working on Blockchain based innovative DNS Security solution, which will try to resolve the issues identified in various solutions mentioned above. They are analyzing various blockchain platforms and data storage methods on Blockchain [13] as well as consensus algorithms, which suits to DNS. This work will be published as a separate research paper soon.

6   Conclusions

DNS threats if exploited can lose all the information and it leads to the major security breach. Organizations are suffering in brand loss as well as huge financial loss due to DNS attacks. The breach may lead to DoS attacks, Packet interception, Name chaining and so on. Though various methods are proposed to overcome the DNS threats, there are few security issues in the proposed methodology and implementation challenges, additional software requirements at all levels or performance issues. Implementation of the above discussed methods may increase the payload affecting the speed and efficiency of the original DNS system.

There is need of a new Blockchain based DNS solution to mitigate the existing flaws mentioned here. Authors are working on Hyperledger based DNS blockchain solution named as DNS-Bchain. DNS-BChain deploys DNSCode as consensus mechanism for DNS Query solutions. This consensus is initiated when the local DNS Server queries DNS-BChain for DNS Name resolution. DNS-BChain will resolve the DNS Query and response is provided to the local DNS Server to communicate further to user. The Image is given to the consensus mechanism and Linear secret sharing scheme is used for consensus verification. This is still in progress and being considered to work without affecting the original DNS systems speed as well as its efficiency.

References

1. Ali, M., et al.: Blockstack: a global naming and storage system secured by blockchains. In: USENIX Annual Technical Conference (2016)
2. Wei-hong, H.U., et al.: Review of blockchain-based DNS alternatives. Chin. J. Netw. Inf. Secur. **3**, 71–77 (2017)
3. Atkins, D., Austein, R.: RFC 3833: Threat Analysis of the Domain Name System (DNS), August 2004. Status: INFORMATIONAL
4. Mockapetris, P.: RFC 1034: Domain names: concepts and facilities, November 1987. Status: Standard 6 (2003)
5. Mockapetris, P.: RFC 1035—Domain names—implementation and specification, November 1987 (2004). http://www.ietf.org/rfc/rfc1035.txt
6. Forte, P., Romano, D., Schmid, G.: Beyond Bitcoin - Part I: a critical look at blockchain-based systems. PA Advice, Naples, Italy (2015)
7. Mohan, A.K., Sethumadhavan, M.: Wireless security auditing: attack vectors and mitigation strategies. Procedia Comput. Sci. **115**, 674–682 (2017)
8. Wang, X., Li, K., et al.: ConsortiumDNS: a distributed domain name service based on consortium chain. In: 2017 IEEE 19th International Conference on High Performance Computing and Communications (2017)
9. Demers, A., Greene D., Hauser C., et al.: Epidemic algorithms for replicated database maintenance. In: Proceedings of the Sixth Annual ACM Symposium on Principles of Distributed Computing, pp. 1–12. ACM (1987)
10. Zou, F., et al.: Survey on domain name system security. In: 2016 IEEE First International Conference on Data Science in Cyberspace (DSC). IEEE (2016)
11. Cao, J., Ma, M., Wang, X., et al.: Wirel. Pers. Commun. **94**, 1263 (2017). https://doi.org/10.1007/s11277-016-3681-2

12. Bushart, J., Rossow, C.: DNS unchained: amplified application-layer DoS attacks against DNS authoritatives. In: Bailey, M., Holz, T., Stamatogiannakis, M., Ioannidis, S. (eds.) RAID 2018. LNCS, vol. 11050, pp. 139–160. Springer, Cham (2018). https://doi.org/10.1007/978-3-030-00470-5_7

13. Liu, J., Li, B., et al.: A data storage method based on blockchain for decentralization DNS. In: 2018 IEEE Third International Conference on Data Science in Cyberspace (DSC) (2018)

14. Kelpen, K., Simo, H.: Privacy and data protection in the domain name system. In: Friedewald, M. (ed.) Privatheit und selbstbestimmtes Leben in der digitalen Welt. D, pp. 253–302. Springer, Wiesbaden (2018). https://doi.org/10.1007/978-3-658-21384-8_8

Hybrid Big Bang-Big Crunch Algorithm for Cluster Analysis

Hakam Singh and Yugal Kumar[✉]

Department of Computer Science and Engineering,
Jaypee University of Information Technology, Solan, H.P., India
hakamsingh011@gmail.com, yugalkumar.14@gmail.com

Abstract. Data clustering is an exploratory technique that organizes the data objects into different clusters in a competent way. There are number of techniques reported in clustering field. Several shortcomings associated with these techniques have been identified and resolved such as initial cluster center selection, number of clusters, slow convergence rate, local optima etc. In present work, a hybrid version of the big bang-big crunch (BB-BC) algorithm is developed to optimize clustering problems. The proposed algorithm work in two stages, initialization and optimization. The K-means algorithm act as initiation arbitrator to generate the initial population. While the big bang-big crunch algorithm acts as an optimizer to obtain the best solution. Here, the cluster centers generated from K-means are treated as preliminary population in BB-BC algorithm. The performance of proposed hybrid BB-BC algorithm is examined over seven benchmark datasets and compared with BB-BC, ACO, GA, PSO and K-means clustering algorithms. From the experimental results, it is clarified that proposed algorithm gives better clustering solution than rest of algorithms.

Keywords: Big bang-big crunch · Hybrid · Optimizer

Abbreviations

ABC:	Artificial Bee Colony
ACO:	Ant Colony Optimization
BB:	Big Bang
BC:	Big Crunch
CSOA:	Cat Swarm Optimization Algorithm
GA:	Genetic Algorithm
GWO:	Grey Wolf Optimization
HS:	Harmony Search
KH:	Krill Herd
KHM:	K-harmonic Means
MOCA:	Magnetic Optimization Algorithm for Data Clustering
PSO:	Particle Swarm Optimization
QCCS:	Quantum chaotic cuckoo search

© Springer Nature Singapore Pte Ltd. 2020
P. K. Singh et al. (Eds.): FTNCT 2019, CCIS 1206, pp. 648–661, 2020.
https://doi.org/10.1007/978-981-15-4451-4_51

1 Introduction

Clustering is a powerful technique that divides the n data objects $X_n = \{X_1, X_2, X_3.....X_n\}$ into K number of clusters $C_K = \{C_1, C_2, C_3.....C_K\}$. The data objects inside the clusters are more similar in nature as compared to that of other clusters [1, 2]. The clustering techniques are mainly characterized into two types viz. hierarchical and partitional clustering [3]. Hierarchal clustering follows the agglomerative and divisive approaches to organize data objects into clusters. While the partitional clustering divides the data objects into several disjoint clusters in an optimized way. Clustering techniques follow some sequence of steps, initialization, selection, evaluation, assignment, optimization and update. Each step is serially accessed and plays a significant role in clustering process. The lack of balance among these steps leads to several problems such as poor population initialization, local optima, slow convergence rate etc. The basic steps of the data clustering algorithm are listed below.

Step 1: Load the dataset and initialize the basic parameters of clustering algorithm such as number of clusters (K), total number of data objects (n), number of attributes (d), maximum number of iterations etc.

Step 2: Select initial cluster centers from the data set.

Step 3: Evaluate the objective function.

Step 4: Assign data objects to clusters using minimum value of objective function.

Step 5: Update the cluster centers.

Step 6: Check the stopping criteria, if met, then stopped. Otherwise repeat steps 3–5.

Step 7: Obtain optimal cluster centers.

Several approaches have been reported in the literature for partitioning and organizing the data objects into clusters. Shelokar et al. have developed an algorithm based on ants' behaviors for clustering [4]. Maulik and Bandyopadhyay have introduced the genetic algorithm in clustering field [5]. Kumar and Pardeep have described a heuristic algorithm inspired from classroom teaching for clustering [6]. Cura has implemented the particle swarm optimization algorithm in the clustering field [7]. Bahrololoum et al. have reported a technique based on Newtonian law of gravity for clustering [8]. Kumar and Pardeep have revealed an improved version of the CSO algorithm for cluster analysis [9]. Cao et al. have disclosed a new initialization method to overcome the drawbacks of random initialization method [10]. Erisoglu et al. have developed an approach to calculate the initial seed points for the K-means algorithm [11]. Chang et al. have proposed an improved version of the genetic algorithm with gene rearrangements to handle the local optima and premature convergence problems [12]. Kumar and Sahoo have hybridized the ICSO with KHM algorithm to enhance its convergence speed [13].

Hatamlou et al. have proposed a heuristic method BB-BC inspired from "universe evolvement theory" for clustering [14]. The BB-BC algorithm works in two phases, BB and BC. The new candidate solutions are generated in BB phase and optimized into single unit in BC phase. It has been observed that BB-BC algorithm suffers from poor initialization issue. In this research work, an effort has been made to address the poor initialization issue of BB-BC algorithm and make it more efficient and robust to solve optimization problem. The proposed algorithm work in two stages, initialization and optimization. Here, K-means algorithm is used to produce initial solution to the clustering problem and then a BB-BC algorithm is applied to optimize the solution by searching around it. The main contribution of this work is highlighted below.

- Incorporated the K-means algorithm as initiation arbitrator to produce an initial solution for BB-BC algorithm and this algorithm analysis optimize these solutions.
- The HBB-BC algorithm is applied to solve partitional clustering problems.

Rest of paper is organized as follows. Section 2 presents related works on clustering problems. Section 3 describes hybrid big bang-big crunch algorithm for cluster analysis. Section 4 discusses the experimental and statistical results of the proposed work. The entire work is concluded in Sect. 5.

2   Related Work

In the past few decades, extensive work has been carried out in the clustering field. Kumar et al. have combined the K-means algorithm with modified artificial bee colony algorithm to optimize clustering problems [15]. In this work, the modified ABS algorithm is used to produce initial seed points for the traditional K-means algorithm. Furthermore, variable tournament selection and worst-case solution replacement policies are also incorporated in this research. The performance of the developed algorithm is examined on six benchmark datasets and perform better as comparison of two well-known clustering algorithms. Abualigah et al. have hybridized the KH with the HS algorithm to solve clustering problems [16]. Leading inspiration of this work is to enhance the global search competence of the traditional KH algorithm by incorporating the global search operator of the HS in it and preserve the best position of krill during the process. The performance is examined on four real-life datasets and on comparison with KHA, PSO, K-mean, HS and Harmony-PSO clustering algorithm showed the better clustering solutions.

Hatamlou et al. have introduced the BB-BC algorithm for cluster analysis [14]. The presented algorithm is inspired from "universe evolvement theory" and works in two phases BB and BC. The big bang phase is accountable for generation of candidate solutions and big crunch phase for optimizing them. The performance of the BB-BC algorithm is examined on four benchmark datasets and compared with K-means, GA and PSO algorithms. Authors have claimed its superiority on other clustering algorithms. In continuation to their work, Hatamlou has also developed a hybrid version of BB-BC with PSO algorithm for clustering [18]. Moreover, Bijari et al. have introduced the concept of memory enrichment in traditional BB-BC algorithm to make balance among local and global search capabilities [19]. As the procedural space of BB-BC algorithm is concentric around the center of mass that is responsible for better results in upcoming iterations. Hence, insight memory enrichment concept is added in BB-BC algorithm. The performance of the developed algorithm is examined on six datasets and compared with BB-BC, GA, K-means, PSO and GWO algorithms. The MBB-BC algorithm provide improved results in the clustering field.

Boushaki et al. have presented a new metaheuristic algorithm named as quantum chaotic cuckoo search (QCCS) for cluster analysis [17]. In this algorithm, quantum theory-based update method is used to extend the global search ability of the cuckoo search algorithm. Further, to enhance the convergence speed the chaotic maps are also incorporated in this work. The performance of the QCCS algorithm is examined on six real-life datasets and compared with eight well-known clustering algorithms. From experimental results, it is observed that the QCCS algorithm work efficiently in clustering field. Yin et al. have modified the gravitational search algorithm with the crossover operator to obtain optimal clusters [20]. In this work, the crossover-based search method is used to rationalize the solution's position and control the search operation. The performance of the QCCS algorithm is examined on several benchmark functions and compared with GSA, GOGSA and DE algorithms. Authors have claimed that the developed algorithm is superior than other clustering algorithms being compared.

To handle the initialization issue of K-means algorithm, Rahman and Islam have presented a hybrid clustering algorithm based on K-means and GA [21]. In this technique, the genetic algorithm is used to produce the initial cluster centers for K-means algorithm. As well the performance of the developed algorithm is examined on twenty datasets and on comparison with five well-known clustering algorithms, it delivers better clustering solutions. Moreover, a cooperative co-evolution framework-based method in order to handle the initialization issue is also reported by Jiang, and Wang [22]. In this method, the original problems in divided into subproblems and exclusively solved by an optimizer. The results are tested on both real-life and artificial dataset and it is seen that proposed algorithm provide better results than rest of algorithm being compared. Furthermore, Zhou et al. have introduced a new metaheuristic approach based on symbiotic interaction for clustering [23]. In this algorithm, new candidate solutions are generated via emulating the biological interaction between organisms. The algorithm works in three phases; (i) mutualism, the interaction benefits both sides in this phase; (ii) commensalism, the interaction benefits only one side and does not affect the other side; and (iii) parasitism, the interaction benefits one side and aggressively harms the other side. It is observed that the developed algorithm is a robust method for solving clustering problems when its performance is examined on ten standard datasets and compared with CS, FPA, PSO, DE, ABC, K-means and MVO algorithms.

3 Hybrid Big Bang-Big Crunch (HBB-BC) Algorithm for Cluster Analysis

In this section, a hybridized version of BB-BC incorporated with K-means algorithm is presented. The HBB-BC algorithm works in two stages, initialization and optimization. The K-means algorithm act as initiation arbitrator to produce the initial population. While, the BB-BC algorithm is act as optimizer to get optimal solution. The solutions generated from K-means are treated as preliminary population in BB-BC algorithm. The detailed description of proposed algorithm is given below.

3.1   Initialization

The initialization is an important aspect in algorithmic space. It is primarily concerned with assignment of initial inputs for algorithm to begin the execution. In this work, we have incorporated K-means algorithm as an initialization arbitrator to select initial population instead of the earlier as random selection of population in BB-BC algorithm. In this work, the Euclidean distance is used as similarity measure and known as the distance between data objects and the cluster center. It is computed for every cluster center and data items. On the basis of minimum Euclidean distance, data objects are associated with clusters. The Euclidean distance can be computed using Eq. (1).

$$D(X_i, C_j) = \sqrt{\sum_{K=1}^{d} (X_{iK}, C_{jK})^2} \qquad (1)$$

Where X_i and C_j denote data points and cluster centers respectively.

3.2   Optimization

The cluster centers generated from K-means are treated as preliminary population in BB-BC algorithm. The operational procedure of the BB-BC algorithm is concentric around the center of mass. Hence, a computation based on center of mass and step size is performed in BB phase to generate new solutions. A repetition of BB phase after BC phase is performed to generate the new solution via retaining the c.o.m using Eqs. 2 and 3.

$$x^c = \frac{\sum_{i=1}^{N} \frac{x_i}{f^i}}{\sum_{i=1}^{N} \frac{1}{f^i}} \qquad (2)$$

Where x^c denote the c.o.m, f_i and x_i are fitness and solution values of *ith* instance respectively.

$$x_{new}^i = x^c + \frac{lr}{k} i = 1, 2, \ldots N \qquad (3)$$

Here, r is a random number between 0 and 1, l is a limit operator functioned to frame the region of search. The algorithmic steps of the HBB-BC algorithm are listed below.

Hybrid BB-BC Clustering Algorithm

Stage 1: Initialization

1.1: Load data set into memory, allocate the number of clusters K_i , where (i = 1,2,...,n)

1.2: Select initial seed points (X_i) using K-means algorithm.

1.3: Evaluate the objective function and organize the data objects into clusters using Equation 1.

1.4: Update the cluster centers.

1.5: Check the "termination criteria", If met stop else, repeat 2-5.

1.6: Optimal Solution.

Stage 2: Optimization

2.1: While (iter_no<max_number of iterations), do   /* iter_no = iteration number

2.2: for i= 1 to K do

2.3: for j= 1 to N do

2.4: Compute the objective function.

2.5: c.o.m[i, j] = Generate new seed point using Equation 3./*BB-Phasee

2.6: c.o.m[i, j] = Compute the c.o.m using Equation 2.   /* BC-Phase

2.7: Update mass

2.8: Check termination condition, If met, Stop algorithm Else, repeat 10-14.

2.9: End while

4   Results and Discussion

This section describes the simulation results of the developed algorithm in clustering field. The proposed algorithm is simulated in MATLAB 2016a environment operated on window 10 operating system. The performance of HBB-BC algorithm is inspected on seven datasets. The illustration of these datasets is given in Table 1. Further, two performance measures, intra-cluster distance and accuracy are measured to assess the efficacy of HBB-BC algorithm. Tables 2 and 3 demonstrates the results of the HBB-BC algorithm in comparison to other well-known clustering algorithms.

Table 1. Datasets description.

Datasets	K	D	N	Description
Iris	3	4	150	Fisher's iris data
CMC	3	9	1,473	Contraceptive method choice
Glass	6	9	214	Glass identification data
Wine	3	13	178	Wine data
Cancer	2	9	683	Wisconsin Breast Cancer
Vowel	6	3	871	Indian Telugu vowel
Seeds	3	7	210	Seeds data

IRIS - The dataset comprises with three variety of iris plant, setosa, virginica andversicolor. It has total 150 instances with three classes (50 instances in each of class) and four attributes.

CMC - Contraceptive method choice is related to survey performed on married women who were either pregnant or not aware about pregnancy. This dataset has three classes with 629, 334 and 510 instances in each class with nine attributes.

GLASS - It contains the results of comparison test conducted by Vina for her rule-based system. The dataset has total 214 instances classified into six classes with nine attributes.

WINE - This dataset is a result of chemical analysis of wine consequential from three different cultivators. It has 178 instances with three classes and thirteen attributes.

CANCER - The cancer dataset contains the result of analysis performed on cancer patients. It holds 683 instances having two classes with nine attributes.

VOWEL - The dataset is composed of Indian Telugu vowel sounds. It has 871 data instances with three features and six classes.

SEEDS - The seed dataset contains three classes of wheat, Kama, Rosa and Canadian having 70 instances in each class and seven attributes.

Table 2. Comparison of the simulation results of HBB-BC and other well-known clustering algorithms using average intra cluster distance and standard deviation (in brackets).

Datasets	Clustering algorithms					
	HBB-BC	BB-BC	ACO	GA	PSO	K-means
Iris	96.58	96.8	98.28	125	97.2	106
	(2.18)	(2.22)	(0.426)	(14.6)	(3.35)	(14.6)
CMC	5670	5740	5831.25	5760	5820	5890
	(23.37)	(28.6)	(44.34)	(50.4)	(47)	(47.2)
Glass	227	664	273.46	239	247	229
	(4.76)	(68.9)	(6.58)	(74.5)	(10.5)	(14.3)
Wine	16300	16700	16530.53	16500	16400	18100
	(1.4)	(2.88)	(48.86)	(78.4)	(85.5)	(793)
Cancer	2896	2960	3178.09	3250	3050	3250
	(438)	(557)	(93.45)	(230)	(264)	(251)
Vowel	149000	194000	158458.14	151000	149000	154000
	(498)	(24400)	(3485.38)	(1480)	(502)	(4220)
Seeds	301	306	326 (38.4)	327	328	313
	(0.19)	(47.9)		(18.7)	(39.7)	(0.27)

From experimental results, it is seen that HBB-BC algorithm acquire minimum intra-cluster distance for most of datasets. Whereas in case of vowel dataset, the values of intra-cluster distance of HBB-BC and PSO algorithm are almost equal. Moreover, SD is also computed to show the lower and upper limits of the optimal solution. It has minimum values for most of cases except iris and cancer datasets. Hence, it is concluded that proposed algorithm performs well in clustering field and produces remarkable results.

Table 3. Comparison of the simulation results of proposed HBB-BC, BB-BC, ACO, GA, PSO and K-Means clustering algorithms using accuracy parameter (average case).

Datasets	Clustering algorithms					
	HBB-BC	BB-BC	ACO	GA	PSO	K-means
Iris	84.29	83.25	77.9	78.34	84.13	78.53
CMC	52.27	44.67	38.8	43.30	44.10	44.53
Glass	58.72	55.53	42.32	48.97	53.73	53.84
Wine	68.09	66.43	62.67	65.73	67.94	67.61
Cancer	64.02	57.04	58.29	55.73	56.94	57.61
Vowel	85.46	84.32	84.70	84.70	84.04	83.45
Seeds	87.41	83.16	76.61	79.00	84.73	87.35

The comparison of accuracy parameter for proposed HBB-BC, BB-BC, ACO, GA, PSO and K-Means clustering algorithms is demonstrated in Table 3. The comparative results are analysed in terms of average accuracy rate. From experimental results, it is noticed that Hybrid BB-BC algorithm attain maximum accuracy than other algorithms. Besides, to reveal the efficacy of the proposed algorithm, the convergence behavior is shown in this section. The intra cluster distance parameter is used to illustrate the convergence of the HBB-BC, BB-BC, ACO, GA, PSO and K-Means clustering algorithm.

The convergence behavior of HBB-BC, BB-BC, ACO, GA, PSO and K-Means on seven clustering problems is shown in Fig. 1(a–g). In the graphical illustration, the X and Y-axis represent the iteration numbers and intra-cluster distance respectively. From the graphical representation, it is clearly seen that HBB-BC algorithm converges on minimum values in comparison to other algorithms. Hence, it is concluded that proposed algorithm has better convergence rate than other algorithms.

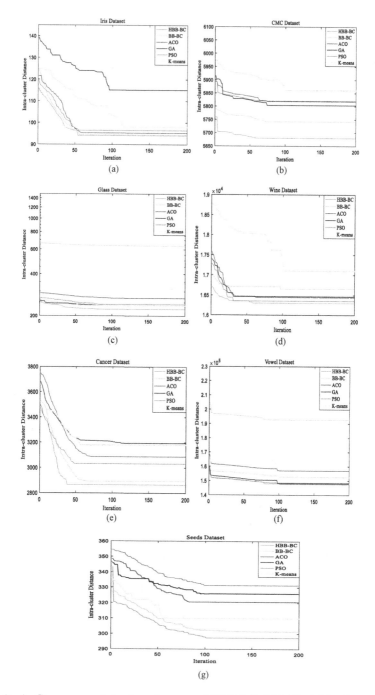

Fig. 1. (a–g): Convergence behavior of proposed HBB-BC, BB-BC, ACO, GA, PSO and K-Means on different datasets using intra cluster distance parameter

4.1   Statistical Results and Discussion

This subsection illustrates the statistical results of HBB-BC and other clustering algorithms. To validate the substantial difference among HBB-BC and compared algorithms, Friedman and Quade tests are applied to evaluate this. The statistical tests are applied on both of performance measures i.e. intra cluster distance and accuracy. The statistical tests are conducted at confidence level (0.5). Two hypotheses are anticipated in this work to notify that the proposed algorithm is statistically better than rest of algorithms. These hypotheses are termed as hypothesis (H_0) and (H_1). The hypothesis (H_0) denotes the population's equivalency while the hypothesis (H_1) stands for inequivalent population.

Table 4. Friedman test performed on intra-cluster distance constraint.

Datasets	Clustering algorithms					
	HBB-BC	BB-BC	ACO	GA	PSO	K-means
Iris	1	2	4	6	3	5
CMC	1	2	5	3	4	6
Glass	1	6	5	3	4	2
Wine	1	5	4	3	2	6
Cancer	1	2	4	5.5	3	5.5
Vowel	1.5	6	5	3	1.5	4
Seeds	1	2	4	5	6	3
Sum	7.5	25	31	28.5	23.5	31.5
Average ranking	1.07	3.57	4.43	4.07	3.36	4.5

Number of observations: 42 Number of problems: 07 Number of algorithms: 06
Sum of squares of ranks: 3999 Correction factor: 514.5 Friedman test statistic: 16.358025
Degree of freedom: 05 p-value: 0.005893 Critical value: 11.070504

Table 4 illustrates the Friedman statistical test using intra-cluster distance. It is observed that the proposed algorithm attains first rank in most cases accept vowel dataset. From these results, the critical value is noted as 11.070504 and p-value is 0.005893 that rejects the null hypothesis and verifies the substantial difference among algorithms.

Table 5. Friedman test performed on accuracy constraint.

Datasets	Clustering algorithms					
	HBB-BC	BB-BC	ACO	GA	PSO	K-means
Iris	1	3	6	5	2	4
CMC	1	2	6	5	4	3
Glass	1	2	6	5	4	3

(continued)

Table 5. (*continued*)

Datasets	Clustering algorithms					
	HBB-BC	BB-BC	ACO	GA	PSO	K-means
Wine	1	4	6	5	2	3
Cancer	1	4	2	6	5	3
Vowel	1	4	2.5	2.5	5	6
Seeds	1	4	6	5	3	2
Sum	7.5	23	34.5	33.5	25	24
Average ranking	1	3.29	4.93	4.79	3.57	3.43

Number of observations: 42 Number of problems: 07 Number of algorithms: 06
Sum of squares of ranks: 4091.5 Correction factor: 514.5 Friedman test statistic: 20.081967
Degree of freedom: 05 p-value: 0.001206 Critical value: 11.070504

Table 5 demonstrates the outcomes of Friedman statistical test conducted using accuracy parameter. It is observed that HBB-BC algorithm achieve best performance whereas ACO algorithm revels worst performance than other algorithms. The p-value is 0.001206 that strongly rejects the null hypothesis and verifies the substantial difference among algorithms. In addition to this, Quade test as a nonparametric test is also conducted in this study. Quade test is an advanced nonparametric test that gives the better result than Friedman test and also the weightage to the size of datasets.

Table 6. Relative size of observation using Quade test on intra-cluster distance constraint.

Datasets	Clustering algorithms					
	HBB-BC	BB-BC	ACO	GA	PSO	K-means
Iris	−5	−3	1	5	−1	3
CMC	−7.5	−4.5	4.5	−1.5	1.5	7.5
Glass	−12.5	12.5	7.5	−2.5	2.5	−7.5
Wine	−15	9	3	−3	−9	15
Cancer	−10	−6	2	8	−2	8
Vowel	−14	17.5	10.5	−3.5	−14	3.5
Seeds	−2.5	−1.5	0.5	1.5	2.5	−0.5
Relative size of observation	−66.5	24	29	4	−19.5	29

Tables 6 and 7 demonstrates the results of Quade test performed on intra-cluster distance parameter. The HBB-BC algorithm have attained the first rank in most cases accept vowel dataset. While the ACO algorithm exhibits worst performance. From statistical outcomes, the critical value and p-value are notified as 2.533555 and 0.004484 respectively that strongly rejects the null hypothesis and verifies the substantial difference among algorithms.

Table 7. Result of Quade test using intra-cluster distance constraint.

Datasets	Clustering algorithms						Relative size of datasets
	HBB-BC	BB-BC	ACO	GA	PSO	K-means	
Iris	1	2	4	6	3	5	2
CMC	1	2	5	3	4	6	3
Glass	1	6	5	3	4	2	5
Wine	1	5	4	3	2	6	6
Cancer	1	2	4	5.5	3	5.5	4
Vowel	1.5	6	5	3	1.5	4	7
Seeds	1	2	4	5	6	3	1
Sum	7.5	25	31	28.5	23.5	31.5	28
Average ranking	1.07	3.57	4.43	4.07	3.36	4.5	4

Quade Statistics = 4.31231 p-value = 0.004484 Critical value = 2.533555

Table 8. Relative size of observation using Quade test on accuracy parameter.

Datasets	Clustering algorithms					
	HBB-BC	BB-BC	ACO	GA	PSO	K-means
Iris	−7.5	−1.5	7.5	4.5	−4.5	1.5
CMC	−15	−9	15	9	3	−3
Glass	−17.5	−10.5	17.5	10.5	3.5	−3.5
Wine	−5	1	5	3	−3	−1
Cancer	−10	2	−6	10	6	−2
Vowel	−2.5	0.5	−1	−1	1.5	2.5
Seeds	−12.5	2.5	12.5	7.5	−2.5	−7.5
Relative size of observation	−70	−15	50.5	43.5	4	−13

Table 9. Results of Quade test on accuracy parameter.

Datasets	Clustering algorithms						Relative Size of datasets
	HBB-BC	BB-BC	ACO	GA	PSO	K-means	
Iris	1	3	6	5	2	4	3
CMC	1	2	6	5	4	3	6
Glass	1	2	6	5	4	3	7
Wine	1	4	6	5	2	3	2
Cancer	1	4	2	6	5	3	4
Vowel	1	4	2.5	2.5	5	6	1
Seeds	1	4	6	5	3	2	5
Sum	7.5	23	34.5	33.5	25	24	28
Average ranking	1	3.29	4.93	4.79	3.57	3.43	4

Quade Statistics = 7.913849 p-value = 7.515e−5 Critical value = 2.533555

Quade test is a progressive nonparametric test, that provide excellent results in compression to parametric tests. The statistical outcomes of Quade test conducted on accuracy parameter is illustrated in Tables 8 and 9. The p-value for Quade test is 7.515e-5 which is much smaller than significant level 0.05. The critical value for Quade test is 2.533555. Overall, it is concluded that the substantial difference is exhibited between the performance of HBB-BC and other clustering algorithm on basis of these statistical tests. Hence, the proposed algorithm is statistically as well as experimentally better than other clustering algorithms.

5 Conclusion

The present work involves the development of a hybrid version of the BB-BC algorithm united with K-means algorithm in order to solve the clustering problems. The proposed algorithm performs two stages working; (i) initialization involves the generation of initial solution through K-means algorithm act as initiation arbitrator; and (ii) optimization includes to obtain the optimal solution using big bang-big crunch algorithm act as an optimizer. The solutions generated from K-means are treated as preliminary population in BB-BC algorithm. The performance of HBB-BC algorithm is tested on seven datasets such as Iris, CMC, Glass, Wine, Cancer, Vowel and Seeds. This hybrid algorithm is compared with BB-BC, K-means, ACO, PSO and GA clustering algorithms using intra-cluster distance and accuracy rate parameters. Additionally, the significance of HBB-BC algorithm also validated by conducting two statistical (Friedman and Quade) tests in this study. Both statistical tests signify the difference between the performance of HBB-BC and other clustering algorithms and validated the existence of the proposed algorithm. Hence, it is concluded that proposed improvement has effectively overwhelmed the limitation of BB-BC algorithm and produces good quality solutions for clustering problems.

References

1. Kant, S., Ansari, I.A.: An improved K means clustering with Atkinson index to classify liver patient dataset. Int. J. Syst. Assur. Eng. Manag. **7**(1), 222–228 (2016)
2. Aggarwal, C.C. (ed.): Data Classification: Algorithms and Applications. CRC Press, Boca Raton (2014)
3. Xu, R., Wunsch, D.C.: Survey of clustering algorithms (2005)
4. Shelokar, P.S., Jayaraman, V.K., Kulkarni, B.D.: An ant colony approach for clustering. Anal. Chim. Acta **509**(2), 187–195 (2004)
5. Maulik, U., Bandyopadhyay, S.: Genetic algorithm-based clustering technique. Pattern Recognit. **33**(9), 1455–1465 (2000)
6. Kumar, Y., Singh, P.K.: A chaotic teaching learning based optimization algorithm for clustering problems. Appl. Intell. **49**(3), 1036–1062 (2019)
7. Cura, T.: A particle swarm optimization approach to clustering. Expert Syst. Appl. **39**(1), 1582–1588 (2012)
8. Bahrololoum, A., Nezamabadi-pour, H., Saryazdi, S.: A data clustering approach based on universal gravity rule. Eng. Appl. Artif. Intell. **45**, 415–428 (2015)

9. Kumar, Y., Singh, P.K.: Improved cat swarm optimization algorithm for solving global optimization problems and its application to clustering. Appl. Intell. **48**(9), 2681–2697 (2018)

10. Cao, F., Liang, J., Jiang, G.: An initialization method for the K-means algorithm using neighborhood model. Comput. Math Appl. **58**(3), 474–483 (2009)

11. Erisoglu, M., Calis, N., Sakallioglu, S.: A new algorithm for initial cluster centers in k-means algorithm. Pattern Recognit. Lett. **32**(14), 1701–1705 (2011)

12. Chang, D.X., Zhang, X.D., Zheng, C.W.: A genetic algorithm with gene rearrangement for K-means clustering. Pattern Recognit. **42**(7), 1210–1222 (2009)

13. Kumar, Y., Sahoo, G.: A hybrid data clustering approach based on improved cat swarm optimization and K-harmonic mean algorithm. AI Commun. **28**(4), 751–764 (2015)

14. Hatamlou, A., Abdullah, S., Hatamlou, M.: Data clustering using big bang–big crunch algorithm. In: Pichappan, P., Ahmadi, H., Ariwa, E. (eds.) INCT 2011. CCIS, vol. 241, pp. 383–388. Springer, Heidelberg (2011). https://doi.org/10.1007/978-3-642-27337-7_36

15. Kumar, A., Kumar, D., Jarial, S.: A novel hybrid K-means and artificial bee colony algorithm approach for data clustering. Decis. Sci. Lett. **7**(1), 65–76 (2018)

16. Abualigah, L.M., Khader, A.T., Al-Betar, M.A., Hanandeh, E.S.: A new hybridization strategy for krill herd algorithm and harmony search algorithm applied to improve the data clustering. Management **9**(11), 1–10 (2017)

17. Boushaki, S.I., Kamel, N., Bendjeghaba, O.: A new quantum chaotic cuckoo search algorithm for data clustering. Expert Syst. Appl. **96**, 358–372 (2018)

18. Hatamlou, A.: A hybrid bio-inspired algorithm and its application. Appl. Intell. **47**(4), 1059–1067 (2017)

19. Bijari, K., Zare, H., Veisi, H., Bobarshad, H.: Memory-enriched big bang–big crunch optimization algorithm for data clustering. Neural Comput. Appl. **29**(6), 111–121 (2018)

20. Yin, B., Guo, Z., Liang, Z., Yue, X.: Improved gravitational search algorithm with crossover. Comput. Electr. Eng. **66**, 505–516 (2018)

21. Rahman, M.A., Islam, M.Z.: A hybrid clustering technique combining a novel genetic algorithm with K-means. Knowl.-Based Syst. **71**, 345–365 (2014)

22. Jiang, B., Wang, N.: Cooperative bare-bone particle swarm optimization for data clustering. Soft. Comput. **18**(6), 1079–1091 (2014)

23. Zhou, Y., Wu, H., Luo, Q., Abdel-Baset, M.: Automatic data clustering using nature-inspired symbiotic organism search algorithm. Knowl.-Based Syst. **163**, 546–557 (2019)

Security Analysis of Cyber Attacks Using Machine Learning Algorithms in eGovernance Projects

Harmeet Malhotra[1(✉)], Meenu Dave[1], and Tripti Lamba[2]

[1] Jagannath University, Jaipur, India
harmeet_hello@yahoomail.com, meenu.s.dave@gmail.com
[2] Institute of Information Technology and Management, New Delhi, India
triptigautam@yahoo.co.in

Abstract. Different nations are striving to implement e-governance on a full scale. The major issue is the problem of secure transactions with high privacy. In order to make sure that the government is functioning properly, there must be a high level of transparency in the system with high accountability, integrity and confidentiality. The risks and challenges that arises by implementing the e-governance are chiefly because of the poor security in free WiFi networks which are given for accessing the e-services. Hence, researchers must develop methods and tools which can react to the attacks and defend themselves autonomously. This paper helps in analysis of few categories of cyber attacks using machine learning algorithms.

Keywords: Cyber security · Risk analysis · Machine learning

1 Introduction

Different systems have different security levels since some people must have more access level than others in order to keep the data in high confidentiality. Previous research has catered to other countries. However, there are very few studies concerning India. The ways of governance change from country to country since they differ with the legal, political, economic situation and also the available technological infrastructure. The computer literacy rate is also important for the implementation level of e-governance, which is very less in developing countries. However, the rapid rise of computer literacy has made it necessary for developing countries to implement e-governance.

Security measures implemented in various e-government projects in different developed countries were evaluated and a strategic framework for e-government security purpose considering both technical and non-technical factors that involve processes, technologies and people has been proposed. The use of Information and Communication Technologies (ICT) has been on the rise and has become common among multiple domains. It is a combination of multiple hardware and software components that creates, stores and interprets information thereby creating communication.

© Springer Nature Singapore Pte Ltd. 2020
P. K. Singh et al. (Eds.): FTNCT 2019, CCIS 1206, pp. 662–672, 2020.
https://doi.org/10.1007/978-981-15-4451-4_52

This rapidly changing technology helps in data management, storage, transmission and dissemination of required information in digital format (Hubackova and Klimova 2014). ICTs have influenced the various economics and polices of the society (Garcia 2015; Visvizi et al. 2017). Similarly, governance has been witnessing a growing connection with technology. The 'twenty tens (2010s)' has envisioned the significant proliferation of technologically advanced devices being installed in government websites and services have been offered, The current trend that has opened new opportunities for development in the government sector using IoT and other techniques. India is a nation that is giving a large emphasis on e-governance improvements. This is common in other developing countries too. It is supporting the usage of Information Technology (IT) in the government sectors where various strategies have been devised to its utilisation (AlGhamdi 2015). Recent programs towards reforming the network connected devices (Nikkei Asian Review 2016) have paved way for the entry of more governance websites. Hence, it is necessary that understanding the perceptions of patients and users of e-governance can provide a better consensus related to the privacy and security.

There are numerous advantages of cloud computing in terms of government. This includes increasing the storage, reducing the cost, improving the automatic process, improving the flexibility and higher levels of mobility among the employees. However, there are large challenges for considering the services (Hashemi et al. 2015). They are segmented into technical, economical and social challenges. Lots of investments are required in order to prepare an efficient e governance system. New environments have to be set up in some cases, whereas the expense of setting up hinders the process in other cases. Other aspects that have to be considered are the privacy and security. It has to be seen whether there will be return on the investments and will be efficient enough to spend the money. Hence, the implementation and operating cost must be very low in order to have a reliable cost and benefit ratio. The system should also be able to be reused by other department of the government. The successful implementation of e-governance requires a high level of involvement by the government.

E-government systems are designed to provide online service to individuals, businesses, and government departments (Carter and Bélanger 2005) like government information to the people. The information may be related to various documents like driver license, birth certificates, marriage certificates, death certificates, income tax payments, etc. It is also enabled for the businesses for communication and documents like policies, rules and regulation, business permits, etc. It is essentially used for transactions between various departments of the government. It may also deal with the international flow of data between different governments. Even though there is huge acceptance of e-government systems for providing effective & efficient services over the Internet, there still remains threat to the privacy and security. A few major threats are privacy violations and identity theft (Bélanger and Carter 2008). There is a lack of trust among the general public on the services offered by the government and this is a huge barrier to adopting the e-government systems (Palanisamy and Mukerji 2012). Attacks on the websites and servers cannot be avoided when the e-government servers are not secured. The most common types of cyber-attacks are Denial of Service (DoS) attacks, accessing the network in an unauthorized manner, stealing personal data, online financial fraud, application layer attacks like cross site scripting (XSS), etc.

(Bélanger and Carter 2008). eGovernance is the concept of delivering government services, data exchange, communication transactions and integration of different services by using ICT. These services are exchanged between the government and other entities like common citizens, businesses, etc. This will enable faster and more efficient delivery of government services to the public. It will also reduce the cost and increase the efficiency of the government thereby improving the transparency and red tapism. The structure of the administration will also change and improve the quality of the service.

2 Literature Review

There were security holes found in TCP/IP network layers and other vulnerable resources both, technical and non-technical and deployment of inadequate and insufficient security laws and standards so the concept of providing security to e-government services gain importance. Moreover, there is no standard technique for detecting the vulnerabilities, where vulnerability might be either known or unknown. The issues faced in providing security to e-governance has been discussed in (Singh and Karaulia 2011). It is seen that there are lots of security issues since lots of sensitive information may be available in the website. There may be lots of documentation in government projects that has to be maintained well in the server. Only authorised people must have access to certain documents and hence enhancement of security is necessary for smoother and safe government undertaking.

The various attacks that the e-governance sites are susceptible to are watering hole attack (Malin et al. 2017), Sybil attack (Vasudeva and Sood 2018), Replay attack (Farha and Chen 2018), Zero day (Tran et al. 2016), Black hole attack, grey hole attack (Tripathi et al. 2013), etc. E-Governance systems need ICT based network for executing the system properly, however, it is different from other online systems especially in-terms of security since legal information has to be protected from the users who are not eligible. If the system is stable, then it may also be used for a wide range of business transactions. Some of the problems in the e-governance are as follows. It has to be ensured that the information is accessible only to those who are authorised. Hence, confidentiality must be maintained. The information must not tampered by unauthorised users. In some cases, even the authorised users may tamper the data by mistake or even purposely and hence integrity should be maintained. The data must be delivered only to those who are intended and hence those send the documents must he accountable. A major problem is authentication where the entities must have valid credentials to access the parts of the system. Most public systems lack trust especially in developing nations, hence a trust must be established and shown to make sure the citizens gain trust of the infrastructure.

A good e-governance website requires multiple security features. Digital Envelope combines the key management using public key encryption and the high speed symmetric encryption. Another necessity is the Digital Signature, which contains features like Hash Algorithms, Key Exchange, etc. for providing Non-repudiation, Data integrity, and Certificate based Authentication. Digital credentials should also be established. Digital Certificates create framework for establishing digital identities.

Pawlak and Wendling (2013) has analysed the advancement in security in government websites and have compared the different security features and have concluded that there should be more government initiatives for defending themselves and their documents. There has to be innovations in various trends like the cloud, IoT, big data, the neuronal interface, mobile internet, quantum computing, and the cyberspace militarisation. Hence, it has been suggested to collaborate the private and public spheres in the future.

To avoid latency in the e-governance websites, the management of time-critical services have to be processed. Hence, a secure cloud environment for effortless management of IoT applications is essential. Hence, it has to be thoroughly investigated. A novel technique for developing an efficient cloud to edge has been proposed in Celesti et al. (2019). A Messaging Oriented Middleware (MOM) on the basis of an Instant Message Protocol (IMP) has provided good performance, however it has overlooked security requirements. This has been solved in this work and has particularly discussed the associated issues related to their improvement for achieving data confidentiality, authenticity, integrity and non-repudiation. A case study considering a MOM architectural model has also been analysed. The experimental results have been performed on a real test bed and have shown how the introduced secure capabilities do not affect the overall performances of the whole middle-ware.

Detecting the anomalies have to deal with a large amount of data; especially, the techniques of detecting the intrusion detection has to detect all of network data. If data dimension is reduced in the data sampling stage and the feature data of network data is obtained automatically, then the efficiency of detection can be improved greatly. SVM has been presented in (Chen et al. 2016) to detect the anomalies on the basis of compressive sampling. Compressed sampling technique has been used in the compressed sensing theory to implement the feature compression for flow in network data so that enhanced sparse representation can be obtained. After that SVM is utilised for classifying the compression results. The proposed technique has been proved to be efficient in detecting the behaviour of network anomalies behaviour quickly without reducing the classification accuracy. Hence, SVM has been proved to be efficient in giving detecting the anomalies in the network. Canonical Correlation Analysis (CCA) has been used for dimensionality reduction (Jendoubi and Strimmer 2018). CCA has been proved to be better than the conventional PCA and LDA approaches.

3 Significance of the Research

- This may bring in more clarity in the policies of cyber security. The security policies that are outdated will also become modernized.
- Since lots of sensitive data is added to the research, adding security features will bring additional security. Hence, the cyber security will be enhanced. This will bring in more confidence in implementing it in all government departments.
- This study will aid the government policies especially in developing countries. This is important since it will bring about more enhancements.

- The purpose of research is to apply the machine learning techniques and choose the best possible method of predicting a particular category of cyber attack by studying the network traffic.

4 Proposed Methodology

From the above literature review, it can be seen that there is a large security issues that must be addressed. The most common types of cyber-attacks are Denial of Service (DoS) attacks, accessing the network in an unauthorized manner, stealing personal data, online financial fraud, application layer attacks like cross site scripting (XSS), etc. (Bélanger and Carter 2008). Hence, privacy and security have to be protected to increase the trust among the users when interacting with e-government services (Alshehri and Drew 2010).

The existing techniques usually take a lot of time in identifying any anomalies in the system. Hence, it is necessary to speed up the process in order to prevent the attacks from taking altogether. Hence a relevant machine learning technique has to be used in order to learn and get trained to automatically deter the attacks. This technique has to be quick and at the same time efficient. It is necessary to predict and prevent the attacks in the e-governance websites. The attacks are predicted by using a learning algorithm. The data about the website is initially obtained and stored. However, pre-processing the data is necessary before being given into the machine learning algorithm. Hence initially, the features are reduced in the data obtained from the website. This is done by combining the data that is similar and identifying the features that are required. Those features that are not required are discarded.

The proposed hybrid framework which is described in the Fig. 1 is known as "Cyber-Attack Prediction" which contains various steps which are as follows:

- Firstly, Boruta is being used as feature reduction technique to identify the relevant features required in the dataset. The reduced features that are obtained are then given as an input to the machine learning algorithm.
- Secondly, attack identification is done on the new filtered dataset. These algorithms were used to classify the data and group the attacks into similar attacks.
- Thirdly, three machine learning algorithms, that is, neural network, support vector machine and Native Bayes, were tried and tested to find the anomaly and accuracy of the proposed framework based on which some mathematical and statistical results are generated.
- Fourthly, these results are being compared and the best algorithm for risk analysis has been chosen.

When the attack takes place next time, the proposed framework will be able to detect the packets received and predict that the attacks are going to take place. This machine learning has to be initially trained. Hence. UNSW NB-15(UNSW 2018) dataset is being used for training the dataset. The layered classification technique is being used to detect the attacks. Firstly, the framework identifies whether there is an attack or not. Once it is ensured that it is an attack, further it tries to identify and classify it into a Fuzzer, DoS or Reconnaissance attack.

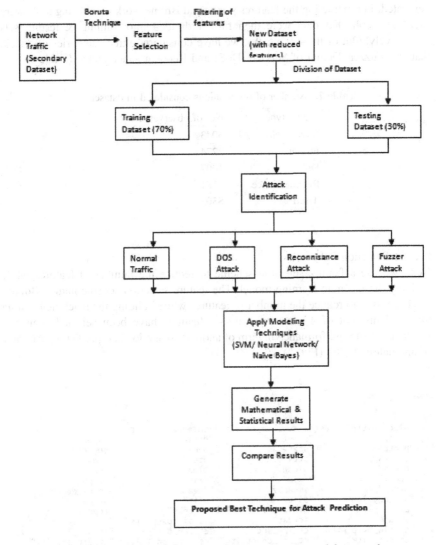

Fig. 1. Implementation of security analysis of proposed framework

The framework generated has undergone various phases which are as follows:

- Description of Dataset
  There are 9 different types of cyber attacks in UNSW dataset. These attacks are common in multi-cloud environment and hence are more suitable for for contemporary anomaly detection schemes. The packets of this dataset were generated using IXIA PerfectStorm tool to monitor normal traffic behavioural patterns and attacks using the network traffic. Then, 49 features were extracted from the tcpdump files

generated. For extracting the features Argus and Bro network monitoring tools were used. The collected data were then further divided into training & testing sets respectively. Out of these 9 attacks, we have considered three categories of attack, that are, Fuzzer, Denial of Service (DoS) and Reconaissance attack (Table 1).

Table 1. Number of observations considered in dataset

Traffic type	No. of observations
Normal(No attack)	3043
Fuzzer	2274
DoS	1007
Reconaissance	2181
Total	**8505**

- Feature Selection Scheme
  Next, we use a feature selection scheme to reduce the number of features while building the machine learning model. The feature selection scheme named **Boruta** has been used to reduce the number of features while building the machine learning model. Thus, out of 49 features only 45 features have been selected. This has resulted in better performance in term of anomaly detection and predicting accuracy of anomalous traffic (Fig. 2).

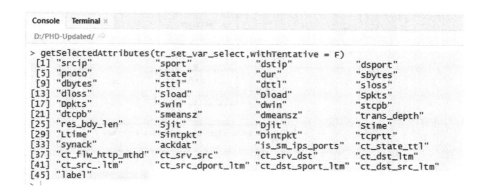

Fig. 2. Result of feature selection technique - Boruta

Boruta algorithm is a feature selection technique that adds randomness to the dataset by creating shuffled copies known as shadow features. Then, it trains a random forest classifier on the extended dataset and calculates the Mean Decrease Accuracy. The features having higher means are more important for the study as compared to others. Finally, the algorithm stops when all features either gets confirmed or are rejected or the algorithm has reached the specified limit of random forest runs.

- Anomaly detection using Machine Learning Models
  Then various machine learning algorithms have been applied for classification of attacks. Firstly, SVM or Support Vector Machine has been applied which is a linear model for classification and regression problems. It can solve linear and non-linear problems and work well for many practical problems. Secondly, Naive Bayes algorithm which is a probabilistic machine learning method has been used for classification tasks. Thirdly, Neural networks algorithm was used which processes one record at a time, and learn by comparing their classification of the record with the known actual classification parameter. The errors found in the initial classification is fed back into the network, and used to modify the networks algorithm for further iterations.
  The work presented in this research focuses mainly on anomaly detection and calculates the overall accuracy of the 3 machine learning models. However, our focus extends to feature selection and categorization of different types of attacks. The training set taken was 70% and testing set 30%. (Training records – 5953, Testing record – 2552).
- Result and Analysis
  In order to justify the result of our framework it has been tried to compare it with other machine learning algorithms and the results found are as follows (Table 2):

Table 2. Comparison of results of machine learning algorithms

	SVM	Naive Bayes	Neural network
Accuracy	90.6	80.05	99.92
95% CI	(0.894, 0.917)	(0.7845, 0.8159)	(0.9972, 0.9999)
No information rate	0.35	0.35	0.36
Kappa	0.86	0.7196	0.9989

The following is the cyber attack wise class statistics

Result of SVM Algorithm

Statistics by Class:

Class:	Fuzzers	DoS	Normal	Reconnaissance
Sensitivity	0.8861	0.72698	1.0000	0.8807
Specificity	0.9388	0.97988	1.0000	0.9584
Pos Pred Value	0.8292	0.83577	1.0000	0.8846
Neg Pred Value	0.9609	0.96225	1.0000	0.9568
Prevalence	0.2512	0.12343	0.3593	0.2661
Detection Rate	0.2226	0.08973	0.3593	0.2343
Detection Prevalence	0.2684	0.10737	0.3593	0.2649
Balanced Accuracy	0.9124	0.85343	1.0000	0.9195

Result of Naive Bayes Algorithm

Statistics by Class:

Class:	Fuzzers	DoS	Normal	Reconnaissance
Sensitivity	0.9483	0.079365	0.9189	0.8351
Specificity	0.7899	0.992848	0.9988	0.9503
Pos Pred Value	0.6106	0.609756	0.9976	0.8591
Neg Pred Value	0.9778	0.884508	0.9576	0.9408
Prevalence	0.2578	0.123433	0.3527	0.2661
Detection Rate	0.2445	0.009796	0.3241	0.2222
Detection Prevalence	0.4005	0.016066	0.3248	0.2586
Balanced Accuracy	0.8691	0.536106	0.9588	0.8927

Result of Neural Network Algorithm

Statistics by Class:

Class:	Fuzzers	DoS	Normal	Reconnaissance
Sensitivity	1.0000	0.9934	1.0000	1.0000
Specificity	0.9995	1.0000	1.0000	0.9995
Pos Pred Value	0.9985	1.0000	1.0000	0.9985
Neg Pred Value	1.0000	0.9991	1.0000	1.0000
Prevalence	0.2637	0.1183	0.3613	0.2567
Detection Rate	0.2637	0.1176	0.3613	0.2567
Detection Prevalence	0.2641	0.1176	0.3613	0.2571
Balanced Accuracy	0.9997	0.9967	1.0000	0.9997

From the above result and analysis, it is clear that Neural Network algorithm is the best possible framework for predicting the cyber attacks as the accuracy is 99% as shown in the above figure.

After the training process, this framework can be implemented in the firmware of the e-governance website server and the network will be constantly monitored for any sign of anomalies. Once an anomaly is seen, the proposed framework will immediately notify the system and take measures to prevent the attack. The parameters will be evaluated, and the obtained results will be compared with existing techniques to find the effectiveness of the proposed system.

5 Conclusion

In the proposed algorithm, we have trained our models to distinguish a particular attack from other types of attacks by studying various types of network traffic. Firstly the normal packets are distinguished from anomalous packets. Then, in further stages the analysis of anomalous traffic is done for different attacks categorization.

Designing and implementing the most effective technique for providing security to e-government is an important issue, since the data available in government websites are normally very sensitive. In this work, combining the existing models for securing the government web services will aid in forming trust among the general public there-by leading to adoption of these services by the general public. Providing security to this service is not only a technical issue, but much more than that. The proposed technique may lead to the rise of electronic government services and improvement of security issues in the government, mainly in the country's development. This will enable a reliable communication between citizens and government and also between different government departments.

References

AlGhamdi, M.A.: Applying innovative ehealth to improve patient experience within healthcare organizations in the Kingdom of Saudi Arabia. In: International Conference on E-health Networking, Application & Services (HealthCom), pp. 346–349 (2015)

Alshehri, M., Drew, S.: E-government fundamentals. In: IADIS International Conference ICT, Society and Human Beings (2010). https://research-repository.griffith.edu.au/bitstream/handle/10072/37709/67525_1.pdf

Bélanger, F., Carter, L.: Trust and risk in e-government adoption. J. Strategic Inf. Syst. **17**(2), 165–176 (2008). https://linkinghub.elsevier.com/retrieve/pii/S0963868707000637

Carter, L., Bélanger, F.: The utilization of e-government services: citizen trust, innovation and acceptance factors. Inf. Syst. J. **15**(1), 5–25 (2005). http://doi.wiley.com/10.1111/j.1365-2575.2005.00183

Celesti, A., Fazio, M., Galletta, A., Carnevale, L., Wan, J., Villari, M.: An approach for the secure management of hybrid cloud–edge environments. Future Gen. Comput. Syst. **90**, 1–19 (2019). https://linkinghub.elsevier.com/retrieve/pii/S0167739X18300682

Chen, S., Peng, M., Xiong, H., Yu, X.: SVM intrusion detection model based on compressed sampling. J. Electr. Comput. Eng. **2016**, 1–6 (2016). http://www.hindawi.com/journals/jece/2016/3095971/

Chopra, L., Lamba, T.: A study of cyber security in web environment. IITM J. Manag. IT **5**(1), 114–120 (2014)

Farha, F., Chen, H.: Mitigating replay attacks with ZigBee solutions. Netw. Secur. **2018**(1), 13–19 (2018). https://linkinghub.elsevier.com/retrieve/pii/S1353485818300084

Garcia, M.: The impact of IoT on economic growth: a multifactor productivity approach. In: 2015 International Conference on Computational Science and Computational Intelligence (CSCI), December 2015, Las Vegas, NV, USA, pp. 855–856. IEEE (2015)

Hashemi, S., Monfaredi, K., Hashemi, S.Y.: Cloud computing for secure services in e-government architecture. J. Inf. Technol. Res. **8**(1), 43–61 (2015). http://dx.doi.org/10.4018/JITR.2015010104

Hubackova, S., Klimova, B.F.: Integration of ICT in lifelong education. Procedia – Soc. Behav. Sci. **116**, 3593–3597 (2014). https://linkinghub.elsevier.com/retrieve/pii/S1877042814008258

Jendoubi, T., Strimmer, K.: A whitening approach to probabilistic canonical correlation analysis for omics data integration. http://arxiv.org/abs/1802.03490 (2018)

Malin, C.H., Gudaitis, T., Holt, T.J., Kilger, M.: Phishing, watering holes, and scareware. In: Deception in the Digital Age, pp. 149–166. Elsevier (2017). https://linkinghub.elsevier.com/retrieve/pii/B9780124116306000050

Nikkei Asian Review: Japan, Saudi Arabia to cooperate on Internet of Things renewables (2016)

Palanisamy, R., Mukerji, B.: Security and privacy issues in E-government. In: E-Government Service Maturity and Development, pp. 236–248. IGI Global (2012). http://services.igi-global.com/resolvedoi/resolve.aspx?doi=10.4018/978-1-60960-848-4.ch013

Pawlak, P., Wendling, C.: Trends in cyberspace: can governments keep up? Environ. Syst. Decis. **33**(4), 536–543 (2013). http://link.springer.com/10.1007/s10669-013-9470-5

Singh, S., Karaulia, S.: E-governance: information security issues. In: International Conference on Computer Science and Information Technology (2011). http://psrcentre.org/images/extraimages/77.1211468.pdf

Tran, H., Campos-Nanez, E., Fomin, P., Wasek, J.: Cyber resilience recovery model to combat zero-day malware attacks. Comput. Secur. **61**, 19–31 (2016). https://linkinghub.elsevier.com/retrieve/pii/S0167404816300505

Tripathi, M., Gaur, M.S., Laxmi, V.: Comparing the impact of black hole and gray hole attack on LEACH in WSN. Procedia Comput. Sci. **19**, 1101–1107. https://linkinghub.elsevier.com/retrieve/pii/S1877050913007631

UNSW. The UNSW-NB15 Dataset Description (2018). https://www.unsw.adfa.edu.au/unsw-canberra-cyber/cybersecurity/ADFA-NB15-Datasets/

Vasudeva, A., Sood, M.: Survey on sybil attack defense mechanisms in wireless ad hoc networks. J. Netw. Comput. Appl. **120**, 78–118 (2018). https://linkinghub.elsevier.com/retrieve/pii/S1084804518302303

Visvizi, A., Mazzucelli, C., Lytras, M.: Irregular migratory flows. J. Sci. Technol. Policy Manag. **8**(2), 227–242 (2017)

Wadhwani, G.K., Khatri, S.K., Muttoo, S.K.: Critical evaluation of secure routing protocols for MANET. In: IEEE International Conference on Advances in Computing, Communication Control and Networking, pp. 202–206 (2018)

Wadhwani, G.K., Khatri, S.K., Muttoo, S.K.: Trust modeling for secure route discovery in mobile ad-hoc networks. In: IEEE International Conference on Reliability, Infocomm Technologies and Optimization, pp. 391–395 (2017)

Techniques for Task Scheduling in Cloud and Fog Environment: A Survey

Raj Mohan Singh[✉], Lalit Kumar Awasthi, and Geeta Sikka

Department of Computer Science and Engineering, Dr B R Ambedkar National
Institute of Technology, Jalandhar, India
rm_singh14@yahoo.com, lalitdec@gmail.com,
sikkag@gmail.com

Abstract. Computing paradigms have evolved over the years in the form of
parallel, distributed, grid, cloud, and fog computing. Scheduling is a fundamental issue in distributed environments where several tasks compete among
available resources. Inefficient scheduling mechanisms lead to underutilization
and overutilization of resources. Scheduling algorithm should strive to maximize performance and optimize crucial parameters for improving the user QoS
(Quality of Service). There is a pressing need to improve resource utilization for
increasing the scheduling efficiency. A number of techniques including
heuristic, metaheuristic, as well as hybrid approaches have been proposed in the
literature to find near-optimum solutions for task scheduling. This paper presents
a survey of various scheduling techniques along with the associated metrics in
cloud and fog computing. Comparison with state of the art techniques is studied
and limitations discussed in order to device more efficient scheduling techniques
in future. Finally, future directions related to research on task scheduling are
discussed.

Keywords: Cloud · Fog · Heuristic · Metaheuristic · Task scheduling

1 Introduction

Computing paradigms have evolved over the years in the form of parallel, distributed,
grid, cloud and fog. Cloud technology provides a multitude of benefits like scalable
infrastructure, on-demand resource allocation, flexible pricing, services provisioning
etc. It encompasses three service models: Infrastructure-as-a-Service (IaaS), Platform-
as-a-Service (PaaS), and Software-as-a-Service (SaaS). However, most of the cloud
data centers are centralized which implies larger separation between devices and the
cloud. To fill this gap fog computing that enables edge computing came into
prominence.

Fog is a distributed paradigm that extends the computing, storage and networking
facilities closer to edge devices. By allowing computation closer to data sources, fog
can reduce latency and cost of sending data to the distant cloud. Fog complements the
cloud by processing of data at the network edge. It comprises a large number of nodes
that are geographically distributed. Fog provides a horizontal as well as hierarchical
architecture that is able to connect anything between the cloud and edge. Fog network

© Springer Nature Singapore Pte Ltd. 2020
P. K. Singh et al. (Eds.): FTNCT 2019, CCIS 1206, pp. 673–685, 2020.
https://doi.org/10.1007/978-981-15-4451-4_53

consists of common networking devices like switches, routers, access points, gateways, base stations, set top boxes, etc. Fog Computing offers numerous advantages like decentralized decision-making, efficient bandwidth usage, lower operational costs, interoperability and continuous operations in situations where reliable network connectivity is a challenging task etc. Cisco initiated the idea of fog computing in 2012 [1]. The increasing number of devices has led to generation of massive amount of data. The data generated by IoT (Internet of Things) devices is usually processed in the cloud environment. However, it is very impractical to transfer such huge amounts of data to the cloud. Additionally, for most of the applications especially latency-sensitive ones, moving such huge amount of data to the cloud adds latency and is not an efficient solution. As a result, analyzing data closer to the source minimizes latency, frees the core network of huge traffic and makes sensitive data secure by keeping it inside the network.

The huge amount of data and the increase in number of devices will raise some issues for cloud computing, like ensuring low latency and supporting high mobility. Fog can withstand this amount of data and enables efficient support of IoT infrastructure. Fog helps in imparting low latency, supports location awareness and supports real time applications. Figure 1 depicts the various capabilities of fog like security, cognition, agility, latency, and efficiency. Comparison between cloud and fog is shown in Table 1.

Table 1. Comparison of cloud and fog by using different features.

Features	Cloud	Fog
Computing model	Centralized	Distributed
Size	Large	Small
Latency	High	Low
Mobility	Limited	Supported
Deployment Cost	High	Low
Storage	High	Low
Access	Fixed and wireless	Wireless
Distance	Far	Near
Power consumption	High	Low
Computing Capacity	High	Low
Target User	Internet users	Mobile users
Real-Time applications	Difficult to support	Supported

The three-layered hierarchical fog architecture is depicted in Fig. 1. It comprises end layer, fog layer, and cloud layer. The end layer is concerned with different IoT devices like mobile phones, sensors, smart vehicles, smart cards etc. This layer is close to users and widely distributed geographically. The devices sense the physical objects or events. Data is gathered and transmitted to upper layers for the purpose of storage and processing. The fog layer comprises routers, gateways, switches, access points, base stations etc. The end devices can obtain services by connecting with the fog nodes. These fog nodes can be static or mobile. Fog nodes are connected with cloud for powerful processing and voluminous storage. Fog layer supports real-time as well as latency-aware applications. The cloud layer includes high-end servers and storage devices. It offers robust computing and storage capabilities. It can support extensive computational analysis and various services like smart home, smart manufacturing, etc.

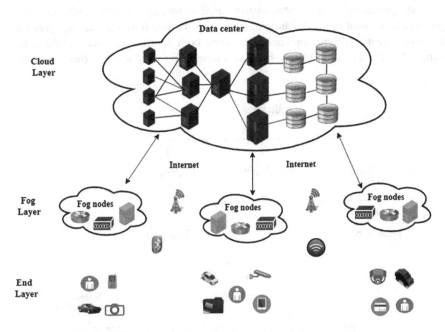

Fig. 1. Three layer architecture for cloud and fog computing.

In this work, a survey of various scheduling techniques in cloud and fog is presented. The organization of this paper is as follows. The second section focuses on the task-scheduling problem in distributed environments along with classification of scheduling algorithms. The third section presents literature review on scheduling techniques along with comparative analysis of existing scheduling techniques. Lastly, conclusion and future directions related to research are discussed.

2 Task Scheduling

Task scheduling is a key issue in distributed environments that need to manage several tasks among existing resources. The aim of all distributed systems is to enhance the throughput and to provide efficient resource utilization. For this purpose, there is a need to sequence the activities for leveraging the performance potential of such computing environments. Optimal scheduling strategies involve mapping of a tasks to resources for efficiently exploiting the capabilities of such computing environments. There exist limited number of resources for serving greater number of user requests in fog. Therefore, optimal task scheduling is required in such an environment. Efficient resource allocation would also result in achieving high throughput.

Task scheduling is an NP complete problem [2]. A number of techniques including heuristic, metaheuristic, as well as hybrid approaches are proposed in the literature to find near-optimum solutions for task scheduling in cloud [3]. Heuristic algorithms employ trial-and-error strategy for generating new solutions but they does not guarantee an optimal solution. Metaheuristics based techniques [4] can handle vast search spaces to reach near optimal solution and as a result, they have gained huge popularity in the past years. Hybrid approaches combine both heuristic and metaheuristic techniques. The classification of metaheuristics scheduling techniques is shown in Fig. 2.

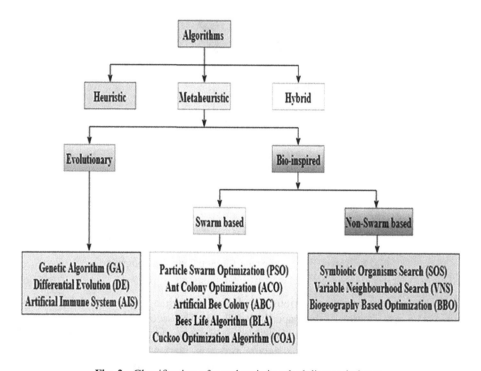

Fig. 2. Classification of metaheuristic scheduling techniques.

Metaheuristics draw inspiration form nature. Biology based algorithms constitute the largest fraction among them. Swarm based category is concerned with collective intelligence of group of agents. The whole system is self-organized and interactions between such agents leads to intelligent global behavior. Many biology-inspired algorithms do not rely on swarming behavior and as such, they constitute a separate category. Evolutionary algorithms are inspired from the process of natural evolution of humans. It should be noted that this classification is not unique. Classifications largely depend on the underlying focus or emphasis and may vary.

3 Related Works

Many researchers are focusing on using metaheuristic techniques [5, 6] for efficient task scheduling in cloud and fog scenarios. A survey of task scheduling techniques applied to cloud as well as fog environment is presented below:

Dhinesh Babu et al. [7] proposed a dynamic honey bee based algorithm for optimizing load balancing as well as considering priorities of tasks in order to minimize waiting time. A comparison with different techniques like Weighted Round Robin (WRR), First-in-First-Out (FIFO), and Dynamic Load Balancing (DLB) is made based upon makespan and degree of imbalance. Although, the proposed approach achieves the desired objectives, it lacks scalability and suffers from starvation in case of low priority jobs. Gu et al. [8] presented a study on distribution of tasks, base station association, and VM placement in fog supported medical cyber-physical systems with the focus on minimizing the overall cost. However, the proposed approach is not suited for cloud–fog environment because of cellular network architecture. Oueis et al. [9] propounded an algorithm for balancing load in fog scenario in which local resources are allocated to small cells. Fog clusters are employed for servicing user requests. The focus is on improving both the performance of the network as well as users Quality of Experience (QoE). Zuo et al. [10] proposed a multi-objective resource cost model that optimizes cost and performance. An improved Ant Colony technique is utilized which solves the problem of falling into local optimum in case of original Ant Colony algorithm. Simulation experiments are conducted based makespan, cost, deadline, and resource utilization. The proposed approach is compared with original Ant Colony algorithm, First cum first Served (FCFS), and Min-Min algorithm. The approach considerably reduces the makespan, but in some application instances the improvement in resource utilization is not satisfactory.

Kimpan et al. [11] combined heuristic approaches with Artificial Bee Colony algorithm with the focus to reduce makespan and balance load in heterogeneous cloud environment. Experiments were conducted using different data sets under varying number of tasks while keeping the Virtual Machines (VMs) fixed. Three different case scenarios are discussed based upon five different parameters. The approach minimizes makespan with increasing number of tasks but does not give satisfactory results in some cases. The authors have not considered Quality-of-Service (QoS) parameters like cost, energy efficiency, etc. The impact of load balancing is not discussed. Abdullahi et al. [12] presented a discrete version of Symbiotic Organism Search (SOS) algorithm named DSOS to schedule independent tasks in cloud. The proposed approach is compared in terms of makespan, response time, and degree of imbalance. Experiments performed on four data sets revealed that performance of DSOS increases with increasing search space. The improved performance of DSOS is due to mutual benefit and parasite vector mechanisms that are distinct to SOS. However, the approach is compared with variants of PSO algorithm only.

Song et al. [13] applied dynamic graph partitioning approach for balancing load in fog environment in which task assignment to fog nodes is carried out on basis of required resources. The motive is to reduce node migrations. However, this approach is not efficient for dynamic load balancing in fog scenario because the graph of redistribution of graph when dealing with the changes. Moon et al. [14] propounded a slave ants based optimization algorithm for efficient allocation of tasks to VMs in cloud. Diversification and reinforcement strategies are employed for enhancing the performance of the algorithm. Resource utilization and cost are not discussed. Mishra et al. [15] proposed an ACO based approach to reduce makespan and average waiting time. This algorithm uses probability function for assigning tasks to VMs to optimize the parameters. The optimal values of the parameters are taken and the performance is compared with Random and Round Robin algorithms. Experiments reveal that the proposed strategy performs satisfactorily. Important issues like load balancing, reliability, and cost are not considered and the proposed approach is not evaluated with respect to other metaheuristic approaches.

Neto et al. [16] introduced a multi-tenancy based load distribution algorithm for fog environments. The metrics used are Tenant Maximum Acceptance Delay (TMAD), and Tenant Priority (TP). Three case studies are discussed. The first case study consists of three different tenants in a small scenario with four fogs connected to each other with four nodes for sending user loads. The second one uses five tenants in the same scenario but the fogs are not connected to each other as in the first and the last one considers a larger scenario with ten fogs connected to each other with each fog having twenty nodes for and two tenants. The algorithm is compared with Delay-Driven Load Distribution (DDLD) strategy and experimental results reveal that in all the cases the proposed approach can distribute load more effectively than DDLD. Rahbari et al. [17] presented a Knapsack based scheduling approach named KnapSOS that is optimized by using Symbiotic Organisms Search (SOS) algorithm. The proposed method is simulated using two case studies using cost, network usage, and energy. The results reveal that KnapSOS performs better than FCFS and Knapsack. Simulation is done in iFogsim.

Kapsalis et al. [18] presented a cooperative for architecture for performing management and execution of tasks by employing a distributed communication method. Fog broker is assigned the task of workload balancing. However, the proposed approach does not consider mobility of fog nodes. In addition, network characteristics like link information, number of hops and path states are not mentioned. Tavana et al. [19] have proposed a Discrete Cuckoo Optimization Algorithm (DCOA) using Group Technology in cloud computing. Since the original COA was designed for dealing with continuous problems, the discrete version redefined the immigration process. A novel technique for grouping the cuckoos using Jaccard index is defined. The objective of the proposed approach is to control operational costs like energy consumption of servers and VMs, penalty cost, and task migration costs. Comparison with popular algorithms like First fit, Round Robin, and GA confirm that DCOA performs better than other algorithms for all the costs and also performs satisfactorily in large problems.

Nasr et al. [20] discussed a scheduling approach named Online Potential Finish Time (OPFT) in order to enhance the cloud broker. The proposed approach assigns the tasks to the VMs in depending on their processing power. PFT of the arrived tasks is calculated and tasks are scheduled based on this value. In this way, each VM gets the best set of tasks. The metrics utilized include schedule length, cost, and balancing degree. The new approach is compared with FCFS, RR, Min-Min, and MCT algorithm. OPFT algorithm performs better in comparison to other approaches.

Authors in [21] presented a hybrid of cuckoo search and oppositional based learning for scheduling in cloud for improving the makespan and cost. The tasks are scheduled based on fitness function. The proposed scheme evaluates better in comparison with other existing algorithms, though it is not suited for real-time applications. Moreover, important issues like resource utilization, load balancing are and energy efficiency are not addressed. Choudhari et al. [22] discussed a priority scheduling algorithm that is an improvement of ERA (Efficient Resource Algorithm) in fog environment. The performance metrics used are response time and cost. The results are simulated in a cloud-only scenario as well as different fog-cloud scenarios and the proposed prioritized scheduling is able to reduce the time as well as cost because it efficiently prioritizes tasks as per delay tolerance levels thus resulting in higher overall output.

Mehmood et al. [23] discussed three load balancing algorithms namely, RR, Throttled, and Odds algorithm in Smart Grid environment. The parameters considered are response time, cost and processing time. Experimental results indicate that: (1) Throttled algorithm performs well than RR. (2) Odds algorithm dominates both RR and Throttled. (3) With increasing number of user requests the Odds algorithm is outperformed by RR and Throttled algorithm. Yin et al. [24] introduced container virtual technology for fog in the intelligent manufacturing environment. Authors focused on task scheduling and resource allocation in order to ensure real-time performance. The reallocation strategy was used for reducing the task delay. Nazar et al. [25] presented a new energy management system in cloud-fog environment. Modified SJF is proposed to manage load between VMs on fog servers. In the proposed scheme there are two fogs and one dedicated cloud server. The evaluation metrics used are processing time, response time, and cost. Comparative analysis of the proposed approach is done with RR and Throttled algorithm. From the experiments, it can be inferred that Modified SJF is not at par with RR and Throttled algorithms because of limitation in network delays.

Zahid et al. [26] discussed a Hill Climbing technique to manage load on VMs with the aim of reducing the response time, processing time and delay. In the proposed framework four different regions are taken with each region containing a fog with a cluster of buildings. Results from simulation reveal that the proposed strategy performs satisfactorily. Kamal et al. [27] addressed the issue of load balancing by employing an heuristic approach for solving a Constraint Satisfaction Problem (CSP). The algorithm first checks the assignment conflicts and then randomly assigns VMs to requests. The proposed approach is compared in terms of processing time, response time, and cost with Throttled and Round Robin algorithms. It helps in allocating optimal resources to requests thereby providing better simulation results.

Bitam et al. [28] presented a new method based on bees swarm for scheduling of jobs in fog environment. The new proposed approach focuses on two main behaviors of bees i.e. food foraging and reproduction. Performance evaluation is done by using two metrics namely CPU execution time and Memory. Experimental studies reveal that BLA fares better than GA and PSO on the basis of scheduling cost. It is also capable of executing all the jobs with a reduced execution time and lesser memory. Natesan et al. [29] discussed an enhanced grey wolf optimization technique to minimize makespan and energy consumption by modifying the hunting and encircling equations. The authors have not focused on parameters like load balancing, reliability, and security. Moreover, the technique is not implemented in real cloud environment. Manju et al. [30] have presented constrained min-min algorithm in their proposed approach with the objective of evenly distributing the load and minimizing response time. The proposed approach is evaluated under different configurations and achieves better results for response time as compared to RR and Priority-Based algorithms. Narendrababu Reddy et al. [31] proposed a task scheduling policy by modifying Ant Colony Optimization (ACO) algorithm with the objective of improving makespan and degree of imbalance. The modified approach is able to decrease makespan values significantly in comparison to other techniques. However, this study lacks in-depth analysis of findings. Nguyen et al. [32] focused on minimizing makespan and cost in cloud-fog environment. The proposed approach has a high fitness value, maintains population diversity and is capable of reaching a more optimal solution. Simulations were performed on different datasets with varying sizes and in different scenarios. Experiments reveal that the proposed GA-based algorithm improves both the makespan and cost and also helps in providing better time optimization.

Table 2. Summary of scheduling works.

Author and year	Technique	Performance metrics	Drawbacks
Nguyen [32] 2019	Genetic Algorithm	Makespan, cost	Does not consider resource utilization, load balancing
Natesan [29] 2019	Grey Wolf Optimization	Makespan, energy consumption	Does not focus on issues like load balancing, reliability, etc.
Narendrababu Reddy [31] 2019	Ant Colony Optimization	Makespan, degree of imbalance	The study lacks in-depth analysis of findings
Manju [30] 2019	Min-Min Algorithm	Response Time	Centralized load balancing Efficient for smaller cluster nodes only
Bitam [28] 2018	Bees Life Algorithm	Execution Time, Memory	Does not consider response time, resource utilization
Nasr [20] 2018	Heuristic	Cost, schedule length, and balancing degree	The impact of resource utilization is not discussed
Tavana [19] 2018	Cuckoo Optimization Algorithm	Cost	Does not consider resource utilization
Kamal [27] 2018	Heuristic	Response time, processing time, cost	Improvement in performance measures not significant as compared to other techniques
Moon [14] 2017	Ant Colony	Makespan	Resource utilization and cost not considered

(continued)

Table 2. (*continued*)

Author and year	Technique	Performance metrics	Drawbacks
Mishra [15] 2017	Ant Colony Optimization	Makespan, average waiting time	Important issues like load balancing, reliability, and cost are not considered Proposed approach is not evaluated with respect to other metaheuristic approaches
Rahbari [17] 2017	Knapsack, Symbiotic Search Algorithm	Energy, Cost, and Network Usage	Results based on comparison with FCFS only
Kapsalis [18] 2017	Message Queue Telemetry Transport	Average execution time, average delay	Fog node mobility not considered
Kimpan [11] 2016	Artificial Bee Colony	Makespan, load balancing	QoS parameters like cost, energy efficiency, etc. not considered
Abdullahi [12] 2016	Symbiotic Search Algorithm	Makespan, response time, degree of imbalance	Energy efficiency and cost are not taken into consideration Comparison is done with variants of PSO only
Ningning [13] 2016	Graph Partitioning Theory	Execution Time	Complexity increases with increasing number of user requests, Fog nodes are considered homogenous
Gu [8] 2015	Heuristic	Cost	Proposed approach is not suited for cloud–fog environment because of cellular network architecture
Oueis [9] 2015	Heuristic	Latency, user satisfaction, power consumption	Complex for large-scale fog infrastructure
Zuo [10] 2015	Ant Colony	Makespan, cost, deadline, resource utilization	Resource utilization does not improve satisfactorily in some of the application instances considered
Dhinesh Babu [7] 2013	Honey Bee Algorithm	Makespan, response time, degree of imbalance	Starvation of low priority tasks Lacks scalability

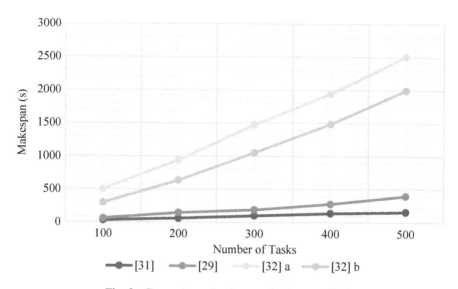

Fig. 3. Comparison of makespan for the year 2019.

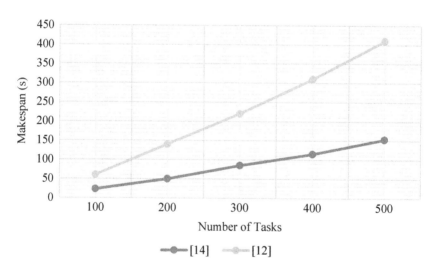

Fig. 4. Comparison of makespan for the years 2016 and 2017.

Table 2 presents the comparison table of the various scheduling techniques studied in literature. The table provides information about various scheduling techniques, performance metrics utilized, and limitations of existing works. Based upon this survey we found that makespan is the most desired scheduling objective as majority of users prefer faster execution of their tasks. Figures 3 and 4 show the makespan with respect to number of tasks by considering latest research works form the years 2016–2019. From the graphs, it can be inferred that with increasing number of tasks the makespan value also increases. Authors in [14] and [31] have reduced makespan values significantly by enhancing their techniques as compared to other approaches.

4 Conclusion and Future Directions

In this study, we have presented a survey of scheduling techniques applied in cloud and fog computing field. Comparative analysis based upon important QoS parameters utilized by algorithms under review is highlighted and limitations of the existing techniques have been discussed. Many task scheduling studies have been conducted in the past. From this survey, we found that most of the techniques focus only on few parameters. Several important metrics like response time, energy efficiency, reliability, scalability etc. are of utmost concern for enhancing efficiency of scheduling. Although few studies have considered these metrics, still there is need for further improvement. Moreover, the use of hybrid techniques can further enhance the scheduling performance. In addition, since fog is in its infancy, metaheuristic techniques offer a lot of scope for improvement in scheduling.

References

1. Bonomi, F., Milito, R., Zhu, J., Addepalli, S.: Fog computing and its role in the Internet of Things. In: Proceedings of the First Edition of the MCC Workshop on Mobile Cloud Computing, pp. 13–16. ACM, Helsinki (2012)
2. Garey, M.R., Johnson, D.S.: Computers and Intractability: A Guide to the Theory of NP-Completeness, pp. 37–79 (1990)
3. Hazra, D., Roy, A., Midya, S., Majumder, K.: Distributed task scheduling in cloud platform: a survey. In: Satapathy, S.C., Bhateja, V., Das, S. (eds.) Smart Computing and Informatics. SIST, vol. 77, pp. 183–191. Springer, Singapore (2018). https://doi.org/10.1007/978-981-10-5544-7_19
4. Potts, C.N., Strusevich, V.A.: Fifty years of scheduling: a survey of milestones. J. Oper. Res. Soc. 60(sup1), S41–S68 (2009)
5. Singh, P., Dutta, M., Aggarwal, N.: A review of task scheduling based on meta-heuristics approach in cloud computing. Knowl. Inf. Syst. 52(1), 1–51 (2017). https://doi.org/10.1007/s10115-017-1044-2
6. Arunarani, A.R., Manjula, D., Sugumaran, V.: Task scheduling techniques in cloud computing: a literature survey. Future Gener. Comput. Syst. 91, 407–415 (2019)
7. Dhinesh Babu, L.D., Krishna, P.V.: Honey bee behavior inspired load balancing of tasks in cloud computing environments. Appl. Soft Comput. 13(5), 2292–2303 (2013)
8. Gu, L., Zeng, D., Guo, S., Barnawi, A., Xiang, Y.: Cost efficient resource management in fog computing supported medical cyber-physical system. IEEE Trans. Emerg. Top. Comput. 5(1), 108–119 (2015)
9. Oueis, J., Strinati, E.C., Barbarossa, S.: The fog balancing: load distribution for small cell cloud computing. In: 2015 IEEE 81st Vehicular Technology Conference (VTC spring), pp. 1–6. IEEE, Glasgow (2015)
10. Zuo, L., Shu, L., Dong, S., Zhu, C., Hara, T.: A multi-objective optimization scheduling method based on the ant colony algorithm in cloud computing. IEEE Access 3, 2687–2699 (2015)

11. Kimpan, W., Kruekaew, B.: Heuristic task scheduling with artificial bee colony algorithm for virtual machines. In: 2016 Joint 8th International Conference on Soft Computing and Intelligent Systems (SCIS) and 17th International Symposium on Advanced Intelligent Systems (ISIS), pp. 281–286. IEEE, Sapporo (2016)

12. Abdullahi, M., Ngadi, M.A.: Symbiotic organism search optimization based task scheduling in cloud computing environment. Future Gener. Comput. Syst. **56**, 640–650 (2016)

13. Song, N., Gong, C., An, X., Zhan, Q.: Fog computing dynamic load balancing mechanism based on graph repartitioning. China Commun. **13**(3), 156–164 (2016)

14. Moon, Y., Yu, H., Gil, J.M., Lim, J.: A slave ants based ant colony optimization algorithm for task scheduling in cloud computing environments. Hum.-Centric Comput. Inf. Sci. **7**(1), 28 (2017)

15. Mishra, S.K., Sahoo, B., Manikyam, P.S.: Adaptive scheduling of cloud tasks using ant colony optimization. In: Proceedings of the 3rd International Conference on Communication and Information Processing, pp. 202–208. ACM, Tokyo (2017)

16. Neto, E.C.P., Callou, G., Aires, F.: An algorithm to optimise the load distribution of fog environments. In: 2017 IEEE International Conference on Systems, Man, and Cybernetics (SMC), pp. 1292–1297. IEEE, Banff (2017)

17. Rahbari, D., Nickray, M.: Scheduling of fog networks with optimized knapsack by symbiotic organisms search. In: 2017 21st Conference of Open Innovations Association (FRUCT), pp. 278–283. IEEE, Helsinki (2017)

18. Kapsalis, A., Kasnesis, P., Venieris, I.S., Kaklamani, D.I., Patrikakis, C.Z.: A cooperative fog approach for effective workload balancing. IEEE Cloud Comput. **4**(2), 36–45 (2017)

19. Tavana, M., Shahdi-Pashaki, S., Teymourian, E., Santos-Arteaga, F.J., Komaki, M.: A discrete cuckoo optimization algorithm for consolidation in cloud computing. Comput. Ind. Eng. **115**, 495–511 (2018)

20. Nasr, A.A., El-Bahnasawy, N.A., Attiya, G., El-Sayed, A.: A new online scheduling approach for enhancing QOS in cloud. Future Comput. Inform. J. **3**(2), 424–435 (2018)

21. Krishnadoss, P., Jacob, P.: OCSA: task scheduling algorithm in cloud computing environment. Int. J. Intell. Eng. Syst. **11**(3), 271–279 (2018)

22. Choudhari, T., Moh, M., Moh, T.S.: Prioritized task scheduling in fog computing. In: Proceedings of the ACMSE 2018 Conference, p. 22. ACM, Richmond (2018)

23. Mehmood, M., Javaid, N., Akram, J., Abbasi, S.H., Rahman, A., Saeed, F.: Efficient resource distribution in cloud and fog computing. In: Barolli, L., Kryvinska, N., Enokido, T., Takizawa, M. (eds.) NBiS 2018. LNDECT, vol. 22, pp. 209–221. Springer, Cham (2019). https://doi.org/10.1007/978-3-319-98530-5_18

24. Yin, L., Luo, J., Luo, H.: Tasks scheduling and resource allocation in fog computing based on containers for smart manufacturing. IEEE Trans. Ind. Inf. **14**(10), 4712–4721 (2018)

25. Nazar, T., Javaid, N., Waheed, M., Fatima, A., Bano, H., Ahmed, N.: Modified shortest job first for load balancing in cloud-fog computing. In: Barolli, L., Leu, F.-Y., Enokido, T., Chen, H.-C. (eds.) BWCCA 2018. LNDECT, vol. 25, pp. 63–76. Springer, Cham (2019). https://doi.org/10.1007/978-3-030-02613-4_6

26. Zahid, M., Javaid, N., Ansar, K., Hassan, K., KaleemUllah Khan, M., Waqas, M.: Hill climbing load balancing algorithm on fog computing. In: Xhafa, F., Leu, F.-Y., Ficco, M., Yang, C.-T. (eds.) 3PGCIC 2018. LNDECT, vol. 24, pp. 238–251. Springer, Cham (2019). https://doi.org/10.1007/978-3-030-02607-3_22

27. Kamal, M.B., Javaid, N., Naqvi, S.A.A., Butt, H., Saif, T., Kamal, M.D.: Heuristic min-conflicts optimizing technique for load balancing on fog computing. In: Xhafa, F., Barolli, L., Greguš, M. (eds.) INCoS 2018. LNDECT, vol. 23, pp. 207–219. Springer, Cham (2019). https://doi.org/10.1007/978-3-319-98557-2_19

28. Bitam, S., Zeadally, S., Mellouk, A.: Fog computing job scheduling optimization based on bees swarm. Enterp. Inf. Syst. **12**(4), 373–397 (2018)
29. Natesan, G., Chokkalingam, A.: Task scheduling in heterogeneous cloud environment using mean grey wolf optimization algorithm. ICT Express **5**(2), 110–114 (2019)
30. Manju, A.B., Sumathy, S.: Efficient load balancing algorithm for task preprocessing in fog computing environment. In: Satapathy, S.C., Bhateja, V., Das, S. (eds.) Smart Intelligent Computing and Applications. SIST, vol. 105, pp. 291–298. Springer, Singapore (2019). https://doi.org/10.1007/978-981-13-1927-3_31
31. Narendrababu Reddy, G., Phani Kumar, S.: Modified ant colony optimization algorithm for task scheduling in cloud computing systems. In: Satapathy, S.C., Bhateja, V., Das, S. (eds.) Smart Intelligent Computing and Applications. SIST, vol. 104, pp. 357–365. Springer, Singapore (2019). https://doi.org/10.1007/978-981-13-1921-1_36
32. Nguyen, B.M., Thi Thanh Binh, H., Do Son, B.: Evolutionary algorithms to optimize task scheduling problem for the IoT based bag-of-tasks application in cloud–fog computing environment. Appl. Sci. **9**(9), 1730 (2019)

Time Improvement of Smith-Waterman Algorithm Using OpenMP and SIMD

Mehak Malik, Srijan Malhotra, and Narayanan Prasanth[(⊠)] [iD]

School of CSE, Vellore Institute of Technology, Vellore, Tamil Nadu, India
{mehak.malik2016,
srijan.malhotra2016}@vitstudent.ac.in,
n.prasanth@vit.ac.in

Abstract. Sequence alignment is a problem in bioinformatics that involves arranging sequences of proteins, RNA or DNA so that similar regions between two or more sequences may be determined. The Smith-Waterman algorithm is a key algorithm for aligning sequences. This paper uses the OpenMP application-programming interface along with the Single-Instruction Multiple-Data (SIMD) instructions. Advanced Vector Instructions 2 (AVX2) is used to implement the SIMD paradigm. It utilizes both fine-level and coarse-level parallelism to improve resource utilization without requiring support from multiple nodes in a distributed memory system. The algorithm shows a multifold decrease in execution time in comparison to an implementation that is sequentially executed.

Keywords: SIMD · OpenMP · Smith-Waterman algorithm · Parallel programming

1 Introduction

One of the most common questions that molecular biologists have to deal with is to decide whether two DNA sequences are related or not. This question is important to understand the functions of different genes and to then determine if these functionalities can be used in any way. Sequence alignment is involves arranging protein, RNA or DNA sequences with the aim of identifying similar regions between them. Local alignment is useful when regions of similarity are to be identified between two sequences. It can be used for sequences of varying lengths and partial similarity as well.

Smith-Waterman algorithm is a sequence alignment algorithm that uses dynamic programming concepts and arranges sequences locally. However, even though it is one of the most used and accurate algorithms in bioinformatics as well as other fields, it has a high computation complexity. Since biological sequences are very large in size, without efficient techniques to implement the algorithm it becomes highly time-consuming for real life applications. Thus, parallel programming techniques are highly useful in executing sequence alignment algorithms for large sequences.

OpenMP is one of the most frequently used application programming interface (API) that equips programmers to add parallelism to sequential applications in Fortran, C++ and C language. It allows for parallelism between cores using threads. It can be used across most platforms and uses shared memory architecture. It consists of

© Springer Nature Singapore Pte Ltd. 2020
P. K. Singh et al. (Eds.): FTNCT 2019, CCIS 1206, pp. 686–697, 2020.
https://doi.org/10.1007/978-981-15-4451-4_54

environmental variables, library routines and compiler directives. OpenMP is easy to understand, scalable and is managed by OpenMP Architecture Review Board, which is a consortium of various software and hardware organizations.

Single Instruction, Multiple Data (SIMD) is a type of computer that allows for data-level parallelism and consists of more than one processing element that can perform the same action on different data values. This classification comes from Flynn's taxonomy. It is important to realize that while algorithms cannot entirely be vectorized, using SIMD for certain operations that are both time consuming and manipulate a large number of data points using repetitive operations can reduce time complexity of algorithms to a great extent. Different vendors provide for instructions sets that can be used to access SIMD capabilities of modern CPUs such as AVX, SSE, MMX, etc.

Advanced Vector Extensions (AVX), developed by Intel is a set of instructions that can be used to access vectorization capabilities of the x86 Instruction Set Architecture (ISA). It was preceded by the Streaming SIMD Extensions (SSE). AVX2 also referred to as Haswell New Instructions in specific extends most integer operations to a vector of size 256 bits along with other additions to the previous instructions, i.e., SSE and AVX. Many compilers such as GCC and Free Pascal provide support for AVX2.

The remaining contents of this paper are organized as follows: Sect. 2 comprises of a detailed description of sequence alignment using the SW algorithm and is followed by the related work. The next section discusses the implementation technique and approach followed by the results. The last section shares the concluding remarks and is followed by the references.

2   Sequence Alignment with Smith-Waterman Algorithm

Smith-Waterman algorithm is a fundamental algorithm that aligns a pair of sequences to find regions of high similarity. Thus it provides local alignment and uses dynamic programming to maximize the alignment score. It was proposed by Smith and Waterman [1]. It evaluates every possible alignment between a pair of sequences and thus is highly accurate. It consists of two parts, which are explained below in the next two sections.

Filling of Matrix: It builds a matrix M with the two sequences defined as $seqA = [a_1 a_2 ... a_m]$ and $seqB = [b_1 b_2 ... b_n]$, which are to be aligned. The initialization of the matrix involves filling the first row and column with zeros. The value of a cell of the matrix is the maximum value of the scores calculated using its left, upper and diagonal neighbor cells. Thus, an element in the matrix cannot be computed until the element to immediately to its left, above it and diagonal to it have been computed. The formula required to compute an element $M_{i,j}$ in the matrix is shown in Eq. (1) where g is the gap penalty, $S_{i,j}$ is the similarity score when the ith element of $seqA$ is compared to the jth element of $seqB$.

$$M_{i,j} = max \begin{cases} M_{i,j-1} - g \\ M_{i-1,j-1} + S_{i,j} \\ M_{i-1,j} - g \end{cases} \tag{1}$$

Locating Highest Score and Backtracking: Once the matrix is filled using the above formula, the cell with the maximum score is found in the matrix it and backtracking is carried out from this position. If the maximum score is found in more than one cell, multiple optimum local alignments may be possible. Backtracking involves moving to the predecessor of each cell or the cell that was used to calculate the maximum score of that particular cell. This process is repeated until a cell of the first row or column has been reached. The chosen cells in the backtracking process represent the local alignment for the pair of sequences. If the cell maximum score was chosen from the cell towards its left or the one above it then a gap is introduced into the final alignment. If the cell maximum score was calculated using its diagonal neighbour then the corresponding row and column sequence elements are aligned with each other. Since the maximum score can be anywhere in the matrix, the alignment will only consist of the sequence from the maximum score till an element of the first row or column is reached and thus, represents local alignment and only finds regions between the two sequences with a high degree of similarity.

The process is illustrated below for sequences *CGTGAATTCA* and *GACTTA* (see Fig. 1) along with the alignment of these two sequences (see Fig. 2). The match score is taken to be $Ma = +5$ and mismatch score $mi = -3$ and gap penalty $g = -4$. The highest score in the matrix is 18 and the particular cell is the starting point of the backtracking process. The shaded cells represent the path obtained by the process of backtracking and each cell points to the previous cell.

	-	C	G	T	G	A	A	T	T	C	A
-	0	0	0	0	0	0	0	0	0	0	0
G	0	0	5	1	5	1	0	0	0	0	0
A	0	0	1	2	1	10	6	2	0	0	5
C	0	5	1	0	0	6	7	3	0	5	1
T	0	1	2	6	2	2	3	12	8	4	2
T	0	0	0	7	3	0	0	8	17	13	9
A	0	0	0	3	4	8	5	4	13	14	18

Fig. 1. Illustration of Smith-Waterman algorithm for sequences CGTGAATTCA and GACTTA

$$G\ A\ A\ T\ T\ C\ A$$
$$G\ A\ C\ T\ T - A$$
$$\overline{+\ +\ -\ +\ +\ -\ +}$$
$$5\ 5\ 3\ 5\ 5\ 4\ 5$$

Fig. 2. Scoring and obtained sequence for CGTGAATTCA and GACTTA

3 Related Work

The SW algorithm is inefficient with respect to memory usage and execution time and thus, even though it is one of the most fundamental algorithms for local sequence alignment, it can be impractical to use for a various applications. Though often-heuristic approaches are used to reduce execution time, the compromise on the accuracy and sensitivity that are an integral part of the algorithm. Hence, approaches towards decreasing execution time and memory utilization involve different architectures and computing platforms.

One such approach involves using an Intel Xeon Phi coprocessor [2], which has a MIC (Many Integrated Core architecture). It consists of 57 to 72 cores along with 512-bit vector units. The series of processors is also equipped for parallel programming models such as MPI and even though they share certain features with GPUs, they can run as an individual computing system. A heterogeneous system involving a divided workload between a CPU with Two Xeon cores and a Xeon Phi coprocessor card provides improved performance.

The algorithm specifically designed for the above system is known as SWAPHI [3] (Smith-Waterman Protein Database Search on Xeon Phi Coprocessors). It involves fine-grained parallelism and coarse-grained parallelism. The former uses a 512-bit vector and the later uses multiple cores of the Xeon coprocessor card. It involves creating unique mapping between Xeon Phi cores and host threads and the threads offload tasks such as memory management and alignment to the cores. Threads wait for each other to coordinate and complete tasks. However this approach is highly energy intensive and energy efficient solutions are required while utilizing such powerful technologies.

Another option for implementation of the SW algorithm is the use of Field Programmable Gate Arrays (FPGAs) as they provide a high performance secure environment. Different techniques can be used to optimize sequence alignment on FGPAs. Dynamic programming [4] is one such solution that breaks down the complex problem into smaller sub-problems. The initialization proves with involves conversion of input sequences to elements that can be processed which uses Ethernet for communication. A side matrix is also generated to reduce workload on the system and proves to be useful for larger sequences. For smaller sequences, backtracking can be used. Matrix calculation uses FGPA based Smith-Waterman processing elements (SWPE). Using different tactics such as linear and lattice techniques for deploying SWPEs will affect the performance of the algorithm. The choice of FPGA architecture also decides speedup and efficiency. Xilinx ZYNQ-7000 is one such FPGA that can be used a parallel implementation of the SW algorithm to provide a multifold increase in efficiency [5]. The suggested architecture also uses a decreased bit size for each base pair to provide speedup and also uses divide and extend for the same. Another architecture involving FPGAs [6] employs an optimized comparator for matching the sequences that compares two bits at time and aims to reduce the number of components necessary for the system. It is adapted to improve the performance using the Altera Cyclone IV

EP4CE115 model for the same. Methods have also been proposed to use FGPAs to reduce memory usage by forgoing the need to store the similarity matrix. One such method [7] achieves this by merging the score calculation and backtracking part of the algorithm to generate the path while calculating the cell values in the matrix.

A number of programming models can be used to improve the speed and re-source utilization of the SW algorithm. One model [8] combines both OpenMP and MPI and thus utilizes both shared and distributed memory paradigms. The dynamic programming technique used in this approach is linear or row wise calculation of the alignment matrix. This method uses memory efficiently as it only keeps track of only two rows. The row being computed and the previous row are stored in the memory, and are deleted as the next row is computed. The MPI is used to have a master node divide tasks between different working cluster nodes and each node applies thread level parallelism using OpenMP. One of the concerns with this implementation is the communication overhead involved between the cluster nodes for and the speedup achieved as opposed to the resources required for the speedup.

Upon evaluation of implementations solely using OpenMP [9], it is observed that if every element is determined independently as a separate task, an increase in the number of threads does not result in a significant speedup since there are a number of small tasks for each thread, but the communication overhead is much higher than the execution time of the tasks. However, when submatrices are used in the matrix calculation there is a significant speedup observed, thus showing that size of tasks for each thread must be significant enough to minimize overhead.

Similarly, when the performance of MPI based approaches was evaluated; it was found that for sequences with length greater than 2000×2000, the number of processors used contributes to the execution time. Finally, when a hybrid approach using both OpenMP and MPI was evaluated, it was observed that this implementation resulted in better performance than the individual OpenMP and MPI based approaches. One of the reasons for this can be that OpenMP provides simpler methods to parallelize sequential programs, MPI is better equipped at handling communication related issues. Thus, a combination of these platforms allows for the reduction of overhead and consequently of execution time.

Another distributed approach [10] involves a Hadoop Distributed File System (HDFS). The sequences are the queries in the model and are mapped to different nodes in the system. The processing of queries happens using threads at each individual node. Finally, a reduced result is produced for the sequences. This approach yields high performance for sequences of much greater length than 3000, but for smaller lengths it is an expensive approach. In order to improve memory utilization, a GPU based approach [11] towards SW algorithm uses a two level tiling method which involves the formation of blocks using tiling and only the points at the boundary of the block horizontally will be stored in the memory to use for the computation of other blocks and vertical points will in turn me used for the determination of the maximum score of the matrix. Such an approach would require proper alignment of the block size to be effective.

To utilize the SIMD paradigm, one recent implementation CloudSW [12], uses Apache Spark, which is an open standard for computing clusters in combination with SIMD instructions. It involves map reduce tasks which are accelerated using SIMD instructions. The mapping process is followed by obtaining K alike alignments using a priority queue. The k results are then reduced during backtracking to give the optimum sequence alignment. This method is highly scalable, especially as it allows for an increase in the number of nodes without affecting performance. It provides a multifold increase in performance for multiple nodes. However, for a single node this technique does not result in a significant speedup in comparison with other OpenMP and MPI based parallel approaches.

4 Methodology

The approach taken towards the paper combines OpenMP and SIMD paradigm, which is implemented using Advanced Vector Extensions 2 (AVX2). This approach was chosen because though there are many OpenMP based parallel implementations that have been developed in the past and the speedup often becomes less after an exponential growth in number of base pairs. Also, there are a number of distributed system-based implementations of SW algorithm. However, these require multiple nodes and prove to be quite expensive to use multiple nodes for sequence alignment.

Since matrix filling comprises of a number of repeated operations such as addition, subtraction and finding maximum value, SIMD would be a useful paradigm for improving time performance of the SW algorithm whereas threads would be useful for managing individual broader tasks. The implementation requires the computation of the values in a matrix M. The matrix consists of points $M_{i,j}$ whose value is calculated to fill the matrix.

4.1 Task Creation

The task creation portion of the implementation primarily deals with dividing the matrix filling process into individual tasks. A block can contain multiple points. The size of each individual block is based on the number of threads and two other constants c_w and c_h, which are used to control the block width and height respectively, so as to provide faster execution of the SW algorithm. The performance for different values of c_w and c_h are evaluated to determine the appropriate block size. The height and width of the block are determined as shown in Eqs. (2) and (3) respectively.

$$h = s1/(t \times c_h) \tag{2}$$

$$w = s2/(t \times c_w) \tag{3}$$

Where $s1$ and $s2$ are the lengths of the two sequences used for local alignment $seqA$ and $seqB$, t is the number of threads. This step is very important for efficiently distributing the load amongst the threads. The pseudocode for task generation can be seen in Listing 1 using the function $generateTask$. This represents coarse-grained parallelism where a different thread is responsible for a block of cells in the matrix. This function uses OpenMP to generate different threads and assign them with different tasks using the *fillBlock* function. Each point consists of a *row* and *column* attribute. The point *maxPoint* is used to restrict task generation to only those blocks whose dependent values are known. Once the required tasks are completed the *row* and *column* values of *maxPoint* are increased. This occurs until all the tasks are generated equal to the number of diagonals, *diagNums*. The *#pragma omp task firstprivate(tmp)* directive is used to assign new tasks to new threads.

Listing 1 generateTask function

```
Function 1: generateTask
Output: call to function fillBlock(block)
for i <- 0 to diagNums do
block <- minLimit
while  block.row >= maxLimit and block.col <= maxLimit.col do
      #pragma omp task firstprivate(tmp)
      fillBlock(block)
      block.row -
      block.row++
end while
waitForTasks
if  maxLimit..col < colNums - 1 then
      maxLimit.col ++
else
      maxLimit.row++
end if
if  minLimit..row < rowNums - 1 then
      maxLimit.row ++
else
      maxLimit.col++
end if
end for
```

4.2 Block Calculation

Block calculation comprises of determining the values of the matrix for all the cells in the block. The formula used for the determination of the score of an individual cell has been explained in Eq. (1). Since the tasks are generated in such a way that all cell dependencies have been taken care of and the scores of all those cells required for a particular cell have been calculated before computing that cell. This portion of the approach is implemented using AVX2 vectorization. This portion of the implementation must be modified on the basis of the size of the vectors that are being used and the processor capabilities since the number of floating point operations that can take place concurrently is determined based on the size of the vectors. The size chosen for the vectors was 256 bits as AVX2 allows for the same. Thus, this allows 8 floating-point operations to be carried out at once. This information is important for loop unrolling that is carried out at a later stage of this portion. Firstly, we require certain vectors to be created to compute the scores for the points in each block. These are for the match score vector *matchVec*, mismatch score *mismatchVec* vector, gap alignment vector *gapVec* and zero vector *zeroVec*, which are required for matrix calculation.

The vectors are then used to calculate diagonal dependent scores. This is done by comparing the sub-sequences for this block using a logical OR operator and storing the result in a *mask* vector. The mask and the match score vector are combined using a logical AND to form *matchScores*. A logical NOT is applied on the mismatch score vector, *mismatchVec* to make the values in it negative, since the mismatch score must be subtracted from the diagonal neighbor cell score in case of a mismatch and then it is also combined with the *mask* vector using a logical AND to form *mismatchScores*. Both of these vectors are combined using a logical OR to provide the *scoresDiagonal*, which are added to the scores of the diagonal neighbors for the points in that particular vector. The row dependent scores, *scoresRow* are calculated by loading the scores of the cells to the left of the concerned cell and subtracting the gap alignment vector. The row dependent and diagonal dependent scores are compared and the returned vector consists of the maximum score, *maxScore* for each cell. The *regSize* is used to define the number or columns that would be computed at once in each task. It is calculated using the required cache alignment and the number of columns. If the total number of columns in the block is not a multiple of *regSize*, then the leftover cells are computed in the unrolled loop.

The column dependent scores are calculated and compared with the maximum of the diagonal and row dependent scores by unrolling the loop based on the size of the registers to improve performance because for a small number of values a loop is an expensive computation and the max score is chosen for each cell and loop is used at the end to calculate score for leftover cells which are lesser in number than the unrolled loop size. The *checkMatch* function is used to find the similarity score for the points in the unrolled loop. The matrix is also aligned to improve speed of the program. The calculation of row and diagonal dependent scores uses Intel Intrinsic instructions for AVX2. *_mm256_set1_ps* is used to create a vector of the required *seqA* character and *_mm256_load_ps* is used to load the required input sequence characters of *seqB* into a vector, *vecB*. *_mm256_cmp_ps* is used to generate the mask vector. *_mm256_add_ps* is used to add the *scoresDiagonal* to the diagonal neighbor for each point and similarly *_mm256_sub_ps* is used to subtract the gap alignment vector, *gapVec* from the element to the left of the concerned point. *_mm256_max_ps* is used to find *max_score* vector between the *scoresDiagonal* and *scoresRow* vectors and is then compared with the column wise scores using the unrolled loop which doesn't require AVX2 instructions. The pseudocode for the *fillBlock* function can be seen in Listing 2.

Listing 2 fillBlock function

```
Function 2 : fillBlock(block, seqA, seqB)
Output matrixBlock(block)
startPoint.row <- block.row * h
startPoint.col <- block.col * w
totalCols <- startPoint.row + h
totalRows <- startPoint.col + w
loopCols <- findFitCols(totalCols)
colsLeft <- findLeftCols(totalCols)
matchVec <- [Ma, Ma, ... , Ma]
mismatchVec <- [mi, mi, ... , mi]
gapVec <- [g, g, ... , g]
zeroVec <- [0, 0, ... ,0]
for i <- startPoint.row +1 to  totalRows do
vecA <- load(seqA)
prev <- M[i][startPoint.col]
for j <- startPoint.col +1 to  loopCols  do
    vecB <- load(seqB)
    scoreMask <- compareOr(vecA, vecB)
    matchScores <- and(matchVec,mask)
    mismatchScores <- and(not(mismatchVec,mask))
    scoreDiagonal <- or(matchScores, mismatch-
    Scores)
    scoreDiagonal    <-    sum(load(M[i-1][j-1],
    scoreDiagonal))
    scoreRow <- diff(load(M[i-1][j], gapVec))
    scoreRow <- max(zeroVec, scoreRow)
    max_score <- max(scoreRow, scoreDiagonal)
    for k <- 0 to k <- regSize -1 do //this loop
    is unrolled
            M[i][j+k]    <-    prev    <-    max(prev-
            g,max_Score[k])
    end for
j <- j+ regSize
end for
for j <- colsLeft +1 to  totalCols do
    seqMatch <- Check_match(seqA[i-1],seqB[j-1])
    M[i][j]   <-   max(prev-g,   M[i-1][j]-g,   M[i-
    i][j-1]+ seqMatch)
end for
end for
```

4.3   Backtracking

Backtracking involves firstly finding the point with the maximum score in the matrix. This is followed by evaluating the previous point, *prevPoint* using the formula explained in Eq. (1). If *prevPoint* is a diagonal point to the current point, *currPoint* then the sequence characters along the row and column are aligned together. If *prevPoint* is in the same row as *currPoint* then a gap is introduced in the alignment of *seqB* and if *prevPoint* is in the same column as *currPoint* then a gap is introduced in the alignment of *seqA*. This process is repeated till *prevPoint* is a point from the first row or column. Finally, the aligned sequences can be printed. The implemented system does not use any parallelization for backtracking, as it is not a very time consuming process, and also always requires that the *currPoint* is known in order to determine *prevPoint*.

5   Results and Discussion

The proposed implementation was tested on a system with Intel Core i7 (2.7 GHz). It is a quad-core processor and supports 8 threads with a 6 MB shared cache. The serial implementation and parallel implementation was compared with minimum number of base pairs as around 256 and the maximum as 65536 base pairs for both sequences. The data set for the evaluation is extracted from NCBI [13] and consists of real sequences in the FASTA format. The values of the constants is taken as $c_w = 128$ and $c_h = 2$ upon multiple trials to provide optimum results.

The performance of both implementations is shown in Table 1. The time taken for the parallel implementation for sequence lengths of 65,336 base pairs is 63.619 s as compared to the serial implementation of SW algorithm, which takes 157.349 s. Evidently the parallel execution time is much lesser than the serial execution time for the SW algorithm even for the larger sequences. Though the time is the same for small number of base pairs, with an increase in base pairs, the parallel implementation performs much better than the

Table 1. Time performance of parallel implementation of SW algorithm in comparison to serial implementation SW algorithm for sequences with different number of base pairs.

Number of base pairs	Serial execution time	Parallel execution time
128	0 ms	0 ms
256	3 ms	1 ms
512	9 ms	3 ms
1024	40 ms	10 ms
2048	135 ms	39 ms
4096	515 ms	166 ms
8192	2160 ms	628 ms
16384	8540 ms	2375 ms
32768	30651 ms	10059 ms
65536	157348 ms	63618 ms

serial execution. The similar performance at lower number of base pairs can be attributed to the overhead associated with vectorization and thread management. A graphical representation of the comparison of performance is shown in Fig. 3.

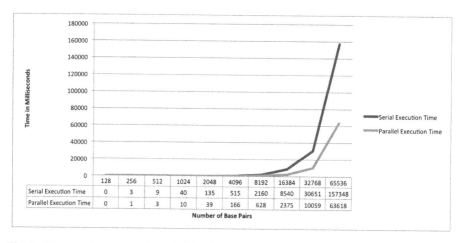

Fig. 3. Time performance of parallel implementation SW algorithm in comparison to serial implementation of SW algorithm for sequences with different number of base pairs.

6 Conclusions and Future Work

Smith-Waterman is one of the most frequently used algorithms by researchers in bioinformatics for local alignment. However, owing to the exponentially increasing size of input sequences, the algorithms are computationally expensive and require other solutions for optimization. The parallel implementation suggested in this paper uses OpenMP API and AVX2 to implement the SIMD paradigm. The technique largely reduces the execution time of the algorithm for different lengths of sequences. The algorithm does not compromise on the detail and sensitivity required in the sequence alignment process while reducing the time taken to carry out the task without the requirement of very expensive hardware.

In the future, we plan to explore different vectorization methods and technologies to optimize the sequence alignment process even further. We would like to explore the use of FGPAs to improve the performance of this approach as determine if backtracking can be parallelized in any way to reduce the time taken for the same. Another direction for the future would be to use AVX-512 using Xeon Phi coprocessors a instead of AVX2 and determine the performance.

References

1. Pearson, W.R.: Searching protein sequence libraries: comparison of the sensitivity and selectivity of the Smith-Waterman and FASTA algorithms. Genomics **11**(3), 635–650 (1991)
2. Rucci, E., et al.: Smith-Waterman algorithm on heterogeneous systems: a case study. In: 2014 IEEE International Conference on Cluster Computing (CLUSTER) (2014)
3. Liu, Y., Schmidt, B.: SWAPHI: smith-waterman protein database search on Xeon Phi coprocessors. In: 2014 IEEE 25th International Conference on Application-Specific Systems, Architectures and Processors (2014)
4. Chang, X. et al.: Optimization strategies for Smith-Waterman algorithm on FPGA platform. In: 2014 International Conference on Computational Science and Computational Intelligence (2014)
5. El-Wafa, W.A., et al.: Hardware acceleration of Smith-Waterman algorithm for short read DNA alignment using FPGA. In: 2016 IEEE 40th Annual Computer Software and Applications Conference (COMPSAC) (2016)
6. Al Junid, S.A.M., et al.: Parallel processing cell score design of linear gap penalty Smith-Waterman algorithm. In: 2017 IEEE 13th International Colloquium on Signal Processing & its Applications (CSPA) (2017)
7. Khaled, H., et al.: Performance improvement of the parallel Smith Waterman algorithm implementation using Hybrid MPI-OpenMP model. In: 2016 SAI Computing Conference (SAI) (2016)
8. Buhagiar, K., et al.: Hardware implementation of efficient path reconstruction for the Smith-Waterman algorithm. In: 2017 4th International Conference on Control, Decision and Information Technologies (CoDIT) (2017)
9. Shafiq, M., et al.: Modeling and performance evaluation of Smith-Waterman algorithm. In: 2016 13th International Bhurban Conference on Applied Sciences and Technology (IBCAST) (2016)
10. Khaire, S.A., Wankhade, N.R.: An efficient implementation of Smith Waterman algorithm using distributed computing. In: 2017 International Conference on Computing, Communication, Control and Automation (ICCUBEA) (2017)
11. Wang, J., et al.: Communication optimization on GPU: a case study of sequence alignment algorithms. In: 2017 IEEE International Parallel and Distributed Processing Symposium (IPDPS) (2017)
12. Xu, B., et al.: Efficient distributed Smith-Waterman algorithm based on Apache Spark. In: 2017 IEEE 10th International Conference on Cloud Computing (CLOUD) (2017)
13. National Center for Biotechnology Information: NCBI. http://www.ncbi.nlm.nih.gov/. Accessed 18 Sept 2019

Synchronization Safety Problem in Quantum Key Distribution System

Anton Pljonkin[(✉)]

Southern Federal University, Taganrog, Rostov Region, Russian Federation
pljonkin@mail.ru

Abstract. The problem of providing secrecy at quantum key distribution was analyzed. A two-pass self-compensation fiber-optic quantum key distribution system (QKDS) with phase coding photons states that operate on the BB84 protocol and implemented by the «plug&play» technology are reviewed. The synchronization process of quantum key distribution system and field test results of quantum cryptographic network basis on the QKDS Clavis2 are analyzed. Abstract strategies of unauthorized access to information in a quantum key distribution system by attacks such as "Trojan horse" and "Brute force" are described. One of the principles of protection the synchronization process of self-compensation quantum key distribution system from unauthorized access was described.

Keywords: Quantum key distribution · Synchronization · Photon impulse · The algorithm · Unauthorized access

1 Introduction

In modern communication systems, the issue of ensuring security is very important. Telecommunications are developing at a tremendous pace and every day more and more communication systems are attacked. The creation of quantum computers raises new questions in the security of communication systems. A quantum computer already solves certain problems much faster than classical algorithms. The latter forces scientists to develop fundamentally new security methods for telecommunication systems. Quantum data protection techniques are known as quantum cryptography. This is today one of the promising ways to protect data. The principles of quantum cryptography are not based on mathematical algorithms, but on the laws of quantum physics. There are several areas of research and most of them are just starting to develop. Scientists are faced with problems in implementation, but it is already becoming clear that quantum cryptography will become the basis for new methods of providing security in telecommunication communication systems. Difficulties in the implementation of quantum communication systems are associated with the requirements for individual components. For example, to implement the protocol of quantum key distribution, it is necessary to register low-energy optical signals. The energy of such single pulses is comparable to the energy of one photon. The task of detecting such pulses is solved by special elements - optical avalanche photodiodes (SAPD). SPAD have many parameters that are highly dependent on external factors and affect the probability of detecting optical signals. One of these parameters is called the

© Springer Nature Singapore Pte Ltd. 2020
P. K. Singh et al. (Eds.): FTNCT 2019, CCIS 1206, pp. 698–707, 2020.
https://doi.org/10.1007/978-981-15-4451-4_55

"dark counts." In avalanche photodiodes, the concept of "noise" differs from the classical concept of "noise" in radio electronics. Note that to date, real-life quantum key distribution systems are already sold and have a high level of secrecy. Such systems are based on the basic principles of absolute secrecy of messages.

To ensure absolute secrecy in the cryptographic system is necessary to satisfy certain conditions: the key should be completely random, the key length should be greater than or equal to the length of the encoded message and a key can be used only once. A solution to ensure secrecy in the key distribution is based on the principles of quantum cryptography and includes coding quantum state of a single particle (photon). There secrecy and the inability to unauthorized access to the messages are based on the laws of quantum physics, as opposed to classical methods of cryptography, which are based on mathematical patterns and potentially indecipherable.

2 Research Objective

2.1 Synchronization of Quantum Key Distribution Channel with Automatic Compensation of Polarization Distortions

The most important part of the QKD complex for the transmission of confidential information is synchronization spaced apart optical transmitter and the photodetector stations Alice and Bob.

Efficient operation of the QKD system is possible only with initial synchronization between Alice and Bob.

The initial synchronization is defined here as the process of fixing the time of reception pulse in receiving station. This is need for supplying a gate signal to the single-photon avalanche photodiodes in transmitting station and pulse coding for controlling the phase shift in coding station. Detection accuracy of the optical synchronization signal ranges of tens picoseconds and strongly affects the overall system performance.

In commercial QKDS the periodic sequence of optical pulses used to synchronize. Temporary markers in this case are the pulses themselves. To ensure accurate synchronization is to be measured total optical path length pulse propagation in a fiber optic link between two QKD stations (quantum channel), and in all functional fiber optic modules within QKDS [1, 2].

2.2 The Process of Measuring the Propagation Time of the Synchronization Signal in Quantum Channel Between QKD Stations

For described self-compensation QKDS, laser diode in transmitting station emits a sequence of optical pulses in synchronization process. Through fiber-optic quantum channel, pulses are sent to Alice station. Note that quantum channel consists of a single-mode optical fiber. In coding station (Alice), two optical pulses sequentially reflected by the Faraday mirror changing polarization by 90°, and follow by the same optical path, but in the opposite direction. After the resulting interference pulses follow to optical modules (SPAD) (Fig. 1).

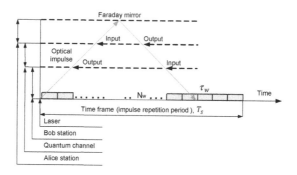

Fig. 1. Timing diagram of the pulse travelling at synchronization

The first preparatory stage of initial synchronization (coarse delay) represents a preliminary measuring the time delay between moment of sending and receiving optical pulses. For this purpose, a time frame τ_{frame1} equal to the repetition period of synchronization pulses $T_s = 1250$ ms is divided into time slots (intervals) of duration $\tau_{w1} \approx 300$ ps. Optical receiving module measures the signal level in each of the time windows $N_{w1} = \tau_{frame1}/\tau_{w1}$. At preliminary stage the time window are analyzed 800 times every time. The time window with the maximum level of the resulting signal is taken as the desired result of the measurement of delay time between sending and receiving the synchronization pulse. The second intermediate stage of initial synchronization (fine delay) implies a divided the time window from first stage on time subintervals $\tau_{w2} \approx 60$ ps. On the second stage the time frame from first stage (detection time window with signal), prior to it and the subsequent time windows are analyzed. Time frame is divided into 51 time window. Each time window is analyzed 800 times. The time window with the maximum signal level is taken as the desired result of the delay time between sending and receiving the synchronization pulse. At the third stage of initial synchronization repeatedly analyzed time windows from second stage. To this end the laser diode emits pulses having a packet structure. The pulses followed by ~ 200 ns packet structure with a duration of 214 μs, consists of a preamble 16 pulses (clock signal used for generator in coding stations), a pause, two pulses of equal duration and subsequent pulses 1049. This stage is the calibration process of synchronization. QKD system is initiated at the beginning of each cycle the formation of quantum keys. Part of this energy in a frame is used to synchronize the clock of the coding station [3].

Note that the first and second stages are initiated at the first start QKD system for calibration purposes, or may be started by the operator in case of a change of physical length of fiber optic links (for example due to temperature or mechanical stress on the optical fiber).

Table 1 summarizes the results of field measurements of optical pulse parameters on the three stages of initial synchronization QKDS Clavis2.

Table 1. Values of optical pulse parameters

Parameter	Synchronization stage		
	First	Second	Third*
Measuring at the output of the laser diode			
Impulse duration**	∼1 ns	∼1 ns	∼1 ns
Impulse frequency	800 Hz	800 Hz	5 MHz
The amplitude of the electrical pulse	140 mV	40 mV	40 mV
Measuring in a quantum channel between stations			
The amplitude of the first electrical pulse	48 mV	13 mV	13 mV
The amplitude of the second electrical pulse	21 mV	6 mV	6 mV

*The measurement results are averaged given the heterogeneity of the package.
**The duration of the optical pulse in the oscillograms is blurring caused by an error when converting from an optical signal into an electric.

2.3   The Relevance of the Problem of Protecting Self-compensation Quantum Key Distribution System

We conducted a series of experimental studies of the self-compensation quantum key distribution system. The experiments included several main stages: investigation of the launch process; research of the synchronization process; investigation of the quantum key formation process with changing external factors. The main purpose of the experiment was to prove the instability of the synchronization process. It is known that in quantum communication systems the synchronization process is separated from the process of forming a quantum key. In some cases, synchronization is carried out on a separate communication channel. In a system with automatic compensation of polarization distortions, synchronization is implemented in the same communication channel as the formation of a quantum key. Recent modifications of quantum key distribution systems operate under the control of one-way quantum protocols. In this case, the synchronization process is modified, but not excluded. Without preliminary synchronization, the key generation process is impossible. It doesn't matter by what principle synchronization is implemented, in general this process should be performed.

In relation to the quantum key distribution system, which works on the principle of phase coding, synchronization is implemented on the same optical fiber as the process of key formation. Under real conditions, an optical fiber that connects two quantum communication systems is called a quantum channel. A quantum channel is a single-mode continuous optical fiber (fiber optic communication line).

During the experiment, normalizing coils with lengths of 4, 24, and 24 km were used as a quantum channel. An energy model of a quantum communication system was built. The energy model allowed us to calculate the loss during the passage of signals along the optical path. At the control points of the experimental stand, the optical power level was measured. As a result of the studies, the values of the introduced attenuation by active and passive equipment are established. The calculations showed that the optical synchronization pulse does not weaken to a low-energy level. Moreover, with the direct passage of the synchronization signal, the pulses have a sufficiently large power (see table). With back propagation, attenuation is introduced only by passive elements. The data obtained show that even with a quantum channel length of 48 km, an optical pulse contains energy equivalent to thousands of photons.

In addition, it was found that the power control algorithms in the quantum communication system are also not involved in the synchronization process. The attenuator in the shoulder with the Faraday mirror does not function and works on the complete transmission of the optical signal. In addition to all this, the results show that avalanche photodetectors operate in linear mode.

The conclusion of the experiment can be consecutive statements: during synchronization, the optical pulse is not one-photon; during the synchronization process, radiation power control algorithms and other algorithms do not work; The synchronization process is vulnerable to certain types of attacks. In published works, we have already described similar types of attacks. Note that such attacks use a quantum channel as a connection point and a multiphoton pulse as a vulnerability.

In [5] describes the main types of attacks on the fiber-optic communication systems. The given methods of attacks aimed at destabilizing the protocols of quantum cryptography. However, the initial synchronization issue is not considered or was thought that at the time of the attack the QKD system is synchronized.

Let us analyze from synchronization positions the "Trojan horse" attack that implements the substitution of key sequences legitimate users transmitted from transmitting station to coding station.

When QKD system using a two-wire fiber line (Fig. 2), signals propagate along a single optical fiber in the direction from transmitting station to coding station, but in the opposite direction from the coding station to transmitting station by other fiber. For attacker enough to secure access to the direct channel optical signal from transmission station to coding station.

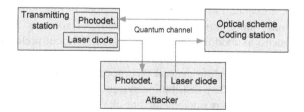

Fig. 2. The scheme of "Trojan horse" attack

Theoretically, an attacker is able to generate copies of optical pulses, intercepted from the station Bob and guide them to the Alice station. It was established that during the attack on this scheme, the percentage of errors in quantum key generation in the presence of the intruder does not exceed the percentage of errors in the absence of the intruder in communication channel. Thus, legitimate users are not able to detect the presence of intruders in quantum channel.

QKD systems with optical radiation transfer in one fiber are complicates, but does not exclude the possibility of unauthorized intruder access to the quantum channel [4]. Breaking procedure is described in 2008 by scientists from Norwegian University of Science and Technology (NTNU). Unauthorized access to the QKD system by the "Trojan horse" or "Brute force" attacks is based on the technical imperfection QKDS optoelectronic components.

The scheme operates on the quantum key distribution stage, and implies that the attacker (Eve) located in a fiber-optic line between the receiving and transmitting stations after the initial synchronization. Synchronization of receiving and transmitting stations before initialize attack to formation of quantum keys in the literature and security documents are not described.

Analysis of the known types of attacks shows that the theoretical possibility of access to the line connecting the QKD and its simulation equipment, an attacker is required to have information about the exact time gating single-photon avalanche photodiodes transmitting station. For this attack the attacker is connecting to the optic line between QKD stations (Fig. 3).

The scheme operates on the quantum key distribution stage, and implies that the attacker (Eve) located in a fiber-optic line between the receiving and transmitting stations after the initial synchronization. Synchronization of receiving and transmitting stations before initialize attack to formation of quantum keys in the literature and security documents are not described.

Analysis of the known types of attacks shows that the theoretical possibility of access to the line connecting the QKD and its simulation equipment, an attacker is required to have information about the exact time gating single-photon avalanche photodiodes transmitting station. For this attack the attacker is connecting to the optic line between QKD stations (Fig. 3).

As the results of experimental studies show, the synchronization process can be represented in the form of an energy diagram with a time distribution. Since optical pulses propagate along a standard optical fiber and the power control algorithms do not work, there is a possibility of losing part of the optical radiation. The classical model of an attacker assumes his actions at the stage of organizing a quantum communication system. Thus, it can be assumed that the attacker will prepare to intercept messages not during the operation of the quantum key distribution system, but at the installation stage (installation of communication lines, installation of equipment, etc.). In this case, it is enough for an attacker to provide fiber access points in a quantum communication channel. When it comes to a short distance (for example, between two neighboring buildings), the intervention is fairly easy to calculate. But if we are talking about 20 km or more, then the detection of an attacker is extremely difficult. Having secured access to the quantum communication channel during the installation of the system, the attacker increases the likelihood of access to the unprotected optical fiber during operation of the quantum key distribution system.

To carry out an attack with two taps, an attacker needs to introduce Y-type taps into the fiber-optic communication channel and use them while the system is running. Two couplers allow the following actions: pulses that follow in the direction from the transmitting station to the coding one fall on the coupler. Most of the pulse follows the quantum channel, while a smaller part of the pulse falls into the arm of the coupler.

Further, this part of the pulse is detected by a classical detector and data on this pulse is recorded in an array. The data includes such parameters as fixation time, pulse power, duration, repetition period, frequency (when fixing several signals). The scheme of an attack on a quantum channel with two taps is shown in Fig. 3.

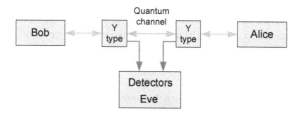

Fig. 3. Block diagram of optical signal withdrawal in two-wire circuit of the radiation

Note that power dividers can be with different division factors. Experimentally, before the introduction of taps, it is necessary to analyze the losses and build an energy model of dividers. The latter allows one to take into account the introduced attenuation when calculating the total losses in the quantum communication channel.

Most of the pulse after the first coupler enters the second coupler and passes through it without significant losses (when the signal passes directly from the transmitting station to the coding one).

Thus, the attacker has data about the sequence of impulses. But this does not provide a complete information chart. To conduct an attack, an attacker needs to obtain data on a sequence of pulses that will be reflected from the Faraday mirror in the coding station and sent to the transmitting station. This data can be obtained using a second Y-type coupler in a quantum channel.

The signal during back propagation is divided into two and sent to the shoulders of the coupler. One of the signals enters the quantum channel, and the other to classical detectors. After detecting the sequence of pulses, the attacker becomes aware of information about the signals. The most important here is information on the time of rereflection of pulses. This information allows you to calculate the distance from the couplers to the Faraday mirror and vice versa. How can this information be used? In practical quantum cryptography, this is used to introduce substitution signals into the system. The original pulses are fed to the first coupler and sent to the detector. Data is captured. With back propagation, information about the reflected pulse is also recorded. Suppose that an attacker has equipment—a coding station of a quantum key distribution system. In this case, it is possible to replace the entire complex of the coding station with an attacker station. Since the attacker already has information about the pulse re-reflection time, he can calculate the delay time and the length of the delay line (quantum channel) to simulate the original coding station.

In this case, the system (transmitting station) will not be able to detect a change in the quantum channel and will work in normal mode.

Note that in some cases it is advisable to use special clothespins instead of taps. They allow you to obtain information about the transmitted optical radiation without cutting the fiber. Such a clothespin is connected in the place where there is a strong bend of the fiber. Sometimes such a bend is formed specifically by an attacker. The disadvantage of this method is the presence of a bare section of the optical fiber.

The experiments performed show that it is not difficult for a telecommunications specialist to integrate into a fiber-optic communication line. Thus, the synchronization process of self-compensating systems of quantum communication under certain conditions can be considered as training for an attacker.

Given that the initial synchronization is performed at the stage of QKDS [9–11] configuring and often long before the start of the main processes for the formation of the quantum key, an attacker could exploit the vulnerability initial synchronization process when multi-photon transmission to provide additional data about the parameters of a quantum channel.

Thus, undetected during the initial synchronization, and possessing the necessary information about the quantum channel, the actions of the phase modulator encoding station and time gating photodetector, the attacker is able to successfully implement the above attacks at quantum protocol stage.

The latter determines the relevance of research and development of methods and algorithms for synchronization QKD systems with automatic compensation of polarization distortions, providing increased security for synchronization against unauthorized access by attacks such as "Trojan horse".

3 Principle of Synchronization with Protection from Unauthorized Access

Based on the above, to enhance security of the initial synchronization from unauthorized access, in [6] was described a new principle using photons as synchronization signals. There, the average number of photons in the impulse does not exceed 0.1. Note that the attenuation of the optical pulse to single-photon level is provided at the reverse direction of propagation sync signal from the coding station Alice to transmitting station Bob. It is realized by controllable optical attenuator in the Alice station. Attenuation level can be adjusted by software and controlled by operator. Proposed in [7, 8] algorithm reduces the probability of making a wrong decision with equal number of accumulated pulses in adjacent signal time windows at distribution of photon pulses energy between them. Advantage proposed algorithm is obvious at a ratio $\tau_w = 2\tau_s$, where τ_w - duration of time window; τ_s - duration of optical pulse.

In [8] shows possibility using analytical expression to calculate the probability of correct detection signal time window at synchronization.

$$P_D = exp(-N_w \cdot \overline{n_{d.N}} + \overline{n_{d.N}}) \langle \overline{n_{w.N}} \cdot exp(-\overline{n_{w.N}}) $$
$$+ [1 - exp(-\overline{n_{w.N}}) - \overline{n_{w.N}} \cdot exp(-\overline{n_{w.N}})](1 + \overline{n_{d.N}})^{N_w - 1} \rangle \tag{1}$$

where $\overline{n_{w.N}}$ - the average number of detected photoelectrons and dark current pulses (DCP) in the signal time window for sampling; N_w - number of time windows in a time frame; $\overline{n_{d.N}}$ - the average number of the DCP detected in the time window.

Thus, we can speak about new principle of synchronization for self-compensation fiber-optic quantum key distribution system with phase coding states of photons with enhanced security from unauthorized access, which is based on the use of single photon pulses as a synchronization signals [12, 13].

4 Conclusion

The self-compensation two pass fiber optic QKDS with phase coding states of photons that operate on the BB84 quantum protocol and implemented by «plug&play» technology are researched. As a result tests of QKDS id3110 Clavis2 found that the transmission of the synchronization signal in the direction to the coding station and back is carried in the multiphoton mode. Showed, that multiphoton mode is potentially facilitates for unauthorized access to information in quantum channel. The latter determines the relevance of search methods and algorithms for QKD systems, providing increased security at synchronization against unauthorized access at attacks such as "Trojan horse" or "Brute force". The algorithm based on principle involving the use of single-photon pulses as a synchronization signal where number of photons per pulse does not exceed 0.1 was proposed.

Acknowledgements. Work is performed within the grant of President of Russian Federation for state support of young Russian scientists MK-2338.2018.9 "Creation of an automated algorithm for integrating quantum keys into the data network while providing enhanced security against unauthorized access to the quantum communication channel".

References

1. Gagliardi, R.M., Karp, S.: Optical Communications. Wiley, New York (1976). 1976; translated to Russian, 1978; translated to Japanese, 1979. (Second Edition, 1995)
2. Gisin, N., Ribordy, G., Tittel, W., Zbinden, H.: Quantum cryptography. Rev. Mod. Phys. 74(1), 145–195 (2002)
3. Rumyantsev, K.E., Pljonkin, A.P.: Preliminary stage synchronization algorithm of auto-compensation quantum key distribution system with an unauthorized access security. In: International Conference on Electronics, Information, and Communications (ICEIC), pp. 1–4, Vietnam, Danang (2016). https://doi.org/10.1109/elinfocom.2016.7562955
4. Kurochkin, V., Zverev, A., Kurochkin, J., Riabtzev, I., Neizvestnyi, I.: Quantum cryptography experimental investigations. In: Photonics, vol. 5, pp. 54–66 (2012)
5. Lydersen, L., Wiechers, C., Wittmann, C., Elser, D., Skaar, J., Makarov, V.: Hacking commercial quantum cryptography systems by tailored bright illumination. Nat. Photonics 4, 686 (2010)
6. Rumyantsev, K.Y., Pljonkin, A.P.: Synchronization of quantum key distribution system using single-photon pulses registration mode to improve the security. Radiotekhnika. 2, 125–134 (2015)
7. Rumyantsev, K.E., Pljonkin, A.P.: Eksperimentalnye ispytaniya telekommunikatsionnoy seti s integrirovannoy sistemoy kvantovogo raspredeleniya klyuchey. Telekommunikatsii, vol. 10, pp. 11–16 (2014)

8. Pljonkin, A.P., Rumyantsev, K.Y.: Single-photon synchronization mode of quantum key distribution system, pp. 531–534, India, New Delhi (2016). https://doi.org/10.1109/icctict.2016.7514637

9. Vidick, T., Watrous, J.: Quantum proofs. Found Trends® Theor. Comput. Sci. 11(1–2), 1–215 (2016). https://doi.org/10.1561/0400000068

10. Rumyantsev, K.Y.: Quantum key distribution systems, 264 p. SFedU, Taganrog (2011)

11. Stucki, D., Gisin, N., Guinnard, O., Ribordy, G., Zbinden, H.: Quantum key distribution over 67 km with a plug&play system. New J. Phys. 4, 4.11–4.18 (2002)

12. Pljonkin, A., Singh, P.K.: The review of the commercial quantum key distribution system. In: Fifth International Conference on Parallel, Distributed and Grid Computing. IEEE (2018). https://doi.org/10.1109/pdgc.2018.8745822

13. Pljonkin, A.P.: Vulnerability of the synchronization process in the quantum key distribution system. Int. J. Cloud Appl. Comput. 9, L. 1 (2019)

Author Index

Printed in the United States
By Bookmasters